PEOPLES AND CULTURES
OF THE CARIBBEAN

The Natural History Press, publisher for The American Museum of Natural History, is a division of Doubleday & Company, Inc. Directed by a joint editorial board made up of members of the staff of both the Museum and Doubleday, the Natural History Press publishes books and periodicals in all branches of the life and earth sciences, including anthropology and astronomy. The Natural History Press has its editorial offices at Doubleday & Company, Inc., 277 Park Avenue, New York, New York 10017, and its business offices at 501 Franklin Avenue, Garden City, New York 11530.

MICHAEL M. HOROWITZ received his doctorate from Columbia University in 1959. The author of the book *Morne-Paysan: Peasant Village in Martinique,* he has published numerous articles on Caribbean and West African anthropology. Since 1967 he has directed a field research project on ethnicity and nomadic-sedentary relationships in the Lake Chad region of the Niger Republic.

Dr. Horowitz has been Visiting Professor at the Institute of Social Anthropology, University of Bergen, Norway, and has taught at the University of Michigan. He is currently Professor and Chairman of the Department of Anthropology, State University of New York at Binghamton, where he specializes in social anthropological theory, comparative political organization, and studies of nomadic and peasant societies.

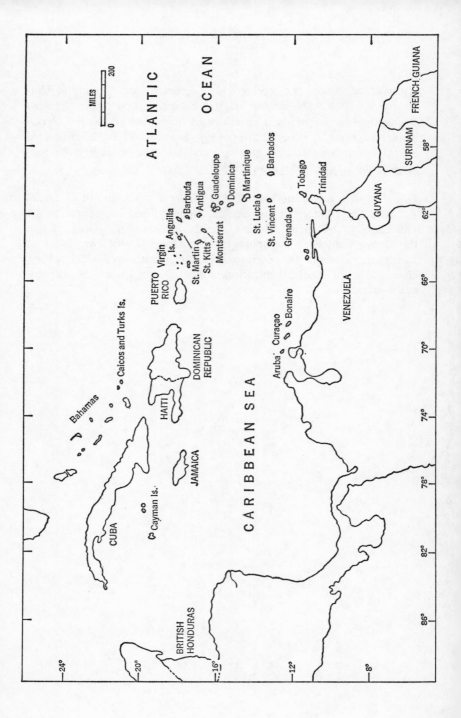

PEOPLES AND CULTURES OF THE CARIBBEAN

AN ANTHROPOLOGICAL READER

EDITED AND WITH AN INTRODUCTION BY
MICHAEL M. HOROWITZ

NHP

PUBLISHED FOR
THE AMERICAN MUSEUM OF NATURAL HISTORY
THE NATURAL HISTORY PRESS
1971 GARDEN CITY, NEW YORK

For Sylvia
who shares it all

Contents

Contents

PEOPLES AND CULTURES
OF THE CARIBBEAN

Introductory Essay

At first glance it is curious that any anthropological work has been done in the West Indies at all, for there are almost no indigenous people, the *sine qua non* of traditional ethnological inquiry. There are no Amerindians in most of the islands, and just a pitiful remnant of the Caribs in Dominica. An early consequence of European colonization during the sixteenth and seventeenth centuries was the almost total destruction of the Indians. The destroyers were Western Europeans: Spaniards, Englishmen, Dutchmen, Scotsmen, Normans, Bretons. Then came the Africans by the millions, captured, transported, sold, and enslaved on New World estates during three hundred years. The slave-based plantation effectively blocked further substantial European migration, for the potential migrant could rarely sustain the capital expenses necessary to acquire the land, labor, and machinery for the cultivation of cane and the production of sugar. Slavery was everywhere abolished during the nineteenth century, and in a number of places new immigrants, indentured workers from India, Africa, China, and other countries, came to labor on the estates. Thus the Caribbean islands were colonial possessions, properties of European states, but with no colonized peoples: the inhabitants were all colonists.

The West Indies are unusual economically also. Most of them at one time or another took the form of vast agrarian factories, producing a very special series of crops designed for overseas consumption: sugar, cacao, tobacco, spices, rum, and coffee, "effective fare for the factory workers of Britain and France, quelling their hunger pangs and numbing their outrage" (Mintz 1964a:xvii). The recurrent pattern of land exploitation was the plantation, worked by Negro

SOURCE: Adapted from Chapter One, "The Anthropology of the West Indies," from *Morne-Paysan: Peasant Village in Martinique,* by Michael M. Horowitz. Copyright © 1967 by Holt, Rinehart and Winston, Inc. Adapted and reprinted by permission of Holt, Rinehart and Winston, Inc.

slaves who had no control over the production and distribution of
the crops. After emancipation the now freedmen were salaried, forming the first great agrarian proletariat in modern times, with no en-
hanced access to economic decisions. Their lot resembled more that
of the wage laborers in the factories of Europe than that of the European peasants, or the peasants of North Africa, South Asia, and the
Far East.

These then are the central facts or common experiences of the
West Indies. First, with the exception, of course, of the mainland
Guianas and British Honduras, they are insular and most of them are
small. Cuba, 90 miles south of Florida as we are so often reminded,
is the largest and most populous, with an area of about 44,000 square
miles and a population of about eight million. The next largest is
Hispaniola, with 28,000 square miles distributed between Haiti and
the Dominican Republic. Jamaica has only a tenth the area of Cuba,
and Puerto Rico, the easternmost of the large islands or Greater Antilles, has a surface of some 3400 square miles. South from Puerto
Rico run the islands of the Lesser Antilles, forming the eastern border
of the Caribbean Sea. They range in size from Trinidad which, with
its dependency Tobago, has slightly less than 2000 square miles,
down to the tiny islets of the Grenadines of a few square miles each.

The Lesser Antilles in particular have two major characteristics of
"island ecosystems" (Fosberg 1963:5): limited size and relative isolation. Martinique, for example, measures about 40 miles by 20 miles
at its greatest extensions, and is separated from its neighbors Dominica to the north and St. Lucia to the south by some 20 miles of rough
seas. By virtue of intensive human occupation for more than four
hundred years, these islands do not have the features of closed, relatively stable biotic communities. Instead the environments are continuously and rapidly changing. Not only has there been a succession
of diverse nonaboriginal human populations—in Martinique, Caribs
replaced Arawaks shortly before the Europeans arrived, then French,
Africans, East Indians, other Europeans, and "Syrians" (a generic
term for immigrants from the French-speaking areas of North Africa
and Southwest Asia); the immigrants brought with them new crops,
new animals, and new planting techniques. Sugar, bananas, pineapples, breadfruit, mangoes, and many other typically West Indian
cultigens were introduced from the Old World, along with cows, pigs,
chickens, sheep, goats, and horses.

The emphasis on monocrop production in a number of the islands has rendered them particularly vulnerable to economic and natural disasters. Hurricanes, endemic in the region, are especially damaging to fragile banana trees. The economic vulnerability of monocrop production is caused by an inability of the colonies to control external events. The major crisis, periodically faced, was the opening up of competitive lands or new sources of the crop. For example, during the nineteenth century Martinique and Guadeloupe suffered the development of the French beet sugar industry. Over the next hundred years increasing amounts of land were shifted from cane to bananas, but here the islands have had to face not only competition from each other, but also from African areas dominated by French commercial interests, such as the Ivory Coast. The metropolitan powers assigned export quotas in relationship to external conditions rather than to domestic capabilities.

The second common experience of the Antilles is their colonial history. With the single exception of Haiti, which achieved its independence by revolution in 1803, all the islands remained colonies until the twentieth century. Many of them changed hands frequently. Spain, the original colonizer, lost much of her empire to England and France in the seventeenth and eighteenth centuries, and the remainder to the United States at the end of the nineteenth century. Of these, Cuba and the Dominican Republic were nominally independent, but in fact were under United States domination for much of the twentieth century. Even Scandinavian countries had colonies. Sweden administered St. Bartélemy for almost a hundred years, before returning it to France in 1877. Denmark sold its little colonies, the Virgin Islands, to the United States in 1917. One consequence of this multiplicity of colonial powers is a tremendously complex legal heritage.

The population, area, and current political affiliations of the more prominent countries are listed in Table 1.

Economically this colonialism made of the islands classic examples of mercantile exploitation. The colonies produce raw materials—food crops, tobacco, and cotton—for export, and import processed and manufactured goods from the mother country and by means of transport controlled by the mother country. Sea-island cotton from the British Leewards is spun into thread, woven into cloth, and cut and sewn into garments in Europe; a shirt of sea-island cotton costs more in Antigua than in England. The sugar exported from most of the islands is brown, with a heavy molasses content. It is refined in Europe and the United States and white sugar is an ex-

TABLE 1

THE CARIBBEAN IN 1968*

Country (Political Affiliation)	Midyear Population Estimate	Area (Square Kilometers)
Cuba (Independent)	8,074,000	114,524
Jamaica (Independent)	1,913,000	10,962
Haiti (Independent)	4,674,000	27,750
Dominican Republic (Independent)	4,029,000	48,734
Puerto Rico (U.S.A.)	2,723,000	8,897
American Virgin Islands (U.S.A.)		
St. Croix	27,000	207
St. John	1,000	52
St. Thomas	30,000	83
Saba, St. Maarten, St. Eustatius (Neth.)	7,000	88
Leeward Islands (United Kingdom)		
British Virgin Islands	9,000	153
St. Kitts, Nevis, Anguilla	56,000	357
Antigua	62,000	442
Montserrat	15,000	98
Guadeloupe and dependencies (France)	318,000	1,779
Martinique (France)	324,000	1,102
Windward Islands (United Kingdom)		
Dominica	72,000	751
St. Lucia	108,000	616
St. Vincent	93,000	388
Grenada and the Grenadines	103,000	344
Barbados (Independent)	253,000	430
Trinidad and Tobago (Independent)	1,021,000	5,128
Aruba, Bonaire, Curaçao (Neth.)	207,000	873
French Guiana (France)	46,000	91,000
Surinam (Netherlands)	375,000	163,265
Guyana (Independent)	710,000	214,969
British Honduras (United Kingdom)	116,000	22,965

* Source: *United Nations Demographic Yearbook, 1968.*

pensive luxury in the Caribbean. West Indian tobacco is processed in European cigarette factories; and so on.

Colonialism has had other effects. Politically it meant that the islands were governed from abroad and administered locally by persons sent from abroad. (Colonial service has been a means for rapid and well-paid advancement through the ranks of the British, French, and Dutch governments.) Although there was perhaps greater use of local personnel in the British administrations, generally the upper levels were effectively closed to all but metropolitans and a handful of creole whites. Educationally, colonialism meant the imposition of metropolitan curricula, texts, and examinations in local schools. Children learned the history and geography of the metropole, and were ignorant of their own. "One hundred years before Christ, the Germans came to our land . . ." begins a textbook used in the Dutch Windwards in 1958 (Keur and Keur 1960:193). British West Indian pupils had to learn arithmetic in terms of pounds, shillings, and pence, even though the local currency employed dollars and cents. Martiniquan students were taught that snow accumulates on fallen leaves in winter, while they were expected to know nothing of the geography of Guadeloupe. West Indian nationalism as it emerged after the Second World War differed from the early nationalisms of Ireland, India, and the Arab lands, for example, and the contemporary nationalisms of Africa and other parts of Asia, in its general avoidance of nativism and the evocation of its own past. The metropolitan colonial country remains the model of intellectual excellence in the Caribbean.

The third common experience of the West Indies is their tendency to be stratified into two great sections: a dominant planter class, owning or managing the estate lands and controlling the import-export trade, and a subordinate agricultural proletariat. With the prominent exceptions of Cuba, Puerto Rico, and the Dominican Republic, these two sections are usually distinguished by color: the darker-skinned descendants of slaves and indentured laborers still form the mass of the proletariat, and the lighter-skinned descendants of the slaveowners form the bulk of the controlling class. (The somewhat different development of the Spanish-speaking colonies had to do, as Mintz points out in his paper in this volume, with Spain focusing its involvement on its mainland possessions, relegating the islands to the status of fueling stations.) In a number of islands there emerged a buffer group of men of color, typically of white fathers and black mothers, in positions intermediate to the top and bottom. Hence the system of stratification resembles a color-class pyramid, dark at the base, and lightening toward the apex. With the advent of local autonomy and independence in some of the islands, there was a separation between political and economic power. Persons of color acceded to those political positions which were open to the ballot, but the whites continued to dominate the economic sector.

While this too simple schema of common facts unites the islands, and permits us to consider them as a culture area, there are important differences among them which should not be obscured. These differences obtain in the peculiar geographic, economic, ethnic, racial, and colonial experiences which they have had. Writing only of the British West Indies, Lowenthal outlines their various productive activities (1958:339):

> Agriculture remains the mainstay of the area, but Jamaica also relies heavily on bauxite and Trinidad on oil. Sugar monopolizes only Barbados, St. Kitts, and to a smaller extent, Antigua; bananas, cacao, coconuts, and citrus fruits occupy more and more land and people in Jamaica, Trinidad, and the Windwards; and several islands depend on unusual specialties—Grenada on nutmegs, St. Vincent on arrowroot, Montserrat on sea-island cotton.

Tobacco is an important crop in Cuba, the Dominican Republic, and Puerto Rico, and coffee is the leading export of Haiti. The Dutch Windwards are exporters of manpower rather than produce, sending men to the oil fields of Aruba and Curaçao and to the merchant marine. St. Thomas is devoted almost exclusively to tourism, and some of the small islands in the Leewards are increasingly geared to visitors.

Colonial political groupings do not neatly define cultural ones. For example, Guadeloupe, Dominica, Martinique, and St. Lucia form a linguistic unit whose populations speak mutually intelligible creoles, similar to the language of Haiti, which are not understood by metropolitan English and French (see the paper by Taylor in this volume). The common tongues of St. Martin, an island administered severally by France and Holland, are English and Papiamento, the creole of Curaçao. Schoolteachers sent to these islands from the mother countries may be unable to communicate with many of their pupils.

What kinds of studies have anthropologists made in the West Indies? M. G. Smith, himself among the most creative Caribbean scholars, brilliantly reviews and criticizes the period up to 1955 in "A Framework for Caribbean Studies" (reprinted in Smith 1965), an essential paper for anyone planning research in the area. I shall merely outline some of the major trends, and refer the reader to that paper, and to those included in this volume, for greater detail.

While studies of folklore predate his work, Melville J. Herskovits was the first American to essay social anthropological field research in the Caribbean. Herskovits was concerned with broad problems of cultural persistence and change. His thesis that New World Negroes were not without a meaningful past, but participated in a culture whose roots lay in the African continent from which they had been stolen, was contrary to much of the opinion of his day. He saw in the values and behaviors of his Dutch Guianan, Haitian, and Trinidadian informants connections which antedated slavery. Not all these connections were simple survivals, in which the African and West Indian instances of the event were to all purposes identical; in fact, Herskovits felt that few such survivals would be found. More often the event was "syncretized" in a new setting, containing elements of both the African and European traditions, as in the Vodun religion of Haiti or the Shango of Trinidad, where West African and Christian pantheons merge at certain points, and the adepts assert clear equations between them. (For examples of this approach, see the papers by Simpson and Bascom in this volume.) Even more remote from the original form are "reinterpretations," in which the African source is discovered substantially beneath the surface. For example, Herskovits felt that the sequence of matings or serial monogamy frequently reported in descriptions of New World Negro families was a reinterpretation of West African polygyny:

> As for the father, he continued to play for the nuclear group the institutionally remote, somewhat secondary role that in Africa was his as the parent shared with the children of other mothers than one's own, a role that was transmuted into the more or less transitory position he holds in so many of the poorer families of New World Negro societies (Herskovits and Herskovits 1947:16). This also explains the importance of the household in the rearing and training of children. In essence, this is based on the retention in Toco [Trinidad] of the nucleus of African kinship structures which . . . consists of a mother and her children living in a hut within her husband's compound, also inhabited by her co-wives and their children. That this nuclear unit has evolved into such a household as the one headed by the elderly woman . . . where her grown daughters are still more or less under her direction and some of their children entirely given over to her care, merely represents in one respect the logical development of this African institution under the

influence of slavery and of the particular socio-economic position of the Negroes after slavery was abolished (*Ibid.*:295–96).

The logic of development was not at all apparent to some of
Herskovits' critics who felt that the conditions of slavery were so
pervasive that continuity with an African past was irrevocably sev-
ered. To them it is slavery itself which accounts for the female-
centered lower-class Negro household.

When sexual taboos and restraints imposed by their original culture were lost, the behavior of the slaves in this regard was subject
at first only to the control of the masters and the wishes of those selected for mates. Hence, on the large plantations, where the slaves
were treated almost entirely as instruments of production and brute
force was relied upon as the chief means of control, sexual relations
were likely to be dissociated on the whole from human sentiments
and feelings. Then too, the constant buying and selling of slaves prevented the development of strong emotional ties between the mates.
But, where slavery became a settled way of life, the slaves were likely
to show preferences in sexual unions, and opportunity was afforded
for the development of strong attachments. The permanence of these
attachments was conditioned by the exigencies of the plantation system and the various types of social control within the world of the
plantation.

Within this world the slave mother held a strategic position and
played a dominant role in the family groupings. The tie between the
mother and her younger children had to be respected not only because of the dependence of the child upon her for survival but often
because of her fierce attachment to her brood (Frazier 1948:360–61).

Herskovits and his colleagues sought survivals, syncretisms, and
reinterpretations of Africanisms in many areas of culture. They were
most successful in music, in dance, and in religion; they were least
successful in economy and politics, though Herskovits argued that cooperative work groups were "directly related to comparable groupings of West Africa, of which a distinctive form is the *dokpwe* of
Dahomey . . ." (Herskovits 1937:257; for a description of Haitian
exchange labor, see the paper by Métraux in this volume). Their
most controversial assertions in the realm of domestic organization,
as cited above, have little currency today, since structural and ecological emphases are now favored over historical ones. But Herskovits
made a great contribution in opening up a whole area to serious in-

quiry. Indeed he established a tradition of scholarship in both the Caribbean and Africa, and a large number of students have followed him in working in the two regions. Mintz's assessment of Herskovits' *Life in a Haitian Valley* may serve as an evaluation of his Caribbean studies in general: "This is pioneering work . . . As ethnography, it does not meet the standards of modern field method, and it leaves many questions unanswered. As a ground-breaking anthropological study of a society previously either ignored or slandered by casual incompetents, it is of first importance" (Mintz 1964b:46).

During the early 1930s anthropologists and rural sociologists began to develop what came to be known as the community-study method, an approach to the study of complex civilizations. Redfield in Mexico, Arensberg in Ireland, the Lynds in the Midwest, and Warner in New England, to name only the leaders, worked in the rural areas and small towns of great nations, treating them as if they had the characteristics of the primitive bands and tribes usually associated with anthropological inquiry. Redfield's approach to communities, the "folk-urban continuum," provided a frame within which these rural villages could be located. It was argued that to know the culture of a modern nation it was necessary to know the kinds of local expressions of culture which were contained within it. Julian Steward's monumental *The People of Puerto Rico* (1956) combined community study and typology with cultural ecology, isolating the major varieties of local organization on the island. He felt that these varieties or subcultures were determined by their commitment to different crops—tobacco, coffee, and sugar—and to concomitant different forms of production, land tenure, and distribution within the limits of a single large tradition:

> We selected the municipalities exemplifying these principal types of farm production and sought to determine whether significant differences in the more important aspects of cultural behavior were associated with the type of production and with the individual's status and role within the community. In the field research, we sought to ascertain subcultural differences between certain classes or categories of rural people by analyzing their methods of making a living, family types, social relations, political and religious forms, practices and attitudes, varieties of recreation, and life values. We paid particular attention to differ-

ences associated with the individual's position in the community, whether as townsman or rural dweller, farm owner, sharecropper, or laborer, merchant, government employee, wage worker, and the like. The lifeways which distinguish the members of these different segments of rural society are presented as subcultures, as self-consistent patterns which prescribe the behavior of the local group of which the individual is a member (Steward 1956:2).

The constituent studies of Robert A. Manners, Sidney W. Mintz, Elena Padilla, and Eric R. Wolf established new standards for ethnographic documentation in the West Indies. The authors brought to prominence the plantation as a social form and the opposed implications of peasant and plantation systems of agriculture, which Ortiz (1947) had earlier called a counterpoint in Cuban history (see the papers by Ortiz, Wolf, Horowitz [1960], and Frucht in this volume).

Edith Clarke's study (1957) of three rural Jamaican villages similarly combined the community-study method with cultural ecology, although her aims were less ambitious than those of Steward and his associates. The villages sampled—Sugartown, an estate-complex of landless cane cutters; Orange Grove, a community based on successful mixed farming on small to medium-sized plots, oriented to local markets; and Mocca, an impoverished village of subsistence cultivators—were selected to show the relationships between land tenure and varieties of mating and domestic organization. Clarke did not deny that slavery, nor even Africa, had a part to play in determining the kinds of alternatives available; rather, she said, within the limits drawn historically, the alternative selected may be understood in terms of variations in economy and community structure.

Clarke made liberal use of quantitative material in arguing her thesis. A quantitative sequential approach is found in the other two major studies of domestic organization in the Caribbean: Raymond T. Smith's *The Negro Family in British Guiana* (1956) and Michael G. Smith's *West Indian Family Structure* (1962). R. T. Smith showed that the several forms of household units coexisting in Guianese villages are actually at different stages of a developmental cycle. The limited role of lower-class adult males as husband-father is related to their marginal economic positions in the larger society. This is particularly the case on plantations, as shown in Clarke's presentation of Sugartown, for the domestic grouping does not assume corporate functions. Different from the peasant household, that of the plantation worker is totally divorced from economic productivity and distribution. The members of the plantation household individually contract to labor for wages; the members of a peasant household may collectively organize for planting and harvesting. The woman in a peasant household has special responsibility in overseeing the sale of the harvest. M. G. Smith's study also evidences, from a much more broadly drawn sample, developmental sequences of domestic organization. M. G. Smith compares households from Carriacou in the Grenadines, and from rural and town areas in Grenada and Jamaica. He believes that the organization of the family is a function of the conjugal pattern chosen by its head: extraresidential mating, coresidential mating or consensual cohabitation, and marriage. He shows further that not all of these patterns are available everywhere, and that a specific pattern is appropriate and sanctioned at a particular stage in the life cycle. (For an alternative explanation of the same data, see the paper by Horowitz [1967] in this volume.)

The complex ethnic and racial character of many of the islands has occasioned studies of social stratification, of race relations, and of cultural pluralism, and has forced into the anthropological consciousness problems which were traditionally associated with sociology. Especially promising has been the extension of research from the large islands of the Greater Antilles and Trinidad, which had been studied for several decades, to the smaller islands forming the arc of the eastern Caribbean. The work now going on and recently completed in the Virgin Islands, Montserrat, Dominica, the Dutch Windwards, Martinique, St. Lucia, the Grenadines, and Barbados, should provide the basis for genuinely comparative analyses. Much of the recent North American research in the Caribbean has been sponsored by the Research Institute for the Study of Man, whose Director, Dr. Vera Rubin, has also made significant scientific contributions. In Jamaica the Institute for Social and Economic Research, with its journal *Social and Economic Studies,* offers Caribbean social scientists a fine forum. Another center at the Institute of Caribbean Studies, University of Puerto Rico, similarly facilitates area research, and publishes the journal *Caribbean Studies.* Other programs exist in Martinique, the Virgin Islands, and elsewhere. From an area so recently unknown to social science, the West Indies are now receiving increasingly competent attention. A sample of that attention is the substance of this volume.

The articles which appear below do not cover all topics considered by social scientists, but were selected rather to expose some of the most important anthropological questions in depth. Thus I have stressed stratification and ethnicity, the opposition between plantation and peasant production, land tenure and internal marketing, the nature of household organization and the structure of affinal relations, and popular religion. In making these selections I have tried also to evidence the various settings in which the studies were made; some of the articles write of the larger islands in the Greater Antilles, some of the Windward and Leeward Islands, and some of the mainland countries of the Guianas in South America and British Honduras in Central America which historically, culturally, and economically belong to the Caribbean. Spanish-speaking and French-speaking countries are included along with English-speaking ones which are perhaps better known to the traveler and student. Because of the effective discontinuity between pre-Columbian and colonial populations, I have included no papers on Amerindian archaeology and culture. The interested student is urged to read, for both these topics, a series of excellent papers by Irving Rouse (1948, 1960, 1964, and Cruxent and Rouse 1969). I have also omitted physical anthropology, and recommend the papers of Jean Benoist, particularly his study of race (1963). There are two other principal omissions. Although political materials are treated in several of the papers (e.g., Mintz, Braithwaite, Kitzinger), there are no studies herein relating specifically to governmental organization, nor to questions of decolonization and the attempts at new forms of government, such as the socialist state in Cuba or the failure of the Federation of the English-speaking islands. Finally, and sadly, there are no selections from the rich body of West Indian literature. To understand the Caribbean fully, one should also read the sensitive portraits of Naipaul, the poetry of Césaire, the biting Calypso of the Great Sparrow. I envy the reader his first discovery of them.

References cited:

Benoist, Jean.
    1963 "Les Martiniquais, anthropologie d'une population métisée," *Bulletin et Mémoire de la Société d'Anthropologie* 4(2):241–432.
Clarke, Edith.
    1957 *My Mother Who Fathered Me*. London, George Allen & Unwin Ltd.
Cruxent, Jose M. and I. Rouse.

1969 "Early man in the West Indies," *Scientific American* 221(5):42–52.
Fosberg, Francis R., ed.
1963 *Man's Place in the Island Ecosystem*. Honolulu, Bishop Museum Press.
Frazier, E. Franklin.
1948 *The Negro Family in the United States*. Rev. ed. New York, Holt, Rinehart and Winston, Inc.
Herskovits, Melville J.
1937 *Life in a Haitian Valley*. New York, Alfred A. Knopf.
Herskovits, M. J. and Frances S.
1947 *Trinidad Village*. New York, Alfred A. Knopf.
Keur, John Y. and Dorothy L.
1960 *Windward Children*. Assen, Netherlands, Royal Vangorcum Ltd.
Lowenthal, David.
1958 "The West Indies Chooses a Capital," *The Geographical Review* 48:336–64.
Mintz, Sidney W.
1964a "Foreword," in *Sugar and Society in the Caribbean,* by R. Guerra y Sánchez. Caribbean Series 7. New Haven, Yale University Press.
1964b "Melville J. Herskovits and Caribbean studies: a retrospective tribute," *Caribbean Studies* 4:42–51.
Ortiz, Fernando.
1947 *Cuban Counterpoint*. New York, Alfred A. Knopf.
Rouse, Irving.
1948 "The West Indies," in J. H. Steward, ed., *Handbook of South American Indians*. Volume 4. Bureau of American Ethnology Bulletin 143. Washington, D.C., Smithsonian Institution.
1960 "The Entry of Man Into the West Indies," *Papers in Caribbean Anthropology,* compiled by S. W. Mintz. Yale University Publications in Anthropology No. 61. New Haven, Yale University Press.
1964 "Prehistory of the West Indies," *Science* 144:499–513.
Smith, M. G.
1962 *West Indian Family Structure*. Seattle, University of Washington Press.
1965 *The Plural Society in the British West Indies*. Berkeley and Los Angeles, University of California Press.
Smith, R. T.
1956 *The Negro Family in British Guiana: Family Structure and Social Status in the Villages*. London, Routledge and Kegan Paul Ltd.
Steward, Julian H. and others.
1956 *The People of Puerto Rico*. Urbana, University of Illinois Press.

A.
The Caribbean:
Culture and History

SIDNEY W. MINTZ

1. The Caribbean as a Socio-cultural Area[1]

The Caribbean islands, a scattering of some fifty inhabited units spanning nearly 2,500 miles of sea between Mexico's Yucatán Peninsula and the north coast of South America, constitute the oldest colonial sphere of western European overseas expansion. By the second decade of the sixteenth century, these territories were circumnavigated and explored, their aborigines had been dominated and Spanish colonies established on the largest islands, and the entire area had been thrust into the consciousness of European monarchs, philosophers, and scientists. As the primordial sphere of Spain's Atlantic imperium, the Caribbean region symbolized the world's beginnings of what Konetzke[2] properly called "planetary" empires, spanning whole oceans; the massive shift from a "thalassic" (Mediterranean) to an "oceanic" (Atlantic) orientation,[3] that would govern Europe's expansive designs for so long thereafter, began with the Caribbean. And when López de Gómara, addressing himself to Charles V in 1552, asserted that, after the Creation and the coming of Christ, the most important event in history had been the discovery of the New World, he was not claiming more than what many informed Europeans of the time would have conceded.[4]

Soon after their discovery, the Caribbean islands became a springboard for the Spanish conquest of the American mainland, and a testing-ground for Reconquista political designs, readapted for use in the administration and control of colonial peoples. After the subjugation of highland Mexico and the Andes, the importance of the islands as areas of settlement in the Spanish imperial system declined

SOURCE: Article prepared for the International Commission for a History of the Scientific and Cultural Development of Mankind, and issued in the *Journal of World History*, Vol. 9, No. 4 (1966):912–37, published by Les Editions de La Baconnière, Boudry-Neuchatel, Switzerland. Reprinted by permission of the author and editor, *Journal of World History*, Division of Cultural Studies, United Nations Educational, Scientific and Cultural Organization.

swiftly. Then, in the seventeenth century, Spain's north European rivals began to carve out overseas empires of their own within the Caribbean area; by the latter part of that century, the importance of the islands to Northern Europe had reached a zenith. After 1800, however, the Caribbean played a less and less significant role in the European scheme of things; only recently has this area taken on new meaning for the West, this time much more political and strategic than economic.

One of the ways to clarify the contemporary importance of the Caribbean islands is to limn their social and cultural characteristics against a backdrop of regional history; much of their commonality, their meaning as a bloc of societies, is the result of demonstrably parallel historical experiences during more than four centuries of powerful (though intermittent and often whimsical) European influence. It can probably be shown that the special distinctiveness of the Caribbean area within the sphere of the "underdeveloped world" inheres in its ancience as a cluster of colonies; what is more, the societies of the Caribbean are only superficially "non-western," taking on their particularity precisely because they are in some ways, and deceptively, among the most "western" of all countries outside the United States and western Europe.

Useful attempts to classify the Caribbean area as a sub-category of some larger culture-bloc have not succeeded either in fully defining its distinctiveness, or in grouping it convincingly with those portions of the Latin American mainland exposed to similar social-historical influences.[5] In spite of certain common historical experiences, the societies of the Caribbean do not form an undifferentiated grouping; and mainland societies similar to those of the islands have not undergone all of the same historical processes. This essay does not propose to replace previous classifications with yet another; in fact, it builds to a large extent on previous work. But perhaps several more points can be made about the societies of the Caribbean, in order to understand better both what sets this area apart from other areas, and what gives it a particular and somewhat distinctive cast; the major points are socio-historical in character. A good general statement of historical relevance comes from M. G. Smith:[6]

> The historical conditions which define the area from Brazil to the United States as the broad comparative context of Caribbean studies are well known. They consist in the expansion of

Europe to the New World, the common historical patterns of conquest, colonization, peonage or slavery, and the development of multi-racial and multi-cultural societies throughout this area. Regional differences of a contemporary or historical nature are of obvious significance for comparative work within so vast a frame of reference. For present purposes the differences of habitat, economy, population composition, political history and status are the most useful general guides in a preliminary subdivision of this wider area.

An attempt will be made here to build on this statement, with the emphasis on the societies of the islands themselves and, only secondarily, on those of the mainland sharing some of the same features. It would undoubtedly be correct to say that each of the characteristics outlined in the following presentation also applies to some other non-Caribbean society or region. Yet whatever utility this classification possesses does not depend upon the uniqueness of any one of the defining features, but rather, upon their collective significance for Caribbean social history. Furthermore, each society within the Caribbean area is of course in some important regards unique; no attempt to generalize about the entire area can deal adequately with the distinctive features of any single component society. But the argument rests on the hope that the generalities that follow will, when taken in aggregate, clarify the extent to which the Caribbean region forms a socio-cultural bloc of some kind. The presentation of relevant data may also make clear some of the principal ways in which the societies of the Caribbean differ among themselves, since they have been subject in different degree to the very forces that have tended to make them similar. It is perhaps particularly important to keep in mind, however, that no one of the points to be made, so much as their interrelated effect, is significant in the following presentation.

In order to advance the argument, one must stress the difference between "culture" and "society," as the terms are employed here. To begin with, it is inaccurate to refer to the Caribbean as a "cultural area," if by "culture" is meant a common body of historical tradition. The very diverse origins of Caribbean populations; the complicated history of European cultural impositions; and the absence in most such societies of any firm continuity of the culture of the colonial power have resulted in a very heterogeneous cultural picture. And yet the *societies* of the Caribbean—taking the word "society" to refer here to forms of social structure and social organization—exhibit similarities that cannot possibly be attributed to mere coincidence. It probably would be more accurate (though stylistically unwieldy) to refer to the Caribbean as a "societal area," since its component societies probably share many more social-structural features than they do cultural features. Pan-Caribbean uniformities turn out to consist largely of parallels of economic and social structure and organization, the consequence of lengthy and rather rigid colonial rule. That many of them also share similar or historically related *cultures,* while important, is treated here as secondary.

According to this analysis, Caribbean regional commonality is expressed in terms of nine major features as follows:

(1) lowland, subtropical, insular ecology;

(2) the swift extirpation of native populations;

(3) the early definition of the islands as a sphere of European overseas agricultural capitalism, based primarily on the sugar-cane, African slaves, and the plantation system;

(4) the concomitant development of insular social structures in which internally differentiated local community organization was slight, and national class groupings usually took on a bipolar form, sustained by overseas domination, sharply differentiated access to land, wealth, and political power, and the use of physical differences as status markers;

(5) the continuous interplay of plantations and small-scale yeoman agriculture, with accompanying social-structural effects;

(6) the successive introduction of massive new "foreign" populations into the lower sectors of insular social structures, under conditions of extremely restricted opportunities for upward economic, social, or political mobility;

(7) the prevailing absence of any ideology of national identity that could serve as a goal for mass acculturation;

(8) the persistence of colonialism, and of the colonial ambiance, longer than in any other area outside western Europe;

(9) a high degree of individualization—particularly economic individualization—as an aspect of Caribbean social organization.

No excuses will be made for the incommensurability of these various points; whatever heuristic value they may have for explaining the special nature of Caribbean societies inheres in their combination. In each case, their combined effects have been somewhat different, so that the various societies of the Caribbean area may be viewed in terms of a multidimensional continuum, rather than in terms of some single abstract model. Furthermore, it is clear that some of these points might be considered "causes" and others "consequences." Since the main objective here is to suggest why Caribbean societies are as they are, no attempt is made to supply any elaborate chronological or causal schema of a sort intended for a more detailed exposition of the same argument.

(1) The Caribbean islands, stretching from the Bahamas and the Greater Antilles in the north, to Trinidad and the Dutch Leeward islands off the Venezuelan coast in the south, are climatically sub-tropical and oceanic, warm in temperature, with few extremes, and with considerable local variation in rainfall. Though some parts of the Greater and Lesser Antilles are ruggedly mountainous, and tropical rain forests are to be found in some interiors, nearly all of the islands possess coastal flatlands. Especially in the Greater Antilles, central mountains are girded by alluvial floodplains, generally well watered along the northern coasts, but sere and dry along the southern littorals. The bigger islands, such as Puerto Rico and Jamaica, have fertile intermontane valleys, often ringed by mountains high enough to support coffee cultivation. The southwestern portions of the Greater Antilles also have uplands and savannas, suitable for cattle-growing and the production of industrial fibers. The Lesser Antilles fall into two geographical groupings, one of flat, dry, and relatively infertile islands, the other of ruggedly mountainous, better watered islands.

The very fact that the Caribbean, as defined by its early western explorers and conquerors, was a sea containing an archipelago, was of course also of considerable importance. The conquest of the Caribbean area took the form of island-hopping, each island a stepping-stone to new conquests. Political control of any island or group of islands had to depend on control of the sea, and the sea inevitably played a significant part in the culture of the settlers. Islands define themselves geographically, so to speak; for the Europeans, each island in turn was a new frontier, until its local aboriginal population was conquered or eliminated, and its total area effectively occupied. On the smaller islands, effective total occupation proved to be relatively easy, though the mountainous character of some—particularly when combined with aboriginal resistance—slowed European expansion. In the larger islands, however, where interior mountain ranges were extensive (and, to judge by what is known, very heavily forested in the sixteenth and seventeenth centuries), European influence tended to be concentrated in coastal settlements, and opportunities for subcultural differentiation were greater.

These few facts, though dangerously over-general, carry considerable significance for the understanding of the Caribbean area. To begin with, all or nearly all of the islands were suitable for commercial tropical agriculture, including the production of food staples for foreign markets, such as sugar, coffee, rum, cocoa, and spices. Where local conditions did not make possible such production, a controlled water supply could sometimes be engineered, in order to put previously uncultivated but fertile lands to agriculture. Moreover, where alluvial floodplains or intermontane valleys were common, such agriculture could be conducted on big estates, since flatness of terrain made possible large-scale organization of enterprise with massed labor, massed machines or both. Finally, the distinction between coastal plain and rugged highland foretold a sharp divergence of enterprise that has typically marked Caribbean agriculture, with plantations concentrated on the coasts and in inland valleys, and small-scale enterprise and some hacienda forms occurring in mountainous sectors. On the smallest and most arid islands, plantations never developed; on those small islands better suited to plantation agriculture, small-scale or "peasant" enterprises have usually remained very marginal; and on the bigger islands, these two differing agricultural systems have competed or co-existed for most of Caribbean history.

(2) Underlying physical conditions thus provide a context within which the differing economic adjustments of the colonists took place. But colonial enterprise, from the very first, also had to take account of the human element in local ecology—that is, of the aboriginal populations of the islands. The Greater Antilles, first discovered, explored, and conquered by Spain, were relatively densely occupied by Island-Arawak peoples practicing slash-and-burn agriculture, and living in settled villages.[7] These peoples caught the full brunt of Spanish power; they were substantially eliminated or genetically absorbed by their conquerors in less than half a century. In the Lesser Antilles, and in a few isolated interiors of the bigger islands, Indian communities survived until the late seventeenth or even eighteenth century. Island-Carib resistance in the smaller islands and the scarcity of metallic resources there limited European interest until the mid-seventeenth century; but even so, the aborigines ceased to be a force

to be reckoned with seriously by 1700 in most places, and before 1800 in all.[8]

During the contact period, many aboriginal cultural features were stabilized as parts of new, synthetic cultures—but cultures in which the native peoples themselves were to play ever less significant roles. Thus the acculturational process in the islands contrasted quite sharply with that characteristic of the European colonizing experience in the highland regions of the New World mainland, and in most of Asia and Africa. For the Spaniards, the early contact situation provided an opportunity to develop administrative and extractive techniques to be reapplied in Mexico, the Andean region, and elsewhere; but it did not require a lengthy, ongoing series of adjustments to a bulking and persistent aboriginal population. Spain's later rivals —Britain, France, Holland, etc.—dealt summarily with the Island-Carib in the smaller islands, not so much assimilating as killing off these aboriginal predecessors. Thus the confrontation of cultures in the islands was one in which European colonizers were able to work out the problems of settlement, adjustment, and development to a very large degree *as if the Antilles were empty lands*. The psychological meaning of this state of affairs—not to mention its economic, social, and political significance—is exceedingly complex. Mannoni, in his psychological analysis of colonialism, tells us that Robinson Crusoe, as the fictive prototype of the European colonizer, feared solitude, but also desired it—what Mannoni calls "the lure of a world without men."[9] As his model, Mannoni deals with Madagascar; but surely the Antilles would have provided him with a better case. For the European experience on the islands was in fact that of creating a world without men soon after original contact. This scourging of the human landscape enabled the Europeans to set the terms of their future colonialism in the Caribbean area in ways very different from those available to them in the densely occupied areas of the non-western world. The significance of this distinction is real; the next stage in Antillean history was set in the absence of subject peoples, for the European colonist had transformed himself from guest into host simply through having eliminated his native predecessors.

(3) The very early development of plantation agriculture can be credited to the Spanish colonists in the Greater Antilles who, in response to the decline in mining enterprises, cast about for alternate sources of livelihood. Small plantations worked with African slave labor were successfully producing sugar for European markets in

the Greater Antilles within less than fifty years of the Discovery.[10] Though other staples were also tried, sugar most dramatically demonstrated its importance by its success on the European market. Almost insignificant in Europe's diet before the thirteenth century, sugar gradually changed from a medicine for royalty into a preservative and confectionery ingredient and, finally, into a basic commodity. By the seventeenth century, sugar was becoming a staple in European cities; soon, even the poor knew sugar and prized it. As a relatively cheap source of quick energy, sugar was valuable more as a substitute for food than as a food itself; in western Europe it probably supplanted other food in proletarian diets. In urban centers, it became the perfect accompaniment to tea, and West Indian sugar production kept perfect pace with Indian tea production. Together with other plantation products such as coffee, rum, and tobacco, sugar formed part of a complex of "proletarian hunger-killers,"[11] and played a crucial role in the linked contribution that Caribbean slaves, Indian peasants, and European urban proletarians were able to make to the growth of western civilization.

But in the first period of Spanish overseas experimentation with sugar-cane and the plantation system, western Europe had barely begun to demand tropical commodities, and the early successes in Santo Domingo, Cuba, Puerto Rico, and Jamaica were soon eclipsed by the immense metallic wealth flowing to the metropolis from the mainland, after 1520. Spanish interest in the islands waned, and the major Hispanic colonies there—Cuba, Española, Puerto Rico and, much less importantly, Jamaica—became fuelling stations and bastions for the treasure fleets. It was Spain's rivals in the Caribbean, especially Britain, France, and the Netherlands, who would revamp and expand the plantation system on a grand scale, beginning about 1640.

The nature of the plantation system was exceedingly complex, and only a few general statements about it may be made here. To begin with, it developed from the outset in a context of scarce labor supply; the plenitude of land relative to labor, and the ability of free laborers to become yeomen in unclaimed land areas, required agricultural entrepreneurs in the Antilles to rely on various forms of forced labor in order to be able to undertake commercial production.[12] Though a variety of forced and contract labor arrangements were employed, the most important labor basis was slavery. Between 1501, when Governor Ovando of Española was first advised to import African slaves to that island,[13] and 1886, when slavery was terminated in Cuba, the Caribbean islands depended almost exclusively on slavery as a source of plantation labor. The numbers of enslaved involved were staggering; though no attempt will be made here to specify, Antillean slavery constituted one of the greatest demographic phenomena in world history.

It was entirely reasonable, according to the political and ideological currents of the time, that the main source of slaves was Africa. Though the enslavement of American Indians in the Antilles was important for a brief period after the Conquest, this resource soon disappeared. European indentured labor was also important, particularly in the early development of the British and French settlements in the Lesser Antilles; but by 1650, this labor supply had diminished sharply, since European labor needs had begun to rise. Furthermore, indentured servants eventually secured their freedom and became yeomen, thus rivalling the plantations, rather than serving them. After the Haitian Revolution and the emancipation acts of the North European powers, other sources of labor besides Africa would reemerge; yet the years 1650–1800 were not only the "core period" for the classic plantation system, but also those during which African slave labor dominated the Caribbean scene.

The irregular development of the plantation system in the Hispanic colonies and its more limited relevance in the smallest, driest, and most mountainous islands signified that these locales would be subject to less "Africanization" than the non-Hispanic islands and those better suited to plantations. As a result, it is not surprising that the distributions of persons of African origin are heavier in some Caribbean islands and countries than in others.[14] In Nevis and Barbados, for example, early settlement by European indentured servants who became yeomen after their terms of service were completed, was followed by a rapid plantation expansion and the virtual end of settlement by Europeans.[15] In such islands, and in Jamaica (seized by Britain in 1655), rural communities of persons of European extraction survived only as tiny enclaves within populations of predominantly African origin. In the remaining Hispanic colonies— Puerto Rico, Cuba, and Santo Domingo—large European populations were stabilized before the reexpansion of the plantation system in the late eighteenth century, and this is still reflected in the populational character of these countries.

The African origin of the populations of many Caribbean islands has had important cultural effects. Though the distribution of cultural forms of African provenience is irregular and in many cases problematical, it is clear that the African cultural impact has been much greater in Haiti, say, than in Puerto Rico; this difference in culture-trait distributions reflects plantation history with some fidelity. At the same time, it should be remembered that the "African cultural impact" did not consist of the diffusion of some undifferentiated, uniform body of beliefs, attitudes, linguistic forms, or other cultural materials. While Herskovits has argued that the majority of New World slaves were drawn from a relatively restricted area of Africa, and while many specific culture elements can be traced with confidence to Africa, it would be extremely difficult to attribute a significant part of the culture of any contemporary Caribbean people to specific African cultures. Moreover, the cultural heterogeneity of the enslaved Africans who reached the islands was apparently reinforced by plantation practices, since attempts were made to prevent any substantial number of slaves of a common tribal background from being concentrated on the same plantation. Hence, while it is perfectly correct to claim that some island societies were more "africanized" than others, the introduction of large numbers of African slaves into one island probably says more about the resulting *societal* arrangements than it does about *cultural* content.

(4) The plantation system was, first of all, an agricultural design for the production of export commodities for foreign markets—a means for introducing agricultural capitalism to subtropical colonial areas, and for integrating those areas with the expanding European economy. But because this system possessed an inner dynamic, in those Caribbean islands where it flourished, it also led to the creation of social and political relationships of a distinctive—and very rigid—sort. Since the populations of "plantation islands" were substantially or predominantly composed of African slaves whose destinies and activities were powerfully controlled by numerically insignificant minorities of European freemen, a fundamentally similar type of social and political system gradually took shape, in one island society after another. Thus the plantation system became much more than an agricultural form; it became in effect the basis of a societal model of a kind.

Plantation growth and spread in the Caribbean area was intimately connected to ecological and physiographic factors, as well as to forces of an economic and political kind, and it is possible to specify in a preliminary way the basic conditions under which plantations spread and grew. First of all, they were confined largely to lowland alluvial floodplain and intermontane valley areas, and their initial expansion occurred in the parts of these areas that also possessed adequate rainfall. Second, their growth was restricted in the Hispanic colonies where they first flourished, declining in the mid-sixteenth century and only reappearing there in strength in the late eighteenth century. Plantations waxed and waned, not only in accord with the competitive spread of colonial power in the hands of European nations and the vagaries of the international markets for tropical commodities, but also in line with changing imperial policies. Third, plantation growth before the mid-nineteenth century was closely linked to questions of labor supply. As we have seen, the major source of labor in the period 1650–1800 was Africa, and the basis for relating that labor to the land was slavery. The production of tropical commodities necessitates large supplies of labor for relatively short periods during the year; the plantation regime hinged on the ability to exercise requisite discipline over the labor force, and slavery facilitated this arrangement.

But as has been suggested, the plantation system was not only an agricultural device; it also became the basis for an entire societal design. This design involved the perpetuation of societies sharply divided at the outset into two segments, one large and unfree, the other small and free, with a monopoly of power in the hands of the latter. The necessity of concentrating a substantial proportion of the available capital of the plantation entrepreneur in human stock—slaves—apparently introduced a certain rigidity into plantation operation. This rigidity was partly economic, especially since plantation demands for labor were so sharply seasonal in character; but the social implications of capital investment in "human machines" were even more serious. The inability of freemen to compete in any local sphere with slave labor complemented and intensified a sort of manorial self-sufficiency in plantation areas, sharply inhibiting the development of occupationally diverse communities of freemen in the same region. In the absence of slave buying power, or slave opportunities for education, religious instruction, medical care, and the like, plantation regions tended to consist of uninterrupted series of manor-like (but *capitalistic*) estates, each with its tiny complement of free European overseers and its massive but politically inert slave population. Since neither the masters nor the slaves were able to transfer to the Caribbean setting any adequate version of their ancestral cultures, and since the slaves in most situations had insufficient opportunity to use the masters' cultural tradition as a model, the cultural forms typifying plantation life were usually contrived out of what the slaves themselves could transfer from Africa and were permitted to retain, combined with those features of European culture that they could learn about as part of the plantation regimen itself.

Especially characteristic of these unusual socio-cultural adjustments to the plantation system was a sexual code that had to take into account the greater proportions of male to female slaves in most cases, the relative lack of free European women, and the sexual defencelessness of the slave female before the master class. Concubinage, informal unions between free Europeans and slave women, and the stabilization of a "mistress pattern" in many Carribbean societies inevitably led to the growth of a group intermediate in physical appearance and, in many cases, in social status as well. Only rarely, however, did this group serve to cement the topmost and bottommost ranks of the social order; much more commonly, the socially intermediate category tended to affiliate itself as best it could with those in power.

The Hispanic colonies deviated to some extent from this generalized picture, allegedly because slaves were better integrated legally and religiously into insular social systems. Of equal or perhaps greater importance, however, was the strength of Spanish overseas control of local policy, the growth of substantial non-African (and non-slave) creole populations, and the very tardy reemergence of the plantation system. Also important was the establishment of creole planter groups in the Hispanic islands, who could provide their slaves with familial and acculturational models of a sort largely lacking in the Caribbean plantation colonies of the North European powers. The Hispanic Caribbean colonies, more than any others, were settled by Europeans who had come to stay and to become "creoles"; nowhere and at no time in the Hispanic islands did African slaves ever outnumber freemen of European origin. The significance of this pattern for the acculturation of the slaves, and for the growth of ideologies of nationhood in the Spanish islands, is very considerable.

(5) The plantation system did not evolve in a vacuum, however. In island after island, this system had to take account either of the pre-existence of other economic adaptations, or of local variations that developed within the sphere of plantation operation. The com-

plementary profile of the plantation system was the precedence, co-occurrence or subsequent development of classes of small-scale cultivators, who either accommodated their style of life to the existence of the plantation system, lived in open opposition to it, or occupied areas where the plantation had flourished, only to wither due to changes in the political or economic scene. In all such cases, the yeoman or peasant adaptation was "artificial," in the sense that there were no autocthonous peasantries upon whom the plantation system was engrafted. The early yeoman communities of the north European settlements in the Lesser Antilles emerged from the groups of indentured laborers there who completed their contracts and became freeholders;[16] the peasant villages of Jamaica were a post-Emancipation development, largely the creation of the missionary churches and composed of ex-slaves who had learned their subsistence skills while still enslaved;[17] the peasantry of Haiti won its security of tenure in revolution;[18] and the runaway slave communities that took up agriculture in such societies as Jamaica, Cuba, and Puerto Rico had to live under daily peril of attack and destruction by the planters.[19] In most of the Lesser Antilles, the early European yeoman villages were eliminated by the spread of the plantation by or before 1700.[20] In the Hispanic Antilles, the reemergence of the plantation at the close of the eighteenth century, and the accompanying repressive labor legislation, undermined highland squatter and peasant adjustments.[21] In these cases and in others, then, the counterposition of plantation and peasantry was essentially negative—a struggle between two differing modes of economic organization:

It might be convenient for some purposes to view the rise of Caribbean peasantries as occurring in three different contexts. First there were the colonists who, early in the settlement of individual possessions, engaged in small-scale agriculture as yeoman cultivators. To a very variable degree, this sort of peasantry took shape in all early settlement of the Antilles, and not merely in the Spanish Antilles. Second, there was—for lack of a better term—the 'protopeasantry' which evolved under slavery, because of the particular circumstances which permitted or compelled the slaves to grow much of their own food, to produce many of their own necessities and, very importantly, to sell their surpluses and dispose more or less freely of their profits. Jamaica is perhaps the best example. Finally, there were the peasantries that evolved during slavery, but in open opposition to it. I refer here to the experiments of Os Palmares, the Bush Negro settlements in British and Dutch Guiana, the Maroons of Jamaica, and the *'palenqueros'* of Cuba, among others. Since the slave owners and the metropolitan governments carried out repeated attempts to destroy these settlements, their inhabitants lived under the constant threat of war, and their economic integration with the outside world was correspondingly impaired. To the extent that they were compelled to maintain complete isolation, these settlements were not, typologically speaking, 'peasant communities.' But the history of such groups was one of extermination, or of transformation into peasantries. This division into three categories is makeshift, and surely does not cover many important variations. Yet it may suggest a preliminary way to fit the description of early Antillean peasantries to the particular social and economic history of that area.[22]

Plantation domination of the most fertile alluvial areas in all of those islands where it flourished has generally persisted up to the present, the major exception being Haiti, where the plantation system never recovered after 1804 and where, even today, the peasant economy dominates the rural landscape.[23] Elsewhere—and again excepting those islands where aridity, low soil fertility, or rugged topography precluded plantation spread—the plantation-yeoman balance continues to this day.

Because the plantation system has invariably received official support and protection while peasant systems have only rarely been supported or protected, the differences between these two sectors in most island societies have always been noticeable on other than purely economic grounds. Generally, transportation and communication, irrigation facilities, and many other benefits are preferentially accorded to plantation enterprises.[24] Caribbean peasantries, meanwhile, have always been regarded as the "backward" and "conservative" sectors of insular economies; because they are also labor-intensive and capital-poor sectors, backwardness and conservatism are in fact characteristic, but not always for the reasons that are conventionally adduced. The origins of Caribbean peasantries in revolution and emancipation, their confinement to the less favorable ecological zones, and their poverty have also meant that they generally perpetuate more cultural materials from the past, perhaps particularly from the African (and much less so, American Indian) past. During the transformation of the plantation sectors into modern factories in the field, particularly after 1900, the peasant sectors fell farther behind, as modern roads, communications systems, and company stores developed in the coastal zones. Thus the contrast between peasants and plantations has to some extent become even sharper in this century.

The particular "balance" of plantation and peasant sectors varies very significantly from country to country; Haiti, for instance, remains a thoroughgoing peasant country, while Puerto Rico has hardly any agricultural producers who could still qualify as "peasants."[25] What distinguishes the Caribbean area in these regards is not a specific mix of two agro-social adaptations, but the fact that nearly every island society has such a mix, engendered by the special social history of the region.

(6) Between 1838, when the British West Indian slave population was manumitted, and 1886, when Cuba freed its slaves, the Caribbean area experienced labor shortages in the sugar industry. These shortages were not absolute, but relative to the wages plantation owners were prepared to pay. In many island societies (though not in all), the solution to labor "shortage" was the massive importation of additional laborers. Though some free Africans came to the Caribbean area on contract, and many laborers were imported from Portugal, the Canary Islands, Madeira, and other parts of Europe, the main new source of labor was Asia. During one century, over 135,000 Chinese and nearly 500,000 Indians were introduced to the Caribbean area. Other laborers came from Indo-China, Java, and elsewhere; the societies most affected by these migrations were Dutch Guiana (Surinam) and British Guiana, Trinidad, Cuba, and Jamaica; but smaller migratory streams reached other Caribbean territories as well. What is more, the shifting destinies of the world sugar industry successively led to new "labor shortages" elsewhere; in thirteen years (1912–24), almost 250,000 Jamaicans and Haitians were imported to Cuba, where the burgeoning sugar industry, under North American tutelage, had created a sudden dearth of sufficiently willing workers.[26] New banana plantations in Central America, and the building of the Panama Canal, created other labor needs on the mainland, which West Indians were to fill. By 1939, Dutch Guiana had received 33,000 Javanese; and Indians shipped to the British islands had begun to drift into the French Antilles and into Dutch Guiana as well.

The effects of these quite massive movements of peoples upon

Caribbean societies and cultures are striking. To begin with, it must be noticed that each such migration meant the introduction of persons of differing culture and, frequently, physical type. Moreover, many such migrations consisted mainly or entirely of males, so that the migrants were usually able to maintain only selected portions of their ancestral cultural forms. But perhaps most important, these migrants were moving into long-established societies still divided for the most part into two major socio-cultural segments: a small class of owners, managers, and professionals, mainly European in ancestry, and a very numerous class of landless people, mainly non-European in ancestry. The bipolar structures of these societies were especially confining to the newcomers, since few opportunities for higher education, development of entrepreneurial skills, or acculturation to the metropolitan culture were available. Hence migration to such societies generally implied a confinement to long-term occupance of working-class status, with very few rewards for special effort or native excellence of any kind. Since the migrants found themselves, willy-nilly, in active competition with their predecessors for the employment opportunities available, it was almost inevitable that mutual acculturation among such groups would be minimal, and ethnic identification would become intensified to some extent. Such has turned out to be the case perhaps particularly with the "East" Indians (that is, Indians—but called "East Indians" to distinguish them from "Amerindians" and from "West Indians") in British Guiana; but similar processes are apparent in other Caribbean lands, and with other ethnic groups.[27]

Comparable migrations have occurred in other areas, such as Southeast Asia and Oceania, and with some parallel consequences. Perhaps one criterion of comparability is that of the extent to which such migrant groups have found themselves jostling others whose pedigrees were not much longer; in the Caribbean region, the lack of a native host population with a homogeneous culture developed *in situ,* has probably slowed down the process of acculturation to a marked degree. The implications of this should become clearer, after the next point is made.

(7) Four parallel historical factors of unequal weight have served both to make Caribbean societies similar and to create detailed socio-cultural differences among them. The processes of ethnic succession and aggregation have varied considerably from one island or territory to another, increasing socio-cultural diversity at a more rapid rate in some cases. At the same time, nearly every Caribbean so-

ciety has experienced one or more phase of the plantation cycle, though the intensities of plantation development and its particular local forms have varied. Another parallel historical force, also with differentiating sociological consequences, has been the varying length and character of metropolitan political control. Thus, while Haiti became independent at the start of the nineteenth century, Santo Domingo in the middle of that century, and Cuba at the start of the twentieth, Trinidad-Tobago and Jamaica were granted their political independence only a few years ago, and the remaining islands and territories are still linked in relations of dependence to their metropolises by a variety of political arrangements. Moreover, the political presence of the United States has been far more pervasive in some societies—such as Puerto Rico, Cuba, and Haiti—than in others. Finally, the cultural patterns of the controlling powers, though conveyed through a grossly uniform colonial design, have differentially affected the nature of local society in these various lands—Dutch, English, French, Spanish, North American and other imperial societies by no means have had the same impact on their respective colonies. These sources of difference, along with other considerations (such as the size, ecology, strategic location, and natural resources of each unit), have created a complex socio-cultural mosaic. It is in the light of this complexity that one seeks to assess the presence of a sense of national identity in any Caribbean society. By "national identity" is meant here a subjective and shared feeling of belonging in the nation-state and regarding it as one's own. Such a feeling in a Caribbean society cannot easily depend, it seems to the writer, on containment within a metropolitan tradition and culture, though it may of course employ that tradition itself. The inhabitants of a Caribbean society, in other words, have a national identity to the extent that they feel themselves to form a separate and independent entity.

Because Caribbean societies are immigrant societies, the ways in which immigrants could become assimilated to local life—their successes and failures in becoming Cuban, Jamaican, British Guianese, etc.—have proved immensely important in affecting the character and strength of national identity in each case. At the same time, whether some national identity had emerged early in the history of a particular island or society, before massive additional migrations occurred, very much affected subsequent processes of assimilation. The assimilative power of a national identity—that is, of a national culture and ideology—hinges upon the presence of a body of values and behaviors that can serve to unite a people in spite of social and economic differences (phrased in terms of class, color, language, and other differentiating variables). A high degree of likeness of conventional understandings, expressed both in the behavior and in the values of a people, ought to signify the existence of a more "solid" or "integrated" national identity than in cases where the degree of likeness is much lower.

But national identity is extremely difficult to specify, largely because the values it carries are fully articulated only rarely, and because different sectors of a national population often make different (though concordant) symbolic uses of the culture. From the perspective of a newly-arrived and massive migrant group, the national culture and ideology can function best as a means for acculturation and assimilation when there is some group or groups within the receiving society that can serve as their model.[28] Hence the initial emergence of a national culture and ideology in Caribbean societies seems to have depended to a great extent on the possibilities for growth of a "creole" group (i.e. of Old World origin, but born in the New World) whose primary identities were with the new society, rather than with their ancestral cultures of origin. Such creole stabilization occurred most clearly in the Hispanic Caribbean, where colonists came to stay and, early on, creole Puerto Ricans, Cubans, and Dominicans—in sharp contrast to Spanish visitors or *peninsulares*—began to create genuine insular cultures. These cultures represented the intermixing of Hispanic, Amerind and African elements in entirely new and distinctive blendings. To some extent, they were frontier cultural adaptations, and represented simplifications of the cultures of their peoples' pasts. Yet these "simple" cultures were suited to local needs, and were not merely "dilutions" or "deculturations"; descriptions of Cuban and Puerto Rican societies in the eighteenth century, for instance, make clear that the national cultures of these islands, each with its special flavor, had emerged in strength.[29]

Something of the same process occurred in the French possessions, but with some significant general differences: the Amerind cultural contribution to French Caribbean creole culture was negligible; the plantation system developed early and in strength, and confined the growth of insular cultural identity to the plantation mold for several centuries; and opportunities for consolidation of new frontier cultures in areas marginal to the plantation system—which were common in the Hispanic Caribbean—were more limited in the French possessions.

The British and Dutch Caribbean, in marked contrast to the Hispanic Caribbean, lacked all of those forces most important in the growth of new cultural identities in the islands. They lacked a missionizing religion, into which slaves could be introduced and through which they could be partly acculturated; they lacked strong overseas control over local decisions affecting the slaves, hence enabling local holders of power to exercise harsher and more arbitrary domination of slave populations, which also slowed acculturation; their planter groups were less likely to come to settle, more likely to regard their lives in the islands as temporary exiles, and—to the extent that there were illicit sexual liaisons with women of the slave group—less responsible as fathers to their bastard offspring. Intermediate social groupings hence grew more slowly in these islands, and when they did, they were not creoles of the Hispanic sort. By the middle of the nineteenth century and thereafter, as the flows of culturally and/or physically different migrants to the Guianas, Trinidad, Jamaica, Cuba, and the Dutch and French islands began once more, these societies differed markedly in their absorptive and acculturational capacities.

Put in these terms, it will be seen that a negative correlation between colonial and plantation regimes and the growth of national identities and ideologies is posited. Such a formulation is admittedly much too simplistic to explain the many variations in contemporary Carribean societal structure; but it may help to explain why cultures such as those of Cuba and Puerto Rico on the one hand, and those of societies such as Jamaica and Surinam on the other, convey such significantly different total impressions to the foreign observer.

(8) The Caribbean picture, then, is very different from that of Nigeria, say, or of India, where the problem of national integration is one of cementing culturally, linguistically, and economically diverse groupings whose existence much predates political independence, into a viable structure. The ethnic groups of the Caribbean have felt the effects of colonial control imposed from afar, implemented more or less literally by small, powerful minorities, often culturally or physically different from themselves; all have experienced the tendency to mesh ethnic and class identities in situations of constricted mobility; all have remarked the relative inaccessibility and alienness of the norms governing the behaviors of the controlling minorities. One way to put the dilemma of creating a national identity in many Caribbean

societies is to note that, in certain cases, the more one acculturates
to the governing norms of the controlling group, the more one is
alienated from local national consciousness and transformed into a
quasi-European in exile:

> For it is that mutual experience of separation from their
> original ground which makes both master and slave colonial.
> To be colonial is to be in a state of exile. And the exile is al-
> ways colonial by circumstances: a man colonised by his incestu-
> ous love of a past whose glory is not worth our total human
> suicide; colonised by a popular whoredom of talents whose
> dividends he knows he does not deserve; colonised by an ab-
> stract conscience which must identify its need with another's
> distress through a process of affection called justice; colonised
> by the barely liveable acceptance of domestic complaint; colo-
> nised, if black in skin, by the agonising assault of another's eye
> whose meanings are based on a way of seeing he vainly tries
> to alter; and ultimately colonised by some absent vision which,
> for want of another faith, he hopefully calls the Future.[30]

It was not, then, some undifferentiated, monolithic "colonialism"
that gave birth to the problem of Caribbean identity. The Caribbean
colonies were not European imperial possessions erected upon massive indigenous bases in areas of declining great literate civilizations,
as was true in India and Indonesia; they were not mere ports of trade,
like Macao or Shanghai, where ancestral cultural hinterlands could
remain surprisingly unaffected in spite of the exercise of considerable
European power; they were not "tribal" mosaics, within which European colonizers carried on their exploitation accompanied by some
curious vision of the "civilizing" function, as in the Congo, or New
Guinea; nor were they areas of intense European settlement, where
new forms of European culture provided an acculturational "anchor"
for other newcomers, as in the United States or Australia. They
were, in fact, the oldest "industrial" colonies of the West outside
Europe, manned almost entirely with introduced populations, and
fitted to European needs with peculiar intensity and pervasiveness.
It is extremely important to note that in the Caribbean region, the
plantation system was a capitalistic form of development, a fact
partly concealed by its dependence on slavery; that its organization
was highly industrial, though this is difficult to discern because

of its basis in agriculture; that the notion of "citizenship" generally did not form part of the imperial intent of the colonizers; and that *with or without political independence,* the formation of any cultural integrity always lagged behind the perpetuation of traditional bipolar social and economic structures, usually established relatively early in the period of settlement of each territory.

Hence the colonial ambiance of the Caribbean region is probably distinctive and, when all of its component features are enumerated, may even be unique in the modern world. While very significant differences mark off the Hispanic Caribbean from the rest, and while early political sovereignty (as in the case of Haiti) may qualify any generalization one sets forth about the Caribbean as a whole, there are some fundamental ways in which the region may be contrasted usefully with such areas as West Africa, Southeast Asia, or the highland portions of Latin America.

(9) The argument is advanced here that Caribbean societies are among the most westernized of the modern world. Westernization in these cases is connected with the ancience of Caribbean societies as colonies; the very early introduction of a capitalistic, agro-industrial form of economic organization; and the break-up both of aboriginal societies and of the ancestral cultures of those migrant groups who supplanted them. "Westernization" is, of course, a term with very imprecise meanings. As it is used here, it refers primarily to the effects of lengthy contact, of the principal mode of economic organization, and of the elimination of the "primitive" from the cultures of Carribean peoples. This "westernization" has been difficult to perceive, to some extent because Caribbean societies have remained preponderantly poor, rural and agrarian—characteristics commonly associated with the non-western world. But the poverty of the region did not originate in the rudimentary technical order of aboriginal peoples, coming instead as an accompaniment to highly-organized agricultural enterprise with a commercial mono-crop orientation, worked by slaves and forced laborers. While the plantation dominated the alluvial plains and intermontane valleys, reconstituted peasant adaptations usually had to take on their typical forms in the less favored agricultural zones in the absence of integrated agricultural traditions, and in the face of plantation (and often, even governmental) resistance. The ruralness of the region, then, is not the ruralness of tribal horticulturists, or of ancient agricultural civilizations, but the consequence of an industrial system that happened to be based on

agriculture rather than on factories. The Thus the Caribbean region makes clear what is well-enough known for retarded agricultural zones within more obviously western societies, as in the United States South: any absence of "westernization" is in fact the by-product of the particular sorts of western control imposed on the inhabitants.

But there is more to the argument. If one attempted to assign Caribbean communities to a continuum such as that developed by Robert Redfield,[31] with the most isolated, homogeneous, and technically retarded community at one pole, and the most urban, heterogeneous, and technically advanced community at the other, it would probably be erroneous to make a city such as Basse-Terre or Pointe à Pitre, Guadeloupe, or Kingston, Jamaica, represent the urban pole. For many Caribbean societies, the most "urban" communities are not cities but plantations.[32] The panoply of modern services—roads, communication, electricity, medical facilities, etc.—and the industrial pattern of life are likely to be as "urban" (if not more so) on a sugar plantation outside Port-au-Prince, Haiti, as they will be within the city itself. In other words, the Caribbean region has been both "urbanized" and "westernized" by its plantations, oil refineries and aluminum mines, more than by its cities; and the very lengthy history of plantation enterprise in the region has made for a very intense and particular sort of westernization.

So far as social interaction is concerned, the processes of urbanization and westernization—at least in some important regards—have hence advanced much further in the plantation countryside than elsewhere, in Caribbean societies. An extremely important aspect of these processes is the extent to which they have individualized Caribbean peoples, particularly with regard to their economic lives. The theoretical implications of this assertion are very serious, and cannot be dealt with adequately in the present paper; but at least some elucidation of this point is required. Many research workers in Caribbean societies have been struck by the relative absence of community-based activity in daily life; such institutional centers as the church, the school, the social club, and the political party office are likely to be entirely absent or at least very unimportant in rural community social life. It seems reasonable to argue that the weakness of community organization in the Caribbean area originated at least in part in plantation domination of island societies, and the long-range effects of this organizational form upon local life. Perhaps particularly important in this connection was the strength of the plantation system in maintaining the division of society into two substantially different segments, and the relative inability of the system to produce or to attract intermediate social groupings that could serve as links between the powerful and the powerless in local community life.[33] We have seen that the growth of creole culture, and the periodic absence or decline of the plantation economy, contributed to the development of national identity in some Caribbean societies, but in many others, these processes have remained retarded. On both the national and local levels, then, forced labor, forced immigration, and the plantation system exacted their toll.

The lack of a developed community life or community spirit, however, is but one aspect of the individualization of Caribbean peoples. Another aspect of such individualization seems to be revealed by the special kinship, mating and domestic forms that typify rural life. Many research workers in the Caribbean area have noted that among rural lower-class persons, consensual or common-law unions are often statistically predominant; that sexual unions are "fragile," and frequently terminated; that serial consensual unions are common; and that uninterrupted and civilly sanctioned monogamous marriages are the exception in many communities. Accompanying these mating practices are kinship systems of a noticeably shallow sort; few relatives are recognized terminologically, and kinship groups acting in concert on issues of common interest, so typical of many non-western or "underdeveloped" societies, are extremely rare, indeed. This very gross and general rendering of the Caribbean situation does serious violence to local variation in form, and evades the technical anthropological issues that are raised; but it is probably correct as far as it goes.[34]

Hence Caribbean communities are noteworthy for their relative lack of two of the most important bases of social assortment: community-based institutional nexuses (such as those provided by churches, schools, political affiliations, etc.) and kinship-group nexuses. It would be entirely incorrect to contend that such bases of group action are wholly missing or inoperative; but the contrast Caribbean rural communities provide, both to western (i.e. European and North American) rural communities on the one hand, and to non-western (i.e. Asian and African) rural communities on the other, is highly provocative. At the same time, to emphasize the feebleness of local institutions and of kinship as assortative and integrative forces in Caribbean rural life is not the same as saying that nothing serves to interrelate local people socially. Probably the main basis of social interaction among rural lower-class people—who make up the bulk of the population in Caribbean societies—is to be found in their ability to establish short- or long-term dyadic social relationships with those around them, either along lines of common interest, or to satisfy particular individual needs. In other words, rather than forming themselves into "groups" around some institution or in terms of kinship rights and obligations, these folk create radial sets of two-person linkages, and at the center of each such series is a single individual. The phrasing of this hypothesis should not be taken too literally; it would be ludicrously inaccurate to contend that there are, in effect, no social groups in Caribbean rural lower-class life other than those based on dyadic ties. But a few examples may give more substance to the argument.

The Catholic custom of selecting godparents for one's children is still socially important and enthusiastically practiced in rural communities in such societies as Puerto Rico and Haiti. This institution—*compadrazgo* in Spanish—gives some protection and security to the newborn child, and to its parents. It could easily be interpreted as a basis for the formation of a "network" or "web" of social ties, uniting many individuals in a group alliance.[35] But this network or web does not, in fact, create a social group in which each participant is actively related to every other. Rather, a father who chooses consecutive sets of *compadres* for his children stands at the center of a radial system, maintaining individual dyadic relationships with each such *compadre*. Again, the market women of Haiti enter into personalized economic relationships with series of clients (*pratik* in Haitian)—both those from whom they buy, and those to whom they sell. These relationships provide a certain amount of security of supply and of demand in situations of glut or scarcity, and are validated by small concessions in profit margin, credit extensions, and the like. Once again, one might suppose that a series of such *pratik* forms a network or web, a social group the individual members of which are drawn together out of common interest.[36] But again, the truth is that each such woman stands at the center of a radial system of clientage ties, and the system is different, consists of a different "group," for each participant in it. Hence the distinctive quality of Caribbean rural social structure may be its heavy emphasis on individual dyadic ties, as opposed to membership in social groups having some corporate institutional or kin basis.[37] Space limitations prevent the citation of other examples to reveal more fully the functioning of social relationships based on ties of this sort. Again, the point is not that group-based or community-based activity does not occur in Caribbean lower-class life, but that the patterns and traditions for such activity differ significantly from what might be expected by observers of poor, rural, agrarian communities in "underdeveloped" societies.

To carry the argument a step further, one must stress the importance of differing cultural traditions, social histories, and contemporary economic and political conditions in affecting the degree of individualism operative in specific cases. Horowitz, in comparing a number of Caribbean communities in terms of their "integration," has suggested that small-scale, private land ownership and operation makes for greater community integration, and contrasts peasant villages with rural proletarian villages in support of his position.[38] It might also be contended that societies which have enjoyed lengthy isolation and possess long-established peasantries, such as Haiti, will probably show less of such individualism than those having lengthy careers as plantation colonies; and that the highland subcultures of countries such as Cuba or Puerto Rico may exhibit less of this sort of individualism than the proletarian subcultures of their coasts. But these assertions will remain almost entirely hypothetical until additional research on such problems is carried out.[39]

Whether these concluding contentions pinpoint some unique quality of Caribbean social organization is doubtful. The view espoused here is that dyadic social forms of the *compadre* and *pratik* sort, as they operate in Caribbean social life, are an adaptive response to the intense westernization, lengthy colonial trajectory, heterogeneous populational origins, and the rather special economic history of the Caribbean area. Furthermore, it can be contended that many other societies, only recently propelled in a "western" direction, are likely to take on more and more similarity to the Caribbean mold, at least in certain sectors of their social systems. Whereas Europe and the United States have been able to develop a heavily individualistic emphasis in social relations, they have done so from the vantage-point of long-established institutional forms of group integration. It is perhaps of some interest, then, that those aspects of modern western society regarded as most depersonalizing and "anti-human"— the view of persons as things and as numbers, interchangeable, expendable, and faceless—have a very lengthy history in the Caribbean area, and developed there in a context of very imperfect transfers of European social institutions.

Notes:

1. The writer is grateful to Jacqueline Wei MINTZ and to Peter J. WILSON, who read and criticized an earlier version of the manuscript. The materials presented here will appear in more elaborate form in a book on the social history and ethnology of the Caribbean islands, now being prepared by the writer.
2. Richard KONETZKE, *El Imperio Español* (Madrid, 1946), p. 9.
3. Albert G. KELLER, *Colonization* (New York, 1908), p. 69.
4. Lewis HANKE, *Aristotle and the American Indians* (London, 1959), p. 2–3, 124.
5. Classifications of the Caribbean islands have placed them within such typological categories as "Afro-America" and "Plantation America," both of which only partially describe the island societies correctly. See John GILLIN, "Mestizo America," in Ralph LINTON (ed.), *Most of the World* (New York, 1941); Werner J. CAHNMAN, "The Mediterranean and Caribbean Regions: a Comparison in Race and Culture Contacts," *Social Forces*, 22 (1943), pp. 209–14; Gilberto FREYRE, *The Masters and the Slaves* (New York, 1946); Charles WAGLEY, "Plantation America: a Culture Sphere," *Caribbean Studies: A Symposium*, Institute of Social and Economic Research, University College of the West Indies, Jamaica, 1957, pp. 3–13; John P. AUGELLI, "The Rimland-mainland Concept of Culture Areas in Middle America," *Annals of the Association of American Geographers*, 52 (1962), pp. 119–29; Eric R. WOLF and Sidney W. MINTZ, "Haciendas and Plantations in Middle America and the Antilles," *Social and Economic Studies*, 6 (1957), pp. 380–412. See also the pathbreaking paper by Rudolph A. J. VAN LIER, "The Development and Nature of Society in the West Indies," *Mededeling No. XCII, Afdeling Culturele en Physische Anthropologie No. 37, Koninklijke Vereeniging Indisch Instituut* (Amsterdam, 1950). To lump the islands indiscriminately with "Latin America" is especially misleading; some foreign area programs for Latin America even have difficulties in deciding whether a fellowship candidate who intends to work in the non-Spanish-speaking (and particularly English-speaking) portions of the Caribbean area really should be considered a "Latin Americanist." Where French (or a creole language of predominantly French lexical origin) is spoken, a feeble argument for "Latin" culture might be made; but "Latin" is not the same as "Latin American," and no tortured logic can justify the inclusion of such societies as Jamaica or Curaçao, for example, within "Latin America." Similarly, the Cayman Islands are hardly part of either "Afro-America" or "Plantation America," and the same could be said of many other parts of the Caribbean area.
6. M. G. SMITH, *The Plural Society in the British West Indies* (Berkeley, 1965), p. 19.
7. Irving ROUSE, "The Arawak," in Julian H. STEWARD (ed.), *Handbook of South American Indians*, Bureau of American Ethnology, The Smithsonian Institution, Bulletin 143, Vol. 4 (1948), pp. 507–46; William C. STURTEVANT, "Taino Agriculture," in Johannes WILBERT (ed.), *The Evolution of Horticultural Systems in Native South America* (Caracas, 1961), pp. 69–82.
8. Douglas TAYLOR, *The Black Carib of British Honduras*, Viking Fund Publications in Anthropology, 17 (1951), pp. 15–26.

9. O. MANNONI, *Prospero and Caliban* (New York, 1956), p. 101. I am grateful to Professor Bruce Mazlish for pointing out to me the relevance of Mannoni's argument.

10. Fernando ORTIZ, *Cuban Counterpoint* (New York, 1947), pp. 254–83; Mervyn RATEKIN, "The Early Sugar Industry in Española," *Hispanic American Historical Review*, 34 (1953), pp. 1–20.

11. It has been fashionable to refer to these items as "dessert crops," but it would be difficult to find another label so ludicrously misleading as this. Coffee, tea, rum, sugar (and tobacco) were the "staple diet" of Europe's proletarians for centuries, and to call them "dessert crops" is to misread a crucial aspect of the Industrial Revolution and of European colonialism. See Sidney W. MINTZ, review of Stanley Elkins, *Slavery*, in *American Anthropologist*, 63 (1961), p. 580.

12. H. J. NIEBOER, *Slavery as an Industrial System* (The Hague, 1900), pp. 420–22; Sidney W. MINTZ, review of Stanley Elkins, *Slavery*, in *American Anthropologist*, 63 (1961), pp. 579–87.

13. José Antonio SACO, *Historia de la Esclavitud* (La Habana, 1937), t. IV, p. 63; Arthur P. NEWTON, *The European Nations in the West Indies* (London, 1933), p. 62.

14. Wilbur ZELINSKY, "The Historical Geography of the Negro Population of Latin America," *The Journal of Negro History*, 34 (1949), pp. 153–221.

15. Ramiro GUERRA, *Sugar and Society in the Caribbean* (New Haven, 1964); Herman MERIVALE, *Lectures on Colonization and Colonies* (London, 1841), pp. 75–76; Sidney W. MINTZ, "The Question of Caribbean Peasantries," *Caribbean Studies*, 1 (1961), pp. 31–34.

16. Sidney W. MINTZ, "The Caribbean," *International Encyclopedia of the Social Sciences*, in press.

17. Sidney W. MINTZ, "Historical Sociology of the Jamaican Church-founded Free Village-System," *De West-Indische Gids*, 38 (1958), pp. 46–70; Sidney W. MINTZ and Douglas HALL, "The Origins of the Jamaican Internal Marketing System," *Yale University Publications in Anthropology*, 57 (1960), pp. 3–26.

18. James G. LEYBURN, *The Haitian People* (New Haven, 1941).

19. See, for instance, Francisco PEREZ DE LA RIVA, "El Negro y la tierra, el conuco, y el palenque," *Revista Bimestre Cubana*, 58 (1946), pp. 97–132; Melville J. HERSKOVITS, *The Myth of the Negro Past* (New York, 1941), p. 94.

20. Herman MERIVALE, *op. cit.*, 1841; Eric WILLIAMS, *Capitalism and Slavery* (Chapel Hill, 1944).

21. Sidney W. MINTZ, "The Role of Forced Labour in Nineteenth-century Puerto Rico," *Caribbean Historical Review*, 2 (1951), pp. 134–41; Sidney W. MINTZ, "Labor and Sugar in Puerto Rico and Jamaica, 1800–1850," *Comparative Studies in Society and History*, 1 (1959), pp. 273–83.

22. Sidney W. MINTZ, "The Question of Caribbean Peasantries," *Caribbean Studies*, 1 (1961), pp. 31–34.

23. Paul MORAL, *Le Paysan Haïtien* (Paris, 1961).

24. Sidney W. MINTZ, "Yeoman Cultivators and Rural Proletarians in the Caribbean Regions," *C.N.R.S. International Colloquium on Agrarian Reform in Latin America*, in press.

25. *Ibid.*

26. Ramiro GUERRA, *op. cit.*, 1964.

27. Michael G. SMITH has applied Furnivall's concept of "the plural society" to the study of the Caribbean, first in his essay "A Framework for Caribbean Studies," *Caribbean Affairs* Series, Extra-Mural Department, University College of the West Indies (n.d. [1955]), and since then in numerous other publi-

cations, including his *Stratification in Grenada* (Berkeley, 1965), and *The Plural Society in the British West Indies* (Berkeley, 1965). Van Lier was the first social scientist to attempt a general theoretical statement concerning the common structural attributes of Caribbean societies (*op. cit.,* 1950); Smith has carried the theme somewhat further.

28. Ease of assimilation is also increased by a receiving society's capacity to assist newcomers in an upward economic direction—as has often happened in the United States, for instance—or by a society's possession of so pervasive an ideology that one's acceptance of the values of the culture does not depend on the achievement of social and economic mobility, as seems to be the case in the United Kingdom.

29. I have avoided dealing with the question of languages in the Caribbean area in this essay. No aboriginal languages are spoken in the islands; the few remaining Island-Carib of Dominica no longer use their ancestral tongue (which was Arawakan, not Cariban). On many islands, Creole languages are spoken by some segments of the population; in Haiti, a Creole is spoken by all classes, and only an upper-class minority employs French as well. In the French and some former French islands, Creole languages of basically French lexical character, but possessing a distinctive syntax, are employed; in the British and formerly British islands, non-standard dialects of English are used by some classes; and in Curaçao, Aruba, and Bonaire, a lexically Spanish/Portuguese Creole called Papiamento is used, as well as Dutch. Sociolinguistics will eventually have much to say concerning the national cultures of the Caribbean from the linguistic point of view, but the study of such problems in the islands is still in its infancy. It may be significant that only in the Hispanic Caribbean are Creole languages or distinctive non-standard dialects of the national languages entirely lacking. See William A. STEWART, "Creole Languages in the Caribbean," in Frank A. RICE (ed.), *Study of the Role of Second Languages* (Washington, 1962), pp. 34–53; Douglas TAYLOR, "New Languages for Old in the West Indies," *Comparative Studies in Society and History,* 3 (1961), pp. 277–88.

30. George LAMMING, *The Pleasures of Exile* (London, 1960), p. 229.

31. Robert REDFIELD, *The Folk Culture of Yucatan* (Chicago, 1941).

32. Sidney W. MINTZ, "The Folk-urban Continuum and the Rural Proletarian Community," *American Journal of Sociology,* 59 (1953), pp. 194–204.

33. Dr. Peter Wilson has suggested that I am overemphasizing the plantation system and underemphasizing the sexual code that governed its social relations in my interpretation. It is certainly correct that the relative weakness of family structure among the slaves in most plantation situations greatly hampered the development of any viable community structure—since community relationships are commonly built outward from the core of the family unit. But I believe the underlying circumstances in the Caribbean area are attributable to the plantation system itself, and the limitations it imposed upon the growth of *any* institutional nexus for community life.

34. The literature on Caribbean social and domestic organization and mating practices has grown very rapidly in the past 15 years. While any attempt to provide a complete bibliography would be unpractical in a brief paper of this sort, the following are some of the principal recent works on these subjects: Rémy BASTIEN, *La Familia Rural Haitiana* (Mexico City, 1951); Rémy BASTIEN, "Haitian Rural Family Organization," *Social and Economic Studies,* 10 (1961), pp. 478–510; Judith BLAKE, "Family Instability and Reproductive Behavior in Jamaica," Milbank Memorial Fund, *Current Research in Human Fertility,* 1955, pp. 24–41; Judith BLAKE, *Family Structure in Jamaica* (New York, 1961);

Edith CLARKE, *My Mother Who Fathered Me* (London, 1957); Yehudi A. COHEN, "Structure and Function: Family Organization and Socialization in a Jamaican Community," *American Anthropologist,* 58 (1956), pp. 664–86; Suzanne COMHAIRE-SYLVAIN, "Courtship, Marriage and Plasaj at Kenscoff, Haiti," *Social and Economic Studies,* 7 (1958), pp. 210–33; Suzanne COMHAIRE-SYLVAIN, "The Household at Kenscoff, Haiti," *Social and Economic Studies,* 10 (1961), pp. 192–222; George E. CUMPER, "The Jamaican Family: Village and Estate," *Social and Economic Studies,* 7 (1958), pp. 76–108; George E. CUMPER, "Household and Occupation in Barbados," *Social and Economic Studies,* 10 (1961), pp. 386–419; William H. DAVENPORT, *A Comparative Study of Two Jamaican Fishing Communities* (unpublished Ph.D. dissertation, Yale University, 1956); William H. DAVENPORT, "Introduction," *Caribbean Social Organization, Social and Economic Studies* (special number), 10 (1961), pp. 380–85; William H. DAVENPORT, "The Family System of Jamaica," *Social and Economic Studies,* 10 (1961), pp. 420–54; William J. GOODE, "Illegitimacy in the Caribbean Social Structure," *American Sociological Review,* 25 (1960), pp. 21–30; William J. GOODE, "Illegitimacy, Anomie, and Cultural Penetration," *American Sociological Review,* 26 (1961), pp. 910–25; Sidney GREENFIELD, *Family Organization in Barbados* (unpublished Ph.D. dissertation, Columbia University, 1958); Sidney M. GREENFIELD, "Socio-economic Factor and Family Form," *Social and Economic Studies,* 10 (1960), pp. 72–85; Fernando HENRIQUES, "West Indian Family Organization," *Caribbean Quarterly,* II (1952), pp. 16–24; Fernando HENRIQUES, *Family and Colour in Jamaica* (London, 1953); Chandra JAYAWARDENA, "Marital Stability in Two Guianese Sugar Estate Communities," *Social and Economic Studies,* 9 (1960), pp. 76–100; Chandra JAYAWARDENA, "Family Organization in Plantations in British Guiana," *International Journal of Comparative Sociology,* III (1962), pp. 43–64; Morton KLASS, *East Indians in Trinidad: A Study of Cultural Persistence* (New York and London, 1961); Miriam KREISELMAN, "The Caribbean Family: A Case Study in Martinique" (unpublished Ph.D. dissertation, Columbia University, 1958); Peter KUNSTADTER, "A Survey of the Consanguine or Matrifocal Family," *American Anthropologist,* 65 (1963), pp. 56–66; Dom Basil MATTHEWS, *Crisis of the West Indian Family* (Trinidad, 1953); Sidney W. MINTZ, "A Final Note," *Caribbean Social Organization, Social and Economic Studies* (special number), 10 (1961), pp. 528–35; Sidney W. MINTZ and William H. DAVENPORT (eds.), *Caribbean Social Organization, Social and Economic Studies* (special number), 10 (1961); John W. MURRA, Discussion of Raymond T. SMITH, "The Family in the Caribbean," *Caribbean Studies: A Symposium,* Institute of Social and Economic Research, University College of the West Indies, Jamaica, 1957, pp. 75–79; Keith F. OTTERBEIN, "The Household Composition of the Andros Islanders," *Social and Economic Studies,* 12 (1963), pp. 78–83; Keith F. OTTERBEIN, "The Courtship and Mating System of the Andros Islanders," *Social and Economic Studies,* 13 (1964), pp. 282–301; Keith F. OTTERBEIN, "Caribbean Family Organization: a Comparative Analysis," *American Anthropologist,* 67 (1965), pp. 66–79; George W. ROBERTS, "Some Aspects of Mating and Fertility in the West Indies," *Population Studies,* VIII (1955), pp. 199–227; George W. ROBERTS, *The Population of Jamaica* (Cambridge, 1957); George W. ROBERTS and Lloyd BRAITHWAITE, "Fertility Differentials by Family Type in Trinidad," *Annals of the New York Academy of Sciences,* Vol. 84 (1960), pp. 963–80; George W. ROBERTS and Lloyd BRAITHWAITE, "Mating Among East Indian and Non-Indian Women in Trinidad," *Social and Economic Studies,* 11 (1962), pp. 203, 240; George E. SIMPSON, "Sexual and Familial Institutions in Northern Haiti," *American Anthropologist,* 44 (1942), pp. 655–74; Michael G. SMITH, "Kinship and Household in Carriacon," *Social and Economic Studies*, 10 (1961), pp. 455–77; Michael G. SMITH, *West Indian Family Structure* (Seattle, Washington, 1962): Michael G. SMITH, *Kinship and Community in Carriacon* (New Haven, 1962); Raymond T. SMITH, "Aspects of Family Organization in a Coastal Negro Community in British Guiana," *Social and Economic Studies*, 1 (1953), pp. 87–111; Raymond T. SMITH, *The Negro Family in British Guiana* (London, 1957); Raymond T. SMITH, "The Family in the Caribbean," *Caribbean Studies: A Symposium*, Institute of Social and Economic Research, University College of the West Indies, Jamaica, 1957, pp. 67–75; Raymond T. SMITH, "Culture and Social Structure in the Caribbean; Some Recent Work on Family and Kinship Studies," *Comparative Studies in Society and History*, VI (1963), pp. 24–46; Raymond T. SMITH and Chandra JAYAWARDENA, "Hindu Marriage Customs in British Guiana," *Social and Economic Studies*, 7 (1958), pp. 178–94; Raymond T. SMITH and Chandra JAYAWARDENA, "Marriage and the Family Amongst East Indians in British Guiana," *Social and Economic Studies*, 8 (1959), pp. 321–76; Nancie L. SOLIEN, "Household and Family in the Caribbean," *Social and Economic Studies*, 9 (1960), pp. 101–6; Nancie L. SOLIEN (DE GONZÁLEZ), "Family Organization in Five Types of Migratory Wage Labor," *American Anthropologist*, 63 (1961), pp. 1264–80; J. Mayone STYCOS, *Family and Fertility in Puerto Rico* (New York, 1955); Lionel VALLÉE, "The Negro Family of St. Thomas: A Study of Role Differentiation" (unpublished doctoral dissertation, Cornell University, 1964); Lionel VALLÉE, "A propos de la légitimité et de la matrifocalité: tentative de ré-interprétation," *Anthropologica* (n.s.), 7 (1965), pp. 163–77; Peter J. WILSON, "The Social Structure of Providencia Isla, Colombia" (unpublished Ph.D. dissertation, Yale University, 1961); Peter J. WILSON, "Household and Family on Providencia," *Social and Economic Studies*, 10 (1961), pp. 511–27.

35. Sidney W. MINTZ and Eric R. WOLF, "An Analysis of Ritual Coparenthood (compadrazgo)," *Southwestern Journal of Anthropology*, 6 (1950), pp. 341–68.

36. Sidney W. MINTZ, "Pratik: Haitian Personal Economic Relationships," *Proceedings of the Annual Spring Meetings of the American Ethnological Society*, 1961, pp. 54–63.

37. This part of the argument owes much to discussions with my colleague, Dr. Peter Wilson.

38. Michael M. HOROWITZ, "A Typology of Rural Community Forms in the Caribbean," *Anthropological Quarterly*, 33 (1960), pp. 177–87.

39. In a provocative paper, George M. FOSTER writes: "The model suggests that where a society is conceived as a network of social relations based on dyadic contracts, in which no two people have exactly the same ties, there can be no blocks to serve as the basis for either positive or negative action." Though written to summarize the description of a Mexican highland peasant village, this phrasing well fits many Caribbean rural communities. The major difference may rest with the extent to which Caribbean peoples lacks any very elaborate constitutional and kinship forms as social-structural background against which dyadic interaction takes place—perhaps making them extreme cases of the sort the author is describing. See George M. FOSTER, "The Dyadic Contract," *American Anthropologist*, 63 (1961), pp. 1173–92, 65 (1963), pp. 1280–94.

2. The Origin of Negro Slavery

When in 1492 Columbus, representing the Spanish monarchy, discovered the New World, he set in train the long and bitter international rivalry over colonial possessions for which, after four and a half centuries, no solution has yet been found. Portugal, which had initiated the movement of international expansion, claimed the new territories on the ground that they fell within the scope of a papal bull of 1455 authorizing her to reduce to servitude all infidel peoples. The two powers, to avoid controversy, sought arbitration and, as Catholics, turned to the Pope—a natural and logical step in an age when the universal claims of the Papacy were still unchallenged by individuals and governments. After carefully sifting the rival claims, the Pope issued in 1493 a series of papal bulls which established a line of demarcation between the colonial possessions of the two states: the East went to Portugal and the West to Spain. The partition, however, failed to satisfy Portuguese aspirations and in the subsequent year the contending parties reached a more satisfactory compromise in the Treaty of Tordesillas, which rectified the papal judgment to permit Portuguese ownership of Brazil.

Neither the papal arbitration nor the formal treaty was intended to be binding on other powers, and both were in fact repudiated. Cabot's voyage to North America in 1497 was England's immediate reply to the partition. Francis I of France voiced his celebrated protest: "The sun shines for me as for others. I should very much like to see the clause in Adam's will that excludes me from a share of the world." The king of Denmark refused to accept the Pope's ruling as far as the East Indies were concerned. Sir William Cecil, the famous Elizabethan statesman, denied the Pope's right "to give and take

SOURCE: Pp. 7–29 of Eric Williams, *Capitalism and Slavery*. Chapel Hill: University of North Carolina Press, 1944. Reprinted by permission of the author and publisher.

kingdoms to whomsoever he pleased." In 1580 the English government countered with the principle of effective occupation as the de-
terminant of sovereignty.[1] Thereafter, in the parlance of the day,
there was "no peace below the line." It was a dispute, in the words
of a later governor of Barbados, as to "whether the King of England
or of France shall be monarch of the West Indies, for the King of
Spain cannot hold it long. . . ."[2] England, France, and even Holland, began to challenge the Iberian Axis and claim their place in the
sun. The Negro, too, was to have his place, though he did not ask
for it: it was the broiling sun of the sugar, tobacco and cotton plantations of the New World.

According to Adam Smith, the prosperity of a new colony depends
upon one simple economic factor—"plenty of good land."[3] The British colonial possessions up to 1776, however, can broadly be divided
into two types. The first is the self-sufficient and diversified economy
of small farmers, "mere earth-scratchers" as Gibbon Wakefield de-
risively called them,[4] living on a soil which, as Canada was described
in 1840, was "no lottery, with a few exorbitant prizes and a large
number of blanks, but a secure and certain investment."[5] The second
type is the colony which has facilities for the production of staple
articles on a large scale for an export market. In the first category
fell the Northern colonies of the American mainland; in the second,
the mainland tobacco colonies and the sugar islands of the Caribbean. In colonies of the latter type, as Merivale pointed out, land
and capital were both useless unless labor could be commanded.[6]
Labor, that is, must be constant and must work, or be made to work,
in co-operation. In such colonies the rugged individualism of the
Massachusetts farmer, practising his intensive agriculture and wring-
ing by the sweat of his brow niggardly returns from a grudging soil,
must yield to the disciplined gang of the big capitalist practising extensive agriculture and producing on a large scale. Without this compulsion, the laborer would otherwise exercise his natural inclination
to work his own land and toil on his own account. The story is frequently told of the great English capitalist, Mr. Peel, who took
£50,000 and three hundred laborers with him to the Swan River
colony in Australia. His plan was that his laborers would work for
him, as in the old country. Arrived in Australia, however, where
land was plentiful—too plentiful—the laborers preferred to work for
themselves as small proprietors, rather than under the capitalist for

wages. Australia was not England, and the capitalist was left without a servant to make his bed or fetch him water.[7]

For the Caribbean colonies the solution for this dispersion and "earth-scratching" was slavery. The lesson of the early history of Georgia is instructive. Prohibited from employing slave labor by trustees who, in some instances, themselves owned slaves in other colonies, the Georgian planters found themselves in the position, as Whitefield phrased it, of people whose legs were tied and were told to walk. So the Georgia magistrates drank toasts "to the one thing needful"—slavery—until the ban was lifted.[8] "Odious resource" though it might be, as Merivale called it,[9] slavery was an economic institution of the first importance. It had been the basis of Greek economy and had built up the Roman Empire. In modern times it provided the sugar for the tea and the coffee cups of the Western world. It produced the cotton to serve as a base for modern capitalism. It made the American South and the Caribbean islands. Seen in historical perspective, it forms a part of that general picture of the harsh treatment of the underprivileged classes, the unsympathetic poor laws and severe feudal laws, and the indifference with which the rising capitalist class was "beginning to reckon prosperity in terms of pounds sterling, and . . . becoming used to the idea of sacrificing human life to the deity of increased production."[10]

Adam Smith, the intellectual champion of the industrial middle class with its new-found doctrine of freedom, later propagated the argument that it was, in general, pride and love of power in the master that led to slavery and that, in those countries where slaves were employed, free labor would be more profitable. Universal experience demonstrated conclusively that "the work done by slaves, though it appears to cost only their maintenance, is in the end the dearest of any. A person who can acquire no property can have no other interest than to eat as much, and to labour as little as possible."[11]

Adam Smith thereby treated as an abstract proposition what is a specific question of time, place, labor and soil. The economic superiority of free hired labor over slave is obvious even to the slave owner. Slave labor is given reluctantly, it is unskilful, it lacks versatility.[12] Other things being equal, free men would be preferred. But in the early stages of colonial development, other things are not equal. When slavery is adopted, it is not adopted as the choice over free labor; there is no choice at all. The reasons for slavery, wrote Gibbon

Wakefield, "are not moral, but economical circumstances; they relate not to vice and virtue, but to production."[13] With the limited population of Europe in the sixteenth century, the free laborers necessary to cultivate the staple crops of sugar, tobacco and cotton in the New World could not have been supplied in quantities adequate to permit large-scale production. Slavery was necessary for this, and to get slaves the Europeans turned first to the aborigines and then to Africa.

Under certain circumstances slavery has some obvious advantages. In the cultivation of crops like sugar, cotton and tobacco, where the cost of production is appreciably reduced on larger units, the slave owner, with his large-scale production and his organized slave gang, can make more profitable use of the land than the small farmer or peasant proprietor. For such staple crops, the vast profits can well stand the greater expense of inefficient slave labor.[14] Where all the knowledge required is simple and a matter of routine, constancy and co-operation in labor—slavery—is essential, until, by importation of new recruits and breeding, the population has reached the point of density and the land available for appropriation has been already apportioned. When that stage is reached, and only then, the expenses of slavery, in the form of the cost and maintenance of slaves, productive and unproductive, exceed the cost of hired laborers. As Merivale wrote: "Slave labour is dearer than free *wherever abundance of free labour can be procured.*"[15]

From the standpoint of the grower, the greatest defect of slavery lies in the fact that it quickly exhausts the soil. The labor supply of low social status, docile and cheap, can be maintained in subjection only by systematic degradation and by deliberate efforts to suppress its intelligence. Rotation of crops and scientific farming are therefore alien to slave societies. As Jefferson wrote of Virginia, "we can buy an acre of new land cheaper than we can manure an old one."[16] The slave planter, in the picturesque nomenclature of the South, is a "land-killer." This serious defect of slavery can be counterbalanced and postponed for a time if fertile soil is practically unlimited. Expansion is a necessity of slave societies; the slave power requires ever fresh conquests.[17] "It is more profitable," wrote Merivale, "to cultivate a fresh soil by the dear labour of slaves, than an exhausted one by the cheap labour of freemen."[18] From Virginia and Maryland to Carolina, Georgia, Texas and the Middle West; from Barbados to Jamaica to Saint Domingue and then to Cuba; the logic was inexorable and the same. It was a relay race; the first to start passed the baton, unwillingly we may be sure, to another and then limped sadly behind.

Slavery in the Caribbean has been too narrowly identified with the Negro. A racial twist has thereby been given to what is basically an economic phenomenon. Slavery was not born of racism: rather, racism was the consequence of slavery. Unfree labor in the New World was brown, white, black, and yellow; Catholic, Protestant and pagan.

The first instance of slave trading and slave labor developed in the New World involved, racially, not the Negro but the Indian. The Indians rapidly succumbed to the excessive labor demanded of them, the insufficient diet, the white man's diseases, and their inability to adjust themselves to the new way of life. Accustomed to a life of liberty, their constitution and temperament were ill-adapted to the rigors of plantation slavery. As Fernando Ortíz writes: "To subject the Indian to the mines, to their monotonous, insane and severe labor, without tribal sense, without religious ritual, . . . was like taking away from him the meaning of his life. . . . It was to enslave not only his muscles but also his collective spirit."[19]

The visitor to Ciudad Trujillo, capital of the Dominican Republic (the present-day name of half of the island formerly called Hispaniola), will see a statue of Columbus, with the figure of an Indian woman gratefully writing (so reads the caption) the name of the Discoverer. The story is told, on the other hand, of the Indian chieftain, Hatuey, who, doomed to die for resisting the invaders, staunchly refused to accept the Christian faith as the gateway to salvation when he learned that his executioners, too, hoped to get to Heaven. It is far more probable that Hatuey, rather than the anonymous woman, represented contemporary Indian opinion of their new overlords.

England and France, in their colonies, followed the Spanish practice of enslavement of the Indians. There was one conspicuous difference—the attempts of the Spanish Crown, however ineffective, to restrict Indian slavery to those who refused to accept Christianity and to the warlike Caribs on the specious plea that they were cannibals. From the standpoint of the British government Indian slavery, unlike later Negro slavery which involved vital imperial interests, was a purely colonial matter. As Lauber writes: "The home government was interested in colonial slave conditions and legislation only when the African slave trade was involved. . . . Since it (Indian slavery) was never sufficiently extensive to interfere with Negro slavery and the slave trade, it never received any attention from the home government, and so existed as legal because never declared illegal."[20]

But Indian slavery never was extensive in the British dominions. Ballagh, writing of Virginia, says that popular sentiment had never "demanded the subjection of the Indian race *per se,* as was practically the case with the Negro in the first slave act of 1661, but only of a portion of it, and that admittedly a very small portion. . . . In the case of the Indian . . . slavery was viewed as of an occasional nature, a preventive penalty and not as a normal and permanent condition."[21] In the New England colonies Indian slavery was unprofitable, for slavery of any kind was unprofitable because it was unsuited to the diversified agriculture of these colonies. In addition the Indian slave was inefficient. The Spaniards discovered that one Negro was worth four Indians.[22] A prominent official in Hispaniola insisted in 1518 that "permission be given to bring Negroes, a race robust for labor, instead of natives, so weak that they can only be employed in tasks requiring little endurance, such as taking care of maize fields or farms."[23] The future staples of the New World, sugar and cotton, required strength which the Indian lacked, and demanded the robust "cotton nigger" as sugar's need of strong mules produced in Louisiana the epithet "sugar mules." According to Lauber, "When compared with sums paid for Negroes at the same time and place the prices of Indian slaves are found to have been considerably lower."[24]

The Indian reservoir, too, was limited, the African inexhaustible. Negroes therefore were stolen in Africa to work the lands stolen from the Indians in America. The voyages of Prince Henry the Navigator complemented those of Columbus, West African history became the complement of West Indian.

The immediate successor of the Indian, however, was not the Negro but the poor white. These white servants included a variety of types. Some were indentured servants, so called because, before departure from the homeland, they had signed a contract, indented by law, binding them to service for a stipulated time in return for their passage. Still others, known as "redemptioners," arranged with the captain of the ship to pay for their passage on arrival or within a specified time thereafter; if they did not, they were sold by the captain to the highest bidder. Others were convicts, sent out by the deliberate policy of the home government, to serve for a specified period.

This emigration was in tune with mercantilist theories of the day which strongly advocated putting the poor to industrious and useful labor and favored emigration, voluntary or involuntary, as relieving the poor rates and finding more profitable occupations abroad for idlers and vagrants at home. "Indentured servitude," writes C. M. Haar, "was called into existence by two different though complementary forces: there was both a positive attraction from the New World and a negative repulsion from the Old."[25] In a state paper delivered to James I in 1606 Bacon emphasized that by emigration England would gain "a double commodity, in the avoidance of people here, and in making use of them there."[26]

This temporary service at the outset denoted no inferiority or degradation. Many of the servants were manorial tenants fleeing from the irksome restrictions of feudalism, Irishmen seeking freedom from the oppression of landlords and bishops, Germans running away from the devastation of the Thirty Years' War. They transplanted in their hearts a burning desire for land, an ardent passion for independence. They came to the land of opportunity to be free men, their imaginations powerfully wrought upon by glowing and extravagant descriptions in the home country.[27] It was only later when, in the words of Dr. Williamson, "all ideals of a decent colonial society, of a better and greater England overseas, were swamped in the pursuit of an immediate gain,"[28] that the introduction of disreputable elements became a general feature of indentured service.

A regular traffic developed in these indentured servants. Between 1654 and 1685 ten thousand sailed from Bristol alone, chiefly for the West Indies and Virginia.[29] In 1683 white servants represented one-sixth of Virginia's population. Two-thirds of the immigrants to Pennsylvania during the eighteenth century were white servants; in four years 25,000 came to Philadelphia alone. It has been estimated that more than a quarter of a million persons were of this class during the colonial period,[30] and that they probably constituted one-half of all English immigrants, the majority going to the middle colonies.[31]

As commercial speculation entered the picture, abuses crept in. Kidnaping was encouraged to a great degree and became a regular business in such towns as London and Bristol. Adults would be plied with liquor, children enticed with sweetmeats. The kidnapers were called "spirits," defined as "one that taketh upp men and women and children and sells them on a shipp to be conveyed beyond the sea." The captain of a ship trading to Jamaica would visit the Clerkenwell House of Correction, ply with drink the girls who had been imprisoned there as disorderly, and "invite" them to go to the West Indies.[32] The temptations held out to the unwary and the credulous were so attractive that, as the mayor of Bristol complained, husbands were induced to forsake their wives, wives their husbands, and apprentices their masters, while wanted criminals found on the transport ships a refuge from the arms of the law.[33] The wave of German immigration developed the "newlander," the labor agent of those days, who traveled up and down the Rhine Valley persuading the feudal peasants to sell their belongings and emigrate to America, receiving a commission for each emigrant.[34]

Much has been written about the trickery these "newlanders" were not averse to employing.[35] But whatever the deceptions practised, it remains true, as Friedrich Kapp has written, that "the real ground for the emigration fever lay in the unhealthy political and economic conditions. . . . The misery and oppression of the conditions of the little (German) states promoted emigration much more dangerously and continuously than the worst 'newlander.' "[36]

Convicts provided another steady source of white labor. The harsh feudal laws of England recognized three hundred capital crimes. Typical hanging offences included: picking a pocket for more than a shilling; shoplifting to the value of five shillings; stealing a horse or a sheep; poaching rabbits on a gentleman's estate.[37] Offences for which the punishment prescribed by law was transportation comprised the stealing of cloth, burning stacks of corn, the maiming and killing of cattle, hindering customs officers in the execution of their duty, and corrupt legal practices.[38] Proposals made in 1664 would have banished to the colonies all vagrants, rogues and idlers, petty thieves, gipsies, and loose persons frequenting unlicensed brothels.[39] A piteous petition in 1667 prayed for transportation instead of the death sentence for a wife convicted of stealing goods valued at three shillings and four pence.[40] In 1745 transportation was the penalty for the theft of a silver spoon and a gold watch.[41] One year after the emancipation of the Negro slaves, transportation was the penalty for trade union activity. It is difficult to resist the conclusion that there was some connection between the law and the labor needs of the plantations, and the marvel is that so few people ended up in the colonies overseas.

Benjamin Franklin opposed this "dumping upon the New World of the outcasts of the Old" as the most cruel insult ever offered by one nation to another, and asked, if England was justified in sending

her convicts to the colonies, whether the latter were justified in sending to England their rattlesnakes in exchange?[42] It is not clear why
Franklin should have been so sensitive. Even if the convicts were
hardened criminals, the great increase of indentured servants and free
emigrants would have tended to render the convict influence innocu-
ous, as increasing quantities of water poured in a glass containing
poison. Without convicts the early development of the Australian
colonies in the nineteenth century would have been impossible. Only
a few of the colonists, however, were so particular. The general attitude was summed up by a contemporary: "Their labor would be more
beneficial in an infant settlement, than their vices could be pernicious."[43] There was nothing strange about this attitude. The great
problem in a new country is the problem of labor, and convict labor,
as Merivale has pointed out, was equivalent to a free present by the
government to the settlers without burdening the latter with the expense of importation.[44] The governor of Virginia in 1611 was willing
to welcome convicts reprieved from death as "a readie way to furnish
us with men and not allways with the worst kind of men."[45] The West
Indies were prepared to accept all and sundry, even the spawn of
Newgate and Bridewell, for "no goalebird [*sic*] can be so incorrigible,
but there is hope of his conformity here, as well as of his preferment,
which some have happily experimented."[46]

The political and civil disturbances in England between 1640 and
1740 augmented the supply of white servants. Political and religious
nonconformists paid for their unorthodoxy by transportation, mostly
to the sugar islands. Such was the fate of many of Cromwell's Irish
prisoners, who were sent to the West Indies.[47] So thoroughly was
this policy pursued that an active verb was added to the English language—to "barbadoes" a person.[48] Montserrat became largely an
Irish colony,[49] and the Irish brogue is still frequently heard today
in many parts of the British West Indies. The Irish, however, were
poor servants. They hated the English, were always ready to aid England's enemies, and in a revolt in the Leeward Islands in 1689[50] we
can already see signs of that burning indignation which, according to
Lecky, gave Washington some of his best soldiers.[51] The vanquished
in Cromwell's Scottish campaigns were treated like the Irish before
them, and Scotsmen came to be regarded as "the general travaillers
and soldiers in most foreign parts."[52] Religious intolerance sent more
workers to the plantations. In 1661 Quakers refusing to take the oath
for the third time were to be transported; in 1664 transportation, to

any plantation except Virginia or New England, or a fine of one hundred pounds was decreed for the third offence for persons over sixteen assembling in groups of five or more under pretence of religion.[53] Many of Monmouth's adherents were sent to Barbados, with orders to be detained as servants for ten years. The prisoners were granted in batches to favorite courtiers, who made handsome profits from the traffic in which, it is alleged, even the Queen shared.[54] A similar policy was resorted to after the Jacobite risings of the eighteenth century.

The transportation of these white servants shows in its true light the horrors of the Middle Passage—not as something unusual or inhuman but as a part of the age. The emigrants were packed like herrings. According to Mittelberger, each servant was allowed about two feet in width and six feet in length in bed.[55] The boats were small, the voyage long, the food, in the absence of refrigeration, bad, disease inevitable. A petition to Parliament in 1659 describes how seventy-two servants had been locked up below deck during the whole voyage of five and a half weeks, "amongst horses, that their souls, through heat and steam under the tropic, fainted in them."[56] Inevitably abuses crept into the system and Fearon was shocked by "the horrible picture of human suffering which this living sepulchre" of an emigrant vessel in Philadelphia afforded.[57] But conditions even for the free passengers were not much better in those days, and the comment of a Lady of Quality describing a voyage from Scotland to the West Indies on a ship full of indentured servants should banish any ideas that the horrors of the slave ship are to be accounted for by the fact that the victims were Negroes. "It is hardly possible," she writes, "to believe that human nature could be so depraved, as to treat fellow creatures in such a manner for so little gain."[58]

The transportation of servants and convicts produced a powerful vested interest in England. When the Colonial Board was created in 1661, not the least important of its duties was the control of the trade in indentured servants. In 1664 a commission was appointed, headed by the King's brother, to examine and report upon the exportation of servants. In 1670 an act prohibiting the transportation of English prisoners overseas was rejected; another bill against the stealing of children came to nothing. In the transportation of felons, a whole hierarchy, from courtly secretaries and grave judges down to the jailors and turnkeys, insisted on having a share in the spoils.[59] It has been suggested that it was humanity for his fellow countrymen and men of his own color which dictated the planter's preference for the Negro slave.[60] Of this humanity there is not a trace in the records of the time, at least as far as the plantation colonies and commercial production were concerned. Attempts to register emigrant servants and regularize the procedure of transportation—thereby giving full legal recognition to the system—were evaded. The leading merchants and public officials were all involved in the practice. The penalty for man-stealing was exposure in the pillory, but no missiles from the spectators were tolerated. Such opposition as there was came from the masses. It was enough to point a finger at a woman in the streets of London and call her a "spirit" to start a riot.

This was the situation in England when Jeffreys came to Bristol on his tour of the West to clean up the remnants of Monmouth's rebellion. Jeffreys has been handed down to posterity as a "butcher," the tyrannical deputy of an arbitrary king, and his legal visitation is recorded in the textbooks as the "Bloody Assizes." They had one redeeming feature. Jeffreys vowed that he had come to Bristol with a broom to sweep the city clean, and his wrath fell on the kidnapers who infested the highest municipal offices. The merchants and justices were in the habit of straining the law to increase the number of felons who could be transported to the sugar plantations they owned in the West Indies. They would terrify petty offenders with the prospect of hanging and then induce them to plead for transportation. Jeffreys turned upon the mayor, complete in scarlet and furs, who was about to sentence a pickpocket to transportation to Jamaica, forced him, to the great astonishment of Bristol's worthy citizens, to enter the prisoners' dock, like a common felon, to plead guilty or not guilty, and hectored him in characteristic language: "Sir, Mr. Mayor, you I meane, Kidnapper, and an old Justice of the Peace on the bench. . . . I doe not knowe him, an old knave: he goes to the taverne, and for a pint of sack he will bind people servants to the Indies at the taverne. A kidnapping knave! I will have his ears off, before I goe forth of towne. . . . Kidnapper, you, I mean, Sir. . . . If it were not in respect of the sword, which is over your head, I would send you to Newgate, you kidnapping knave. You are worse than the pick-pockett who stands there. . . . I hear the trade of kidnapping is of great request. They can discharge a felon or a traitor, provided they will go to Mr. Alderman's plantation at the West Indies." The mayor was fined one thousand pounds, but apart from the loss

of dignity and the fear aroused in their hearts, the merchants lost
nothing—their gains were left inviolate.[61]

According to one explanation, Jeffreys' insults were the result of
intoxication or insanity.[62] It is not improbable that they were connected with a complete reversal of mercantilist thought on the question of emigration, as a result of the internal development of Britain
herself. By the end of the seventeenth century the stress had shifted
from the accumulation of the precious metals as the aim of national
economic policy to the development of industry within the country,
the promotion of employment and the encouragement of exports.
The mercantilists argued that the best way to reduce costs, and
thereby compete with other countries, was to pay low wages, which a
large population tended to ensure. The fear of overpopulation at the
beginning of the seventeenth century gave way to a fear of under-
population in the middle of the same century. The essential condition
of colonization—emigration from the home country—now ran counter
to the principle that national interest demanded a large population at
home. Sir Josiah Child denied that emigration to America had weakened England, but he was forced to admit that in this view he was in a
minority of possibly one in a thousand, while he endorsed the general
opinion that "whatever tends to the depopulating of a kingdom tends
to the impoverishment of it."[63] Jeffreys' unusual humanitarianism
appears less strange and may be attributed rather to economic than
to spirituous considerations. His patrons, the Royal Family, had already given their patronage to the Royal African Company and the
Negro slave trade. For the surplus population needed to people the
colonies in the New World the British had turned to Africa, and by
1680 they already had positive evidence, in Barbados, that the African was satisfying the necessities of production better than the European.

The status of these servants became progressively worse in the
plantation colonies. Servitude, originally a free personal relation
based on voluntary contract for a definite period of service, in lieu
of transportation and maintenance, tended to pass into a property
relation which asserted a control of varying extent over the bodies and
liberties of the person during service as if he were a thing.[64] Eddis,
writing on the eve of the Revolution, found the servants groaning
"beneath a worse than Egyptian bondage."[65] In Maryland servitude
developed into an institution approaching in some respects chattel
slavery.[66] Of Pennsylvania it has been said that "no matter how

kindly they may have been treated in particular cases, or how voluntarily they may have entered into the relation, as a class and when once bound, indentured servants were temporarily chattels."[67] On the sugar plantations of Barbados the servants spent their time "grinding at the mills and attending the furnaces, or digging in this scorching island; having nothing to feed on (notwithstanding their hard labour) but potatoe roots, nor to drink, but water with such roots washed in it, besides the bread and tears of their own afflictions; being bought and sold still from one planter to another, or attached as horses and beasts for the debts of their masters, being whipt at the whipping posts (as rogues,) for their masters' pleasure, and sleeping in sties worse than hogs in England. . . ."[68] As Professor Harlow concludes, the weight of evidence proves incontestably that the conditions under which white labor was procured and utilized in Barbados were "persistently severe, occasionally dishonourable, and generally a disgrace to the English name."[69]

English officialdom, however, took the view that servitude was not too bad, and the servant in Jamaica was better off than the husbandman in England. "It is a place as grateful to you for trade as any part of the world. It is not so odious as it is represented."[70] But there was some sensitiveness on the question. The Lords of Trade and Plantations, in 1676, opposed the use of the word "servitude" as a mark of bondage and slavery, and suggested "service" instead.[71] The institution was not affected by the change. The hope has been expressed that the white servants were spared the lash so liberally bestowed upon their Negro comrades.[72] They had no such good fortune. Since they were bound for a limited period, the planter had less interest in their welfare than in that of the Negroes who were perpetual servants and therefore "The most useful appurtenances" of a plantation.[73] Eddis found the Negroes "almost in every instance, under more comfortable circumstances than the miserable European, over whom the rigid planter exercises an inflexible severity."[74] The servants were regarded by the planters as "white trash," and were bracketed with the Negroes as laborers. "Not one of these colonies ever was or ever can be brought to any considerable improvement without a supply of white servants and Negroes," declared the Council of Montserrat in 1680.[75] In a European society in which subordination was considered essential, in which Burke could speak of the working classes as "miserable sheep" and Voltaire as "canaille," and Linguet condemn the worker to the use of his physical strength alone, for "everything would be lost once he knew that he had a mind"[76]—in such a society it is unnecessary to seek for apologies for the condition of the white servant in the colonies.

Defoe bluntly stated that the white servant was a slave.[77] He was not. The servant's loss of liberty was of limited duration, the Negro was slave for life. The servant's status could not descend to his offspring, Negro children took the status of the mother. The master at no time had absolute control over the person and liberty of his servant as he had over his slave. The servant had rights, limited but recognized by law and inserted in a contract. He enjoyed, for instance, a limited right to property. In actual law the conception of the servant as a piece of property never went beyond that of personal estate and never reached the stage of a chattel or real estate. The laws in the colonies maintained this rigid distinction and visited cohabitation between the races with severe penalties. The servant could aspire, at the end of his term, to a plot of land, though, as Wertenbaker points out for Virginia, it was not a legal right,[78] and conditions varied from colony to colony. The serf in Europe could therefore hope for an early freedom in America which villenage could not afford. The freed servants became small yeomen farmers, settled in the back country, a democratic force in a society of large aristocratic plantation owners, and were the pioneers in westward expansion. That was why Jefferson in America, as Saco in Cuba, favored the introduction of European servants instead of African slaves—as tending to democracy rather than aristocracy.[79]

The institution of white servitude, however, had grave disadvantages. Postlethwayt, a rigid mercantilist, argued that white laborers in the colonies would tend to create rivalry with the mother country in manufacturing. Better black slaves on plantations than white servants in industry, which would encourage aspirations to independence.[80] The supply moreover was becoming increasingly difficult, and the need of the plantations outstripped the English convictions. In addition, merchants were involved in many vexatious and costly proceedings arising from people signifying their willingness to emigrate, accepting food and clothes in advance, and then sueing for unlawful detention.[81] Indentured servants were not forthcoming in sufficient quantities to replace those who had served their term. On the plantations, escape was easy for the white servant; less easy for the Negro who, if freed, tended, in self-defence, to stay in his locality where he was well known and less likely to be apprehended as a vagrant or runaway slave. The servant expected land at the end of his contract; the Negro, in a strange environment, conspicuous by his color and features, and ignorant of the white man's language and ways, could be kept permanently divorced from the land. Racial differences made it easier to justify and rationalize Negro slavery, to exact the mechanical obedience of a plough-ox or a cart-horse, to demand that resignation and that complete moral and intellectual subjection which alone make slave labor possible. Finally, and this was the decisive factor, the Negro slave was cheaper. The money which procured a white man's services for ten years could buy a Negro for life.[82] As the governor of Barbados stated, the Barbadian planters found by experience that "three blacks work better and cheaper than one white man."[83]

But the experience with white servitude had been invaluable. Kidnaping in Africa encountered no such difficulties as were encountered in England. Captains and ships had the experience of the one trade to guide them in the other. Bristol, the center of the servant trade, became one of the centers of the slave trade. Capital accumulated from the one financed the other. White servitude was the historic base upon which Negro slavery was constructed. The felon-drivers in the plantations became without effort slave-drivers. "In significant numbers," writes Professor Phillips, "the Africans were latecomers fitted into a system already developed."[84]

Here, then, is the origin of Negro slavery. The reason was economic, not racial; it had to do not with the color of the laborer, but the cheapness of the labor. As compared with Indian and white labor, Negro slavery was eminently superior. "In each case," writes Bassett, discussing North Carolina, "it was a survival of the fittest. Both Indian slavery and white servitude were to go down before the black man's superior endurance, docility, and labor capacity."[85] The features of the man, his hair, color and dentifrice, his "subhuman" characteristics so widely pleaded, were only the later rationalizations to justify a simple economic fact: that the colonies needed labor and resorted to Negro labor because it was cheapest and best. This was not a theory, it was a practical conclusion deduced from the personal experience of the planter. He would have gone to the moon, if necessary, for labor. Africa was nearer than the moon, nearer too than the more populous countries of India and China. But their turn was to come.

This white servitude is of cardinal importance for an understanding of the development of the New World and the Negro's place in that development. It completely explodes the old myth that the whites could not stand the strain of manual labor in the climate of the New World and that, for this reason and this reason alone, the European powers had recourse to Africans. The argument is quite untenable. A Mississippi dictum will have it that "only black men and mules can face the sun in July." But the whites faced the sun for well over a hundred years in Barbados, and the Salzburgers of Georgia indignantly denied that rice cultivation was harmful to them.[86] The Caribbean islands are well within the tropical zone, but their climate is more equable than tropical, the temperature rarely exceeds 80 degrees though it remains uniform the whole year round, and they are exposed to the gentle winds from the sea. The unbearable humidity of an August day in some parts of the United States has no equal in the islands. Moreover only the southern tip of Florida in the United States is actually tropical, yet Negro labor flourished in Virginia and Carolina. The southern parts of the United States are not hotter than South Italy or Spain, and de Tocqueville asked why the European could not work there as well as in those two countries?[87] When Whitney invented his cotton gin, it was confidently expected that cotton would be produced by free labor on small farms, and it was, in fact, so produced.[88] Where the white farmer was ousted, the enemy was not the climate but the slave plantation, and the white farmer moved westward, until the expanding plantation sent him on his wanderings again. Writing in 1857, Weston pointed out that labor in the fields of the extreme South and all the heavy outdoor work in New Orleans were performed by whites, without any ill consequences. "No part of the continental borders of the Gulf of Mexico," he wrote, "and none of the islands which separate it from the ocean, need be abandoned to the barbarism of negro slavery."[89] In our own time we who have witnessed the dispossession of Negroes by white sharecroppers in the South and the mass migration of Negroes from the South to the colder climates of Detroit, New York, Pittsburgh and other industrial centers of the North, can no longer accept the convenient rationalization that Negro labor was employed on the slave plantations because the climate was too rigorous for the constitution of the white man.

A constant and steady emigration of poor whites from Spain to Cuba, to the very end of Spanish dominion, characterized Spanish colonial policy. Fernando Ortíz has drawn a striking contrast between the role of tobacco and sugar in Cuban history. Tobacco was a free white industry intensively cultivated on small farms; sugar was a black slave industry extensively cultivated on large plantations. He further compared the free Cuban tobacco industry with its slave Virginian counterpart.[90] What determined the difference was not climate but the economic structure of the two areas. The whites could hardly have endured the tropical heat of Cuba and succumbed to the tropical heat of Barbados. In Puerto Rico, the jíbaro, the poor white peasant, is still the basic type, demonstrating, in the words of Grenfell Price, how erroneous is the belief that after three generations the white man cannot breed in the tropics.[91] Similar white communities have survived in the Caribbean, from the earliest settlements right down to our own times, in the Dutch West Indian islands of Saba and St. Martin. For some sixty years French settlers have lived in St. Thomas not only as fishermen but as agriculturalists, forming today the "largest single farming class" in the island.[92] As Dr. Price concludes: "It appears that northern whites can retain a fair standard for generations in the trade-wind tropics if the location is free from the worst forms of tropical disease, if the economic return is adequate, and if the community is prepared to undertake hard, physical work."[93] Over one hundred years ago a number of German emigrants settled in Seaford, Jamaica. They survive today, with no visible signs of deterioration, flatly contradicting the popular belief as to the possibility of survival of the northern white in the tropics.[94] Wherever, in short, tropical agriculture remained on a small farming basis, whites not only survived but prospered. Where the whites disappeared, the cause was not the climate but the supersession of the small farm by the large plantation, with its consequent demand for a large and steady supply of labor.

The climatic theory of the plantation is thus nothing but a rationalization. In an excellent essay on the subject Professor Edgar Thompson writes: "The plantation is not to be accounted for by climate. It is a political institution." It is, we might add, more: it is an economic institution. The climatic theory "is part of an ideology which rationalizes and naturalizes an existing social and economic order, and this everywhere seems to be an order in which there is a race problem."[95]

The history of Australia clinches the argument. Nearly half of this island continent lies within the tropical zone. In part of this tropical area, the state of Queensland, the chief crop is sugar. When the industry began to develop, Australia had a choice of two alternatives: black labor or white labor. The commonwealth began its sugar cultivation in the usual way—with imported black labor from the Pacific islands. Increasing demands, however, were made for a white Australia policy, and in the twentieth century non-white immigration was prohibited. It is irrelevant to consider here that as a result the cost of production of Australian sugar is prohibitive, that the industry is artificial and survives only behind the Chinese wall of Australian autarchy. Australia was willing to pay a high price in order to remain a white man's country. Our sole concern here with the question is that this price was paid from the pockets of the Australian consumer and not in the physical degeneration of the Australian worker.

Labor in the Queensland sugar industry today is wholly white. "Queensland," writes H. L. Wilkinson, "affords the only example in the world of European colonization in the tropics on an extensive scale. It does more; it shows a large European population doing the whole of the work of its civilization from the meanest service, and most exacting manual labor, to the highest form of intellectualism."[96] To such an extent has science exploded superstition that Australian scientists today argue that the only condition on which white men and women can remain healthy in the tropics is that they must engage in hard manual work. Where they have done so, as in Queensland, "the most rigorous scientific examination," according to the Australian Medical Congress in 1920, "failed to show any organic changes in white residents which enabled them to be distinguished from residents of temperate climates."[97]

Negro slavery, thus, had nothing to do with climate. Its origin can be expressed in three words: in the Caribbean, Sugar; on the mainland, Tobacco and Cotton. A change in the economic structure produced a corresponding change in the labor supply. The fundamental fact was "the creation of an inferior social and economic organization of exploiters and exploited."[98] Sugar, tobacco, and cotton required the large plantation and hordes of cheap labor, and the small farm of the ex-indentured white servant could not possibly survive. The tobacco of the small farm in Barbados was displaced by the sugar of the large plantation. The rise of the sugar industry in the Caribbean was the signal for a gigantic dispossession of the small farmer. Barbados in 1645 had 11,200 small white farmers and 5,680 Negro slaves; in 1667 there were 745 large plantation owners and 82,023 slaves. In 1645 the island had 18,300 whites fit to bear arms, in 1667 only 8,300.[99] The white farmers were squeezed out. The planters continued to offer inducements to newcomers, but they could no longer offer the main inducement, land. White servants preferred the other islands where they could hope for land, to Barbados, where they were sure there was none.[100] In desperation the planters proposed legislation which would prevent a landowner from purchasing more land, compel Negroes and servants to wear dimity manufactured in Barbados (what would English mercantilists have said?) to provide employment for the poor whites, and prevent Negroes from being taught to trade.[101] The governor of Barbados in 1695 drew a pitiful picture of these ex-servants. Without fresh meat or rum, "they are domineered over and used like dogs, and this in time will undoubtedly drive away all the commonalty of the white people." His only suggestion was to give the right to elect members of the Assembly to every white man owning two acres of land. Candidates for election would "sometimes give the poor miserable creatures a little rum and fresh provisions and such things as would be of nourishment to them," in order to get their votes—and elections were held every year.[102] It is not surprising that the exodus continued.

The poor whites began their travels, disputing their way all over the Caribbean, from Barbados to Nevis, to Antigua, and thence to Guiana and Trinidad, and ultimately Carolina. Everywhere they were pursued and dispossessed by the same inexorable economic force, sugar; and in Carolina they were safe from cotton only for a hundred years. Between 1672 and 1708 the white men in Nevis decreased by more than three-fifths, the black population more than doubled. Between 1672 and 1727 the white males of Montserrat declined by more than two-thirds, in the same period the black population increased more than eleven times.[103] "The more they buie," said the Barbadians, referring to their slaves, "the more they are able to buye, for in a yeare and a halfe they will earne with God's blessing as much as they cost."[104] King Sugar had begun his depredations, changing flourishing commonwealths of small farmers into vast sugar factories owned by a camarilla of absentee capitalist magnates and worked by a mass of alien proletarians. The plantation economy had no room for poor whites; the proprietor or overseer, a physician on the more prosperous plantations, possibly their families, these were sufficient.

"If a state," wrote Weston, "could be supposed to be made up of continuous plantations, the white race would be not merely starved out, but literally squeezed out."[105] The resident planters, apprehensive of the growing disproportion between whites and blacks, passed Deficiency Laws to compel absentees, under penalty of fines, to keep white servants. The absentees preferred to pay the fines. In the West Indies today the poor whites survive in the "Red-legs" of Barbados, pallid, weak and depraved from in-breeding, strong rum, insufficient food and abstinence from manual labor. For, as Merivale wrote, "in a country where Negro slavery prevails extensively, no white is industrious."[106]

It was the triumph, not of geographical conditions, as Harlow contends,[107] but of economic. The victims were the Negroes in Africa and the small white farmers. The increase of wealth for the few whites was as phenomenal as the increase of misery for the many blacks. The Barbados crops in 1650, over a twenty-month period, were worth over three million pounds,[108] about fifteen millions in modern money. In 1666 Barbados was computed to be seventeen times as rich as it had been before the planting of sugar. "The buildings in 1643 were mean, with things only for necessity, but in 1666, plate, jewels, and household stuff were estimated at £500,000, their buildings very fair and beautiful, and their houses like castles, their sugar houses and negroes huts show themselves from the sea like so many small towns, each defended by its castle."[109] The price of land skyrocketed. A plantation of five hundred acres which sold for £400 in 1640 fetched £7,000 for a half-share in 1648.[110] The estate of one Captain Waterman, comprising eight hundred acres, had at one time been split up among no less than forty proprietors.[111] For sugar was and is essentially a capitalist undertaking, involving not only agricultural operations but the crude stages of refining as well. A report on the French sugar islands stated that to make ten hogsheads of sugar required as great an expenditure in beasts of burden, mills and utensils as to make a hundred.[112] James Knight of Jamaica estimated that it required four hundred acres to start a sugar plantation.[113] According to Edward Long, another planter and the historian of the island, it needed £5,000 to start a small plantation of three hundred acres, producing from thirty to fifty hogsheads of sugar a year, £14,000 for a plantation of the same size producing one hundred hogsheads.[114] There could be only two classes in such a society, wealthy planters and oppressed slaves.

The moral is reinforced by a consideration of the history of Virginia, where the plantation economy was based not on sugar but on tobacco. The researches of Professor Wertenbaker have exploded the legend that Virginia from the outset was an aristocratic dominion. In the early seventeenth century about two-thirds of the landholders had neither slaves nor indentured servants. The strength of the colony lay in its numerous white yeomanry. Conditions became worse as the market for tobacco was glutted by Spanish competition and the Virginians demanded in wrath that something be done about "those petty English plantations in the savage islands in the West Indies" through which quantities of Spanish tobacco reached England.[115] None the less, though prices continued to fall, the exports of Virginia and Maryland increased more than six times between 1663 and 1699. The explanation lay in two words—Negro slavery, which cheapened the cost of production. Negro slaves, one-twentieth of the population in 1670, were one-fourth in 1730. "Slavery, from being an insignificant factor in the economic life of the colony, had become the very foundation upon which it was established." There was still room in Virginia, as there was not in Barbados, for the small farmer, but land was useless to him if he could not compete with slave labor. So the Virginian peasant, like the Barbadian, was squeezed out. "The Virginia which had formerly been so largely the land of the little farmer, had become the land of Masters and Slaves. For aught else there was no room."[116]

The whole future history of the Caribbean is nothing more than a dotting of the i's and a crossing of the t's. It happened earlier in the British and French than in the Spanish islands, where the process was delayed until the advent of the dollar diplomacy of our own time. Under American capital we have witnessed the transformation of Cuba, Puerto Rico and the Dominican Republic into huge sugar factories (though the large plantation, especially in Cuba, was not unknown under the Spanish regime), owned abroad and operated by alien labor, on the British West Indian pattern. That this process is taking place with free labor and in nominally independent areas (Puerto Rico excepted) helps us to see in its true light the first importation of Negro slave labor in the British Caribbean—a phase in the history of the plantation. In the words of Professor Phillips, the plantation system was "less dependent upon slavery than slavery was upon it. . . . The plantation system formed, so to speak, the in-

dustrial and social frame of government . . . , while slavery was a
code of written laws enacted for that purpose."[117]

Where the plantation did not develop, as in the Cuban tobacco
industry, Negro labor was rare and white labor predominated. The
liberal section of the Cuban population consistently advocated the
cessation of the Negro slave trade and the introduction of white immigrants. Saco, mouthpiece of the liberals, called for the immigration
of workers "white and free, from all parts of the world, of all races,
provided they have a white face and can do honest labor."[118] Sugar
defeated Saco. It was the sugar plantation, with its servile base, which
retarded white immigration in nineteenth century Cuba as it had
banned it in seventeenth century Barbados and eighteenth century
Saint Domingue. No sugar, no Negroes. In Puerto Rico, which developed relatively late as a genuine plantation, and where, before
the American regime, sugar never dominated the lives and thoughts
of the population as it did elsewhere, the poor white peasants survived and the Negro slaves never exceeded fourteen per cent of the
population.[119] Saco wanted to "whiten" the Cuban social structure.[120]
Negro slavery blackened that structure all over the Caribbean while
the blood of the Negro slaves reddened the Atlantic and both its
shores. Strange that an article like sugar, so sweet and necessary to
human existence, should have occasioned such crimes and blood-
shed!

After emancipation the British planters thought of white immigration, even convicts. The governor of British Guiana wrote in glowing
terms in 1845 about Portuguese immigrants from Madeira.[121] But
though the Portuguese came in large numbers, as is attested by their
strength even today in Trinidad and British Guiana, they preferred
retail trade to plantation labor. The governor of Jamaica was somewhat more cautious in his opinion of British and Irish immigrants.
Sickness had broken out, wages were too low, the experiment could
only be partially useful in making an immediate addition to the laboring population, and therefore indiscriminate importation was in-
advisable.[122] The European immigrants in St. Christopher bewailed
their fate piteously, and begged to be permitted to return home.
"There is not the slightest reluctance on our part to continue in the
island for an honest livelihood by pleasing our employers by our
industrious labour if the climate agreed with us, but unfortunately it
do not; and we are much afraid if we continue longer in this injurious

hot climate (the West Indies) death will be the consequence to the principal part of us. . . ."[123]

It was not the climate which was against the experiment. Slavery had created the pernicious tradition that manual labor was the badge of the slave and the sphere of influence of the Negro. The first thought of the Negro slave after emancipation was to desert the plantation, where he could, and set up for himself where land was available. White plantation workers could hardly have existed in a society side by side with Negro peasants. The whites would have prospered if small farms had been encouraged. But the abolition of slavery did not mean the destruction of the sugar plantation. The emancipation of the Negro and the inadequacy of the white worker put the sugar planter back to where he had been in the seventeenth century. He still needed labor. Then he had moved from Indian to white to Negro. Now, deprived of his Negro, he turned back to white and then to Indian, this time the Indian from the East. India replaced Africa; between 1833 and 1917, Trinidad imported 145,000 East Indians* and British Guiana 238,000. The pattern was the same for the other Caribbean colonies. Between 1854 and 1883 39,000 Indians were introduced into Guadeloupe; between 1853 and 1924, over 22,000 laborers from the Dutch East Indies and 34,000 from British India were carried to Dutch Guiana.[124] Cuba, faced with a shortage of Negro slaves, adopted the interesting experiment of using Negro slaves side by side with indentured Chinese coolies,[125] and after emancipation turned to the teeming thousands of Haiti and the British West Indies. Between 1913 and 1924 Cuba imported 217,000 laborers from Haiti, Jamaica and Puerto Rico.[126] What Saco wrote a hundred years ago was still true, sixty years after Cuba's abolition of slavery.

Negro slavery therefore was only a solution, in certain historical circumstances, of the Caribbean labor problem. Sugar meant labor— at times that labor has been slave, at other times nominally free; at times black, at other times white or brown or yellow. Slavery in no way implied, in any scientific sense, the inferiority of the Negro. Without it the great development of the Caribbean sugar plantations, between 1650 and 1850, would have been impossible.

* This is the correct West Indian description. It is quite incorrect to call them, as is done in this country, "Hindus." Not all East Indians are Hindus. There are many Moslems in the West Indies.

Notes:

1. C. M. Andrews, *The Colonial Period of American History* (New Haven, 1934–1938), I, 12–14, 19–20.
2. N. M. Crouse, *The French Struggle for the West Indies, 1665–1713* (New York, 1943), 7.
3. Adam Smith, *The Wealth of Nations* (Cannan edition, New York, 1937), 538. To this Smith added a political factor, "liberty to manage their own affairs in their own way."
4. H. Merivale, *Lectures on Colonization and Colonies* (Oxford, 1928 edition), 262.
5. *Ibid.*, 385. The description is Lord Sydenham's, Governor-General of Canada.
6. Merivale, *op. cit.*, 256.
7. *Ibid.*
8. R. B. Flanders, *Plantation Slavery in Georgia* (Chapel Hill, 1933), 15–16, 20.
9. Merivale, *op. cit.*, 269.
10. M. James, *Social Problems and Policy during the Puritan Revolution, 1640–1660* (London, 1930), 111.
11. Adam Smith, *op. cit.*, 365.
12. J. Cairnes, *The Slave Power* (New York, 1862), 39.
13. G. Wakefield, *A View of the Art of Colonization* (London, 1849), 323.
14. Adam Smith, *op. cit.*, 365–66.
15. Merivale, *op. cit.*, 303. Italics Merivale's.
16. M. B. Hammond, *The Cotton Industry: An Essay in American Economic History* (New York, 1897), 39.
17. Cairnes, *op. cit.*, 44; Merivale, *op. cit.*, 305–6. On soil exhaustion and the expansion of slavery in the United States see W. C. Bagley, *Soil Exhaustion and the Civil War* (Washington, D.C., 1942).
18. Merivale, *op. cit.*, 307–8.
19. J. A. Saco, *Historia de la Esclavitud de los Indios en el Nuevo Mundo* (La Habana, 1932 edition), I, Introduction, p. xxxviii. The Introduction is written by Fernando Ortíz.
20. A. W. Lauber, *Indian Slavery in Colonial Times within the Present Limits of the United States* (New York, 1913), 214–15.
21. J. C. Ballagh, *A History of Slavery in Virginia* (Baltimore, 1902), 51.
22. F. Ortíz, *Contrapunteo Cubano del Tabaco y el Azúcar* (La Habana, 1940), 353.
23. *Ibid.*, 359.
24. Lauber, *op. cit.*, 302.
25. C. M. Haar, "White Indentured Servants in Colonial New York," *Americana* (July, 1940), 371.
26. *Cambridge History of the British Empire* (Cambridge, 1929), I, 69.
27. See Andrews, *op. cit.*, I, 59; K. F. Geiser, *Redemptioners and Indentured Servants in the Colony and Commonwealth of Pennsylvania* (New Haven, 1901), 18.
28. *Cambridge History of the British Empire*, I, 236.
29. C. M. MacInnes, *Bristol, a Gateway of Empire* (Bristol, 1939), 158–59.
30. M. W. Jernegan, *Laboring and Dependent Classes in Colonial America, 1607–1783* (Chicago, 1931), 45.

31. H. E. Bolton and T. M. Marshall, *The Colonization of North America, 1492–1783* (New York, 1936), 336.

32. J. W. Bready, *England Before and After Wesley—The Evangelical Revival and Social Reform* (London, 1938), 106.

33. *Calendar of State Papers, Colonial Series,* V, 98. July 16, 1662.

34. Geiser, *op. cit.,* 18.

35. See G. Mittelberger, *Journey to Pennsylvania in the year 1750* (Philadelphia, 1898), 16; E. I. McCormac, *White Servitude in Maryland* (Baltimore, 1904), 44, 49; "Diary of John Harrower, 1773–1776," *American Historical Review* (Oct., 1900), 77.

36. E. Abbott, *Historical Aspects of the Immigration Problem, Select Documents* (Chicago, 1926), 12 n.

37. Bready, *op. cit.,* 127.

38. L. F. Stock (ed.), *Proceedings and Debates in the British Parliament respecting North America* (Washington, D.C., 1924–1941), I, 353 n, 355; III, 437 n, 494.

39. *Calendar of State Papers, Colonial Series,* V, 221.

40. *Ibid.,* V, 463. April, 1667(?).

41. Stock, *op. cit.,* V, 229 n.

42. Jernegan, *op. cit.,* 49.

43. J. D. Lang, *Transportation and Colonization* (London, 1837), 10.

44. Merivale, *op. cit.,* 125.

45. J. D. Butler, "British Convicts Shipped to American Colonies," *American Historical Review* (Oct., 1896), 25.

46. J. C. Jeaffreson (ed.), *A Young Squire of the Seventeenth Century. From the Papers (A.D. 1676–1686) of Christopher Jeaffreson* (London, 1878), I, 258. Jeaffreson to Poyntz, May 6, 1681.

47. For Cromwell's own assurance for this, see Stock, *op. cit.,* I, 211. Cromwell to Speaker Lenthall, Sept. 17, 1649.

48. V. T. Harlow, *A History of Barbados, 1625–1685* (Oxford, 1926), 295.

49. J. A. Williamson, *The Caribbee Islands Under the Proprietary Patents* (Oxford, 1926), 95.

50. *Calendar of State Papers, Colonial Series,* XIII, 65. Joseph Crispe to Col. Bayer, June 10, 1689, from St. Christopher: "Besides the French we have a still worse enemy in the Irish Catholics." In Montserrat the Irish, three to every one of the English, threatened to turn over the island to the French (*Ibid.,* 73. June 27, 1689). Governor Codrington from Antigua preferred to trust the defence of Montserrat to the few English and their slaves rather than rely on the "doubtful fidelity" of the Irish (*Ibid.,* 112–13. July 31, 1689). He disarmed the Irish in Nevis and sent them to Jamaica (*Ibid.,* 123. Aug. 15, 1689).

51. H. J. Ford, *The Scotch-Irish in America* (New York, 1941), 208.

52. *Calendar of State Papers, Colonial Series,* V, 495. Petition of Barbados, Sept. 5, 1667.

53. Stock, *op. cit.,* I, 288 n, 321 n, 327.

54. Harlow, *op. cit.,* 297–98.

55. Mittelberger, *op. cit.,* 19.

56. Stock, *op. cit.,* I, 249. March 25, 1659.

57. Geiser, *op. cit.,* 57.

58. E. W. Andrews (ed.), *Journal of a Lady of Quality; Being the Narrative of a Journey from Scotland to the West Indies, North Carolina and Portugal, in the years 1774–1776* (New Haven, 1923), 33.

59. Jeaffreson, *op. cit.,* II, 4.

60. J. A. Doyle, *English Colonies in America—Virginia, Maryland, and the Carolinas* (New York, 1889), 387.

61. MacInnes, *op. cit.*, 164–65; S. Seyer, *Memoirs Historical and Topographical of Bristol and its Neighbourhood* (Bristol, 1821–1823), II, 531; R. North, *The Life of the Rt. Hon. Francis North, Baron Guildford* (London, 1826), II, 24–27.

62. Seyer, *op. cit.*, II, 532.

63. *Cambridge History of the British Empire*, I, 563–65.

64. Ballagh, *op. cit.*, 42.

65. McCormac, *op. cit.*, 75.

66. *Ibid.*, 111.

67. C. A. Herrick, *White Servitude in Pennsylvania* (Philadelphia, 1926), 3.

68. Stock, *op. cit.*, I, 249.

69. Harlow, *op. cit.*, 306.

70. Stock, *op. cit.*, I, 250. March 25, 1659.

71. *Calendar of State Papers, Colonial Series*, IX, 394. May 30, 1676.

72. Sir W. Besant, *London in the Eighteenth Century* (London, 1902).

73. *Calendar of State Papers, Colonial Series*, V, 229. Report of Committee of Council for Foreign Plantations, Aug., 1664(?).

74. G. S. Callender, *Selections from the Economic History of the United States, 1765–1860* (New York, 1909), 48.

75. *Calendar of State Papers, Colonial Series*, X, 574. July 13, 1680.

76. H. J. Laski, *The Rise of European Liberalism* (London, 1936), 199, 215, 221.

77. Daniel Defoe, *Moll Flanders* (Abbey Classics edition, London, n.d.), 71.

78. T. J. Wertenbaker, *The Planters of Colonial Virginia* (Princeton, 1922), 61.

79. Herrick, *op. cit.*, 278.

80. *Ibid.*, 12.

81. *Calendar of State Papers, Colonial Series*, V, 220. Petition of Merchants, Planters and Masters of Ships trading to the Plantations, July 12, 1664.

82. Harlow, *op. cit.*, 307.

83. *Calendar of State Papers, Colonial Series*, IX, 445. Aug. 15, 1676.

84. U. B. Phillips, *Life and Labor in the Old South* (Boston, 1929), 25.

85. J. S. Bassett, *Slavery and Servitude in the Colony of North Carolina* (Baltimore, 1896), 77. On the docility of the Negro slave, see *infra*, pp. 201–8.

86. Flanders, *op. cit.*, 14.

87. Cairnes, *op. cit.*, 35 n.

88. Callender, *op. cit.*, 764 n.

89. Cairnes, *op. cit.*, 36.

90. Ortíz, *op. cit.*, 6, 84.

91. A. G. Price, *White Settlers in the Tropics* (New York, 1939), 83.

92. *Ibid.*, 83, 95.

93. *Ibid.*, 92.

94. *Ibid.*, 94.

95. E. T. Thompson, "The Climatic Theory of the Plantation," *Agricultural History* (Jan., 1941), 60.

96. H. L. Wilkinson, *The World's Population Problems and a White Australia* (London, 1930), 250.

97. *Ibid.*, 251.

98. R. Guerra, *Azúcar y Población en Las Antillas* (La Habana, 1935), 20.

99. Williamson, *op. cit.*, 157–58.

100. *Calendar of State Papers, Colonial Series*, X, 503. Governor Atkins, March 26, 1680.

101. *Ibid.*, VII, 141. Sir Peter Colleton to Governor Codrington, Dec. 14, 1670. A similar suggestion came from Jamaica in 1686. Permission was requested for the introduction of cotton manufacture, to provide employment for the poor whites. The reply of the British Customs authorities was that "the more such manufactures are encouraged in the Colonies the less they will be dependent on England." F. Cundall, *The Governors of Jamaica in the Seventeenth Century* (London, 1936), 102–3.

102. *Calendar of State Papers, Colonial Series*, XIV, 446–47. Governor Russell, March 23, 1695.

103. C. S. S. Higham, *The Development of the Leeward Islands under the Restoration, 1660–1688* (Cambridge, 1921), 145.

104. Harlow, *op. cit.*, 44.

105. Callender, *op. cit.*, 762.

106. Merivale, *op. cit.*, 62.

107. Harlow, *op. cit.*, 293.

108. *Ibid.*, 41.

109. *Calendar of State Papers, Colonial Series*, V, 529. "Some Observations on the Island of Barbadoes," 1667.

110. Harlow, *op. cit.*, 41.

111. *Ibid.*, 43.

112. Merivale, *op. cit.*, 81.

113. F. W. Pitman, "The Settlement and Financing of British West India Plantations in the Eighteenth Century," in *Essays in Colonial History by Students of C. M. Andrews* (New Haven, 1931), 267.

114. *Ibid.*, 267–69.

115. *Calendar of State Papers, Colonial Series*, I, 79. Governor Sir Francis Wyatt and Council of Virginia, April 6, 1626.

116. Wertenbaker, *op. cit.*, 59, 115, 122–23, 131, 151.

117. R. B. Vance, *Human Factors in Cotton Culture: A Study in the Social Geography of the American South* (Chapel Hill, 1929), 36.

118. J. A. Saco, *Historia de la Esclavitud de la Raza Africana en el Nuevo Mundo y en especial en los Países America-Hispanos* (La Habana, 1938), I, Introduction, p. xxviii. The Introduction is by Fernando Ortíz.

119. T. Blanco, "El Prejuicio Racial en Puerto Rico," *Estudios Afrocubanos*, II (1938), 26.

120. Saco, *Historia de la Esclavitud de la Raza Africana* . . . Introduction, p. xxx.

121. *Immigration of Labourers into the West Indian Colonies and the Mauritius*, Part II, *Parliamentary Papers*, Aug. 26, 1846, 60. Henry Light to Lord Stanley, Sept. 17, 1845: "As labourers they are invaluable, as citizens they are amongst the best, and rarely are brought before the courts of justice or the police."

122. *Papers Relative to the West Indies, 1841–1842, Jamaica-Barbados*, 18. C. T. Metcalfe to Lord John Russell, Oct. 27, 1841.

123. *Immigration of Labourers into the West Indian Colonies* . . . , 111. William Reynolds to C. A. Fitzroy, August 20, 1845.

124. These figures are taken from tables in I. Ferenczi, *International Migrations* (New York, 1929), I, 506–9, 516–18, 520, 534, 537.

125. The following table illustrates the use of Chinese labor on Cuban sugar plantations in 1857:

Plantation	Negroes	Chinese
Flor de Cuba	409	170
San Martín	452	125
El Progreso	550	40
Armonía	330	20
Santa Rosa	300	30
San Rafael	260	20
Santa Susana	632	200

The last plantation was truly cosmopolitan; the slave gang included 34 natives of Yucatan. These figures are taken from J. G. Cantero, *Los Ingenios de la Isla de Cuba* (La Habana, 1857). The book is not paged. There was some opposition to this Chinese labor, on the ground that it increased the heterogeneity of the population. "And what shall we lose thereby?" was the retort. *Anales de la Real Junta de Fomento y Sociedad Económica de La Habana* (La Habana, 1851), 187.

126. Ferenczi, *op. cit.*, I, 527.

B.
Language

Although European languages are official in all Caribbean countries, in a number of them the majority of the people speak them only slightly or at best secondarily, and prefer to communicate in local languages which have been called "creole" or "patois." While these originally may have been pidgins, facilitating contact between members of different speech communities, they have for several hundred years been the first and often the only language of the rural black people in Haiti, the French Antilles, Curaçao, Surinam, the Windward Islands of Dominica, St. Lucia, and Grenada, and in some of the other islands. These languages have attracted the interest of linguists because they seem to combine a European-derived lexicon with an African-derived syntax. Some of the problems which Douglas Taylor discusses in the following paper are more technically treated in his "Language Contacts in the West Indies," *Word* 12:399–414, 1956. Different approaches were taken by R. A. Hall, "Creolized Languages and 'Genetic Relationships,'" *Word* 14:367–73, 1958, and by Uriel Weinreich, "On the Compatibility of Genetic Relationship and Convergent Development," *Ibid.:* 374–79. Taylor replies to his critics in "The Origin of West Indian Creole Languages: Evidence From Grammatical Categories," *American Anthropologist* 65:800–14, 1963.

DOUGLAS TAYLOR

3. New Languages for Old in the West Indies

It is usually assumed that most if not all "natural" languages spoken today are the products of slow but continual change, obsolescence, innovation and borrowing; and that divergence among members of a clearly related group, like the Romance languages, can be fully accounted for by the gradual fragmentation of what once was, to all intents and purposes, a single linguistic community. This assumption, though well founded, is rarely susceptible of positive proof, even in the comparatively rare case of languages with a long written record; for writing is always more conservative than speech, and especially so at times and places in which this skill is acquired only by a small minority; so that the presumably gradual transition from late Latin to, let us say, Old French is largely undocumented. On the other hand we know of some languages, like Sabir or Lingua Franca (once used in the Levant), that began—and often ended—as nobody's mother tongue, but serve or served to facilitate communication between members of different speech communities who became—often rather suddenly as the result of some historical accident—interdependent. Such most likely had been (but no longer was) the so-called "men's speech" of the 17th-century Island Carib, which largely consisted of Karina (Cariban family) lexemes articulated by means of phonemes, inflexion and syntax belonging to the indigenous Arawakan language; for if it be true, as tradition had it, that the Carib conquerors of the Lesser Antilles killed all the indigenous males and took the women to wife, some sort of linguistic compromise must have been an urgent necessity.[1] In what follows I shall attempt to discuss the occurrence and development of other such languages in the West Indies subsequent to the introduction of Negro slaves, and

SOURCE: Reprinted from *Comparative Studies in Society and History*, Vol. 3 (1960):277–88, by permission of the author and the Cambridge University Press.

the part that they play or played in the life of the communities concerned.

In Guiana, the Caribbean and Louisiana various new languages such as Sranan (Negro English), Saramakkan, Papiamentu, Negro Dutch and several forms of French Creole have emerged within the past three hundred years, and, for the most part, prospered. At first "pidgins" or jargons employed only between African and European, and between Africans of different provenance, all of them later became "creolized"—adopted, that is to say, as the first and in general only language of whole communities; and with the exception of Negro Dutch (formerly spoken in the Virgin Islands, but probably now extinct), they remain that to this day. These languages are peculiar in combining rather similar grammatical structures of a non-Indo-European and seemingly West African type with vocabularies that are preponderantly of English, Portuguese or Spanish, Dutch and French ancestries respectively. By far the most widespread and diversified of them is French Creole, whose four main dialects (excluding those of Mauritius and Réunion in the Indian Ocean), each containing an indeterminate number of mutually intelligible subdialects, are spoken in French Guiana, certain of the Lesser Antilles (Trinidad, Grenada, St. Lucia, Martinique, Dominica, Guadeloupe and dependencies and St. Thomas), Haiti and Louisiana. Sranan is spoken mainly in Surinam, as the name implies; but as a second or trade language it is also used to some extent, by Amerindians and others, in the neighbouring French and British territories to the east and west. Saramakkan is spoken only by the Bush Negroes on the upper reaches of the Surinam or "Saramakka" river. It has not yet been thoroughly investigated; but appears to be a tone language containing Portuguese, English and African elements. Papiamentu is confined to the three Dutch islands of Curaçao, Aruba and Bonaire. It is usually assumed to be the only Spanish Creole in the Americas; but Tomás Navarro and, more recently, H. L. A. van Wijk have shown that the many Portuguese items in its lexicon are basic, and that its hispanicization must have taken place at a time long after the Spaniards and other Spanish speakers had left Curaçao for the mainland.[2]

A *pidgin* may then be defined as a linguistic compromise that is nobody's mother tongue; and a *creole* as a mother tongue that began in a pidgin, and has not come to be identified with any previously existing traditional language (see now footnote 14). I think it was

Voltaire who said that while a foreign language may be learnt in two or three years, it takes half a lifetime to master one's own; and in the same sense it seems obvious that the process of creolization presupposes and entails considerable enrichment and regulation of the original pidgin, whose formation for the requirements of a rapidly learnt second language necessarily involved a notable reduction of two or more speech communities' means of expression and communication. All creoles are therefore "regular" languages in that each has its own pattern of distinctive units of sound, its own grammatical signs and conventions, and a vocabulary adequate for the cultural demands of its native speakers. Moreover, such languages evolve, once creolization has taken place, in much the same ways as do other idioms, and in accordance with their native speakers' changing needs of communication. But they differ from languages with a longer tradition in having basic grammars whose source cannot clearly be identified with that of their basic vocabularies, and in being comparatively free from such fossilized historical débris as result in our own irregular noun plurals and verbal conjugations.

Of these creolized languages' short history little, unfortunately, is known; for few writers of the past took any serious interest in them, and the slaves themselves were, almost without exception, illiterate. However, we know that the first French settlers and missionaries employed a sort of *petit-nègre* in their attempt to make themselves understood by the slaves; for toward the middle of the 17th century, Father Chevillard wrote: "Les nègres . . . se familiarisent rapidement avec le langage de l'européen, langage volontairement corrompu pour faciliter sa compréhension"; and at about the same time Father Pelleprat remarked: "Nous nous accomodons à leur façon de parler qui est ordinairement par l'infinitif du verbe, comme par exemple: 'moi prier Dieu, moi aller à l'Eglise, moi point manger'; et y ajoutant un mot qui marque le temps à venir ou le passé, ils disent: demain moi manger, hier moi prier, et ainsi de suite." Moreover, both these priests have left us samples of the language in which religious instruction was given to slaves in their time.[3] So, from Chevillard:

> Toy sçavoir qu'il y a un Dieu: Luy grand Capitou, luy sçavoir tout faire sans autre l'aider: luy donner à tous patates; luy mouche manigat pour tout faire, non point comme luy. Vouloir faire maison, non faire comme homme, car toy aller chercher

hache pour bois, puis couper roseaux, prendre mahoc et lianes
et ainsi pequins faire case. Or Dieu mouche manigat, luy dit en
son esprit, moy vouloir homme, luy preste miré homme. Enfin
luy envoyé meschant en bas en enfer, au feu avec maboya et
autres sauvages qui n'ont vouloir vivre en bons chrétiens. Mais
tous bons chrétiens, luy bons pour mettre en son paradis où se
trouve tout contentement, nul mal, nul travail, et nulle servitude
ou esclavage, mais une entière joye et parfaite liberté.

And from Pelleprat:

Seigneur, toi bien savé que mon frère lui point mentir, point
lui jurer, point dérober, point lui méchant. Pourquoi toi le
voulé faire mourir!
Mon frère, toi te confesser, toi dire comme moi: Seigneur, si
moi mentir, moi demander à toi pardon; si moi dérober, si
moi jurer, si moi faire autre mal à toi, moi bien faché, moi demander pardon.

But this is something very different—apart from a couple of resemblances such as the absence of a copula (*luy grand Capitou*) and the
employment of *moi, lui,* etc. as subject (*moi demander, lui envoyé*)
—from the language used a hundred years later as portrayed in the
first French Creole texts, and which differs little from that current at
the present time.[4] So, for example, no French Creole employs the
objective personal pronouns *me, te, le* or *se* (*toi te confesser, toi le
voulé, où se trouve*), the auxiliary verb *avoir* (*qui n'ont vouloir*),
or the conjunction *que* (*toi bien savé que*); while Chevillard's *toi
savoir* and *moi vouloir* vs. Pelleprat's *toi bien savé* and *toi le voulé*
suggest a jargon in the making rather than one already established.
    Then was this incipient jargon a model, as is usually assumed,
imitated and modified by the African slaves; or itself a kind of imitation of these Africans' speech, as we are told ("We adapt ourselves
to their manner of speaking . . .")? Most probably both. Surely
Fr. Pelleprat was not claiming, for himself and others who had never
before come into contact with Negroes, a familiarity with West African languages. But the first French settlers and missionaries got their
slaves from the Spaniards and, more especially, from the Dutch; who
in their turn got them from the Portuguese settlements or "factories"
on the west coast of Africa, where a Portuguese pidgin had been

in use since the 15th century. And as Van Wijk has shown, slaves bought or captured in the interior usually remained in these "collecting centres" quite long enough to learn the pidgin, which served henceforth not only in their dealings with Europeans of whatever nationality engaged in the slave-trade, but also as a lingua franca between fellow slaves whose mother tongues were not mutually intelligible. It was, I suggest, this "façon de parler" to which the first French settlers and missionaries sought to adapt themselves, and whose vocabulary they sought to gallicize.

There can be no doubt that they succeeded in the latter part of this enterprise; for few words of Ibero-Romance ancestry are to be found in modern French Creole, except in the Guianese and Haitian dialects, where they are a little more common (*cf.* Guianese *briga* "to fight" and *fika* "to be in a situation or state", from Ptg. *brigar, ficar*; and Haitian *kachimbo* "pipe" and *mantèg* "lard", from Ptg. *cachimbo, manteiga*—or Sp. *manteca*). However, Portuguese *pai, compai* and *mãe,* which have been naturalized in the "normal" Spanish dialects of Trinidad, Puerto Rico and probably other of the Spanish-speaking Antilles,[5] are also employed—though only as friendly or endearing terms of address, without any reference to kinship—in French Creole of the Lesser Antilles, whose *iche* (French spelling) "son(s), offspring" apparently derives from an early dialectal form (with hushing sibilant but no *f* or aspirate *h*) of Sp. *hijo, -ja* or Ptg. *filho, -lha*. And had the slaves arrived in the French islands speaking nothing but their native African languages, it is most unlikely that Frenchmen there should have taught them words like: *capitou* (cf. Ptg. *capitão*) "chieftain, leader", *pequins* (cf. Ptg. *pequeno*) "little ones", *miré* (cf. Ptg. & Sp. *mirar*) "look at" and *mouche* (cf. Sp. *mucho,* Ptg. *muito*) "very, much, many".[6]

The importance of the Portuguese elements in Papiamentu, beginning with the name of the language itself (*papia* "speak" < Ptg. *papear* "chat" + nominalizing *-mentu,* a fully productive suffix, < Ptg. *-mento*), has never been denied; but their presence has usually been attributed to the Sephardic Jews who sought refuge in Curaçao in the second half of the 17th century and later. Van Wijk argues that these refugees were not at that time either numerous or powerful enough to have exerted such an influence; although they most probably helped to de-africanize the Portuguese pidgin spoken by the incoming slaves. Moreover, he has found in the vocabulary of Curaçao: "more than 70 Portuguese words that occur also in the

Negro English of Surinam [Sranan] in the same characteristic shapes
as in Papiamentu". This is not the place to argue either for or against
such a hypothesis; but if a Portuguese pidgin or creole spoken in a
Dutch island could be hispanicized to the extent that is seen in modern Papiamentu by visiting missionaries and others coming from the
adjacent mainland of South America, it would not be surprising if an
originally Afro-Portuguese pidgin left still fewer remnants of its vocabulary in creolized languages that emerged among slaves belonging
to English and French masters. Finally we may mention, as not irrelevant to our discussion, Whinnom's opinion that the Spanish Creole dialects now spoken in the Philippine Islands evolved from the
imitation, by Spanish soldiers, of a Portuguese pidgin that was widely
used as a trade language in the Eastern Seas during the 16th, 17th and
early 18th centuries, not only by the Portuguese themselves, but also
by the Dutch and English.[7]

The West Indian slave-owners' precautionary policy of mixing together Africans belonging to different tribes must have led to general
use of the local pidgin, and to its creolization in the second or third
generation born in the American colonies. But the importation of
African slaves continued, with some interruptions, throughout the
18th and early 19th centuries; and in Martinique, where 5,435 individuals of African birth were reported to be living as recently as
1905, it was renewed between 1857 and 1860 under the new label
of "indentured labour (engagés)".[8] It therefore seems justified to
say that these new West Indian languages have been throughout
most of their history the mother tongue of some, but a second language for other of their speakers.

Understandably, their importance has varied enormously with
time and place. Father Labat, who was in the islands (principally
Martinique) between 1693 and 1705, appears not to have considered
them worthy of mention; though he discusses the speech of the Island Carib, and tells us that he learnt the African language of his
"Arada" slaves. A hundred years later ("Paris, 17 Brimer, an 10 Ré-
piblique francé, yon et indivisible"), Bonaparte and Leclerc considered French Creole important enough to have their proclamation
"a tout zabitans Saint-Domingue" translated into it; and during the
second half of the 19th century, the indigenous (Island-Carib) Indians of Dominica gradually gave up their own language for it. At
the present time, French Creole is the mother tongue of more than
95% of the population in Dominica and St. Lucia (not more than a

third of whom can express themselves in English) and Haiti (where less than a third can express themselves in French); while it is rapidly dying out in Trinidad and Grenada, where it is probably not understood by more than 10% of the inhabitants. It is probably safe to say that in French Guiana and the French islands every native inhabitant (excepting perhaps some Amerindians in the former) is now more or less bilingual in French and Creole; a circumstance which tends to bring their dialects of Creole much closer to 'normal' French than they were even fifty years ago. And owing to the prestige of Spanish, something of the same sort appears to be happening—or to have already happened—to Papiamentu; which is, according to Van Wijk:

> casi el único idioma criollo—más exactamente idioma semi-criollo—que tiene además valor cultural, pues en él se escriben no sólo diarios y revistas, sino también novelas, cuentos y hasta poesía. Lamentable es que el papiamentu carezca de una ortografía uniforme, ya que las distintas ortografías basadas en argumentos etimológicos vacilan entre la transcripción española y la holandesa de los sonidos.

The first part of this statement, if not altogether exact, shows that the social aspects of the several creoles are very different. Some stories and more poems have been written and published, during the past two hundred years, in various dialects of French Creole and in Sranan; though the earlier writings were not—understandably, in view of the slaves' enforced illiteracy—produced by what we should call native speakers. They employ, for the most part, an inconsistent spelling that leans heavily on the conventional orthography of one or another "national" language. This also is understandable; for only in Haiti and within the past decade, so far as I know, have the schools begun to teach reading and writing in a creole mother tongue; and even there the standardized orthography based on a phonological analysis of Haitian Creole has had to be abandoned under pressure from people who think that their language should at least "look like" French!

But native speakers of French Creole (of whatever dialect) who also possess a modicum of French or English have come to regard the use of their mother tongue in much the same light as speakers of standard French do the use of *tu* instead of *vous*—with this difference, that the former will often change from the "intimate" to the "polite" form with the same interlocutor when coming within earshot of "respectable" strangers. Some years ago, in Dominica, a very good variety show, composed and performed in Creole by local talent, was rather widely deplored as being "unprogressive". I myself have served, by request, as interpreter between a Dominican and a Martiniquais whose mother tongues, always employed in the family circle, differed less than those of a Bostonian and a Baltimorean; but who, being hitherto unacquainted, both felt it incumbent on them to converse only in their respective "national" languages. And from Guadeloupe to St. Lucia, if not elsewhere, many people who themselves habitually speak Creole are wont to chide any children whom they hear using it in the street.

The antecedents for this attitude are sufficiently clear. The various pidgins arose, persisted and became creolized under conditions in which social status was determined mainly by racial identity; the ratio of "white" to "black" was constantly decreasing;[9] and the former, once they themselves had become bilingual, actively discouraged the latter from learning the "masters' language". The abolition of slavery brought no immediate change in these conditions; but with the decline of the old plantation system (Fr. *habitation*) it soon became evident that these coloured populations would be a burden on the mother country unless and until they became literate and learnt the national language. It was hoped to accomplish this end by the introduction, several generations ago, of public schools (whose numbers and equipment are still inadequate). But the attainment of bilingualism in a community where there is little opportunity of practising the second language in contacts with its native speakers is always and everywhere a difficult task; and it has been rendered particularly arduous in English islands like St. Lucia and Dominica, where children have been—and are—taught that their mother tongue is "only a monkey language"—or no language at all, that it "has no grammar", cannot be written and is a mark of social inferiority.[10] Poorly trained and poorly paid local teachers might be excused for spreading such false doctrine; but as recently as 1945 the Educational Adviser to the Comptroller for Development and Welfare in the West Indies published a report in which he stated his opinion that: "The aim should be not to make the children bilingual, but ultimately to make English the mother tongue." I cannot conceive how a shift of language without an interim period of bilingualism might be achieved—except by removing all infants from their homes and parents, and taking full charge of them until the age of puberty! Moreover, most educationalists are now agreed that children who learn to read and write first in their mother tongue subsequently make better progress in the second language than those others whose schooling is in the latter from the start.[11]

Some readers may ask why it is that no pidgin or creole is current in the Spanish-speaking Antilles, or in English islands such as Jamaica, Barbados and St. Vincent. So far as the former territories are concerned, R. W. Thompson has answered the question as follows:[12]

> In addition, a more serious effort was made by the Spaniards and Portuguese to plant their New World territories with peasants of European stock. As a result, their subjects of African descent did not greatly overwhelm in numbers those who spoke a European language in conformity with native usage, as happened in the English, French and Dutch colonies of the West Indies. Today there is no Spanish *creole* dialect in the New World, where the negroes of Cuba, of the Dominican Republic and of Porto Rico pronounce the voiced dental fricative ð every bit as well as their white or mulatto compatriots.

On the other hand, Cromwell did make a serious effort to provide the English planters (no island south of Montserrat other than Barbados was at that time in English hands) with the enforced labour of as many "convicts, vagabonds and light women" of British stock as he could lay his hands on; the last two categories designating, in the main, Catholic priests, boys and girls. "In four years", we are told, "sixty-four hundred white slaves rounded up in Ireland and Scotland were sent out to the West Indies. The population of Jamaica seven years after its conquest was fifteen thousand."[13] But though black slaves proved more efficient than white, and gradually replaced the latter in the English islands, the Africans had time to learn from their British fellow sufferers, and to pass on, a dialect which, though far from standard English, is not in my opinion a creole.[14] Nevertheless, there are some remarkable correspondences between the Negro English creole of Surinam (Sranan)—which colony the Dutch received in compensation for the theft of New Amsterdam, alias New York—and the English dialects of Barbados and Jamaica.[15]

The linguistic history of St. Vincent is another story. Until 1763 this island was, like Dominica, in the hands of the Caribs; and its language was Island Carib. But in 1635 (the year in which the French occupied Guadeloupe and Martinique), the living cargoes of two wrecked slave-ships had sought refuge there; and been joined in the course of the years by numerous fugitives from neighbouring islands, particularly Barbados. These Negroes soon adopted the language and customs of their Indian hosts, and stole as many of their women as possible; the more readily, no doubt, because only identification with the indigenous Caribs preserved them from recapture. After the Treaty of Paris in 1763, the English moved in, bringing their own slaves; and ten years later the Caribs, "red" and "black" alike, were confined to the northernmost quarter of the island. But the black outbred the red to such an extent that after the unsuccessful Carib war of liberation (1795–96), very few pure Indians were left in St. Vincent; and the modern descendants of the 5000-odd Caribs who were deported to Central America in 1797, now numbering some 30,000, are of preponderantly negroid stock, although they alone today have retained the Island-Carib language.[16]

Though prediction is impossible, it seems likely that the future fortunes of the West Indian creoles will largely depend on their speakers' ability to adapt them to new requirements of communication—with regard to both speech and writing—in a changing world. So far as speech is concerned, this should offer little difficulty in places where the present national or official language is a later stage of that from which the creole's basic vocabulary was drawn, as in the French territories and in Haiti. But elsewhere, lexical borrowing is apt to be replaced by "code switching"—by the use, that is to say, of whole phrases or sentences lifted from the source-language. In Dominica, this is particularly common among chauffeurs, truck-drivers, clerks, typists and salesmen; while the introduction of such things as fertilizers, spraying and contour draining have made it not infrequent even among peasants. On the other hand, fishermen, hunters, sawyers and other woodsmen, sugar-cane workers in field and factory, bakers, carpenters, coopers and others who practise a conservative handicraft usually have, pertaining to their occupation, a rich Creole vocabulary that has been passed on without change throughout many generations, and that differs little—and if at all, then only by greater conservatism—from its counterpart in Martinique or Guadeloupe. Moreover, native speakers of Dominican Creole are not given to extending the meaning of a word as they know it; so, *hwazwè* (Fr. *rasoir*) "razor" is replaced by *réza* (Eng. *razor*) when a "safety razor" is referred to, *vè* (Fr. *verre*) "glass drinking-vessel" and *vè butey* (Fr. *bouteille*) "broken glass" are replaced by *glas* (Eng. *glass*) in any other reference, and *dis nwè* (Fr. *dix noirs*) "sixpence" has not been extended to "ten cents" of the new currency, which is called *tensens*.

The net result of numerous such changes and innovations, which have been gaining ground during the past forty—and especially the past fifteen—years, is that conversation between native speakers of French Creole belonging, respectively, to the English and to the French islands (of the Lesser Antilles) is today much more hampered and restricted than was the case only a generation ago; hampered because, in the French islands, the phonology is becoming closer to that of French (introduction of front rounded vowels, loss of the aspirate *h* and its replacement by velar *r*; whereas in the English islands *h* has been retained and velar *r* merged, for most speakers, in a non-distinctively velarized *w*); restricted because there is not and has never been a common vocabulary pertaining to things and institutions unknown in the islands before the present century, but which have recently become commonplace.

As for writing, so long as only those who have first become literate in another language can attempt to write and read a creole mother tongue, there will continue to be some wavering between an 'etymological' spelling (mainly where the second or school language was the source of the creole's lexicon) and one that is "phonetic"—not in a scientific sense, but in terms of the second language's conventional orthography (mainly where the second language was not the source of the Creole's lexicon). So, perhaps, for Papiamentu: *gaap* or *haap* from Dutch *gapen, loer* or *lur* from Dutch *loeren, yuda* or *joeda* from Spanish *ayudar, joven* or *hoben* from Spanish *joven, bij* from Dutch *bij* but *bai* from Portuguese *vai*. And in the case of a French Creole dialect some of whose speakers have French and others English as the language of literacy, the situation is much more serious. So, one and the same utterance, which might be transcribed phonematically: *se joomu yon ki sav fòs kuto ki ã cè-y* "it's the pumpkin alone that knows the strength of the knife in its heart", would be likely to appear, when written by a Martiniquais, as: *c'est geo'omon yonne qui save fò'ce couteau qui en tchoeu'-y*; and when written by a Dominican or a St. Lucian ignorant of French as: *say zhowomoo yon kee sahv force cootow kee ahn chair ee.* But were a Creole word of English ancestry to be recorded, "etymologist" and "phonetician" would most probably change places, the one writing, for example, *saïbòte* and the other *sideboard* for what is, phonologically, *saybod.*

Under the circumstances, it is hardly surprising that even personal correspondence is usually written—often by the intermediary of an interpreter-scribe—in what passes for the national language. But a better and more general knowledge of the latter, spoken and written, could, I suggest, be achieved most rapidly and painlessly by way of literacy in the creole mother tongue; for writing which some adequate, consistent and simple orthography should be agreed upon. Conventional French spelling clearly has none of these qualities; but since the vast majority of those who speak a French Creole have or wish to acquire French as a second language, some concessions should be made by the others; and it would be wise for the educational authorities of the W. I. Federation to adopt such digraphs and trigraphs as are or may be used to represent similar distinctive sounds of both English and French; for example, *ou* as in *you* and *vous, tch* as in *clutch* and *tchèque.* Thus the Creole proverb cited in the preceding paragraph would appear as orthographic: *se joomou yon ki sav fôs kouto ki ã tchê-y.*

In conclusion I should perhaps apologize for having given what may be a disproportionate place in my discussion to French Creole. But though I have done so mainly because I know most about it, having spoken one of its dialects almost daily for the past twenty years, there are reasons why it may be considered more important than some of the others of its kind, in respect to the rôle that it has played in the past, and may still play in the future. French Creole as a whole is more widespread and diversified and has a greater number of native speakers (between three and four million in Haiti alone) than any other creole language. However, size is no guarantee of longevity when the ability or the will to adapt is lacking; and there can be little doubt that, thanks to encouragement from Holland and to native speakers' own volition, the creoles now spoken in Dutch territories have made most progress in that direction. In token of which I shall end with a poem by Trefossa, written in Sranen (Negro English), and for whose translation I must plead guilty.[17]

wan tru puëma na wan skretji-sani.	a real poem is a frightening thing.
wan tru puëma na wan stree te	a real poem is a strife with death.
[f'dede.	
wan tru puëma na wan tra kondre,	a real poem is another land,
pe ju kan go	where you can go
te ju psa dede fosi.	once death has been outrun.
wan tru puëma na den wortu d'e tan	a real poem is the words that stay
[abra	
te ala trawan n'in ju libi wasi gwe;	when others from your life are
wan koko soso,	a naked kernel, [washed away;
ma wan di kan sproiti	but one that can put forth
njun libi.	new life.
lon na mi abra dan,	then let pour over me
Arusubanja fu grontapu.	the world's Arusubanya.
kande wandee, wandee	perhaps one day, one day
mofo fu mi sa broko opo	my mouth will open up
fu tatji dji onoosruwan tu wortu	to tell for simple souls a double tale
di, te den gro, sa trowe lepi stari,	which, when it grows, will cast ripe
di mi suku noo.	that now I seek. [stars

Notes:

1. See, s. v. "Galíbi" (p. 229) et passim: Raymond Breton *Dictionnaire caraïbe-français* (Auxerre, 1665); réimprimé par Jules Platzmann, édition fac-simile (Leipzig, 1892).

2. Tomás Navarro, "Observaciones sobre el papiamento", *NRFH*, VII (1951), p. 188 ff., and H. L. A. van Wijk, "Orígenes y evolución del papiamentu", *Neophilologus*, XLII (1958), p. 169 ff.

3. Citations from Chevillard and Pelleprat are both taken from L. Calvert, "Histoire de la formation du langage créole", *Martinique*, December 1944. The latter author himself took them from, respectively: C. A. Banbuck, *Histoire politique, économique et sociale de la Martinique* (Paris, 1935), and Pierre Pelleprat, *Relation des missions des pp. de la Cie. de Jésus dans les isles, et dans la Terre Ferme de l'Amérique méridionale* (Paris, 1656). Calvert does not say what edition of the latter he used; but the spelling—evidently modernized in the case of Pelleprat, and not (or less) in that of Chevillard—is as given by him.

4. On p. 234 of her *Du français aux parlers créoles* (Paris, 1956), Élodie Jourdain gives the text of a message sent by a Guianese Amerindian, pupil of the Jesuits, to the French Governor d'Orvilliers in 1744; and which she believed to be the oldest monument of French Creole: *Anglai pran Yapok, yé méné mon père allé, toute blang foulkan maron dans bois* "(the) English have taken (the) Oyapok (post), they have carried off (the) priest, all (the) white (people) have cleared out (and) taken refuge in (the) woods". The same message would be conveyed in the same words in the Guianese dialect of today.

5. See: Robert Wallace Thompson, "A Preliminary Survey of the Spanish Dialect of Trinidad", *Orbis*, VI (1957), p. 353 ff., and Manuel Álvarez

Nazario, *El arcaísmo vulgar en el español de Puerto Rico* (Mayagüez, Puerto Rico, 1957).

6. It is true that *mouche manigat* "very skilful" is said to have occurred also in the jargon used between Europeans and Island Caribs; and some have attributed *manigat* to the latter's language. Breton denies this; but if he was mistaken, these Indians must have had a peculiar sense of humour; for the most similar word in their language, *maníkati*, means "unable or not disposed to do (something)".

7. Keith Whinnom, *Spanish Contact Vernaculars in the Philippine Islands* (Hong Kong–London, 1956). In a review of this book, in *Word*, 13 (1957), p. 489 ff., I have mentioned some similarities between the languages therein described and the West Indian creoles.

8. L. Calvert, *op. cit., Martinique*, June 1944.

9. L. Calvert (*op. et loc. cit.*), citing Martineau & May, *Trois siècles d'histoire Antillaise*, says: "Les noirs sont moins nombreux en 1652, avec Pelleprat. Ils tendent à l'égalité en 1658, avec Rochefort; ils sont supérieurs en nombre en 1660, d'après la relation des îles. C'est donc entre 1658 et 1660 que la population noire dépasse la blanche pour suivre un mouvement continuellement ascendant. Elle la double en 1720, la quadruple en 1740, époque à laquelle les blancs étaient eux-mêmes cinq fois plus nombreux qu'en 1660. Le nombre des noirs augmentait sans cesse: Il atteignait 70,000 en 1763 et 90,000 en 1789."

10. See: Pierre Vérin, "The Rivalry of French Creole and English in the British West Indies", *De West-Indische Gids*, 38 (1958), p. 163 ff.

11. See: UNESCO, *The Use of Vernacular Languages in Education* (= *Monographs on Fundamental Education,* No. VII) (Paris, 1953).

12. Robert Wallace Thompson, "The 'th-Sounds' and Genetics", *Phonetica* I, 3/4 (1957).

13. Germán Arciniegas, *Caribbean Sea of the New World* (New York, 1946), p. 213 ff.

14. *Pāce* Professor Robert Le Page formerly of the UCWI (and others), who holds that "broad Jamaican Creole stands in much the same relationship to English as does Haitian Creole to French" (personal communication). The clue to what I regard as an essential difference is the qualification, "broad". So far as I could ascertain, there is a continuous gradation in the speech of Jamaicans—such as exists within perhaps most fairly large speech communities—from the broadest dialect to the local variety of standard English; and everybody normally uses the nearest approximation to the latter with which he or she is familiar. But there is not and cannot be any such gradation from a French Creole to any dialect of French because of great differences in basic grammar; and it is always clear which language is being spoken, even though it be a variety of Creole that is full of gallicisms or a variety of French that is full of creolisms. I do not doubt that "broad" Jamaican (or Barbadian) began in a pidgin that became the mother tongue of some; but this mother tongue has evolved continuously in the direction of "normal" English, as which it should now be identified for the reasons stated above.

15. For some examples of such correspondences, see: Melville J. Herskovits, *The Myth of the Negro Past* (New York, 1941), p. 282.

16. For further details of this people's history, see the Introduction to my monograph, *The Black Carib of British Honduras* (= *Viking Fund Publications in Anthropology,* No. 17) (New York, 1951).

17. From: Trefossa (puëma fu), *Trotji*; p. 19. Published for the Bureau of Linguistic Research in Surinam (University of Amsterdam) (Amsterdam, 1957). Arusubanja is the name of a rapid in the Surinam river; and means, literally "shakes the ribs loose".

C.
Race, Ethnicity, and Class

In the Introductory Essay, I said that stratification in the Carribean frequently has the form of a color-class pyramid, with dark-skinned laborers and peasants at the bottom, lighter-skinned service and lower professional and government people in the middle, and white-skinned landowners at the top. This is too simple a model, not only because there are so many exceptions, but also because it sidesteps the problem of cultural complexity. When M. G. Smith speaks of pluralism in the West Indies it is not because color seems to correlate with class, but because, in a number of the countries, the component ethnic groups are committed to quite disparate sets of basic institutions: ". . . the plurality is a discontinuous status order, lacking any foundation in a system of common interests and values, while its component sections are genuine status continua, distinguished by their differing systems of value, action, and social relations" ("Social and cultural pluralism," *Annals of the New York Academy of Sciences*, 83(5):769, 1960). What we now need in the Caribbean, indeed in any situation of ethnic complexity, are concrete specifications of how ethnic boundaries are generated and maintained, and of how ethnicity provides a set of resources upon which the person draws in interaction.

LLOYD BRAITHWAITE

4. Social Stratification and Cultural Pluralism

The discussion of social stratification in relation to cultural pluralism is important because these two approaches to the phenomena of social stratification and to the so-called plural society have for the most part developed quite separately. What is proposed here is to show briefly and, consequently, perhaps inadequately, the manner of approach of those primarily interested in one or the other of these phenomena and to examine concretely the society of the island of Trinidad. Such an approach would appear to have two merits: first, Trinidad rivals in cultural complexity any other island or territory in the Caribbean and, second, it permits the possibility of examining the limitations of the existing approaches to the problems and of uniting two large areas of sociological interest within some broad framework of sociological theory.

For the purposes of this paper, social stratification is regarded as a form of social differentiation in which social groups or quasi-organized groups (social classes) are differentiated in terms of status within a hierarchically arranged social order. The empirical study of social stratification has had two important points of impetus: one was the study of "socioeconomic status" by sociologists; the other impulse, possibly more important, was given by the attempts of the social anthropologist to describe modern Western society. Strangely enough, it is the anthropological approach to the problems of social class and social status that has stimulated the greatest theoretical interest. Unsurprisingly, these approaches are by no means mutually incompatible; some of the pioneers attempted (some might say reverted to) sociological techniques of objective measurement.

The approach of the anthropologist seems to have sprung largely

SOURCE: *Annals of the New York Academy of Sciences,* Vol. 83, Art. 5 (1960):816–31. Copyright The New York Academy of Sciences; 1960. Reprinted by permission of the author and The New York Academy of Sciences.

from a desire to discover, in his study of modern Western society, some principle of social structure that would serve to reduce the complexity of its culture to some order. The principles of social class, status, and stratification are roughly comparable, at first glance, in simplicity and "explanatory value" to those of kinship, locality, age-group, and the others with which the anthropologist is accustomed to deal.

The anthropological concern with the problems of Western society has not been paralleled by a like concern of the sociologists with the problems of colonial societies. Sociologists do not appear to have realized how culture-bound have been their concerns, particularly among empirically minded sociologists addicted to the production of *ad hoc* theoretical schemes. Until recently American sociologists, for instance, appear to the outsider to have been concerned primarily with empirical and quantitative analysis of segments or aspects of American social structure.

One consequence of this is that the analysis and understanding of multiracial and multicultural societies is relatively undeveloped. The comparative research that has been done in the field of race relations, for instance, has been concerned chiefly with the problems of prejudice, discrimination, and the measurement of relevant attitudes and with the so-called race-relations cycle, and much of the export of sociology has been in the international extension of such projects.

Moreover in the United States, where empirical sociology has achieved its highest development, it has been the anthropologists who have worked most clearly and distinctly with the concept of culture. Consequently, sociological concerns have not proved to be particularly relevant to the analysis of multicultural or multiracial societies in which gross differences in culture coincide or coexist with racial differences.

In default of an adequate sociological theory (notions of the plantation, the race-relations cycle, and the concept of the frontier notwithstanding) the phenomenon of cultural pluralism has been fruitfully examined by political scientists concerned with the problem of nationalism and national minorities or by persons interested primarily in problems of colonial administration and, more especially, with those problems that arise where there is a transition to self-government. The dearth of theoretical formulations in this field has been met largely by the concept of the plural society, which has attracted much attention and uncritical use. The notion was transferred from the field of economics, where the "dual economy" of Western enterprise and traditional native production formed a striking contrast.

The chief advocate of the theory of the plural society has been, of course, Furnivall.[1] Although he was interested primarily in problems of colonial administration, his views are by no means those of an orthodox colonialist. Rather, they appear to stem from a somewhat naive acceptance of the radical criticism of the social order. The colonial society, the radical claimed, is held together by force, which is harmful and disruptive in its consequences. The theory really differs from the conventional stereotype portrayal of imperialism only in that it declares that the imperialists are not to blame.

This suspicion as to the genesis of the theory has, of course, nothing to do with its intrinsic adequacy. It is of interest only because the theory of the plural society is logically unacceptable; therefore its widespread acceptance must be explained on other than logical grounds.

THE PLURAL SOCIETY

The plural society has been defined by Furnivall as one lacking in social will. According to him, under modern conditions all tropical countries tend to be plural societies. That is, a European or "Western" power creates a superstructure that leads to the destruction of the former established pattern of social relationships. The cultural homogeneity of society (as it existed before Western contact) is replaced by a culturally and racially heterogeneous society. The one common feature that all groups in the plural society share is the desire for economic advancement. Hence arises the lack of a common social will.

It is convenient to bear in mind the brief description of the plural society given by Furnivall in his essay *Tropical Economy*:

"I. The plural society has come into existence because the only factor common to all groups and members has been the economic factor. Trying to cure its defects by purely economic measures is like casting out devils in the name of Beelzebub. The *first* problem is to find some principle transcending material ends, some moral principle, that *all* can accept as valid.

"II. The economic factor predominates because the colonial power, exercising political control, is primarily concerned for its economic interests. The *second* problem is then to dissociate as far as possible economic and political control; to find some moral and not solely material authority.

"III. The predominance of economic forces is prejudicial to social and individual welfare because these forces sacrifice social to individual demand. The *third* problem, accordingly, is to devise some machinery for the organization of demand.

"IV. The plural society is inconsistent with political welfare because it is unable to stand alone for lack of a common social will. The *fourth* problem therefore is to devise some means of creating a common social will."[2]

The problem faced in creating an autonomous community and self-governing country is thus seen as, basically, one of creating such a social will as will be capable of sustaining a self-governing country. A people must be capable of wanting what it needs and doing what it wants.

It is clear from the foregoing description that Trinidad to some extent falls into the category of a plural society. Here the heterogeneous cultural elements have been drawn together because of the dominant political structure of the British Empire, which facilitates movement on a broad Empire-wide scale.

Furnivall has obviously pointed with a great deal of insight to some of the problems of such a society. However, it can be doubted whether the term plural society is sufficiently clear theoretically to throw much light on the problem.

Indeed, Furnivall claims that all tropical societies are plural societies, and cites the case of the Indians in East Africa and the Syrian merchants in West Africa. However, the mere existence of a national or ethnic minority such as the Syrians in West Africa does not create the characteristic problems of the plural society. In some respects the nation states of West Africa with racially homogeneous groups form a similar type of social structure to that found in a so-called plural society.

Furnivall himself sees that the term "plural society," when used too loosely, becomes debased, and he contrasts a plural society with a society with pluralistic aspects. It is my belief that, rich though Furnivall's insight is, the conceptual framework he employs is not adequate to deal with the phenomenon he is analyzing. Even the terms used by Sorokin[3] of differentiation between unibonded and multibonded groups goes a little further. It at least leads to a study of what are the particular bonds that unite the social groups in question and suggests a range extending from these societies or groups with one single common value to those that share many major values in common.

If we use the more general sociological theory of Parsons and Shils, we get a better picture.[4] A plural society is one composed of such varying groups, each with its own subculture, that only a few cultural symbols are shared by all. Under these circumstances there are consequently tendencies toward disintegration. In those societies usually referred to as plural we see societies in which the dominant ties of particularism and ascription,* especially those of the large kinship group, are largely replaced by those of universalism and achievement.

The position is complicated further by the fact that this is not an indigenous process, but part of the disruption of a subordinate social system by one which is superordinate. To a very large extent the values of particularism and ascription still remain strong, but have an entirely new content: the acceptance of the superiority, as such, of the superordinate system. By and large, however, this process of acculturation implies the introduction and partial acceptance of universal and achievement values in spheres in which particularistic and ascriptive values were previously dominant.

The concentration of the phenomenon of the lack of social will of which Furnivall speaks obscures the really important fact that no society can exist without a minimum sharing of common values, without a certain amount of "social will." This may be responsible for the fact that, although Furnivall shows a great deal of insight into so many of the problems involved in the metropolitan-colonial relationship, he tends to lay too great stress on the economic factors affecting policy and too little on the necessary existence of sentiments favorable to the metropolitan power and the ways and means by which such sentiments are inculcated and encouraged. It is impos-

* "Ascription: the normative pattern which prescribes that an actor in a given type of situation should, in his selections for differential treatment of social objects, give priority to certain attributes that they possess (including collectivity memberships and possessions) over any specific performances (past, present, or prospective) of the objects . . . the role-expectation that the role incumbent, in orienting himself to social objects in the relevant choice situation, will accord to the objects' given attributes (whether universalistically or particularistically defined) over their actual or potential performances" (Parsons and Shils, pages 82 and 83).[4]

sible to understand the sociological evolution of colonial societies without taking this factor into account.

A major need of the individual in a subordinate social system whose particularistic-ascriptive values have been torn asunder would appear to be acceptance of another such set of values. Hence it comes about that the first reactions of many colonials is toward the acceptance of the superiority of the scale of values of the superordinate social system. After a time there is a sufficient acquaintance with this scale of values and a sufficiently general incorporation of them into the subordinate society for this relationship of superior to subordinate to be questioned, even when the common yardstick of generally accepted values is used.

When this relationship is questioned, the problem of the integration of the subordinate system also comes into question. When there are heterogeneous cultural elements in the population, the position is particularly acute. With the breakdown of the system of integrative values that holds the subordinate community in position, there are no other system integrative values to take their place.

Furnivall, in his discussion of the political features of the plural society, states that it has these characteristic aspects: the society as a whole comprises separate racial sections; each section is an aggregate of individuals rather than an organic whole and, as individuals, their social life is incomplete. However, in point of fact the breakdown of the power and prestige of the metropolitan power shows that these separate racial sections that are thought of as being atomistic under colonialism have a very strong group consciousness of their own. It is true that the breakdown of the integration of the colonial society with the metropolitan society tends to create a set of disparate individuals, but this is a feature of all societies that have accepted the Western democratic scale of values without possessing the political and economic conditions and the psychological attitudes necessary to ensure the working of a democratic regime. The interesting feature about the special case of the multiracial, multicultural, or plural society is that, in addition to this, we have the development and accentuation of antagonism between subordinate groups.

The cases that spring most readily to mind are those of Palestine, Malaya, and India. There can be little doubt that, at the time of transfer of power, neither the proponents of partition nor the advocates of a united India were able to assess at all accurately the explosive forces that they were unleashing. It was the dominant power, directly concerned as it was with the integration of the previous system, that made the most realistic appraisal of the situation. In all the other societies of which Furnivall wrote intimately we see the same disparate tendencies manifesting themselves.

In this connection we must note the emergence of somewhat similar problems in places such as Nigeria, which is not a multiracial society, but a multicultural one. Here, as the society moves in the direction of self-government, the separate self-conscious groups have become somewhat more antagonistic to one another. It is not that the "union is not voluntary but is imposed by the colonial power and by the force of economic circumstances,"[1] it is that the identification with the superior social system has ceased, and subordinate identification (whose strength has not been appreciated, precisely because of this subordination) now assumes a major importance.

The colonial system, far from placing economic considerations first, is in fact dominantly based on ascriptive ones. That is why the characteristic colonial response in revolt takes on a certain common form. The answer to ascription is ascription; to nationalism, nationalism. When the need to replace the system's integrative values becomes paramount, the tendency is to look for similar values elsewhere. If the country has a culturally homogeneous tradition, this is revived, and colonial nationalism tends to result; if the country is a plural society, sectional and racial antagonism tend to preponderate.

This need for system integration throws some light on the much-noted appeal of communism to underdeveloped peoples. Marxism not only furnishes an ideology that allows the acceptance (albeit partial) of universalistic-achievement values to which people have become accustomed with Westernization, but it also makes for system integration. It replaces a fragmented scale of values with an integrated and unified one. It presents a philosophy that appears to have all the answers, and this exerts a powerful attraction on the individual. Even more important, however, is the fact that it permits of a certain degree of identification with a metropolitan power. Hence it comes about that the combination of "nationalism" with communism becomes feasible. The nationalism allows the working off of aggressive feelings against the dominant power in control, while communism allows for the identification with both a foreign and a metropolitan power. Of course, such an identification is not inevitable. Sometimes the separate ethnic groups seek the same psychological comfort from identification with the foreign power from which the ethnic group originally came. To some extent this is the case with the Indians of Trinidad, and to the extent that this occurs the crisis in the integration of the society is deepened. Even in this case, however, there is still often to be found a marked tendency to identify with that metropolitan power which is in opposition to the dominant power. For, insofar as people seek to obtain a new integration of the society as a whole, they find the appeal of communism with its subtle blend of universalism and particularism extremely powerful.

It has been suggested that not merely places with distinctive ethnic pockets, such as Trinidad and British Guiana, but the society characteristic of all the West Indian islands can be described best as a plural society. The danger here is that the differences between the subcultures of the different social groups come to be stressed, and this is contrasted with a so-called unitary or homogeneous society that does not exist in reality, but that is an ideal type to which no society in fact corresponds in total detail.

In a sense every society has pluralistic aspects. Indeed, one of the main problems that recent advances in sociological theory elucidate is the fact that different values and attitudes are necessarily produced by any functioning social system, so that the integration of these diverse values is one of the important tasks of the social system to which energies must be allocated. In addition to this, however, there enter into the functioning of groups geographical and other factors that may correspond with special cultural traits and either raise or lower the prospects of such groups functioning as separate independent entities. The mere existence of cultural pluralism does not necessarily threaten the existence of the social order.

Furthermore, in any social system the values to which people aspire must be in short supply, otherwise we are forced to believe in the possibility of a classless society. If these values were unlimited and in supply as free goods, they would cease to be a central focus of attention. It is for this reason that all attempts to create classless societies, whether in small Utopian communities or on the grand scale, as in the Soviet Union, have collapsed. This fact in itself makes the existence of pluralistic or subcultural elements an inevitable product of any social system.

Nevertheless, societies can be characterized by the number of values that are shared as desirable by all; insofar as they are diverse, we can speak of cultural pluralism. In this sense it is clear that the society of Creole Trinidad could be accurately described as in some sense a plural society.* As shown elsewhere, the main common value element has been the sharing of the value of ethnic superiority and inferiority.[5] Other values, however, were shared only by the middle and the upper classes, yet others by the whole society except the upper class, and so on. The fact that there was only one common value strongly held by the whole society, of a type inherently productive of tensions, created a certain tendency to "disintegration" within the social system, particularly when this main common value was challenged. This disintegration was reflected in the political life of the community as the lower class, with its own subculture, became dominant, and again in socially deviant behavior, as in the case of the steel-band movement.

We have in the case of the various ethnic-group cultures within the island (the more usual sense in which the term plural society has been used) a more complicated case. With the breakdown of the common-value element ("the political and social superiority of the Englishman and the European") we find the same assertion of disparate tendencies within the social group. There was to be observed, for instance, not merely an increased tension between Indians and non-Indians, but between Hindu and Moslem as well. The splits within the Chinese community, too, became more public and important. Our chief concern, however, is not whether to use the term plural so-

---

* Trinidad society (contemporary population approximately 780,000) has been described in terms of social stratification as a society in which the dominant values have been those of racial origin and skin color, and one in which the social ascendancy and high status of the white group was broadly accepted. It was further characterized as a colonial society in which the hierarchic grouping of social classes was reinforced through the subordinate nature of the colonial society in relation to the metropolitan power. However, it was pointed out further that sharp social changes were taking place in that ascriptive values of race were being replaced by those of achievement in the economic and political fields, and one in which the goals of an independent democratic society were replacing the old colonial relationship.

While such an analysis is essential, and later developments have emphasized the validity of this position, it was incomplete in that it ignored much of the cultural complexity of the island. It was confined to the Creole section (about 55 per cent of the society). There can be no doubt that acceptance of these values was widespread among the rest of the population in spite of the persistence of subcultural patterns. These values are, however, not so firmly implanted among the Indian section (about 35 per cent of the population) largely because of the tenacity of certain aspects of Hindu and Moslem culture. What we therefore see in the case of the acculturation of the Indian ethnic groups is a process of acculturation in which large aspects of Hindu and Moslem culture were shed and the dominant features of the host society, such as we have described, accepted.[4]

ciety to characterize either or both situations. The point of substance is that we must be careful not to stress the culturally pluralistic elements of the society without appreciating the fact that there must be a certain minimum of common, shared values if the unity of the society is to be maintained. In the case of Furnivall this led to the neglect of ties of sentiment with the imperial power, to an overstressing of economic elements, and to an over-all view of the political structure as essentially one of force. In the case of an analysis of Trinidad society there is also the possibility that these same elements may be neglected.

In the case of Furnivall there seems to be a tendency to misunderstand the existing hierarchy of values by stressing the equality of the plural elements and the importance of the ethnic cultures. This leads to an over-idealization of the subordinate cultures as compared with the dominant scale of values with its corresponding lack of social will. Something of the same sort may be seen in the West Indies by those who stress the pluralistic elements in the situation. We have seen, for instance, the development of the concept of lower-class family life as equally viable with that of the middle and the upper classes. Here one of the basic problems in the integration of the society tends to be overlooked. The concept of pluralism, considered outside of a sociological theory, leads also to a definition of the social system purely in terms of cultural institutions and of the adherence of the different groups to different institutions. The confusion in meanings which surrounds the term "institution" is thus introduced into the confusion that surrounds the term "plural society."

One alternative to an analysis in sociological terms of the social structure is to divide these institutions into "core" institutions and "peripheral" ones. However, if these institutions are not defined in "structural-functional" terms, that is, in terms of the functional tasks of the social system itself, they tend to reduce sociology to a mere department of biology. Hence the attempt to create order by the use of an institutional treatment eventually ends by creating even greater theoretical disorder.

In the analysis of social stratification in relation to pluralism, the homogeneity of a culture or social system is differentiated from a plural society by the institutionalists as follows: the homogeneous society shows among different social classes an allegiance to the same forms of institutions, the plural society shows among different social classes allegiance to different forms of the same institution.

Two objections may be raised here. In the first place, it is usually more appropriate to regard social classes as quasi-organized groups. It is not the interaction among themselves as a group that defines the membership of any given social class, but more particularly their place in a hierarchy defined in relation to other groups. Therefore, it is somewhat incorrect to look upon these groups as if they were self-contained societies. The definition of such a group as a society depends upon the interaction among its own members, and it is clear in the case of the West Indies that, while the existence of a subculture shared by so many of the lower class renders concerted action possible, there is in fact very little unity of action precisely because of the fact that such a group is only quasi-organized; it is, in a sense, a category created by the research worker rather than a separately functioning social system. The problem of the plural society is indeed a problem of social structure posed by the existence of marked differences of culture, but a society or social system cannot be defined in cultural terms by merely observing the presence or absence of cultural traits; it must be done in terms of social action, that is, the interaction of social roles. The approach that defines society in terms of culture is fundamentally at variance with the approach that, while recognizing the importance of cultural items, stresses the viewpoint of social action. All the most important developments in sociological theory will appear to revolve around this important distinction about social action.

In the second place, differences in social class must depend on a difference in the spread of certain values among different groups. The important differences may be few or many. The contrast between homogeneity and heterogeneity would tend to ignore this important theoretical point. Furthermore, it tends to encourage a merely quantitative estimate of what are "similar" and "different" in institutional practices and beliefs and to ignore the main point, which is that certain of these values are central and others peripheral to the social system. Thus, notwithstanding the concept of cultural core and cultural focus, sociology becomes reduced to cultural anthropology.

Consequent upon this definition of society in terms of culture or in terms of institutions is the view of the integration of the society as a matter of holding the institutions of the society together. Such a view leads to the conception of the integration of homogeneous societies as essentially different from and less difficult than that of heterogeneous societies. This view of the plural society or the culturally diverse community as essentially unstable appears to ignore some of the most important facts. The most significant of the plural societies, the caste system of India, has shown a stability not shared by "homogeneous" Western societies. Similarly, conditions of revolution and other forms of political instability appear not to depend upon homogeneity of culture alone, although this may be a relevant factor. For instance, the threat to the social order in the West Indies in the postemancipation period appears to lie not only in the cultural differences of the social groups, but in the fact that such differences came to be hinged around and identified with racial and color symbols that were cardinal to the values held by the society. At the same time these values were threatened by the introduction from outside the West Indian community (viewed as a separate social system) of ideas and values as congenial to the subordinate groups in the society as they were uncongenial to the West Indian ruling class; these ideas and values were derived from the superior social system (the United Kingdom) to which there was a common allegiance.

The allegiance to different institutions may or may not threaten the integration of the entire social structure dependent upon a variety of conditions. The shared cultural characteristic facilitates, under certain circumstances, unity of action as organized groups. However, whether such unity of action develops a form that can be contained within the larger social structure depends on the strength or wealth of the shared common values, as well as of a variety of other features. Some of these are discussed below in connection with the differences between the lower class and the Indian community. Among many persons who use the concept of the plural society there is a tendency to underestimate the bonds of sentiment and a stress on the power and authority aspects of the society that leads to the obscuring of some crucial issues. An uncritical use of the term instituion vitiates the functional approach. An adequate functional analysis cannot be made on the basis of a classification of institutions that is haphazard or based on external appearance. Structure must be defined in terms of function.

The limitations of the concept of the plural society as contrasted with the unitary society can be seen from the fact that nearly all national societies, even the most homogeneous of them, show significant regional, ethnic, rural-urban, and social class differences among themselves. Another society appears highly unitary when we do not know it, but all the research that has been done in the more highly developed societies has gone to show that a rich cultural variation can subsist within an apparently highly unified national society. Indeed, from an historical point of view, it is the homogeneous society that appears exceptional. In this sense Furnivall, for instance, is forced to classify nearly all the societies he mentions as plural societies. He is forced to rely upon Great Britain as an essentially homogeneous society.* While disagreeing with his formulations, we must agree that Furnivall showed a great deal of insight even when he pointed to the "absence of social will" as one of the characteristics of this plural society. Those areas in which groups of markedly different cultures are found to exist within a larger structure, such as the modern empire state, pose extremely important problems because, as a consequence of the breakdown of the belief in European superiority and of European dominance, there is indeed a relative absence of social will. What is needed is the study of a range of societies so that it becomes clear what are the minimum common values that must be shared in order that a viable social structure may exist.

In this respect it should be noted that in Trinidad, although the cultural framework of the Indian and Creole peoples appears to be fundamentally different, nevertheless there are more values held in common than appears at first sight. For instance, the acceptance of the British social system and its scale of values as a superior one led to the partial incorporation of a whole series of values and attitudes characteristic of that system. These values and attitudes are more or less incompatible with the culture of the system of values of the subordinate ethnic groups, and a process of gradual shedding of the latter has consequently taken place.

Thus, although the ascriptive color values were the dominant ones in the island, the universalistic-achievement values of the larger social system also invaded the island society. This was reflected not only in the increasing incorporation of a "democratic" scale of values, but also in the system of administration. The elementary principle of democracy, "each one to count as one and not more than one," was applied to the various groups in a large variety of situations, as in the religious question, in the question of the control of education, and in the suppression of carnival. The dominant de-

---

* Sharp differences in class cultures in British society are clearly recognized both on the empirical and popular levels.

mands of the subordinate social groups, both lower-class Creole and Indian, came to be expressed in this demand for equality of treatment, a demand that was at least not incompatible with the new goals that the society has come to accept. The one case in which there was a striking difference of treatment was that of the regulation of marriage. There has never been any attempt to accept the lower-class Creole family structure as worthy of legal existence in its own right, while in the case of the Indian family there was always some respect, and eventually legal recognition, shown to the existing social customs of the group.

That is a reflection of the fact that the Creole populations were accepted as belonging essentially to a national community and therefore could be expected to live up to the more general standards of the society. Such cultural differences as there were did not lead to a conception of a lower class eternally destined to be different from the other classes. Although some biological and other rationalizations developed to justify their inferior position, this did not in fact prevent a definition of the goals of the society as universalistic in the sense that there were no legal barriers to economic opportunity. Following the abolition of slavery the eventual evolution of West Indians toward the acceptance of democratic political participation was logically compatible with that position. To some, indeed, it seemed its inevitable fulfillment.

On the other hand, the Indian group was considered as almost outside the social system. The dominant conception of the upper group was economic in relation to the Indian problem, but even here the control from abroad tended to modify the purely economic outlook and to that extent incorporated the Indian into a universalistic scale of values; indenture was temporary, and the loss of freedom was compensated by the removal of all those legal restrictions that tended to perpetuate the caste system. Indeed, so much of the culture was shed that the recognition of Hindu and Moslem marriage and divorce created as many problems as it solved.

It is the incorporation of these universalistic values that makes it possible to conceive of a system of common values shared by Indian and Creole alike that may overcome the tendencies toward disintegration already apparent in the social system.

In this respect it is interesting to compare the situation with that in the United States. Although the United States has been conceived as a unitary society by some, there seems to be greater wisdom in

Furnivall, who pointed to the United States as an example of his plural society. There, as is well known, wave after wave of different groups possessing somewhat different cultures swept into the country, particularly during the Nineteenth and early Twentieth Centuries. The existence and persistence of these divergent nationalities, while posing special problems of their own, have not hindered the overriding loyalty to the "American way of life" that renders the national system viable; in part, the problem has been met by the theory of the melting pot. All immigrants were to be subjected to a process of Americanization by which their cultural traits were to be replaced by American ways. On the other hand, the resistance of the immigrant cultures to Americanization has led to the conception, in Louis Adamic's colorful phraseology, of "a nation of nations."[6] In other words, the idea of a unitary or homogeneous society has been replaced by the acceptance of cultural pluralism. An interesting analysis of these aspects of the social structure of the United States is made in an article by M. M. Gordon[7] in which he points out that these problems have not been given the attention they deserve. Gordon seeks to go beyond the popular conceptions of the melting pot and the nation of nations. In his opinion there are at least five possible conceptions of cultural pluralism that are nonetheless compatible with an overriding sense of national loyalty.

First, there is the goal of complete assimilation, which is impossible of achievement.

Second, there is a possible recognition of subcultures, of various features of cultural pluralism. Gordon defines a subculture as "a social division of a national culture made up by a combination of ethnic group [used here as a generic term covering race, religion, or national origin], social class, region and rural-urban residence."[7] These subcultures may all be permitted to coexist, but with the contacts between them secondary and not primary, and limited in number. Such groups would have tolerant attitudes toward one another and maintain such relationships as would be necessary to meet the demands of a common legal system and allegiance to a common government. This Gordon calls "cultural pluralism: the tolerance level."[7]

Third, there is a form of "cultural pluralism: the good group relations level." This is characterized as one in which the subcultures continue to exist, but secondary contacts increase in number, and a limited number of primary contacts then takes place. Relations on this level imply employment integration, common use of public accommodations, interethnic composition of civic organizations, and frequent symbolic demonstrations of intergroup harmony to emphasize common goals and values. Primary contacts are not such as to endanger the endogamous system and therefore the ethnic subculture as a whole. This, in his opinion, is the position that obtains in the United States at present.

Fourth, there is the "community integration level." In this there is an acceptance of all ethnic backgrounds as equally valid and a positive encouragement of primary group relationships. This level accepts diverse ethnic backgrounds that presumably need be shed only insofar as they affect social participation. In this respect the goal differs from the previous goal in the acceptance of ethnic approbation as in itself a positive value. This is a goal envisaged as possible in America, because the brotherhood of man takes a higher place in the hierarchy over every subcultural system of the individual nation and of the values of the subculture itself.

Finally, there is conceived as a possibility a mixed type or "pluralistic integrative" level. In this case the common allegiance and common values remain, but ethnic groups are permitted to retain their special heritage. However, unlike the present position there would be a subcultural system in which the individuals who wished to rise above ethnic affiliation would be allowed to participate.

The limitation of this analysis is that it seems to center its attention so largely upon the United States. It takes into consideration only situations conceivable within that country and within a national framework. There is a much wider range of possibilities which needs to be taken into account. The importance of the phenomenon of the plural society lies precisely in pointing to the minimum common values that must be shared if a viable social structure is to exist: in other words, the implications of cultural diversity for the integration of the social structure and the larger national framework. The introduction of the concepts of the dominant systems and subsystems of culture is insufficient if no basic change in the relationship of these systems is considered.

Nevertheless, this recognition of a variety of situations in a continuum is helpful, and we may consider how far in Trinidad the social structure in any way resembles one or another of these types. The assimilationist ideal was present to a certain extent in the attitudes toward the lower class, since in the postemancipation period it was considered desirable that the exslaves and their descendants should be educated to a truly Christian way of life. In the case of the Indians, on the other hand, although there was intermittent concern for the problem posed by the existence of a large number of heathens and aliens in the social order, there was never any serious concern with stripping the Indians of their cultural heritage and replacing it by something self-consciously new. The acculturation of the Indians took place largely as a "natural" and not as a planned process. The fact that Trinidad society was not autonomous but subordinate to the larger British social system meant that there would not be any conscious attempt at Trinidadization in the same way that people were Americanized. Insofar as Indians adopt the ways of other Trinidadians they are described as being Creolized. However, the Creole culture was considered to be in many respects an inferior one.

On the whole, the relations between the non-Indian and the Indian communities approached in its position most closely Gordon's second category, that of cultural pluralism: the tolerance level. Although a certain amount of friction between Indian and Creole developed, and although there was a tendency to exploit the less sophisticated of the Indians, there was an over-all tolerance of the ethnic group and its culture.

Primary group contacts between the Indian and other ethnic groups were limited. This situation arose not only because of mutual prejudice, but also because of certain special aspects of the culture of the Indian group. The recreational life of Creole society centered around the mixing of the sexes; the particular dietary customs of the Indians made the usual dinner invitation a difficult problem, for the taboos on drinking possessed a great if diminished force among the Indians, while drinking was a major form of recreation among the Creoles.

The secondary contacts of the Indian group, however, eventually produced a middle class possessing many of the attributes of the colored middle class and the white upper class. Even here, however, we are still dealing with a subcultural group since, although its subculture of achievement is middle class, its primary contacts are still mainly with other individuals of the same subculture of origin and ascriptive status. Development along separate lines has continued in spite of the increasing Creolization of the Indian professional class. However many persons still conscious of their Indian origin have sought to retain a certain ethnic exclusiveness in their social clubs while mixing in the rest of Creole society. This has been resented by members of the Creole middle class, who envisage them as seeking to obtain the best of both worlds.

The third phase, cultural pluralism, the "good group-relations level," represents the ideal possibility toward which Trinidadians can now aim. The crucial problem is how far universalistic standards have reached down among the masses of the population so that a common loyalty can override the particularistic ethnic affiliations.

The "community-integration" type of society is clearly not within possibility of achievement in contemporary Trinidad, and the best that can be hoped for is the evolution of the second type into the third and then the fifth type of culturally pluralistic society.

There are two other points in connection with the coexistence of several subcultures within a social structure that must be noted. First, the fact that values are shared does not mean that they are common in the sense of being widespread; there may be a common acceptance of the superiority of a particular scale of values and a particular type of action, although the social groups that hold these values may not aspire to them. This is the case in most caste societies and in all highly stratified societies in which there is little mobility.

On the other hand, in a society in which there are varying cultural traditions there may still be an over-all awareness of the values of the superior group and an acceptance of the desirability of striving for them. In the first case there is a more-or-less total acceptance of the pattern of stratification as more or less permanent; in the second case there is a great deal of ambivalence because of the fact that there is the acceptance of mutually incompatible cultural traditions. Hence there is the characteristic cleavage between the "level of aspiration" on the one hand, and the "level of expectation" on the other. As long as the levels of aspiration and expectation are more or less the same for the lower-class individual and diverge sharply from those accepted as superior, there is no threat to the disintegration of the larger social structure. Again it would appear that, as long as the level of aspiration and the level of expectation are so much at variance that the level of expectation of the subordinate group is unrelated to the values accepted as superior, there is no serious problem. However, when the levels of expectation and levels of aspiration approach those of the superior group the problem of the integration of the social structure becomes acute. Then there arises the characteristic demand for equality of treatment.

In the case of the lower class of Creole Trinidad, the levels of aspiration were "national," the levels of expectation subcultural; in the case of the Indian community, both level of aspiration and level of expectation tended until recent years to be subcultural. In understanding the development of the society special attention must be paid to those groups of both cultures that have most completely incorporated upper-class values. It is through them that the attack against the dominant upper class becomes most vocal. In Trinidad society this revolt showed itself both in Negro nationalist movements that expressed an alternative to the dominant system and, when the revolt became stronger, in the political movements for self-government. These developments are more fully discussed elsewhere, but here it is essential to note that the movements came from those groups that had to a large extent shed subcultural characteristics. As a result of this there is a confusion on the part of the leaders of their own position with that of the masses to whom they turn for support. Consequently, it is not necessary that there be a total acceptance or striving for the upper-class values by the masses for a mass movement to develop. In order that a threat to the stability of the social order may develop there must be merely sufficient of that merging of level of "national" aspiration and level of personal expectation to lead to an identification of the mass of the people with the new leadership.*

To the extent that leadership is unable to establish such roots, it fails through lack of support. The crisis arises when through continued Western rule the disruption of the subcultures is such that they become incorporated into a system of "national" striving. Thus leadership in Trinidad arose directly or indirectly from those groups that had traveled abroad and imbibed the best of Western culture and therefore demanded equality of treatment. The lower-class subculture, with its ambivalent cultural traditions, could never become a focus for the political movement because, when the lower class thought in national terms, it evaluated itself and its problems according to national standards; hence the much-noted political apathy of the mass of the people. When, however, the acceptance of upper-class values came within the level of expectation of a sufficient number of lower-class individuals, there was a response to political

* Stonequist, in *The Marginal Man*[8] long ago showed the role of the marginal group in effecting leadership of nationalist movements. However, the insight expressed in that book, because of inadequate theoretical foundation, led to an indiscriminate use of the term "marginal," so that "marginal man" became, like "plural society," a source of more confusion than help.

leadership. The demand for adult suffrage, in its emotional origin, at any rate, was one for economic and social equality on the part of middle-class persons who felt they had been subjected to discrimination.

On the other hand, it is an indication of the difference of the problem of the integration of the Indian group that there has begun to develop a fear of the general economic dominance of the latter. The fact is that the Indian group, far from being a minority, bids fair to become a majority of the population. However, this factor of numerical preponderance applied as well to the Creole lower-class group. Besides this, however, the Indian community, possessing so many elements of a different culture, is less appreciative of the national tradition than is the Creole lower class. This group is growing more powerfully in terms of economic strength and is throwing up a sufficiency of leaders in the economic field. It is conceivable therefore that a tie-up can develop between the economic and political fields that may lead to an eventual challenge to the general economic dominance of the white group.

While the situation is a complex one, it appears that in recent elections overriding loyalty to the Indian ethnic group and its culture has led to the return of Indian members in all those constituencies in which Indians predominate. In the case of the Indian group, however, there has not developed such a disparity between the middle-class leader advocating the Indian cause and the leaders actually thrown up by the masses.

One hypothesis that has been advanced is that the persistence of the caste pattern led to the success of Indians of high-caste origin. If these ethnic values persist over the general universalistic achievement values and democratic political forms to which the society has become committed, then the future of Trinidad is likely to be quite different from that envisaged by those who planned the future and initiated political change.

One feature that may lead us to a too optimistic view of the spread of universalistic ideas is the fact that the principle of equality of treatment developed as between the different subcultural groups in the society. This principle is not necessarily in line with the conception of a democratic universalistically oriented society. The system unit of such a society tends to be the individual and the primary group, that at a minimum is compatible with a continuously functioning social system, namely the conjugal family. The principle of equality of treatment of groups recognizes larger particularistic ties to the ethnic group as a whole, and the individual tends to become subordinated to this ethnic tie. It is this replacement of the individual by the group as the system-unit that differentiates the society whose main principle is equality of rights of the individual from the multicultural society that gives formal recognition to its component cultural groups.

SOCIAL STRATIFICATION AND SUBCULTURAL GROUPS

A discussion of the various groups on the island would show a varying degree of assimilation to the dominant social values and culture. The analysis in terms of social stratification serves the useful purpose of stressing the common values of the society. However, there are of course severe limitations to analysis in terms of social stratification. The basic problem is not whether the approach to the society is through a theory of pluralism or through a theory of stratification, but one of levels of analysis. Insofar as the various ethnic groups in the islands comprise social subsystems of their own, these subsystems are themselves also capable of analysis in terms of stratification and even of cultural pluralism. For instance, although we have been speaking of the Indian group as a single entity, the relations between Hindu and Moslem are of great importance. Again, in terms of social stratification the Hindu group can be analyzed in terms of the partial persistence of hierarchically organized caste groups and in the way in which this original form of social stratification (and its associated cultural pluralism) has been modified and subordinated to the more general norms of the society.

What is needed, therefore, appears to be not a commitment to any particular form of approach, but the relation of these forms of approach to some sort of general sociological theory that will render the inevitably partial empirical analyses meaningful. Without this we are likely to fall into doctrinaire disputation with selective perception and selective presentation of the facts. This is all the more important because, while some features of cultural pluralism (such as urbanism and its effects on the mingling of cultures) will respond readily to quantitative analysis, the most meaningful problems of the plural society are much less susceptible to such treatment. The basic problem is the implication of cultural pluralism to the integration and viability of the social order, but in the analysis of the phenomenon we may easily find that the group of leaders, numerically small and culturally assimilated, is of critical significance.

References cited:

1. Furnivall, J. S.
   1948 *Colonial Policy and Practice.* Cambridge Univ. Press, Cambridge, England.
2. Furnivall, J. S.
   1945 *Tropical Economy.* In *Fabian Colonial Essays.* R. Hinden, ed. Allen & Unwin, London, England.
3. Sorokin, P. A.
   1947 *Society, Culture, and Personality, Their Structure and Dynamics: A System of General Sociology.* Harper, New York, N.Y.
4. Parsons, T. & E. A. Shils, eds.
   1952 *Toward a General Theory of Action.* Harvard Univ. Press, Cambridge, Mass.
5. Braithwaite, L.
   1952 *Social Stratification in Trinidad. Social and Economic Studies* 2(2, 3): 5–175.
6. Adamic, L.
   1945 *A Nation of Nations.* Harper, New York, N.Y.
7. Gordon, M. M.
   1954 *Social Structures and Goals in Group Relations.* In *Freedom and Control: Essays Presented to Robert MacIver.* M. Berger, ed. Van Nostrand, Princeton, N.J.
8. Stonequist, E. V.
   1937 *The Marginal Man: A Study in Personality and Culture Conflict.* Scribner, New York, N.Y.

5. Social Stratification and Ethnic Identification

STATUS RIVALRY BETWEEN THE ETHNIC GROUPS

Social stratification in Canalville must be analyzed against the background of the historical positions of the different ethnic groups within the community as well as throughout the colony. When the upper-class whites and middle-class mulattoes left the plantations after the abolition of slavery, the ex-slaves who bought the plantations and converted them into villages, such as Canalville, remained as the only social group. There were differences in wealth between the rural blacks, and as already described, those blacks who owned land and houses in the villages spoke with "conscious superiority" of the laborers who had no homes of their own and who still lived on the plantations. These differences were not so great nor were they sustained for a period long enough to create permanent class divisions within the black group. At the time the other immigrants began to enter the colony, the blacks considered themselves a unified group.

The blacks based their group's status on its "civilization" which was "essentially British in its characteristics." They were Christian, educated in accordance with British ideas and conceptions. Their tastes in food and clothing was approximately that of the British, and most important of all, the blacks believe that they thought and acted in harmony with the British of whose civilization they were the products. In the social hierarchy of the colony the freeholding black farmers occupied the lowest stratum, but in their villages they were the only group and were secure in their position.

The riots between the blacks and Portuguese some years after the

SOURCE: Pp. 179–203 of Elliott P. Skinner, "Ethnic Interaction in a British Guiana Rural Community: A Study in Secondary Acculturation and Group Dynamics," Ph.D. Dissertation, Columbia University, 1955. Reprinted by permission of the author.

migration of the latter group to Georgetown, and the rural villages such as Canalville, grew out of the rivalry between the two groups for superior status. The blacks because of their "civilization," considered themselves superior to the Portuguese. But the superior economic position, skin color, and basically European (although not British) culture of the Portuguese gave them a higher status than the blacks. Today in the colony blacks acknowledge the higher position of the Portuguese but still feel that no deference need be paid to them. The British, who place this group in the social category "Portuguese" as against "Other Europeans" (which includes most Europeans), have the same attitude.

As the Portuguese left the rural villages, such as Canalville, rivalry for status shifted to the blacks and Chinese. No overt conflicts arose between these groups, mainly because the Chinese were few in number and easily established intimate social relationships with the blacks. Moreover, as soon as the Chinese became wealthy and acculturated they too moved into the cities. Thus, the black group was again left dominant in the villages until the East Indian group began to compete with them for higher status. It is this rivalry which will be analyzed.

The main difficulty in dealing with social stratification in Canalville is that individuals, whatever their economic, educational, and political position, regard themselves, and are regarded by others, primarily as members of ethnic groups. Though the wealthiest man in the village is an East Indian, there are many poorer East Indians than there are blacks. Thus, with regard to wealth as a criterion, the status of the East Indian group *qua* group is lower than that of the blacks. Similarly the black group includes more educated people than the East Indian group although the only illiterate young person in the village is a black man. Furthermore, the black group has had control of the political apparatus of the village since its inception. It is interesting to note in this context that none of the East Indians has even attempted to attain a seat on the village council although their numbers should entitle them to one at the very least.

A serious challenge to the present hierarchy in the village is now developing. More East Indians are acquiring the "valuable" traits which were the basis of the black group's status and which are still necessary for high status in the community. The position of the black group is threatened because the East Indian group, through the process of secondary acculturation, has acquired and is still acquiring the desired traits. These traits, in combination with the important trait of "thrift," are enabling the East Indians to compete with the blacks for status.

As a group blacks are ambivalent about the importance of thrift and wealth as factors in achieving or maintaining group status. While some of them try to emulate the East Indians, many of them regard thrift not as a desirable trait but as one indicative of low status position.

The blacks believe that the East Indians would do anything for money and that among them money is carefully saved instead of being used for food and clothing. A black man points to an East Indian and says: "Me know that man when he had nothing; today he is a big man." The reason for this, he would tell you, is that while the black man eats and drinks well, the East Indian saves his money. An example of the "cheapness" of an East Indian was pointed out to me when an East Indian man who had just purchased a plot of land from an African, approached another African to ask him whether a full quart of rum or a half quart would be adequate to seal the bargain. My African companion replied: "Man, if you can't buy a bottle of rum tell the people that." This East Indian man had just paid $2000 for the plot of land so it was doubtful that he lacked the money to buy a full quart of rum; more probably the East Indian, not knowing the etiquette of the situation, sought this information from the black man. His behavior was not viewed in the light of one who was willing to learn the customary practice, but in terms of the prevailing stereotype.

Whenever possible a black person indicates his dislike of the East Indian's "cheapness." A group of Africans and East Indians were discussing a murder trial which was taking place in Georgetown and concluded that "there is no justice in the colony"; but although agreeing in part with this consensus, an East Indian said that his friends misunderstood a certain abstruse point of law. An old African man took offense at this statement and replied, "No coolie know more than any African. The only thing a coolie has more than an African is money, because they cheap." The East Indian replied that he was not talking about "nation" (meaning ethnic group) but pointed out that India was governed by Indians, a fact which he thought indicated that there were intelligent among Indians. This rather sharp exchange between an African and an East Indian characteristically brought forth no comment from the assembled East Indians and Africans since both groups openly discuss racial matters and each other's cultural characteristics. There is no taboo on the subject of ethnic peculiarities.

The wealthier Africans in the village make it a point to see that no East Indian "let his eye pass" them, meaning that they would not allow an East Indian to do them any favors which might be considered to confer on him equality of status, or worse, superiority. Mr. N., an East Indian, insisted on paying for a piece of mutton which Mr. P., an African, had sent him as a present. Mr. P. never forgot what he thought was a slight and from that day has refused to accept drinks from Mr. N. Most of the Africans in Canalville did not approve of black girls working as domestics in the homes of wealthy East Indians. They thought that this tended to "lowdown" the status of the group, for as one said, "Me won't let my relative work for no coolie, for me believe a black man better than a coolie anytime."

The East Indians in the village still pay deference to the superior status of the blacks. They refer to themselves as "coolies" although they are aware that the term is a derogatory one. Nowadays, East Indians grudgingly admit that the blacks taught them many things, but point with pride to India to show that East Indians can do more than make money. The charge of a black man that only now East Indians were learning from Africans how to build houses brought the significant retort that there were no black men in India but Indians built the Taj Mahal.

The East Indians in their turn say the blacks are spendthrifts and spend their money on entertainment rather than on anything else, even food. This stereotype of the blacks held by the East Indians is interesting since it is complementary to the one held by the blacks of the East Indians. The East Indians, in addition, hold that the blacks are uncooperative and ungrateful; thus for an East Indian to tell another East Indian that "he is just like a black man" means that the disparaged individual has refused to repay a debt of gratitude.

East Indians often hesitate to invite black men to their homes because they don't quite trust the black men with their wives. I overheard an East Indian telling a black man, "Your nation can't come to my home because you na know how to act." This widespread stereotype is also indicated in the epithet which the East Indian uses to signify black people. They call the black people "Ravan." Ravan, in Hindu mythology, is the lustful, curly-haired king of Ceylon who kidnapped the beautiful and chaste Sita, the wife of Rama, the hero of the *Ramayana*. Since Sita represents to the Hindus the ideal of feminine chastity and wifely devotion, her abductor is held in contempt by them. Ravan was, however, a Brahmin—so by calling the blacks Ravan, the less-informed East Indians, much to the chagrin of the pandits, unknowingly admit the higher status of the blacks.

The fact that the Africans and East Indians consider themselves primarily as members of ethnic groups conditions the interaction of individuals within the groups. For example, there is almost no intermarriage between the groups, since an East Indian looks for a husband for his marriageable daughter only among members of his own ethnic group. Mr. S., a Hindu, told me that he was a "nationalist" and did not believe in intermarriage. He said that every "nation" should confine its marriages to its own women, and that if he married a black woman he would be "robbing" his own group. When a black man enumerated the traits he looked for in a wife, I asked him whether he might not sooner find them in an East Indian woman than in a black woman. He admitted that this was so, but said he would never marry a "coolie," mainly because there was some indefinable difference between her and a black woman. This young man later qualified his statement by saying that he would marry only an "Englishified" East Indian girl because only such know how to conduct herself among blacks. He pointed out that the "ordinary" East Indian girl was too shy.

This reluctance to intermarry does not mean that sexual relations do not occur between the groups or that there is a complete absence of intermarriage. When asked about the incidence of mixed marriages in the village, an informant said that there were not more than two or three, but laughingly added: "There is more mixing than that." Asked what he meant, he replied: "Some people thief some," meaning, of course, that surreptitious sexual relations existed between the groups. I discovered that the black man, referred to above, who told me that he would never marry an East Indian woman was the paramour of an East Indian married woman. East Indian men, too, cross the ethnic boundary in search of sexual gratification, and there are at least three East Indian men in the village who have children by black women. One of them admitted to me that he "played with the [African] girl but would never married she."

Given the East Indian practice of marrying their female children off at an early age within the ethnic group, it is easy to understand why few East Indian girls have black men as their first husbands.

But a woman whose husband is dead cannot marry again according to Hindu rites and is undesirable as a spouse. Thus, many East Indian women "take up" with African men and, in order to attain the status of married women, often get married in Christian churches. Again, some East Indian girls who have been able to escape parental control (or somehow manage to secure parental authority) marry black men. These marriages, although accepted by both groups, are not approved of by many. Mr. S., the Hindu referred to above, did not like the fact that most of the intermarriages were between black men and East Indian females. He intimated that the black men who married East Indian women so appreciated this fact that they performed such "unmanly acts" as bringing water for their spouses. A black man, Mr. A., did not care whether people intermarried or not, but was gratified to see that nowadays, unlike a few decades ago, the black men were marrying East Indian women instead of East Indian men marrying black women.

Marriage and sex is not the focal point of rivalry between African and East Indian. For example, during a discussion in the village at which both East Indians and blacks were present it was brought out that an African youth, the unmarried father of twins by an African girl, turned around and married an East Indian girl. The speaker concluded with the statement: "An to think that his father and mother stayed around and see he married a coolie girl." This statement had all the overtones of disapproval but none of the East Indians present took offense at it. In the "mock courts" (games played by the people in the village in which they pretended to conduct trials) held in the village some time ago, it was revealed to me that East Indian women used to have African men brought before the "judge" for child support. This could not be done if there was sexual taboo between the groups. Both groups believe that the blacks are "superior" sexually but instead of this fact being used as an added point of friction the blacks are simply envied for it. An East Indian man, seeing a naked African boy bathing in the river said: "Black man bless. Look at that *anaconda* [a large boa-constrictor]."

Circumscribed by status position, East Indians and Africans interact successfully and unsuccessfully as individuals. Here the "real" worth of a man is taken into account, and by "real" is meant the man's share of those traits which, when taken as a whole and attached to ethnic group, mean high status. Those East Indian and black families who live near each other maintain friendly relations and often share food and utensils. The black man who would object if a person, black or East Indian, used his donkey cart without permission, did not object when the East Indian owner of a large shop used it without asking for it. The black man felt that his permission should have been obtained and said that the East Indian considered himself a "big man," but at the same time, the African did not question the action. On the other hand, when this black man was ill, he called in the same East Indian (and not a black man) and asked him to "watch out for" his children if he should die.

The East Indian man who owned a rum shop in the village often did not sell rum on credit to East Indians, but accepted the note of credit which an East Indian brought from an African requesting the rum. In these cases, the East Indians who wanted the rum were better known to the African than to the rum-shopkeeper. One informant bragged that he was the only black man in the village who could walk up to any East Indian man and receive monetary or nonmonetary assistance. The truth of this statement was brought home when, after trying in vain to raise the money among the blacks, he was able to borrow money from an East Indian man to bail out one of his relatives from jail. On the other hand, I have seen this black man lend money without interest to individual East Indians and give them fruits and vegetables from his farms. The same informant thought it necessary to visit a sick East Indian man who was on his way to the hospital because though he was not himself on speaking terms with the man he was a good friend of the family. When the sick man died, the black man spent a good part of the day consoling the bereaved family.

In many cases the personal relations between members of the East Indian and African ethnic groups modify or take precedence over the type of behavior expected of them as members of different status groups. One evening, about 7 P.M., I heard a disturbance down at the crossroads in the village and hurried down only to hear a black man shouting: "Na provoke me, man, or a'll bust your tail." The disturbance originated when an East Indian man threatened to kick the speaker's nephew because the boy had allowed a cow to stray into the East Indian's yard. The speaker had gone to the East Indian's house to ask the reason for the threat to the boy, but, instead of responding, the East Indian had started to abuse the black man. Thereupon the black man collared him and started to thrash him. They were soon parted, but the black man, being very angry, kept on cursing. Shouting at the top of his voice he said: "Me don't eat you coolie dahl [a form of sauce made from peas] and rice. You good for nothing coolie!" After he had kept on in this vein for some time he suddenly stopped and said: "Me can't talk over much, cause this boy here [referring to an East Indian] is me neighbor and it go hurt he."

Some black people in the village say that their fellow blacks betray their ethnic and status affiliations by making common cause with the East Indians against other blacks. A case in point was the attitude of the blacks in the village toward a black man who was having a boundary dispute with an East Indian. The East Indian had bought a grocery shop on a fairly large piece of land and not being too concerned with the land but mainly with the shop made no effort to fence the land. The village officials, believing that there was enough land for a house lot between the East Indian's property and the government-owned land, sold the piece to this black man. The black man, when told by other villagers that he might be trespassing on the East Indian's land, accused them of jealousy and boasted that he would show them how to run a business and compete with the coolies in Canalville. The East Indians, primarily because they did not want a competitor in the black man, and partly because they were peeved at such remarks as, "Me wouldn't let any coolie make a fool of me," had their land resurveyed and built a fence right up to the black man's shop, a deed which placed the black man in a position of having violated the building laws by not allowing distance between his building and the boundary of his property. For days afterwards the black man raved. Not being able to get any satisfaction from the helpless village officials (they were wrong to sell him an inadequate piece of land in the first place), he said: "Black man is going down; because black man is for coolie; and coolie is for coolie." What he did not know, and moreover could not discover, because of his poor relations with both blacks and East Indians, was that many people in the village were sorry for him. One black remarked: "Me know he wrong, but me still think it is advantage [unfair]."

RANKING WITHIN ETHNIC GROUPS

Although a person's position in the village hierarchy is primarily determined by his membership in an ethnic group and its relative rank in the status hierarchy, one cannot ignore the relative ranking of the individual within his own group. His rank is determined by his possession of few or many of these strategic traits on which the status position of his group is based. Most of the blacks are farmers, but some are "big" farmers possessing up to ten acres of land while others possess not more than one acre. The differential income of these groups determine, in part, their capacity to participate in the *style of life* ideally associated with their status group. For example, only those farmers with large incomes send their children to school in Georgetown, run for office in village politics, and provide for their families adequate food, clothes, and shelter. They are respected by the rest of the population and reciprocate by serving in the churches, acting as sponsors for children at baptism, and helping poorer families by giving them plots of land to farm.

The more prosperous farmers are the only ones who are concerned with ranking within the group. Thus, a feud is still going on between two of the most important families in the village, although one of the main protagonists is now dead. The moves and countermoves which characterize this feud reveal where the source of village prestige lies. There was a big struggle over the village chairmanship, during which each family marshaled its friends in an effort to retain or gain the office. The head of one of the feuding families was headmaster of the village school. He declared that as long as he lived, the daughter of his antagonist, who was quite well qualified, would never teach in the village school. This stand, directed against a family which was very high in the church hierarchy, and, as such, had a voice in school affairs, was grievously felt. It meant, among other things, that the family under attack lost a coveted prize—teaching jobs often being given even to unqualified individuals by virtue of family connections. Also it made it necessary for their daughter to leave home and community in order to get a teaching job.

Unity among high-ranking African families is not conspicuous. Of course, they speak to each other and sometimes visit with each other, but they have no more social or economic interaction with each other than with lower-ranking members of their group. The wife of the village chairman, the wives of the village councillors, and the wives of those farmers with less than one acre of land, all huckster alike in the market place at Georgetown.

A really serious problem for families of higher rank in the African ethnic-status group lies in getting their daughters married. Their sons, of course, take care of themselves by following the local pattern of begetting children and then setting up households. Their daughters, indeed, are usually well educated, read good books, and often know how to play the piano. They are, in reality, educated for city life and not for life in the village as farmers' wives. They are not allowed to live in the city because their parents, like most of the people in Canalville, fear the riotous life of the city. Their chances of meeting young men of suitable rank from other villages are not good because usually these young men have already made the "customary" arrangements. The result is that they make local alliances—propinquity being a strong factor in romantic affairs—which are not only below their rank, but often unsanctioned by religious rites; or they become bitter old maids. The latter possibility does not often occur because, on the dissolution of their families of orientation, the females frequently make some sort of arrangement that the family would have attempted to prevent. Today many people in the community are anxiously waiting to see what will become of the several unmarried, and presumably chaste, daughters of an important family in the village when its head eventually dies.

Social ranking within the East Indian group is similar to that in the African group. Caste, which was so characteristic of these people in India, is insignificant in the village, and only detailed inquiry brings out any evidence that the East Indian villagers recognize or observe rules of caste. The Hindu villagers say that there are six castes among themselves: Brahmin, Chatri, Bye, Sudra, Chamar, and Done (Doan). They are, however, not sure whether each caste is represented in the village. When they discuss caste with me, they took the same attitude many Americans do who are asked about their genealogy—interesting but not too relevant. There is only one Brahmin family in the village. By occupation the head of it is a vendor of ices, and one sees him daily on his little donkey cart stopping from time to time to sell refreshments to crowds of children and young people. He does a little farming, the products of which are sold by his daughter. This man does not observe the caste prohibition against eating with members of lower castes; nor does he indulge in ritual purification after such contact. As a Brahmin he is entitled to perform certain religious rites for the other Indians in the community, but except for the Di Vahlie festival on which he lights up his whole house and yard and gives a feast for all the people in the village, he is not interested in playing any religious role. Curiously enough, this man had icons of the Virgin Mary and of the Sacred Heart of Jesus on the walls of his house but none of the more colorful Hindu deities. This puzzled me, so I asked him for an explanation. His only reply was a vague sentiment of wanting to conform to local "Christian" conditions. The difficulty, however, is that he did not have to go this far in his attempt to conform. This man also had a Christian priest perform a marriage ceremony for himself and his wife to "protect my wife and children." He could not explain, however, why he did not simply go to Georgetown and register his traditional marriage as a means of accomplishing the same thing. The reason why he did so is clear; his family, being one of the oldest East Indian families in Canalville, is the most "Englishified" and needed the prestige which comes from a Christian wedding.

The older East Indians in the village remember when people married according to caste rules. In those days a male Brahmin was free to marry within any caste—even Chamars, and his children took his caste status. His daughters, however, could only marry a Brahmin or a Chatri. The Brahmin in the village told me that one of his daughters was married to a Chatri and that although he would not "look for" a Chamar for his daughter he would consider other factors such as character, wealth, and family connections before allowing his daughter to marry any man regardless of his caste. Another East Indian, a Chatri, when asked about the traits he looked for in a husband for his daughter, listed good character, industry, wealth, and good family. When asked about caste he disclosed that his first wife was a member of his own caste, but that today he was married to a woman of a lower caste.

By and large, Hindus and Moslems who live in the village say they do not like to intermarry with each other. I have already discussed the case of a Moslem young woman who, although she had had an affair with a young Hindu, could not marry him and finally married a Moslem like herself. Discussing this case with the villagers brought out the information that "today people don't bother too much with that stupidness." Case after case of couples in such positions were related in which one or both of them changed religions. Incidentally, the Hindus and Moslems, while sharing common status as East Indians, have stereotypes of each other. A young Moslem girl, without being asked, said that she would never marry a Hindu as she was of a higher "nation"; she said that she would sooner marry a black man. An unmarried Hindu girl maintained that she would not marry a Moslem man because "Moslem men are cruel; they get drunk and don't work." She too said that she would marry a black man before she would marry a Moslem.

Except for these negative attitudes between the Hindu and Moslem East Indians, the two groups get along very well together and the observer scarcely noticed the difference between them. They visit each other, and attend each other's ceremonies. In British Guiana, an East Indian ceremony is an East Indian ceremony and during the rituals, except that the main participants must play their religious roles, the Hindu and Moslem men sit together and their women sit together as well. A Moslem of means refrains from using beef at any of his festivities because his Hindu friends could not eat it and thus could not be invited to the ceremony. A poorer Moslem buys a young steer (it is more economical to use beef than mutton or goat meat), but he serves his Hindu guests mutton that has been cooked in a different house with different utensils. At a Moslem wedding in the village the meals for the Hindus were prepared at the house of a black woman.

Irrespective of caste and religion, major differences between members of the East Indian ethnic group are based on factors similar to those which operate among the blacks; wealth and all that which it brings, and education. The owners of the shops in the village do not have much in common with the people who work on the plantations. Relations between these people are limited to commercial affairs and to activities which show ethnic affiliation. The East Indian shopkeeper who attends the wedding of an East Indian of lower rank does so in the name of patronage, but does not invite low-ranking East Indians to his own house. The children of the wealthier East Indians in the village go to school in Georgetown while the children of the poorer ones go to the plantations. It is taken for granted that educated East Indians (regardless of caste as there is no correlation between caste and wealth among them) will marry people of their own rank and they may even marry outside of the ethnic group.

The marginality of the Chinese ethnic group in the village is evident in their interaction with the other groups in the village. They are cordial to the other villagers and one of the Chinese usually attends any functions given by the villagers; but this interaction is not spontaneous and has an air of patronage. This behavior of the Chinese group is necessary, for as commercial people they have to be friendly so as to survive in a village where there are only two Chinese families.

Biologically, the Chinese in Canalville are a mixed group with only one individual claiming both a Chinese mother and father. The others are descended from Chinese, East Indians, and blacks. Culturally they do not differ from the blacks and more acculturated East Indians in the village. None of these Chinese speak the Chinese language and the eldest Chinese could not recognize his name when written in Chinese characters. All of their clothes, meals, and household furnishings are Guianese and not too different, except in elegance, from those of the local blacks. Despite this similarity in culture, the Chinese still remain to themselves.

The Chinese when possible marry people like themselves. No black young man in the village believes that he has the opportunity to become familiar with the young Chinese females, not only because of their relative seclusion but because of the ethnic barrier. Attempting to get an idea of how the Chinese felt about their status in the village I asked a young Chinese woman if she feared she would not be accepted by the villagers if she tried to become more friendly with them. The question amused her because she could not think of wishing to mingle with the bulk of the villagers on any terms, and thus could not conceive of being rebuffed if she tried to do so. The Chinese stereotype of the blacks sees them as being improvident and unable to pay their bills because of too much frivolity, and they regard the East Indians as being "too cheap." Both the East Indians and the blacks think the Chinese are crafty and when one Chinese man attempted to cultivate the friendship of a wealthy young East Indian, the young man's father objected because he feared that the Chinese had an ulterior motive.

It can be said with assurance that the Chinese are outward-looking in terms of their relationship with the other groups in the village. They visit their relatives in the other villages and towns and sometimes remain away for long periods. Their friends come from other villages and from the towns, and it was not surprising to see several autos of outside Chinese around the Chinese homes during the holidays or on Sundays.

The attitude of the villagers to the Chinese in their midst was best summed up by a black man who asked: "Me wonder what go happen when Y. [a Chinese man] dies." This question is of great significance because the pattern of reaction to a death in the village is a fairly standard one. As soon as the death is announced, both East Indians and blacks rush to the house of the dead person to offer condolences, even if they do not attend the wake or funeral. The East Indian who answered the question was not too sure of himself and simply stated: "Me think me would go see the old lady."

THE PROBLEMS OF STRATIFICATION

In treating problems of social stratification in the village of Canalville I have to eschew the categories of class and also the categories of caste (as used by Warner and his followers) for they simply do not apply. If class is defined in the strictly economic sense as differential access to the strategic resources of the community then we find that there are no sharp lines of division between the inhabitants of Canalville. Most are subsistence farmers and although some have more land than others, this added wealth is not enough to separate categories of farmers. Using as an index of social class the largest group of people whose members have intimate access to each other, taking part in such informal activities as visiting, dancing, receptions, and larger informal affairs (Davis and Gardners, 1941:59), we discover that not only are there no such exclusive groups in the village but that the only cliques are based on political affiliations. Most social functions in the village are attended by the entire population.

The use of the category of caste could not be used to distinguish the different ethnic groups in Canalville even in the Warnerian sense: social groups, often in a superordinate and subordinate position between which there are no marriages or social intimacies (*Ibid.*, p. 59). Not only are there intermarriages between the groups in the village but considerable social intimacy exists between them. The traditional caste relationship among the East Indians has lost much of its religious sanction and the Brahmin, who is not a religious leader, is not shown any special deference. Money, position, and education are the new cultural values which the East Indians now use for social ranking within their ethnic group. Marriage does not often take place between the East Indian and other groups, not so much on account of that group's status but because of the persistence of marriage patterns from India. The marriage patterns of this group are changing with acculturation, and increasing incidence of intermarriage results. The differences between the ethnic groups are based on recognizable cultural differences. With the breakdown of these cultural differences, the question of intermarriage loses its significance and the way is opened toward assimilation which is the end result of successful acculturation.

The pattern of social stratification in Canalville shows something else: fluidity of the social structure when individuals belonging to disparate status groups acquire or lose those strategic qualities which maintain the status of the group. Thus the Africans in Canalville when informed, in answer to their inquiry, that the anthropologist was served an "English" dinner (with the proper use of silver and crystal) at the home of a wealthy East Indian reacted first with disbelief, and later attempted to prove that the reason for this was that the hostess had lived among blacks all her life and had their ways. This fact was not checked so I do not know whether it was true or not; but it is revealing to note that the Africans also discounted the East Indians when the question as to the identity of the best-dressed women in the village was discussed. Both of these illustrations point to the unwillingness of the Africans to reward the East Indian women for their acquisition of "English" ways. East Indians are still regarded as "cheap" though the younger East Indians consume as conspicuously as blacks. When the African speaks of the social mobility of the East Indian it is in these terms: "Black man is falling. When the black man used to wear feathers in his cap, the coolie was eating water-rice. Black man used to say, 'Go way, you water-rice coolie!' Today the coolie think they are big people. After one time will be a next. Today is time for coolie. I don't mind cause the Lord say, 'In the last days race will rise against race, and nation will rise against nation, and there will be wars and rumors of wars.' "

The dilemma of the African group, as revealed in the analysis of social stratification in Canalville, is that although the Africans possessed most of these attributes necessary for high status in the community, they lacked the acquisitive trait. The possession of this trait in a colony with a market economy is of utmost importance. The East Indians had this trait when they came to the colony and they have acquired through their contact with the blacks the other traits needed for high status. The blacks although boasting on the one hand that they taught the "coolies all they know," refuse, on the other hand, to reward the East Indian for the acquisition of new cultural traits. The black man must refuse this or admit the possibility of a higher or equal status for the East Indians.

Despite the problems of the blacks which were brought about by the acculturation of the East Indians, there is a growing awareness among both groups of the similarity of individuals based, not on ethnic affiliations, but on similar life goals. An East Indian man said

to me: "When me was a child, Indian and African children na want
to see each other tall [at all]. Now me can be a koker-keeper
[watchman for the dikes] and me no have nothing to do with an
African who is a farmer. If me son become a hunter and the African
son become a hunter, they go together and forget all about we old
people and we ideas." Thus in these words a local inhabitant of the
village has discovered for himself the cultural and social changes
which are taking place in his own society.

In Canalville there is taking place the formation of class groups
based on such criteria as wealth, education, and an outlook (this can
be called a *style of life*) which is the result of acculturation. There
is a movement away from social stratification based on a hierarchy
of ethnic groups in the community to one based on class groups
which cut across ethnic boundaries. Of course, there is always the
possibility that the East Indian ethnic group in Canalville might
supersede the African ethnic group. This, if it ever comes about,
will be due mainly to influence on the community from the colony as
a whole. The growth of nationalism in the colony, and in the whole
Caribbean—a nationalism which has as one of its major aspects racial
and ethnic equality—is likely to counteract any ethnically divisive
forces at work in the society.

NANCIE L. SOLIEN

6. West Indian Characteristics
of the Black Carib[1]

Since the year 1797 there has been living on the Caribbean coast of Central America a group of people known as "Black Carib." They are the descendants of the Red Caribs who occupied the Lesser Antilles at the time of Columbus, and of Africans brought to the New World during the seventeenth and eighteenth centuries. Taylor has outlined the history of this group in detail up to the time of their arrival on the Central American mainland.[2] These people, originally having landed at Trujillo, Honduras, have now spread up and down the coast and live in a series of towns and villages from Stann Creek, British Honduras, to the Black River in Honduras.

Studies of Black Carib culture in the past have stressed its similarity to the Tropical Forest type of culture of their Red Carib ancestors. In fact, in Taylor's opinion, "It is in its imponderable aspects that the culture of the Black Carib differs most from that of their Indian forbears in the Lesser Antilles, so as to constitute, as it were, a Negro cake composed of Amerindian ingredients."[3]

The present writer conducted field work among the Black Carib from July 1956 to July 1957. Livingston, Guatemala, was the community studied most intensively, but survey trips of one month each were made in British Honduras and the Republic of Honduras. During this study many striking similarities between the culture of the Black Caribs and that of their Negro neighbors were noted. Especially were there resemblances to the British Honduran Creole culture.[4] This finding led to a comparative study of materials published on West Indian Negro cultures. The purpose of this paper is to suggest that the culture of the Black Carib, though differing in many

SOURCE: Reprinted from the *Southwestern Journal of Anthropology*, Vol. 15, No. 3 (1959):300–7, by permission of the author and the editors of the *Southwestern Journal of Anthropology*.

ways from that of other New World Negroes, nevertheless should be considered as a variant of West Indian Negro culture. It will also demonstrate that the most probable sources of the West Indian traits in Carib culture were the non-Carib Negro groups living on the coastline of Central America during the nineteenth century. In other words, the evidence indicates that the Black Carib were more similar, both racially and culturally, to the Red Carib upon their arrival on the mainland than they are at the present time.

The groups with which the Black Carib have been compared here are the rural Creole of British Honduras, the Haitians and Trinidadians as reported by Herskovits, and Jamaica as studied by Beckwith and Henriques.[5] In addition, historical accounts of the customs of slaves during the eighteenth and nineteenth centuries in the various West Indian islands have been drawn upon freely.

In the realms of economics and social organization there are great similarities throughout the Caribbean, including the Black Carib area. Wage labor, whether on plantations, road-building gangs, loading bananas, etc., has high prestige value, and is generally sought by most men, even though the work is often of a periodic or seasonal nature. Among the Black Carib horticulture has been traditionally women's work, the men assisting with clearing and burning, but in recent years many men have become small farmers. They grow crops different from those of the women, and usually sell the greater portion of their yield. The most important of these crops are rice, beans, coconuts (for copra), and formerly, bananas. All of these are products which enter into the national economies of the countries in which the Caribs live.

Women, on the other hand, grow cassava, sugarcane, plantains, yams, and various other roots, primarily for home consumption or local sale. Here, as elsewhere in the West Indies, the woman has exclusive right to her own earnings.

Fishing, formerly one of the main bases of the Carib economy, is still important, but now tends to be done either by specialists or by other men at irregular times when they have nothing else to do or when the fish are said to be plentiful and biting. Women do not fish, but they play an important role in distribution, since they preserve the fish by salting and drying, after which they carry them to market.

Home industries, especially dressmaking done by women and tailoring by men, contribute greatly to the domestic economy. Both sexes, but especially men, tend to dress in fashions copied from certain segments of the Negro population in the United States. Many Carib men have traveled to New Orleans, New York, San Francisco, and other United States ports while working on steamships. From these places they have brought back articles of clothing which have then been copied by their less fortunate brethren. For everyday wear, however, the women still use a one-piece smock-like dress over which is worn a full gathered skirt. On their heads they invariably wear a cotton cloth knotted at the nape of the neck and/or a wide-brimmed straw hat. All of these clothes, except the straw hats, are made locally and follow patterns which bear a close resemblance to those worn in other parts of the Caribbean. They are quite different from the clothing worn by mestizo peasants in Central America.

Basketmaking, woodworking, and canoe-building are all men's specialty occupations. Basketry items still manufactured include the water-tight *pataki,* or travel-basket, also made by the Creoles of British Honduras. Presses and sifters used in processing the bitter manioc into cassava cakes are obviously of Tropical Forest origin, but it is interesting to note that certain West Indian Negroes also adopted this equipment.[6] Beckwith noted the manufacture of fishtraps in Jamaica which she likened to those of the Tropical Forest Carib illustrated by Roth.[7] The Black Carib still make these fishtraps today. Woodworkers make mortars and pestles for grinding plantains and husking rice, as well as various bowls and troughs, all of which have their counterparts among the Creole of British Honduras.

The manufacture of dug-out canoes has now also become specialists' work, the methods employed and the finished products being undistinguishable from the industry among the Creoles, and similar to those described by Beckwith.[8]

The present-day family form among the Black Carib shows all the characteristic traits noted by investigators in other areas in the West Indies. Within the household consanguineal ties are far more important than affinal. Marital relationships are unstable and primarily consensual, though in later years couples may be joined in legal marriage as a means of gaining prestige within the community. A strong emphasis on the maternal kin, continued association of the children with the mother after divorce or separation, plus adoption of children for economic reasons, generally by some member of the mother's kindred, are all common features of this organization.

Another institution prominent throughout the Negro Caribbean is that known as the "caretaker" system.[9] In this, a young child is sent to live with a family of higher social position and greater means, exchanging its services for food, shelter, education, and other advantages which its own family could not provide. In most cases, if not all, the host family is non-Carib and non-Negro.

Carib religious beliefs and rituals stem from at least three general traditions—the African, the European, and the American Indian. This statement, of course, can be made concerning most or nearly all peoples living in Latin America today. However, the religion of any local group usually shows a predominance of one of these traditions over the others. Among the Carib there is no good reason to doubt that the African is the most important. There is great emphasis on the importance of the family ancestors, although Taylor believes that the cult which surrounds this may have been as typical of the Island Arawaks as of Africa.[10] However, Coelho has recently pointed out resemblances between Black Carib rituals and those of Negroes in Brazil.[11]

Customs surrounding death correspond almost exactly to those described in Jamaica, Trinidad, and British Honduras.[12] As soon as the death is announced relatives and friends begin to gather at the home of the deceased. Wailing begins then and continues throughout the first night wake. At this and again on the ninth night after death, the friends and relatives keep vigil by praying, singing, dancing, playing games such as checkers, forfeits, and bingo, and listening to stories of the Anansi type. Refreshments are served several times during the night, gifts of food, rum, and coffee having been brought by the guests.

Christianity, among the Black Carib universally Roman Catholicism, has had a great effect on ritual and custom, though these still retain a flavor of non-Christian sources. For example, masses for the dead are as important as elsewhere in Catholic America, but they are given at irregular intervals and usually in response to dreams in which the dead ancestors request such rites.

The belief in and practice of obeah, or black magic, are of vital concern to most Black Caribs today. Significant also is the fact that the term "obeah" itself is in general usage among them. Most deaths are attributed to the magic of obeah-men, whose services have been purchased by some enemy of the deceased. In addition to causing death, magic may have an effect on the course of a love affair, the well-being of one's crops, one's animals, etc.

There is also a belief in spirits, both of the dead and those of the "bush." Although such beliefs are so widespread both in Africa and in the New World that it is impossible to trace their exact provenience, there are a number of parallels between Carib culture and other West Indian cultures. For example, the Black Caribs paint an indigo cross (using household bluing) on the forehead of infants to ward off evil spirits. Beckwith reports the identical custom in Jamaica.[13] Although fear of the evil eye is undoubtedly European in origin, the Caribs have a preventive measure not generally found among the mestizo peoples of Latin America. A charm consisting of a closed fist with the thumb inserted between the index and middle fingers is worn, commonly incorporated into a bracelet. Pierson notes the same charm worn for the same purpose among Negroes in Brazil.[14]

It is in the realms of folk-lore, music, and dancing that the most specific resemblances to the West Indies may be seen. Thus, as Taylor has mentioned, the proverbs, riddles, and folk-tales nearly all have themes identical to those recorded in Trinidad, Guadaloupe, Martinique, and elsewhere.[15] Folk-tales are now generally told only at wakes by men who specialize in this art.

Music is an integral part of their life, and one encounters a number of types of songs and dance, each appropriate for a different occasion. Work songs are sung by women as they coöperate in grinding cassava or working in the fields, while other songs are used with drums as accompaniment in various dances. All of these songs have in common the element that they are comments on current happenings, although many of them are so old that the people no longer remember the events for which they were composed. They serve as moral instruction, as a form of social control, and as a means of broadcasting the latest events.

One of the most popular dances is that called *punta*. This is performed primarily at wakes, and appears to be very similar to the "plays" described by early writers among the slaves.[16] It is still danced in other parts of the Caribbean, though to the writer's knowledge it carries the name *punta* only among the Caribs and the Creoles of British Honduras. One couple occupies the center of a ring of onlookers who aid the drummers' accompaniment with singing and handclapping. The man and woman alternately pursue each other about the floor, at times attempting to get as close as possible to the other without actually touching. During the dance the feet move rapidly in a kind of sideways shuffle, the hips shimmy, and the arms are held alternately outstretched over the head, akimbo, or extended backwards. Occasionally a partner will drop out, leaving the other circling alone about the floor until some other person from the audience enters the circle. Often too, one person, usually a woman, will dance alone with no attempt to draw a partner out onto the floor. Although the word *punta* generally refers to the above complex of singing, dancing, and drumming, the Caribs also think of it as applying to the rhythm involved and to the *kind* of song sung in accompaniment to it. The themes are often derisive or critical, never naming the subject, but making his or her identity entirely clear. Herskovits notes that in Haiti women who share the same mate may sing derisive songs against each other, and that these songs are referred to as "point."[17] Conzemius believed it likely that the Caribs had adopted certain dance elements from Haiti.[18]

During the Christmas season there are a number of dances using costumes and masks held in the streets. Some of these have not yet been identified or linked by this writer to customs elsewhere, but most of them are suggestive of dances described in the Caribbean. The Caribs themselves have no knowledge of their origin or meaning. The first group to appear, about December 24, are called *warín*. This consists of a number of men dressed in costumes made of dried plantain leaves, with masks of papier-mâché or wire-screening material. They dance in various houses or yards to the accompaniment of drums, receiving small amounts of money, a drink of rum or wine, and perhaps a bit of food in return. This type of costume has been described by Crowley as one of the traditional masques of the Trinidadian carnival.[19] The type of behavior involved in this dance complex will readily be recognized as typical of many Negro groups in the Caribbean both during the days of slavery and at the present time.

On Christmas Day, and again on January 1, another male dance group appears dressed in short full skirts, blouses with yokes and long full sleeves, flesh-colored stockings, masks, and elaborate headdresses built up something like a crown decorated with feathers and ribbons. Colored ribbons are also attached to the dress and stream out on all sides when the body is in motion. The dance has two names —one is *wanáragua,* which merely means "mask," according to Taylor.[20] The other name, and the one more commonly used, is "John Canoe." This is the name of a character widely portrayed in masked dances in Jamaica. In the 1830's the dance was described as follows: ". . . rapid crossings of the legs . . . terminating in a sudden stoppage."[21] Although hardly a complete description, this is also true of the dance as performed by the Black Caribs today.

Throughout the Christmas season there appear from time to time other performers, whom the Caribs call *pia manádi*. These characters always go about in pairs, one dressed as a man, the other as a woman with pillows placed to emphasize the secondary sexual characteristics. These two are thought of as clowns. The most important aspect of their performance is verbal, consisting of repartee designed to amuse. It is always somewhat lewd, and the accompanying actions are often obscene. At times they beat each other with sticks. Part of the Carnival in Trinidad today involves a similar character called Pierrot Grenade, though it would be pushing the similarity too far to say the two are identical.[22]

Regardless of where the Black Caribs live today, they form a separate ethnic group which some social scientists might choose to call a caste. They tend to be endogamous, and though they mix freely with other people on many levels of daily intercourse, they usually prefer to return to their own group for the more intimate functions of life, including recreation, marriage, birth, and death.

In spite of the outcast status which they tend to hold today, it should not necessarily be assumed that the Black Caribs have been placed in such a position throughout their residence on the Central American shore. References to the Black Caribs during the first century after their arrival there make frequent mention of their friendly relations with other ethnic groups—in particular with other Negro groups.

The history of Negro occupation of the coast of Honduras goes back to the early sixteenth century when slaves were imported to work in the silver mines. In 1641 a slave ship direct from Africa was lost near Cape Gracias a Dios; the passengers escaped and settled on the coast all the way from the San Juan River to Trujillo.[23] In 1795 a group of Negroes from Santo Domingo was transported to Trujillo after the revolt in their country made it dangerous for them to remain there.[24] These references show that when the Black Caribs arrived on the mainland in 1797 it was already inhabited by numerous Negroes from various areas. In later years, especially during the first half of the twentieth century, thousands of Negroes came from all over the West Indies to work in the banana industry.[25]

It is this writer's opinion that economic competition, among other factors, contributed toward forming the present-day situation in which the Black Caribs are set apart as being "different," and therefore "inferior" to other Negro groups of the area.

Another early contact which the Black Caribs made with Negroes was in British Honduras. As early as 1802, only five years after their arrival on the mainland, we know that they were making frequent trips to that colony for the purpose of smuggling British goods to Honduras.[26] Some of them remained for longer periods to work in the mahogany plantations along with the Negroes who resided in British Honduras. In 1832 large numbers of Black Caribs left Honduras to settle permanently in the British colony after they had coöperated in an unsuccessful attempt by the Royalists to overthrow the Republican government in Honduras.

Several Black Carib genealogies were collected by the writer along the northern coast of Honduras, as well as in Livingston, Guatemala, which indicate non-Carib ancestors two to three generations back—usually Negroes from Haiti, Jamaica, or British Honduras. In Livingston they claim that their village was founded by a group of Black Caribs from Trujillo led by a Haitian. Although many of the details of this story are fantastic and show its myth-like character, it is not altogether improbable since we know that there was a group of Negroes from Haiti living in Trujillo when the Caribs arrived there (see above).

In summary, an analysis of Black Carib culture combined with the evidence available concerning the group's recent history indicates that during the past 160 years they have become more similar culturally and racially to other Negro groups in the Caribbean than they were at the time of their deportation from the island of St. Vincent in the Lesser Antilles. Since the culture traits were adopted piecemeal from a variety of different Negro groups, their total culture resembles no one New World African pattern, but rather presents a configuration unique to the Black Carib. Nevertheless, this pattern should be considered as a variant of Afroamerican, rather than American Indian culture.

Because they have since become a more isolated in-group, if not to say a caste, these people have retained many traits which have changed or disappeared among their neighbors—traits which have generally been assumed to be strictly "Carib" by both Caribs and non-Caribs today.

Notes:

1. Materials from this article have been presented in two papers—one read at the Annual Meeting of the American Anthropological Association, December 1957, and the other at the International Congress of Americanists, July 1958. I wish to thank the Henry L. and Grace Doherty Foundation and the University of Michigan for grants which made the field work among the Black Carib possible.

2. Douglas M. Taylor, *The Black Carib of British Honduras* (New York, 1951), pp. 15–27.

3. *Idem*, p. 143. Also see Eduard Conzemius, "Ethnographical Notes on the Black Carib (Garif)" (*American Anthropologist*, vol. 30, pp. 183–205, 1928).

4. The term "Creole" as used here with respect to British Honduras refers to any person born in the Colony of Negro or mixed-Negro blood. This is the meaning currently attached to the term in the Colony itself. Although no studies of British Honduran culture have been published, the writer's own observations there indicate that it is similar in many ways to the cultures of other Negro groups in the Caribbean, especially in areas which are or have been British colonies. On the other hand, it does seem to exhibit many distinctive characteristics and would form an excellent field for study.

5. Melville J. Herskovits, *Life in a Haitian Valley* (New York, 1937); Melville J. Herskovits and Frances S. Herskovits, *Trinidad Village* (New York, 1947); Martha Warren Beckwith, *Black Roadways* (Chapel Hill, 1929); Fernando M. Henriques, *Family and Colour in Jamaica* (London, 1953).

6. Charles Kingsley, *At Last: A Christmas in the West Indies* (London, 1887).

7. Beckwith, *op. cit.,* p. 30.

8. *Ibid.*

9. Herskovits and Herskovits, *op. cit.,* p. 290.

10. Taylor, *op. cit.,* pp. 140–42.

11. Ruy Galvao de Andrade Coelho, "The Black Carib of Honduras: A Study in Acculturation" (Ph.D. dissertation, Northwestern University, 1955).

12. Beckwith, *op. cit.,* pp. 78–84; Herskovits and Herskovits, *op. cit.,* pp. 134–41; *The Honduras Almanack* (Belize, 1830), p. 17.

13. *Idem*, p. 57.

14. Donald Pierson, *Negroes in Brazil* (Chicago, 1942), p. 257.

15. Taylor, *op. cit.,* p. 152.

16. James M. Phillippo, *Jamaica: Its Past and Present State* (Philadelphia, 1843), p. 93.

17. Herskovits, *op. cit.,* p. 115.

18. Conzemius, *op. cit.,* p. 192.

19. Daniel J. Crowley, "The Traditional Masques of Carnival" (*Caribbean Quarterly*, vol. 4, 1954, p. 198).

20. Taylor, *op. cit.,* p. 7.

21. P. M. Sherlock, "West Indian Society a Century Ago" (*Caribbean Quarterly*, vol. 2, 1954, p. 47).

22. See Andrew T. Carr, "Pierrot Grenade" (*Caribbean Quarterly*, vol. 4, 1954, p. 281).

23. *Comisión de Las Islas del Cisne* (Tegucigalpa, 1926), p. 18.

24. Jacques Houdaille, "Negroes Franceses en America Central a fines del Siglo XVIII" (*Antropología e Historia de Guatemala*, vol. 6, 1954, p. 65).

25. For information on this see Malcolm J. Proudfoot, *Population Movements in the Caribbean* (Port-of-Spain, 1950).

26. See John Alder Burdon, ed., *Archives of British Honduras* (London, 1934), vol. 2, pp. 57, 60. Also Antonio R. Vallejo, *Primer Anuario Estadistico Correspondiente al Año de 1889* (Tegucigalpa, 1893), p. 123.

D.
Plantations, Peasants, and Communities

7. Cuban Counterpoint: Tobacco and Sugar

Sugar cane and tobacco are all contrast. It would seem that they were moved by a rivalry that separates them from their very origins. One is a gramineous plant, the other a solanaceous; one grows from cuttings of stalk rooted down, the other from tiny seeds that germinate. The value of one is in its stalk, not in its leaves, which are thrown away; that of the other in its foliage, not its stalk, which is discarded. Sugar cane lives for years, the tobacco plant only a few months. The former seeks the light, the latter shade; day and night, sun and moon. The former loves the rain that falls from the heavens; the latter the heat that comes from the earth. The sugar cane is ground for its juice; the tobacco leaves are dried to get rid of the sap. Sugar achieves its destiny through liquid, which melts it, turns it into syrup; tobacco through fire, which volatilizes it, converted into smoke. The one is white, the other dark. Sugar is sweet and odorless; tobacco bitter and aromatic. Always in contrast! Food and poison, waking and drowsing, energy and dream, delight of the flesh and delight of the spirit, sensuality and thought, the satisfaction of an appetite and the contemplation of a moment's illusion, calories of nourishment and puffs of fantasy, undifferentiated and commonplace anonymity from the cradle and aristocratic individuality recognized wherever it goes, medicine and magic, reality and deception, virtue and vice. Sugar is *she;* tobacco is *he.* Sugar cane was the gift of the gods, tobacco of the devils; she is the daughter of Apollo, he is the offspring of Persephone.

In the economy of Cuba there are also striking contrasts in the cultivation, the processing, and the human connotations of the two products. Tobacco requires delicate care, sugar can look after itself; the one requires continual attention, the other involves seasonal

SOURCE: Excerpts from pp. 6–7, 30–34, 41, 46–59 of Fernando Ortiz, *Cuban Counterpoint: Tobacco and Sugar.* New York: Alfred A. Knopf, Inc., 1947. Reprinted by permission of the publisher.

work; intensive versus extensive cultivation; steady work on the part of a few, intermittent jobs for many; the immigration of whites on the one hand, the slave trade on the other; liberty and slavery; skilled and unskilled labor; hands versus arms; men versus machines; delicacy versus brute force. The cultivation of tobacco gave rise to the small holding; that of sugar brought about the great land grants. In their industrial aspects tobacco belongs to the city, sugar to the country. Commercially the whole world is the market for our tobacco, while our sugar has only a single market. Centripetence and centrifugence. The native versus the foreigner. National sovereignty as against colonial status. The proud cigar band as against the lowly sack.

Tobacco and sugar cane are two gigantic plants, two members of the vegetable kingdom which both flourish in Cuba and are both perfectly adapted, climatically and ecologically, to the country. The territory of Cuba has in its different zones the best land for the cultivation of both plants. And the same happens in the combinations of the climate with the chemistry of the soil.

The special requirements of tobacco cultivation have made it necessary (a most imperative economic need) for tobacco to be grown in small plots, like vegetable gardens, and not on great acreage like the canefields of the sugar plantations. Each of these tobacco fields was called, and should still be called a *tabacal;* but the preferred name is *vega,* which was applied to the river bottom lands, which were the best for the growing of tobacco because of their fertility, the ease with which they could be watered, and their sheltered location. *Veguerío* now is used to designate all the vegas of a region.

Each vega is a unit in itself, where the complete agricultural cycle of tobacco begins and ends. It is in no way connected with the subsequent operations of the tobacco industry. The vega is independent, unlike the canefields and the colony that springs up about them, which is dependent upon the industrial processing and the marketing of sugar through its final stage. The vega is not the slave of a mechanical installation whose voracity it must feed as is the sugar plantation of the tentacled structure of the mill. In the tobacco industry there are no centrals.

With the cutting of the cane the work of the sugar-raiser is finished. It is loaded, weighed, and all his work is turned into a figure that tells him the number of arrobas he has delivered and a voucher for the money due him. But the work of the tobacco-raiser is not over with the cutting of the leaves from the plant. On the contrary, it is now redoubled, and requires great skill. The drying of the leaves involves delicate and patient handling. And once more weather conditions become a factor. The *enmatulado,* for instance, must be done at daybreak and under the right conditions, for the wrong temperature could spoil the whole crop. The tobacco leaves then go through three stages, in the *cujes,* in the *pilones,* and in the *tercios,* and in all of them the tobacco is cured or fermented more or less, depending on the quality of the leaf and the amount of sap in it, and the help given it. On the care and success of the curing much of the value of the product depends, its aroma, taste, appearance, flexibility, combustibility.

The grower visits his treasure every day, first to touch the leaves and gauge their degree of dryness, then to smell them and judge the progress of curing by their scent. If the tobacco gets too dry it may crumble to powder in handling. It is here that the painstaking skill of the grower comes into play to keep the leaves at the right degree of flexibility. Thus they wait for the *pilón,* which consists in piling up the tobacco leaves, one by one and one on top of another, in prescribed formation and with many precautions to beautify and make uniform the color of the leaf, get rid of the excess of resin, attenuate its bitterness, and soften it so it will be more flexible and silky.

Then comes the stripping, which is removing from each leaf the stem left on it. After this comes the tedious process of selection, in which, after pulling out all the threads on which they have been strung together, those leaves to be used for filler must be separated from the wrappers, which are like fillets of tobacco. These are delicate operations, generally performed by women, *abridoras, rezagadoras* or *apartadoras,* and *repasadoras.* And finally the leaves must be reclassified, according to whether they are fillers or wrappers, in hands, hanks, bunches, and bales, prepared and ready for the market. There is no exaggeration in saying that in the cultivation and harvesting of tobacco in Cuba the human contribution is the most important element because of the great variety of special skills, physical and mental, involved in achieving the best results, as though it were a question of a work of art, the miracle of an ever changing and harmonious symphony of smells, tastes, and stimuli.

After the selection of each tobacco crop, or, to be more exact, after the selection of each leaf of each plant of each field, tobacco emerges from its agricultural cycle into that of industry, business, pleasure;

it goes forth, as Martí wrote, "to employ workmen, to enrich merchants, to amuse the idle, while away sorrow, accompany lonely thoughts."

In the olden days the selection of leaf tobacco was made by the planter himself. But even before the war of independence (1895) a division of labor was introduced and the selection was made in the towns nearest the fields, where it was easier and cheaper to find adequate space and workers. In this, too, the production of tobacco differs from that of sugar. The only centers of population with which the latter is concerned is the *batey,* the mill yard around the central, and the port of embarkation alongside the warehouses. The tobacco industry, on the contrary, gives life to selected rural centers. Guanajay, Pinar del Río, Consolación, and other towns in the Pinar del Río section, and Artemisa, Alquízar, San Antonio de los Baños, Santiago de las Vegas, and Bejucal have been selected locations for Vueltabajo; Camajuaní, Remedios, and others for Vueltarriba.

In the canefields and in the mills there is no selection. All canes go to the conveyor belt and the grinder together, and all the juice is mixed together in the same syrup, the same evaporating-dishes, the same filters, the same centrifugals, and the same sacks.

Whereas the steps in the harvesting and selection of tobacco are slow and studied, those connected with sugar cane always demand haste. The cane must be ground as soon as it is cut or else the yield of juice shrinks, ferments, and spoils. This characteristic of the sugar cane is responsible for social and historical consequences of incalculable importance. The workmen who do the cutting cannot be the same as those who, later on, carry out the grinding and boiling of the syrup. With tobacco, as with wheat, the agro-industrial operations are consecutive over a whole cycle. The same farmers can carry out the different phases of the work one after another. This is not the case with sugar cane. The offhand manner in which it can be treated in the field is transformed into the most breathless haste once it has been mutilated to steal its juice, and not a moment can be lost. Cut cane begins to ferment and rot in a few days. The operations of cutting, hauling, grinding, clarification, filtration, evaporation, and crystallization must theoretically be carried out one after the other, but without interruption; nearly all of them are going on at the same time in the mill. While one field of cane is being cut, others are being converted into sacks of sugar. And all at top speed. From the time the machete fells the cane until the receptacle of the sugar is closed, there is only a short lapse, a few hours. The grinding season of a plantation lasts months because of the volume of cane, but the conversion of each stalk into sugar is always quick. For this reason the milling season requires the simultaneous co-operation of many workers for a short time. The rapidity with which the cane must be ground after cutting and milled in an unavoidably brief space of time gave rise to the need for having on hand plenty of cheap, stable, and available labor for work that is irregular and seasonal. The intermittent concentration of cheap and abundant labor is a fundamental factor in the economy of Cuban sugar production. And as there was not sufficient labor available in Cuba, for centuries it was necessary to go outside the country to find it in the amount, cheapness, ignorance, and permanence necessary. The result has been that this urgent agricultural-chemical nature of the sugar industry has been the fundamental factor in all the demogenic and social evolution of Cuba. It was due principally to these conditions governing the production of sugar that slave-trading and slavery endured there to such a late date.

It was not the existence of latifundia that was responsible for the large Negro population of Cuba, as has been erroneously supposed, but the lack of native labor, of Indians and white men, and the difficulty of bringing in from other parts of the world except Africa workers who would be equally cheap, permanent, and submissive. The latifundium in Cuba was only a consequence of stock-raising first, and then of cane cultivation, and of other concomitant factors, just as was the influx of Negro population. Both have been the almost parallel effects of the same basic causes, sugar being mainly responsible, and the Africanoid population is not a direct result of latifundism. There was an abundance of Negroes in Cuba even when there was no shortage of land, and the great sugar plantations did not constitute a primordial economic factor.

For this reason, also, the division of labor in a sugar factory is different from that in a tobacco workshop. In the sugar central many workmen are needed to carry on the different industrial operations necessary from the time the cane is put on the conveyor belt to the grinder until the sugar comes out of the centrifugals into the sacks in which it is packed. In the making of sugar certain workmen tend to the fires, others to the grinding, others to the syrup, others to the chemical clarification, others to the filtering, others to the evaporating, and so on, through the successive steps involved in the sugar cycle. Each workman attends to one single job. No workman of the mill can by himself make sugar out of the cane; but each cigar worker can make a cigar out of a leaf of tobacco unassisted. The same tobacco worker can take charge of making each cigar from beginning to end, from cutting with his own knife the leaf for the filler to twisting the wrapper to its final turn. And any smoker can do it, too, as the tobacco-planter does with the leaf of his own harvest for his own smoking. He can cut the leaf, dry it, shred it, stuff it into a pipe or roll it in a cigarette paper, and light it and smoke it, as he pleases. At the mill many work together in joint and successive operations, which in their totality produce sugar in great quantities. In the tobacco industry many workers are occupied in individual but identical tasks, all of which when added together produce many cigars. The manufacture of sugar is a collective job; that of tobacco is by individual efforts.

Sugar is to be found in the cradle, in the kitchen, and on the table; tobacco in the drawing-room, the bedroom, and the study. With tobacco one works and dreams; sugar is repose and satisfaction. Sugar is the capable matron, tobacco the dreaming youth. Sugar is an investment, tobacco an amusement; sugar enters the body as nourishment, tobacco enters the spirit as a cathartic. The former contributes to the good and the useful; the latter seeks beauty and personality.

Tobacco is a magic gift of the savage world; sugar is a scientific gift of civilization.

Tobacco was taken to the rest of the world from America; sugar was brought to America. Tobacco is a native plant, which the Europeans who came with Columbus discovered, in Cuba, to be exact, at the beginning of November of the year 1492. Sugar cane is a foreign plant of remote origin that was brought to Europe from the Orient, thence to the Canary Islands, and it was from there that Columbus brought it to the Antilles in 1493. The discovery of tobacco in Cuba was a surprise, but the introduction of sugar was planned.

It has been said, though I do not know on what authority the statement is based, that when Columbus returned from his second voyage he took tobacco seed with him to Andalusia, as did the Catalonian friar Ramón Pané later, and planted it, but without success. It would seem that it was Dr. Francisco Hernández de Toledo who gave a scientific account of tobacco half a century later in a report to King Philip II, who had sent him to Mexico to study the flora of that country. The cultivation of tobacco was spread less through a desire for gain than through the spontaneous and subversive propaganda of temptation. Tobacco was the delight of the people before it became that of the upper classes. Its appeal was natural and traditional rather than studied and commercial. It was the sailors who spread its use through the ports of Europe in the forms in which they used it aboard ship, either for chewing or for pipe smoking. The courtiers of Europe made its acquaintance later through travelers returning from America.

Centuries and even millenniums went by before sugar left Asiatic India, passing into Arabia and Egypt, then traveling along the islands and shoreline of the Mediterranean to the Atlantic Ocean and the Indies of America. A few decades after a handful of adventurers discovered it in Cuba, tobacco had already been carried not only through America, where the Indians used it before the arrival of the Spaniards, but through Europe, Africa, and Asia, to the distant confines of Muscovy, the heart of darkest Africa, and Japan. In 1605 the Sultan Murad had to place severe penalties on the cultivation of tobacco in Turkey, and the Japanese Emperor ordered the acreage that had been given over to its cultivation reduced. Even today many nations still lack sugar, but hardly any lack tobacco or some substitute for it, however unworthy. Tobacco is today the most universal plant, more so than either corn or wheat. Today the world lives and dreams in a haze of blue smoke spirals that evoke the old Cuban gods. In the spread of this habit of smoking the island of Cuba has played a large part, not only because tobacco and its rites were native to it, but because of the incomparable excellence of its product, which is universally recognized by all discerning smokers, and because Havana happened to be the port of the West Indies most frequented by sailors in bygone days. Even today to speak of a Havana cigar is to refer to the best cigar in the world. And that is why, as a general thing, in lands remote from the Antilles the geographical name of Havana is better known than that of Cuba.

The economy of sugar was from the start capitalistic in contrast to that of tobacco. From the earliest days of the economic exploitation of these West Indies this was perfectly evident to Columbus and his successors who settled the islands. Aside from the fertility of the land and the favorable climate, the efficient production of sugar always required large acreage for plantations, pastures, timberland, and reserves of land—in a word, extensions that verged upon the latifundium. As the historian Oviedo said, "an ample supply of water" and accessible "forests for the hot and continuous fires" and, in addition, "a large and well-constructed building for making the sugar and another in which to store it." And, besides, a great number of "wagons for hauling the cane to the mill and to fetch wood, and an uninterrupted supply of workers to wash the sugarloaves and tend and water the cane." Even all this was not enough, for there was the investment in the required number of those automotive machines known as slaves, on which Oviedo commented: "At least from eighty to one hundred Negroes must be on hand all the time, or even a hundred and twenty and more to keep things running smoothly," and, besides, other people, "overseers and skilled workmen to make the sugar." And to feed all this crew still another and larger investment. According to Oviedo, "a good herd of cattle, from one thousand to three thousand head, close by the mill to feed the workers" was necessary. For this reason he concludes logically enough that "the man who owns a plantation free from mortgage and well equipped has a property of great value." Sugar is not made from patches of cane but from plantations of it; cane is not cultivated by the plant but in mass. The industry was not developed for private or domestic consumption, nor even for that of the locality, but for large-scale production and foreign exportation.

Tobacco is born complete. It is nature's gift to man, and his work with tobacco is merely that of selection. Sugar does not spring full-fledged; it is a gift man makes to himself through the creative effort of his labor. Sugar is the fruit of man's ingenuity and the mill's engines. Ingenuity where sugar is concerned consists in the human and mechanical power of creation. In the case of tobacco it is rather in the personal selection of that which has been naturally created.

Of the tobacco leaves, the invention and gift of nature, the knowing countryman selects the best, and, with the simple effort of his hands to roll them into shape, he can smoke the best cigar that can be made. Just with the hands, without tools, machinery, or capital, one can enjoy the finest tobacco in the world; but one cannot get sugar that way, not even the poorest grade.

There can be no manufacture of sugar without machinery, without milling apparatus to grind the cane and get out its sweet juice, from which saccharose is obtained. The mill may be an Indian *cunyaya*—a pump-handle device resting against the branch of a tree, which as it moves up and down presses the cane against the trunk—or a simple two-cylinder roller moved by animal or human power, or a titanic system of mills, wheels, cogs, pumps, evaporating-pans, boilers, and ovens, powered by water, steam, or electricity; but it is always a machine, fundamentally a lever that squeezes. Sugar is made by man and power. Tobacco is the voluntary offering of nature.

It is possible for the *guajiro* living on his small farm to make a little sugar squeezing the juice out of the cane by the pressure of the *cunyaya,* that simple device with its single lever which the Indians used, simpler even than the *cibucán* with which they pressed the yucca. Probably it was with the Indian *cunyaya* that the first juice was squeezed out in America, from the cane planted in Hispaniola by Christopher Columbus. But it was impossible to develop production on a commercial scale with so rudimentary an instrument. The first settlers in Hispaniola devised and set up grinding mills operated by water or horse power.

To be sure, these mills which were known in Europe before the discovery of America were all of wood, including the rollers. The maximum of juice that could be extracted from the cane was thirty-five per cent, and the sugar yield was only six per cent. But in the manufacture of sugar the grinder was always as essential as the evaporating-dishes and the other vessels for the filtration of the settlings and the clarification of the syrup.

For centuries sugar was manufactured in these *cachimbos*. In the year 1827 Cuba had over one thousand centrals. The limited capacity of the mills was the cause of the small scale of their operations. At this time the average size of the numerous plantations in Matanzas, for example, was only about 167 acres of cane, and some 750 in wood and pasture land. For a good central 1,000 acres was enough.

In 1820 the steam engine was introduced into Cuba and marked the beginning of an industrial revolution. The steam engine changed everything on the central. The process of the penetration of the steam engine into the sugar industry was slow; half a century went by from the time it was first employed in the grinding mill in 1820 until 1878, when it was applied to the last step of the process—that is, in the separation centrifugals. By the end of the nineteenth century everything about the central was mechanical, nothing was done by hand. Everything about the organism was new. The framework continued the same, but the organs, the joints, the viscera had been adapted to new functions and new dimensions. For as a result of the introduction of steam not only was completely new machinery installed, but everything grew in size. The increased potential of energy called for enlarged grinding capacity of the mills, and this, in turn, made it necessary for all the other apparatus in the sugar-milling process to expand. But only in the last third of the nineteenth century did the Cuban sugar central begin that intense growth which has brought it to its present-day dimensions.

The Cuban sugar mill, despite the complete transformation of its machinery brought about by the steam engine, grew slowly in productive capacity, both in machinery and in acreage. As late as 1880 the size of the centrals was not extremely large. At that time the centrals of Matanzas Province, for example, averaged some 1,650 acres all together, of which only about 770 were planted to cane. This delay in the growth in size of the centrals, despite the possibilities afforded by the introduction of steam-powered machinery, was not due so much to the revolutions and wars that harassed the colony and laid much of its land waste for years as to the economic difficulties that impeded the development of transportation by steam—that is, the railroads. Railways were first introduced into Cuba in the year 1837, before Spain had them, by a company of wealthy Creoles. But it was after the ten-year revolution that steel rails were invented and that they became cheap enough so they could be used on a large scale on the centrals, not only on lines from the mill yard to the canefields, but to link up the mills and the cane-growing zones with each other and with the ports where sugar was stored and shipped. From this time on, the railway lines reached out steadily toward the sugar cane and wrapped themselves about it like the tentacles of a great iron spider. The centrals began to grow in size, giving way to the great latifundium. By 1890 there was a central in Cuba, the Constancia, that produced a yield as high as 135,000 sacks of sugar, at that time the largest in the world.

The machine won a complete victory in the sugar-manufacturing process. Hand labor has almost completely disappeared. The mechanization has been so thorough that it has brought about a transformation in the industrial, territorial, judicial, political, and social structure of the sugar economy of Cuba through an interlinked chain of phenomena which have not been fully appreciated by Cuban sociologists.

In the twentieth century the sugar production of Cuba reached the peak of its historical process of industrialization, even though it has not yet passed through all the phases necessary for its perfect evolutionary integration. Mechanization, which reached Cuba in the nineteenth century with the steam engine, began to triumph in that century and created the central; but it is in this twentieth century that the machine has given rise to the typical present-day organization, the *supercentral*. This type of mill has been the logical outgrowth of mechanization, and from it have streamed a whole series of derivations that because of their complicated interlocking structure and the relation of cause and effect have not been clearly understood or properly analyzed. It is sufficient to point out here that the principal characteristics typical of the Cuban sugar industry today, and the same holds true in a greater or lesser degree of the other islands of the Antilles, and happens to a certain extent in other similar industries, are the following: mechanization, latifundism, sharecropping, wage-fixing, supercapitalism, absentee landlordism, foreign ownership, corporate control, and imperialism.

Mechanization is the factor that has made possible and necessary the increased size of the centrals. Prior to this the central's radius of activity was the distance suitable for animal-drawn haulage. Now, with railroads, the limits of extension of a central are measured by the cost of transportation. It is a known fact that cane cut in Santo Domingo is milled in Puerto Rico and transported to the mill in ships. The mill and the railroad have developed simultaneously and their growth has made necessary planting on a larger scale, which explains the need for vast areas for cane plantations. This phenomenon also gave rise to the occupation of virgin lands in the provinces of Camagüey and Oriente and the consequent shifting of the agricultural center of Cuba. These Cyclopean machines and those great tentacles of railways that have turned the centrals into monstrous iron octopuses have created the demand for more and more land to feed the insatiable voracity of the mills with canefields, pasture land, and woodland.

On the heels of the mechanization came the great latifundism—that is, the use of a great extension of land by a single private owner. Latifundism was the economic basis of feudalism, and it has often reproduced this state. The struggle of the modern age has always been, particularly since the eighteenth century, to give man freedom and sever him from his bondage to the land, and for the freedom of the land, liberating it from the monopolistic tyranny of man. Today this process is on the way to being repeated in the Antilles, and one day we shall see agrarian laws enacted to disentail the lands held in the grasp of mortmain. The agrarian latifundism today is a fatal consequence of the present universal system of the concentration of capital. Every day industry needs more and more means of production, and the land is the most important of them all.

The central is now more than a mere plantation; there are no longer any real planters in Cuba. The modern central is not a simple agricultural enterprise, nor even a factory whose production is based on the raw materials at hand. Today it is a complicated "system of land, machinery, transportation, technicians, workers, capital, and people to produce sugar." It is a complete social organism, as live and complex as a city or municipality, or a baronial keep with its surrounding fief of vassals, tenants, and serfs. The latifundium is only the territorial base, the visible expression of this. The central is vertebrated by an economic and legal structure that combines masses of land, masses of machinery, masses of men, and masses of money, all in proportion to the integral scope of the huge organism for sugar production.

Today the sugar latifundium is so constituted that it is not necessary for the tracts of land or farms that constitute it to be contiguous. It is generally made up of a nuclear center around the mill yard, a sort of town, and of outlying lands, adjacent or distant, linked by railroads and under the same general control, all forming a complete empire with subject colonies covered with canefields and forests, with houses and villages. And all this huge feudal territory is practically outside the jurisdiction of public law; the norms of private property hold sway there. The owner's power is as complete over this immense estate as though it were just a small plantation or farm. Everything there is private—ownership, industry, mill, houses, stores, police, railroad, port. Until the year 1886 the workers, too, were chattels like other property.

The sugar latifundium was the cause of important agro-social developments, such as the monopolizing of land that is not cultivated but lies fallow; the scarcity of garden produce or fruits that would complement the basic crop, which is sugar—the reason for the latifundium's existence—because the effort required for this can be turned to more profitable use from the economic standpoint; the depreciation in value of land that it does not need within the zone monopolized by the central, and so on.

Within the territorial scope of the central, economic liberty suffers serious restrictions. There is not a small holding of land nor a dwelling that does not belong to the owner of the central, nor a fruit orchard or vegetable patch or store or shop that does not form part of the owner's domain. The small Cuban landowner, independent and prosperous, the backbone of a strong rural middle class, is gradually disappearing. The farmer is becoming a member of the proletariat, just another laborer, without roots in the soil, shifted from one district to another. The whole life of the central is permeated by this provisional quality of dependence, which is a characteristic of colonial populations whose members have lost their stake in their country.

The economic organization of the latifundium in Cuba has been blamed for consequences that are not properly attributable to it, such as the importation of cheap labor, especially colored. First Negro slaves were brought into the country, then laborers from Haiti and Jamaica. But this immigration, which lowers the wage level of the whole Cuban proletariat and the living standard of Cuban society and upsets its racial balance, thus retarding the fusion of its component elements into a national whole, is not the result of the latifundium system. The use of colored slaves or laborers has never been nor is it a social phenomenon due to latifundism or to the monopolizing of the land. Both these economic developments are essentially identical: with the concentration of the ownership of land comes the concentration of laborers, and both depend directly upon the concentration of capital resulting from industry, especially when the process of mechanization demands more land for the plantations upon whose crop it depends, more labor to harvest it, and, in an endless progression, more machines and more and more money. The land and the laborer, like the machine itself, are only means of production, which, as a rule, are simultaneously augmented, but often the increment of one is followed by that of the others. When there was an abundance of land and before the machines had reached their full development, sugar-planting used large numbers of Negro slaves brought in from Africa; at this time the latifundium had not yet come into being. Later, as the machines grew in power, they demanded more and more cane plantations, and these, in turn, more and more labor, which was supplied by white immigration and the natural growth of population. But as the speed of the development of the sugar industry outpaced that of the population, and great centrals were established on vast tracts of virgin land, everything had to be brought in: machines, plantations, and—population. It was the swift occupation of large and new sections of Camagüey and Oriente that, aside from other secondary economic considerations such as the scale of wages, brought about a revival of "traffic in Negroes," who were now hired on terms of miserable peonage instead of being bought outright, as under the earlier system of slavery. In Puerto Rico the latifundium developed after its great demographic expansion, and as it has a dense and poverty-stricken white population, it has not been necessary to bring in cheap labor from the other islands.

In the tobacco industry the process is exactly the reverse. It was an industry without machinery. In the beginning it used very few manual devices, and these of the simplest, to twist the tobacco or grind it to powder or shred it. The largest of these apparatuses was a simple wheel. At the Quinta de los Molinos in Havana one can still see the insignificant stream of water that turned the little mills, from which it derived its name, that were formerly used to make the snuff that was exported. In addition to the preparation of snuff and cut tobacco, it was in the manufacture of cigarettes that the machine began to be used; but for hundreds of years these were made by hand at home. Machinery did not come into the life of tobacco with the invention of the steam engine, but years after the Jamaica engines had been invented for the sugar mills and were introduced into Cuba.

There is always a stationary quality to sugar. Where the canefields are planted, there they stay and last for years, around the mill installation, which is permanent and immovable. The canefields are vast plantings and the central is a great plant. Tobacco is a volatile thing. The seeds are planted in a seed-bed, then transplanted to another spot; sometimes even from one vega to another, and tobacco's cycle ends with the year's harvest. Nothing is left in the field, and it has to be planted all over again.

The rental arrangements for tobacco lands are usually for a brief period; the crop-sharing may be on an annual basis. In the case of sugar they are of lengthy duration, depending on how long the root stock continues to produce cane before it turns into worthless stubble.

Without a large investment of money in lasting plantations and powerful machinery it is impossible to set up a central or produce any form of sugar, unless one excepts the honey produced by the communistic bees in their hives. Tobacco's economical arrangements could be limited to a small patch of fertile land and a pair of skillful hands to twist the leaf into cigars or shred it for pipe smoking. For the widespread distribution of sugar great advances had to be made first in the secrets of chemistry, in machinery, in maritime shipping capacity, in tropical colonization, in the securing of slave labor, and, above all, in the accumulation of capital and in banking organization. In the case of tobacco all that was required was for a few sailors and traders to scatter about the world a few handfuls of seed, which are so small they will fit anywhere, even in a cabin-boy's duffel-bag.

The social consequences deriving from tobacco and sugar in Cuba and originating in the different conditions under which the two crops are produced can be easily grasped. The contrast between the vegas where tobacco is grown and the sugar plantation, particularly if it is a modern central, is striking. Tobacco gave origin to a special type of agricultural life. There is not the great human agglomeration in the tobacco region that is to be found around the sugar plants. This is due to the fact that tobacco requires no machinery; it needs no mills, nor elaborate physical and chemical equipment, nor railway transport systems. The vega is a geographical term; the central is a term of mechanics.

In the production of tobacco intelligence is the prime factor; we have already observed that tobacco is liberal, not to say revolutionary. In the production of sugar it is a question of power; sugar is conservative, if not reactionary.

I repeat, the production of sugar was always a capitalistic venture because of its great territorial and industrial scope and the size of its long-term investments. Tobacco, child of the savage Indian and the virgin earth, is a free being, bowing its neck to no mechanical yoke, unlike sugar, which is ground to bits by the mill. This has occasioned profound economic and social consequences.

In the first place, tobacco was raised on the land best suited for the purpose, without being bound to a great indispensable industrial plant that was stationary and remained "planted" even after it had impoverished all the land about it. This gave rise to the central, which even in olden times was at least a village, and today is a city. The vega was never anything but a rural holding, like a garden. The vega was small; it was never the site of latifundia, but belonged to small property-owners. The central required a plantation; in the vega a small farm was enough. The owners of a central are known as *hacendados* and live in the city; those of the vegas remained *monteros, sitieros,* or *guajiros* and never left their rural homes.

The cultivation of tobacco demands a yearly cycle of steady work by persons who are skilled and specialized in this activity. Tobacco is often smoked to kill time, but in the tobacco industry there is no such thing as "dead time," as is the case with sugar. This, together with the circumstance that the vega was a small holding, has developed in the *veguero* a strong attachment to his land, as in the rancher of old, and made it possible for him to carry on his tasks with the help of members of his family. Only when this is not feasible does he hire workers, but in small groups, never in gangs or by the hundred, as happens with sugar cane. The vega, I repeat, is merely a topographical denomination; the *colonia* is a term having complex political and social connotations.

For these same reasons, while during slavery Negroes were employed as sugar-plantation hands, the cultivation of the vegas was based on free, white labor. Thus tobacco and sugar each have racial connections. Tobacco is an inheritance received from the Indian, which was immediately used and esteemed by the Negro, but cultivated and commercialized by the white man. The Indians at the time of the discovery raised tobacco in their gardens, considering it "a very holy thing," in the words of Oviedo, distinguishing between the mild cultivated variety and the stronger wild species, according to Cobo. The whites were familiar with it, but did not develop a taste for it at once. "It is a thing for savages." The historians of the Indies did not smoke, and some abominated the habit. Benzoni tells that the smell of tobacco was so offensive to him that he would run to get away from it. When Las Casas wrote his *Apologética Historia de las Indias,* in the second quarter of the sixteenth century, he called attention to the unusual fact that he had known "an upright, married Spaniard on this island who was in the habit of using tobacco and the smoke from it, just as the Indians did, and who said that because of the great benefit he derived from it he would not give it up for anything."

It was the Negroes of Hispaniola who quickly came to esteem the qualities of tobacco and not only copied from the Indians the habit of smoking it, but were the first to cultivate it on their owners' plantations. They said it "took away their weariness," to use Oviedo's words. But the Spaniards still looked askance at it. "Negro stuff."

In Cuba the same thing probably happened; tobacco was a thing "for Indians and Negroes," and only later, as it worked its way up from the lower strata of society, did the whites develop a taste for it.

But by the middle of the sixteenth century in Havana, where each year the Spanish fleets assembled and set out across the ocean in convoy, tobacco had already become an article of trade, and it was the Negroes who carried on the business. The whites realized that they were missing a good venture, and the authorities issued ordinances forbidding the Negroes to go on selling tobacco to the fleets. The Negro could no longer sell or cultivate tobacco except for his own use; the Negro could not be a merchant. From then on, the cultivation and trade in tobacco was the economic privilege of the white man.

Sugar was mulatto from the start, for the energies of black men and white always went into its production. Even though it was Columbus who brought the first sugar cane into the Antilles from the Canary Islands, sugar was not a Spanish plant, nor even European. It was native to Asia, and from there it was carried along the Mediterranean by the Arabs and Moors. For the cultivation of the cane and the extraction of its juice the help of stout slaves and serfs was required, and in Portugal, as in Spain and Sicily in Europe, in Mauritania and Egypt in Africa, in Arabia, Mesopotamia, Persia, and India in Asia, these workers were as a rule of Negroid stock, those dark people who from prehistoric times had penetrated into that long strip of supertropical areas and gave them their permanent dark coloring, the same stock that in the Middle Ages invaded it anew with the waves of Moslems, who never felt any hostile racial prejudice toward the Negro. Sugar cane and Negro slaves arrived together in the island of Cuba, and possibly in Hispaniola, from across the sea. And since then Negro labor and sugar cane have been two factors in the same economic binomial of the social equation of our country.

For centuries the workers in the centrals were exclusively Negroes; often even the overseers were colored. This was true of the mill workers as well as of the field workers, with the exception of the technicians and the management. It was not until the abolishment of slavery, the influx of Spanish immigrants after the Ten Years' War, and the introduction of the share-cropping system that white farmers were to be found on the Cuban sugar plantations.

The nineteenth century in Cuba was marked by the change in the labor system brought about by the prohibition of the slave trade and, much later, by the abolition of slavery and the substitution for it of hired workers. The abolition was proclaimed by the Cubans fighting a war of secession against the mother country, and later by Spain in

1880–6. The cessation of the slave trade coincided with the introduction of the steam engine, which increased the productive capacity of the mills, and the abolition of slavery (1886) was simultaneous with the use of steel rails and the development of the railroads, which increased the radius of activity of the centrals. Cheap labor was an imperative need, so Spain, no longer able to smuggle in slaves or bring in more Chinese coolies or peons from Yucatán, began to export her own white laborers. As a result the proportion of Negroes in the Cuban population began to diminish. In the distribution of colored population in Cuba today the greatest density is to be found in the old sugar-growing sections, not in the tobacco-raising areas, which were settled in the main by white immigrants from the Canary Islands and peasants of old Cuban stock. Tobacco drew upon the free white population, whereas for sugar cane black slaves were imported. This also explains why there are no invasions of migrant seasonal workers in the tobacco industry, and still less of Haitians and Jamaicans, who were brought in to make the harvesting of cane cheaper.

It should be noted that this process which took place in Cuba was not paralleled in other countries, such as Virginia, for example, whose early economy was based on tobacco. In Virginia, at that time an English colony, when the settlers began to raise tobacco they depended wholly on slave labor to cultivate it—white or black slaves, but preferably black.

This was due to the fact that the growing of tobacco there did not follow the same pattern as in Cuba, where, just as the Indians had done, it was treated as a small-scale, garden product, but in Virginia it employed the system of large plantations. The reason for this was that from the start the growing of tobacco in Virginia was a business, and the product was for foreign export, with the largest possible profit. That is to say, from its beginnings it was a capitalistic enterprise. For this reason, in the Anglo-American colonies there were never small growers nor any concern with the distinctive qualities of the leaf. There capitalism was in control of tobacco production from the first moment, and its objective was quantity rather than quality.

ERIC R. WOLF

8. Specific Aspects of Plantation Systems in the New World: Community Sub-cultures and Social Classes

PLANTATIONS: CLASS STRUCTURE

It is important, I think, to begin a discussion of community, sub-cultures and social classes on the plantation by underlining the fact that the plantation is by definition a class-structured system of organization. Technologically, it enables the laborer to produce more than he needs to satisfy his own culturally prescribed standards of consumption. Economically, the owners of the plantation appropriate that surplus in culturally sanctioned ways. The individual members of the labor force cannot sell the goods they produce, nor consume the proceeds of such sales. The entrepreneurs who operate the plantation monopolize the right to sell in a market, to reinvest the proceeds realized, to appropriate the profits obtained for investment elsewhere, or to siphon off the surplus for culturally sanctioned individual ends. The worker sells his muscular energy and is paid for its use in the services of surplus production. This basic distinction between owners and workers is supported by a complex system of political and legal sanctions. I want to stress these factors—so obvious to those of us who have grown up in the capitalist tradition—because they are culturally relative. That is, they operate in some cultures but not in all cultures, a fact most evident in areas where plantations are set up among people who possess different notions of production, appropriation and distribution. Wherever the plantation has arisen, or wherever it was imported from the outside, it always destroyed antecedent cultural norms and imposed its own dictates, sometimes by

SOURCE: *Plantation Systems of the New World,* Social Science Monograph 7 (1959):136–46. Washington, D.C.: Pan American Union. Reprinted by permission of the author and the General Secretariat of the Organization of American States.

persuasion, sometimes by compulsion, yet always in conflict with the cultural definitions of the affected population. The plantation therefore is also an instrument of force, wielded to create and to maintain a class-structure of workers and owners, connected hierarchically by a staff-line of overseers and managers.

Conversely, wherever it has spread, it has affected the social groups established in the areas before its advent. Due to its tendency to amass capital, land and labor, it has frequently brought about the decline and atrophy of semi-independent groups of owners of small property, such as small farmers, or store-keepers, or sellers of services to farmers and store-keepers. Through the use of bound labor under conditions of labor scarcity or the employment of cheap labor under conditions of labor surplus, moreover, it has tended to inhibit the rise of small property owners from the ranks of its own labor force. It thus tended to push rival social groups towards the periphery of its sphere of influence, to eke out a marginal existence in Indian *pueblo, caboclo* village, or Tobacco Road. The plantation thus not only produces its own class-structure, but has an inhibiting effect on the formation of any alternate class-structures within its area of control.

PLANTATIONS: SPATIAL ASPECTS

This class-structure finds expression not only in social terms, but also in spatial relationships. Invariably the plantation creates new communities. In the highland areas of the New World it drew the Indian from his community into life near the hacienda, and made him an *acasillado*. In the lowlands of the New World, it ringed the big house with the huts of African slaves. When population grew to a point where labor became plentiful, cheap and readily available, new settlements of laborers grew up in the vicinity of the fields, inhabited by men eager to find employment in cultivation and harvest.

Everywhere these new communities also follow a basic plan which translates into spatial terms the chain of command of owners, managers, overseers, permanent laborers and seasonal workers. At the core of each enterprise we invariably find the technical nucleus of the plantation, the processing machines; its administrative nucleus, the house of the owner or manager; and its nucleus of distribution, the store-houses, pay-booth and company store. Distributed about this plantation nucleus are the settlements of the permanent employees, the backbone of the labor force. Beyond the settlements of the permanent workers lie the scattered settlements of the occasional workers who report for work in time of need. If there is a town in the vicinity of the plantation, it is usually small and stunted in growth, for the real center of power and wealth lies on the plantation. The town is rarely more than a subsidiary center of political services, often under the direct or indirect influence of the plantation owners.

PLANTATION: LABOR

If all plantations are class-structured and conform to a basic spatial plan, they nevertheless differ in the character of this class-structure and in the characteristic sub-cultures of these classes. In an anthropological analysis of these differences, two variables appear to be crucial. The first of these is the way in which the labor supply is geared to the enterprise. Plantations either make use of some mechanism of outright coercion such as slavery, or peonage, or indentured servitude, or labor forced to work under vagrancy laws; or they employ free labor which is remunerated with wages. The factors which govern the degree of servitude are many, but undoubtedly the most important is the sheer availability of labor in the area occupied by the plantation, or the willingness of the population within the area to subject itself to the new cultural regime of the plantation. Where there is no labor, it must be imported, and coercion has been frequent in such cases. Where potential labor is unwilling, coercion can—up to a point—ensure at least a measure of compliance. Nor is bondage exercised wholly through force. Where labor is bound we tend to also encounter mechanisms designed to attract and hold the laborer beyond the power of compulsion. The worker may receive a plot on which to grow some of his own food; he may receive the right to sell some of this food on the open market; he may, to some degree, be led to expect aid and succor from the owner of the plantation in time of need. Often some small part of the surplus produced by the plantation will be re-distributed to him, frequently in lieu of wages.

Where labor is plentiful, on the other hand, these mechanisms of direct or indirect bondage tend to fall by the board. No outside mechanism of coercion is needed to drive the worker in search of a job: the worker will seek out the job himself, in search of subsistence and wages to meet cultural standards of consumption. Under conditions of labor surplus, he will work under double pressure: the pressure of his own need, and that of competition with his fellows. Increasingly, in the New World, systems using external coercion to exact work performance have tended to give way to systems utilizing the worker's own drive for subsistence. It is thus possible to refer to plantations using bound labor as old-style plantations, to plantations using free labor as new-style plantations.

PLANTATIONS: DISPOSAL OF SURPLUS

If the manner of gearing labor to the enterprise is one crucial variable distinguishing one type of plantation from another, the second crucial variable—crucial for anthropological analysis—lies in the way in which the plantation disposes of its surplus. Here again we can draw a distinction between old-style and new-style plantations. The new-style plantation is an organization which uses money to make more money. Its operation is governed by "rational" cost-accounting, and the consumption needs of both owners and workers are irrelevant to its operation. The price of labor is set by the number of laborers competing for available jobs, or by other factors which affect this competition, such as labor organization. The subsistence needs of the labor force are irrelevant to the concerns of the enterprise. Similarly, it may or may not produce dividends for its owners. The dividends may be consumed or plowed back into the concern, but the manner of consumption is of no interest to the management. On the old-style plantation, however, labor is not only employed in the fields. A considerable amount of labor-time goes into both feeding the owner and his family, and into the provision of services which may enable him to live in the style demanded by his social position. His workers not only plow and reap; they also serve at table, or curry his horses, or play music on festive occasions. In turn, part of the resources of the plantation and part of the surplus produced is used to cover the subsistence needs of the labor force. Here labor does not feed itself outside the boundaries of the plantation. Part of the cost of bondage is due to the fact that the owner must expend some of his substance to maintain and augment the supply of labor. Put in another way, we may say that the new-style plantation is single-minded in its pursuit of profit; the fate of its labor-force is of no concern to it as long as enough workers are available to do the necessary work. The old-style plantation, on the contrary, has a split personality. It produces goods for a market, but part of its energy goes into self-maintenance and status consumption. Old-style and new-style plantation, then, differ in the ways in which they dispose of surpluses and in the ways in which they bind labor to the enterprise. The patterning of sub-cultures in the two kinds of enterprise is expectably different.

OLD-STYLE PLANTATION: PERSONALIZED RELATIONSHIPS

In discussing the sub-cultures of social groups in any class-structured society, we must remember that the sub-cultures bear close relationship to the network of social relations. Sub-cultures cannot be divided into near watertight compartments, or separated on the model of a layer cake. At least one of their functions is to relate the different subordinate and superordinate groups to each other. Therefore, we must inquire into the characteristics of these different relationships.

It is often said that the old-style plantation is or was characterized by a predominance of personal face-to-face relationships, as opposed to the impersonal relationships which predominate on the new-style plantation. If we inquire more closely however, it becomes clear that these personal relationships are not the same kind of personal relationships which occur in tribal or peasant communities with which anthropologists are most familiar. They differ from kin and other face-to-face relationships in that they retain the *form* of personal relationships, but serve different *functions*. When a plantation owner returns to the plantation at Christmas to give presents to the children of his workers, or when he lends money to a worker whose wife stands in need of expert medical care, or when in the past he supervised the flogging of a recalcitrant peon at the plantation whipping post, he is using the form of personal relationships, while carrying out functions which maintain the plantation as a system of labor organization.

In these acts he carries out operations of a technical order (to use a phrase of Robert Redfield's) which are still mediated through cultural forms that bear the personal stamp. He involves himself in relationships which carry affect, either positive or negative, in order to underline the dependent position of the laborer in contrast to his own status of dominance. He thus reinforces the managerial relation between the worker and himself. This hybrid wedding of form and function also characterizes the periodic plantation ceremonies which involve the entire labor force and which serve to underline the role of the plantation owner as a symbolic "father," who distributes food and favors to his symbolic "children." This occurred in the daily distribution of rum on the slave plantations of the Antilles and the Southern United States, or of *pulque* on the Mexican haciendas, as it still occurs in the distribution of coca in the haciendas of highland Peru and Bolivia. This was also the function of the annual harvest festivals or celebrations of Christmas in which common festivities provided an occasion for unification on the ritual level.

The worker, in turn, must seek personal relationships with the plantation owner. He will attempt, whenever possible, to translate issues of the technical order into personal or moral terms. This he does *not* because he is incapable of behaving in non-personal terms, but because the social system of the old-style plantation forces him to adopt this manner of behavior. The owner is the source of his daily bread and of any improvement in his life chances. He is thus the only one capable of reducing the worker's life risks and materially raising his prospects. The worker therefore addresses his pleas to him, and the culturally sanctioned way to do this is through a ritual pantomime of dependence. The worker must strive to attend to the personal needs of the owner, above and beyond the tasks required of him as a hand in the field. He may place the labor and services of his family at the owner's disposal. He may even welcome the owner's entry into a network of quasifamiliar sexual relationships with his dependents, a subject so brilliantly explored by Gilberto Freyre in his *Casa Grande e Senzala*. All of these acts of dependence draw the owner into the worker's personal debt, and surround the technical relationship of master and dependent with the threads of personalized ritual exchanges. These ritual acts that symbolize dependence and dominance cannot, of course, involve all the workers on the plantation in equal measure. Many may be called, but only a few will be chosen; most must remain outside the personalized circle. Nevertheless, this social selection furthers the maintenance of the plantation as a going concern, since it builds up in the labor force general expectations that personal contact with the owner will help ease the burdens of life.

As a corollary, these personalized ritual exchanges on the old-style plantation tend to inhibit the growth of a consciousness of kind among the labor force. The individual family, rather than the labor force as a whole, becomes the carrier of the ritualized exchange with the owner. Since the individual families compete for a place in the sun, close to the dominant source of distribution, we must expect to encounter, on this type of plantation, worker communities that are heavily differentiated into social groups that vie with each other for the stakes of an improved livelihood.

NEW-STYLE PLANTATION: IMPERSONAL RELATIONSHIPS

The new-style plantation, in contrast, dispenses altogether with personalized phrasings of its technical requirements. Guided by the idea of rational efficiency in the interests of maximum production, it views the labor force as a reservoir of available muscular energy, with each laborer representing a roughly equivalent amount of such energy. This view of muscular energy or labor power apart from the person who carries and sustains it, is, of course, as Polanyi has shown, a culturally developed and culturally relative fiction. The worker who provides a given amount of muscular energy is remunerated in wages. Otherwise his life risks or life chances are of no moment to the planners and managers of production and distribution. The human reality of the system is of course very different from the fiction which guides its operation. The human carrier of muscular energy required by the plantation has a family to feed and other social relations to keep up in the midst of a setting where labor is plentiful and the wages paid for it correspondingly low. The plantation at this point divorces itself from any responsibility to its labor supply. It does not extend credit to individual workers, nor differentiate between workers according to their different needs, or the urgency of their respective needs. It assumes no risks for the physical or psychological survival of the people who power its operation. At the same time, the new-style plantation is not an apparatus for the servicing of the status needs of its owners or managers. It thus bars the worker effectively from entering into personalized relationships with the administrative personnel.

NEW-STYLE PLANTATION: PROLETARIAN SUB-CULTURE

Within such a regime of labor use, in which men are paid equally for equal work the life chances of men are roughly equal, as are the risks of life which they share. Since there is no way in which the worker can assuage his needs by establishing personalized and differentiated ties with the owner, he can find security only or primarily in those of his own status: he can reduce his risks largely through adequate social relationships with his fellow-workers. We should, therefore, expect to find on the new-style plantation the growth of a homogeneous sub-culture, in which individuals learn to respond similarly to like signals and symbols, and in which self-esteem is built up in social intercourse with like-minded and like-positioned men. We have an excellent picture of such proletarian homogeneity in the study of a community of sugar-workers on the south coast of Puerto Rico (Mintz, 1956). Mintz has shown how homogeneity of sub-culture has not only embraced house types, food preferences and linguistic behavior, but also child-training practices, ritual kinship practices, political attitudes, attitudes towards the land, towards the position of women, towards race and religion. The corollary of this sub-cultural homogeneity is a strong consciousness of kind in which the behavior and norms of the proletarian sub-culture are counterposed to the behavior and norms of the managerial group, and, by extension, to the behavior and norms of all those who are thought to occupy similar positions of wealth and power in the larger society of which these sugar-workers form a part.

To date, this study remains the most complete and imaginative anthropological account of a plantation population, and many of us see it as a type case of proletarian sub-culture. Yet, at this point in the discussion, we would do well to have second thoughts about the typological rating we have given to this particular case. We should, I think, ask ourselves whether Cañamelar (op. cit.) is typical in the sense of representing a norm of plantation situations everywhere; or whether it is typical because it represents a culmination of processes which have run their course here, but have been denied full expression elsewhere. If Cañamelar represents a plantation climax—and I incline in that direction—and if such climaxes are rare rather than common the world over, then Cañamelar will be of interest to us primarily as an extreme case in which the relevant processes stand forth with less ambiguity than elsewhere. How, then, do we appraise the more numerous cases which do not exhibit the clarity of the Cañamelar sample? Are they to be judged simply by the yardstick of the extreme case, and written off as cases which have not yet reached fruition? Or are they worth investigating in their own right?

SPECIALIZED VERSUS GENERALIZED ADAPTATIONS

These considerations lead me to a further train of thought. In biological evolution we often encounter the results of specialization where an organism has become strongly organized along a particular line, in terms of a particular set of environmental conditions. The organism is highly efficient in terms of this particular set of conditions, but at the same time highly "exposed," should its conditions of life undergo basic change. Specialization is, as Howells puts it, "a disguised straight jacket." The organism has abandoned all alternative modes of adaptation in order to ensure its optimum survival along some special line.

Specialized organisms contrast with generalized organisms, which lack specific adaptation to a particular set of conditions, and the advantages of such specificity. At the same time, they retain a potential for greater versatility and greater plasticity under changed conditions. Evolutionary processes continuously produce both more specialized and more generalized forms.

It is always dangerous to extend biological analogies into the analysis of human groups, but I do want to take advantage of the image I have just used to draw attention to a point which seems to me to be of considerable moment. It is certainly true that human beings with culture are never as specialized as a sightless worm in an underground cave. Cultures are plastic; organic specializations are not. At the same time, it seems to me that we err when we assign but one culture to each human group, or one sub-culture to each social segment. For, in doing so, we implicitly assume that every human group tends towards specialization, towards the development of one way of life to the exclusion of alternative ways. This, I think, has drained our capacity for dynamic analysis. I do not wish to advocate the opposite point, that all human groups will tend to generalized adaptations. No, both kinds of phenomena occur, but neither is self-evident. We should assume that specialization and generalization in culture are both problems, and we should begin to inquire into the reasons for these different modes of adaptation. I should like to ask, for instance, just what happened at Cañamelar to cause the worker group to develop such a specialized sub-culture, just as I would like to ask why this has not occurred in some other plantation areas.

CAÑAMELAR: EXTREME CASE

A thorough examination of the forces which created Cañamelar are beyond the scope of this paper, but I should like to indicate where I, for one, would be prompted to seek the answers. It is a community which suffered so massive an impact of corporate capital organized in new-style plantations, that all feasible cultural alternatives and all alternatives for social action on the part of the worker group were destroyed. At the same time, the sugar cutters had no "frontier" during the crucial years when the old-style plantations of the south coast were converted into new-style plantations, and for some fifty years thereafter. The Cañamelar proletariat thus had to abandon all hopes of bettering its life chances through social or geographical mobility for well over half a century. Such conditions can occur again, and in all parts of the world; yet it seems to me that the possibilities for a repeated recurrence are quite limited. The giant new-style plantation forces its workers to develop a highly specialized sub-culture; but the giant new-style plantation is itself a highly specialized form of capital investment in which a lot of nest eggs are concentrated in one very large basket. Not all world areas offer the particular combination of land resources, technological requirements, labor and other factors of production to make such specialized investment profitable, nor is the search for returns on invested capital served everywhere by the establishment of such highly specialized forms. This would seem to be especially true in a world which suffers from overproduction of agricultural commodities as well as from political reactions against the past sins of unilateral imperialism. I should thus expect to find few other Cañamelars.

CULTURE VERSUS SOCIETY

It is time to return to theoretical considerations. I believe we have erred in thinking of one culture per society, one sub-culture per social segment, and that this error has weakened our ability to see things dynamically. To put this in a way familiar to anthropologists, I think we have failed to draw a proper distinction between culture and society, and to make proper use of this conceptual polarity in our analyses. By culture I mean the historically developed forms through which the members of a given society relate to each other. By society I mean the element of action, of human manoeuver within the field provided by cultural forms, human manoeuver which aims either at preserving a given balance of life chances and life risks or at changing it. Most "cultural" anthropologists have seen cultural forms as so limiting that they have tended to neglect entirely the element of human manoeuver which flows through these forms or around them, presses against their limits or plays several sets of forms against the middle. It is possible, for instance, to study the cultural phenomenon of ritual co-parenthood (*compadrazgo*) in general terms: to make note of its typical form and general functions. At the same time, dynamic analysis should not omit note of the different uses to which the form is put by different individuals, of the ways in which people explore the possibilities of a form, or of the ways in which they circumvent it. Most social anthropologists, on the other hand, have seen action or maneouver as primary, and thus neglect to explore the limiting influence of cultural forms. Cultural form not only dictates the limits of the field for the social play, it also limits the direction in which the play can go in order to change the rules of the game, when this becomes necessary. Once more using co-parenthood in Cañamelar as an illustration, it can be said that it functions to link worker families together in their joint efforts to better their life chances. At the same time, it can link families in one way, but not in another. Using Talcott Parson's terminology, ritual co-parenthood links them particularistically, and therefore proves ill-adapted to human manoeuver in the case of a plantation-wide strike which requires action through an organization like a labor union with universalistic characteristics. On one level of action, the two forms and the play they make possible are supplementary in function; on another level of action, however, they interfere and contradict each other. In such a situation, both forms may survive, and survive also in their combined potential for tension and interference. Past culture certainly structures the process of perception, nor is human manoeuver always conscious and rational: by taking both views—a view of cultural forms as defining fields for human manoeuver, and a view of human manoeuver always pressing against the inherent limitations of cultural forms—we shall have a more dynamic manner of apprehending the real tensions of life.

Following the logic of this point of view, I believe that it is possible for a human group to carry more than one culture, to diversify its approach to life, to widen its field of manoeuver through a process of generalization, just as it is possible for a human group to specialize, to restrict itself to one set of cultural forms and to eschew all possible alternatives. This point, it seems to me, is crucial to an understanding both of the specialized case of Cañamelar as well as of the many cases in which plantation workers straddle more than one cultural adaptation. For the purposes of this paper, therefore, I want to define a sub-culture as those several sets of cultural forms through which a human group that forms part of a larger society manoeuvers—consciously and unconsciously—to maintain or improve its particular balance of life risks and life chances.

NEW-STYLE PLANTATION: GENERALIZED ADAPTATIONS

Looking beyond specialized adaptation to other possible adaptations to life on the new-style plantation, we may distinguish three generalized modes of adaptation.

The first kind of double adaptation—involves the possession of at least two sets of cultural forms and thus two fields of manoeuver for a better balance of chances and risks: this is discernible in areas where peasants work on plantations, and step with one foot into the plantation way of life, while keeping the other foot on the peasant holding. Jamaica seems to be an example of an area where this occurs. Yet faint traces of this kind of double life are discernible even in culturally specialized Cañamelar where recent immigrants from the highlands retain some material traits, marriage customs and religious attitudes of their highland peasant relatives. These should not, I believe, be interpreted as survivals. They are, on the contrary, ways of maintaining two alternative sets of ties which can be played against the middle for the important end of improving the balance of life. We may hazard a guess that this kind of cultural straddling will acquire a permanent character, if economic development is at once too slow to provide many opportunities for social and geographical mobility, and too weak to eliminate other cultural and social alternatives. In this kind of adaptation, the alternate activation of first one set of cultural forms and then another does not mean that some people are rising out of their class; rather, it signifies an attempt by people in the same condition of life to widen the base of their opportunities.

With the opening of some sort of "frontier," some room for increased manoeuver, we should expect to find the second type of multiple adaptation. Here again people will activate first one set of cultural forms and then another, but this time in the services of social and economic mobility. In this kind of adaptation, the individual begins his play with one set of cultural forms. Later, he learns another through a gradual process of acculturation, and attempts—for a period of time—to operate with two. Gradually, however, he severs his connections with his original cultural possessions, until he finally emerges from the chrysalis of the double adaptation when his newly-won sphere of manoeuver is secure. Within the Caribbean, this seems to have been the pattern adopted by the Barbadians, who have made effective use of their system of education to propel members of the plantation-peasant groups into professional positions throughout the British West Indies. The pattern may also be characteristic of Italian immigrants, both in South and North America. In these groups—as in others who adopt this second pattern, we should expect to find a break between generations, sharp cultural discontinuity between the parent group and the filial generation, not only in the cultural forms utilized, but in the expectations provided by the new fields for manoeuver.

There is a third kind of multiple adaptation which appears to involve greater complexities. It certainly has important bearing on the character of the society in which it is attempted. Like the previous one, it occurs when a group with a different culture is settled among populations with distinct cultural patterns. The phenomenon is highly characteristic of plantation areas which have imported workers from different parts of the world. At the same time, the motives which propel the migrant group to choose adaptation 3 rather than 2 remain obscure. I shall therefore describe it briefly, and offer some comments on a possible line of investigation which might help us understand the problem. In this third kind of multiple adaptation, the migrant group attempts to strike a balance between the cultural forms offered by the host group and its own particular heritage of forms. Two sets of processes seem to be involved in this balance or compromise solution. First, the migrant group may strive to increase its sense of security, reduce its risks and improve its life chances, by retaining measurable cultural identity and thus enforcing group cohesion in a new and strange environment. This process may be aided materially if the host group is hostile. Second, migrants are often able to see opportunities, fields for manoeuver, in the host culture which the local inhabitants fail to perceive. This sharpened perception on the part of the migrant group is due partly to their possession of a distinct cultural lens through which they view the outside world, partly to their need to strive for an improved balance of risks and chances in a situation in which they have cut their connections with an established way of life. They may thus find and create new niches in the local ecology, and then stake their claims to these niches in terms of cultural forms which differ from those of the local population.

This kind of double adaptation in which a migrant group straddles two sets of cultural forms can occur both in societies with restricted opportunities for mobility and in "open" societies. The Jewish ghetto of the European Middle Ages comes readily to mind as an example of such a group, contained within a relatively static social structure. The East Indians of Jamaica may perhaps serve as still another example, though adapted to the more mobile characteristics of modern Jamaican society. Yet this kind of double adaptation can also occur under conditions of accelerated mobility, where indeed it may serve a special function. For it would seem possible for a migrant group of this kind to utilize its double adaptation as a means for "short-circuiting" the process of social circulation. The Chinese in Jamaica, the Japanese in North and South America, as well as Jewish groups of many countries, have developed patterns of using the channels of education and other devices of mobility to push members of the next filial generation into the top professional strata. In contrast to the adaptation of the second type, however, mobility here does not cause a break between successive generations. The parent generation may indeed sacrifice itself to allow the filial generation to fulfill its own parental expectations of increased mobility. Both the success of this adaptation at the outset, and its continuous maintenance, seem to depend on very tight family organization in which the familial group always remains the last stronghold of cultural differentiation. Familial patterns, especially group endogamy, play a large part in this process.

SUMMARY

First, we spoke of the plantation as a class-structured form of organization, set up along hierarchical lines which are expressed both socially and spatially. Then we differentiated two kinds of plantations. On the old-style plantation, labor is bound and part of the resources of the enterprise are employed to underwrite the consumption needs of the workers and the status needs of the owner. On the new-style plantation, in contrast, labor is free, and all consumption needs are divorced from the operation of the enterprise. We then examined the social matrix of these two kinds of plantation: the dominance of personalized ties on the old-style plantation, the dominance of impersonal ties on the new-style plantation. We noted that,

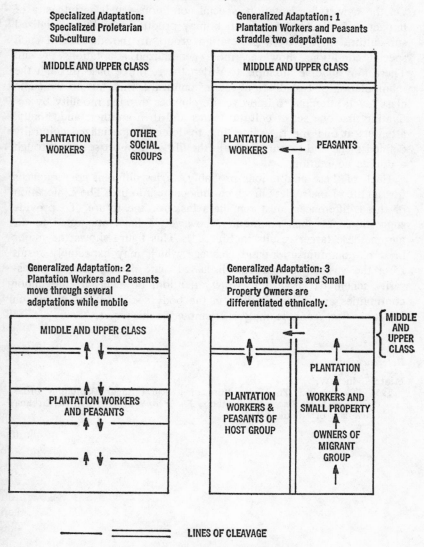

FIGURE 1

Diagrammatic Representation of Lines of Cleavage and Communication, Produced by the Various Adaptations to Life on New-style Plantations

on the old-style plantation, workers competed strongly for access to favors and goods from the same source. In such a setting, I should expect to find generalized rather than specialized cultural adaptations. On the new-style plantation, special conditions—such as intensity of impact and absence of a frontier—may produce a highly specialized sub-culture carried by a proletarian group. In the absence of such special conditions, however, more generalized adaptations prevail. These may involve attempts to widen the resource base through the manipulation of two different sets of cultural forms, but on the same class level; attempts to improve life chances through mobility by activating first one set of cultural forms and then another; and, finally, attempts at one and the same time to defend a specialized culturally defined niche and to participate in the life of the host society through a double adaptation.

Each of these adaptations probably carries different consequences for the life of the society in which they come into use. The exploration of these differences must remain a task for the future. To provide suggestions for such an inquiry, however, I have attempted to diagram these larger results in Figure 1. This figure shows the major lines of communication and cleavage which may expectably result from the various adaptations discussed. The presentation is necessarily schematic. I wish to draw attention, however, to the major continuities and discontinuities in the body social and politic which appear to flow from the analysis attempted in this paper.

Reference cited:

Mintz, Sidney W.
   1956 "Cañamelar: The Sub-culture of a Rural Sugar Plantation Proletariat," in J. H. Steward and others, *The People of Puerto Rico*. Urbana, University of Illinois Press.

MICHAEL M. HOROWITZ

9. *A Typology of Rural Community Forms in the Caribbean*[1]

In every society known to the ethnographic record there are social systems which provide for the socialization of all members to the behavioral patterns of their ancestors. These systems include all the categories of culture—i.e., family, kinship, religion, economics, politics, *rites de passages,* etc.—that are necessary for the continuance of the culture and its transmission to the next generation. They function to teach the young of the culture how to be participating adults. Similar, in a sense, to the isolate of biology, they are the smallest units in the society which provide for sustained cultural transmission and variation, and which permit the emergence of new forms which will themselves be sustained and transmitted. Such systems are termed "communities."

In complex societies the community is no longer coterminous with the society itself. Therefore, as anthropology turns increasingly to the study of such societies, we must have some means of identifying and comparing the constituent kinds of communities. We must have a meaningful taxonomy of them based on a set of conventions of description which insure the comparison of like events. We find most useful the indices of space, time, and personnel, as formulated by Conrad Arensberg in his classification of American communities (1955:1146). They are not formal or arbitrary boundaries but are natural parameters of interaction.

We shall attempt to identify the range of community forms which are found in so limited an area as the insular Caribbean and British Guiana, the region which Charles Wagley has aptly termed "Plantation America." "Throughout this sphere," he writes, "there seems to be a weak sense of community cohesion, and local communities

SOURCE: Reprinted from the *Anthropological Quarterly,* Vol. 33, No. 4 (1960): 177–87, by permission of the *Anthropological Quarterly.*

are but loosely organized" (1957:8). He suggests that this may be responsible for the lack of community description in the ethnographic reporting for the area; although we have considerable information about such problems as acculturation, family organization, race and ethnic relations, and historical survivals, we are seldom presented with a clear statement of the community in which these problems were investigated.

The peasant *commune* of Morne-Paysan in Martinique appears to represent a community which has a high degree of integration. It can be located on a continuum with other communities in the West Indies which range from the rather tightly "closed" to the relatively "open," of the kind Wagley had in mind. These types do not seem to be randomly distributed but are in relationship to particular socioeconomic organizations. The hypothesis advanced is that peasant life is associated with the tightly integrated kind of community, while that of the plantation workers is associated with the open community. The broad categories of community organization are related to the productive technology and economy of the people. Within these categories there are subtypes or classes finer drawn, sharing a greater number of qualitative similarities. These specifics of form within the broad categories have to do with the particular culture history of the people, especially in terms of specific derivations in Europe.

A tightly integrated community is one in which the great majority of significant interactions of its members occurs within its bounds. It is probably endogamous, or in a relationship of spouse exchange with a narrowly restricted number of other communities. In an open community a marital partner may come from anywhere, with the result that the community location of any member's affinal kin may be different from that of any other's. There is, then, an independence and potential conflict between community and affinal kinship.

Membership is free and easy in the open community, restricted in the tightly integrated. The former requires only a partial involvement of the person in its activities. One may be a member for limited periods of time, for example, during the crop season only, and then move on. There is here a greater degree of subcultural variation for it makes less demands on the total loyalty of its members. Thus, it may include groups in active competition for scarce goods, competing political and religious groups. In this sense, the open community is more "urban" than the tightly integrated, for there is greater possibility for anonymity on the part of its members.

The elusive attribute of *esprit de corps* is pronounced in the tightly integrated community, where the members have a vested interest in the perpetuation of their way of life and identification with it. They are more likely to have developed a sense of "weness" and a recognition of their differences from other communities. As long as a member maintains a stake in the community, for example, continues to own a piece of land, he may leave and yet have a guaranteed right to return to full participation at any time. The open community provides little distinction between the person who returns and the one who enters for the first time.

Before turning to the comparative material, we shall comment on the terms "peasant" and "plantation." Redfield follows Wolf's definition of the peasant as one for whom "agriculture is a livelihood and a way of life, not a business for profit," and adds Kroeber's observation that the peasant community always stands in some relationship to urban centers, which serve them as markets for the disposal of their surplus produce (Redfield 1956:27,29). Thus defined, the peasant community differs from his earlier conceptualization of it as having an "all-providing self-sufficiency" (1955:4). Wolf distinguishes between peasant owners and tenants, seeing the two as each having distinct implications (1955:453). My research in Morne-Paysan does not necessitate the dichotomy. Most persons are at the same time owners and tenants, and the alternatives do not appear to have important structural correlatives.

In my definition of the peasant the amount of land under his control is relatively small, and surplus production limited or nonexistent. The primary purpose in agriculture is to feed himself and his family. In addition, land is a scarce commodity, and cannot be abandoned or allowed to lie fallow for very long, even though productivity may decline as a consequence of uninterrupted cultivation.

Plantation workers form the vast agricultural proletariat of the Caribbean. Their labor is a commodity which is exchanged for cash. They have no control over the production or distribution of the crop. The nature of the crop provides only seasonal employment, so that for much of the year plantation workers have only occasional work. Most must provide for their own lodging, but each plantation in Martinique maintains a small group, called *gens casés,* housed rent-free on the estate, and in a paternalistic relationship with the *patron* reminiscent of that of slavery.

The large number of studies which have been done in recent years in the West Indies precludes reference to anything more than a sample in the present paper. We have selected for comparison reports, from eight areas within the region, which have been specifically concerned with the nature of the community itself. We have neglected, of necessity, several excellent studies which concentrate rather on specific problems, such as on family organization, or religious cults, or race relations, or African retentions and reinterpretations.

The charts at the end of this paper list what appear to be the salient facts—both structural and attributional—which are relevant to the typology. Unfortunately, not all of the reports are sufficiently complete to allow a full listing for each community. There is, however, enough information to enable us to suggest a tentative classification as to degree of integration:

1. Most integrated: Morne-Paysan (Martinique); Orange Grove (Jamaica); Mocca (Jamaica).
2. Moderately integrated: August Town (British Guiana); Canalville (British Guiana); Tabara (Puerto Rico).
3. Least integrated: Sugartown (Jamaica); Cañamelar (Puerto Rico).

The first three are characterized by a high degree of communal activity, corporateness of household groupings, and a wide extension of extra-household kinship obligations. In addition, they have limited stratification and a relatively stable population. All three are ethnically homogeneous. The members do not migrate seasonally for outside employment, nor do outsiders enter in search of work. This seems to be related to the fact that although all three are in close proximity to sugar estates, they are able to derive enough income from work on their own lands throughout the year so that there is little incentive to leave. In Canalville the peasant is likewise accorded higher status than the cane laborer, but there the individual plots do not provide enough return to permit a total devotion to horticulture.

The second three are characterized by populations much more mobile, with constant movement from the town to the sugar estates and, in August Town, to the bauxite fields. Although they are all peasant areas, in August Town and Tabara concentration is on a cash crop (rice in the former, tobacco in the latter), rather than on provisions. Canalville is the only one of the three in which there is any development of exchange labor groups, a feature which characterizes both Morne-Paysan and Orange Grove. (The plots in Mocca are too small to require exploitation by any group beyond the household).

Tabara has a well-developed class system, with attendant activities restricted to the members of a given class. Canalville is ethnically complex, restricting, through limited intermarriage, a wide extension of kinship ties which would serve further to integrate the community.

Finally, Sugartown and Cañamelar are devoted to plantation cane production. Here there is no peasantry, but an agrarian proletariat with no control over the process of production beyond organization into labor unions. Not only are there differences in orientation among the rigidly distinct classes in these communities, but these orientations are in direct conflict: the elite is concerned with producing cane as efficiently and economically as possible; the workers are interested in raising wages and prolonging the cutting season. The frequency of strikes in these areas is an index of the lack of integration in the sugar fields.

While there appear to be no West Indian communities which approach the degree of integration achieved in the Central American "closed corporate community" reported by Wolf, the data available indicate that the major factor in determining the relative degree of integration in the West Indies is the kind of tenure and exploitation of land. Where land is held in relatively small holdings, exploited by the household group, and sold in local markets, there seems to emerge a community structure which unites the population by bonds of kinship (real and ritual) and mutual assistance. Where the land is held in great estates, or where the population is forced to sell its labor in an industrial situation, the associated community structure does not serve to join all the members in a common matrix. Rather, it results in a stratified system which opposes the establishment of a wide range of mutual assistance. In the peasant community, the emphasis is on the household and larger groupings for economic and other activities; in the plantation community the emphasis is on the individual. Among West Indian peasants, labor is generally not a commodity. The plantation worker, however, has nothing else to sell.

Such sentiments as "we are all one family" do not seem to appear in the literature for the plantation towns. In the three highly integrated communities the statement is literally true; descended from the original settlers, joined again through intermarriage, the people are kin to each other. Until kin ties are established, outsiders remain outsiders, although they may have lived in the community for many years.

Religion does not appear to be an important factor except where a plurality of cults competing for membership tends to divide the community. Neither is ethnic descent, as such, an important element, although again it may become significant in those communities characterized by a plurality of ethnic groups in which the members of each view themselves as distinct from the others. In Canalville, for example, persons of East Indian ancestry tend to see themselves as separate from those of African descent, and vice versa.

The settlement pattern appears to have more to do with the historical antecedents of the community than with the kind of integration which developed. This is an area in which more study is needed. Careful descriptions of the patterns which obtain in the West Indies should be made and culture-historical studies would indicate continuities with similar patterns in other areas. Conrad Arensberg (1955) has demonstrated connections between various community patterns in the United States and those of the Old World. We have tried to point out the relationship between the settlement use of space in Morne-Paysan and in Brittany (1959). Such work will require the joint efforts of the ethnographer and historian.

Population size and density are factors which influence the kinds of community structure found. The West Indian islands are among the most densely populated rural areas in the world. It is unnecessary to elaborate on the increasing poverty caused by a continual expansion of population without an expansion in the opportunities for employment. In Morne-Paysan, the increasing demographic pressure has forced an immigration from the community to the city, with some movement of the young to the sugar fields. This has the effect of making labor a commodity which, although not yet an important factor within the community, may make for modifications in the system of exchange labor. Sheer size is also important, for people in towns as large as the Puerto Rican *Municipios* cannot experience the extensive face-to-face relationships which are characteristic of the other areas. The effective interpersonal area for these people is something much smaller than the *municipio* as a whole: the *barrio, poblado* or *colonia*. But these units do not provide the total range of services necessary for full cultural participation; the result seems to be that in Puerto Rico the *municipios* themselves are internally divided into rural and urban elements, with attendant divergencies in orientation.

To summarize, West Indian rural community structures range from tightly integrated, corporate-like systems to open, loosely integrated ones. Associated with the former is a peasant economy, based upon exploitation by household units of small plots. Associated with the latter is a plantation economy, based upon modern techniques of sugar cultivation with labor supplied by landless workers. I have argued that the demands of these two types of agricultural activities have much to do with the kind of integration extant in the community.

CHART ONE

Community	Population to nearest 50	Form of Settlement	Source of Income	Ethnic composition (Primary ancestry of residents)
Morne-Paysan	1650	*bourg*—administrative center (non urban) *quartiers*—dispersed farms and homesteads	Sale of produce from own holdings in urban markets	African
August Town	1750	Line village of houses with all lands behind village	1) wage labor on sugar estate and in bauxite fields 2) own farms	African
Canalville	700	Line village of houses with all lands behind village	1) market sale from own lands 2) wage labor on sugar estates	African East Indian
Tabara	17000	*Municipio Pueblo*—urban center *barrio poblado*	1) wage labor on farms 2) sale of tobacco to cooperatives and produce to urban markets	European
Cañamelar	20000	*Municipio pueblo barrio colonia* Factory-in-field	Wage labor on sugar estates	African European
Sugartown	1200	Factory-in-field Class segregated housing Barracks for estate laborers	Wage labor on sugar estates	African European Chinese East Indian
Orange Grove	700	*Village with surrounding dispersed household clusters	Sale of produce from own holdings in urban markets	African
Mocca	400	*Village with surrounding dispersed household clusters	Subsistence horticulture	African

* information from M. G. Smith (1956:297–98)

CHART TWO

Community	Stratification	Exploiting Unit	Tenure of Productive Holdings	Religion
Morne-Paysan	Limited	Household Exchange labor groups	1) Fee simple: individual and undivided family. All children (legitimate) inherit. 2) Share tenancy ("fifty-fifty") 3) Rent tenancy	Roman Catholic
August Town	Consid-erable	Individual	1) Productive lands in fee simple 2) Pasturage rented from Crown	Congregational Anglican and other groups Few Roman Catholics
Canalville	Limited	1) Household exchange labor groups 2) Individual	Fee simple	Various Protestant groups Hindu Moslem
Tabara	Consid-erable but fluid	1) Household 2) Individual (wage laborers)	1) Fee simple—lands bought rather than inherited 2) Share tenancy (*a medias*)	Roman Catholic Various Protestant groups
Cañamelar	Rigid	Individual (wage laborers)	(Housed free on estates or on government lands) Corporate owned estate	Roman Catholic Various Protestant groups
Sugartown	Rigid	Individual (wage laborers)	1) Fee simple—all children inherit. "Family lands" and "bought lands" 2) Corporate owned estates	Jehovah's Witnesses Various Protestant groups Pocomania
Orange Grove	Limited	1) Household 2) Exchange labor groups	Fee simple—all children inherit. "Family lands" and "bought lands"	Protestant
Mocca	Slight	Household	Fee simple—all children inherit. "Family lands" and "bought lands"	Protestant

CHART THREE

Community	Population Stability	Expressions of community solidarity and tensions
Morne-Paysan	Few outsiders enter community Endogamous Few leave to work on sugar estates	"Tout le monde est parent." Collective building of town hall. Limited recourse to courts to settle internal disputes. All households represented at wakes. Households are corporate.
August Town	Endogamous Migration to sugar estates and bauxite fields	"All one family." "Black folks' village" All households represented at wakes. Families and households not corporate.
Canalville	Constant turnover of personnel	Extensive use of courts to settle internal disputes. Ethnic stereotypes. "No trespassing" signs. "Boxes"
Tabara	Continual movement in and out of area. Seasonal migration of *agregados* to coastal estates.	Class differences in religion. Upper class clubs.
Cañamelar	Large number of outsiders enter during crop time.	"Nosostros del barrio." Restricted social interaction among classes.
Sugartown	Large number of outsiders enter during crop time.	Household not corporate. Class differences in residential areas.
Orange Grove	Do not migrate for wage labor.	Household is corporate. Collective building of town hall.
Mocca	Do not migrate for wage labor.	Household is corporate. Stranger indentified as "Bluefoot" even after several generations.

CHART FOUR

Community	Kin and Ritual Kin Ties	Times
Morne-Paysan	Both well-developed. Market role for women.	Short dead (dry) season. Many times of total assemblage: wakes, special masses, patron saint. Saturday market.
August Town	"Little development of . . . reciprocal kinship obligations."	Migration of young out during sugar crop season.
Canalville	Market role for women. Some development of godparent ties.	Regular cultivation throughout year with some daily movement to plantation and back to village during crop time.
Tabara	Weak *compadrazgo*.	1) 3 months dead time in tobacco. 2) Commerce active from November through April, season of sale of tobacco.
Cañamelar	Limited kin ties. Strong *compadrazgo*.	1) 6 months dead time. 6 months crop time. 2) No times of total assemblage.
Sugartown	Resident core of persons related by ties of kinship.	1) 6 months dead time. 6 months crop time. 2) No times of total assemblage.
Orange Grove	Well-developed kin ties.	Saturday market. Regular times of total assemblage.
Mocca	Well-developed kin ties.	Regular cultivation throughout year.

Note:

1. This paper was presented at the annual meeting of the Central States Anthropological Society held at the University of Indiana in April, 1960. Field research in Martinique during 1956, 7, and 8 was supported by fellowships from the Social Science Research Council and the Department of Anthropology, Columbia University, to which grateful acknowledgment is hereby recorded.

References cited:

Arensberg, C. M.
1955 "American Communities." *American Anthropologist* 57.
Clark, Edith (Sugartown, Orange Grove, and Mocca).
1957 *My Mother Who Fathered Me.* George Allen and Unwin Ltd., London.
Horowitz, Michael M. (Morne-Paysan).
1959 "Morne-Paysan: Peasant Community in Martinique." Ph.D. dissertation, Columbia University, New York.
Manners, Robert (Tabara).
1956 "Tabara: Subcultures of a Tobacco and Mixed Crops Municipality," in J. Steward (ed.), *The People of Puerto Rico.* University of Illinois Press, Urbana.
Mintz, Sidney (Cañamelar).
1956 "Cañamelar: The Subculture of a Rural Sugar Plantation Proletariat," in J. Steward (ed.), *The People of Puerto Rico.* University of Illinois Press, Urbana.
Redfield, Robert.
1955 *The Little Community.* University of Chicago Press, Chicago.
1956 *Peasant Society and Culture.* University of Chicago Press, Chicago.
Skinner, Elliott P. (Canalville).
1955 "Ethnic Interaction in a British Guiana Rural Community." Ph.D. dissertation, Columbia University, New York.
Smith, M. G.
1956 "Community Organization in Rural Jamaica." *Social and Economic Studies* 5.
Smith, R. T. (August Town).
1956 *The Negro Family in British Guiana.* Grove Press, New York.
Wagley, Charles.
1957 "Plantation America: A Culture Sphere," in V. Rubin (ed.), *Caribbean Studies, a Symposium.* Institute of Social and Economic Research, Jamaica.
Wolf, E.
1955 "Types of Latin American Peasantry: A Preliminary Discussion." *American Anthropologist* 57.

RICHARD FRUCHT

10. A Caribbean Social Type: Neither "Peasant" nor "Proletarian"[1]

Studies and commentaries on Caribbean societies have made it clear that such concepts as "peasant" and "proletarian" are not categorical, but variable.[2] In this paper I attempt to show that what may also be of importance in understanding Caribbean societies besides the nature of the category ("peasant" or "proletarian") is the nature of the variable relationships characterizing the society. I want to show that particularly for the smaller islands, such as Nevis,[3] the people are categorically neither peasants nor proletarians. Rather the situation may be comprehended by making use of Marx's analytic distinction between the *means of production,* that is, the tools and techniques, *and relations of production,* that is, what we usually mean by the social division of labour as well as the articulation of the productive economy and the social organization, including property and power relations. More specifically, I want to show that during the period after slave emancipation in 1834 and until the end of the second World War, Nevisian society could be characterized as exhibiting a *peasant-like* means of production along with *proletarian-like* relations of production. The argument here rests on discriminating between kinds of sharecropping or *metayage* relationships.

Most of our discussions about peasantry and proletariat in the Caribbean have been based on work carried out in the Greater Antilles[4]—Jamaica, Haiti and Puerto Rico—and in some of the more important Lesser or Eastern Antilles[5] such as Martinique and Trinidad, as well as Guyana. At the risk of over-simplifying, such peasantries are to be found in communities on lands marginal to the needs of the plantations, in the highlands and sometimes in the arid lowlands. A primary characteristic of peasantry is household production

SOURCE: Reprinted from *Social and Economic Studies,* Vol. 13, No. 3 (1967):295–300, by permission of the author and publisher.

of subsistence crops on small plots, with cash crops produced according to location and market conditions.[6] Occasional involvement in wage labour on plantations in order to supplement cash needs is also a feature of Caribbean peasantries. They are usually contrasted with the part-societies of plantation labourers, the rural proletariat, who live on or near plantations and whose livelihood depends primarily upon the sale of their labour to the plantations and supplemented by desultory cultivation of subsistence crops on garden plots, when and if available.[7]

I want to point out that the word "peasant" is not to be here understood as a categorical concept describing a subculture or kind of community. It is not to be so understood because the so-called peasantry of Nevis has always been inextricably bound to the plantation system or to some other system of wage labour in more than an occasional sense. This is an artifact of geography, of economic history, and of the economic and political predominance of the industrial, colonial power.[8]

In essence I want to make what I hope is not a too simplified distinction: that in Nevis, whereas there is a peasant-like *means* of production, which includes cultivation of small plots with the use of household labour and traditional manual technology,[9] the *relations* of production are proletarian, that is, based on the sale of labour for wages either paid in cash or in kind, and the latter through systems of sharecropping, farming-out, and under conditions of male labour emigration. Finally, the existence together and in alternation of seemingly disparate *means* and *relations* of production is an adaptation to the vicissitudes of a marginal economy.

The development of a peasant-like means of production—household production—began after the emancipation of slaves in 1834, because of geographical and economic factors. In the first place, free villages of the type founded in Jamaica, for instance, did not develop in the Leeward Islands since there was no land available either for slaves or freedmen. All the land was alienated and under the control of the plantation-owners. The post-emancipation villages established on free-hold or lease-hold tenure grew on estate boundaries, along the sides of steep ravines, too steep for profitable sugar cane cultivation, on the arid lowlands, and on the steep upper slopes of the central mountain masses. In short, the villages were founded on land marginal to the plantations' uses, but on or near them so that they served, in effect, as dormitories for the labourers. Such villages are still found in St. Kitts and Antigua where plantations predominate. In Nevis, however, the plantation economy slowly became a small-holders' economy through the failings of the sugar—and, later, the cotton—markets. But the small-holders' economy in this island is not a peasant economy—that is, it is *not always* and has never been *only* a peasant economy.

To some extent, the economy based on household production of subsistence and cash crops on small plots was instituted in order to preserve a way of life based on the social relations of plantation production. In Nevis, for instance, the end of the apprenticeship period in 1838 and the final emancipation of slaves, together with the threatened position of the entire West Indian sugar industry led to a call for debt payments on the part of the factors and creditors of plantation operators. The resulting cash shortage and the necessity of maintaining plantation operations for the benefit of the planters and absentee-owners resident in England led to the adoption of forms of sharecropping as the means by which sugar cane cultivation could be carried on. The hallmark of sharecropping is the use of household labour, but the share which remains with the labourer can be considered a form of wage payment—not in cash, but in kind. In other words, the freed slaves were forced to remain on plantation lands, and the lack of cash with which to pay these freedmen even low wages impelled the planters to pay their labourers in kind—through the means of what may be referred to as the share-wage.

The share-wage is one form of sharecropping. It refers to a situation in which the cropper, or labourer, supplies the tools—in this case hoe and pitch-fork—and the labour—his own and that of his household. The landowner, on the other hand, supplies the seed, the fertilizer, the insecticide, and supervision in the person of a "chargehand" or overseer. Furthermore, within this relationship it is the owner who decides which crop shall be cultivated. In this way the share which remains with the sharecropper or labourer can be considered a form of wages in kind.[10]

The other form of sharecropping is what I refer to as the share-rent, and is similar to the share-tenant relationship characteristic of the American south.[11] Under these conditions, the tenant supplies tools, seed, fertilizer, labour, etc., the landowner merely lets the use of his land. The decision as to what to cultivate remains with the tenant, and he may hire labourers to work his plot for him. The share given to the landowner, then, can be considered a form of rent in kind. In Nevis, the share-rent relationship was engaged in primarily and perhaps only by what I have previously referred to as Special People[12]—an upper lower class composed of millhands, carters, overseers, mechanics and other skilled or semi-skilled individuals able to accumulate cash wages. The share-wage relationship was never engaged in by this type, but always by households of agricultural labourers.

The use of household labour on small plots for the benefit of the plantation was further reinforced during the middle of the nineteenth century in spite of conditions of available cash, because of new techniques of intensive cultivation of sugar cane introduced from Barbados. Under this farming-out system, sugar cane planting was carried out by gangs hired by the estate after which households were given one- to two-acre plots to care for, for which they were paid a weekly wage. The cane cutting was done by gangs which invariably included men from the households who were given farms. This system gave the advantage of intensive care which produced greater yields and was even more eminently suited to the cultivation of cotton, a more delicate crop, which was introduced at the beginning of this century. But the farming-out system was common on the few large, well-capitalized estates, while the many smaller estates still relied on share-cropping.

Finally, another factor in the instituting of peasant-like adaptations or household production is the emigration of male labourers which began during the depression of the 1880's and which continued to the end of the first quarter of this century. During the eighties and nineties there was emigration to the gold fields of Venezuela, and to other islands in search of employment. According to the 1891 census there were 83 males for every 100 females in Nevis. After the turn of the century, opportunities for overseas male employment increased. In 1911 there were 74 males for every 100 females in Nevis, and in 1921, 68 males per 100 females. Female predominance under sharecropping and farming-out worked as well if not better with cotton, which was introduced in 1904. Demands of cotton cultivation are not as great as those of sugar cane. Weeding and picking cotton was primarily the work of women, children and elderly men; a division of labour which exists to this day. In a real sense, during the early part of this century women engaged in peasant-like means of production, although both they and the emigrant male labourers were engaged in proletarian *relations* of production: wage labour, either for cash or for kind.

The co-existence of peasant means of production and proletarian relations of production continued until the end of the Second World War, which saw the end of sharecropping and farming-out as predominant systems of production due to the slump in the sugar and cotton markets and the selling out of plantations to local speculators who then divided these estates and sold to small holders for the wealth which the latter were able to accumulate during the wartime prosperity and high wages. Opportunities for emigration were reduced; Nevisian males stayed at home on their small plots and cultivated subsistence crops, some sugar cane, and some cotton for whatever price they were able to receive. Household labour predominated, pitch-fork and hoe were still used. The government bought defunct estates and initiated expanded land settlement schemes in order to encourage the development of a yeomanry. The immediate post-war period of Nevis was the season of peasantry, both in modes and means of production.

After 1955 opportunities for emigration opened up again, not only to England, but to the U.S. Virgin Islands, where the tourist industry had begun to flower and, with it, demands for labourers in construction and the service occupations multiplied. And, as the cotton market rose for a short time and subsequently went into a steady decline, Nevisian labouring class households were again dependent upon cash remittances sent by emigrants, this time both male and female, while desultory cultivation of cotton and subsistence crops was carried on by the grandmothers, grandfathers and youngsters left behind. In 1962, more than 70 per cent of the adult population was not cultivating at all, save for a garden plot of yams, sweet potatoes, and garden vegetables on freehold and leasehold land. In the same year well over $600,000 BWI in postal and money orders were cashed, an amount greater than the proceeds cotton growers received during their biggest crop year since 1942. As I have stated elsewhere, remittances replace agricultural production as the main and most important source of wealth, by a wide margin.[13]

Accompanying this trend towards agricultural non-production and the increasing influx of wealth is the increasing availability of land. Estates are purchased, divided and resold in small parcels to foreign speculators in the tourist business as well as to Nevisians. To the latter, it would appear, land is considered more as a commodity rather than as capital for further productive use. Land is an investment, not only insuring social prestige, but economic independence, in the way of ensuring bank loans for further emigration. In this present period of Nevisian social and economic history, the means of peasant production are present, but are not used; the source of wealth is the cash wages of emigrant labourers. The cash is often invested in land, in shops, in cars and other consumer goods. Today in Nevis there is a curious mixture of dependence upon proletarian-like relationships, peasant-like holdings, and bourgeois aspirations and consumer behaviour. In any event, theirs is a marginal economy, and since there is now some question about whether they can continue to send emigrants abroad—to say nothing of the ability of the emigrants to continue to send remittances—they will be forced to seek out any means of making a livelihood by their own labour, whether for themselves or for others.

In the foregoing pages I have tried to point out that the development of seemingly disparate means and relations of production is possible, especially within the context of marginal, and perhaps only capitalist, economies. In the specific case of Nevis, a former British Caribbean colony, my argument has not been with the *concepts* of peasantry or proletarian *per se,* but with the categorical use of such concepts, since certain forms of production, e.g., sharecropping, may yield proletarian-like relationships in association with peasant-like techniques. In a different context this argument has been already made. Sidney Mintz suggests three historical contexts for the development of Caribbean peasantries: the early yeomen cultivators; a "'proto-peasantry' which evolved under slavery," i.e., slaves who were allowed to cultivate and market food crops, and peasantries which developed in opposition to the slave plantation, e.g., Bush Negroes and Maroons.[14] There is some evidence that a "proto-peasantry" developed in the Leeward Islands and especially on Nevis,[15] but it did not become a "reconstituted peasantry"[16] after emancipation as in Jamaica. The small size of the Leeward Islands and the lack of open areas into which they could go forced the freed slaves/"proto-peasants" into wage labour and sharecropping relations. In terms of the means of production they remained "proto-peasants". Peasant-like production and marketing in these situations may be interpreted as the means by which planters reduced their costs of production by having the slaves provide for themselves, and later, under sharecropping, as the means by which plantation production was carried on in the face of cash shortage. In terms of the relations of production and the social division of labour, the slaves remain slaves, and the sharecroppers remain proletarian.

Furthermore, I am not arguing that Nevisian society is wholly proletarian (though because of its historic tradition and its pattern of labour migration a strong argument could be made for this case), but that the increasing wealth and rising standard of living invites thinking of the present day situation in terms of a *petit bourgeois* style of life. Such circumstances make it difficult categorically to apply terms like "peasant" or "proletarian." The special conditions noted here have to be taken into account, for instance, if attempts are made to organize Nevisian sentiment into political action. The rise of new, non- or anti-Labour Government political parties might be expected under these conditions.

Finally, comparisons of these materials for Nevis with those for other islands such as Montserrat, or even other areas, such as the lower Danubian basin described by Doreen Warriner,[17] may enable us to stipulate other sociological and ideological components accompanying the apparent disparities between peasant-like means of production and proletarian-like relations of production. One possible implication of such an attempt is that we will have to shift our attention from peasant and proletarian *community*, and describe and analyze peasant and proletarian *relations* in all their variety. This is to reiterate the point that peasantry and proletariat can be conceived of as both class *and* culture.[18]

Notes:

1. The data on which this article is based were collected in 1961 and 1962–63 during fieldwork supported by Brandeis University and the Research Institute for the Study of Man. This article was read as a paper before the American Anthropological Association in Pittsburgh, 1966.

2. See, for instance, Sidney Mintz, Foreword to *Sugar and Society in the Caribbean,* by R. Guerra y Sanchez. Yale University Press, New Haven, 1964, especially pages xxiv–xxxviii, also, A. Norton and G. Cumper, " 'Peasant,' 'Plantation' and 'Urban' Communities in Rural Jamaica: A Test of the Validity of the Classification," *Social and Economic Studies,* 15:4:338–52, 1966.

3. Nevis is a unit of the former British Caribbean colony of St. Kitts-Nevis-Anguilla in the northern Lesser Antilles. It has an area of 36 square miles, and a population of approximately 13,000. Sugar-cane and Sea Island cotton were the major cash crops.

4. A comprehensive bibliography of the British and formerly British Caribbean, edited by Lambros Comitas is forthcoming. Herewith are some references

I have found useful. M. Horowitz, "A Typology of Rural Community Forms in the Caribbean," *Anthropological Quarterly* 33:4:177–87, 1960; S. Mintz, "Historical Sociology of the Jamaican Church-Founded Free Village System," *De West Indische Gids* 38:46–70, 1958; A. Metraux, *Making a Living in the Marbial Valley* (Haiti), UNESCO, 1951; J. Steward (ed.), *The People of Puerto Rico*, University of Illinois Press, 1956.

5. M. Horowitz, *Morne-Paysan: Peasant Village in Martinique*, Holt, Rinehart and Winston, Inc., New York, 1967; M. Freilich, "Cultural Diversity Among Trinidadian Peasants," Ph.D. Dissertation, Columbia University, 1960; R. Farley, "Rise of a Peasantry in British Guiana," *Social and Economic Studies* 2:4, 1954.

6. Support for this emphasis on household production within the peasant type can be found in: Eric Wolf, *Peasants*, Prentice-Hall Englewood Cliffs, 1966, especially pages 13–15; Janet Fitchin, "Peasantry As A Social Type," in *Proceedings of the 1961 Annual Spring Meeting of the American Ethnological Society*, Seattle, 1961, especially page 115; Teodor Shanin, "The Peasantry as a Political Factor," *Sociological Review* 14:1:5–27, 1966, especially pages 6–10.

7. Sidney Mintz, "The Folk-Urban Continuum and the Rural Proletarian Community," *American Journal of Sociology* 59:136–43, 1953; Eric Wolf and Sidney Mintz, "Haciendas and Plantations in Middle America and the Antilles," *Social and Economic Studies* 6:3:380–412, 1957.

8. This theme is elaborated in R. Frucht, "Community and Context in a Colonial Society," Ph.D. Dissertation, Brandeis University, 1966.

9. Based on use of pitch-fork and hoe, wielded equally well by men and women.

10. See C. Y. Shephard, *Peasant Agriculture in the Leeward and Windward Islands*, Imperial College of Tropical Agriculture, Trinidad, 1945, pp. 5–10.

11. R. Vance, *Human Factors in Cotton Culture*, University of North Carolina Press, 1929, pp. 253–71.

12. R. Frucht, "Remittances and the Economy in a Small West Indian Island," read before the American Anthropological Association, 1963.

13. *Ibid.;* see also R. Manners, "Remittances and the Unit of Analysis in Anthropological Research," *Southwestern Journal of Anthropology* 21:3:179–95, 1965.

14. Sidney Mintz, "The Question of Caribbean Peasantries: A Comment," *Caribbean Studies* 1:31–34, 1961, especially page 34.

15. See, for instance, Elsa Goveia, *Slave Society in the British Leeward Islands at the End of the Eighteenth Century*, Yale University Press, New Haven, 1965.

16. Sidney Mintz, Foreword to R. Guerra y Sanchez, *op. cit.*, p. xx.

17. D. Warriner, *The Economics of Peasant Farming*, Oxford University Press, 1939.

18. Sidney Mintz, "The Folk-Urban Continuum and the Rural Proletarian Community," *op. cit.*, especially page 141; T. Shanin, *op. cit.*, especially page 17; Eric Wolf, *op. cit.*, especially pages 91–92.

E.
Land Tenure

EDITH CLARKE

11. Land Tenure and the Family in Four Selected Communities in Jamaica

(i)

The following account of land tenure in its relation to family structure and organization is based on original field research in four communities in Jamaica selected as being together representative of rural working-class and small farmer communities.

Three of the villages to which the fictitious names of *Orange Grove, Mocca* and *Patentville* have been given, represent three types of farming communities based on three different modes of tenure and land use common throughout Jamaica. Orange Grove lies in a fertile valley and is a settlement of progressive farmers, owning their own holdings ranging from 5 and 10 to one hundred acres and practising mixed farming based on citrus and cattle. The standard of agriculture is high; the majority of the homes, built of local stone and hardwood, are commodious permanent structures and living approximates middle-class standards. Patentville is an example of the effect of short term leases on family structure and agricultural practice. The erection of permanent houses on the holdings is prohibited by the terms of the lease; homes are usually one-room grass huts, sometimes divided by a bamboo screen. Cultivation is largely of local foodstuffs and there is no animal husbandry nor are permanent crops grown on the rented lands. Mocca is a tiny isolated village, on the fringe of the sugar area but aloof from it, consisting of a handful of families descended from common ancestors, living on land given them before and just after Emancipation, and getting a precarious living from cattle which they run on waste land, by fishing, and casual day labour on the surrounding large properties. Sugartown as the name indicates,

SOURCE: Reprinted from *Social and Economic Studies,* Vol. 1, No. 4 (1953): 81–118, by permission of the author and publisher.

is an example of a community wholly dependent on the sugar industry.

It is clear from our research that there is, common to all these communities, a customary system of family tenure, inheritance and use, supported by a body of traditional beliefs and a system of values and reinforced by strong social sanctions. If this is so, the facts which we endeavour to set out here, cannot safely be ignored altogether in any programme of land reform, nor in such a far-reaching survey of tenure, agricultural practice and resources (both in soil and in people) as has recently been recommended by the World Bank Mission[1] and appears likely to be accepted by the Government of Jamaica.

Unless these current beliefs and practices, common throughout the farming communities, and equally strongly held by the landless population dependent primarily upon wage labour in the towns and sugar estates, are fully understood and due attention paid to the tenacity with which they are held and the sentiment which attaches to them, changes which in themselves seem admirable enough and which in any case are inevitable under the pressure of modern economic conditions and population growth, may be unduly held up, if not ultimately defeated. It will also be appreciated from what follows that reforms such as are recommended are bound to have far-reaching effects on the structure of family life and on the system of kinship relationships and roles.

The current ideas in regard to land profoundly affect the family— the form it takes, the constitution of the household, and the kinship roles. The concept of *family land* and the principles of inheritance and use, not by one individual member but by a group within a prescribed lineage, is a vital factor in preserving the sense of relationship and mutual responsibility and interdependence of the kin, and in keeping the family together.

The primary concern of this study, therefore, is to describe the system of customary law with particular reference to its effect upon family structure and kinship roles. This is all the more necessary since any attempt to change the system, which has survived in spite of the fact that it is largely unrecognized in the legal code, and in spite of changing economic conditions and pressure on the land available for small settlers, will also affect the pattern of this family structure and the kinship roles.

As an example, to insist "once for all" on Registered titles for all holdings as a preliminary to any sponsored system of agricultural loans or credit, raises, not only the practical problem of high cost and excessive delays (which is relatively easily soluble) but the probable effect on family organization of insistence (a) on the principle of individual ownership (and use) where it runs contrary to the current theory of the rights of a group of kin; and (b) on defining an heir in terms of legitimacy or illegitimacy.

According to customary belief and practice family land passes to "all the family" or "all the children" and may be used jointly by a group of kindred who together subscribe towards the "tax money". Alienation outside "the blood" on the one hand or the paternal kin on the other is prohibited. It is a wrong against the family. If this is as deeply rooted an idea as we believe, and if the concept of "family land" attaches, in the process of transmission, to "bought" land then there is a further difficulty (which challenges this "once-and-for-all") of how to perpetuate the reform and control subsequent fragmentation or partition.

Even the principle of joint-registration of holdings which is legally permissible, is not as simple as it sounds if it requires the agreement of large numbers of kin, not only scattered about Jamaica, but living in other parts of the world.

There is another complex question: the principle to be followed in determining the rightful heir in the case of intestacy, or where the family, or any member of it, resorts to litigation to settle an attempt at innovation or attempted exploitation by one member of the kin. In current practice "all the children" may include descendants of both or of one parent only; it may also include siblings or lateral kin on the relevant side. There is no recognition of an exclusive right to inheritance, or use, by any one member of the family, no prior right based on sex, or seniority or "legitimacy". Any such principle would seem to our informants to strike at the very root of kinship solidarity.

There is general acceptance that a will may override the "rights" of succession of "all the family" in favour of one member. Thus a man (or woman) may will all or a portion of his holding to a son or daughter who (alone of all his children) stayed in the home and cared for him in his old age. Such a will would be accepted though there may be bitter resentment at its terms.

There is also, in practice, non-exercise by kin of their "rights" for one reason or another—the fact that they have got on in the world and have better land or prospects elsewhere or that they live too far away to use the land. Even in such cases, we were told they would have the right to return at any time and build on the site, and there were many instances of gifts of produce from family holdings being sent to kindred in Kingston or other parts of the island.

It is impossible in a short article to condense conclusions arrived at in a long and comprehensive study of social institutions and some of the findings in this paper are dependent on or reinforced by evidence which I give elsewhere. Our evidence goes to show that the kindred, the blood relatives and in particular the maternal kin, as distinct from the conjugal or the household group, is the most important institution in our communities and often the only vital one. Nor is it by any means as weak and disorganized as appears if we make the mistake of identifying the family with marriage and confuse kin or family with conjugal relationships.

The second point which our research brings out is the degree to which the strength of the kinship group (as also of the conjugal family wherever it has strength, permanence and stability) is associated with ownership of land and the customary procedure of transmission with its implicit acknowledgement of parental responsibility for all children.

It is not accidental that marriage and the family as an institution is at its strongest and most stable in Orange Grove, the farming community where the holdings are (at present at any rate) adequate to support and hold together wives, husbands and their children in a highly integrated society; that it is equally strong (if economically less well-placed) in Mocca where, in spite of a lower ratio of marriage, concubinage was generally a life-long institution based on family homes and land; and that in Sugartown there is the highest proportion of unstable unions, promiscuity and irresponsible parenthood.

In Mocca the family is, in fact, *the* chief social institution, the only other of any importance (apart from the religious cults) being the Trade Union organization, leadership in which was exercised by the head of the leading family as part of his natural leadership in the village. As he dramatically informed us: "I rule Mocca!"

Sugartown was in its original form similar to Mocca and there is still the core of the old village with its Old Families living on family land inherited from ancestors who were granted it after Emancipation, upon which the new industrial community has been superimposed. Few of the members of these Old Families work on the estate

In spite of the higher income to be derived from this, they regard fieldwork as beneath them and are either tradesmen, barbers, butchers or tailors, or depend on the rent of their rooms (and of thatched huts which they erect on the family land) to new-comers seeking work in the factory or in the cane fields during crop. Family land here has no agricultural value—it consists of "yards" of beaten earth between crowded huts containing households of linked families and tenants.

(ii)

After annexation by the British, all land in Jamaica became the property of the Crown and was granted by Royal Patents to English colonists subject to the payment of Quit Rents. Hundreds of acres of these properties were forfeited to the Crown owing to non-payment of these rents and at Emancipation, although there was no official attempt to create a small-farmers' community, there were three categories of land on which a peasantry might establish itself: the forfeited lands which might be purchased from the Crown and which attracted many of the most independent and ambitious of the freed slaves who had saved money; the marginal lands which might be purchased or leased from land-owners; and the mountainous forest reserves which might be squatted on.[2]

The British colonists who received grants of land by Letters Patent from the Crown were given Common Law Titles. (Patentville is one of the few properties which remain to this day intact and in the possession of the descendants of the original Patentee). Although there was no complete registration of these titles in Jamaica, I am informed that they were subsequently recorded. (The Registration of Titles Law was not introduced until 1888.)

It is not possible to state what happened in the case of the small parcels of land which were bought by slaves prior to and after Emancipation. It is known that such transfers took place and there is evidence in our own work in Jamaica, that at least some slaveowners made free grants of land to their slaves. If these pieces of land were formally conveyed, and if Registered or Common Law titles were obtained, it should be possible to trace these transactions in the archives at Spanish Town and the figures would give an indication of the extent of early peasant settlement. In our own fieldwork we never came across any such documents although some of the land in our "old districts" had been inherited by the present occupiers from forbears who received it as a grant at the beginning of the 19th Century. Considering the importance attached to any official "paper" and the way such "proofs" of ownership are treasured, these would undoubtedly have been shown us had they survived. It is probable that in most of these original purchases or free grants, there was a conveyance from the landowner. There is evidence, however, that a good deal of "squatting" took place on the back lands of properties, and on the Crown lands in the pockets of soil in the Cockpit Country. With the large proportion of absentee landlords in the years following Emancipation, and the absence of adequate patrolling of the Crown forest reserves, these "free tenants" were left unmolested for years and in some cases established squatters rights which could be upheld under the terms of the Statute of Limitations.[3]

Where a man has neither a Title nor a Conveyance for his land he may, under this Statute, establish ownership by proving undisputed possession for a minimum of twelve years.

As will be seen from the account which follows, very few of the holdings "owned" or occupied by the peasants, were more than a few acres in extent and many more are measured in "squares".* The value of the land in terms of money (apart from its social value) is small. The cost of taking out a Registered Title, which entails paying for a survey and employing a lawyer, is prohibitive in the majority of these cases.

According to the Law of Inheritance, in the case of intestacy, the eldest legitimate son is the legal heir to all property. Illegitimate children are not recognised as having any legal rights. Failing the establishment of a legitimate heir, the land is forfeited to the Crown and is administered or disposed of by the Administrator General.

There is a considerable body of current belief in our community which does not easily adapt itself to this legal framework.

We found, for instance, that three documents are popularly believed to establish proof of ownership: (i) *a Receipt* from the vendor when the land is purchased, stating the amount paid and the area, and, in some cases, setting out the natural boundaries: (ii) *a Tax Receipt* in the name of the man or woman for payment of the Land Tax: and (iii) *a Will,* bequeathing the land to a particular member of the family.

---

* i.e. square chains

The only real value or use of the first two of these documents in a Court of Law would be as evidence of possession. A Will indicates nothing more than the testamentary desire of the previous owner and does not, as is popularly believed *per se* establish anything. But, if proved, it would be a good source of title.[4]

This may not seem very important; few laymen in any country fully understand the intricacies of their own legal system. But English Common Law, based on precedents, in so far as it relates to land tenure, which is what we are here concerned with, grew out of the native theory and practice over generations of evolutionary experience in Britain. In its translation to Jamaica, it was a comprehensible system to the English settlers. Once however, peasants began to buy and use land, another layer of experience, and a different set of traditional beliefs in regard to land, handed down from father to child, began to appear in the practice of inheritance and transmission of land, and, among the peasantry where it operated, to give a specific (and as we shall show, a different) meaning to such terms as "ownership", "right", "claim", which do not easily fit into the pattern of English experience as expressed in the legal code.

Thus we found that a distinction exists in the meaning of the word "ownership" when applied to land which a man acquires by purchase (*bought land*) and land which he, generally together with other members of his family, inherits (*family land*). There is also another distinction within this category of inherited land. Thus not *all* inherited land is family land, though there appears to be a tendency so far as the controls on transmission and alienation are affected, for it to become so in the second and third generation.

Again, in contradistinction to the Law which does not recognise any right of illegitimate children to inherit land, and recognises the eldest son as the rightful heir where there is no testamentary disposition we found the principle of joint inheritance by "all the children" generally recognised and it is by no means apparent that any discrimination is practised against "outside" children. But the peasant theory of land tenure, reflecting West African principles, came into conflict with English Law chiefly in the matter of the local importance attached to joint inheritance and of what are regarded as the equal rights of all the family where family land is concerned, and its corollary that family land is not "owned" by any one member of the family but belongs to all the family, and secondly, in the traditional proscription on the alienation of family land.

Moreover, temporary non-exercise of a claim on family land does not, in the traditional system, preclude a subsequent exercise of that right. For example, a brother may return to the family land, occupied by his other brothers and sisters, after years of residence elsewhere and it would still be recognized by his family that he had the right "if he had the need", to erect his house on the land and share in the crops of any fruit trees planted by his forbears on the property.

It is admittedly a confused situation, and not always clear in individual cases, but the evidence of a consistent system and of its social sanction is, I think, irrefutable. The position is not made happier by the fact that among the younger generation one member of the family may attempt, and succeed, in enforcing a claim based on the legal code, in violation of the customary theory, and strong as public opinion may be against such procedure it is inevitably ineffectual where there is recourse to law. But it is obvious that the difference between the customary theory and the legal code creates a situation in which there is plenty of room for dissension to arise.

It is now necessary to examine the material on this subject collected in our Communities and endeavour to set out the theory more specifically on the basis of the evidence.

(iii)

The first indication that there exists a customary theory of land tenure emerges from the accounts given us of the founding of the old districts in two of the communities in which we worked; Sugartown and Mocca. Later we find the same theory restated in the history of the transmission of family land generation by generation from the original head of the family to the present holders.

In Sugartown, when we arrived and were trying to distinguish the ecological features and differentiate between the new Estate village and the old settlements, we were told that three of the districts— Yaccatown, Springfield and Mountainview—had been founded after Emancipation.

The account given by a member of one of the old families of the origin of the old districts is as follows:—

"The whole of Yaccatown had originally been land granted after slavery to the freed Negroes. The people then were not very wise which was why we (the descendants) have not got enough land. They did not look ahead (he touched his fore-head with his finger). The lower part of Springfield and of the village into which it runs, has the same history. You could say it was all family land for it had been handed down from genera-tion to generation. It could never be sold. Family land could not be sold. The members of the family had a right to a house spot on it and to reap the produce. Even though one member paid the taxes and had it registered in his name, he was only a trustee and he could not dispose of it. They would say 'too many people are involved'."

On another occasion he stated:—

"Family land cannot be sold. It is inherited. It cannot be willed by the descendants. If the original owner left a will then that would be followed . . . People have a right to come and live and use the land if they are of the family. If there is room they would be given a house site. For instance if one of my family came here and asked permission to stay on my land, and if there was room for him to put up a little house, he would ask to do so, until he could find his own place, and I would let him . . . You know, my brother lives here."

The origin of Mocca is similar to that of the old parts of Sugar-town. The whole land area is owned by a number of families, closely knit by kinship or inter-marriage or inter-concubinage.

The lower part of the village is still called "Bungotown" or "Africa land". This land is administered by the head of the family whose grandparents were given an acre of land by their mistress after Emancipation. The old man himself did not live in the village but in an adjacent one on another piece of family land. None the less, he was still in control of the family settlement in our village. While some of it was inhabited by his descendants he retained his own claim to a share of it by leasing a portion and collecting the rents.

"His grandparents came as slaves from Africa. He did not re-member what part they came from. But when they were free his mistress (whose name he took) gave them a piece of land which they have free of taxes forever. It is about an acre. This land is situated in Mocca. Part of it he leases to tenants. One tenant

pays rent because he is a stranger, but the others do not pay
rent because they are living with women of the family.

"He would never sell the land. 'You see I don't pay taxes. The
mistress on the property give it to my people free. I am not free
to sell it. When there is nobody [of the family] to live on it, it
[will] stay as no man's land if the property don't take it. The
land is left to reap generations. If X [his son by his present
concubine] have a son by the name, the name will stay. If the
name pass the land will stay no man's land.'"

The forbears are invariably buried on family land and, where this
is the case, it is another bulwark against alienation. These graves
are generally "tombed" and, even where the family now lives in
considerable poverty, these tombstones are often expensive and
elaborate, engraved with the person's name and age at death and
including a text from the Bible.

In one of the old districts in Sugartown we discussed the subject
of the inheritance of family land with an old lady who traced her
ancestry back to grandparents who came from Africa. The land and
house belonged to her father who inherited them from his father and
in turn left them to her. In addition to this piece on which she lives
there are also two-and-a-half acres in one of the adjoining villages
which she and her brother cultivate and jointly reap the produce.

"They regard this land as family land in the old tradition.
Neither piece of land could or would ever be sold by her or her
brother. Her father taught her that in their country the land
would always be for the family—they would come there and
reap anything. That is why she had [built] the second room in
her house so that any of the family coming would have a room
to stay. With the younger ones it might be different. They might
not want to live there. Here her daughter (who is married and
lives with her husband and infant child in a room in a house)
said that [that was because] they might not want to live in the
country. The younger ones, she said, preferred to live in Kingston. The old lady said yes, but that was not so in the old times.
They had the African tradition. For instance, any of the family
who came to see her would be free to go and pick a coconut

[from the tree on the land]. 'That is how the older people tell we.' "

In spite of the general theory against alienation, family land may be sold by agreement between the joint heirs. Even so, it is regarded as a bad thing to do.

"Her parents died many years ago. They left half an acre of land and a house on it to their children—a son and four daughters. Two of the daughters married and live elsewhere. The two unmarried sisters live in separate houses on the land. The brother is a shoemaker and lives in an adjoining parish.

Her brother wrote and asked her sister and herself to allow him to sell a square of the land to pay off some debts and to buy some leather for his trade. He owed some money to a man which he either could not or would not pay. Her sister and herself gave him permission and he sold a square of the land in front of the house for £10, paid the man to whom he owed the money £4, and took the £6 away with him. By that he had forfeited a right to any more of the land and they could keep him away if they wanted but she herself did not care very much as she was prepared to die any time. She said he was a bad brother."

There was a case in Sugartown where the head of the family sold family land to his nephew. After his death the right to the sale was disputed and the family took the land back:—

"He bought an acre of land for £9 from his uncle. He cultivated the land but he had no title for it and after his uncle's death, the other members of the family said it was family land and all should be allowed to live on it and cultivate it, so he left it without making any fuss."

The restrictions on family land, and the personal problems of joint use, often lead to disagreement among the members of the family herded together on it, and to their renunciation of their shares. Sometimes there were expressions of discontent at these restrictions.

"His mother's father died and left 1½ acres of land for his children. His mother is now living on the land. There are two two-roomed houses on the land. His mother and some of his brothers and sisters live in them. After his mother's death the land will pass to the other sisters and then to his mother's children. His other sisters pay no taxes, only the mother does, so it is almost hers alone. Her father told them not to sell it, it should go from children to children. That is a foolish idea. Suppose they should get into serious trouble, what would happen? They would have to go to prison, when everybody would agree to sell."

Her maternal grandfather left the land when he died, which is now family land. Her uncle and his wife live on it. She could live there if she desired, but "she does not like family place".

(iv)

Even when the couple are married there is no bar against inheritance by any of their illegitimate children. In the case just cited our informant's parents and grandparents were all married and she gave no record of their having had any outside children. She herself is the eldest of their five children. Her eldest brother died without leaving issue. The other has two children, both living abroad. The rest of the family consists of two younger sisters, both married; one living in Kingston, the other in America. They have no children. Her younger brother lives in the same parish and visited her only that week. She said "he keeps in touch with me all the time". He and she are trustees for the family in the matter of the land although she herself never married and her three children are illegitimate. Her eldest daughter is married and lives with her husband and their infant son in a well-built cottage recently erected on the family land. Her eldest son lives in one of the neighbourhood villages and she has charge of his twin children. Her other son lives in barracks. Both she and her brother recognise that any of these siblings or their descendants who desire to settle on the land will have the right to do so.

In another case in Sugartown where a woman was living on family land her genealogy showed that her parents lived in concubinage but she and her siblings were all children of the union and there was no mention of any outside issue. Her mother inherited the land from her grandfather and she has inherited as the sole surviving child. Her mother and four of her ancestors are buried on the land. Her father is buried elsewhere. She herself has not married and her four children are by two different fathers. The only boy, issue of the first union, is dead. By the second union she had three girls. One lives abroad; one lives in the home with her. The third died, leaving a boy and girl of different paternity. These grandchildren and the girl's infant child, also born out of wedlock, live with her. The land is only large enough for a house site and contains a two-roomed cottage in very bad repair.

Here again the inheritance passed to illegitimate children. It is also noticeable that the land passed from father to daughter and daughter's daughter.

A grandchild does not normally attempt to make any claim on family land until after the death of the grandparent and parent, and his or her rights may be subject to the equal rights of descendants of siblings of the parents.

"Miss Jane's father . . . had a big cultivation and was well off. He died . . . Her mother could not manage the cultivation so she had to leave it to Miss Jane's father's family for the land was a family land. Her mother died. Miss Jane could not claim the land because it had been inherited from her father's father and her father had brothers and sisters who were more entitled to the land than she was, since it was a legacy from their own father and she was only a grandchild.

Miss Jane added that she was not concerned with family land. 'Mother have, father have, blessed be the child that have her own.' And she had nothing of her own."

The wife has usually only a life interest. If a woman's husband had land of his own, however, her family would expect her to go and live out and leave the family land to the other heirs:—

"Miss Thomas inherited her house and land from her father who she thinks bought it. No will was made and her father's grandson is also entitled to live on the land. 'They must live till they die and after their death it will go to their children. It is a good thing no will was made or she wouldn't be here. They would tell her to go to her husband's land and he had none.'"

Where a grandchild inherits during the children's lifetime it would appear to be in cases where there has been a legal distribution of family land, or where the people concerned are out of the usual peasant class and are dissatisfied with the traditional system. One of the better off householders in Sugartown furnishes an example.

Our informant, Mr. Campbell, now in his middle thirties, began work as an apprentice at the Estate. During the war he went to America as a farm labourer. He is regularly employed during crop; and out of crop he "trades". He buys goods—toilet articles and haberdashery from the wholesale firms at a discount and travels on his bicycle from house to house in the villages selling the goods at the best price he can get. He has built himself one of the best homes in the village, consisting of a sitting room, two bedrooms and hall with a verandah overlooking a trim, well-kept flower garden. It was expensively equipped with shop furniture and a radio. The house is on one of three adjoining plots, the other two pieces of which are "owned" by Mr. Campbell's mother's sister (Sara) and his maternal grand aunt's son's daughter, Mrs. Murray. Mrs. Murray referred to it as family land and said that it could not be sold. Mr. Campbell, on the other hand, did not use the expression in describing it.

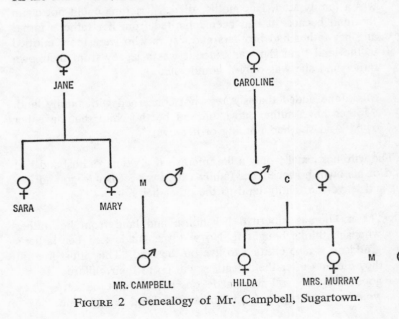

Figure 2   Genealogy of Mr. Campbell, Sugartown.

Both Mr. Campbell and Mrs. Murray were brought up by their grandmothers. Mr. Campbell's mother after an unsatisfactory love affair went abroad leaving her son with her mother. Mrs. Murray's mother died when she was a baby and she was brought up by Caroline. The two sisters, Jane and Caroline, were "caretakers" for the old man who owned the land and on his death he left it to them both. They erected their own homes and on their deaths Caroline left her share to Mrs. Murray. Hilda was not said to have been included in the inheritance, though no reason was given. She "lives outside the district and has a family". Jane left her share to Sara, Mary *and* Mr. Campbell. Both Mr. Campbell and Mrs. Murray erected modern bungalows on their plots, fenced them off and took out titles for them. Sara "lives elsewhere" and from Mr. Campbell's guarded references to her, I got the impression that they were not on good terms and that possibly she disapproved his action in sub-dividing the land. Her section is not fenced and I was not told that she had taken out a title.

Such a subdivision would be impossible where the land was family land *in the sense in which the term is used for the old holdings* in Sugartown and Mocca. Two facts emerge therefore from this example: that, in the traditional view (as expressed by Mrs. Murray, and possibly by Sara), even land recently inherited becomes family land in the second generation of transmission and cannot be alienated, subdivided or individually owned. Mrs. Murray's paternal grandmother, her own father and her mother's sister are buried on her plot. The second fact is that where land is recently inherited, where there are only a few members of the family involved, and where agreement can be reached or the objection of dissenting members over-ruled, subdivision does occur. It is, however, always regarded as a breach of custom and, as in this case, leads to family friction.

In Sugartown land has a special value for the workers as house sites and when left to "all the family" soon becomes a congeries of homes of brothers and sisters and their children.

> "The house is on family land. It was left to Mrs. Chambers by her husband who died leaving no will. She will live in it for her life. Then all the brothers and sisters have the right to a share in it. A number of these are already living in their own houses on it. All the families have their own kitchen gardens on the land which is well stocked with fruit trees: breadfruit, ackee, jim-

blings, avocado pears, coconuts and a few bananas, under which the crops are grown."

The right to build houses on family land and rent them out may be exercised by members of the family who live elsewhere. The following is a description of one of the Family Compounds in our sugar centre, where each of the families has a separate house on the "land". The land, one-third of an acre in extent, with "three small cottages" was left to all her children by their mother who inherited it from her mother and mother's mother before her. One cottage was left to each child. At the time of our visit there were on it five two-roomed houses, and one three-roomed one; one double kitchen and two single ones.

The mother had seven children by her husband, six of whom are alive. Her husband had two outside children, one of whom is alive but does not participate in the inheritance. Only the two younger sisters live on the land, the elder of whom occupies a two-roomed cottage (A) and is erecting another two-roomed cottage (B). She has her own kitchen. Her household consists of herself, her concubine and their son aged 5, the man's adult sister, and an adopted son aged 16. The second sister and her son aged 12 occupy one room in a third cottage (D); she rents out a fourth (E) which she also owns, and one of the rooms in (F), a fifth three-roomed cottage which she inherited. She has her own kitchen. The other siblings, three sisters and a brother, live in other parishes and rent out their rooms; the brother rents out the second room in cottage (D); the two eldest sisters get the rent from yet another two-roomed cottage (G) and the third from the remaining two rooms in (F). These siblings send their own "agent to collect the rent for them".

Where there is a large family house on family land and this is also left to all the family, the children who do not live in the home may rent the rooms which fall to their share.

"The house and land is belonging to the family (ten children of whom seven are alive). They inherited it from their mother who bought it herself. There are five apartments, of these four are rented and one daughter (our informant) occupies the fifth with her husband and her outside child.

"The family contribute for the paying of the taxes which amount to £1. 2. 1. per year. Because she occupies one of the rooms her 'bad family' do not give her any of the rent."

Although we have seen that a childless woman may leave family land to her husband, she would not do this if she has even an illegitimate child. B. in one of our records, had been living with a man for a year when interviewed. Prior to this she had had three illegitimate children, one of whom, aged 6 was alive:—

"The land was left to her by her father and is not to be sold. Immediately he died she built her house on it. If she should die, the land would immediately be turned over to her son. Her father had called her before he died and told her that under no circumstances should she do away with the land and that it should go to her children and her children's children. (The land is three-quarters of an acre.)"

A man may leave his land to his wife, but in these cases she has generally a life interest only:—

"The house and land is hers, willed to her for her lifetime by her husband. (Their two children died in infancy.) She has the right to the house and land for her lifetime provided she does not marry again. If she marries she must leave it. She cannot marry and stay there. Her husband left the land (except for her life-interest) to his three brothers and sisters."

She is now living in concubinage with a man and apparently wishes to marry him but the terms of her husband's will stand in their way:—

"If she married he (i.e., her present concubine) would have to carry her to *his* land. Asked whether he had any land she replied in a dispirited, somewhat bitter tone, 'so he says!' mentioning two distant parishes as where the land was situated."

In an example already quoted when the husband died leaving no will, it was recognized that his widow, even though she took a concubine, had the right to live in the house for her life, but after that her husband's brothers and sisters came into the inheritance.

Another case which is interesting because it brings out the distinc-

tion between children of different paternity is the following where
we are told that "all the children" inherited land left by the father.
In the enumeration it is evident that two of these were by the mother
but not by her husband. Later in the record, however, we ascertained
that the mother is still living and that these two were children born
subsequent to her husband's death by the man with whom she now
cohabits. She still lives in the house her husband built, and her concubine lives there with her.

In the following example a woman's children by a second union
inherited to the exclusion of the children of the first union:—

> "Her mother inherited land from her father. Informant was
> born in the house (wattle and thatch), on the land, which her
> mother built. Her mother had two families: by the first man,
> whom she began to live with in her mother's house, to which
> he came to live, she had 14 children. 'They were making up to
> be married when he died.' The eldest son living has his own
> land. Seven of the others died in childhood; two sons are now
> dead. Of the remaining five she remembers four. None of them
> came in for the mother's land. After the first man's death the
> mother 'got in with another man' by whom she had informant
> and one son. The son is now in Panama. Her father had two out-
> side children: they are grown men living at Mountainview
> and in a neighbourhood village. They do not enter into the pic-
> ture. The land apparently went to the mother's two children by
> the second union and to her since her brother is abroad."

In spite of the theory that "all the family inherit" there is evidence
to show that in practice a selection may be made of one member to
the exclusion of another. This is generally done in a will as in the two
following examples:—

> "Miss M inherited land from her mother, whose mother left her
> both house and land. Miss M's mother died and left the land to
> her by will. She has the will. Her mother did not will any of the
> land to her son because he was much older and had already
> bought land of his own."

In the other case a woman had two daughters: one with a daughter; the other with four sons by different men. She left a will bequeath-

ing one acre to be divided between the grandchild of the eldest daughter and the second son of her younger daughter. She also left three-quarters of an acre to two of this daughter's other children but left nothing to the fourth grandchild because she was married and "her husband had vast amounts of land".

If this descendant were ever "to make claims for the land she would be defeated before the trial of the case because her grandmother had made a will before she died". Nevertheless, "if it happened that she became destitute" her half-brother assured us that "he would gladly assist her by giving her a house spot on his half acre". He also asserted that his cousin could not sell her land or any part of it without his consent.

Sharing, though it does take place where family land is involved is however more usual where the land has been bought or acquired by an immediate forbear:—

> "A bought thirteen acres of land and at his death left them to his son. This son had eight children, four sons and four daughters. He left the land at his death to all the children, and their offspring. However, the youngest son was given by his father a piece of land two and one-fourth square acres all to himself, plus his share of the remainder . . . The land is not divided up but worked on, each according to his need and ability."

It would appear that even where "bought land" is concerned once it is left to "all the children" it passes into the category of family land and the traditional proscription against alienation is applicable.

It is not uncommon for two brothers to club together and purchase a piece of land and in such cases we get joint occupation of land by the kindred:—

> "The land on which (our informant) lives was bought by her father and his brother. After their death it was left for herself and her uncle's children. She was given a square on which she built her house."

(v)

There appear thus to be two principles of distribution of family land: the first where the land is left to all the children (or "family") and where it is used by them, according to their need, as a group. This more commonly happens where the land has ceased to have agricultural value (except for the economic trees planted by the ancestors) and is used primarily for house sites. On this family land there may be found a number of houses, or more usually grass huts, all occupied by kin who trace their descent from a common ancestor. With them are their children, often by "outside" unions, and their spouses. The group included in all these households may, therefore, at any one time cover three or four generations and a wide range of kin and connections by marriage or concubinage.

Secondly, there may be individual inheritance, but this is, in theory, limited to land which has been bought, not inherited. Selection of a particular member of the family, son or daughter, is often in gratitude by the parent or donor, for "care" bestowed on them in their old age. This explains some of the cases where a younger son inherits to the exclusion of his elder brothers who have by that time moved out into their own homes, leaving him as a young man in the parents' home:—

> "A was born on this land . . . He was not the first child of his parents but he looked after his father and so inherited the land."

In another record, a woman was left half an acre of land by her "cousin":—

> "who had cared for her (raised her) and at her death left her . . . the land. She has a house on it which she rents out for 10/- a month . . ."

In another case there was evidence of a desire on the part of a woman living on family land, to leave her portion outside the immediate line of inheritance:—

> "The land and the house (she said) were hers. She would like her step-daughter to get something after she is dead. But it depends who cares her. She does not know who will at the end. Even if somebody (else) gets something she won't leave the step-daughter out."

The "step-daughter" in this case was her uncle's daughter. The woman had her own house, but the evidence (though not conclusive as she was a very reluctant informant) seemed to show that the land was family land. She and her brother, the next claimant, were on bad terms, hence her doubt whether she would be able to leave her step-daughter anything. There was all the making here of a serious family quarrel.

Even where the land has agricultural value, there are cases where each child was given his "share". In some cases the father or mother leaving the land may define each child's share, more commonly the children themselves agree on a definition of their share.

Where division is by "share", there is further fragmentation in the next generation until there arrives the stage (which has been reached in the case of most family land in Jamaica) where the congestion of homes on the site makes agricultural usage impossible. In any case, the possibility of members of the family living in other parts of the island, returning to exercise their claim, either to cultivate the land, or erect their home on it, or to reap the produce of the trees, acts as a deterrent on economic use.

The following are examples of land being inherited by the group, but where, because it is still used agriculturally, there is the beginning of a distinction between what the occupier cultivates for his own use, and what the absent members of the family may claim, or be given as a gift:—

"He also cultivates an acre of family land. He paid the taxes. He was solely responsible for all his brothers and sisters, 'and whenever I reap I distribute and who feel (i.e. wish to do so) can come and reap'. In reply to questions he said that he cultivated 'his part'. His brothers and sisters also came and cultivated. His sister (who lives outside the parish) never comes. 'But I give her all the time off my land and off what I don't cultivate too.' "

Here we would seem to have common ownership of the land by the group, with no right of disposal, but the right of inheritance by their children; individual cultivation and right to all crops individually grown; common ownership by all siblings of economic trees (in this case, bananas, coconuts, plantains and breadfruit).

The same record brings out the complexity of this whole problem of family land. Our informant was a married man with seven children. Besides this piece of family land he had acquired one-and-a-half acres of land which, although family land, he was permitted first to lease, and then buy from his brother's children, while he lives on his wife's family land.

> "Informant also said that he had one-and-a-half acres 'of his own'. It had belonged to his brother who was sick. He cared him and his three children till he died. After his death the children said he must take the land because of his care of the old man and his children. He said he would not take it but he would lease it. After a while they told him he must buy it. So he paid £2 and still has £2 to pay.

> "The land on which his home is built belongs to his concubine. Her father died and left it to his brother, and he died and left it to his niece, and his two sisters and one brother. It is about four acres. One piece was found to be about one acre and belongs to one sister. The top piece, where informant has his house, was found to be three acres, and was divided into two lots. Lot one, of one-and-a-half acres, went to one of the sisters and lot two of one-and-a-half acres to the brother. On this last lot informant's concubine was living, where, before that her father had lived. On it, at the father's death, lived also another of his daughters. Informant's concubine's father also owned another piece of land at Top Hill where she was born. This land also belonged to her family (i.e. was family land). It was there, in 1927, that informant and his concubine first began to live together. ('They had been together before but began to be steady together since then.') His eldest child was born there. 'The rest of (her) family robbed her of this land.'"

The inability to use family land, owing to the necessity of living or working elsewhere, may lead to its occupation by another member of the family.

> "His mother inherited land from her mother. During her lifetime the mother lived there. On her death she left it for her children. She had two families. By the first she had a son and a daughter. The daughter is dead. The son lives in another parish.

The only other child, by the second union lives elsewhere. His mother's sister's son lives on the land, pays the taxes and is responsible for it."

An example of the extent to which the system results in non-use or insufficient use of land is given in the following account by a sugar worker who lives in a barrack-room with his wife and their nine children, whose ages range from 2 to 22 years:—

"In addition to one-and-a-half acres given to him by his parents' request and which 'is solely his' he is, even though he is the youngest child, in charge of ten acres of family land which his father left to all his children. All this land is in another parish and though it is his ambition to go back there and work on it he has to have the money first (hence his seeking employment on the Estate), . . . Since most of his brothers and sisters are dead, the two sisters who are left take care of the ten acres on which they live and work it as they please. They pay the taxes both on his piece and on the ten acres. It is no worry to him. They plant and eat, there are lots of coconuts and coffee but the sisters use it all."

Inability or unwillingness to use, may even result, as we saw, in alienation of family land, with the consent of the co-heirs, but even so it is regarded as an indication of a breach of family faith and a "bad thing".

Alienation of land—even when it is of the category of "bought" land, of which the owner admittedly has the right of free disposal—is always resented because it deprives the children of their heritage.

"His parents are both dead. They had fourteen children of (whom) seven are alive. His mother had a place of her own in . . . . She sold this place—one acre—to spite her children. He does not know why she wanted to spite them. When she got old they had to rent a room for her to live in. She died in the Poor House. His father also had four-and-a-half acres of land which he sold before his death. The children inherited nothing. When he saw that he had nothing left, that his parents had sold their places, he left home."

In any case land has such high social, as distinct from economic, value that only in dire necessity would it be sold.

(vi)

We have already given evidence to show that not only land but houses may be inherited by all the children. In some cases the parents' house passed to one child, and the other members of the family erected their own homes on the land.

> "House and land were inherited from their father by all his children. One daughter built her house on it and so did a son. Another (daughter) who lives at................ is entitled to build here if she wants to. The house in which he lives is a two-apartment wooden structure (the old home)."

While a life-interest in family land is one of the most evident bonds in the family pattern, there are obvious sources of conflict in the crowding together of numbers of adults and their children on a small piece of land. Paradoxically, the element of conflict or discord between members of the inheriting group, may be at least as strong a factor, in perpetuating the system, and keeping the group together, as complete trust and amity. In the latter case, the members can afford to live where it suits them and rely on the recognition by the land-using group, of their "claim" and "right". Where there is any question of infringement or an intention to exploit the non-exercise of these claims or rights, then joint residence becomes necessary.

The following is an example of such a case. Incidentally it is also an illustration—though admittedly an extreme one—of the effect which this joint inheritance of family land and houses by all the children may have *on the type of household*. It occurs in Sugartown.

As it is a complicated family organization, comprising two household records the diagram may help to clarify the story of the inheritance.

Our informants were Nesta and Winston in Household 1 and Mr. and Mrs. Brown and Celeste in Household 2. Although we had many interviews with all the interested parties, saw them continually in our rounds of the village, and went over the ground (both literally and figuratively) many times, the statements remain contradictory.

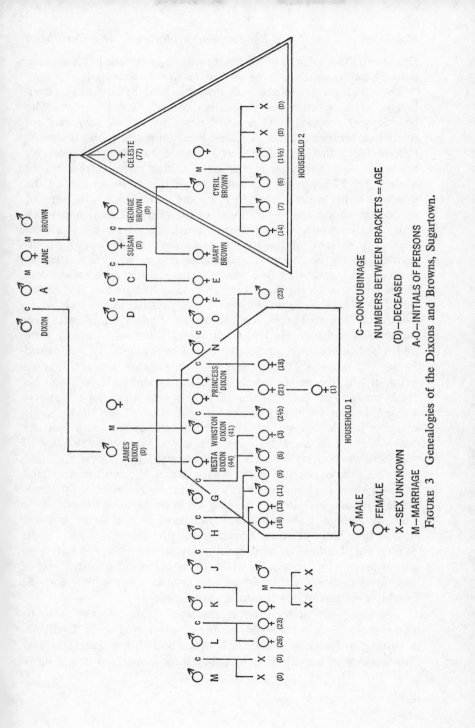

FIGURE 3 Genealogies of the Dixons and Browns, Sugartown.

♂ MALE
♀ FEMALE
X–SEX UNKNOWN
M–MARRIAGE

C–CONCUBINAGE
NUMBERS BETWEEN BRACKETS = AGE
(D)–DECEASED
A–O–INITIALS OF PERSONS

Even as to the total area of land there was disagreement but it appears unlikely that more than three or four acres were involved.

Both Winston and Nesta said that this land had originally been bought by their father and "a brother of his", George Brown. The genealogy as supplied by Cyril and Celeste, shows that they were actually half-brothers, James the elder, being an outside child of Jane's. Celeste added that Jane had been a co-purchaser with her sons. We are left to decide whether to discount Celeste's statement because of her age (at 77 she spent most of her days dozing in the sun on the doorway of her room) or credit it, on the ground that, like many of our oldest informants, her memory of the past was clear and vivid. The point is important, as if James and George were the sole "ancestors" a division of the land between their descendants each individual having his "share" would be in accord with the customary practice, and, except by their grace, Celeste would have no share in the inheritance. If, on the other hand, Jane had participated in the purchase, then Celeste would have a claim on the inheritance.

James Dixon died when Winston was eight years old, his wife having predeceased him. He left, according to Winston, an apiary from which he had been making nine barrels of honey annually, and owned horses and donkeys. Winston was left in his uncle's care and they all continued to live on the family land. But according to Winston his uncle treated him badly. Although he was sent to school till he was thirteen he was frequently beaten, and worst of all, his uncle "made away" with the apiary including the machines for extracting the honey, and all the stock his father had left so that "when he came of age there was nothing left". This was the beginning of discord.

At the time of our stay in the village, Nesta, Winston, Princess and their children (or some of them) lived in the house built by James while Cyril and his wife and family lived in the three apartment house built by George. Celeste had her own room in this house, but had at one time had "her own house on the premises" . . . i.e. on the family site. During our nine-month stay in the village, Cyril completed fencing off the site on which his house stood from the rest of the family property, but could not be drawn into any explanation. He would never discuss his cousins in Household 1.

The ownership of the "rest of the land" (said by Princess to be two-and-a-half acres) was not at any time referred to by Cyril but, according to Nesta, it is divided between herself, her sister and their brother. Again, according to her, they three alone "are bound up in this" . . . i.e. the inheritance was between them equally and does not concern Cyril or any descendant of George.

Winston, on the contrary, claims that "all this land" is really his "as the only son of his father" (his only brother being dead) and that his sisters live there "rent free" . . . the implication being that this is by his good will. In regard to his cousin's share, Winston considers that all Cyril has a right to is the house site which James gave to George during his lifetime. This again conflicts with the statement that George and James together bought the land which would give Cyril every right to inherit his father's portion.

It is certain, however, that it is the brother and sisters in Household 1 who solely *use* this "remainder". Princess told us that her share was one square and that she leases it at 7/6 per quarter. Winston rents out five house sites, of one square each, at 9/- per quarter and it is indicative of his ignoring of kinship claims that one of the tenants from whom he exacts rent is his cousin—"the son of another brother of his father".

Apart from exemplifying the difficulty of getting the facts in regard to tenure, this record is a striking example of the effect which an interest in family land has on keeping the family together, as much where the conflict is overt or suppressed as when there is solidarity. It is also an example of the effect of family land on the *type* of household.

The family inheritance includes a home, and the fear of the sisters that, if they do not occupy and use the home, their brother may attempt and even succeed in establishing individual ownership, has its result in their separation from the several fathers of their children. For both sisters are at present consorting with men (G and O in the diagram) whom they cannot bring into the home because it is already full to capacity. Yet they cannot go and live with them because they are fully aware of their brother's intention to oust them, especially now that he has taken a concubine, has one child and "another on the way".

Princess's eldest son "would live with her if he could but the home is not convenient" so he rents a room in the village. But although he works at the factory:

> "She is still responsible for him. She cooks his food for him and he gives her something. It is not a definite amount but last Saturday he gave her 12/-."

She has been out of work for three months,

> "but she has a gentleman with whom she is friendly. He helps
> her with the children though they are not his. He is a carpenter,
> although he is not trained. In crop he gets work at the Dump.
> The Dump is the deep place in the factory where they dump
> the cane for feeding the machine. It is deep, deep . . . when
> they dig it out they find it is floored with boards. His house is
> small, so small that they cannot live there. She prepares his food
> and sends it to him and he comes to visit her but does not sleep
> at the home. He gives her 15/- a week . . . she hasn't got a
> garden but around the house she reaps from the plantains, the
> bananas and the coconuts, when there are any. Also she has her
> share of one square of the family land at Springfield."

Nesta is also still in company with the father of her two youngest
children. He lives in Springfield.

> "While the interview was going on his young daughter (by an-
> other woman) came and stood at the kitchen door, waiting for
> her father's dinner while Nesta fried the fish."

It was very noticeable in Nesta's account that although she knew
the whereabouts of all her children and chatted about them at length,
visits them and is visited by them, she volunteered nothing about the
formidable number of their fathers. It is almost certain that these
unions were matrilocal and, in this particular, follow the practice
where the woman has an interest in family land.

Where a woman has such an interest, but does not own a house,
the house may be built by her concubine, so that there is the further
complication that the man owns the home but that it is erected on the
woman's family land.

The genealogy shows that besides her children by George, Cyril's
mother had children by two other men who are not said to have any
part in the land left by George. This ties in with the statement by the
Patriarch of Mocca, already quoted, that inheritance follows "the
name", i.e. goes in the paternal line. This underlies much of the conflict between Winston and his sisters. Nesta's children bear no less
than six family names and all that Nesta would be able to transmit
to any of them would be *her own individual share* if she could estab-

lish to everyone's satisfaction that her father had in fact made any such bequest, verbally or by will. The respect paid to a verbal bequest during a lifetime, or to a will, may override normal accepted procedure.

Although a wife or concubine has no "right" in her spouse's family land and this must pass to his children, she is regarded as having the right to live in the family home or on the land during her lifetime. Any children whom she might bear to other men would not, however, have any claims on the family land. According to our Patriarch of Mocca, "men who cohabited with women of the family" had the privilege of living rent-free on the land.

And here we are involved in a complication of the system of joint inheritance when the sharing up is not done by the siblings by agreement after their parents' death, but each child is allotted its own portion by the father or mother. In such cases a daughter who had inherited her own "share" may bequeath such land to her children. The blood line is then counted through her, and the fact that these children may be by a number of different fathers does not affect their right to the inheritance.

(vii)

We come now to two confusing aspects of this subject. In the first place not *all* inherited land is described as family land. Historically speaking the term applies properly to land inherited from forbears who were given it at or before Emancipation. It is this category of land, represented in the Old Settlements of Mocca and Sugartown and in those abutting on Orange Grove proper, which is regarded as inalienable, as "belonging to the family" "to reap generations". There seems little doubt that all the children "of the name" or "of the family" inherited and equally, though there is at least one statement that even in regard to this category of land there might be differentiation, or "sharing". If the intention to divide the holdings between some members of the family was expressed in a will of the original owner, its provisions would, we were told, be accepted by the family. There is a possible explanation for this development. The purpose of these gifts of tracts of land adjoining the Estates was to ensure a labour supply for the Estates. It is reasonable to assume that where a block of land was granted by the Estate proprietors, the gift was made to the male head of the family. The statement by the Patriarch of Mocca which we have already quoted at length asserts the principle of legitimacy in the male line: "If my son has a son by the name he will stay on the land. If the name passes, the land will stay no-man's land." If this were followed in all cases, daughters might inherit with sons, but their offspring would be debarred in the next generation. This is not however the case, as has already been established by cases cited. The fact could be still further documented if necessary, that where a daughter inherits she can and does bequeath the land to her descendants, though probably only when either there has been the process of division and she has her own share, or when there is no effective claim exercised by male heirs either siblings or in a lower generation.

The second complication concerns the creation of "family land", in more recent times, out of "bought land".

It appears to be generally accepted that when a man (or woman) purchases land (a) alienation is permissible, or within the rights of the owner, although it is always resented as cutting across the natural expectation of all the children to inherit; and (b) nomination of one or more members of the family, siblings or own children, is permissible.

In Orange Grove, where the bulk of the land owned by the farmers had been purchased within half a century, either by our informants or by their father, the term family land in the sense in which it is used here, occurs only rarely in our records. Prior to this, there had been old settlements running up into the mountains within which the valley of Orange Grove proper lies, and some of our farmers had inherited land from these ancestors. One such farmer, who, incidentally, was one of our largest landowners, told us that in addition to his bought land, he had inherited three acres from his maternal grandmother, Victoria. According to him, he had "passed it on to Mrs. Sutherland, whom he described as his sister". Mrs. Sutherland, however, told a different story. According to her, the farmer was her cousin, not her brother, and she, he and another of Victoria's grandsons had all been raised by their grandmother. But the two grandsons "grew up and went their ways while she remained at home with the old lady. She nursed the old lady till her death to find that she had willed the land to her".

In this community there appeared to be two processes at work. One is that family land, where inherited by the well-to-do middle class farmers, tends to become individually owned.[5] But there is a second process at work, arising out of the expectation both on the part of parents and children that land will be left to the children, which can only lead to one of two things: fragmentation or joint inheritance by the family, and the resuscitation of the concept of family land in this progressive community.

The process of fragmentation is illustrated in the following account from Orange Grove. Our informant in this case we will call Sam Willis. His father, John Willis, had ten children, nine by his wife and an illegitimate son.

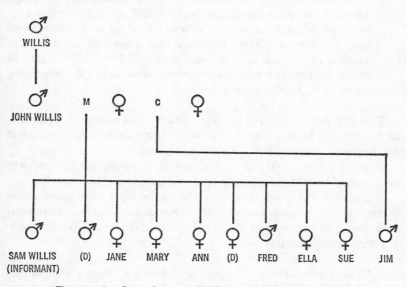

FIGURE 4   Genealogy of Willis family, Orange Grove.

John Willis inherited five acres of land from his father and he also purchased eight acres; two acres he bought in the name of his son Fred, and two for one of his daughters, Ann. At the same time he also bought eight acres from his brothers and sisters, which they had received as an inheritance from their father. During his lifetime John sold three-quarters of an acre to Ella's husband.

"The reason for this was that Ella's husband came from another district and her father did not want his daughter to go away. She was the only child of his who had not yet gone out on her own. He and his wife were failing in their strength and they needed someone to be near them, to help them with their cultivation and the housekeeping."

He also sold an acre to Fred and an acre to Mary's husband.

When the old man died his will was read and it was found that he had disposed of his remaining property as follows:—

"To Ella one acre adjoining the threequarter acre already sold to her husband. To Sam two acres (which he later sold to Fred). To Fred two acres. To Jim one-and-a-half acres. Jim was a bastard and when he died Sam allowed Fred to take one acre of this. To Sue one acre, to Mary one-and-a-half acres, three-quarters of an acre each to Jane, Ann and Ella, half an acre to his illegitimate son and three-quarters of an acre (the remaining portion) to Fred—the heir at law."

This description of Fred as heir at law is interesting as according to our records he is younger than Sam. Accuracy in regard to age is not however a strong point with our informants.

It will be noted that the land disposed of during his lifetime was land he had bought. The family land was distributed in the will.

The practice of giving land to a son or daughter during one's own lifetime is by no means uncommon in Orange Grove. One of the most respected and progressive farmers expressed his views on this subject to me very forcibly:—

"You know there is a custom in Jamaica to keep your children [dependent on you] so that they have no strength to give you when you are old. I give them from now. I gave land to my daughter (who lives in the home) and she cultivates it herself alone. She makes up the land and plants without assistance."

He has also given her four coconut trees and four breadfruit trees. He values these trees at £5 each so he has given her £40. This he has told her is her dowry.

An interesting fact in the previous record is that Jim, the illegitimate son, received his portion out of the inherited land, but at his death it reverted to the legitimate brothers. He was not given anything in his father's lifetime, nor any of the land his father had purchased.

The complication of this distinction between some inherited land which is not "family land" and the difficulty in arriving at the concept is brought out in records which link a number of households and families in Sugartown and Mocca.

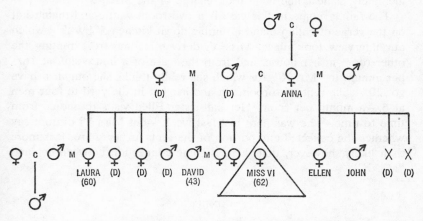

FIGURE 5   Genealogy of "Miss Vi", Sugartown.

Our informant (Miss Vi in the figure) was the only child of her parents living in concubinage. Both her father and mother married and had legitimate children, only four of whom survive: her mother's son, John, who lives in one of the South American Republics and a daughter, Ellen, who is married and lives in Kingston; and, on her father's side, by his wife, Laura, who lives with her husband in an adjoining village, and David, who is married and lives with his wife and her sister on their family land in Mocca.

Miss Vi herself lives on an acre of land in Sugartown. According to her this land was bought by her maternal grandfather and left by him, at his death, to his concubine (Anna) who, in turn, left it to Miss Vi and her children, Ellen and John, by her marriage.

Miss Vi was emphatic that "this is NOT family land. It's only me and my sister, Ellen, who rule here. If my eyes were shut (i.e. if I were to die) today there is only one person can take charge here. That is my sister, Ellen. She was here last week. She is married and has children. Or my brother, John, in America, if he should come back."

Miss Vi's insistence that "this is not family land" and concerns no one but their three selves, is almost academic since they are the only three survivors in the mother's line. In fact, they are the only "family" since Miss Vi's father's children by his wife bear neither "the name" nor do they inherit "the blood" of the original donors of the land. She was working in Portland when her mother died and immediately came home and "took charge of the place".

The family home in this case is a two-room wattle-and-thatch hut on the verge of collapse and a tumble-down kitchen 5′ by 8′ in which our interview took place. Miss Vi derives income from renting the other room in her house, and from the lease of a house site, at 16/- per annum to "Mr. X", for which she really thinks she ought to have got 20/-. She rents two rooms in another hut in the yard to four men at 6/- a month per room. Her half-sister Ellen visits the home from time to time—"she was here just last week"—but Miss Vi did not say whether she collected any portion of the rents as her share. It is more than likely, however, that there is some connection between her and "Mr. X".

(viii)

We may conclude therefore that, unrecognised though it may be in legal practice, there is a traditional system of tenure which distinguishes three categories of land (family land, inherited land and bought land) and governs the process of their transmission and inheritance.

It will be useful at this stage to summarize our findings and proceed to see what effect the system has (a) on the organization of the family, both in its primary sense as a household unit, and its wider extensions as a group of kindred, and (b) on the use of land.

First let us deal with the distinction between family land and the other two categories.

The term family land is applicable to all land inherited from the ancestors. In its historical sense it takes its origin from the pre- or post-Emancipation grants of land to freed slaves, grants made by the donors probably to individuals but interpreted by the recipient and the members of that family as including all the family in perpetuity.

The principle governing "ownership" and transmission of *family land* is explicitly stated. It belongs to all the family and it is held in trust by one member for the family; is inalienable and is transmitted to "all the family". We shall have to return to the question of the precise meaning here of the term family, complicated as it is by the high incidence of multiple unions and step-relationships.

Bought land, a generic term in common use applied to land purchased by a man or woman, is not in theory subject to any restriction on alienation or transmission. This freedom tends however to become qualified in practice as a result of two things: one is the high place of land in the scale of social values; the other the deep-rooted sentiment (on the part, let it be said of both parents and children) in the "right" of all the children to inherit. In practice, therefore, bought land is as often left to "all the children" as to a selected member and when this happens the land may be said to acquire the character in the next generation of family land and be subject to the appropriate restrictions.[6]

We had thus, in recording the distinction explicitly made by some of our informants, to recognise a third category of land, viz., "inherited land which was not family land", where both the theory and the practice of tenure and inheritance is complicated by its traditional character. Thus there are cases where a man or woman inheriting bought land leaves it to all his or her children and others where a selection is made.

We have seen however, that even where the principle of joint inheritance is applicable, in practice only one or some of the heirs might in fact inherit. This was generally the result of conditions which make effective occupation or use by some members impossible or unattractive, and does not invalidate the principle. It was unequivocally asserted that members who did not exercise their right to live on land did not thereby lose their right to do so at a later period. Non-residential heirs might draw on the land by reaping the fruit of permanent crops on the holdings (such as breadfruit or coconut) or by renting rooms or house sites upon it. And always their right to return and live on it was acknowledged. These privileges also extended to their recognised heirs.

This brings us to the next problem of defining "legitimate heirs". Is descent bilateral or unilateral; what precisely is meant by "all the family" inheriting—a particularly confusing aspect of the problem in view of the numbers of step-brothers and -sisters in any one home?

We can get rid of one complicating element without much difficulty and assert with confidence that the question of legitimacy (whether legal or social, that is between children of married parents or parents living in concubinage) does not affect the inheritance.

Secondly, there is no sex discrimination: daughters are equally eligible with sons to inherit. Thirdly, there is no hint of primogeniture.

It is not so easy to resolve the statements we have in regard to the tracing of descent either "by the name" (i.e. through the father) or "through the blood" (i.e. through the mother). Here theory is apt to be obscure at times.

In practice it would appear that where a woman inherits family or bought land (or is co-purchaser in the latter) the inheritance passes to children "of her blood". Thereafter, in the case of her sons, succession is "by the name", regardless of the status of his spouse or spouses and the legitimacy or illegitimacy of his children.

In Mocca, where we had the advantage of drawing on the aged descendants of the original ancestors, the pattern was predominantly unilateral and patriarchal at that. Descent and inheritance are traced "through the name" and since children take the name of the father even when illegitimate, this excludes children of daughters from the line of succession. In practice, even in Mocca, this breaks down when the inheritance passes through a woman.

In Sugartown where on the face of it most of the occupiers and trustees of family land seem to be women, it is the blood that counts and not the name. Thus a woman's heirs may be of two or more different names (i.e. fathers). What I have not found, however, is any assertion that children having neither the blood nor the name of the ancestor to whom the land belonged, have any presumptive right to inherit, even when brought up in the home. And this has nothing to do with the fact that they are or may be illegitimate.

In other words where land is inherited from the father it passes to sons and daughters of the name, i.e. any of his children by any woman: but children of any of his spouses by another man, even though they may live in the home, would not be regarded as eligible for the inheritance. In the same way if the land is transmitted by the mother, her children, whatever their paternity, would be of the family but outside children of her husband and concubine would not be. In this sense therefore outside[7] children in a home may be under a disability. It can be seen that there is no question of legitimate children having a prior claim over illegitimate children. Such a proscription on the contrary, conflicts with the traditional system and in cases where it has been enforced in the courts creates a deep sense of injustice and indignation.

In fact were any such principle generally enforced it is obvious that a large portion of small-holders in possession of inherited land might be discovered to have no title to their land which could be upheld in a court of law except such as they were able to establish under the Statute of Limitations.[8]

We pass thus to the need for a definition of the term "family" so often used in statements quoted in this paper to refer to the heirs to family land. This term is obviously not extended indefinitely to all members of the name or the blood. Apart from what we may call fortuitous limitation, that is, where members for one reason or another refrain voluntarily, or by force of circumstances are prevented, from exercising rights, there is also the limitation imposed by the size of the inheritance and the physical possibility of its containing all the potential heirs. From the examples which we have quoted it is clear that the inheriting unit is the offspring in line of descent, whether through the mother or the father, of the progenitor from whom the land is inherited. Thus for the purpose of inheritance of land, the term family excludes "outside" children of the spouse of the parent through whom the inheritance passes. Where brothers jointly own land, and the children of both siblings inherit, the process of individual division is unusually accelerated.

Finally we have shown that the theory of joint inheritance by all the family, specific in land inherited from the ancestors who are buried on the land, tends to become attached to all land acquired, and that once there has been joint inheritance by all the family, the principle of inalienability is also involved.

The traditional concepts when applied to this category of inherited land become, however, attenuated: and the practice (permitted in the case of bought land) of sharing the inheritance between the children is more common.

(ix)

It is clear from the foregoing evidence that the position in regard to Land Tenure is not a static one and that there are continual pressures both from within and without, operating, on the one hand to reinforce the traditional beliefs and practices and on the other to modify or undermine them.

The system of family land and joint inheritance by all the children may be regarded from the functional point of view as a conservative force, directed to ensure that the inheritance is kept intact and contributing also to family cohesion and solidarity. Joint occupation and use not only keeps the kinship group together but links the individual members of the family in a series of repetitive activities which of necessity call for co-operation and mutual adjustments. Agreement must be reached in regard to living accommodation; sharing of the economic trees planted by the ancestors; amicable sharing of the area which can be planted in food crops for the separate households; the sharing of kitchen and toilet or provision of these facilities (as is more usual) by each household. The children of the families play together in the yard, while their mothers perform their daily individual and separate household tasks within sight and sound of each other. There is the continual "borrowing" and "sharing" that is so much part of the pattern of Jamaican life and the ideas of hospitality.

Contact is also maintained with absent members of the family, involved in joint ownership of the land, living in other parts of the island. When the crops are reaped baskets of foodstuffs are sent from the home cultivation to these relatives working in Kingston or other parts of the island, and in return those who can reciprocate with small sums of money or gifts of clothing.

The possession of an interest in family land or a family house produces a sense of security out of all proportion to the actual economic security, which at best is slight. The word home, as a place one can go back to, may be said to be synonymous with a family holding. One might not inappropriately paraphrase the dictum about marriage (that "One does not marry and live in a rented house") and say "One does not *go home* to a rented house". The nostalgia in the tone of the sugar worker who longed to "go home" to his mother's land in a distant parish but could not until he had made good and could return with money in his pocket is also reflected in this account of a woman then living in a rented room and working in the canefields, whose longing is for the time when she can go back with her sons to her parents' land and make her home there:—

"When she goes back her sons will go with her. They are all in sympathy with her. In their father's yard they regard themselves as being in the enemy's camp. At present she goes and comes and when she is coming she brings with her bags of food. When coconuts are reaped she gets her share of the net after taxes have been paid. Her brother and sister look after the land.

When (she and her sons) go away to look after the land they will cultivate it and build houses in which to live. She already has a zinc house on her mother's land but (the sons) will have to build thatch houses. She and her sons will come down to Sugartown to work in the Crop and when the Crop is over they will go back to their land."

With the increasing scarcity and irregularity of employment and the corresponding insecurity of the wage earner and with the pressure of population on the land which the small man can buy or rent, a few squares of family land in which one has an interest come to have great importance and the internal forces are all against any division of family holdings or enforced consolidation. The few pounds received in compensation is no recompense for the satisfaction a man gets from the knowledge that there is somewhere he can go when the worst happens and be permitted "to build his house and live there."

At the same time there is an equally active pressure from within directed against joint inheritance and towards individual ownership, illustrated by the process, where family land is concerned, of the heirs being given their individual shares either in a will or by joint agreement among themselves. The traditional practice of joint inheritance runs counter to the very strong ambition of the peasant to own his own land and house. This emphasis on ownership colours the whole attitude to land use under tenancy systems. The strength—one might almost say the passion—which attaches to the concept of ownership is undoubtedly in part due to the conditions under which rented land is available; that is, for limited periods, with proscriptions against the erection of a permanent home and without compensation for improvement. In part this explains the antipathy to leasehold. But it would be unwise to assume that mere remedy of the defects in the system (necessary as this is) would satisfy the peasant for whom land has not only a real but an almost mystic significance. It may be said that in this desire to own his land, the Jamaican peasant is no different from peasants in Britain, or Europe, or any other part of the world. There are, however, intensifying elements in the Jamaican situation. First, as we suggested in the historical analysis we give elsewhere, land during slavery acquired a social and status value, and, after slavery, became in a sense both the symbol and the reality of freedom. Secondly, the religious association of land is strong: the spot on which the ancestors are buried is sacred and land containing their graves should not be permitted to pass into alien hands. Thirdly, in the economy of the island, ownership of land is believed to be the only real and permanent source of security and of the means of satisfying the normal expectations which operate between men and women as prospective parents and between them and their children. And this has no connection, be it stated, with the income which the land can provide. There is a deeply ingrained suspicion that jobs, however well paid, are insecurely held. This feeling of insecurity grows with the increasing pressure of population on available jobs; with the inability of education and practical training to keep pace with this increase of population; and with the steep climb in the rates both of unemployment and of unemployability.

We see that from within there come therefore pressure both to conserve the traditional system of joint inheritance and inalienability and, at the same time, movements towards division into shares and individual ownership.

The external forces are all against conservation of the traditional system. First, it is unrecognized by the law of the country and, I am told, unknown in all its complex implications to most practising lawyers and solicitors.

From another angle, the system is discreditable as a perpetual source of dispute. We have referred to the stabilizing and cohesive effects of the system on the family, but we have equally shown that the congregation of families on family land and in family houses with communal ownership is also a frequent source of contention and disagreement, although, from our point of view, even these disagreements were a factor in keeping the group together. There is thus, where the desire is to effect amicable agreement (and the monetary value of the inheritance is rarely sufficient to make litigation worth while to anyone), a great temptation to do this by cutting the Gordian knot and forcing a division or sale.[9]

Secondly, the legal recognition of legitimacy as a principle governing inheritance, which has no counterpart or reality in customary ideology or behaviour, and the legal concept of an individual heir-at-law, defined in terms of age and sex, all militate against the social stability of the traditional system in a society where the several subcultures are continually encroaching and reacting on one another.

Thirdly, there is the impracticability of the system in the modern social evolution of Jamaica. From the aspect of land use it is inevitably wasteful and incompetent. A good deal of family land is under-used, occupied by the old people who are physically unable to develop it. Other multiple-owned holdings are completely unproductive save for the food trees planted by the ancestors. When adjacent to a town or an industrial centre (such as Sugartown) they fully justify their existence as house sites. But in rural or depressed areas where they are expected to carry a large kinship group having no other means of subsistence, they may, and do, keep the family together, but for no profitable purpose. Misuse of land in the form of exhaustion or neglect, under-use because of lack of capital, or multiple ownership restricting development, are all practical results which have to be weighed against the strong sentiment and the high values attached to the system.

On the other hand we have, as illustrated in Orange Grove, the opposite practice of division of land among the children—not to mention sales at lower than economic prices to landless kin. Although the Settlement in its present form is only some three or four decades old, our records show that few of the original holdings are intact. Considering the size of the families and the strength of family sentiment this process of fragmentation gives rise to some anxiety for the future of what is, at the moment, one of the most prosperous, progressive and well-integrated farming communities in Jamaica.

Notes:

The research upon which this paper is based was financed by the Colonial Social Science Research Council and supervised by a small committee representing the London School of Economics. I am indebted to both for kind permission to publish this here.

1. Mission of the International Bank for Reconstruction and Development, 1952, *The Economic Development of Jamaica.* Johns Hopkins Press, Baltimore, Chapter 2.
2. For much valuable information on the subject see *"The Blessed Isle"* and *"The Myth of Governor Eyre"*, pp. 170 et seq., by Lord Oliver.
3. The Statute of Limitations provides that squatters' rights are established on Freehold Estates and Crown Lands by undisputed possession for 60 years. I am not aware if there is any available information as to the acreage of land so alienated.
4. The Wills Act of Jamaica is based on the English Act.
5. The process is undoubtedly made easier by the fact that (a) there is at present no pressure on the land and (b) the old land as compared with that purchased some 30 odd years ago is on the hill slopes, much eroded and ex-

hausted and hence of low agricultural value compared to the holdings acquired 35 years ago.

6. When there is joint purchase by two brothers this may involve two sets of siblings: it may also (where one brother is childless) make the other brother the heir.

7. I have used the term "outside" throughout my paper to describe children of a man or woman living together (whether in marriage or concubinage) born to them in previous unions, i.e. "outside" the current union. These are not necessarily illegitimate children since the current union may be based on concubinage and the previous unions legal marriages. The question of legitimacy does not in itself, in customary theory and practice, affect the inheritance since illegitimate children take the name of the father and therefore are "of the name".

8. The Intestates' Estates and Property Charges Law, Cap. 372 of the Laws of Jamaica (Law 35 of 1936) provides in Section 11 of Part 11 as follows:—

> *Sub-section (1)* when the mother of an illegitimate child dies intestate and has no legitimate issue the illegitimate child or his issue shall be entitled to take any interest in that property to which he or they would have been entitled if he had been legitimate.

> *Sub-section (2)* entitles the mother of an illegitimate child dying intestate to the interest to which the sole surviving parent of a legitimate child would be entitled.

9. I am informed that The Partition Law (Cap. 360 of the Revised Laws of Jamaica) gives the Court power to direct a sale instead of a division of the land.

RAYMOND T. SMITH

12. Land Tenure in Three Negro Villages in British Guiana

INTRODUCTION

This paper describes the system of land tenure in three Negro village communities in the coastal area of British Guiana. It is intended as a preliminary statement of the situation and does not deal with the subject from a comparative theoretical point of view. All three villages are fairly long-established and came into being when groups of ex-slaves purchased the land shortly after emancipation around the middle of the nineteenth century. The information presented here was collected in the course of eighteen months' field study in 1951–53.

The three villages are situated in the counties of Berbice, Demerara and Essequibo, and will be referred to by the fictitious names of August Town, Perseverance and Better Hope. Whilst they are referred to as 'Negro' villages, they all contain a small proportion of persons who are either East Indian, Portuguese, Chinese or Coloured, the latter term being used for persons of mixed descent (except mixed East Indian-Negro). August Town has the largest population with approximately 1,700 persons; Better Hope has approximately 1,000 persons; and Perseverance is the smallest with approximately 700 persons.

Most of the inhabitants of all three villages derive their livelihood partly from farming activities within the village, and partly from working as unskilled labourers on the sugar estates, at the bauxite mines, and in the gold and diamond fields. There is also unskilled work available with the Public Works Department, and a small proportion of the men have steady employment in Government Service or in the

SOURCE: Reprinted from *Social and Economic Studies,* Vol. 4, No. 1 (1955): 64–82, by permission of the author and publisher.

sugar factories.* Despite this, one is justified in regarding the villages as solidary localized groupings with relatively little internal hierarchical social differentiation, but being themselves differentiated as lower class Negro communities in the system of social stratification of the colony as a whole.

Each village is a territorial as well as a social unit, and this paper will deal with the relations between the people and the land they live on and cultivate. A part of this relationship consists of the way in which interests in land are controlled, exchanged and transmitted, and of course these transactions are governed by systems of control which have general social acceptance. In an admirable article on land tenure, Simpson says:

'I suggest that a simple and understandable approach is, like the English lawyer's, to regard land itself as incapable of ownership and that it is only interests in land which can be owned. The interests in land can be likened to a bundle of sticks, not all of the same length or thickness. All the sticks (i.e. the whole bundle) can be owned by one man, or separate sticks can be owned by separate persons. Two or more persons can own one stick or the owner can be a group of persons such as a family, a clan, a village or a tribe. There can in fact be many interests in land ranging from the right, say, of a village to collect nuts from a nearby forest right up to what the English lawyer would call "a fee simple absolute in possession". Each interest can be precisely described in simple plain language and will correspond with or be comparable to some type of interest in land familiar to land-lawyers, but called by different names in different systems of law' (6).

It is proposed to adopt Simpson's approach and describe interests, or rights, without using legal terminology.

The major portion of the land occupied by all three villages was originally alienated by the Dutch to private individuals prior to 1803. There are 607 square miles of such land along the coast and banks of the principal rivers, but practically none of it is in the hands

---

* Better Hope is the only one of the three villages where persons work regularly in the sugar factories. In this village there is a group of highly skilled technicians known as sugar boilers who earn relatively high wages and enjoy positions of prestige in the village on this account.

of the descendants of the original proprietors. This land was disposed of long ago either to groups of ex-slaves, to large corporations operating the present day sugar estates, or to the Government which has established several large land settlements. The ancestors of our present day villagers acquired freehold title after emancipation by purchasing it from the previous estate owners. The way in which these sales came to be made, and the general method of purchase have been described by Farley (*3*). This freehold land forms the main territorial *locus* of the villages and leasehold Crown lands extend the farming boundaries inland in the case of August Town.

COLONY LAW IN RELATION TO LAND

A brief description of the legal system of land tenure in British Guiana is given in *Caribbean Land Tenure Symposium* (*1*), but the outlines will be recapitulated here.

In 1916 by the passing of the *Civil Law of British Guiana Ordinance*, effect was given to the adoption of English common law for the whole colony, but exception was made in the case of the law relating to movable and immovable property, which remained essentially the same as under the Roman-Dutch code. This latter is much simpler than the traditional English system, and its main features are that all conveyances of land must be registered in an office called the Registry of Deeds, and that registration of title is normal proof of its ownership. This system is essentially the same as the Torrens system (*6*, p. 57), and the title 'Registry of Deeds' is perhaps confusing if the function of this office is to maintain a register showing title. Both the transferor and the transferee have to sign a document of transfer, or transport, which is registered.

Whenever title to land is changed by the normal method of transport, and registered with the Registry of Deeds, provision is made for the transfer to be advertised in one daily newspaper, and in the Official Gazette, in order to ensure publicity.

Joint ownership of rights in land is visualized as two or more persons holding shares in a piece of land, the shares not being defined by any dividing line in the property itself. This is an important concept of joint ownership which is widely held in the villages.

There are various other provisions in law relating to encumbrances of property, leases, rental, prescriptive rights and so on, but these are not of immediate concern at this point. Rights of possession are enforced by the Supreme Court and litigation over disputed rights can be an expensive process. In practice Negro villagers rarely take disputes to court, and there are other mechanisms of control which operate with effect.

DEVELOPMENT OF VILLAGE ADMINISTRATION
AND THE WORKING OF THE LOCAL GOVERNMENT SYSTEM

We may begin by considering the case of August Town. When the village lands were first acquired in 1841, title was granted for the joint possession of all the shareholders represented by two of their number who signed the transport on behalf of all the others. This was the common practice throughout the colony. So far as title was concerned, all the shareholders enjoyed joint freehold rights of tenure, and there was no registered sub-division of the property. However, the villagers divided the land between themselves, each shareholder being allotted rectangular portions of land in the cultivation and dwelling areas, and retaining undivided rights in the burial ground, pasture and 'wood-bush' where firewood could be gathered. All the drainage trenches, dams, sluices and so on were joint property and their maintenance was a joint responsibility.*

Individual rights in village lands always carried a responsibility to contribute labour or money towards village works. The plots of land allotted to individual proprietors were defined by small drainage trenches and natural objects such as clumps of bush or trees, and the rights in these plots were defined by custom. As time went by it became increasingly difficult to enforce the obligations binding upon proprietors. The original 'shares' consisting of a definite number of lots in the cultivation and dwelling areas, gradually became divided amongst a number of descendants, and disputes within the community became more frequent. Neglect of the drainage and irrigation system was almost inevitable when men's interests lay primarily in working for cash wages outside the village, and the cultivation area was almost completely abandoned in August Town at one stage in its history. This had been the experience of most similar villages at one time or another, and indeed of most similar agricultural blocks in British Guiana where financial resources on the one hand and unified control on the other have not been combined to exclude sea water from the front and flood water from the back.

* For a description of the lay-out of Guianese villages see Smith, R. T. (7).

In 1925 August Town was brought into the local Government system when over 50 per cent of the proprietors (i.e. persons having rights of possession in the village lands) applied to the colonial Government for incorporation. When this happened two major steps were taken. The central Government made monetary grants and loans for the rehabilitation of the drainage and irrigation system, and the village lands were partitioned and assessed. A land partition is exactly the same as Simpson's 'Systematic Adjudication' (*6*, p.53). A sworn land surveyor employed by the Department of Lands and Mines measures each bed and after hearing all claims and examining documentary evidence such as wills and bills of sale, he determines who shall be registered as the title holder. It should be made clear that he does not 'grant' title; he merely determines who is the rightful title holder. Where disputes arise, provision is made for appeals against the decisions of the partitioning officer. When the partition is complete a cadastral plan is prepared showing every plot of land, and this serves as a basic reference for assessment of rates and so forth. Each freeholder is given documentary evidence of his or her title, and this is registered both in the Deeds Registry and in the village Assessment Book. A partition such as this effectively destroys the old original divisions of the village lands, defines the existing state of land holdings and makes explicit at one point in time the rights and claims of living individuals in the village land. Provision is made in law for the continuing re-definition of these rights to title through the processes of registration of transport, but it is not always resorted to, for the customary ways of doing things do not die easily.

Incorporation into the local Government system implies more than the making of a grant or loan, and the partition of the village lands. Primarily it means the introduction of a legally sanctioned system of village administration controlled by the central Government. The basis of the system had been worked out in August Town under the previous regime where elected village headmen kept a register of 'proprietors' who were liable to contribute labour or cash to the upkeep of the village dams, trenches, sluices, etc. These headmen were responsible to all the proprietors, who occasionally held meetings to discuss village affairs, and so on. Under the new system a council of nine persons was appointed by the central Government, the value of each bed of land was assessed and entered in the Assessment Book, and the council was empowered to levy a rate, the proceeds from which were to be used to pay the wages of an overseer, a sluice watchman and two rangers, and to pay for labour to carry out any necessary communal works in the village. Although this merely represents a rationalization of the previous system it involves certain fundamental changes, amongst which the transfer of managerial function from the elected headmen to the new chairman and councillors is the most important. The old headmen were farmers and proprietors, whereas the new chairman and leading men on the council tended to be school-teachers or even persons not belonging to the village at all, though this was rare.

Both Perseverance and Better Hope went through the same processes of development as August Town, though Perseverance was partitioned as recently as 1950, and Better Hope was administered by a chairman and council as an incorporated village before 1900.

It will be useful now to examine the main outlines of the Local Government system as it exists today, and the powers of the village councils in relation to the land within the boundaries of their jurisdiction.

The whole of the rural areas of the coastlands come under the jurisdiction of a Central Board, known as the Local Government Board, whose members are appointed by the Governor of the colony. This Board has the power to declare any district to be a 'village district', a 'country district' or a 'rural district', as it thinks fit. A village district has a partially elected and partially nominated council (usually 6 elected and 3 nominated members), a country district has a wholly nominated council and a rural district comes under the direct control of the Board. At the time of the 1946 census there were 32 village districts with a total population of 61,361, and 63 country districts with a total population of 44,267. Superficially at least, this would seem to indicate that the larger communities are more likely to have attained village district status. There are many small settlements which remain fairly autonomous as regards their administration, if any, and the communities resident on sugar plantations are managed by the company controlling the plantation (often advised by a joint committee of residents and company representatives).

August Town and Perseverance are both country districts, and Better Hope is a village district. The council, whether nominated or partially elected, is known as the 'Local Authority' and it is invested with power to levy rates on land and/or buildings within its boundaries, and to take action to recover rates in case of non-payment. Rates are monies payable by title holders and/or owners of buildings, to the Local Authority to enable it to administer the village and maintain the drainage and irrigation works in good order. Section 121 of the *Local Government Ordinance* (*1945*) lays down the liability for and mode of recovery of rates (*5*). The principal instrument provided by this Ordinance is the power to seize either buildings or land and put them up for public auction in order to recover outstanding rates. The powers granted to the Local Authority under this section of the Ordinance are used sparingly, but the threat of loss of land is often enough to enforce payment of rates. It is clear from the foregoing that rights in village land are subject to considerable limitation, and the individual title holder is by no means free to use his land or neglect it as he wishes, for the interests of the whole community are held to over-ride individual interests in this respect.

In point of fact it is usually the District Commissioner, acting as the agent of the Local Government Board who puts pressure to bear on the Local Authorities to take proceedings for the recovery of rates. This Central Board has almost absolute power in that it can take over completely the management of any village which does not fulfil the requirements of the Ordinance, and it uses its powers quite extensively in bringing pressure to bear on inefficient councils. The Board has to approve every estimate made by a Local Authority, and it very often amends these before approving them. The District Commissioner, acting as the servant of the Board, is responsible for holding the funds of each Local Authority within his area, and all expenditure has to be authorized by his office. In practice the District Commissioner is forced to exercise the closest supervision over the Local Authorities in his area in order to ensure that they carry out the wishes of the Local Government Board. Many local authorities do manage their affairs to the satisfaction of the Board, of course, but so long as there is an hierarchy of control, situations must arise in which the superordinate body has to over-rule the decisions of the subordinate ones.

In a famous minute written in 1930 (*2*), Sir Edward Denham, then Governor of the colony, laid down that the function of the District Commissioner was to exercise the maximum of persuasion with the minimum of coercion, so far as the local authorities were concerned. This nice distinction may be of some use in directing the District Commissioner toward the path of diplomacy, but it does not alter the fact that his efficiency is judged to some extent by the efficiency of the rate collections in his district. It is quite clear that the villages are incapable of complete self-government, not because of the quality of their inhabitants but because they are too small to support the necessary administrative machinery and to provide the drainage works necessary for agricultural occupation. This has always been their handicap and it is fully realized by many persons in and out of the Government. Village councils would have some functions to perform under any system of administration, but it would be more realistic to build up the Unions of Local Authorities* into fully democratic institutions controlling the administrative machinery of the Local Government Department in the various districts. There would be many difficulties involved, not least of which is the solidarity and separatism of the various villages, but since the majority of villagers already regard their village council as little more than the tool of 'Government', the transition may not be too difficult. Once relieved of the onerous responsibility of maintaining drainage and irrigation works, the village councils would be free to devote their energies to the provision of other local amenities, and they could be granted a fixed proportion of the local rate for this purpose.

In theory then, each village is divided into plots of land, each individually held by one or more persons possessing legal title, and there is a residue of land comprising pasture, drainage trenches, dams, streets, burial ground and playing field, title to which is held by the Local Authority, and rights to the use of which are possessed by all rate-paying villagers. The village is taken to be the natural unit of local government and its council has authority to impose restrictions on the use of land and to require each proprietor to contribute towards the upkeep of communal resources, particularly drainage and irrigation works. In turn the village council is subject to the direction of the Local Government Board whose officers exercise supervisory functions. The philosophy underlying the whole local government system is that the villagers are not yet capable of managing their own affairs, and that until such time as they are more 'advanced' the central Government has to exercise supervision. This is a dubious philosophy, and the real problem lies in establishing a hier-

* These are district bodies formed with a view to enabling members of all the local authorities in a district to meet and discuss common problems. They have no executive functions at the present time, but their quarterly meetings provide an occasion for all the Government officers in the district (such as the District Commissioner, Agricultural Officer, Social Welfare Officer, Sanitary Inspector, etc.) to meet representatives of the local authorities and hear their problems and suggestions.

archy of control in which each level will be equipped with the necessary resources both in money and administrative machinery to deal effectively with the tasks it is expected to perform.

METHODS OF TRANSMISSION OF RIGHTS OVER VILLAGE LANDS

(a) By Sale.

The buying and selling of land between villagers is fairly common, and during his lifetime an individual may accumulate a considerable number of scattered plots. Plots rarely amount to more than about one acre in any of the villages and the majority are still smaller. There is very little tendency to acquire possession of a number of adjacent holdings in order to have a consolidated large holding, but in the case of rice land which produces a cash crop some consolidation does seem to be taking place. The possession of land does not in itself confer status within the village, but on the other hand the absence of large differentials in the size of land holdings reflects the egalitarian status structure of the village group, and it is only outside the village community proper that persons holding large areas of land and possessing a pronounced difference in wealth are found. The few persons living in these villages who operate large areas of land are usually non-Negroes, and their land holdings do not form part of the village freehold lands, and so need not be considered here.

Prior to the partition of the village lands, the two parties to a sale would often draw up a 'paper' or receipt for the money passed over, and this would suffice to effect the transfer. Often the transfer would be by mutual agreement only. Even today, no other formality than the drawing up of a receipt may be entered into, but in the great majority of cases an attempt is made to effect a legal transfer of title. Because the expenses of retaining a lawyer to draw up a bill of sale and apply for the transaction to be registered in the Deeds Registry is quite high, a customary method of securing registered title, which involves the co-operation of the Local Authority, has developed and is described below. This method is often used whenever it is desired to effect a change of title, and not only in cases where a sale has been made.

The person wishing to acquire title makes an arrangement with the village overseer to allow the rates due on the land in question to fall into arrears. The overseer then exercises the authority conferred under Section 121 of the *Local Government Ordinance* (*1945*) to arrange for the lot to be executed upon and put up for public auction for the recovery of the outstanding rates. The person wishing to acquire title goes along to the sale, purchases the land (virtually from himself) and is granted a legal title at a very small cost. There are certain hazards involved in this procedure since one can never be quite sure what may happen at a public auction, but the method is widely used. Strictly speaking this involves the use of government machinery by private individuals for the transaction of private business; but it is clear that some provision for the proper transfer of title is necessary without involving poor people in unduly heavy legal expenses and this method serves quite well, and is understood by the majority of villagers.

(b) By Gift.

When a young man sets up a household in the village he will normally require a lot on which to build a house. He may buy a vacant lot, or he may be given a plot on which to build by a member of his family, and more usually by a member on whose property he would normally have a claim if that person were to die intestate.

The spatial distribution of households shows quite clearly that the tendency is for a young couple to build their house away from the lots occupied by both the man's and the woman's parents. The ability to purchase house lots facilitates this scatter and helps to prevent the development of extended families occupying a close cluster of house lots. The multi-lateral nature of the operative kinship ties in the village, and the fact that women both own and inherit land, means that it is quite likely that any individual landholder has acquired beds of land which are widely scattered, having been held by many different households at one time and another.

A man who is getting old, and has acquired a collection of parcels of land during his lifetime often decides to distribute them before his death, usually amongst his potential heirs. This relieves him of the burden of paying the rates on land which he is no longer able to work.

Legal title to land transferred by gift is usually acquired though the transfer may not be recorded at all, the recipients merely taking over the responsibility for the payment of rates. This responsibility may be recognized by the village overseer, but officially he cannot alter the name in the Assessment Book until the new title has been made legal.

(c) *By Will.*

This method of transfer is essentially the same as transfer by gift, except that it does not take place until after the donor has died. In practice, only a few villagers make wills, for a part of the property may have been disposed of before death, and as the customary rules of inheritance are usually adhered to, serious disputes rarely arise. Where disputes seem likely to occur, a potential heir may persuade an ageing person to make a will in order to ensure amity later on. Testamentary succession will be upheld by the courts if the will is properly made, but it is rarely found necessary to apply to the courts in order to have the terms of a will enforced.

(d) *Inheritance.*

By inheritance is meant that transfer of rights over property which takes place when a property holder dies intestate. Rules of inheritance are those rules defining the manner in which such rights should be distributed.

The rules of inheritance with which this study is concerned are primarily customary rules sanctioned by tradition and public opinion in the villages. The basic concept in these rules is the idea that all full siblings have equal rights to equal shares of the property of their parents, if those parents die intestate. However, this is merely the foundation of the rules and there are many elaborations on it. If a man dies intestate leaving a widow and adult children, then, according to the law, his estate should be divided in the proportion of one-third to his widow and two-thirds to be divided equally amongst his legitimate children. In fact what usually happens is that the widow takes control of the estate and divides it according to customary practice. Certainly all the man's legitimate children have a customary right to equal shares, but the land may be divided according to 'need', those whose needs are less receiving merely a token share. If she is a reasonable woman the widow may decide to give a portion of land to one or more of the man's 'outside' children (i.e. his illegitimate children by women other than the one with whom he has actually been living). The property may be divided according to 'need' while the title may be retained as joint ownership, so that those who do not need to use the land at the time, may still retain undivided rights in it which they can transmit by will or inheritance to their own children.

A further modification is introduced when the deceased has reared a child which may not be his own begotten child, but may nevertheless be treated as one for the purposes of inheritance. This most frequently occurs when a man and woman have reared a daughter's child, and then treat it as a full heir to the property, and the customary rules of inheritance definitely recognize that such a grandchild has a right to a share in the property.

The principal inheritors are those persons who have stood in the relationship of son or daughter to the deceased by virtue of having been reared by him, irrespective of exact biological or legal relationship. Inheritance follows the same pattern whether the deceased is a man or a woman, and the surviving spouse acts for the children as a trustee of that portion of the estate which is not transmitted directly to them.

Where a couple live together in a common-law marriage and the male partner dies intestate, the same customary rules apply, but the common-law wife and her children cannot, strictly speaking, invoke the law to substantiate their claim. If the common-law union has been of short duration, it sometimes happens that the siblings of the deceased may step in and claim the dead man's property, but this would be a marginal case. Where the union has been long established, such a situation would not arise, and if it did then in all probability the courts would uphold the claims of the widow, as would public opinion in the village.

With such a large number of heirs it would be reasonable to expect a high degree of fragmentation of land holdings. This is certainly the case, for even before lots are subdivided they are, technically speaking, little more than 'fragments'. But excessive sub-division is circumvented in several ways. Because there is no great pressure on land,* it is possible to acquire lots in ways other than by sub-division of existing lots, and the continual transference of lots by purchase, gift, etc., bears this out. There is also a legal ban on dividing any registered lot into more than four equal portions or into pieces of less than one fifteenth of an acre. This legal provision only refers to division for the purpose of granting individual title, and it would still be possible for persons to be using smaller areas than this, but in fact they rarely do. The Roman-Dutch system of allowing persons to retain undivided rights in a plot of land also means that one heir may be using the land whilst his co-heirs retain their rights with the pos-

* This reference is to the particular villages being considered here, not to the colony or coastlands as a whole.

sibility of exercising them at some future date, or passing them on to someone else.

With regard to the inheritance of houses, the surviving spouse continues to own and occupy the house. When there is no surviving spouse the person will usually give an indication of who shall succeed to possession, and in the vast majority of cases this is the person who has 'cared' for the deceased prior to death. In a few cases the house may be regarded as the joint property of the surviving legitimate children, and may even be dismantled and the timber distributed amongst them, but this is rare. It is an accepted custom that occupation of the house constitutes a basis for rights of possession, and so the person living with the deceased prior to death has first claim.

The lack of strong feelings about rights of inheritance is illustrated by the fact that there are no explicit rules forbidding alienation of rights over property which the potential heirs would have a just expectation of acquiring on the death of the owner. It is true that children would feel aggrieved if their parents disposed of all their land to 'strangers' but if it had been sold to meet the needs of ordinary living they would show little concern. There is no conception of a collection of parcels of land being passed intact from one generation to another, except at the level of the village itself, where there is a feeling that the village as a whole should pass intact from generation to generation of its Negro inhabitants; but we shall deal with this later.

(e) By Prescription.

Acquisition of prescriptive rights to property is of little significance within the village, since a person could hardly occupy land for the required period of 33⅓ years without the title holder's consent, or without his knowing of it, and if the title holder did not take action to recover his rights then the matter would be treated as if a gift had been made. It may happen that a person has a better claim to title than another but has not been in occupation of the land, and so forfeits his claim to the person who has been in occupation and who has thereby acquired prescriptive rights. Such cases, however, are rare.

(f) Lending and Renting of Land.

It is a common practice for persons to allow fellow villagers, and particularly kinsmen, to use a plot of land for the purpose of growing a crop or building a house; and in the case of a loan of this kind there is no transfer of title rights. The borrower will normally pay the rates due on the land for the period during which he is using it, and very often he will present the lender with a small part of any crop that is grown as a token of appreciation.

A distinction must be drawn between those cases where a person has borrowed and is using a piece of land, and those cases where a person has been given a piece of land without having acquired legal title. In the former case there is a definite expectation that the person holding title will claim back the land at a future date, whereas in the latter case a transfer of rights of possession has been made and there is no expectation of return. However, this distinction may be difficult to make in many cases, since loaned land may eventually be given to the borrower when the title holder decides he has no further use for it himself. This would normally depend on the borrower's relationship to the holder, and whether or not he were a potential heir.

The renting of land between villagers is not common, since by and large, there is no real land shortage. Land outside the village boundaries is sometimes rented by villagers, particularly for rice cultivation, and much of it is Crown land. So far as freehold land is concerned, the few cases of renting that do occur are principally cases where beds of land are rented to 'outsiders', and this is a more frequent practice in Better Hope than in the other two villages. The rents charged are not high, and usually just cover the amount of the rates which have to be paid, leaving very little margin of profit to the owner.

ALIENATION OF RIGHTS OVER LAND
TO PERSONS NOT BORN IN THE VILLAGE

It has been stated that there is a definite feeling in all three villages that rights over village lands should be retained by the members of the village community and not alienated to outsiders, particularly East Indians.* This is most pronounced in August Town, where definite measures are taken to prevent such alienation. If a man marries a village girl and comes to live in the village he is at first regarded as a

---

* The same feeling is common in East Indian villages *vis-a-vis* Negroes, but the expansion of East Indian land holding and the Indians' greater interest in farming means that attention is usually focussed on Negro resistance to alienation.

'stranger', but of course he will need land on which to build a house and start a farm, and he will experience no difficulty in getting it. He will, however, experience difficulty in acquiring title to the land until such time as he has become relatively well assimilated to the village group. Title will normally be given in his wife's name at first, so that there will be no danger of the rights of possession being alienated to an 'outsider', and particularly to a speculative East Indian, without her knowledge and that of her 'family'. This control as to which persons should be granted title is possible because of the manner in which title is normally obtained and it may be imposed as a condition of sale or gift.

In actual pactice, title to some plots of land in all three villages is held by East Indians or by persons who do not live in the village and were not born there. In Better Hope this process of alienation of rights to 'outsiders' has gone farthest, but this is compatible with the fact that this village is the least cohesive of the three as a distinct local group. It has also a much higher proportion of non-Negro inhabitants.

FACTORS ASSOCIATED WITH ACTUAL UTILIZATION OF VILLAGE LANDS

So far this paper has been concerned with the system of rights of possession and rights to title, and the various methods by which these rights may be transferred. It will now be useful to consider the question of how the land in the village is actually used, and by whom it is used. Malinowski made this distinction between possession and use long ago *(4)*. This can best be illustrated by reference to Perseverance, for in this village a partition was effected, and titles to individuals' holdings given, only one year before the field work was carried out, so that one would expect the least number of anomalous titles in this village. (Fewer persons will actually have rights of possession over land which is registered in other people's names.)

Perseverance farm lands are divided into two distinct areas, one comprising 213.76 acres on which rice is grown, and one comprising 357.88 acres of which part is used for growing 'provisions', etc., the other part being under bush. Rice land is in greater demand than the other type of land, and so the two areas will be treated separately.

In Tables 1 and 2 the situation is summarized. In the rice area (Table 1) all the land is under cultivation, none of it being abandoned to bush, so that there are no cases where only a part of a bed is under cultivation. A 'bed' is taken to be a portion of land which is separately registered as one unit, i.e. some person or group of persons possess title to it, and it is registered in the village Assessment Book against their name or names. An 'individual planting' is a portion of land being worked as a distinct unit by one person, or very infrequently by a group of persons; one registered 'bed' may comprise several 'individual plantings', but not *vice-versa* for the purposes of these tables. (In practice one person may be cultivating two or more adjacent beds as one unit but they are taken as separate plantings for the purpose of these tables.)

TABLE 1. RIGHTS OF POSSESSION AND
USE OF RICE LAND: PERSEVERANCE

No. of registered beds	119
No. of individual plantings (aver. size = 1.25 acres)	179
No. of persons planting (aver. area per person = 1.54 acres)	139
No. of beds used solely by registered title holder	36
No. of beds or parts of beds rented	22
No. of beds or parts of beds lent to kinsfolk	40
No. of beds which are subdivided	40
No. of beds with joint title*	22

* Includes beds registered in name of a deceased person.

TABLE 2. RIGHTS OF POSSESSION AND
USE OF PROVISION LAND: PERSEVERANCE

No. of registered beds	324
No. of individual plantings*	137
(Total area under cultivation = 76 acres; aver. area per planting = .55 acres, approx.)	
No. of beds totally abandoned**	180
No. of beds or parts of beds worked by title holder	41
No. of beds or parts of beds rented	13
No. of beds or parts of beds lent to kinsfolk	56
No. of beds with joint title	38

* These are on 117 registered beds. In the majority of cases only a part of the lot is under cultivation. There are 27 beds or parts of beds planted in coconuts which have not been included. The crop on all except a few of the beds is 'mixed provisions'. One bed (1.76 acres) is planted in oranges.
** One or two of these beds have a few scattered fruit trees growing on them (mainly mangoes).

Several points emerge from these tables. In the rice area there are 60 more individual plantings than there are separately registered beds, and of the registered beds only 36 are used solely by the registered title holder, the rest either being wholly lent or rented, or being subdivided into several plantings, some of which are lent or rented. It is clear that the lending of land is common, and more frequent than is renting, even though rice land is in fairly high demand, and many people have to go outside the village to rent it. 40 beds are subdivided into two or more portions. All land in both sections which is lent, is lent to kinsfolk. In the provision section 180 beds are totally abandoned to bush, but of the rest many are only partially cultivated. Again the number of cases where a piece of land is lent to kinsfolk is far in excess of the number of cases where land is rented, and only 41 cases occur where the land is actually being worked by the person having legal title to it. In a few cases the land will actually have been given to the person using it, or it may reasonably be expected that it will be given to, willed to, or inherited by that person.

In regard to the type of kinship relations obtaining between title holders and users of land the following table shows quite clearly that

TABLE 3. RELATIONSHIP OF USERS TO TITLE HOLDERS
OF RICE AND PROVISION LAND: PERSEVERANCE*

Relationship	No. of cases	
	Where title holder is female	Where title holder is male
Son	6	18
Daughter	2	10
Brother or brother's child	2	40
Sister or sister's child	6	13
Son's wife	0	1
Daughter's husband	1	6
Son's son	0	3
Son's daughter	1	0
Daughter's son	0	6
Daughter's daughter	0	2
Spouse	0	2
Husband's brother	2	0
Wife's father	0	1
Wife's brothers	0	2
Matri-lateral kinsman	5	7
Patri-lateral kinsman	0	3

* Includes cases where land is held on joint title and indicates relationship to deceased person in whose name land is registered.

sons, daughters, brothers and sisters are the persons to whom land is most frequently lent. It should be noted that these numbers refer to the number of lots held and used by various kin and not to the number of persons involved. Thus the large number of male-held lots lent to brothers is partially accounted for by one man who holds a large number of beds which are being used by his two brothers while he is in the United States.

The largest category of kin relations after siblings, children and grandchildren is that of matri-lateral kin which corresponds with the general pattern of kinship ties (7). Although at the time of the field study the land mentioned in this table was being 'lent' it is reasonable to expect that in a number of cases it would eventually be given, willed to or inherited by the user. This is particularly true in the case of sons, daughters and grandchildren of the title holder, who may be considered as potential heirs according to the rules of inheritance. In some cases this had already happened at the time of the enquiry, but the land was still registered in the name of the deceased person.

Table 4 gives some idea of the size of the units of land under discussion and it is clear that individual plantings are usually quite small in area, and generally less than one acre.

TABLE 4. SIZE OF ALL FARM BEDS
(RICE, PROVISIONS, ABANDONED, ETC.): PERSEVERANCE

Under .5 acre	66	
.5 to 1 acre	144	
1 to 2 acres	143	
2 to 3 acres	64	Total no.
3 to 4 acres	21	registered
4 to 5 acres	1	lots = 443
5 to 6 acres	3	
6 to 7 acres	1	

N.B. Larger lots are usually subdivided for purposes of cultivation.

VILLAGERS RIGHTS OVER LANDS OUTSIDE THE VILLAGE BOUNDARIES

Apart from their freehold land, villagers use a certain amount of land which does not form part of the village lands proper. August Town rice growers rent large blocks of land just behind the village back dam. This is Crown land and the lease is held communally in the same way as the original transport to the village lands was held, two men being appointed as representatives and the names of all the other lessees being entered on the lease (*3*). The lands are then allotted in strips. There are three blocks of this type of rice land, one behind each section of the village, and the one behind Belle Vue section is leased in the name of the village council.

Behind Troy section 189 acres of Crown land are leased by 64 people, represented by two of their members. The lease was officially granted in 1941, although rice had been planted on the land for about 17 years prior to this date. Although the terms of the lease state that there should be no sub-letting of this land, it does in fact take place, and there are far more than 64 individual cultivations. The sub-letting is mainly between kinsfolk, and it is difficult to see how this kind of sub-division could be prevented. Even on Land Settlements where economic holdings of 5 acres or more are leased to settlers, no efficient method of preventing sub-division of holdings between kinsfolk has been found. The same conditions obtain in regard to 94 acres behind St. Paul's section which are leased by 49 persons, some of them also being shareholders in the Troy and Belle Vue Crown lands. The 253 acres behind Belle Vue are leased in the name of the village council and have 44 official shareholders. Thus the total area of Crown land under rice cultivation is 536 acres and this is theoretically divided between 157 shareholders. In fact some persons hold shares in all three sections, and there are more persons actually cultivating portions of land than is indicated by the number of shareholders, so that the average of 3.41 acres per share over the three sections, can serve as no more than a rough guide to the amount of rice land cultivated by each farmer.

The rental for this land is only 20 cents* per acre per annum, but the shareholders have to bear the expense of empoldering and fencing the land. They usually hold a meeting under the chairmanship of their representatives, decide what work shall be done, and raise the money by contributing bags of 'padi' after the harvest. This padi is sold by the representative and the money used to pay for materials and labour.

Behind these three blocks of rice land, further blocks of Crown land are rented for cattle grazing. These lands are rented in exactly the same way, and all persons holding a share are entitled to graze their cattle in this area.

* \$ (B.W.I.) = 4/2d.

Neither Perseverance nor Better Hope has this type of co-operative renting of Crown lands, but 14 men from Perseverance rent large blocks of Crown land about 5½ miles from the village. This is relatively undeveloped land which costs them 30 cents per acre per annum and it is used in the following way:

CROWN LAND RENTED AT LOCATION A, 5½ MILES FROM PERSEVERANCE

Mr. Z rents 40 acres	8 acres planted in rice
	20 acres used for cattle grazing
Mr. Y rents 30 acres	9 acres planted in rice
Mr. X rents 5 acres	5 acres planted in rice
Mr. W rents 5 acres	5 acres planted in rice
Mr. V rents 15 acres	15 acres planted in rice
Mr. U rents 15 acres	15 acres planted in rice

CROWN LAND RENTED AT LOCATION B, 5½ MILES FROM PERSEVERANCE

Mr. X and		
2 brothers	rent 100 acres	not used
Mr. T	rents 100 acres	a few coconuts planted recently
Mr. S	rents 25 acres	one acre planted in coconuts

This land has neither drainage on the landward side nor sea defence.

CROWN LAND RENTED AT LOCATION C, ADJOINING PERSEVERANCE

Mr. R rents 5 acres	all planted in rice
Mr. Q rents 5 acres	all planted in rice
Mr. P rents 10 acres	all planted in rice
Mr. O rents 10 acres	all planted in rice

So far freehold land and Crown land alone have been considered, and the renting of this land had almost invariably been between villagers. The inhabitants of August Town and Perseverance also rent land from other private landholders outside the village, mainly for rice cultivation and for cattle grazing. There is a privately owned estate 'within' the borders of August Town, and one on its western boundary.* The one 'within' August Town has 188 acres of rice grown on it, and of this, 36 acres is grown by the owners. The other

* These are blocks of land which were purchased by single buyers and they do not constitute a part of the village lands. Both estates are owned by non-Negro families.

152 acres are rented out at $6.00 per acre per year, most of it being rented by August Town residents. They also rent land from other private estate owners in the immediate vicinity, the terms being about the same. There is practically no share-cropping type of rental in any of the villages.

Perseverance residents rent this kind of land and use it as follows:

PRIVATE ESTATE AT LOCATION D, 3¼ MILES FROM PERSEVERANCE:

Rice Land:
5 villagers (3 men and 2 women) rent the following 5 areas of land which are totally planted in rice:
(i) 4¼ acres   (ii) 2 acres   (iii) 8 acres   (iv) 1 acre
(v) 2½ acres .
Rent for this land is $8.00 per acre per crop.

Provision Land:
4 villagers (all men) rent the following 4 areas of land which are planted in provisions:
(i) 3 acres   (ii) 1½ acres   (iii) 1 acre   (iv) ½ acre.
Rent for this land is $4.00 per acre per crop (½ year).

PRIVATE ESTATE AT LOCATION E, 1 MILE FROM PERSEVERANCE:

3 villagers (all men) rent the following 3 areas of land which are totally planted in rice:
(i) 1 acre   (ii) ½ acre   (iii) 1 acre.
Rent for this land is $8.00 per acre per crop.

PRIVATE ESTATE AT LOCATION F, 1 MILE FROM PERSEVERANCE:

13 villagers (11 men and 2 women) rent the following 13 areas of land which are totally planted in rice:
(i) 1½ acres   (ii) 2½ acres   (iii) ½ acre   (iv) ½ acre
(v) 1½ acres   (vi) 1½ acres   (vii) ½ acre   (viii) 1 acre
(ix) 1½ acres   (x) 1 acre   (xi) 1 acre   (xii) 1 acre   (xiii) 1 acre.
Rent for this land is $8.06 per acre per crop.

PRIVATE ESTATE AT LOCATION G, 2 MILES FROM PERSEVERANCE:

6 villagers (5 men and 1 woman) rent the following 6 areas of land which are totally planted in rice:
(i) 2½ acres   (ii) 1½ acres   (iii) 1½ acres
(iv) 1½ acres   (v) 1 acre   (vi) 1 acre.
Rent for this land is $8.00 per acre per crop.

PRIVATE ESTATE AT LOCATION H, ADJOINING PERSEVERANCE:

5 villagers (all men) rent the following 5 areas of land which are planted in rice:
(i) 3 acres   (ii) 2 acres   (iii) 2 acres   (iv) 1 acre   (v) 1 acre.
Rent on this land is $4.00 to $5.00 per acre depending on how good the crop is. There is no drainage or irrigation provided on this land.

Perseverance cattle owners have either to graze their cattle on the rice fields after the harvest and on their own rented Crown lands as already enumerated, or they have to pay agistment fees to the owner of an adjoining estate, which charges 60 cents per head per month. August Town has no such difficulties over pasturage, and few in Better Hope keep cattle so there is no difficulty involved in their relative lack of grazing land.

CONCLUSION

At the present stage of development of these villages there is a tendency for the freehold lands of the village as a whole to be regarded as the main land unit, and the very strong feeling against alienation of permanent rights over this land to 'outsiders' is a reflection of the social solidarity of the village group. In the case of Better Hope, strong public opinion against alienation is much less evident than in the other two villages, and this fact is of particular interest, since Better Hope is a much more socially diversified community than either August Town or Perseverance. It is more diversified both in terms of racial composition (having a substantial proportion of East Indian inhabitants) and in terms of occupation and social status of its members. In fact this village contains within itself more of the social elements of the total social system of British Guiana as a whole, whereas the other two are primarily local groups of lower-class Negroes who all share a common position in the total social system, forming a solidary sub-group of the total society. There is no space here to elaborate this statement but the important fact is that in both August Town and Perseverance, and to a large extent in Better Hope, the continuing occupation of the village lands by an ethnically and kinship-defined group is correlated with the continuing existence of the group itself as a differentiated unit in the total system. The reluctance to alienate land to 'outsiders' is an index of the lack of status mobility in the social system, and where mobility is slightly increased, as in the case of Better Hope, there is a corresponding increase in land alienation.

In other villages not covered by this survey alienation may imply nothing more than a change over from permanent rights of tenure to temporary renting rights, resulting in the creation of a less securely fixed solidary group. In one such village a great deal of land had been alienated to East Indian shop-keepers and speculators, and was being rented back to the Negroes, but the villagers still referred to it as "our land originally bought by our forefathers" and since they were still occupying and using the land it could still serve as a focus of the group's identity. In this case the community itself had not become internally diversified, and the proportion of East Indian inhabitants of the village was very low.

This conception of the village lands being vested in the village as a social group through the title rights of the individuals comprising the group, is probably the most important aspect of the whole system of land tenure and has much to do with the belief that the village is the most suitable unit of local government.

In this paper an attempt has been made to show how land is actually held and used and the fact has been made clear that ownership of rights in land is not closely tied to the family system, and does not tend to act as a stabilizing factor so far as domestic groups are concerned. It is at the level of the local community itself that land becomes an important symbol; and as the local community loses its strongly *solidaire* characteristics one would expect the emergence of a situation where land is more important as the basis for the economic support and continuing stability of smaller, probably domestic groups.

References cited:

1. Caribbean Commission.
   1946 *Caribbean Land Tenure Symposium.* Washington, D.C.
2. Denham, Sir Edward B.
   1930 *Minute on District Administration.* Georgetown, British Guiana.
3. Farley, Rawle.
   1954 "The Rise of the Peasantry in British Guiana," *Social and Economic Studies,* Vol. 2, No. 4. Institute of Social and Economic Research, University College of the West Indies, Jamaica.
4. Malinowski, Bronislaw.
   1935 *Coral Gardens and Their Magic* (2 Vols.) George Allen and Unwin Ltd., London.
5. *Ordinance No. 14 of 1945.*
   1945 Argosy Co. Ltd. Georgetown, British Guiana.

6. Simpson, S. Rowton.
   1954 "Land Tenure: Some Explanations and Definitions," *Journal of African Administration*, Vol. VI, No. 2. H.M.S.O., London.
7. Smith, R. T.
   1953 "Aspects of Family Organization in a Coastal Negro Community in British Guiana: a Preliminary Report," *Social and Economic Studies*, Vol. 1, No. 1. Institute of Social and Economic Research, University College of the West Indies, Jamaica.

DON R. HOY

13. Changing Agricultural Land Use on Guadeloupe, French West Indies[1]

Within the Caribbean region, there is an ever-growing awareness of problems which have been brought about by increasing population pressures and limited economic development. Guadeloupe, French West Indies,[2] exemplifies many of the existing problems of the region. In addition, Guadeloupe is of geographic importance for the following reasons. First, it is the largest island of the Lesser Antilles, comprising some 570 square miles within which are examples of nearly every physical setting of the Caribbean zone. Second, Guadeloupe is a faithful miniature of the causes and consequences of land use patterns which in varying degrees are duplicated virtually everywhere in the Antilles. Third, there is a striking localization of agricultural production into separate regions with a sharp boundary zone between crop areas. Fourth, since French settlement in 1635, significant land use changes have occurred at different times. Fifth, Guadeloupe is an area which has received scant attention from American geographers.

This study attempts to analyze the underlying cultural conditions—especially French governmental policies and social structure of Guadeloupean society—that affect, and have affected, agricultural production on Guadeloupe. The study illustrates how these conditions have changed in their impact from time to time, creating different circumstances of crop production. It will show how such crops as tobacco and cotton which were prevalent during the initial stages of French settlement were replaced by sugar cane, coffee, and cacao, and how these in turn were superseded by other crops to form the present agricultural landscape of sugar cane, bananas, and provisions.[3] Stress will be placed on showing that within a given set of

SOURCE: Reproduced by permission of the author and publisher from the *Annals* of the Association of American Geographers, Vol. 52, No. 4 (1962): 441–54.

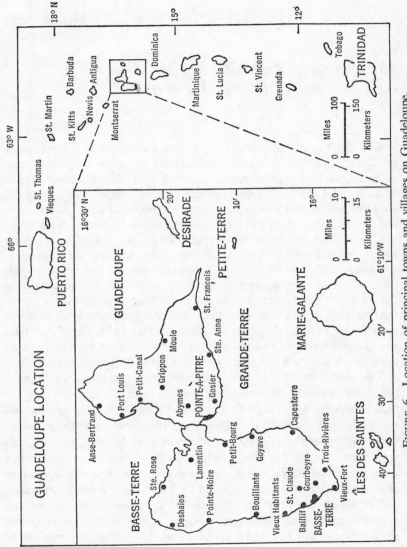

FIGURE 6 Location of principal towns and villages on Guadeloupe.

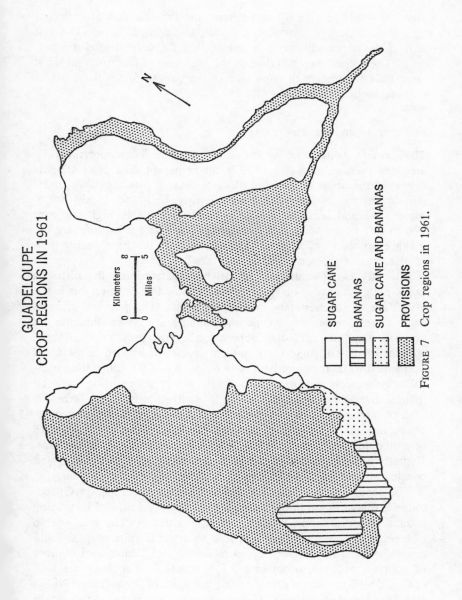

GUADELOUPE
CROP REGIONS IN 1961

Kilometers
0 ___ 5 ___ 8
0 ___ 5
Miles

SUGAR CANE
BANANAS
SUGAR CANE AND BANANAS
PROVISIONS

FIGURE 7 Crop regions in 1961.

physical conditions, land use patterns are dynamic and are affected by a wide variety of historical, political, and cultural forces. The first part of the paper will describe and analyze the current land use patterns. The second part will discuss the evolution of land use and show more fully the impact through time of the various forces listed above on Guadeloupe.

PRESENT LAND USE PATTERN

The present pattern of agricultural land use is characterized by localized monoculture (Fig. 7). In all areas but one, production is devoted to a single crop; in most cases that crop occupies 70 to 80 per cent of the total cultivated area. On the best land, export crops, sugar cane and bananas, dominate, and a relatively high per cent (70 to 90) of the total area is cropped; but where provisions are the major crop, the physical characteristics are such that rarely more than 25 per cent of the total area is cultivated.

Presently two factors are operative in determining the distributional pattern of crops on Guadeloupe. The first of these factors is the utilization of the best land for export crops. The physical circumstances under which sugar cane and bananas are grown illustrate the primary emphasis of Guadeloupe upon export production. Almost without exception, sugar cane and bananas are cultivated in the areas best suited to their respective needs (Figs. 8 and 9). Since the physical requirements for these two crops differ, competition between them for land rarely occurs. Only in southeastern Basse-Terre, an area of increasing banana production, is there any significant competition, and this area is now marginal for sugar cane. Provisions are relegated to areas generally unsuitable for either cane or bananas. Partially as a result, local food crops are relatively low yielding, and considerable amounts of foodstuffs must be imported each year.

The second factor affecting the distribution of crops on Guadeloupe is the variation in the local physical environment and its varying suitability for different kinds of crop production. The relationship of topography, precipitation, and soils to crops is quite simple. Sugar cane, the most important crop in terms of area, value, and number of people employed, occupies the low, relatively flat limestone soils of Grande-Terre and the gently rolling volcanics of Basse-Terre. Within this area terrain, soil, and climatic conditions for cane production are the most favorable on Guadeloupe. The land is generally flat,

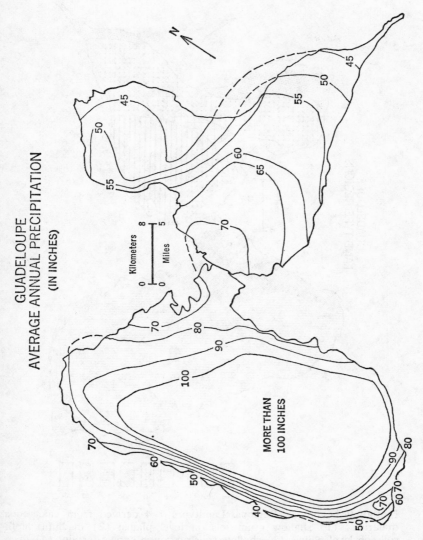

FIGURE 8 Average annual precipitation. Isohyets on Grande-Terre at 5-inch intervals, on Basse-Terre at 10-inch intervals. (Source: *Climatological Data: West Indies and Caribbean Section,* and weather records at Raizet, Guadeloupe.)

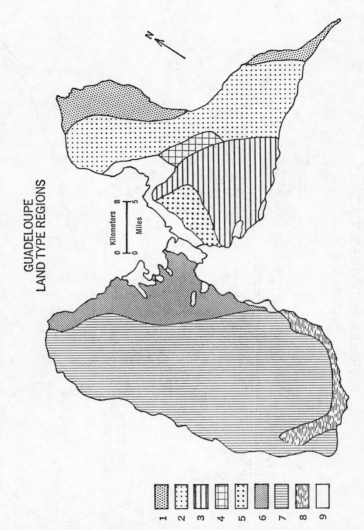

FIGURE 9 Landtype Regions. Landtypes 1–4 derived from calcareous materials: (1) shallow grumusols on level plains; (2) medium depth soils on level plains; (3) shallow soils on rough karstic terrain; (4) deep coluvial soils on level plains. Landtypes 5–8 derived principally from andesitic materials; (5) heavy ferruginous soils on level plains; (6) deep ferrallitics on rolling plains; (7) shallow soils on mountainous terrain; (8) rust-brown ferruginous soils on mountainous terrain; and (9) mangrove swamps.

and the soils are thick and fertile. Annual precipitation varies from 45 inches on the east to 90 inches on the west, with a distinct dry season from December to June. The dry season not only allows for the development of a high sugar content in the cane but also permits the use of trucks and tractors in the field for the harvest period, and, when necessary, for preparing the land for replanting.

Commercial banana production is situated on the lower mountain slopes of southern Basse-Terre, where, although the land is in considerable slope (one banana field is on a 40° slope), the soils are relatively deep and fertile (Fig. 10). Precipitation within the banana zone averages 90 to 120 inches per year; and while there is a less wet season from December to June, rainfall is usually sufficient for near-optimum banana growth. There are also a few banana fields in other areas of Guadeloupe, but these are presently experimental and must be irrigated.

Provisions occupy the remaining parts of Guadeloupe. The physical circumstances under which these food crops are produced vary greatly. On the eastern littoral of Grande-Terre, rainfall is so low that plant desiccation in summer is common. In south-central Grande-Terre, karst topography forms a maze of ridges and valleys with little or no soil on the sloping surfaces. In the area between Grande-Terre and Basse-Terre, low, swampy mangrove forests prevail. In the central part of Basse-Terre, short steep slopes with impoverished soils and high amounts of rainfall and cloud cover create unfavorable circumstances for most crops; and finally on the west coast of Basse-Terre, a leeward situation, steep slopes and moisture deficiency inhibit agricultural development. It is not strange therefore, that within the provisions regions, crop production is limited to a small percentage of the total area, and yields are very low.

Sugar Cane Regions

Each of the major crop regions has characteristic differences in farm size, tenure arrangements, and secondary crops. Within the sugar cane regions there are three basic farm types: the large integrated sugar plantations, the plantation sharecroppers' holdings, and the small owner-operated farms.

Nine sugar plantations[4] with holdings ranging from 2,800 to 20,-000 acres own over one-half of the land of the sugar regions and crop all but the least suitable parts; suitability is determined by the

physical condition of the land and relation to the plantation's processing plant. The plantations employ the most modern methods of sugar
production of any farm type on Guadeloupe; however, in comparison with other parts of the world, these methods must be classed as
relatively archaic and inefficient. While mechanization is increasing,
most operations are still accomplished with manual labor and oxen.

On these plantations sugar cane is the only crop of significance.
There are small areas of pasture upon which oxen are grazed and
still smaller areas on which bananas are produced. The importance
of pasture lands is constantly declining as mechanization is increased.
Bananas are a relatively new crop. Presently most of the plantations
are experimenting with bananas under irrigation in an attempt to diversify their production. The government has recently established a
quota system on sugar production which in the future may curtail the
amount of land devoted to cane.

The less desirable parts of the plantations are divided into small
farms, each operated by a sharecropper (*colon*) who uses only a
few crude hand tools. The *colons* must cultivate a specified amount
of cane and pay as rent one-half of the crop to the plantation. Often
they supplement their income by working as wage laborers on the
plantation. The sharecropper's farm has, in addition to cane, various provisions which are used for the subsistence of the family and,
when a surplus is available, for sale in a nearby market. In addition,
many farmers have a few head of cattle which they pasture around
their dwellings on unused plantation land and between fields.

The land not owned by the plantations is held by several thousand
owner-operators who individually crop very small areas, usually less
than 3 acres (Fig. 11). These farms are similar in appearance to
those of the sharecroppers, although provisions are slightly more
important. Often the owner or members of his family work for the
plantations at various times of the year.

For some time it has been necessary to import foodstuffs for the
local population, and at intervals in the past this situation has
prompted some of the larger farm operators to attempt commercial
truck gardening for the local market. Each time, however, such ven-
tures have failed, the principal cause being the adverse and occasionally violent reaction of the *colons* and small farmers who feel that
provisions production is their exclusive right. Any encroachment
upon this monopoly is met with strikes at harvest time, and for more
harmonious labor relations the plantations, especially since they are

controlled by Metropolitan French and Martiniquian capital, have not in recent years attempted to compete on the local market with their *colons* and wage laborers.

In addition to differences in secondary crops between the plantations and the land held by the *colons* and small farmers, differences exist in sugar yields. In part, this difference can be attributed to the generally poorer physical conditions and cruder techniques of the *colons* and small planters, but the French Government also plays a role in causing differences in yields. Under present statutes, the plantation sugar mills must buy cane on the basis of weight and not on sugar content. These laws encourage the growth of cane varieties which produce a great deal of matter but not necessarily much sugar. As a result, yields of sugar on the *colon* and small properties are often one-third to one-half those of nearby plantations.

It will be noted from the above that both latifundia and minifundia are common within the sugar cane regions. Currently there exist few "medium-sized" farms between 3 and 200 acres within the cane region, and the number of such farms is continually decreasing due indirectly to the actions of the French Government and to the social attitudes of the Guadeloupeans. In 1946, Guadeloupe was made an overseas department; and with the change in political status, the wage laws of France became effective in Guadeloupe, resulting in substantial pay increases and benefits to all salaried workers. While these increased wages were partially compensated for by higher subsidies for sugar, profits from cane production were reduced. The medium-sized farms were unable to improve their cultivation techniques and hence became progressively submarginal. On the plantations, plant modernization and greater mechanization in part compensated for increased rates. On small farms, the family supplied the labor, and thus these were unaffected by the wage laws.

Social conditions within Gaudeloupe have led to the destruction of medium-sized cane farms in two ways. First, in spite of repeated attempts by the government and employers to improve labor efficiency, antiquated and uneconomical production methods are still used. Illustrative of the tenacity with which the cane worker clings to tradition is his method of harvesting cane. Formerly when cane was processed in small sugar mills, it had to be cut in one-meter lengths. By the end of the nineteenth century, more advanced mills had been erected and the necessity of short cane lengths was removed. The workers, however, refused to change from the traditional method of cane cutting and today still harvest as their ancestors did, resulting in low productivity per worker. Because of this trait and the increased labor costs brought about by the government in 1946, many medium-sized farms have not been able to produce cane on a competitive basis with either the small family farms or the large, more mechanized plantations.

Second, the Guadeloupean worker places a premium upon leisure time and is not greatly motivated by the desire for economic gain. Frequently these laborers work only long enough to buy a particular item, such as a suit, a hat, or a dress. In spite of a dense rural population within the cane regions, there is often a critical shortage of labor during the latter part of the harvesting season; absenteeism is prevalent and only one-half of the original labor force may remain. The plantations have partly solved this problem by renting some of their land to *colons,* who may be required to work on plantation-cultivated land if needed. The small family farms do not have this labor problem; it is the medium-sized farms which suffer from this social condition, for they are not large enough to develop effectively a *colon*-owner relationship and still produce an adequate profit.

Banana Region

For years, sugar cane has been the traditional export crop of Guadeloupe, but recently the development of bananas for export has lessened the island's dependence upon sugar. In the banana region, farm size varies from less than 5 acres to as much as 600 acres, with a considerable portion between 5 and 200 acres. The smaller farms are normally owner-operated with the owner supplying the required labor. On the larger farms, absentee ownership is common, and a resident manager is responsible for maintaining an adequate supply of labor and producing and marketing the crops.

The rugged topography of the banana zone prohibits mechanization, and no advantage results to the large units over medium-sized farms as in the sugar cane regions. Care and cultivation of bananas are spread relatively evenly throughout the year, and hence there is no seasonal labor demand as in the cane areas. On both large- and medium-sized farms, the problem of labor shortage is partially solved by allowing a substantial proportion of the workers to live on the farm and raise provisions among the banana plants. While the growth of provisions and bananas within the same field lowers banana yields, the entrepreneur accepts this loss for the advantage of a permanent labor supply.

Actually farms within the region are undergoing both consolidation and parcelling. In the areas where transportation facilities are well developed, farms tend to increase in size. In the more remote areas, however, small units predominate, and some of the large farms are undergoing morselling.

Bananas and provisions are not the only crops grown. On almost every farm regardless of size, coffee and, to a lesser extent, cacao are intertilled with bananas. These plants are relics of past land use in the region. While profits from coffee and cacao are not as great as profits from bananas, the farm operators prefer to place at least part of their production in these "insurance" crops. When droughts or winds severely damage the banana plants, a complete crop loss is averted by harvesting coffee and cacao. Where moisture conditions are better for banana growth, however, coffee and cacao yields are normally so low that the crops may not even be harvested.

Provisions Regions

In contrast to the banana and sugar cane areas, which yield the principal exports of Guadeloupe, only a small amount of the total land within the provisions regions is effectively used. Much of the area is incapable under present economic conditions of any substantial production and is allowed to remain idle or is used sparingly for grazing.

Within the provisions regions, farms are small and are owned or squatted upon by agriculturists who intertill a multitude of various foodstuffs in small gardens with the aid of only a few tools. As in many tropical and subtropical areas the composition of plants within gardens varies seasonally, but the most important ones include varieties of beans, peas, and yams, and manioc, yautia (*Xanthosoma sagittifolium*), sweet potato, eggplant, and bananas. Around the farmer's house and within the garden are normally several fruit trees such as breadfruit, mango, and guava. Throughout Guadeloupe, the basic composition of the provisions garden is the same, although there are differences in the relative importance of the plants depending in part upon the physical circumstances of the area.

As indicated earlier, provisions production on Guadeloupe is insufficient to supply the needs of the population. This situation exists primarily because of past and present French governmental actions.

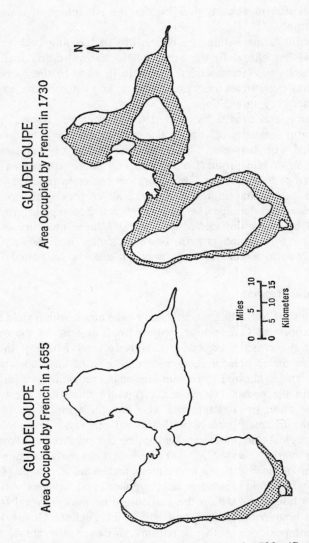

FIGURE 10   Area occupied by French in 1655 and 1730. (Source: *Histoire de la Guadeloupe sous l'Ancien Régime* [Paris, 1928].)

Traditionally the government has encouraged export crop cultivation and in effect, by acts of omission, has hindered the production of local foodstuffs. This situation has been created by the desire of the French Government to keep Guadeloupe and other French territories dependent upon Metropolitan France and to supply France with an outlet for agricultural surplus.

HISTORICAL SEQUENCE OF AGRICULTURAL LAND USE

While the above analysis of recent conditions of agricultural land use and their attendant ramifications leads to a partial explanation of crop distribution and agricultural characteristics of Guadeloupe, a much greater insight may be gained by an examination of the origin of land use patterns. It is also possible that certain apparently inappropriate land use characteristics of the present can be more logically explained through their historical development. The following section will discuss the principal characteristics and patterns of land use on Guadeloupe at five different periods of time, and will illustrate the dynamic nature of land use upon a static physical setting.

Early French Colonization

The first land use period began in 1635 with French colonization on Guadeloupe, and ended in the latter part of the 1660's (Fig. 10A). Prior to the arrival of the French, the indigenes had cultivated small gardens in Basse-Terre. These gardens were composed of a number of plants native to the Americas including maize, manioc, pineapple, cotton, peanuts, and tobacco, and Old World crops including bananas, sugar cane, and coconuts, which the Indians had obtained through contacts with European colonies in other parts of the Caribbean.[5] Although the Indians were quickly decimated, their system of gardens was preserved on the small farms of nearly every colonist and became the antecedent of the provisions gardens of today.

As colonization continued, commercial agriculture developed, oriented toward the production of tobacco for export to France. Tobacco became the leading crop on Guadeloupe primarily through acts of the French Government. Taxes were paid in tobacco and for a time it was used in place of coin for money. Every colonist was required to produce on his farm, in addition to his own provisions crops, a specified amount of either cotton or tobacco.[6] Cotton, however, was not important in this period, since tobacco proved to be a much more profitable crop; and many ship captains refused to carry cotton as cargo because of the fire hazard. When it appeared in the 1640's that colonial production of tobacco would saturate the French market, the government attempted by various decrees to limit and in some cases prohibit the production of tobacco in the Caribbean territories and directed the farmers to increase their plantings of cotton and annato (*Bixa orellana*).[7] These decrees were only moderately successful, but in 1674, the sale of tobacco became a monopoly of the government. Strict controls were effected, and tobacco production on Guadeloupe steadily declined. Tobacco production presently is prohibited by law.

The development of tobacco illustrated the general attitude of the French towards their Caribbean possessions and indicated the power of the government to direct agricultural production. One purpose for colonizing Guadeloupe and other parts of the Caribbean was to develop trade between this region and France. It was implicit that the economy of the area be supplementary to that of France, and that the resulting trade be beneficial to France though not necessarily to the territories. The official instrument by which France regulated the economies of her territories was the *Pacte Colonial*.[8] In essence, the pact had five major provisos, which were: (1) the territory must produce commodities suitable for the French market not already produced in France, (2) the territory must act as a market for French products, (3) the territory must not produce commodities which could be supplied by France, (4) the territory must not develop any industry which could create competition with French industries, and (5) transportation of products between France and the territory must be accomplished by French nationals.[9] These provisos formed the basic framework by which the Guadeloupean economy was regulated, although for short periods some departures were permitted. They also isolated Guadeloupe from other parts of the world, even from other French colonies. Officially the pact was abolished in 1861; in practice, however, it is still operative.

Development of Sugar Cane

As restrictions on tobacco production were increased, rapid changes occurred in the agricultural pattern of Guadeloupe during the second land use period, 1670–1730's. By 1730, sugar cane had become the principal export crop, and all of coastal Basse-Terre and most of Grande-Terre were parcelled into farms in association with the extension of cane (Fig. 10B).

Sugar, like tobacco, was developed through the efforts of the French Government. While the plant itself had been introduced into the area by the Indians, its importance as an export crop was not fully realized until the 1650's, when a group of farmers of Dutch background, who came from Brazil and possessed improved techniques of cane raising and sugar processing, were granted land by the government for the express purpose of producing cane and teaching the Guadeloupeans the essentials of cane culture. (After the Guadeloupeans had learned cane culture, the Dutch were forced to move from the island.)[10]

Associated with the arrival of the Dutch was the introduction of slave trade, also under government auspices. The influx of slaves permitted the rapid development of Grande-Terre and hastened the extension of cane cultivation in preference to other crops, for relatively unskilled labor could be used in sugar production, but greater skills were necessary with tobacco and cotton.

As a corollary to the arrival of the Dutch and the slaves, immigrants from France during this period were generally wealthier than the original colonists. Both the Dutch and the more wealthy French immigrants were granted concessions of land ranging from 250 to 750 acres on much of Grande-Terre and the eastern littoral of Basse-Terre. These large units were established in previously unoccupied areas and were devoted almost exclusively to the production of sugar for export, although provisions also were cultivated for the slaves and laborers on the farms. Each farm was organized for manufacture as well as agriculture, and the cane was processed in the farm's small sugar mill.

Diversification of Agriculture

As the second land use period progressed, there was a greater and greater tendency towards the exclusive production of sugar cane in preference to other crops for export. Between 1730 and 1790, the third land use period, the development of cotton and coffee retarded the trend toward a sugar monoculture. It is within this period that Guadeloupe experienced its greatest crop diversification (Fig. 11).

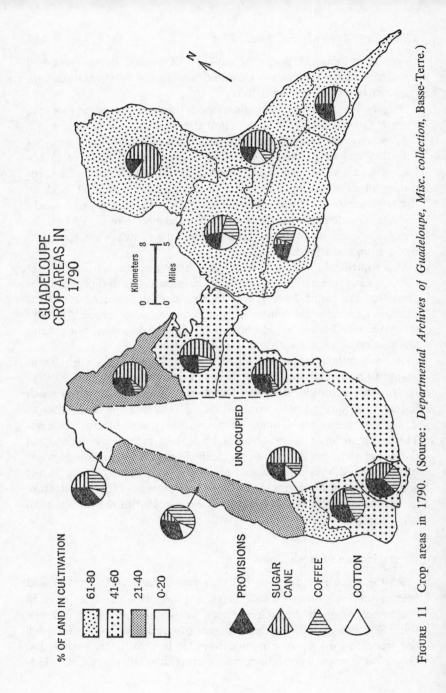

FIGURE 11 Crop areas in 1790. (Source: *Departmental Archives of Guadeloupe, Misc. collection*, Basse-Terre.)

Throughout the period, the area devoted to sugar cane continued to increase, and by 1790 approximately 52,000 acres were in cane, nearly the same amount as at present. Most of the sugar cane, however, was produced on large farms with a general reduction of cane on the smaller units. With the decline of cane as an important crop on the small farms, its area of dominance was slightly contracted to Grande-Terre and eastern Basse-Terre.

As sugar cane decreased in importance on the smaller farms, cotton and coffee replaced it. Until 1760, cotton on Guadeloupe was of little importance for export, since it was considered a fire hazard on board ship. As the price of cotton increased in France, however, greater demands by the French Government were made on the ship captains; and finally the captains were ordered to accept cotton as cargo. While cotton was produced for the French market in other territories, it appears that Guadeloupean cotton brought premium prices, since it was of the long-staple Sea Island variety.

The second crop which retarded the movement towards a sugar monoculture was coffee. In the 1720's, the local Guadeloupean Government sponsored the introduction of coffee from Martinique with the reservation that coffee production should in no way interfere with sugar cane.[11] Coffee did usurp some land from sugar cane, and through the 1720's and early 1730's, coffee production within the French Caribbean greatly expanded. In order to protect the new crop, an import duty was placed on foreign coffee entering France, and under the protection of tariffs, the area devoted to coffee on Guadeloupe steadily increased until the 1790's.

During the 1790's, the period of the French Revolution, the instability of the government both on Guadeloupe and in France affected Guadeloupean agriculture. As in France, an approach to anarchy existed in her territories of the Caribbean. Slavery was abolished only to be reinstated when Napoleon became the head of state; battles were fought between the monarchists, who were in a majority on Guadeloupe, and various expeditionary forces sent by the revolutionary government of France; there were several revolts by the Negroes on Guadeloupe and a general exodus of these people from the more settled portions of the island; crop production dropped severely; many fields were destroyed; numerous whites were killed or fled, and farms were abandoned. Furthermore, the transportation lines between Guadeloupe and France were harassed by the British. As a result of these conditions, agricultural production was severely cur-

tailed and crops such as cotton and coffee, which required a great
deal of care and a considerable time to mature, were largely discontinued.

Crop Specialization

With the rise of Napoleon, the fourth land use period on Guadeloupe was inaugurated and lasted until the 1920's. During this time
several changes occurred in the agricultural landscape of Guadeloupe; two changes were most fundamental. First, there was a general
decrease in the production of all crops except provisions, although
sugar cane was less affected than other export crops. Second, beginning in the 1850's, the farms devoted to sugar cane on Grande-Terre
and eastern Basse-Terre underwent either consolidation or morselling.

The first change was brought about by shifting French policies
and governments that seriously deterred the production of crops,
such as cotton and coffee, which required a considerable time to mature. Government policies changed so rapidly that the colonial farmer
was unable to determine whether his crop would be protected by
tariffs in the French market by the time it was ready for harvest.[12] As
a result, crops which required a long time to mature and hence required greater foresight tended to be abandoned. The uncertainty
was as great for sugar cane; however, since sugar cane required only
a relatively short time to mature and since it already had become a
"traditional" crop of Guadeloupe, its position became progressively
more important.

An example of the effect of shifting governmental policies is noted
with sugar cane. Between 1791 and 1810, eighteen different laws
were passed in France affecting duties on colonial and foreign sugar;
the net result was to increase duties on all sugar.[13] In 1814, the
import duty on colonial sugar was made the same as that on foreign
sugar, but in 1816 colonial sugar again gained protection in France
when the foreign duty was increased. By 1821, duties on foreign
sugar had become so high that their imports no longer offered competition to the colonial producers. The colonial producers soon faced
a new challenge to their market in France, which was much more
fundamental and serious. In 1826, the beet sugar industry of France
began a rapid extension under government support. Increased beet
sugar production from 3,400 metric tons in 1828 to 50,000 metric

tons in 1836 brought serious repercussion to the colonial producer, for the tax-free beet sugar was able to undersell the cheaper but heavily taxed colonial sugar. Throughout the remainder of the nineteenth century, a continual battle was waged between the colonial cane producers and the proponents of beet sugar in France. Sometimes there was a general equalization of duties so that neither faction gained an advantage, but most of the time the beet sugar producers had a favored position.

The second fundamental change of the period was also related to shifting governmental policies. From French settlement to about 1850, farms underwent little change, but beginning in the latter half of the nineteenth century, the sugar cane farms between 250 and 750 acres were either consolidated into larger holdings gradually evolving into the present nine large plantations, or were morselled into many thousand small farms. Consolidation occurred on the best cane lands and parcelling in the poorer areas.

These changes, although precipitated by the government, were not brought about intentionally. As the conditions of the Guadeloupean cane producer worsened through competition on the French market, the French Government established the *Crédit Foncier Colonial,* a bank designed to aid the cane growers by granting them loans at fairly low interest rates. Very few farmers were able to repay these loans, and within a few years the bank controlled most of the cane area.[14] The land was offered for sale; and since the population of Guadeloupe was almost completely destitute, the best lands were bought at low prices by companies based largely in France. Land not suitable for sugar cane was divided into small farms and distributed among local inhabitants.

Another factor which led to the destruction of farms was the emancipation of the slaves in 1848.[15] The proclamation freeing the slaves precipitated the already imminent ruin of most slave-using farms. Many of the newly freed slaves refused to work for their former owners, and many owners refused to pay their former slaves. Some Negroes moved to areas ineffectively occupied, principally in the south-central portion of Grande-Terre where they subsisted, and still subsist, on provision gardens. Most became squatters in the cane regions; and where this land was not effectively controlled by the plantations, because of its distance from the processing plant or unfavorable physical setting for cane production, they gained possession by default. There has never been a cadastral survey of Guadeloupe.

With the outflow of workers, the plantations were severely pressed for a labor supply, and it was during this time that the system of sharecroppers was begun in order to obtain the needed labor.

TABLE 1.—PRINCIPAL EXPORTS OF GUADELOUPE
FOR 1955 TO 1958 (METRIC TONS)*

Item	1955	1956	1957	1958
Sugar	125,672	123,287	113,028	113,661
Bananas	66,416	57,045	79,427	94,097
Molasses	17,551	15,390	10,966	12,325
Rum	7,206	8,287	9,766	8,558
Coffee	226	386	64	196
Cacao	132	161	47	109
Vanilla	4	6	0	3
Others	3,484	3,291	1,234	1,909
Total	220,691	207,853	214,532	230,858

* Compiled from information given by the Service des Douanes de la Guadeloupe.

Another result of these changes was a disassociation of cane and provisions production. Where plantations developed, the area of provisions was greatly decreased and the production of sugar cane augmented. In the areas where parcelling of the farms occurred, the sugar acreage was reduced; and the amount of provisions was greatly increased, leading to the present-day distribution within the sugar cane and provisions regions of Grande-Terre and eastern Basse-Terre.

Development of Banana Cultivation

By 1920, the current land use patterns were essentially established on all but southern Basse-Terre (Fig. 12). Prior to the 1920's, southern Basse-Terre was characterized by small farms devoted to provisions, coffee, and, to a much lesser extent, cacao; commonly, these crops were intertilled and shaded by bananas. After World War I, however, coffee and cacao production became increasingly uneconomical through increased competition on the French market from African colonies, and export banana production began. Between the two world wars, the production of bananas constantly increased, accomplished in some cases by the removal of coffee and cacao trees,

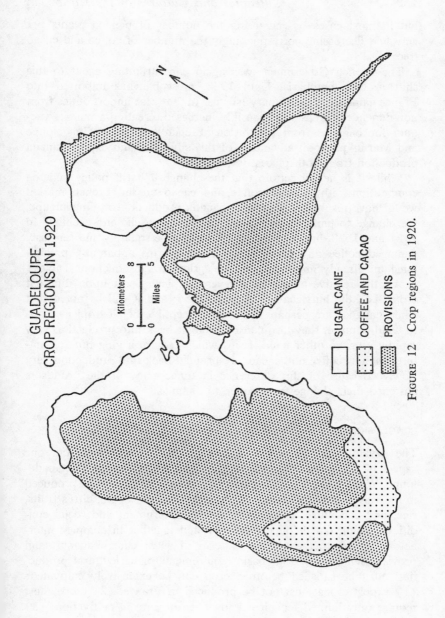

GUADELOUPE
CROP REGIONS IN 1920

N

Kilometers
0   8
0   5
Miles

☐ SUGAR CANE

∴ COFFEE AND CACAO

▓ PROVISIONS

FIGURE 12   Crop regions in 1920.

but in most cases by increasing the number of banana plants per acre and decreasing correspondingly the number of coffee and cacao trees.

The French Government was again a contributing agent to this shift in crop emphasis. Until 1928, most bananas imported into France came from the Canary Islands. In that year import duties from non-dependent areas were sensibly increased, creating a market vacuum for bananas from the various French territories. Guadeloupe and Martinique took advantage of this situation, and export banana production from both places developed.

While it is nearly certain that the change in tariff policy and the competition with African coffee and cacao on the French market would have resulted in increased banana production on Guadeloupe, the change to bananas was greatly hastened by climatic events.[16] In 1921 and 1928, hurricanes struck Guadeloupe squarely and seriously damaged coffee and cacao trees. These storms apparently precipitated an already imminent shift in agricultural production. Table 1 shows the relative effects of a severe tropical storm upon different crops, i.e., the hurricane of August, 1956; and it will be noted that while bananas are perhaps the most susceptible of all tropical crops to wind damage, they also can be brought back into production very rapidly. On the other hand, crops which require a long time to mature, such as coffee and cacao, are brought back into production very slowly. Because of this difference in time, many of the producers hastened their change from coffee to bananas.

CONCLUSIONS

The development of export banana production represents but one aspect of the constantly changing agricultural landscape on Guadeloupe. While there is a wide variety of crops which could be produced in the varied physical setting of the area (i.e., pineapple, citrus fruits, rice, and coconuts), the policies of the government and social conditions within Guadeloupe have operated together in complex interactions to create the current patterns of sugar cane, bananas, and provisions. Presently four basic requirements of agricultural production must be satisfied before a crop can be extensively cultivated: (1) export crops must not be produced in France, (2) crops must require only limited technical knowledge or care in cultivation, (3) crops must be quick-maturing and yield a rapid financial return on the initial investment, and (4) crops must be adaptable to the varied tropical environment of Guadeloupe and quickly return to production after storm damage. The cultivation of sugar cane, bananas, and provisions readily fits the above requirements.

There are several general conclusions which can be drawn from the above study. First, the study shows that a proper appreciation of present agricultural characteristics must be the result not only of present land use conditions but also those of the past. Second, agricultural land use is dynamic, and within Guadeloupe, the direction of agricultural development has been effectively directed by a variety of political, social, and cultural forces. Third, Guadeloupe characterizes many of the agricultural conditions common throughout the Antilles and other dependent areas of the tropics. A study of other areas should lead to fuller understanding of these conditions.

Notes:

1. Data for this study were collected while the writer was engaged in field research supported by the Foreign Research Program and under the direction of the Division of Earth Sciences, National Academy of Sciences–National Research Council, and financed by the Geography Branch of the Office of Naval Research under contract Nonr-2300(09).

2. For the purposes of this study, the term "Guadeloupe" is confined to the islands of Grande- and Basse-Terre. Politically Guadeloupe encompasses several other much smaller islands such as la Desirade, les Saintes, and Marie Galente. On these small islands, agriculture is limited to subsistence crops, except on Marie Galente where small amounts of sugar cane are produced.

3. Crops used for subsistence by the local population are grouped under the term "provisions," for they may be cultivated either on the subsistence level or for sale in a local market. The various plants are intertilled, and the composition of the provisions fields varies seasonally.

4. Guy Lasserre, "Une Plantation de canne aux Antilles: La Sucrerie Beauport," *Les Cahiers d'Outre-Mer, V* (October–December, 1952), pp. 297–329, gives an analysis of one of these plantations.

5. Maurice Satineau, *Histoire de la Guadeloupe sous l'Ancien Régime* (Paris: Payot, 1928), pp. 21–22.

6. Stewart L. Mims, *Colbert's West India Policy* (New Haven: Yale University Press, 1912), p. 25.

7. *Ibid.*

8. Auguste Rochette, *Étude sur les Rapports Commerciaux de la France et de ses Colonies* (Paris: A. Pedone, 1897), pp. 43–44.

9. Rochette, *op. cit.*, pp. 8–10.

10. Satineau, *op. cit.*, pp. 120–21.

11. Jules Ballet, "The Ballet Manuscripts" (Departmental Archives of Guadeloupe), Vol. VII, p. 128.

12. Shepard B. Clough, *France: A History of National Economics; 1789–1939* (New York: Charles Scribner's Sons, 1939), pp. 42 *et passim.*

13. Rochette, *op. cit.*, pp. 28–29.

14. Charles Robequain, "Le Sucre dans l'Union Française," *Annales de Géographie*, LVII (October–December, 1948), p. 328.

15. Louis Joubert, "Les Conséquences Géographiques de l'Emancipation des Noirs aux Antilles (1848)," *Les Cahiers d'Outre-Mer, I* (April–June, 1948), pp. 105–18.

16. A. Kopp, "L'Agriculture a la Guadeloupe," *Annales de Géographie*, XXXIX (1929), p. 490, believes that the hurricane of 1775 led to a shift in production from coffee to sugar.

HERMAN J. FINKEL

14. Patterns of Land Tenure in the Leeward and Windward Islands and Their Relevance to Problems of Agricultural Development in the West Indies

The Leewards and the Windwards in the British West Indies are facing a problem common to many newly developing countries, namely, the fuller development of their agricultural potential for the purpose of raising the standard of living. Agricultural development is predicated as being prior to industrial development because of the dearth of materials and sources of power for the latter and because of the inadequate levels of education and technical training. The existing agricultural resources of these islands include fertile soils, mild climate, long growing seasons, adequate rainfall in many parts of the islands, topographic and climatic variations permitting a certain amount of crop diversification, a potential labor supply, and potential markets. Many of these resources are far from fully utilized at the present time, however. The author was asked to outline a program of agricultural development for the region with special emphasis on the utilization of soil and water resources. As typical islands representing the range of natural conditions prevalent in the Caribbean chain, the following were chosen: St. Kitts and Nevis in the Leewards, and Dominica and St. Lucia in the Windwards.

It became obvious during the field work that it would be difficult to separate the technical considerations of agricultural development from certain basic problems arising out of the various prevailing systems of land tenure or correlated with them. Each of the four islands studied was characterized by a different pattern of land settlement, the readjustment of which appeared to be a prerequisite to

SOURCE: Reprinted from *Economic Geography*, Vol. 40, No. 2 (1964):163–72, by permission of the author and publisher.

further agricultural progress. A program of soil and water development divorced from the considerations of land tenure would lead to
economically unjustified investments, and would ultimately fail. The
problems of these tiny islands are of general interest because they
represent, in miniature, the problems of many larger countries.

GENERAL DESCRIPTION OF THE ISLANDS

For purposes of general background, the essential geographical information about the four islands is summarized in Table I. Some idea
of the pressure of the population on the land in each of the four
islands may be gained from the densities given in Table II.

By way of comparison, the population densities per square mile
of total and cultivable areas, respectively, for various parts of the
world are as follows: India—114 and 250; Japan—243 and 1775;
China—65 and 570; the countries of the European Common Market
—140 and 208; and the United States—22 and 32. It is seen, therefore,
that all of the islands except Dominica have relatively high gross
population densities, and the net density (in terms of arable land)
is high in all four of the islands. This pressure on the land serves to
intensify the importance of the land tenure patterns.

PATTERNS OF LAND TENURE AND LAND USE
IN THE FOUR ISLANDS

Although part of the same geographical group, each of the four islands studied is characterized by a distinct pattern of land tenure
and land use. These differences are partly the result of climatic and
topographic characteristics, which dictate choice of crops. No less
influential, however, are the socioeconomic factors which, in each
case, have resulted in unique and distinctive forms of land settlement
and tenure which may be described as follows.

St. Kitts

St. Kitts is one of the few remaining examples of the almost pure
estate economy of the 19th century. Most of the 27,000 acres of
total arable land is held by 74 private estates ranging in size from
100 to 600 acres. They are grouped around the central mountain
range in more or less irregular sectors, each containing a portion of
the gently sloping coastal plain and an area of the wooded upland.
The lower areas are all planted to sugar cane and in some cases the

cane fields are pushed up the slopes toward the center. Much of the forest land above the line of cultivation also belongs to the estates. The total sugar area is 16,000 acres producing from 400,000 to 430,-000 tons of canes annually, yielding approximately 50,000 tons of sugar. The estates all belong to the association of sugar planters which operates a central sugar factory near the capital, Basseterre. There is a narrow gauge railroad which encircles the island and collects the canes from every estate. This organization of field and factory functions efficiently and has maintained a high level of productivity over many years. Some of the estates are worked by resident owners while others are operated by professional managers with the owners absent. The latter type are often owned by partnerships or corporations located abroad.

There are practically no small landowners on the island. The Government has attempted a few small land settlement schemes by which small tracts of land were made available to the cane workers for the growing of provisions, but these schemes have met with very limited success so far. It is remarkable that in these times of worldwide agrarian reform there has been little demand on the part of the Kittitians for land redistribution. They have also evinced very little enthusiasm for the growing of either food crops or sugar cane on small plots. There have been instances where the small farmer would not bother to reap the harvest *on his own tract of land,* which had been planted with the aid and persuasion of the Ministry of Agriculture. The popular indifference to the growing of food crops has been explained partly by the lack of adequate market facilities, partly by the existence of unrealistically low ceiling prices on farm produce, especially proteins, and partly because of the prevalence of praedial larceny in the fields.

The anachronism of a pure estate economy in the latter half of the 20th century has, on St. Kitts, given rise to several paradoxes which are not easy to explain. Of a population of 37,000, less than 100 own agricultural land, and yet there is no appreciable land hunger or desire on the part of many to become landowners. Although the dense population and lack of industrial development have caused considerable unemployment, the sugar planters have difficulty in finding enough hands to reap the canes. Last year a fair part of the crop was left unharvested in the field because of the labor shortage. However, despite a general disinclination toward agricultural work on the part of a large segment of the population, there is a general demand for a higher standard of living which has prompted the usual trend from the villages to the town, where employment is sought in commerce and the services. The great hope of those islanders with aspirations toward self-betterment, is migration to England, Canada, or the United States. Unfortunately, the sense of partnership between the people and the land, in St. Kitts, seems to have been broken. The majority see no future in agriculture and express little desire for land ownership. This attitude may be an outgrowth of the old system of slavery, under which man was linked to the land by forced labor, often under conditions of privation and cruelty. Although the slaves were emancipated in 1830 in the West Indies, the association of agricultural work with compulsory and menial servitude has persisted in the minds of subsequent generations until this day. This is a difficult sociological and psychological problem of far-reaching implications.

If the 74 estate owners are prepared to continue their present operations, and there is little land hunger among the bulk of the population, the question may well be asked: why change anything? What is wrong with the *status quo?* Cane has been grown on this island continuously for over 300 years and the economy has remained viable. With proper fertilization, maintenance of trash cover, and selection of new genetic varieties the productivity of the soil and protection against erosion have been well provided for. Why, then, should not the present land use pattern be encouraged to persist? Unfortunately, however, the economic future of sugar growing is no longer assured. The danger threatening the prevailing monoculture is not agricultural but economic. The cost of sugar production is steadily rising because of increased labor costs. With the organization of strong trade unions, wages have gone up but labor productivity has fallen.[1] Despite the improved wages, the workers gravitate to town. Moreover, emigration has depleted both the sugar factory and the estates of the most skilled workers and much time and money must be invested in the training of new workers in the technical phases of the work. Coupled with these rising costs of production the sugar industry is faced with the threat of falling prices due to a decline in the world price of sugar and the reduction in the size of the preferential quota offered to St. Kitts by Great Britain. The European Common Market poses an even more serious threat to future sugar exports from the West Indies. The margin of profit is very narrow at the present time and in some estates the break-even point has already been reached and operations are at a loss. If the sugar industry should continue to grow less profitable it would spell the complete economic collapse of the island. Most of the food and all of the consumers' goods are imported and paid for with earnings from sugar. The economic situation is therefore one of extreme vulnerability.

The danger could be averted, to a certain extent, by greater agricultural diversification, toward vegetable growing, citrus fruits, meat, and dairy products. The gradual changeover toward other crops could actually be more easily accomplished under the present estate system, given the recognition on the part of the planters of the need for diversification. The cooperative aspects of the sugar growers association could also be put to good use in sharing the initial risks of introduction of new crops. On the other hand, the prevailing land tenure system also has certain distinct disadvantages to the process of diversification. With the concentration of the land in the hands of a few, the general population of the island would tend to be indifferent to the success of the new agricultural enterprises, since they do not appreciate the clear connection between the profitability of the island's agriculture and their own economic welfare. Diversification would thus not become the common concern of the islanders, and the necessary labor force would be hard to recruit, and internal markets would be difficult to organize. The demand for locally-grown products would be slow to develop since the people have grown accustomed, over generations, to consume imported foods purchased with sugar.

Nevis

The island of Nevis belongs to the same administrative unit as St. Kitts, and is separated from it by straits two miles wide. Nevertheless, the patterns of land tenure and land use in the two sister islands are as different as though they were located in separate continents. Nevis also was, at one time, a predominantly sugar estate economy. The hundred or more estates which covered the island each had its own grinding mill and boiling works for the production of muscovado sugar. Life centered around the Great House, with its conical windmill tower of beautifully wrought cut-stone, its tall, masonry smokestack, its independent water supply, and its surrounding cluster of cabins for the workers, formerly slaves. The landscape of Nevis is dotted with the ruins of these structures. Sugar has been produced on the island from 1697 to modern times with annual yields varying from 1000 to 4000 tons. However, with the opening of the modern sugar factory in Basseterre, St. Kitts, it suddenly became uneconomical to produce sugar in the old individual boiling houses, and production fell off sharply in Nevis. Since it was necessary to ship the canes across the straits by launch most of the estates found this too expensive, and went out of sugar growing completely. Subsequently, attempts were made to introduce Sea Island cotton as a substitute cash crop, but in recent years the acreage of this crop has continuously declined. As a result of this collapse most of the estates have been abandoned by their owners, and the government has taken over 15 farms, having a total acreage of 5129 (out of a total island area of 23,000 acres). On some of this former estate land the government is attempting to develop herds of cattle and improved communal pastures. On the other areas, land settlement schemes have been started for small farmers, but so far with only limited success.

Table III indicates the prevailing land tenure pattern of the island, as reported by the agricultural census of 1956–1958. From this table it can be seen that 94 per cent of the farmers own less than 5 acres apiece, totaling only 27 per cent of the land. Of the large holdings, 64 per cent of the land is in blocks of over 50 acres, most of which have been taken over by the government. (There is also a certain area of Crown Land not subdivided, and not included in the above table.) This picture represents, on the one hand, the typical *minifundia,* or fragmentation of small holdings so well known throughout Latin America. But on the other end of the scale we do not find the typical *latifundia,* or concentration of larger area in a few hands since the estates have been, for the most part, abandoned. This is a curious situation since the government is quite prepared, and even anxious, to redistribute this land to the small holders, but cannot find many takers. There are several reasons which may possibly explain this reluctance on the part of the islanders to acquire land. Primarily, there seems to be a lack of a basic plan for profitable agricultural production in Nevis. Although there is a great need for vegetable, dairy, and meat products, which could be raised on the island, the people see little hope for profit in these branches because of inadequate technical training coupled with a lack of adequate distribution and marketing facilities. The second reason is historical. The sugar estates, in their heyday, were far more than mere cane plantations. Each one was a centralized socio-economic unit which encompassed every aspect of life. The workers lived in small cabins around a Great House, where the social activities of the planter class provided a focus of interest and excitement for all of the people, even though most of them had no share in these events. The planter had a paternalistic concern for the welfare of his workers and their families and relieved them of a large measure of responsibility for their daily problems. The standard of living was not high, and the degree of exploitation of labor was considerable, but the rule was generally accepted willingly and cheerfully. Today, after the complete breakdown of the estate economy, many people are still inclined to yearn nostalgically for the good old days of the Great House, rather than assuming with ambition and enthusiasm the responsibility for working out their own destinies.

It may be said that Nevis is suffering from the burden of a glorious past. Everywhere on the island the ruins of the old windmills and boiling houses cast long shadows across the now derelict fields and remind the people of former days of thriving plantocracy when there was work for all. The once elegant spa at Bath Estate now stands empty and silent. The land, shorn of its protective cover of sugar cane, reveals, in all its harshness, the eroded, stony soil and the boulders which are the heritage of ancient volcanic eruptions. The streams are dry and the wells brackish. The few coconut plantations are neglected, and the pastures are little more than rocky wasteland. The islanders are permeated with a sense of discouragement and defeat alleviated occasionally by the expression of the idle hope that one day, when a sugar factory will be built on the island, Nevis will be liberated from the oppressive alliance with St. Kitts, and will regenerate some of her past grandeur. This dream of salvation is, of course, doomed to frustration since even St. Kitts is actively searching for an alternative to sugar monoculture.

Dominica

Dominica is one of the largest islands in the Windwards, and is characterized by steep, rough topography, heavy forests, and few roads. The land tenure pattern is indicated in Table IV, based on the 1958 Census. This table shows that the majority of the farms are operated by farmers on their own account (whether tenants or landlords) and only a few farms are operated by professional managers. These few, however, include 38 farms of over 100 acres each totaling almost 24,000 acres. This represents 0.4 per cent of the total number of farms and 33 per cent of the total farm area. Together, the 85 large estates (100 acres+) include 40,000 acres of a total land area in farms of 72,408 acres, or 55 per cent, which are operated by less than 1 per cent of the farmers. At the other end of the scale there are 8027 farmers with less than 5 acres each, totaling

16,293 acres. This represents 91 per cent of the farmers and 22.4 per cent of the land. The intermediate size farms, from 10 to 50 acres, are held by 680 farmers (7.7 per cent) covering 16,043 acres of land (22 per cent).

The larger farms are located in the few, narrow alluvial valleys, and are served by the sparse network of existing roads. The smaller farms are in the steep, inaccessible hinterland, for the most part. Field inspection reveals that the majority of the large estates are operating well below their potential productive capacity. In some, large tracts of good land are not worked at all. In others the trees are neglected and weeds, plant disease, and soil erosion are making rapid inroads. The farming methods are outdated and inefficient. Many of the large estates are owned by absentee landlords, or by importers and storekeepers who are more interested in commerce than in agriculture. Their land is managed by local overseers who have been described as little more than glorified laborers, with limited agricultural knowledge and managerial skill. There seems, however, to be little incentive for the absentee owners to strive for higher productivity and fuller land utilization since that portion of the land which is worked yields sufficient profit for the owners' needs, in addition to their much larger incomes from commercial operations. Furthermore, there are no land taxes in Dominica, and hence there is no deterrent to letting good lands lie idle.

As a result of the low productivity of much of the good estate land, the many small farmers are applying great pressure to the steep slopes, and are continually pushing the line of cultivation higher up the mountains and deeper into the forests. Their method of settlement is simply one of squatting on Crown Land with little subsequent possibility of their eviction. Whoever chooses goes into the steep, wooded hills and clears a patch of public land on which he plants a few bananas and other fruit trees. At harvest time he carries out the produce on his head over great distances and across rough terrain. This haphazard and completely uncontrolled type of land settlement leads to serious soil erosion and depletion of fertility, which is followed by shifting cultivation. Inordinately high investments of labor produce relatively low yields, and the land is gradually being destroyed.

It is obvious to the objective observer that the first step in a rational program of agricultural development in Dominica is to correct the faults of the prevailing land tenure pattern at both ends of the scale. The large estates must be encouraged to either increase production or redistribute their land. This may be accomplished by a system of progressive taxation on land which is idle, but potentially productive. If it is expensive to hold idle land, the estates may be willing to sell to the small farmers and thus reduce the pressure on the steep hinterland. The small farmers, in turn, should be discouraged from indiscriminate squatting, unplanned and disorganized settlement, and heedless depletion of the island's limited soil resources. Only in the wake of such land reforms can consideration be given to the host of other measures which would lead toward greater and more balanced agricultural production, such as soil conservation techniques, pasture improvement, crop diversification, increase in livestock, development of credit and marketing facilities, and farmers' cooperatives. Without the prerequisite changes in the land tenure pattern, most of these measures would be of little permanent value.

St. Lucia

Unlike any of the other British West Indies, St. Lucia still operates under an old system of land tenure, which is a legacy of the former French occupation, and known as the Community Property System. By this system there is compulsory joint ownership by the husband and wife of all property acquired after marriage, but not inherited from one side or the other. Upon the decease of one of the partners of the marriage the surviving spouse acquires half of the land and all the children acquire equal rights to the other half. When the second parent dies, rights to the entire land are equally divided among the children. It should be noted that the land itself is not necessarily divided, but the *rights* to the land are equally shared, and the legacy of the land becomes the communal property of the entire family. Thus, for example, if one of the heirs clears a field and plants a crop on it there is nothing to prevent all the other members of the family (including brothers, sisters, nephews, and nieces) from harvesting the crop when it is mature. This arrangement of communal land rights within the family serves as a strong deterrent to agricultural development since the more ambitious and enterprising farmers feel that it is not worthwhile planting crops under these conditions.

A typical case was related to the author by one of the ministers of the government. A St. Lucian farmer had recently become so disgusted by the fact that the oranges on his orange tree were always being picked by his relatives that he chopped it down when it was in full fruit. (A piquant detail of this incident was the fact that the man chopped down the tree precisely while his young nephew was still up in the branches, picking fruit.)

The Community Property System is further complicated by the fact that many of the children on the island are illegitimate and as such barred from inheritance rights. The exception occurs in the frequent case where a woman, in the absence of a legal spouse, may specifically leave her land to all her illegitimate children, who hold it as common property. As a result of the very confused state of land titles in all of the island, there are no complete statistics of the pattern of land tenure, such as are available for the other islands of the West Indies. The registry of land is still based upon the old French cadastral survey made in the 18th century which is incomplete, and often incorrect. It is interesting to note that the other Windward Islands which had once been under French rule abandoned the doctrine of Community Property in 1925 and have revised land tenure and inheritance laws to conform, more or less, with the English system. (A minor exception to this is a small region on the north coast of the island of Dominica.) St. Lucia has not yet taken this step, although the authorities are well aware of the deleterious effects which the system has upon agricultural development. A land tenure specialist from England has been invited to survey the situation and propose a program of legislation leading to land reform. His report has, up to the present, not been acted upon.

Under the present system there is very little incentive among the farmers to develop their land, and the agricultural extension services have great difficulties in promoting improved farming practices such as the use of fertilizers, soil erosion control, better planting stock, disease and pest control, etc. Suggestions leading to long-range profits, but involving immediate expenditures of time, effort, and money, are likely to fall upon deaf ears, except among those few farmers who hold a clear and solitary title to the land, unencumbered by the rights and claims of numerous relatives. The chief enterprise in which some progress has been made toward more scientific methods has been in the banana plantations where, thanks to the efforts of the Banana Growers Association, many farmers have been persuaded to use better plant stock, sprays, fertilization, and a certain amount of supplementary irrigation. The quick turnover of the banana crop and the prospect of immediate cash returns have, in this instance, helped to overcome the difficulties created by the land tenure system.

SUMMARY

It has been found in four small islands of the West Indies that the existing patterns of land tenure are distinctly different, and in each case exert a decisive influence upon the agricultural development and prevailing patterns of land use. In St. Kitts almost all of the land is estate owned and there is no small peasantry. The prevailing agricultural system is sugar monoculture which is eminently successful but seriously threatened by increasingly narrower margins of profit. In Nevis the old sugar estates have been abandoned and most of the arable land is in the hands of the government which is both willing and anxious to redistribute it to the small farmers. The latter, however, are reluctant to acquire this land since no profitable systems of farming, distribution, and marketing have been developed to replace the collapsed sugar economy. In Dominica, on the other hand, the pressure on the land is very great and the small farmers are exceedingly anxious to acquire good plots to grow bananas, limes, and other fruits, for which there are good potential markets. Good, workable land is very limited because of the steep, broken topography of the island, and is largely in the hands of a few estates where it is operated far below capacity or allowed to lie fallow. The absence of land tax encourages the large owners to hold idle land for an indefinite period, while the small farmers are forced to push into the interior and squat on Crown Lands which are far too steep for safe cultivation. In St. Lucia, finally, the survival of the old French system of joint family ownership has led to fragmentation, and has discouraged initiative and progress.

The unifying generalization which may be drawn from this heterogeneous picture is that technical programs for agricultural development, such as are proposed by agronomists and engineers, are often dependent for their success upon the prior solution of fundamental socio-economic problems, such as faulty land tenure patterns. Attempts on the part of technicians to proceed with specific development plans while ignoring basic weaknesses in the underlying social and economic structure may result in fruitless effort and wasted expense. The essence of the modern approach to the development problems in the newly emerging states is the *integration* of the cultural, economic, social, and technical phases of the program, coupled with a degree of boldness to propose the alteration of basic, traditional, but deleterious, aspects of the existing order.

Note:

1. The prevailing field wage is now BWI$0.36 per hour or BWI$2.88 per day. Cane is usually cut as piece work at BWI$1.2, per ton, with an average of 3 tons per day or more per worker. (BWI$1.00 = US$0.60.)

TABLE I

SUMMARY OF GEOGRAPHICAL INFORMATION ON THE FOUR ISLANDS

Feature	St. Kitts	Nevis	Dominica	St. Lucia
Area (sq. mi.)	68	36	304	233
Dimensions (mi.)	19 × 5	6.5 diam.	29 × 16	25 × 13
Peak elevation (ft.)	3700	3600	4747	3145
Geological structure	Old volcanic	Single central volcano	Recent volcanic. Many peaks	Multi-peaked volcanic. Recent
Topography	Central ridge and gentle coastal plain	Central cone and flat perimeter	Steep, broken. Few alluvial valleys	Moderately steep. Some plains and valleys
Soils:				
Good types (%)	70	28	35	20
Poor types (%)	30	72	65	80
Rainfall, annual:				
In center of island (")	60	150	250	150
Average on coast (")	40	30–40	50–100	50–70
Months of rain	All year	July to December	July to December	July to December
Miles of primary roads	32	20	107	
Farming systems	Pure estate	Abandoned estates and small peasants	Few estates, many small farmers and squatters	Mixed small farming. Very few estates
Principal crops	Sugar	Cotton Vegetables Pastures Coconuts	Bananas Coconuts Cacao Limes Coffee	Bananas Coconuts Sugar Cacao Coffee Food Crops Pastures

TABLE II

LAND AREAS AND POPULATION DENSITIES IN THE FOUR ISLANDS

Island	Total area sq. mi.	Cultivable area sq. mi.	Population in thousands	Density per sq. mi. total area	Density per sq. mi. cultivable area
St. Kitts	68	42	37	544	880
Nevis	36	22	13	360	580
Dominica	304	115	60	200	523
St. Lucia	233	120	86	370	715
Total	641	299	196	302	655

TABLE III

NUMBER AND SITE OF AGRICULTURAL HOLDINGS IN NEVIS

Size group (acres)	Less than 1	1 to 5	5 to 50	Over 50	Total
Number of holdings	954	1,747	148	33	2,882
Total size of holdings (acres)	381	3,501	1,261	9,164	14,312

TABLE IV

NUMBER AND ACREAGE OF FARMS IN DOMINICA

(Acreage indicated in parentheses)

Size group (acres)	0–1	1–5	5–10	10–50	50–100	100+	Total
Own account	3,049 (1,216)	3,471 (7,926)	1,144 (6,931)	547 (8,996)	87 (5,713)	47 (16,221)	8,615 (47,003)
Managed	34 (3)	40 (101)	19 (116)	38 (773)	8 (561)	38 (23,851)	177 (25,405)
Total	3,083 (1,219)	3,511 (8,027)	1,163 (7,047)	585 (9,769)	95 (6,274)	85 (40,072)	8,792 (72,408)

F.
Labor, Economics, and Internal Marketing

Three of the papers in this section deal with internal marketing of locally produced goods, for it is through local markets that the West Indian peasant makes contact with a cash economy. Anthropologists have been especially interested in these markets for, as Sidney Mintz writes, "to follow the movement of marketers and stock through the system is an ideal way to begin to study the economy and to trace the distribution of economic and political power in the society" ("Peasant markets," *Scientific American,* 203(2):112, 1960). Students have particularly noted the prominence of women in these markets; Lafcadio Hearn, traveling in the 1880's, wrote a delightful, sometimes fanciful portrait of women bearers, *porteuses,* who were the main transporters as well as sellers of produce before they were almost everywhere replaced in the former capacity by trucks and buses:

> At a very early age—perhaps at five years—she learns to carry small articles upon her head,—a bowl of rice,—a *dobanne,* or red earth decanter, full of water,—even an orange on a plate; and before long she is able to balance these perfectly without using her hands to steady them. . . . At nine or ten she is able to carry thus a tolerably heavy basket, or a *trait* . . . containing a weight of from twenty to thirty pounds; and is able to accompany her mother, sister, or cousin on long peddling journeys,—walking barefoot twelve or fifteen miles a day. At sixteen or seventeen she is a tall robust girl,—lithe, vigorous, tough,—all tendon and hard flesh;—she carries a tray or a basket of the largest size, and a burden of one hundred and twenty to one hundred and fifty pounds weight;—she can now earn about thirty francs (about six dollars) a month, *by walking fifty miles a day,* as an itinerant seller (*Two Years in the French West Indies.* New York: Harper and Brothers, 1890, pp. 104–5).

The significance of women in the market to conjugal patterns is explored by Horowitz (1967) in this volume.

The reader interested in West Indian fishing should also read Richard Price, "Caribbean Fishing and Fishermen: A Historical Sketch," *American Anthropologist* 68(6):1363–83, 1966. The mathematics of Davenport's article have been criticized by R. Kozelka ("A Bayesian approach to Jamaican fishing," in I. R. Buchler and H. G. Nutini, eds., *Game Theory in the Behavioral Sciences*. Pittsburgh: University of Pittsburgh Press, 1969) and by D. W. Read and C. E. Read ("A Critique of Davenport's Game Theory Analysis," *American Anthropologist* 72(2):351–55, 1970). It is pointed out that the sea cannot legitimately be considered a rational opponent attempting to maximize gain in a game situation.

WILLIAM C. DAVENPORT

15. Jamaican Fishing: A Game Theory Analysis

At first glance the theory of games of strategy[1] would not appear to have any value for cultural anthropology, for it is not only a highly mathematical theory, but its direct application is intended to be in the field of quantified economics, not to the qualitative aspects of human culture. But game theory, as it is more usually called, is a theory of human behavior, and more particularly, of human behavior in certain kinds of decision-making or problem-solving situations. If we can assume that human culture, or some of it at least, is a set of patterned solutions to problems which has accreted through trial and error, then such a nonpsychological theory of problem solving should have some relevance to the study of culture. At least it should be of interest to see whether or not its application does have any real value to problems in cultural anthropology.

The analysis to follow is a direct application of game theory, in that it deals with economic behavior, but it is also an ecological application, in that it is concerned with the pattern of responses which a group of people have evolved in coping with some of the combined physical, biological, and social forces of their environment. Let it be quite clear that the writer in no way professes to understand the mathematics of proof of the theory of games as set forth by its authors. Yet the assumptions and solutions of some simple game types can be understood readily by anyone when they are explained in nonmathematical language.[2] Unfortunately, the data to be used here were not collected for a game theory application, and for this reason alone the results will be something less than perfect. But this shortcoming has one slight advantage in that there is no danger of a theo-

SOURCE: From *Papers in Caribbean Anthropology*, compiled by S. W. Mintz, Yale University Publications in Anthropology No. 59 (1960):3–11. New Haven: Yale University Press. Reprinted by permission of the author, the Department of Anthropology, Yale University, and Yale University Publications in Anthropology.

retical bias having been introduced in the collection of the materials.[3]

The group to be considered is a fishing village of about 200 persons, located on the south shore of Jamaica. The male villagers are all fishermen, and they make their living exclusively by fishing in the local waters and selling their catches into the general marketing system of the island. The fishing grounds used by them extend out from shore to the 100-fathom line, about 22 miles, and comprise about 168 square sea miles. Twenty-six fishing crews in sailing, dugout canoes fish this area by setting fish pots, which are drawn and reset, weather and sea permitting, on three regular fishing days each week. The fishing crews are composed of a captain, who owns the canoe, and two or three crewmen. Some of the crewmen own and set their own fish pots, some do not. The captains do not allow their crewmen to set more than four pots each, and not all crewmen are even given this privilege. The economic reason for this restriction is that a canoe and its crew can comfortably handle a maximum of only 20 to 25 pots, and each pot set by a crewman amounts to one less for the captain, who has a considerable investment in his canoe and sailing gear. The crewmen who own no fish pots are paid a small, variable wage for each trip, and they are allowed to take as many fish as they need for home consumption. A captain also has an obligation to pay the crewmen who own their own fish pots when they catch nothing, even though he himself may have caught no fish either. The total number of fish pots set by the 94 fishermen who make up the 26 crews is 572, of which slightly more than one half is owned by the captains.

The fishing grounds are divided into inside and outside banks. The inside banks lie from 5 to 15 miles offshore, while the outside banks all lie beyond. The distinction between inside and outside banks is not made on the basis of their distance from shore alone, but more importantly, on the basis of the strength of the currents which flow across them. Because of special underwater contours and the location of one prominent headland, very strong currents set across the outside banks at frequent intervals in both easterly and westerly directions. These currents run up to a velocity of five knots, and they are not related in any apparent way to weather and sea conditions of the local region. The inside banks are almost fully protected from the currents, and the sea there never gets as rough as it does on the outside banks, so canoes going outside must be both sound and well managed.

In setting the fish pots, the captain alone decides where they shall be put. He selects a series of likely places which are removed as far as possible from the localities where other fishermen have set theirs. Several pots are set a short distance apart at one location, and locations are spaced several miles apart in a line extending out from shore. Captains are very secretive about their locations, and they keep their range marks on shore by which the pots are located secret even from their own crews. This secrecy and avoidance of other captains' locations is related to the very competitive spirit between fishermen and strong fears of theft and of being accused of theft.

When strong currents run across the outside fishing banks, the bamboo floats which mark the hauling lines are dragged under the water, and the fishermen cannot find them to draw their fish pots. If this continues for several days, the floats become waterlogged and sink, and the pots are lost forever. Strong current also moves the pots around on the bottom, smashing them against outcrops of rock and coral, causing considerable damage and loss. Even when the currents come and go without damage to the pots, there is loss, for fish that enter them under one condition of water do not long survive under changed conditions. Thus fish which are caught under no-current conditions are killed by temperature and other changes brought on by the current, and vice versa. As indicated above, there is absolutely no way for the fishermen to predict when the current will come or go, nor can they tell from shore if the current is running or not. In short, current is the scourge of the outside fishing banks, while the inside banks are free from this unpredictable menace.

The advantage of fishing on the outside banks as compared with fishing on the inside banks is that more quality grades of fish, both as to varieties and size, are caught outside. In general, too, larger catches are obtained outside than inside. These differences between the current-ridden outside banks and the safe inside banks constitutes a choice situation for the captains as to where they will fish. These are not mutually exclusive alternatives, so the choices are: (1) all pots set inside, (2) all pots set outside, (3) some pots set inside and some set outside. These three alternatives, or strategies, will be called *inside, outside,* and *in-out.*

Actually, no fisherman chooses the outside alternative, for it is entirely too risky. But we are going to ask game theory to predict the proportions of captains (or crews) which choose each strategy, and so we can expect it to predict this fact.

The fact that there are captains pursuing different alternatives in fishing has important relationships to other aspects of the social and economic organization of the village. Ecologically, different varieties and species are caught on the inside and outside banks, which means that the exploitation of both banks is a full utilization of the available resources. When the size of the catch declines in one place, pots are shifted to another. This selection and the avoidance of each others' locations prevents any one location from being overfished. The fact that larger fish and bigger catches are obtained on the outside banks than on the inside is a direct reflection of the less intensive fishing on these outside banks. Thus we see that a special kind of exploitive balance is maintained on the fishing grounds.

Since the captains who are fishing the in-out alternative must cope with much more difficult sailing conditions, they need good canoes, and they must replace them after only a few years use. In contrast, the inside captains need less sturdy craft, so they purchase the used, but still serviceable, canoes which the in-out captains can no longer use with safety. And since the in-out captains own the newest and finest canoes, they dominate the sport of canoe racing, which is one of the most important recreational interests of the village. Canoe races with very large purses for the winner and heavy side betting take place between fishermen of the village and also between captains of this village and other villages along the south coast. There are still other relationships to these alternative fishing strategies, but these just cited are enough to show that they are related to the culture in a variety of ways and are not isolated patterns.

Although the proportion of captains choosing each of these alternatives seems to have remained fairly constant over the past four or five years, the actual persons choosing each have not. Captains and crewmen who are fishing the in-out alternative frequently get disheartened by their constant losses from the current, and they shift their gear over to the inside banks. Inside fishermen sometimes decide to gamble a bit, and they shift some of their gear to the outside banks, in hopes of making more money.

Game theory is supposed to be applied to situations of choice such as this, where two or more "players" are set against each other to win as much as they can and to lose as little as possible. In this game, the village as a whole is one player, or team of players, while the other team consists of all the uncontrollable forces of the environment which affect the outcome of fishing. It is assumed that each player or team will take full cognizance of every alternative open to his opponent when making his own choice of strategy, and that, over time, the opponents will pursue the only possible pattern of choices which seeks the maximum gain with a minimum of risk. This is called minimaxing, and it is the crucial utility, or function, as a structural anthropologist would call it, of the theory. Whatever one might think of this motivational scheme as applied to individual behavior, and there is room for controversy,[4] it is possible that such assumptions do characterize the cumulative effect of individual choices in groups.

Let us examine the advantages and disadvantages of the three fishing strategies of the village in greater detail. Since strong currents do not cross the inside banks, the men fishing there entirely (inside strategy) do not have days when they cannot find and draw their pots. Thus on days when the current is running across the outside banks, the inside fishermen still get full advantage of all their fishing equipment, while those men fishing partly inside and partly outside (in-out strategy) can draw only their inside pots. Canoes which go to the outside banks must also leave the beach first, and they are usually the last to return after a day's fishing. The time factor here is important, since it enables the crews fishing inside only to handle a few more pots than the crews fishing both the inside and outside banks. The net effect is a difference of 10 per cent in the mean number of pots per canoe which the in-out canoes manage when compared with the inside canoes. This reduction, in combination with the losses due to days of current, amounts to a considerable reduction in the productive potential of the in-out canoes, if this were measured by the total number of pots multiplied by the number of times each is drawn and reset.

The inside fishermen must replace about 90 per cent of their pots each year, while the in-out fishermen average 220 per cent more than this. In money, this amounts to £17.0 and £37.4. The canoes and sailing equipment used by the inside captains have a mean value of £39.0, as compared with £70.0 for the in-out captains. The yearly depreciation of this equipment is about the same for both, and, as estimated from the sale and resale values, is assumed to be £10.0 for inside canoes and £11.0 for in-out canoes. The total annual equipment cost for inside fishermen, then, amounts to £27.0 and for in-out fishermen, £48.4.

The advantages and disadvantages of the two alternate fishing strategies do not end with these costs which have just been summarized, for the reactions and trends of the market are also important. The fishermen sell their fish to vendors who come to the beach and pay cash at the canoe. The price of different grades of fish varies, according to the familiar forces of supply and demand. The seasonal fluctuation in employment on the sugar estates has the most important influence on the demand, while weather and month-to-month changes in the habits of fish affect the supply. Both of these factors are irrelevant here, for they affect all fishing strategies alike. But what is relevant is that when canoes fishing outside bring in large catches of quality grades of fish, it drives the price of the fish of lesser quality down, by driving them off the market. This means the inside fishermen suffer when the in-out fishermen make good catches from their outside pots. Conversely, when the current prevents the in-out canoes from drawing their outside pots, the absence of quality fish enables the inside fishermen to force the price of their poor-quality fish up. On these days the men fishing the in-out strategy have only their fish caught in their inside pots to sell, since the current prevents them from drawing their outside pots. In summary, regardless of the over-all level of the market, a day of current means a severe loss in income for the in-out fishermen, while it is a gain for the inside fishermen. The reverse holds true for days when there is no current.

The average annual income, less the amounts paid to crewmen as wages, for the inside captains is £190.8, and for the in-out captains is £197.6, which by substracting the equipment costs listed above yields net incomes of £163.8 and £149.2.[5] These means do not give a very adequate picture of the income distributions, for there is great individual variation due to luck, skill, and amount of productive equipment controlled by captains. There is both greater variation and greater maximum incomes in the in-out incomes than in those of the inside alternative.

From fishermen's estimates, the percentage of days with current for each calendar month was calculated. Combining this with the annual income and observed differentials for current and no-current days, mean values of income for inside and in-out fishing for current and no-current periods were computed. The period used is one-twelfth of a year, or what will be called a *fishing month*. Since the fishing month does not correspond to the calendar month, the seasonal fluctuations in income due to over-all market conditions and variations in the supply of fish, as described above, are averaged out.

The values thus computed on the basis of the fishing month are as follows:[6]

	Current	No-current
Inside	£17.3	£11.5
In-out	5.2	17.0

This matrix is to be read as follows: if current ran for a whole month, the captains fishing inside only would average £17.3 net income, while the captains fishing the in-out alternative would earn £5.2 net. For a month of fishing with no current, the captains fishing inside only would average £11.5 net, while the captains fishing the in-out strategy would average £17.0 income, net. These are the conditions for a two-person-two-strategy, zero sum game in game theory. The village as a whole is one player and the environment, consisting of all the forces which affect fishing, is the other.[7]

It will be recalled that there is actually a third strategy, fishing entirely outside, even though no one in the village chooses it. To make this analysis complete, estimates of what incomes might be derived from this alternative will be computed. On no-current days, the outside captains would do extremely well, and the increase in income over the in-out captains would be proportionate to the number of pots the latter set on the inside banks. According to observations, the in-out captains set about one-third of their pots there, and the best estimate of the net increase in income is £3.6.[8] In the case of current, the outside captains would not only make no cash, but they would have additional wage expenses for their crews. This expense is calculated to be at least £4.4 per fishing month of current days. The complete matrix is now as follows:[9]

		Environment	
		Current	No-current
	Inside	£17.3	£11.5
Village	In-out	5.2	17.0
	Outside	−4.4	20.6

This now changes the game model to a two-person-three-strategy, zero sum game in which the village has three alternative strategies and the environment has two.[10] The theory should predict the proportion of the 26 captains which selects each strategy and the proportion of the time that the current runs across the outer banks.

The solution of this matrix lies in first applying the minimax principle to each of the possible pairs of the three village strategies. If one of the strategies in any pair turns out to be absolutely preferable over another, it is said to be dominant, and a zero proportion is assigned to the one over which the other is dominant. Let us start by comparing the outside with the in-out strategy. Since the maximum-of-the-row-minimums (5.2) is equal to the minimum-of-the-column-maximums (5.2), the in-out alternative is dominant over the outside, and a proportion of zero is assigned to the outside strategy.[11]

Comparing the remaining two strategies (inside and in-out) by the same method, the maximum-of-the-row-minimums (11.5) is not equal to the minimum-of-the-column-maximums (17.0), so neither is dominant over the other, and the theory predicts that the village will use a mixture of these two alternatives. This is called mixed strategies.[12] Computing the proportions in which these two strategies will be mixed, the matrix yields 5.8 in-out to 11.8 inside, or 67 per cent of the captains will be fishing inside only.[13] During the periods of observation, 18 of the 26 captains, or 69 per cent, were fishing inside.

In summary, the theory predicts that 00 per cent of the captains will be fishing outside, that 67 per cent (or 17 captains) will be fishing inside, and that 33 per cent (or 9 captains) will be fishing the in-out strategy. The observations yielded 00, 69 (or 18 captains), and 31 (or 8 captains) respectively.

Predicting the proportion of time in which there is current, the matrix yields 5.5 current periods to 12.1 no-current periods, or the current runs 31 per cent of the time.[14] Averaged estimates by fishermen for the years from June 1953 to June 1955 yielded an "observed" proportion of 25 per cent for the current. Although there is a 6 per cent discrepancy between the predicted and the observed, it is to be remembered that these observed data are subject to distortion, since they are based upon fishermen's memories alone, and also the period over which the current was calculated may be too short. We can say, however, that the theory and the observed agree to the extent that the current runs less than one-half but not less than one-quarter of the time.

When the minimax test for dominance between the village strategies was made above, we did not compare the inside and outside alternatives with each other. If we do so, we will find that the maximum-of-the-row-minimums (11.5) is not equal to the minimum-of-the-column-maximums (17.3), which indicates this is a situation of mixed strategies. At first glance this might seem to contradict the behavior of the fishermen, for did we not say that no captains chose the outside alternative? But in making this paired comparison, we assume there are only two strategies, setting pots inside or setting them outside. The theory, then, predicts that some pots will be set in each place, and our observations confirm this much of the prediction. In other words, by assuming only these two strategies, we are maintaining the same level of analysis—the village vs. the environment—but we are shifting the unit of behavior from the total strategy of captains to the placement of individual fish pots. We can ask the theory to predict the proportion of pots set in each of the two areas, and, as before, the proportion of time which the current sets across the outside banks. Computations yield a predicted proportion of 0.811 of the pots will be set inside and the current runs 0.30 of the time.[15] The observations are: 452/572 pots, or 0.790, are set by all fishermen on the inside banks and the current runs 0.25 of the time.

The outcome of this application of game theory to a case of economic anthropology, although not perfect, is rewarding enough to warrant a close look at exactly what assumptions are being tested. More than anything else, they are the assumptions that the fishermen, as a group, are behaving according to the minimax utility. This probably arises from the fact that in their pursuit of fishing, some fishermen behave very conservatively, while others do not. The group effect of this distribution is a utility which approaches minimaximization. If this kind of function is characteristic of groups or patterns in which choice is permitted, then the naive assumptions of complete conformity which certain structure-functionalists make about groups and patterns must be taken under further advisement.

Notes:

1. Von Neumann and Morgenstern, *Theory of Games and Economic Behavior* (1953).

2. See Williams, *Compleat Strategyst* (1954), and Luce and Raiffa, *Games and Decisions* (1957).

3. These data were taken from unpublished field notes and Davenport, *A Comparative Study of Two Jamaican Fishing Communities* (1956). The writer wishes to thank Dr. Omar Khayyam Moore for reading and criticizing an earlier version of the paper. While some of his valuable suggestions have been incorporated here, his reservations concerning the application of game theory have

been ignored, since the main purpose is to test whether or not this kind of application works out. For a highly imaginative application of derivations from game theory to cultural phenomena, see Moore, *Divination* (1957).

4. See Simon, *A Comparison of Game Theory and Learning Theory* (1956).

5. These were computed from daily observations made from June to September 1954 and from fishermen's estimates of their month-by-month incomes from June 1953 to June 1955. The latter were taken twice, in September 1954 and again in June 1955. These, in combination with income figures computed for the short observation period, gave a check on the consistency and reliability of the informants' estimates. Although some men gave inconsistent data and some information did not check with the observations, when the fishermen's estimates were averaged, there was a remarkable correspondence between estimates and between the estimates and the observations. Calculations are given in decimal parts of the pound rather than in shillings and pence.

6. Obviously, the current never runs for a whole month, but this unit of the *fishing month* was adopted, because the field data were collected for calendar months, and they could not be reduced to smaller units for this analysis. Figures are given for captains only, because these data were taken from all 26 of them, while data for crewmen were obtained only for a sample. This does not alter the results, for the same results would be obtained if the figures in the cells of the matrices were those for entire crews. See Williams, *Compleat Strategyst* (1954), 43–46.

7. See von Neumann and Morgenstern, *Theory of Games and Economic Behavior* (1953), 85–168 and Williams, *Compleat Strategyst* (1954), 13, 29–63.

8. This estimate is made as follows: in-out captains set about one-third of their pots inside. This one-third is equal to less than one-third of the number of pots the inside captains set on the inside banks, for the in-out captains set fewer pots altogether. It was determined that this one-third of the in-out captains' pots are equal to .30 of what the average inside captain sets inside. In no-current periods the in-out captains' income from their outside pots alone would be $(.30)$ $(11.5) + X = 17.0$ and $X = £13.55$. By setting all his pots outside, an outside captain would increase this potential ($£13.55$) by one-half, since he is adding approximately one-half more pots there. Thus, the outside income would be $13.55 + (13.55/2) = £20.57$.

9. For reasons which need not be discussed here, both these figures for the outside strategy may be too low. Even with such an error, however, the results of this first test would not be affected, for any other larger figures in the cells will still make the outside alternative less advantageous than the in-out strategy. See Footnote 11.

10. See Williams, *Compleat Strategyst* (1954), 65–81.

11. The procedures for solution are those from Williams, *Compleat Strategyst* (1954), and they will not be explained in detail here. In general, however, the simple solution of a 2 × 3 game of this sort lies in reducing it to a series of 2 × 2 games, then eliminating one of the strategies when another is dominant over it. Thus: $5.2 > -4.4$ and 5.2 is the maximum-of-the-row-minimums. $5.2 < 20.6$ and 5.2 is the minimum-of-the-column-maximums. Since these are equal, the better of the two strategies for the village is the in-out, and the outside alternative is eliminated.

12. See Moore, *Divination* (1957), 73 and Williams, *Compleat Strategyst* (1954), 36–39.

13. The method for finding these proportions is as follows: subtract the right figure in each row from the left, ignore the sign, and apply the result to the other

strategy. The same procedure is used for the columns, subtracting the bottom figure from the top. See Williams, *Compleat Strategyst* (1954), 39–44.

	Current	No-current
Inside (p = −11.8)	17.3	11.5
In-out (p = 5.8)	5.2	17.0
(p = −5.5	12.1)

14. See Footnote 13.
15. See Footnote 13 for method of solution.

	Current	No-current
Inside (p = −25.0)	17.3	11.5
Outside (p = 5.8)	−4.4	20.6
(p = −9.1	21.7)

References cited:

Davenport, W. C.
  1956 "A Comparative Study of Two Jamaican Fishing Communities." Unpublished doctoral dissertation, Yale University, New Haven.
Luce, D. R., and H. Raiffa.
  1957 *Games and Decisions: Introduction and Critical Survey*. New York.
Moore, O. K.
  1957 "Divination—a New Perspective." *American Anthropologist*, n.s. vol. 59, pp. 69–74, Menasha.
Simon, H. A.
  1956 "A Comparison of Game Theory and Learning Theory." *Psychometrika*, vol. 21, pp. 267–72, Richmond.
Von Neumann, J., and O. Morgenstern.
  1953 *Theory of Games and Economic Behavior*. 3rd edition, Princeton.
Williams, J. D.
  1954 *The Compleat Strategyst*. New York.

16. Cooperative Labor Groups in Haiti

This eroded soil, which has been mercilessly exploited, now gives a very low yield. In order to gain a living from it, the peasant has to cultivate an area too large for his own and his family's working capacity. To attain a certain standard of comfort, he should really be able to cultivate four or five "carreaux";[1] but for this purpose he must have considerable manpower at his disposal at the necessary periods, which recur several times during the year.

He must also overcome an obstacle which is characteristic of tropical countries: shortage of time. The rainy seasons are brief, and the various phases of agricultural work follow each other in rapid succession. Clearing operations, for instance, are confined to a relatively short period, the beginning and end of which vary from year to year. If the ground is cleared too early, the weeds will come back in force; if clearing is too long delayed, the heavy downpours of the rainy season will hamper the work, and the peasant will lose valuable weeks.[2] Therefore, he needs the help of his neighbors in overcoming the difficulties that are due to space and time.

The status of a Marbial peasant cannot be judged *a priori* by the number or extent of his holdings, although the owner of ten or more "carreaux" is assured of a very comfortable subsistence. In the case of the average peasant, the area of ground he owns is less important than his facilities for exploiting it. Even the owner of a quite small plot, of a quarter "carreau," may live in considerable comfort if he is able to cultivate land which he leases or holds on *pòtèk*.

There is a close relationship between agricultural output and the income in hard cash which the peasant obtains by selling livestock or coffee, or by working as a craftsman or trader.

SOURCE: Pp. 67–86 of Alfred Métraux, *Making of a Living in the Marbial Valley (Haiti)*. Educational Clearing House Occasional Paper in Education. Paris: United Nations Educational, Scientific and Cultural Organization, 1951. Reprinted with permission of UNESCO.

His method of cultivating his property varies not only according to his resources, but also according to his rank and age. He may work alone, with members of his family, in cooperation with his neighbors (cooperative work group, association, or society), as a wage laborer, or as an employer. The choice between these different methods is sometimes left to his taste or personal inclination, or may even depend upon the weather. One single agricultural operation may be carried out, in successive stages, by manpower recruited according to the principle of mutual assistance, by wage labor, and, finally, by the concerted efforts of the landowner and his family. We may take as an example the case of a peasant who owns two "carreaux." During the first season, he will try to plant an area of about one and a half car. The simplest and quickest method is to call successively upon four or five cooperative work groups of twenty to thirty men each, who will do nearly all the work within a relatively short space of time, and to finish it with the help of his family or of two or three associates. It is estimated that twenty to thirty men are needed, according to the nature of the ground, to clear and hoe half a "carreau" in one day. Other peasants, who cannot afford the cost of several work groups make do with one, and clear their remaining "carreau" with help from neighbors—which they later reciprocate—or by calling upon four or five poorer peasants who, by a sort of contract, undertake to clear a given area.

A young man at the beginning of his career, or a poor peasant, has to join up with a group of neighbors who help each other in turn.

If the group of associates consists of fifteen persons, they can clear 0.15 car. in one morning's work, which is the normal duration of a "ronde."[3] The area the owner can cultivate will depend upon the number of "rondes" that he can arrange during the brief period that precedes the spring. Working alone, it would be difficult for him to exploit more than one or two tenths car.

In the Marbial region, only the "Chefs de section"—who, owing to the fear they inspire, have abundant labor, often unpaid, at their disposal—and a few rich peasants are in a position to cultivate ten or more "carreaux" in the year. Most landowners prefer to farm out their land on a leasehold or share-crop basis, rather than exploit it themselves.

INSTITUTIONALIZED FORMS OF COOPERATIVE WORK

Collective labor, several forms of which exist at Marbial, goes by various names in the peasants' speech, according to the basis on which it is organized and the time for which it lasts. We will examine each form separately.

The labor team (corvée)

The "corvée" (*kové*)[4] or "combite" (*kôbit*) is, in theory, the day's work done by a group of men for a landowner who, for his part, is responsible for feeding them. Nowadays the term cannot be so exactly defined, for one often hears the expression "bought corvées" ("corvées achetées") used to describe the work done, for money payments, by groups of peasants organized in a "society."

Teamwork which ends with a distribution of food is, undoubtedly, the favorite type of cooperative labor. Though it has some drawbacks, it satisfies certain deeply rooted psychological requirements, both in him who calls upon his friends and neighbors for help, and in those who offer that help.

Foremost among the advantages of the system is the ease with which it enables a large labor force to be raised for an urgent task. People accept a neighbor's invitation with alacrity, for when one is dependent upon others it is wise to show a helpful spirit. Besides, there are compensations for the effort required. The prospect of a copious meal at the day's end is accompanied by the pleasure of meeting friends, singing, and enjoying oneself in many other ways.

Cooperative group work enables its organizer to increase his prestige and to win fresh authority by showing himself a generous host, grudging no expense. If he does things handsomely, he will be spoken of with respect, and he will always be able, henceforth, to rely on his neighbors' goodwill. If the host has a stock of provisions in reserve, he will have the satisfaction of dispatching a great proportion of the season's agricultural work in one day, without the need to spend a great sum in cash.

There are flaws in the system, however. Landowners often complain that, despite the bustle and gaiety that accompany working parties, its yield is inclined to be low. Many of those invited arrive late, others waste time in chatting, and the host cannot reprimand them too sharply, since they have come as friends. From the peasant's point of view, the little glasses of *clairin* (white rum) that are handed round, and the copious meal served about halfway through the afternoon, are not payment for the work he is doing, but simply a mark of consideration, a courtesy on the part of the landowner.

The organization of a labor team is by no means a simple matter. First of all, the quantity of food that will be needed for the whole party has to be calculated. This is not always easy, when fifty to a hundred people are expected. Once the supplies have been laid in, the host is faced with the problem of cooking them. If he cannot afford to buy the huge cast-iron caldrons necessary for this purpose, he borrows them from some well-to-do peasant who is in the habit of organizing big cooperative work groups and to whom such utensils are indispensable. As nobody, however wealthy, has enough plates, etc., to go round, neighbors are appealed to and are usually quite willing to lend them—on a reciprocal basis, of course.

The heavy responsibility of preparing and serving the food naturally rests with the women of the household, who, if they are too few for the task, call in their female relatives or friends.

Not many peasants, even if they have reserves in their own storehouses to draw upon, manage to arrange a big "combite" without some financial outlay. Very often the host is obliged, not only to kill a pig or a goat, but to go to great expense in buying maize meal, beans, fat, and the other foods usually served on such occasions, not to mention drink. It is not sufficient to have enough for everybody; some must be left over, as a sign of the host's prosperity and generosity. Nothing flatters a peasant more than to have it said of his labor team that: *Moun lignê pèd vi. Mâjé rèté a tè kô sa! Nèg té kôn fè, wi* . . . (The rows of people stretched as far as one could see. There was that much food left on the ground. He's a man who does things properly . . .)

The host's reputation will suffer if the portions are too strictly calculated, or if there are complaints about the quantity or quality of the food. All those present must be able to gorge themselves, and some will even expect to take scraps home in their *makout* (bags).

So a labor team is usually an expensive affair. Most of the peasants we questioned agreed that even without extravagance, it cost them from 1 to 1.50 gdes per head. The traditional form of labor team is thus more costly than the bought "corvée" or than laborers who are paid piece rates.

The peasants are too close-fisted and shrewd not to have perceived this difference in cost. If they still prefer this form of collective labor to all other systems, it is because it enables a given task to be completed in one operation, and frees the landowner from the uncertainties attendant upon hiring labor on any other basis. This attitude toward the labor team was clearly defined by one man who, when the point was raised, exclaimed almost violently: "Even if the labor teams were to cost three times as much, they would still be more satisfactory than hired workers, who never hurry and only come when they want to." He might have added that the labor team system is better than that of the "ronde," since the beneficiary does not contract any further obligation toward his guests.

Nothing points more clearly to the economic decadence of the Marbial region than the decline in the number of these working parties. Peasants who can afford to organize them are becoming fewer and fewer; and whereas in the old days they were glad to help a neighbor in return for a good meal, their chief wish nowadays is to get money with which to buy seed or pay their debts. During seed time in 1948, at the end of a long drought, the Marbial peasants arranged only very few of these traditional working parties with a meal to follow.

The members of such a team start work about 7 A.M., after a light meal usually consisting of bread and coffee. During the morning they drink several glasses of *clairin,* and another snack is sometimes served to them toward noon.

The day's work ends at about 3 P.M. and all the members of the team gather round the caldrons, to partake of the big meal. After which, well primed with food and *clairin* and feeling in excellent form, they often improvise a dance which goes on far into the night.

The work party now sing while they work, instead of being accompanied by drums, as in former times. The Catholic and Protestant clergy have managed to convince their flocks that the drums have something of the satanic character of the voodoo ceremonies in which they are used. The Protestants even go so far as to insist that only hymns shall be sung to accompany the work.

Among the peasants on the "cool lands," who are more conservative than those in the lower valley, the "sambas"—that is, the men who "start the songs"—also lead and guide the lines of workers.

The "combite" songs are often drawn from the repertory of the voodoo shrines, but as a general rule they are improvised on the spot and deal with some recent local scandal or with something ridiculous that has been done by one of the company. They may also be based on a political event, such as the fall of a President.

Here, by way of example, are the words of some work songs which we noted in Marbial.

A man who has been deceived by his wife is advised to make the best of it:

Fò ou résigné ou	You must be resigned
Mwê di X fò ou résigné ou	I tell you, X . . . , you must be resigned
Apolin, bèl fâm, vòlò	Apoline, a beautiful woman, has stolen
kôfiâs ou	your confidence.

To an unmarried girl who is pregnant:

M'pral di mâmâ-m a ya	I'll go and tell your mother, a ya (repeat)
M'pral di mâmâ-m, si la lin	I'll go and tell your mother if I don't
sa m'pa wè li	see the moon (menstruation)
Si la lin sa m'pa wè li	If I don't see the moon,
sé vré	it's true.

Against prostitutes:

Levé, levé o, levé pou alé-o	Get up, get up o to go
Arona di la krazé kay la-o	The prostitute says she has broken the home
Levé pou'n alé-o	Get up to go

About the voodoo sea-god Agoué:

Agwé, Agwé	Agoué, Agoué
Rété sou lâmè	He dwells on the sea
Li tiré kanô-a	He fires his guns

About the fall of President Lescot:

Lesko ou alé, ou alé, ou alé   Lescot, you've gone, you've gone,
                                            you've gone
Ou alé Lesko, ou pa di-m âyê   You've gone Lescot, you didn't
                                            say anything to me

In the old days there were certain men well known for their gift of improvisation, who spread merriment and good humor around them whenever they took part in a working party. Their high spirits infected the workers and staved off quarrels and complaints.

The Marbial cooperative work groups place little reliance on the spirit of competition or rivalry as a means of stimulating the workers. A game practiced in northern Haiti, and which consists in trying to get ahead of a rival team and encircle it, is unknown here. The Marbial peasants are content to urge on their idlers by means of banter and quips. The energy of a few young men, eager to display their "courage," sets a sufficient example to their companions. However, anyone who is too obviously reluctant to work runs the risk of hearing himself satirized in song by his companions.

The landowner exhorts them to work with exclamations and encouraging remarks: *"Lévé mê nou pou nou fini, mâjé sou difé, mésyé, dam."* (Lift a hand to finish, the food is cooking, ladies and gentlemen.)

The Work Societies

An association of peasants accustomed to helping each other by the "ronde" system becomes a "society" when it adopts an order of rank and obeys certain fixed rules.

The principal attribute of these societies is an orchestra composed of four or five musicians who play the drum (*mazòn*) or trumpets (*vaxin*) while the work goes on. The peasants name the different societies according to their instruments or their favorite drum-rhythm —*mazòn, vaxin, kôgo, pistô,* or *zizipâ, kalâmplâm,* etc. In addition to this, each society chooses a name for itself: *Flè di ròz, Résigné, Flè Komâs,* etc.

The peasants' taste for complicated orders of rank and high-sounding titles finds free vent in these societies, whose inspiration is entirely military and political. Each society is like a miniature army or republic which, as in the "days of the bayonets," is liberally supplied with officers and higher officials.

The higher grades often outnumber the rank and file. In the *Flè di ròz* society, ten out of the fifteen members bore titles and the others grumbled about their humble position and aspired to similar dignities. One must, of course, make allowance for the playful element that forms part of this masquerading, and remember that, with a few exceptions, the dignitaries themselves do not take their lofty status very seriously. When the Morne Rouge cooperative was established, titles were distributed with fantastic generosity.

The military spirit that animates these societies finds expression in other ways. Each society has a General, who drills his soldiers at will and shouts orders at them as though on the parade ground. "Right, right," "Dress," "Shoulder arms," etc. These drill-ground interludes are repeated each time the society meets as a working party and, above all, at public celebrations. The societies of a region regard each other as rival armies. They are quick to accuse each other of hostile intentions, and pretend to be afraid that their neighbors will entice away their "soldiers."

One of our informants at Cap-Rouge said that if the President did not treat his soldiers well, they were entitled to "capsize him." The peasants are aware that all this military display has come down to them from the civil war period, when they used to be pressed into one or another of the revolutionary armies.

Like many other peasant institutions in the Marbial region, the Work Societies are gradually disappearing or changing their character. Only three survive, to our knowledge, in the whole area of our inquiry.

Owing to the general poverty, the present societies are a mere shadow of what they used to be. They consist, at most, of some twenty members, the majority of whom are poor peasants who sell their day's work to such landowners as are able to buy it. The ceremonies connected with the activities of a working party are also tending to die out. Hence, when describing the functions of the various dignitaries of a society, or its rules, we are often obliged to use the past tense.

Nature and Functions of the Work Societies

The society is first and foremost an association for mutual assistance in agricultural work. Each member is entitled to a due share of the help of his comrades, who give it to him in the form of a "ronde" lasting about four hours. If he wishes, he can sell his "turn," receiving his companions' salaries as well as his own. If ten or fifteen peasants form a working party, the "master" of the work—i.e., the member of the society entitled to the cooperative work of his associates—is paid from 4 to 6 gdes by the owner of the field.* If a member of a society sells not a half day's but a whole day's work, he receives only half the lump sum agreed upon with the employer. He draws his share of the other half which is divided equally between all the members of the working party. Sometimes the money paid to the society is set aside and used to buy a goat, to be eaten when a dance is held. The societies are always ready to undertake a task for which a good meal will be the sole payment (*kôbit pou bay mâjé*).**

The system of cooperative work groups is becoming increasingly commercialized. The individual no longer has to find a purchaser for his "turn"; the society itself sells "turns," the payment for which is handed over to each member in succession.

If a member of a society is ill, his comrades tend his ground, come to visit him, and bring him remedies. The Congo Society of Cap-Rouge even has a health insurance fund. This is kept up by small sums deducted from money earned by bought teams.

To draw attention only to the utilitarian aspect of these societies would be to misjudge their spirit and their nature. They are intended also to provide entertainment for their members and enable them to satisfy their taste for pomp and pageantry. In the "good old days," it seems, the societies used to arrange weekly balls. The cost was

* One of our informants, Charitable Cyprien, who wanted to clear the grass off a piece of ground and sow it, applied to the Governor of a *vaxin* society with twenty-one members. These latter worked for a whole afternoon, and the Governor gave the *mèt-kòvé* (master of the working party) the sum of 6.30 gdes.

** For instance, the society known as *La sous* (The Spring), which has twenty-four members, did a morning "ronde" which lasted five hours. It was rewarded by a meal for which the owner of the field had made the following outlay:

27 "godets" of maize	3.60	gdes.
7 "godets" of beans	2.00	"
fat	0.75	"
coffee	0.35	"
sugar	0.40	"
spices	0.15	"
	7.25	"

He also made a lavish distribution of mangoes grown on his own ground.

covered by the sale of a day's work or by subscriptions. The President and the Queen made up the sum needed for these rejoicings, if the society was short of funds. All the "big members," who are not liable for work, have to give a ball for the society now and again.

The life of these societies is short. They are "got up" during the period of the earliest sowings, and disperse during the "dead season" of the following year. The President of a defunct society may call a meeting to form a new society, which often, but not necessarily, takes over the name of the old one.

Formation of the Societies

The initiative in forming a society is usually taken by a few enterprising peasants who, after working together for some time, decide to enlarge their group so as to put it on a firmer basis.

They call a meeting of their friends and neighbors, and put forward their suggestion of founding a society. If they obtain enough supporters, they immediately proceed to elect the authorities. The first to be appointed is the "President of the Council," usually the person with whom the idea of a society originated. He is elected by acclamation, after having been proposed by his friends. This President of the Council, or another notability, then puts before the members a series of candidates for the remaining offices. Pointing to them each in turn, he asks the audience *"Eské nou kôtâ?"* (Are you pleased?). If the audience agrees, it responds by cries of "Vive . . ." or "Yes"; if the candidate is not welcome, it remains silent. The entire hierarchy of dignitaries, from the President to the humblest officials, is put to the vote in this way.

As will be readily suspected, these elections conducted by word of mouth do not always take place along strictly democratic lines. An energetic President can "put over" his own candidates, as did the President of Morne Rouge.

At the inaugural meeting of *La Flè Komâs* (The Flower is Commencing) Society, which we attended, the authorities were chosen by general agreement, under the guidance of an old peasant who had had a long and active career as head governor of such societies. The *gouverneur-la-place* was appointed automatically by the organizer's request to him to install the "majors de la batterie"—the *vaxin* players who make up the society's orchestra. The *la-place* made a speech to them, addressing each by his rank. (The major who plays the biggest *vaxin,* the *mamâ,* is the leader of the musicians.)

The old man who was presiding over the assembly and giving it the benefit of his experience, next chose two *général-la-police* each of whom in turn declined the offered post—one because he did not feel he would be energetic enough to keep delinquents in order, and the other for the opposite reason, that he knew he had a tendency to wield the *kokomakak* (cudgel) too violently. The first of the two agreed, however, to become *général-la-place*. The "dirigeur," the "war minister," and the *reine-drapeau* (flag queen) were appointed in the same manner; the last of the three made no secret of her ambition to be a *grâ chef*. Another woman resentfully refused the offer of a post as *reine dirigeuse,* and was mollified only by being raised to the rank of *reine-la-place*. The old man was then asked to choose his own title. He proclaimed himself to be *président bayonnette,* and made a point of reminding everyone that this status dispensed him from working and from accompanying the society—in contrast to the head governor, who has to be active and cannot evade his obligations.

Several new officials asked to have their "duties" defined, but the President confined himself in most cases to very vague explanations. Each time a title was conferred upon a new dignitary, the orchestra, acting as spokesman for the rank and file, responded with a "roule-ment"—a brisk tune ending with a long drawn-out note.

When the "elections" were over, the *gouverneur-la-place* gave the signal for a dance, which he himself led off. Before the meeting broke up, the members of the society acclaimed each of the dignitaries in turn, with cries of "Vive . . ." interspersed with "roulements" on the *vaxin*.

Duties of the dignitaries

The high-sounding titles so dear to the members of the work so-cieties do not always correspond to any definite function, and are interpreted in widely differing fashions in the different groups. The information we collected on this point was most contradictory. The best way to define the prerogatives of these dignitaries will be to de-scribe, so far as possible, the part they are called upon to play in the normal life of a society.

The President. His position is chiefly an honorary one. On all oc-casions, and especially during festivities, he is treated with the great-est deference. He does not have to work with the society but is expected to make a brief appearance during the day, in order to speak a few words of encouragement to the society's members and inquire how the work is going on. He must, however, attend balls; even illness does not dispense him from this duty.

His other tasks are few and their nature rather vague. If he hears of some disagreeable incident that has occurred in the society, he goes to the "President of the Council" and asks him to convene a general meeting for the following Sunday. There, in the presence of the rank and file, he asks the "President of the Council" to clear the matter up, and the latter, in his turn, refers it to the governors and to those officials who bear the title of *la-place*. In the presence of the other members, all the authorities then discuss the disciplinary measures to be applied to the guilty party or parties.

In some societies the President is responsible for the upkeep of the musical instruments, especially the drums, and must also buy the flag that is the society's emblem.

As we have already said, the President is expected to meet the expense of one or more balls. In return for this, he is entitled to one or more days of unpaid work by the team. One of our informants, who had formerly been President of a society for a considerable time, was fond of recalling the balls he used to give every Saturday, and which were so keenly appreciated that the entire society would turn out each week to work for him with a zeal and vigor in keeping with his generosity.

The Council. The President is assisted by a "Council," whose most prominent member, the chairman ("président conseil" or *kôsit*), is perhaps the most influential personage in the society. The other members of the Council are the "people's governor" ("gouverneur du peuple"), the *gouverneur-la-place,* and the supervisor ("dirigeur").

The "President of the Council" is kept informed of everything concerning the society, down to the smallest detail. He is its mentor, and it is he who convenes the assembly whenever necessary, to restore order or make some important decision.

At the inaugural meeting of *La Flè Komâs* Society one member, having been invited to choose his own title, asked to be appointed Deputy—an office which had never been mentioned to us before. It was probably a new one, for its holder immediately proceeded to describe it. In his view, it was something very lofty. The Deputy, he explained, is a *grâ tèt,* capable of expounding their duties to all the other officials. He accompanies the President, and has a right to the general salute ("aux champs") accorded to every important dignitary on his arrival. He went so far as to add that even if he went away and came back again ten times running, the orchestra would have to play the salute to him each time. He ended his speech with the hope that the society would not refuse him the right to one unpaid working party.

"Governor of the people," "supervisor" (dirigeur-la-place), *etc.* The "head governor" is a sort of foreman. He fixes the objectives for the day's work, and reserves certain tasks for himself—that, for instance, of cutting through thickets with the machete, or rectifying whatever may be badly done. His assistant and occasional substitute is the *gouverneur-la-place* who lines up his "soldiers" facing the section of field (*kouch*) on which they are to work, and takes up a position as file-closer on the right, from which he directs them. A governor is privileged to leave off work when he chooses.

When one *kouch* has been cleared or hoed, the team rests and the governor arranges for *clairin* to be passed round, or a snack to be served. The *gouverneur-la-place* gives the signal for the workers to reassemble and start on a new section of field.

The dignitaries bearing the title of *la-place* include, as well as the *gouverneur-la-place,* the *général-la-place* and the *adjoint* (adjutant or deputy) *la-place.*

In former times, anyone who needed the society's help—in picking his coffee, for instance—made his request to the governor of the people "gouverneur peuple," to whom he sent a bottle of *clairin* and a head of maize, wrapped in a white napkin. The "governor" or the "President" then informed the Council of the request, and the Council passed it on to the society at the next general meeting. The "President of the Council" then announced the date on which the members were to assemble at the dwelling of the landowner who had asked for the team. The society met there very early on the appointed day, and were greeted by the host, who served them with coffee.

These formalities are now no longer observed. Anyone wishing to buy a day's work from a member of the society must still, however, apply to the governor. If the landowner is paying in cash for the society's work, he gives the money, at the end of the day, to the *gouverneur-la-place* who hands it to the governor; the latter passes it on to the member who has sold his "turn."

Certain ceremonies are still kept up, and among those mentioned to us was the symbolic gesture of the landowner in presenting the "governor" with a pitcher of water and a piece of charred wood, to indicate that he intends to provide the society with food and drink. In return, the "governor" gives him a notched stick or a number of coffee berries, to show the exact number of workers in the team.

Every society has, too, its exploring general ("général-découvert," or *zòlié*), who acts as its scout and spy. He reconnoiters the ground on which the society is to work. He inspects its irregularities of surface and notes all thorny thickets, rotten tree trunks, and rubbish liable to hamper his comrades in their task. He also beats the bounds of the field, in search of hypothetical "enemies"—i.e., a rival society, disposed to open hostilities. The "exploring general" carries his investigations even into the kitchen. He prowls round the cooking-pots, lifting their lids to take a discreet peep at their contents. He then makes his report to the "governor of the people."

When the food is ready, the "supervisor" ("dirigeur") goes to taste it, in order to get a more definite idea of its quality, and more particularly its quantity. If he decides that it is insufficient or bad, he complains to the "governor" who calls a council to decide whether the meal is to be accepted or refused. If the dignitaries take the latter course, the humiliation suffered by the landowner is especially cruel. It is, therefore, not lightly resorted to. In examining his case, the council takes his means into account, and tries to discover whether he has or has not been guilty of meanness. If a doubt persists, the "President of the Council" is asked for his opinion, which is final.

If the meal is considered to be acceptable, the musicians sound the assembly, and the "governor" and "supervisors" proceed to distribute the food. This is served out by the various *la-place* officials, who are also responsible for the plates and cutlery, for which they must account to the master of the house. The governor is always careful to set aside a portion for the host. He serves himself last, but if he has reserved too little for himself, the master of the house hastens to send him a generous portion from his own share.

In former times, at the end of a day's work that had given general satisfaction, the *gouverneur-la-place,* who had brought along the bottle of *clairin* sent to him by the landowner, would offer a glass of it to the latter, as a sign of his pleasure. The host, on receiving this honor, would dance a few steps and join the members of the society in their festivities.

The order to stop work is given by the *gouverneur-la-place* who tells the orchestra to sound the assembly.

Female dignitaries. Certain ranks in the society are given to women, who all receive the title of "queen," followed by some epithet such as "bayonet," "flag," "basket," or "supervisor" ("dirigeur"). Their duties are even less precise than those of the men. It is chiefly at balls and other festivities that the "queens" come to the fore, but they also play a very active part in the big working parties organized for coffee picking. The "bayonet queen" (*reine-bayonette*) who is the most important of them, is the female equivalent of the president. Like him, she has to give one or more dances, in return for which the society gives her certain days of unpaid work. The queen sometimes presents the society with an embroidered flag.

The "flag queen" (*reine-drapeau*) carries a banner whenever the society marches in military formation at the end of a day's work or before a dance. She is also to be seen—accompanied by the "flag guide" (*guide-drapeau*), who carries a staff—ceremoniously escorting some distinguished guest or high dignitary of the society on his way to take the drummers' "general salute." This queen, like her colleague the "queen-supervisor," helps the "governor" and his associates to divide up and pass round the food at the end of a big day's team work or at a party.

The "flag queen" is under a moral obligation to bear the cost of a dance or, if she cannot afford this, to contribute a few liters of *clairin* or some food. The society gives her a day's "work" in return for this generosity.

The "basket queen" (*reine-corbeille*) is so called because it is she who hands round the basket in which members of the society place their contributions when a dance is to be organized, or new skins bought for the drums. This "queen" is also responsible for the money collected, and is thus the treasurer of the association.

La Flè Komâs Society has a *kôsit* (consul) queen who, like her male counterpart, is entitled to give shelter to any member who has broken the society's rules, and can also intercede to have his penalty reduced.

Lower ranks. There is a long series of other dignitaries, but they have no special duties, except perhaps for the "secretary" who, in some societies, keeps the list of members up to date. Among the quainter titles we may mention the "General-silence" (*Jal-silâs*), who restores quiet in the society when bursts of untimely chattering occur; the various "ministers," including the war minister and the finance minister; the "district officers" ("arrondissements") and "assistant district officers" (adjoints-arrondissements), etc.

It is evident that the peasants have adopted whatever sonorous titles and administrative terms happened to appeal to their imagination. When it comes to explaining the duties of the bearers, the interpretations offered are sheer puns. For instance, the President of one society told us that the "finance minister" is the man who "finishes everything" (*finances finir*). The "arrondissement" (district officer) is described as a dignitary who "goes round and round" the society, to make sure the work is being done properly, etc. To take these functions seriously would be, in most cases, to misinterpret the spirit of the societies. As one very experienced peasant pointed out to us, in a cooperative work group "the people work all together, and everyone does the same thing, digging or hoeing." The only members of the hierarchy whose task is clearly defined are the "governor of the people" and the "dirigeur" who keep order in the society and are responsible for sharing and distributing the food provided by the host at the end of a day's team work.

Discipline

There are definite rules, accompanied by penalties, for maintaining order and discipline in the societies. The gravest lapse of which a member can be guilty is to absent himself without good reason from work. When it is over, the entire society betakes itself to his house, to carry out a "seizure." An official waving a white flag walks round the house to warn him that the other members are on their way. The society's flag is set up at his door, and the *gouverneur-la-place* goes inside, to ask the reason for his absence and warn him of the penalties he is to incur. The culprit may get off comparatively lightly if he is repentant and humble, and treats the society's envoy courteously: *"Si sé nâmi pa puni moun-la"* (If he's a friend we must not punish him). He will only be required to supply some *clairin* and a little food—just enough for a small dance, which then takes place beneath an impromptu arbor in the yard. But if the offender shows signs of "swelled head" and refuses to apologize, the *la-place* officials carry out the seizure, slaughtering one of his animals and cutting some branches of bananas for a feast at his expense. It should be added, however, that as a consolation prize the society gives its victim a day's free work, either on the very next day or on whatever date suits him.

A delinquent can, if he wishes, take refuge with the "President of the Council" (*kôsit*)—like a defeated politician seeking shelter in a foreign consulate. He then tries to interest the *kôsit* in his case, and to persuade him to intercede and placate the society. The culprit can also obtain pardon by paying the price of his day's work to the head of the labor team.

Any member who, during team work, disturbs discipline and picks a quarrel with a comrade is called to order by the "war minister." If he defies the reprimand, he is arrested by the "police." In the case of a serious incident being provoked by anyone regarded as dangerous, the Council is summoned and, in the presence of the other ministers (war, justice, finance), decides whether or not the offender is to be expelled. If there has been any violence or actual criminal offense, the culprit is handed over to the "Chef de Section" who takes him to the town.

According to the society's rules, no one may be expelled until he has received the day's work to which he is entitled.

A worker who arrives late is "sent to the stake" (*mis au piquet*) by the "stake chief" (*chèf pikêt*); that is, he is made to stand on one foot and rest the other on the point of a sharp stick that is thrust into the ground. He must remain in this awkward position until his comrades have obtained forgiveness for him from the "governor of the people."

The members of the Congo Society of Cap Rouge hold their President responsible for all affronts they may suffer. When they have been badly entertained by some landowner who had asked for their help, they make up for it by going to "bivouac" at the President's house. To "bivouac"—the expression has come down from the civil wars—is the equivalent of making a seizure, and implies that the unfortunate President will have to submit to some degree of robbery.

Relations between rival societies

A society, being modeled on the lines of a little army, was bound to have enemies. These took the form of rival societies, who were the objects of envy; and when two hostile societies met on a road or in a field, a free fight would ensue. At the approach of a society with whom there was no feud, an envoy with a white flag would be sent to circle around in its path, as a sign of peaceful intentions. When the envoys returned to their respective groups, if nothing seemed likely to disturb the peace, each society would delegate its

"General" to bear greetings and assurances of goodwill to the other party. Despite this exchange of courtesies, "war" would break out if one society suspected the other of putting on airs and trying to humiliate it. Another duty of "war ministers" was to maintain peace. This role of peacemaker was also discharged within the society itself. They seem, in theory, to have had authority to mobilize the society— or, to quote one of our informants, to "bring it to its feet," to say "forces, to arms." They are said also to have been entitled to disband it if it became unruly.

A society at work

The foregoing general information is based on the evidence of informants, most of whom were high dignitaries of various societies; but the picture would be incomplete without the description of a society at work. The various details are culled from what we observed during a "ronde" (half day's work) done by *La Flè Komâs* Society for a peasant whose son was one of its most active members.

The *vaxin* players are the first to reach the plot that the society is to clear. They begin playing at daybreak, to remind the other members of their obligations. The others arrive in leisurely fashion, some of them very late, and work does not begin until practically everyone is there.

The workers gather behind the orchestra, which alternately marks time and goes forward with small steps. Everyone tries to adjust his movements to the rhythm of the songs struck up ("envoyés") by a sort of chorus master, who beats time with a stone on the blade of his billhook. The musicians accompany him by striking their bamboo trumpets with long sticks, and do not begin to blow into them until the team has quite picked up the tune and words of the song.

The work is done in a jerky manner, without much coordination. One group will stop for a chat, another will break into a few dance steps. Sometimes a worker will feel inspired to improvise a song about some trivial happening—as when, on catching sight of my camera, one of them composed the following:

> *Yo vini tiré pòtré nou*
> (They've come to photograph us)

About halfway through the morning, the landowner tells the "governor" that he is going to offer some fruit by way of refreshment. The "governor" then goes over to the orchestra, takes off his hat, and bows with a sweeping gesture. At this signal the musicians break off whatever tune they are playing, and begin to make muted sounds which they draw out or cut short at the direction of the "governor," who acts as conductor. These moaning sounds are a summons to the society to stop work and gather together as there is something to tell them. The "governor" then announces that mangoes are to be handed round and that there will be a pause while they are eaten. Everyone goes to sit down in the shade. When the pause seems to be lasting too long, the landowner, feeling uneasy, begins to dig all alone, in the hope that the others will follow his example. The "war minister" gets up and reminds his people of their duties: "Will you never finish eating? Your work is not over. Don't go to sleep over your refreshments." He orders the musicians to "roll, roll" a *levé mach*, a stimulating air played in an abrupt rhythm.

The "governor" then gives further instructions concerning the work, and faces the workers toward the section they are to hoe. Some protest, and suggest that the company shall work in closer ranks on a smaller piece of ground. The "governor," his authority thus threatened, refuses to listen to this criticism.

The society sets to work again with some show of energy, but this zeal does not last long. The orchestra "sounds the rally" once more. This time everyone is convoked to discuss the society's business. Inquiries are made about absentees, and severe strictures are passed on those who have sent no excuse. There are threats of a "seizure" to be operated forthwith at the house of one man who has already failed several times to answer the society's call.

The "governor" takes this opportunity of calling the members to order. He stresses the need for punctuality and diligence and asks them not to swear or use bad language during work. The orchestra marks its approval by greeting each of his statements with long drawn-out, low-pitched notes.

Work is resumed. But the "queen" is now seen approaching, which provides an excuse for a fresh interruption. They escort her, holding a billhook above her head, and the orchestra plays a "salute" in her honor. It is then realized that the queen is late. There is some talk of putting her at the stake, and a sharpened stick is thrust into the ground as a symbol of the punishment awaiting her. When she finally arrives, she is at first reproached, but then forgiven.

The president next makes his appearance on the field. Two dignitaries take up their station behind him and cross their billhooks like swords. They escort him in this fashion to the orchestra, which plays a second "salute" ("aux champs") and blows its trumpets in acknowledgment of the president's raising his hat. With no change in his solemn expression, the president then amuses himself by uttering a series of sharp-toned military commands: "Column, halt"; "Shoulder arms"; "Slope arms on the right shoulder"; "Present arms"; "Long live The Flower Is Commencing Society." Nobody, of course, moves an inch.

After this display of authority, the president withdraws and the "war minister" puts himself at the head of the musicians, whom he leads to a new section of the field where they are joined by all the rest.

At the end of the morning, the *gouverneur-la-place* signs to the orchestra to "sound the rally." The president shouts: "Division . . ." All the members of the society raise their arms and answer him with a long "Ha." At a further order from the president, the men line up and follow the musicians, who are guided by the *gouverneur-la-place* holding his billhook clutched against his chest.

When the entire society is reassembled, it cheers the president, who asks whether there are any complaints. If everyone is satisfied, he orders the trumpet (*vaxin*) players to "roll, keep on rolling." It is now the landowner's turn to come and thank the society for its help.

The musicians show their approval and thank him by sounding their instruments.

The president resumes his series of martial commands. The orchestra plays a quick tune, a "march," and the whole society sets out in military formation for the spot where the meal or light refreshment is to be served.

The "queen" and the host's wife serve the food and drink. When everyone has finished eating, the *gouverneur-la-place* asks the orchestra to play a few tunes, while he conducts, using his billhook as a baton. He then goes to fetch the president, whom he escorts, crossing two billhooks above his head. The president bows ceremoniously to the orchestra and asks three times: "What do you want?" The *la-place* then informs him that the day's work is over and that the society is about to disperse. The president signifies his approval and takes the opportunity to make a long speech. Before the society breaks up, the members come to agreement about the "combites" or "rondes" to be worked in the next few days.

The "ronde"

The "ronde" is a system of mutual aid in agriculture, by which a group of peasants band together to work on each member's land in turn. As the members of a turn only give one another a morning's or afternoon's work, the word is also used to signify any task which takes up only part of the day.

The associations based on this principle of the "turn" are often formed by only a very small group of neighbors, who agree to pool their energies at certain times during the season. There are, however, some more permanent associations, many of which have from fifteen to twenty members, organized into a mutual assistance group. The larger cooperative groups are made up chiefly of young or poor peasants who cannot afford any other form of manpower. The wealthier peasants, who have a great sense of their own importance, will not join these associations, partly because of the time lost in going to work for each member in succession, and partly out of regard for their own dignity, because the atmosphere of a "ronde" is one of familiarity, and the general tone such as no respectable man could endure.

When there is urgent work to be done, a group of associates will often carry out two turns a day. When a member receives help from the team before his turn is due, this is known as a "double" (*ré-doub*). The agricultural tasks which are considered most suitable to the "ronde" system are clearing, sowing, and above all, weeding. The cooperatives organized by Unesco intend to carry out various improvements on the land of each of their members by using the "ronde" system.

Vâjou (before daylight)

The *vâjou* is, speaking accurately, the collective work which begins at daybreak and ends halfway through the morning—whatever the type of cooperation adopted. Thus a *vâjou* may be teamwork done for food; a bought "corvée" or a "ronde" in the true sense of the word. In certain parts of Haiti the afternoon working party is known as the *diné-mâchèt*.

Notes:

1. A "carreau" equals 1.20 hectares, approximately 3.33 acres.
2. The more rapidly the peasant works, the greater his likelihood of obtaining a good crop, for "the spring" may last only a short time and give a bad yield unless the plants enjoy the two months' rain that they need. If the rainy season sets in early and promises well, planting continues until the end of May or even, in exceptional cases, into June.
3. The "ronde" (*rôd*) is the amount of collective work that can be done, usually on a reciprocal basis, by a small group of men in the space of half a day.
4. In the Marbial region the word "corvée" is used in preference to "combite," which is employed in the rest of the country. As is well known, the latter word is derived from the Spanish "convite" (invitation).

MARGARET FISHER KATZIN

17. The Business of Higglering in Jamaica[1]

The purpose of this paper is to describe the internal distribution system of Jamaica, by which produce grown on small farms for sale locally moves from producer to ultimate consumer, and to assess its efficiency as a marketing device.[2] The system functions mainly through middlemen, nearly all women, who are variously called "higglers", "vendors", "speculators", or "wholesalers", but the first designation is most commonly used as a generic term to describe any trader in agricultural produce. Actually a chain of middlemen, of varying lengths, handles agricultural produce as it goes from rural producer to consumer. Some middlemen grow at least part of the goods that they sell and nearly all consume some part of the goods that they buy. The term "higgler", as used here, refers to a trader who is a true middleman in that she buys almost everything that she sells and her trade purchases are made for resale.

Internal exchange takes place mainly at markets, of which there are three types: government-supervised, "free" and roadside. There are 87 government-supervised markets, all of which are enclosed and assess fees from sellers. Of these, Coronation Market in West Kingston is by far the largest and functions as the hub of the internal exchange system. It serves Kingston and the surrounding area, which has the island's greatest concentration of population, and also is a distributive centre for goods circulating in the internal distribution system. Since most goods are accompanied by the trader who sells them, Coronation is the one place where all types of traders from all parts of the island may be found.

SOURCE: Reprinted from *Social and Economic Studies,* Vol. 9, No. 3 (1960): 297–331, by permission of the author and publisher.

TYPES OF HIGGLERS

After three months of interviewing in all parts of the market on all days of the week and the important nights for wholesale trading, most sellers were found to fit into the following groups on the basis of place of residence of the seller, source of goods, regular occupation, number of hours spent in buying and selling and the amount of invested capital. The following classification does not claim to be exhaustive, for there is no limit to the ingenuity of Jamaicans in finding ways to earn a few shillings in trade.

    A. Rural Residents.

      1. *Country People;* women who sell produce grown by someone in their own households.

      2. *Weekend Country Higglers;* women from areas within 25 miles of Kingston, who buy wholesale in Coronation and sell there at retail.

      3. *Country Higglers;* women who buy produce from growers near their rural homes and sell it in Coronation.

      4. *Planter Higglers* or *Speculators;* mostly men who may grow part of their stock, but differ from country higglers principally because they cover wider distances to buy a large quantity of one commodity and transport it a greater distance, often over 50 miles, to market.

    B. Kingston Residents.

      1. *Tray Girls;* women who carry their total stock on a tray or flat basket.

      2. *Weekend Town Higglers;* women who buy wholesale in Coronation and sell there at retail on Thursdays, Fridays and Saturdays.

      3. *Town Higglers;* women who rent market stalls for which they pay a weekly fee that entitles them to sell at any time the market is open.

      4. *Vendors;* town higglers who rent several stalls and specialize in one item, such as tomatoes.

Country people are found principally in country markets, but many come to Kingston if they live within a radius of 25 miles. While they sell at retail in country markets, few do so in Coronation. They prefer to give their goods to one or more town higglers, whom they know, on their arrival at the market and wait to collect until a few hours before they intend to leave the city. Nearly all Jamaican children learn to sell by accompanying their mothers to market. If the best market is more than 20 miles away, few rural women have enough produce to make a regular trip worth while, but nearly all go several times each year. The rest of the time they sell their small weekly surpluses to country higglers or ask a neighbour to sell it. Country people might be called planter higglers but, strictly speaking, they are not higglers since they do not buy the goods that they sell.

Weekend country higglers are poor rural women who need to earn cash to supplement the family income. They come to the market on Thursday afternoons, bringing any small quantities of produce that they may have for sale, and buy goods, on credit if possible, from country people or country higglers and sell at retail in the market. As they sell out one lot, they buy more, and continue the process until noon on Saturday. By that time, if they have been lucky, they will have made a profit of a few shillings with which to buy necessities and to pay the expenses of the trip. Most weekend country higglers live within a 10-mile radius of Kingston, as their earnings are too small to pay the costs of a longer trip.

Country higglers are an essential link in the internal distribution system because they buy produce in remote rural areas and take it to urban markets. The growers may let the country higgler take the goods and wait for payment until she returns or until the following week, or may demand all of the agreed price, or part of it, at the time of sale. The amount of credit extended varies with the customs of the particular locality, the type of produce and the relationship between higgler and grower. Most country higglers take their loads to markets at some distance from their homes because they could be undersold in the local market by country people selling their own crops.

All country higglers have regular customers[3] among growers and town higglers and weekend town higglers. The number of customers waiting to buy from any particular country higgler on any given trip will vary with the scarcity of the goods that she is known to sell, but, if she comes to the market regularly, there will always be some who will buy from her even if her goods are plentiful, because they want to keep her as a source of supply in time of scarcity. The experienced country higgler deals with town higglers with sympathy and understanding so that they will continue to buy from her, but, at the same time, she guards her own interest against them.

A country higgler may sell to town higglers or at retail, depending on the contacts she has built up and the method she has found best. One who regularly sells to town higglers will give out her entire load within an hour of her arrival at the market, unless there is a glut. She only sells at retail if the demand for her goods is so low that town higglers will not take it all. Such a woman prefers a smaller but certain quick profit to the greater profit and also greater risk of selling at retail. Those who sell at retail have built up a dependable group of house buyers who take most of their goods on every trip, but they must depend on passing buyers to sell the rest. Most of those who sell at retail come in on Thursday to allow themselves two full days to dispose of their goods. They are much more at the mercy of thieves and ruffians than are those who sell at wholesale, for they sit long hours with their goods spread out before them.

Country higglers co-operate with other types of traders in several ways. They always extend credit to town higglers and weekend town higglers, as do country people, and only collect for their goods just before they leave the market. Country higglers buy their household supplies, whenever possible, from town higglers who let them use stall space, help guard the country higgler's goods or sell for her in her absence. They may lend money to each other and often belong to the same "partners".[4] Both weekend and town higglers co-operate with each other in much the same ways and all exchange market information.[5]

Tray girls are mostly poor, young women who sell garlic, guinea pepper, black pepper and other spices in penny and two-penny packages. The spices are purchased by the pound from wholesale merchants and broken up into smaller units. Usually a girl sells from a tray only until she has made enough contacts and accumulated enough money to buy stock to sell from a station or stall. A few almost destitute older women eke out a bare living selling from trays.

Weekend town higglers buy regularly from country people or country higglers and sell at regular places in the market, many in space that was originally intended for the use of country people. A few weekend town higglers specialize in a particular line if they can arrange for an assured supply, but even these diversify their stock to reduce the risk. One weekend town higgler, whose operating statements were recorded, specializes in country peppers, but she also handles carrots, escallion, thyme and, intermittently, coconut oil. When her supply is sufficient, she sells at wholesale to other higglers.

Town higglers are the regular stall holders whose names are listed in the books of the market and who pay a weekly fee which entitles them to sell from the stall at any time that the market is open and to use the storage space beneath the stall. The basic stock of a town higgler is semi-perishables, but most of them will buy nearly any type of produce from country sellers, if the price is right. Except for some "Irish" potatoes, dry onions and red kidney beans, which may be bought from importers, the town higgler's entire stock is purchased from country people or country higglers. Established stall holders have built up a clientèle among country people who come directly to them each time they come to the market, rather than search among town higglers whom they do not know for the highest price obtainable.

Most town higglers are in the market six days of the week and at least two nights, but if goods are scarce they will stay more nights to be on hand to buy from any country people who might come in. They buy their meals from the vendors of cooked foods or have them brought from their yards.

Town higglers vary in capital, experience, business ability and size of clientèle. At one end of the scale are those like Miss T, who occupies one stall, has a small clientèle and has been selling in the market for eight years. She has little capital and a total stock of a few quarts of beans, some dry onion and garlic and a few bunches of vegetables that she obtains on credit. At the top of the scale are the most prominent "King Street" stall holders who have a large clientèle, three or four stalls advantageously located, a large and diverse stock and thirty years or more of experience in successful higglering.

"Vendor" is the term preferred by the larger operators, mostly men who specialize in one item, such as tomatoes, and sell both retail and wholesale from the four or five stalls which they rent. Since most of the tomatoes are grown in the distant parish of St. Elizabeth, vendors have standing arrangements with speculators and planter higglers who bring in hundreds of pounds of tomatoes at one time. The speculator could not bring large quantities of perishable items like tomatoes into town unless he were certain that a vendor would take them off his hands. The vendor keeps a notebook with a record of his receipts from each speculator and does not pay him until the following week.

Of these different kinds of traders, those most essential to the internal distribution system are the country higglers, the town higglers and the weekend town higglers. Although some goods are marketed by other means,[6] the fundamental structure of the internal distribution system can be described by a detailed analysis of the business activities of these three types of higglers.

THE BUSINESS OF HIGGLERING

The following analysis of the business of higglering is drawn mainly from the operating statements, covering more than a year, of five country higglers and a weekend town higgler, that were collected and recorded.[7]

Country Higglers

The operations of the five country higglers can be taken as representative of the pattern of higglering practice for their rural area because the five of them have bought goods in the region for an average of 30 years each. They live in three communities that are located within a radius of 8 miles in the uplands of Eastern St. Andrew and across the border in St. Thomas and draw their goods from the same geographical region, but each buys from a different district within the area. All of them have dealt for years in the root vegetables that are grown by small farmers to be sold in the internal distribution system, and all take the truck to town from a spot near the St. Thomas boundary.

The five country higglers are: Miss A, who buys in three communities at an average distance of 6 miles from her home and sells wholesale in Coronation on Friday nights; Miss B, who buys from farmers in her home district and in two other communities each 5 miles distant from her home and sells wholesale and retail in Coronation on Thursday nights, Fridays and Saturdays; Miss C, who buys in her home district and sells wholesale in Coronation on Friday nights; Miss D, who buys in her home district and sells wholesale and retail in Coronation on Friday nights and Saturday mornings; and Miss E, who walks with a donkey and buys from three hilltop communities that are, on the average, 6 miles from her home, and sells wholesale and retail in Cross Roads Market on Thursday nights, Fridays and Saturday mornings. If her load is too large for her to take on Thursday, her 22-year-old son sends part of it to her by truck on Friday. However, it should be emphasized that in the hills of Eastern St. Andrew and bordering St. Thomas, as in most of Jamaica, the distance in miles between two points is no indication of the time and effort required to carry loads from one point to another. Paths are narrow, precipitous, irregular and slippery both in wet and dry weather.

TABLE 1. DATA ON FIVE COUNTRY HIGGLERS.

	Miss A	Miss B	Miss C	Miss D	Miss E
Age of higgler	53	45	47	42	54
Years of higglering regularly	38	28	31	14	39
Buying days per week	2	2	2	2	2
Selling days per week	1	2	1	1	2
Help of others:					
Buying and preparing load	2d.; husband	2d.; husband	husband	husband	son; mule
Market trip	1d.	1d.	—	—	1 girl
Conjugal condition	Married	Married	Com. law 3 years	Married	Widow
Contributions to household	Over half	Over half	Half	Half	Over half
Number of children	4	3	2	0	2
Taught higglering by:	Mother	Mother	Mother	Sister	Friend

As shown in Table No. 1, all five higglers spend two days of each week, Wednesday and Thursday, walking and buying. Each has the help of at least one other person in the household in carrying the goods, washing and preparing them for market. Three of them spend one full day each week on the market trip; two spend two full days each week. All five have had many years of experience at successful higglering. All went to market with their mothers as young children, but Miss B and Miss D did not take up higglering until after they were fully adult. Miss D worked for six years for wages in the fields before she began to sell with her sister, who was a higgler, and only later did Miss D take up higglering as a regular occupation. None of the others has ever earned money at any other occupation. Miss A, Miss B and Miss C learned higglering from their mothers, all of whom were higglers. Miss E has a sister, two years younger than herself, who also is a higgler.

Miss A takes her 13-year-old daughter to the market with her, as she used to take another daughter, who is three years older, but she does not plan that either of them will become higglers. She expects to stop taking this daughter, as she did the other, when she is old enough to be influenced by the bad market environment. Miss B has no definite plans for the daughter who regularly goes to market with her, but it is probable that she will start higglering for herself within a year or two. She has been so well schooled in every aspect of higglering that her mother sometimes sends her alone to the market with her load. Miss C has no daughters, Miss D has no children and the one daughter of Miss E is a dressmaker.

Before proceeding to the analysis of the operating statements, the meaning of the categories should be made explicit. The operating statements, as recorded in the field, included supporting data that has not been reproduced here because of lack of space. The complete statements include a record of each buying transaction, specifying the type of goods, the quantity, the price and the name and place of residence of the producer; a breakdown of total expenses into the components of passenger fare, freight charge, market gate fee and handcart fee; details of business transactions completed in town for rural neighbours and suppliers, specifically, the name of the owner, value and type of goods sold for others together with the price of each item, and a listing of the value and types of goods purchased for others; and personal business for the higgler and her family aside from the dealings involving the market load.

In order that the data of business operations would include only items purchased for sale, we have subtracted the value of goods taken from the higglers' fields and sold with the load and goods sold on consignment for others, on which the higgler did not receive her usual margin of gross profit. However, it is impossible to subtract the extra expense incurred by the higgler in taking such goods to market because expenses were not recorded separately for such items. Therefore, the total expense that is shown as being incurred with each week's market load is, in some cases, overstated. The additional freight, market and carriage fees seldom aggregate more than 2/-, but each higgler is careful to keep these items separate and to collect the proper amount from the owner of the goods. The higgler incurs no additional monetary expense by purchasing goods for others in town because no freight fee is charged on the return trip.[8]

Analysis of the operating statements of the five higglers, combined with information garnered from other sources, reveals eight basic facts about their business activities.

1. All five pay cash for all goods, with the exception of large quantities of red peas.

2. The time spent in higglering is almost exactly the same for a small load as for a large one.

3. Minimum operating expenses are very high.

4. Operating expenses are relatively constant and do not vary proportionately with the value of the load.

5. Current market prices are known to grower and higgler alike.

6. Growers grant that the higgler is entitled to a certain gross profit as compensation for her time and expense.

7. The gross profit margin accrues to each unit, i.e., 6d. per bundle of carrots. The margin per unit remains the same regardless of the number of units.

8. Therefore, *the larger the load the larger the higgler's net profit*.

1. None of these five country higglers routinely buys goods on credit or borrows money, entailing the payment of interest, with which to buy load. Each of them built up her operating capital by starting with only a few shillings and adding profits to capital over the years. Miss C currently borrows money for higglering, but in lieu of interest, she purchases supplies for the lender's shop in town and takes the goods to him in the country, saving him the freight charges. Other higglers in the area report that they have borrowed money from friends, relatives or a shopkeeper without paying interest. Only when they (other higglers in the area) are desperate do they borrow from a woman of the district who charges interest. The five higglers take goods on consignment only when they are offered a large quantity of a high-priced item, such as red peas, when they are out buying load without sufficient funds to pay for it. If the grower lives at an inconvenient distance from the higgler's house she gives him the money on the next trip, but if he lives nearby, she sends it to him the day following her return from the market.

2. The time spent in higglering is almost exactly the same for a small load as it is for a large one. As shown by Table 1, all five higglers spend the same amount of time and effort each week calling at the yards of their suppliers and going to the market regardless of the size of the load, because the time and effort are mainly expended in travelling. The same ground must be covered to call upon each of the suppliers regardless of the quantity of produce they have to sell.

The truck schedules are the most important factor determining the time spent away from home on the trip to the market. Each woman must leave her home in time to be at the truck stop well in advance of the scheduled departure time, wait patiently during the long periods required to allow other passengers to board, and remain in Kingston until the truck leaves for the last return trip of the day on Saturday, because only on that run does the truck go all the way to the end of the road. All five of the higglers buy large quantities of groceries in town, in addition to purchases made for others, so that their baskets are very heavy on the return trip and all want to ride on the truck to the point nearest their homes. Thus, Miss A does not leave the city until three o'clock on Saturday afternoon, although she usually finishes selling within an hour of her arrival at the market and could complete all of her purchases within an hour or two in the morning.

3. Minimum operating expenses are high because of the irreducible item of 5/- passenger fare and the fact that freight charges are very high for the 19-mile distance. Therefore, the minimum load which a higgler can take to market and be certain that the gross profit will exceed the expenses is large.[9] Years ago, when three of the five higglers began to trade regularly with very little capital and, therefore, small loads, they walked to town carrying the load to minimize their operating expenses. In the operating statements, the few instances when a load barely covered the expenses were invariably those showing a very small load. The graphs of the business operations of all five higglers indicate that a load which costs less than £4 is likely to yield little profit and one less than £3 probably will yield none. With smaller loads, the higgler must resign herself to receiving little or no compensation for her time. That higglers are aware of the risk involved in taking small loads to market is indicated by the fact that the number of higglers decreases very sharply when vegetables are scarce.

4. The total operating expenses do not vary proportionately with the value of the load, as is shown by all of the graphs. For loads varying in value from £3 to £11, Miss C incurred expenses fluctuating between 10/- and 15/-, and the other four graphs show a corresponding relationship. For instance, Miss A took a load to market on January 19th for which she paid £2. 9. 0 on which she incurred a total expense of 10/-, and another on November 23rd costing £9. 0. 4 on which the expenses were 12/6. Thus, for a load over three times greater in value, the expenses were only 21 per cent greater.

5. Farmers are at no disadvantage when discussing prices with higglers because of the efficiency of the informal market intelligence

network. Farmers congregate at the truck stops on Fridays and Saturdays where the principal topic of conversation is the prices of locally-grown goods in town markets. Also, some country people always go to the market every week and return with information about prices. Thus, the growers often know the prices received by the higglers for their goods before the higglers return.

6. All higglers, growers and others in the community with whom the matter was discussed, agreed that the higgler is entitled to a specific margin of gross profit to defray expenses and to compensate her for her time and effort.[10] A particular gross profit margin is associated with every commodity that is sold to higglers in the region. Thus, if carrots are selling in the market for 1/6, growers consider 1/- to be the proper price that the higgler should pay them. They do not try to play one higgler off against another to increase the price that they receive and higglers do not bid against each other by offering to give part of the gross profit to the growers.

Where cash is paid for the load, the grower does not expect to share in the extra profit if the higgler should find the market "running bright" and receive more than the margin, but neither does he consider it his responsibility if she should "meet bad market" and be forced to sell for less than the customary margin.

According to the records of the five higglers, the customary margins of the commodities which constitute most of their stock are: 6d. per bundle for carrots, thyme and beets; 3d. per bundle for turnips; 6d. per quart for red peas; and the margin for escallion varies between 6d. and 1/- per bundle. Other commodities that do not come into crop as regularly as the above listed items yield gross profits that are not so constant, rather they fluctuate about a certain amount. Usually the gross profit is greater near the beginning and end of the crop season. Two of the latter type of commodities are salad tomatoes, which yield an average gross profit of 3d. per pound, and cabbage, which brings an average gross profit of 2d. per pound.

The graphs of the commodity prices indicate that the prices paid to farmers and those received by the four higglers in Coronation and the one in Cross Roads Market were remarkably uniform for long periods.[11] The gross profit for escallion remained at 1/- for several months and then reverted to 6d. per bundle; carrots and thyme prices were stable for even longer periods. It appears that the larger margin can be maintained for escallion for some time without resulting in an increase in the price paid to the growers. During the first six months of the year, loads were small and prices were low, but the customary margins for each type of produce were maintained, with very few exceptions.

Supporting data in the operating statements reveal that, whenever a higgler makes an unusually high profit on a load, it is due to the fact that, while most of the load yields the customary gross profit, one or more commodities bring unusually high prices. For example, on February 8, 1958, Miss A made a net profit of £3. 4. 0, over 50 per cent, on a load for which she paid £6. 10. 6. The prices were:

	Paid			Received			Gross Profit		
Carrots	1/-	per	bundle	1/9	per	bundle	9d.	per	bundle
Escallion	2/-	"	"	2/9	"	"	9d.	"	"
Thyme	1/-	"	"	1/6	"	"	6d.	"	"
Beets	1/-	"	"	2/-	"	"	1/-	"	"
Salad	9d.	"	"	1/3	"	"	6d.	"	"

Though the gross profit per unit for escallion was near the average for the year and that for thyme at the customary level, that yielded by the other load components was unusually high. The gross profit for carrots was 3d. above the usual figure, beets 6d. above and salad tomatoes, 4d. Other higglers did not show correspondingly high profits because none of them took salad tomatoes to the market and only Miss D was able to sell beets for 2/- per bundle, as did Miss A. Miss E sold beets for 1/9 per bundle, and all of them except Miss A sold carrots for the usual 1/6 per bundle.

7. The fact that the gross profit accrues to the higgler on each unit of goods is extremely significant, for it gives the higgler an incentive to maximize her load. The price graphs for all five higglers shows that the gross profit margins for each unit of each commodity held remarkably constant throughout the year. Under these conditions, the higgler is encouraged to take as large a load as possible commensurate with her ability to dispose of it, because, for all goods beyond the minimum required to defray expenses, gross profit becomes net profit.

8. Therefore, the larger the load, the greater the net profit. This is borne out by the fact that the profit curve for each of the five women almost parallels the curve for the cost of the load. Further evidence is contained in Table 2, which sets forth the average of the higgler's weekly operating statements for the year. In each case, the greater the average value of the load, the higher the average net profit.

Whenever there is an extremely valuable load without a proportionately high profit, which occurred in some weeks during the end of the year for all five higglers, the explanation lies in the composition of the load. Nearly all of the peak loads included one or two bushels of red peas in addition to the usual root vegetables. Red peas yield a customary gross profit that is only 20 per cent of the unit price when the price is at its lowest, while the customary margin for carrots is 50 per cent of the unit cost to the higgler. Therefore, two loads costing identical amounts would yield different gross profits if one were made up entirely of red peas and the other of carrots. The latter yield would be almost three times greater than the former. Thus, the net profit gained from loads made up largely of red peas is a much smaller proportion of the cost of the load than is the case when vegetables make up the entire load.

TABLE 2. AVERAGE OF HIGGLERS' WEEKLY BUSINESS OPERATING STATEMENTS FOR ONE YEAR BEGINNING FEBRUARY 2, 1957.

Name of Higgler	Miss A			Miss B			Miss C			Miss D			Miss E			Miss F		
	£	s.	d.	£	s.	d.	£	s.	d.	£	s.	d.	£	s.	d.	£	s.	d.
Average total sales per week	6	18	11	6	0	0	8	16	11	4	10	6	8	1	10	10	6	1
Average cost of sales per week	4	15	7	4	6	4	6	6	6	3	0	7	5	17	10	8	1	6
Average gross profit per week	2	3	4	1	14	5	2	10	5	1	9	11	2	4	0	2	4	7
Average total expenses per week		11	8		12	0		13	6		11	0		13	3		1	0
Average net profit per week	1	11	8	1	2	5	1	16	9		18	11	1	10	9	2	3	7

Judging from the data, it appears that the above general facts of higglering apply to higglers who sell in other nearby markets as well as those who sell in Coronation. Though Miss E sells at Cross Roads and Miss C occasionally takes her load to the Morant Bay market in St. Thomas, there are no significant differences between their operating statements and those of the three who sell at Coronation. Gross profit margins and selling prices are almost identical with those obtained at Coronation for the corresponding weeks. On the one occasion, February 22nd, 1958, when Miss E sold escallion for 2/- per bundle at Cross Roads, receiving no gross profit, while the others obtained the customary margin at Coronation by selling escallion for 2/6 or 2/9 per bundle, the difference was not due to a lower market price at Cross Roads. Miss E's escallion that week was of such poor quality that she was forced to sell below the market price. On both the preceding and succeeding weeks, she obtained the usual gross profit for escallion, as did those who sold at Coronation.

This indicates that wholesale prices are nearly uniform for markets near the area of production, even though retail prices are generally higher in other markets than at Coronation.[12] Higher retail prices in other markets do not signify that town higglers there obtain higher gross profit margins than Coronation town higglers, but reflect the fact that their costs, generally speaking, are higher. Much of the fresh produce sold in other Corporate Area markets is purchased at Coronation by the town higglers who sell in those markets. Consequently, they incur additional handcart and market fees in transporting the goods to their stalls in other markets.

Analysis of the operating statements shows a discrepancy between the actual freight charges for red peas and the opinions held about them by higglers, farmers and truck drivers. All three types of informants report that the freight charge for red peas is much higher than would be justified on the basis of their bulk because they are a very high-priced commodity. Truckers and higglers report that higglers try to conceal red peas from the driver by hiding them among the vegetables or carrying them in a hand basket. The data show that red peas are not as profitable to the higgler as are vegetables and the statements show that freight charges do not increase markedly when the higgler is carrying red peas.

A possible explanation might be that the driver does charge a high fee when the red peas are taken to market by the grower, because she will realize a large sum of money from the sale, but that his charges are more reasonable when a higgler takes them, because the driver knows that her profit margin is not large. Unfortunately, this evidence that truck drivers are sympathetic to higglers cannot be verified, because no information is available on the expenses incurred by country people taking red peas to market.

An additional general fact shown by the operating statements is that each of the higglers specializes in a few crops which are her principal load components throughout the year. Other related items are added to the basic components as they are available, but there is no evidence that country higglers make a practice of searching for different types of load components as a means of diversifying the load and thereby minimizing the risk of a loss in the case of a glut of one item in the market. It would seem to be a valid inference that the basic components, in the cases of the five higglers, are not a matter of choice, since they are the same for all five—carrots, escallion and thyme—and these three vegetables are the only crops grown in the region that are ready for market almost every week of the year. However, an incident involving the marketing of flowers occurred during the field stay which demonstrated that higglers with long experience in certain types of goods and well-established contacts with farmers and buyers, do not readily add a different kind of load component, even when it is available and has been demonstrated to be profitable. In other words, they do not seek to diversify their loads by adding unrelated commodities that would entail developing a different group of suppliers and buyers, and also require them to learn to interpret market conditions for another line.

The process by which the cultivation and marketing of flowers were adopted by Riverside residents demonstrates their reluctance to incorporate new lines. In 1940, farmers in a community 6 miles from Riverside began to grow flowers which were taken to Kingston markets by higglers of that community and sold at prices that yielded high returns to both growers and higglers. The higglers had previously traded in vegetables, but gradually changed to flowers as the farmers began to grow more flowers and fewer vegetables. They established trading relations with town flower higglers and retail customers and sold in the markets, in a street flower market in the main business district, and to florists.

Though they knew flowers to be a profitable crop, many Riverside farmers were reluctant to cultivate them for several reasons. They require more capital investment than vegetables, are more likely to be damaged by adverse weather conditions, and, probably most important, if the demand for flowers should suddenly fall off, the grower cannot utilize them by feeding them to his family or domestic animals, as he can do with vegetables. However, by 1947 a few Riverside farmers had begun to grow flowers which they sold to the distant flower higglers, since those higglers were anxious to take more flowers to market and no Riverside higglers displayed interest.

More and more Riverside farmers began to grow flowers as it became evident, from the success of the earlier plantings, that the climate and soil were well suited to them. Also, those who had first cultivated flowers enlarged their plots. As flower production increased, the outside higglers continued to monopolize the marketing. Each Wednesday, they walked to Riverside with their double flower baskets and carried away the crop for the week. It was common knowledge that the flower higglers earned higher profits than vegetable higglers and always had sufficient cash to buy quantities of flowers, but established Riverside higglers refused to take flowers to market even when requested to do so by growers. Also, everyone knew that the risk of taking flowers to market was less than other goods that would yield a comparable profit, because the customary freight charge for flowers was only 2/- per basket and there was almost no danger of damage to the load, since flower baskets were always placed on top of all other freight.

In late 1956, one young, inexperienced Riverside higgler began to buy flowers, but she had difficulty obtaining them because the farmers did not wish to antagonize the regular flower higglers who could be depended on to take all of their flowers throughout most of the year. However, she made the rounds of the growers every week, bought whatever flowers they were willing to sell to her and, to keep her expenses low, walked the 25 miles to Coronation with the flowers in a basket on her head. By May, 1957, she had been able to increase the size of her weekly load somewhat, but she was still walking to the market.

In June of 1957, Miss B began to take flowers to Coronation along with her usual vegetable load, only because her husband had begun to grow them. After she had established trading relations with town flower higglers, she began to buy from other Riverside growers. Since that time, when flowers are available, her entire load may be made up of flowers. Subsequently, the other higglers, with the exception of Miss C, took flowers from their own fields to market on rare occasions, but none of them, other than Miss B, had bought flowers to sell by May of 1958.

The other four country higglers continued to specialize in root vegetables, adding other related items as they became available. They took their loads, as made up in the country, to the market and sold them to their customers. They made no effort to diversify their loads beyond the variation that comes easily to hand in the rural district. Under certain weather conditions at some times of the year, a load may be almost entirely thyme or escallion because that crop is the only one that growers have to sell. At such times, the higgler takes that load to the market and sells it, buys her groceries and other household items and returns home.

From these facts revealed by analysis of higglers' operating statements, extensive interviews with higglers and prolonged periods of observing them at work, it is apparent that the first requisite of successful higglering over a period of time is the establishment and maintenance of a large pool of farmers as suppliers and of town higglers or retail customers in the market, because these two factors determine the size of a higgler's weekly load and, consequently, her net profits. When a farmer has become one of her "customers", a higgler does not risk losing him to another higgler by deceiving him, taking advantage of him or indulging in aggressively hostile behaviour toward him. Rather, she is fair and responsible in all of her dealings with him and never neglects an opportunity to cement the relationship by doing any favours that lie within her power. All country higglers shop, scrupulously and carefully, for their suppliers and their suppliers' families.

One very successful higgler, whose home is near the end of the main road used by all upland farmers on their way to town, always greets them from her yard, invites them in to rest, offers them food and drink and "when bad weather catch dem" lends them dry clothes or puts them up for the night. As a result, three sidemen are required to lift her weekly load onto the truck. The neighbours say of her: "If she can do a favour for the littlest pickney, she will do it."

Each of the five country higglers is as careful to establish and maintain trading relations with higglers in town and retail customers, if she sells at retail, as she is with farmers. She deals with them with sympathy and understanding, seldom hesitating long to accept a little less than the agreed price, if, in her considered judgment, the town higgler will not be able to obtain her usual margin of gross profit. If any of her regular buyers do not come to her place soon after she arrives in the market, she will send to let them know that she is there and keeps the goods that they usually buy until she hears from them, even if others who are not regular buyers clamour to take them.

She knows that her group of town higglers depend upon her for a part of their goods every weekend and she considers it to be her responsibility to get the load to them. If she is unable to come to the market for any reason, such as illness, she will send someone to buy the load and take it to her regular customers.

This affords an explanation for the story, often heard in Jamaica, which alleges that higglers and country people make the trip to market every week, not out of economic necessity, but because they enjoy it.[13] As the story goes, if one meets a country higgler on her way to the market with a big load while she is still near her home, and offers to buy the whole load and pay more than she can expect to get for it in the market, she will refuse to sell. The reason for the refusal, according to those who tell the story, is that she wants to go to Kingston for some high life, to be able to do things that would not be approved by her rural neighbours. Such incidents have rarely been documented, but if they ever occurred, the reason for the higgler's refusal is obvious. The higgler wanted to preserve her trading relations with town higglers and knew that, if she failed to come to the market, they might well begin to buy from someone else and probably would not readily return to her. If any of those who tell the tale had guaranteed to buy the higgler's entire load every week, the answer might have been different.

Rural women, generally speaking, like to go to Kingston occasionally, to buy clothing or even groceries because they believe that things are somehow better and fresher if they are purchased in town instead of the nearby shop. Also, a much more varied selection is always to be had in Kingston. But they would not carry heavy loads over precipitous trails for two days each week in all kinds of weather and go to Kingston on a crowded truck and sleep for a night, or even two nights, on a hard bench in the market merely for pleasure.

After a country higgler has established trading relations with a town higgler, there is little bargaining over prices because both know the costs and usual gross profit of the other and the state of the market. Neither tries to enlarge her own gross profit at the expense of the other. However, when the market is slow and the goods which they handle are plentiful, each will be forced to take a little less than her usual margin. At such times, they bargain over the amount to be cut from the country higgler's gross profit. Usually, final settlement is not made until the town higgler has had time to sell some of the goods and make a fairly accurate estimate of the price that she will obtain for the remainder. Each of the higglers is interested in preserving the good will of the other and the final settlement is one to which both can agree. A country or town higgler who insisted on preserving her own margin of gross profit at the expense of the other would be unable to maintain her trading relations over a period of time.

Since a country higgler considers it to be her responsibility to supply her customers, she does not search in the market for the highest price obtainable, but goes immediately to her place, judging the state of the market from information gained on the trip to town and in or near the market, and sells her load to her regular customers. When goods in her line are scarce, she knows that she could sell her load to almost any town higgler, but she makes no effort to do so, but rather, takes the opportunity of cementing her relations with her regular customers. As a result, when the country higgler's goods are plentiful, they feel obligated to take some from her, giving her as much of her usual margin as possible. However, in such cases, both buyer and seller are well aware of the market price and, if the price on which they agree departs at all from the market price, it will be by a very small amount, probably not exceeding 3d. per unit. To both buyer and seller, the most important feature of the trading relationship is the fact that through it the town higgler is assured of a supply of goods and the country higgler is certain of a market for her load. This is always a matter of concern, but it becomes vital during periods of scarcity or glut.

Some sellers favour their regular customers in other ways. To give "brawta" or "make-up" is the practice, all along the line from rural producer to retail buyer. This is identical with the British and American practice of giving something additional in a transaction which is called, for example, "giving an extra unit or more to boot" as in the "baker's dozen".

The judicious giving of "brawta" is a mark of the successful higgler. She considers it a good investment in customer relations, saying: "That's why they come back to me," or "I give brawta to encourage them" (to make it profitable for the customer to continue to deal with her). Some country people and country higglers who sell to town higglers say: "I don't give it, but dem take it." Country higglers who specialize in oranges report that their customers always take one "to taste" before they buy, and expect at least one extra for every dozen that they buy. One or two extra "fingers" are given with every dozen bananas. However, a higgler only gives "brawta" to her customers if she has received it from her suppliers; she does not give away goods for which she has paid.

The amount given as "brawta" is, in many regions, established by local custom, sometimes through variations in the quantity represented by the same unit of measurement. Thus, a country higgler is able to sell ten dozen oranges for every "hundred" that she buys because the "hundred" that she buys exceeds one hundred units. In some rural areas, oranges and grapefruit are counted by the "trose". Twenty "trose" make one "hundred", but in the country, six units equal one "trose". Furthermore, when a country higgler buys a commodity that is easily injured, such as oranges or grapefruit, she is usually given an additional quantity, which may run to as much as twenty extra units for every "hundred" that she buys, in case "the load mash".

In practice, a hundredweight is not invariably 112 pounds. In the yam trade, one "hundredweight" is 135 pounds. The custom of giving extra weight arose as an allowance for the dirt that clings to yams, and, at first, was quite small. However, dealers began to compete with each other, not in the price per pound, but in giving more over-allowance in weight, until the present figure of 23 pounds became established practice.

At present the same type of goods are sold using different units of measure. Grains, pulses and coffee are sold by the quart, pint, gill and also by the pound. Some ground produce, such as carrots and escallion is sold by the bundle, but the same type of goods is also sold by the pound. Before the Second World War, it was customary to sell by the "heap", though the size of the heap could be varied, allowing for manipulation of the price. On completion of a sale, the higgler usually threw a little more on the heap and many of them became adept at making the gesture without adding anything to the heap. Selling by the heap has largely disappeared, but the cry: "Penny-a-heap" can still be heard in Coronation Market, for tray girls customarily sell dry onions in small mounds which they spread out before them on the ground.

Weekend Town Higglers. Operating statements for the year were also obtained from Miss F, a weekend town higgler, who is a customer of two of the five country higglers and sells, both retail and wholesale, on Fridays and Saturdays in Coronation Market. She is 26 years old and has been higglering for six years, having started after coming to Kingston at 18 and working as a domestic servant for one year and then selling cooked food in a bar. She prefers higglering to her previous occupations because she earns more money in less time and is free four days each week to care for her 10-year-old daughter, with whom she lives in a small room in a yard in the slum district of West Kingston. Her daughter sometimes comes to the market on Fridays and Saturdays to run errands or sell for her mother in her absence.

Miss F specializes in country peppers, which she sells both at retail and wholesale when she has sufficient supplies, but she also sells carrots, escallion and thyme. Escallion and carrots are bought by the bundle from Eastern St. Andrew country higglers and by the pound from those who come from South St. Elizabeth. Country peppers are usually purchased by the pound and sold by the dozen.

The goods which she sells at wholesale are sold in the same condition in which they were purchased, but at a price that yields her a particular gross profit. For her retail business, she breaks up the large bundles that she buys from country higglers into smaller bundles that she sells at a price that will yield the particular gross profit per unit for the original bundle. The graph of her buying and selling prices shows that the retail price for any item is determined by adding her customary gross profit to the price that she paid for it. For example, if she buys escallion for 2/- per bundle, she breaks each bundle into five small ones, each of which she sells for 6d.; but, if she also bought other escallion for 3/- per bundle, she divides the latter into seven small bundles, each of which she sells for 6d. In both cases, she receives her customary gross profit per bundle, which is 6d. She follows a similar practice with all goods in which she deals. The carrots that she buys by the pound, she sells by the pound, after adding 2d. per pound to the price. When she buys country peppers by the pound and sells them by the dozen, she translates the price per pound into a price per dozen and adds the amount of her customary gross profit. For example, on April 20, 1957, she bought peppers at 9d. per pound. Each pound contained 12 dozen, so she sold them for 1d. per dozen, earning a gross profit of 3d. per pound.

Weekend town higglering differs from country higglering in several respects other than the fact that the country higgler goes to the farmer to buy while the weekend town higgler buys in the same market where she sells. Some of the basic facts of country higglering must be modified to apply to the weekend town higgler.

1. Weekend town higglers obtain most, if not all, of their goods on credit, while country higglers risk their own capital.

2. Both country and weekend town higglers spend the same amount of time on small loads as on large ones.

3. Whereas minimum operating expenses of the country higgler are very high, those for the weekend town higgler are very low.

4. The country higgler's operating expenses do not vary proportionately to the value of the load, but those of the weekend town higgler do not vary at all.

5. As in the case of the country higgler, current market prices are known to buyer and seller alike.

6. As in the case of the country higgler, both buyer and seller grant that each is entitled to a certain gross profit margin.

7. The customary gross profit accrues to each unit of goods handled, as it does for the country higgler.

8. In both cases, the larger the load, the higher the net profit.

1. The custom of country people and country higglers granting credit to town higglers and weekend town higglers until a few hours before they intend to leave Kingston has been discussed above. As a consequence, a weekend town higgler must have capital only when she is setting up in business and has not yet established a reputation in the market. After trading relations have been instituted with a sufficient number of country higglers, she needs very little capital, if any.

2. Miss F spends two nights and two days in the market each week regardless of the size of her load, as do most weekend town higglers. However, a few weekend town higglers begin to sell on Thursdays and thus spend three days each week in the market. After a weekend town higgler has become a regular customer of country higglers, she may not be compelled to stay in the market at night to buy during times of normal supply or of "plenty", for she can ask her suppliers to set aside whatever goods she thinks she will need and then call for them in the early morning. However, most weekend town higglers only do this occasionally, because they prefer to be in the market where they can judge the state of supply and demand for their lines before they buy. They also have another advantage over the country higgler, for they need not wait for a truck, but can return to their homes if they finish selling early.

3. Operating expenses for the weekend town higgler are very low. They consist of a 6d. station fee for each day that she sells, but if she should buy any goods outside the market, she would have to pay the market gate fee. She does not have the handicap of a high mini-

mum operating expense. A load of even a very small size is almost
certain to yield her some compensation for her time.

4. Miss F's total business expense remained at 1/- per week
throughout the year, although her loads varied in value from
£3. 11. 3 to £15. 6. 8. Business expenses for weekend town higglers are greater only if they sell more days and, therefore, pay the
6d. daily station fee for each day, or if they buy part of their stock
outside the market and thus become liable for the market gate fee
when they bring them into the market.

5. Current prices are known to country higglers and town higglers
alike. Though the town higgler knows more about the current state
of the market than the country higgler who has just arrived, the country higgler is not ignorant about them, and final settlement is not
made until she has had adequate time to judge them.

6. The willingness of the country higgler to grant that the town
higgler is entitled to a certain gross profit has been discussed above.
The one point on which country higglers sometimes express envy of
town higglers is that the town higglers can be in the market for as
long as they choose and can, therefore, afford to wait until they get
their price, while country higglers must sometimes sell for lower
prices because they must leave the city.

7 and 8. The fact that the gross profit margin accrues to each unit
of goods handled has the same significance for the country higgler
and the weekend town higgler, specifically, the larger the load, the
greater the profit. The principle is more applicable to the latter than
to the former because a larger load does not increase the weekend
town higgler's operating expenses. All gross profit, beyond the 1/-
station fee for two selling days, is net profit. This accounts for the
fact that Miss F's net profit curve parallels her "cost of load" curve
very closely throughout the year. The discrepancy during the late
months of the year, when the load was at its greatest and net profits
did not increase proportionately, was due to the presence of the
same load component, red peas, that caused the same effect in the
graphs of the business operations of country higglers.

Town Higglers

Operating statements of the type obtained from country higglers
and the weekend town higgler, were not obtainable from stall holders, the regular town higglers, because of the nature of their business
and their manner of conducting it.[14] Their business hours are from

six in the morning until five in the afternoon six days each week, and from six to ten on Sunday mornings and at least two nights each week. Most retail sales are of small quantities, such as one-half pint or a big gill, and their purchases are comparatively small, such as one or two quarts of beans. No record is kept of purchases, sales or cash balances. During the week, cash realized from sales is paid out for purchases and foodstuffs are taken from stock to feed the higgler's family. She feels that she is doing well if her stock remains near the usual level, while her sales yield enough cash to purchase new stock and to meet her living expenses and her obligations in her savings pool. If she should find herself with a lump sum above her usual cash reserve needed to buy from country people, say from £1 to £5, she usually purchases imported goods, such as red kidney beans, Irish potatoes or dry onions, from a wholesaler. Such purchases are always for cash because wholesale merchants do not ordinarily extend credit to higglers. Town higglers whose volume of business does not permit them to accumulate cash surpluses sufficient to purchase imported commodities in the quantities in which wholesalers sell them, combine their cash to buy a bag of potatoes or onions and divide the contents.

Town higglers obtain most of their stock from country people and country higglers, but prefer to buy from the former because country people sometimes sell at lower prices than country higglers since they have grown the goods themselves. Country people bring goods to them to sell at any time during the week and the higglers pay cash at the time of purchase, if the seller is leaving the city immediately. Those who are staying in town for several days wait for payment until they are ready to leave. Some, who are a town higgler's regular suppliers, accept part payment and wait until the next trip for the remainder. Therefore, in order to conduct her business properly, a town higgler must have a quantity of cash on hand and tend her stall throughout the week, buying and selling as the opportunity arises.

One town higgler agreed to keep a complete record of her daily transactions. Her accounts were checked by taking an inventory of her stock at the beginning of each week and again at the end of the week and comparing the book inventory with the physical inventory. In five different weeks, it was never possible to find one in which the book inventory, obtained by adding the week's purchases to the physical inventory at the beginning of the week and subtracting the week's sales, agreed with the physical inventory at the end of the week. The amount of the difference ranged from £2 to £3. Possible explanations for the discrepancy are: first, she failed to record some of her transactions, or, more likely, she was deliberately understating her volume of business in order to understate her net profits.

Judging from the operating statements that were recorded, it is undoubtedly correct to infer that the same fundamental considerations govern the business activities of the stall holders, the weekend town higglers and the country higglers. These are a primary concern with building trading relations with as many suppliers and customers as possible, because the larger the volume of business the greater the net profit. Expenses for the town higgler are relatively constant, consisting of the 2/- per week fee for each stall, plus the market gate fee for any goods purchased outside and brought into the market for resale. Although data are not in hand to prove the point, it is safe to infer that a relatively fixed gross profit is earned on each item sold.

Town higglers obtain their original capital to stock their stalls in various ways. Some work at another occupation, such as domestic service, to earn money to participate in a mutual savings group until they have the needed amount, and others enter into an economic partnership with a common-law husband.

Until a few years ago, both women and men worked as banana loaders at the Kingston docks and many were common-law mates, the man and woman sharing living expenses. However, banana ships discontinued loading at Kingston, and although men continue to work as stevedores loading and unloading other types of cargo, this type of employment ceased for women. At that time many of the men gave their mates enough money to stock a stall in the market and the business partnership continued on a healthier basis than before. When they were both loading bananas, each could work only when a banana boat was loading, but under the new arrangement, the woman has a more regular source of income, even though her weekly earnings are less than those of the man when he is working. The household is thus assured of food and necessities during the frequent periods of unemployment that are characteristic of work on the docks.

When a town higgler is short of operating capital, she usually borrows from one of the successful town higglers who always have cash on hand. Town higglers who have sold from adjacent stalls for some time often lend each other small amounts, such as £1, without charging interest, but in most cases, interest is charged. One town higgler described the general practice: "I lend money to a few honest higglers in the market. I lend out a person £5 on Monday and that person must give back the £5 and 5/- for the week on Saturday. It mustn't sleep out over the weekend and they can take the £5 next Monday. Some people charge more—2/- on the pound. I know a woman; she lets a girl take £4 from Thursday to Saturday and every weekend give her back 5/- and her £4. But sales are slow now, so I just take what I believe they should pay."

Undoubtedly some higglers obtained their original capital and amounts of operating capital, from time to time, from relatives or common-law husbands, but this is not an important source for higglers as a group, because, in most higgler families, the higgler is the principal contributor, if not the only one, to the support of the household.

PRICES

Some of the factors entering into the determination of prices have been discussed above in the description of the business operations of higglers, but the determination of prices in the higglering system, as a whole, merits a fuller account.

Retail prices for the same type of goods exhibit variations at a given time in Coronation Market. Customary prices to growers and customary gross profit margins to wholesalers and retailers tend toward uniform supply prices. However, within this framework of comparatively uniform supply prices, the following factors operate to bring about variations in retail prices.

1. Goods of the same type but varying in quality will usually be priced differently.

2. Anywhere along the line from grower to ultimate consumer, a seller may demand and get a price that is somewhat higher than the customary one. Nearly always, unless there is an extreme glut, she will be able to get the higher price if she waits long enough and her goods are of high quality. Thereafter, every higgler who handles part of that load will be forced to ask a higher price than others are asking at that particular point in the chain of transactions, unless she is willing to reduce her gross profit. Town higglers who sell in the market every day can buy such over-priced goods with less risk than a country or weekend town higgler. Stall holders buy on the assumption that, if the item is attractive and sound, a buyer will eventually

come who will pay the price. One "King Street" higgler said: "Everybody doesn't sell the same price. Everybody asks her own price according to how she bought it. If your customer come with it a 3d. higher than somebody else, you pay it. You wouldn't stop buying from her and buy from somebody else for a 3d. If it is pretty and nice, somebody will come and buy it from you. You pay her price to keep her selling to you."

3. Conversely, if a higgler is able to make a particularly fortunate purchase at less than the prevailing price, she may sell the goods below the usual retail price, taking only her customary gross profit. One higgler, who did not customarily sell coconut oil, received 32 quarts at a low price from a friend. She began to sell it below the going market price, adding only the customary margin to the low purchase price. Very soon regular coconut oil higglers, who had heard from their customers that she was underselling them, came to test the quality of her oil. They did not dispute her right to sell at the lower price, but neither did they reduce their own prices to meet hers.

4. Waiting is the usual response of higglers when they see their line being sold cheaper than they are able to sell it. Stall holders demonstrate by their buying and selling practices that they are astute judges of the supply and demand schedules of the goods in which they deal. Because they are aware of the constant factors in the supply prices of produce entering the market and know very well the seasonal variations in quantity and price of each commodity, they can be quite certain that goods being sold below the market price at a given time will soon be exhausted, and then buyers will have to pay the going market price.[15] If the majority of higglers are selling at the lower price, so that nearly all of a commodity in the market is affected, a country higgler or weekend town higgler will usually assume that there is a glut of that item and reduce her gross profit margin, after waiting for a reasonable time. But town higglers almost never reduce prices in the face of lower ones elsewhere, but instead, wait either for a particular buyer or for a turn in the market. However, if the glut endures, they will insist on paying lower prices to their suppliers so that they can meet the changed retail prices.

5. If the market is slow, leaving many country higglers with unsold goods near the truck's departure time, they may take them back to the country to feed their families or livestock or leave them with

a town higgler to sell for them, but if it is possible to sell them, even at a loss, they usually do so.[16]

The retail price in any given transaction is further influenced by the fact that all higglers ask different prices from different types of buyers, whom they classify as follows:

1. Buyers of the higgler's socio-economic status.
2. Middle-class buyers or maids buying for middle-class households.
3. Non-Jamaican middle- or upper-class housewives and tourists.

Higglers are adept at classifying buyers. They can tell when a woman of their own socio-economic class is buying for a middle-class household and when she is buying for her own use. In the latter case, she will buy in very small quantities, since her own cash is limited and she has no place to store food. Hence, if she buys in quantity, filling a large basket, the higglers know that she is buying for someone else.

The price to one of the higgler's own class, when the customer is buying for her own use, will almost never exceed the higgler's cost plus her usual margin, and she is more likely to reduce the price for a poor woman than for others. As one stall holder put it: "The hungry feed the starving." Furthermore, this type of buyer is always well acquainted with prices and is forced, by her meagre resources, to try to drive the best bargain she can. From a maid who is shopping for a middle-class household, a higgler demands her usual price, but she may give the buyer some small items for her own use.

The price to the middle-class housewife will not only always be high enough to cover costs and the usual margin, but the higgler routinely asks slightly more, 3d. or 6d. on each item, of most buyers in this class. However, a shrewd Jamaican housewife who is an experienced shopper knows that many higglers demand a higher price of her than they are willing to take. Thus, if she is persistent in bargaining, she may get the goods at a price very near the higgler's cost plus her margin.

A regular customer of the higgler would not try so hard to induce her to reduce her price because the two of them would have arrived at an understanding and both would be anxious to continue the relationship. Regular customers receive "brawta" and, usually, the choicest items in the higgler's load. Also, in times of scarcity, rather

than sell her entire load quickly to strangers, the higgler favours her
regular customers by reserving all of her supply for them.[17]

An extra 6d. or more is almost always asked of non-Jamaican
housewives or tourists because higglers assume that they are able
to pay more and that most of them are unfamiliar with the usual
prices and have little knowledge of or experience in bargaining. For
example, a higgler who sold large, sweet navel oranges to another
higgler for 3d. each and to a market cleaner for 4d. each, immediately afterward demanded 6d. each from a non-Jamaican for the
same type of fruit. However, few Coronation higglers ever have an
opportunity to sell to non-Jamaicans, so that their total gross profit
is little affected by this type of buyer.

From the above data, it is plain that no formal or informal price-
fixing arrangements exist between higglers who sell in competition
with each other in Coronation Market. Each town higgler sets her
own retail price, taking into consideration her costs, the going market price and her estimate of her ability to sell at least a part of her
stock at a price somewhat above the going market price. In the Jamaican system of distribution of fresh produce, most goods move
through chains, varying in length, of higglers from the rural grower
to the ultimate consumer. Over a long period of time, a certain price
at each juncture, which has been established by custom, dominates
the expectations of both buyer and seller. During periods of price
stability, after the goods are taken from the site of production, the
price at which each subsequent exchange takes place consists of two
elements, both determined by custom, the cost of each unit of goods
to the seller plus a specific gross profit margin per unit. For a number of commodities of different unit values, this gross profit margin
per unit is fixed at 6d.

Price changes in the entire chain of transactions are initiated at
the retail level in response to changes in supply and demand in the
market. The change is reflected back to the producer through successive changes in the price at each juncture in the chain. At each
level the unit gross profit margin, 6d., is maintained, while the cost
of the goods changes by an amount corresponding to the change in
the retail price, until finally, the price to the grower is changed by
that amount. The new price structure may remain constant for some
time until another change is initiated at the retail level. Thus, a competitively determined retail price dominates a structure in which
other prices are determined largely by custom. Price competition

between buyers or between sellers does not obtain at levels in the chain other than retail.

Only during the transition from one customary price structure to a new one do the traders bargain to determine the amount of the change to be absorbed by each of them. For example, if a country higgler arrives at the market with carrots, for which she has paid the grower 1/-, anticipating that the previous wholesale market price of 1/6 would continue, to find that retail higglers cannot pay 1/6 because the retail price has fallen from 2/- to 1/9, the country higgler and town higgler may agree to share the loss by each reducing her gross profit margin by 1½d. But, the following week, the country higgler will try to buy carrots for 9d. so as to restore her 6d. gross profit margin. More than one week may be required to establish a new price structure because the grower must be convinced that the reduction is relatively permanent and not confined to one week's market.

Within the general pattern of price stability punctuated by orderly change, other factors that were discussed above produce variations in prices. Producers sometimes take their goods to market and sell to town higglers or consumers at a lower price than prevails in the higgler system. Also, country higglers without an established group of suppliers and buyers bring loads at irregular intervals and often sell at a lower price than the regular higglers receive. The price at which some retail transactions are completed departs from that expected when customary costs and profit margins dominate, because of the higglers' discrimination between different types of buyers. Though the above types of exchanges may be made at prices other than the going market price, the range of variation seldom exceeds 6d. per unit. The price in a given transaction ordinarily departs from the market price no more than 3d. in either direction. All sellers and almost all buyers know the customary prices of the goods that they buy and bargaining centres around that figure.

As stated above, retail prices are determined by conditions of supply and demand in Coronation, under conditions that appear to be purely competitive. A market in pure competition must be atomistic, open, free and its trade must be conducted by buyers and sellers who act rationally. Coronation is atomistic because there are numerous buyers and sellers and the operations of each are so small that no one of them can influence the general market price; it is open in that no barriers are erected against additional sellers; and it is free since prices, with the exception of a few items, are not fixed by authority and no informal price-fixing arrangements exist.

The final criterion of a competitive market, that of rational behaviour of the participants, requires a somewhat fuller discussion. In the Jamaican economy, where markets and monetary exchange obtain, all that rationality requires is that, when presented with alternative choices, a buyer will select that choice which will maximize his utility, roughly speaking, and a seller will select that choice which maximizes his gain or profit, and, in general, this may be thought of as a long-term proposition. From this point of view, the behaviour of both town and country higglers is perfectly rational in the sense that each seeks to maximize her long term gain. Given the conditions and structure of the market, the greatest chance to accomplish this is by cementing long-term buyer-seller relationships.

In a competitive market, according to standard price theory, the supply prices of the different sellers will vary according to the cost of the goods that they bring to the market and their expenses, plus the amount of profit that they expect to make. Demand prices will be determined by the number of buyers in the market and the intensity of the desire of each for the goods in question. The market price will tend toward the point where the curves, representing the demand and supply prices of the various traders, meet. Unit retail prices in Coronation are, in most cases, identical with the costs of the seller plus a customary margin of gross profit which covers the seller's business expenses and yields a small return to her. Effective demand, at that price, is sufficient to clear the market, as a rule. The presumption is that market price, in the long run, does not rest very much, if at all, above the lowest point of minimum cost. Thus, since it satisfies these conditions, Coronation appears to approach a market in pure competition.

As far as could be ascertained, similar conditions prevail at other markets in the Kingston area and in rural government-supervised markets. Therefore, the probability is that the prices that obtain in the higglering system are determined largely by the conditions of supply and demand in the markets.

RELATIVE EFFICIENCY OF THE HIGGLERING SYSTEM[18]

The problem of assessing the relative efficiency of the higglering system for the Jamaican economy as a whole involves consideration of several factors. The higglering system does, in fact, perform an essential function by making available to consumers goods that are produced in small quantities on scattered, relatively inaccessible, outlying farms. An evaluation of its efficiency depends upon a judgment as to whether, in doing so, it consumes an undue amount of the resources of labour and capital available in the Jamaican economy. Generally speaking, if labour or capital is devoted to marketing activities when it would yield a higher return if otherwise employed, the community is poorer by the amount of the difference. As Galbraith has pointed out (*4*, p. 1–2), much of the marketing research in the United States proceeds on the assumption that an excess amount of resources is consumed in marketing activity and concentrates on labour because that factor is scarce as compared to capital. As a consequence of the relative proportions of labour and capital, marketing facilities that require a maximum of capital and a minimum of labour have proved to be most efficient in the United States. But it is an error to apply this specialized definition of efficiency to countries in which the factors are present in different proportions.

Research in the economies of countries with limited technological development has shown that their problems require a different approach because the relative availability of capital and labour is the reverse of the situation that obtains in the United States (*4; 1,* p. 25; *2; 7*). Therefore, facilities that utilize a greater proportion of labour and a lesser proportion of capital are likely to be more efficient for such underdeveloped economies. However, such facilities should be examined to determine whether they consume an undue amount of the factors available in the economy.

The business routine of country higglers may be uniquely adapted to the present conditions of agricultural production and transportation in Jamaica. Most regular country higglers pay for produce when they collect it and later transport it to market. In the process, much of the gross profit is paid out as expense which serves as income to other economic units, such as transport services, markets and handcart men. The remainder of the gross profit which the higgler retains as a return on invested capital and compensation for her time, is seldom large but, more important, each market trip entails the risk of a net loss.[19]

Stall holders in Coronation Market invest more capital in stock for longer periods than the average country higgler and are available in the market at nearly all times to country people who wish to sell and consumers who wish to buy. The net return to a stall holder is proportionate to her volume of business, since expenses are relatively constant. Though the typical stall holder probably earns less than £2 per week, on the average, the most successful ones with large stocks and many years of experience in which they have developed large groups of suppliers and buyers and skill in judging trends in the market, undoubtedly earn more.[20] However, their invested capital is much greater and they must keep large amounts of cash on hand to buy in bulk from country people. It is improbable that their greater return is derived from unduly high prices exacted from consumers because Coronation prices are generally acknowledged to be the lowest in the city.

As concerns the weekend town and country higglers who crowd the market on Fridays and Saturdays and concentrate their activities on trade in highly perishable produce, they buy, or preferably obtain on consignment, stock from country people and country higglers and sell at retail. An astute woman who is able to gain the confidence of enough country higglers to obtain a substantial quantity of goods can earn, on the average, £2 per week with the investment of little or no capital and only two days working time, but the great majority of weekend higglers probably earn less than 10/- in an average week. Undoubtedly some additional sellers are required to supplement the stall holders in disposing of the large quantities of perishable produce that is usually brought to Coronation on Thursdays and Fridays, but many more come to the market than are necessary to effect distribution of the goods. However, the fact should not be neglected that they probably perform an important service to the community. It may be that their presence in such numbers is responsible for the fact that prices in Coronation Market are competitively determined, with consequent benefits to the community as a whole.

Higglering requires a minimum of capital investment by the community because no special facilities are provided for higglers. They use public transportation facilities and public markets which, presumably, would be maintained if distribution were effected by other means.

It would seem, then, that under the conditions that obtain in Jamaica, the higglering system is a relatively efficient means of effecting the internal distribution of locally-grown produce. Though more labour is utilized than is required to accomplish the task, this does not constitute faulty allocation of resources, since a resource is mis-

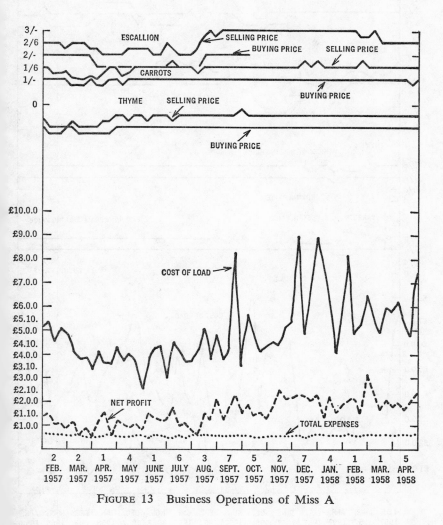

FIGURE 13   Business Operations of Miss A

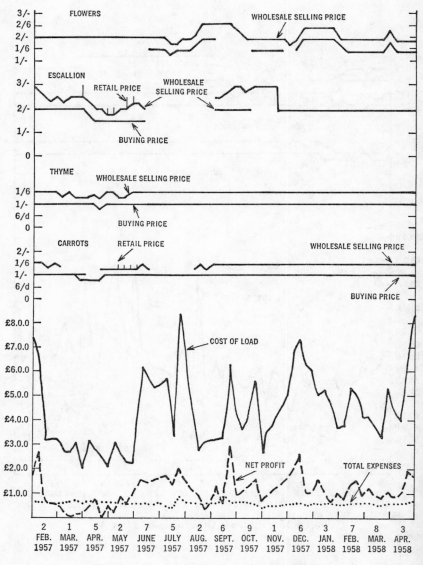

FIGURE 14   Business Operations of Miss B

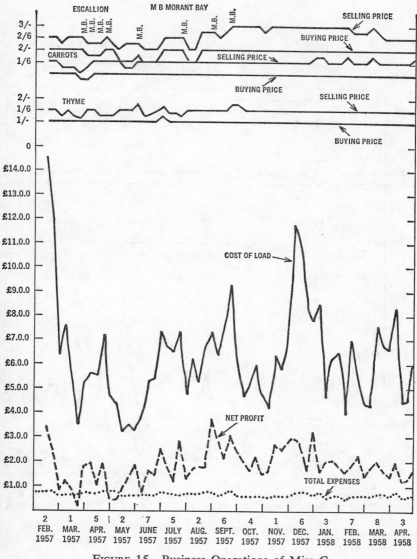

FIGURE 15   Business Operations of Miss C

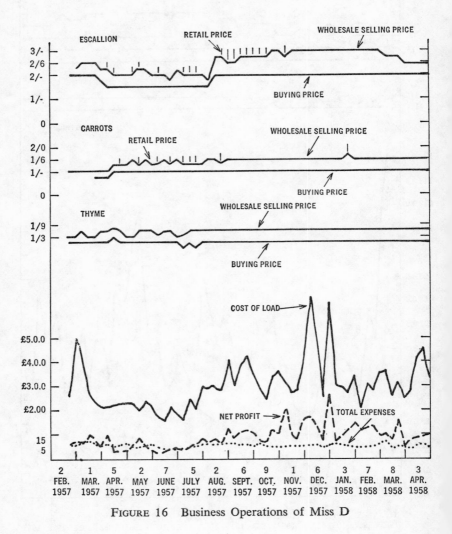

FIGURE 16   Business Operations of Miss D

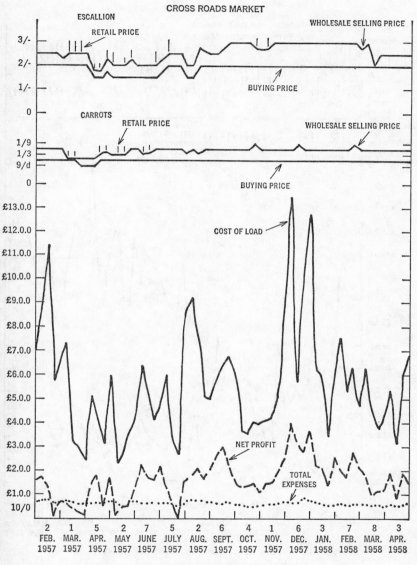

CROSS ROADS MARKET

FIGURE 17   Business Operations of Miss E

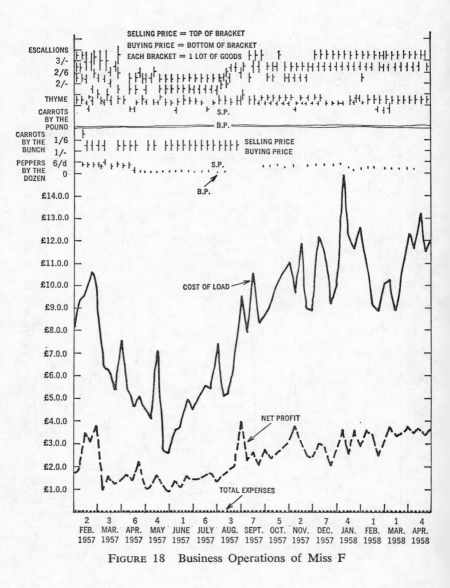

FIGURE 18   Business Operations of Miss F

used only if it is consumed in one activity when it would yield a higher real return if otherwise employed. Almost all labour in the higglering system is supplied by women and children who, as productive workers, are redundant in Jamaica. If another marketing system were adopted that eliminated higglers and did not, at the same time, provide alternative employment for the women who were displaced, most of them would swell the numbers of the unemployed. Some might find employment as domestic servants or agricultural labourers and some displaced country higglers might spend more time in their homes or cultivating their fields, but their contribution to national income in such occupations would be less than it is when they are occupied as higglers.

The essential points to be kept in mind in assessing the relative efficiency of the higglering system are: first, the contribution of higglers to the national income is sufficiently important to warrant the existence of the system and, second, their contribution to national income in alternative employment, under existing conditions, would be less than it is under the higglering system.

Notes:

1. This paper is a part of the writer's doctoral dissertation, entitled "Higglers of Jamaica", for which data were collected during a nine-month field study in the fall of 1956 and the spring of 1957. Many persons in Jamaica, in addition to a number of higglers, gave valuable assistance to the writer, particularly Prof. H. D. Huggins, Dr. M. G. Smith, Mr. Russell LeWars, and Mr. W. D. Burrowes. Dr. Sidney Mintz, of Yale University, also made helpful suggestions.

2. Most of the material for this paper was gathered at Coronation Market and in a rural community, that is here called "Riverside", which is approximately 20 miles from Kingston in rural St. Andrew. Other markets were also studied for short periods both in Kingston and some rural areas.

3. The term "customer" is used by Jamaicans as a generic term applied to anyone with whom one has regular business dealings. Higglers call both those who sell to them and those who buy from them "my customers". One town higgler said: "The house buyers who buy from us are our customers, but country people call us 'customer' and we call them 'customer'. We are really the customer because we do the buying, but I don't know what we would call them, so we still call them 'customer'." M. G. Smith cites a farmer who calls his regular workers his "customers" (9).

4. An informal mutual savings institution that is widespread in Jamaica. An account of "partners" is given in (5).

5. This refers only to higglers on nearly the same level of experience and business ability. It is well known that some town higglers take advantage of the ignorance and naivete of country people.

6. Two vegetable producers' co-operatives were operating in Jamaica at the

time of the field study, one in St. Elizabeth and one in St. Thomas, but they marketed a very small quantity of goods compared with that which moves through the higglering system.

7. In late 1956 and early 1957, many lower-class Jamaicans displayed hostility to and distrust of the political party then in power to the extent of being reluctant to co-operate in any way with outsiders seeking information. To most higglers, a stranger in the market asking questions and recording information about expenses, costs, turnover and earnings could only be gathering material for the government to utilize in some way to their disadvantage. Worse still, interviewing of higglers selected at random was made impossible by market idlers who followed the interviewer about making violent threats toward any higgler who appeared to be willing to answer questions. In the search for data on business operations, many town and country higglers were approached. Several, besides the six agreed to submit a record of their transactions, but the statements were not used because checking revealed them to be inaccurate.

8. This is not true for other parts of the island where freight charges are assessed and collected on the return trip.

9. Mintz states that a woman who takes a load from St. Ann to Kingston "estimates that she must gross about £5 to make her trip worth while; that is, £1 or less profit, £1 or more for expenses, and £3 for reinvestment in the next trip". In this quotation "gross" is used for "total sales". We use "gross" for total sales less cost of goods sold. Thus, the above higgler's "gross" is not £5 but £2, which is not significantly different from the operations of St. Andrew country higglers (6, p. 21).

10. This is also true in other parts of the island. "If the person who has come to buy is a higgler . . . bargaining is prohibited. If, for example, the commodities in question are chickens and eggs, the seller will set his price in accordance with the prevailing market price. Chickens will sell by the pound and eggs by the dozen, and custom dictates that the higgler shall not earn more than 6d. profit on the pound or dozen. If eggs are retailing at market at 2/-, the higgler will buy them at 1/6. If the higgler can get more than his 6d. profit by selling the eggs at more than 2/-, then it is his good fortune" (3).

11. Although the price per bundle may remain constant, fluctuations in value of these goods may be reflected in variations in the size of the bundles.

12. Coronation retail prices are generally recognized to be the lowest in the city.

13. In an article condemning the practice of women marketing produce, a columnist for *The Farmers' Weekly*, which is a supplement to *The Gleaner*, referred to the women as "fun-seeking farm wives" who squander money earned by their husbands by buying "ice-cream, snowballs, yeast-punch and fried fish on week-end jaunts." June 1, 1957, p. 2.

14. The following paragraph refers to the typical town higgler. The few who occupy several stalls stocked with bushels of grains usually have sufficient cash on hand to buy in large quantities.

15. If an item is being sold in the market well below its known value, it is certain to be reported to the market police, who investigate on the assumption that the goods have probably been stolen.

16. In the full year's operating statements, none of the five country higglers reported an instance of selling below cost or leaving goods with town higglers because of inability to dispose of it. However, other higglers reported doing so at an indefinite time in the past.

17. Some housewives have well-established trading relationships with par-

ticular country higglers in which consideration of each for the other is taken for granted to the extent that, not only do they refrain from bargaining over price, but the housewife may send someone else to the market for the things she wants.

18. The following argument and conclusions are similar to those advanced by Mintz (*6*, p. 21–23).

19. It has been suggested that some Caribbean communities, including Jamaica, purchase the services of self-employed higglers at a lower cost than would be approved for wage-employed labour. On those occasions when the higgler's gross profit is approximately equal to her business expense, she is working for zero wages; when she loses money, her wages are a negative quantity. The community countenances this condition when it would not tolerate employers utilizing the labour of others at such wages (*8*).

20. Bauer states that to the extent that luck does not enter into the results, the superior knowledge, skill and effort of some traders give them higher returns than are enjoyed by other traders, and "such skill should be rewarded. In under-developed areas it is one way of encouraging the development of some of the qualities which are necessary if members of the rural population are to become fitted to take an active part in economic advancement." (*1*), p. 226.

References cited:

1. Bauer, P. T.
   1954 *West African Trade,* Cambridge.
2. Bauer, P. T.
   1957 *Economic Analysis and Policy in Under-developed Countries,* p. 117–18. London.
3. Cohen, Y.
   1953 "A Study of Interpersonal Relations in a Jamaican Community", p. 55. Ph.D. thesis, Yale, Unpublished Ms.
4. Galbraith, J. K., and Holton, R. H.
   1955 *Marketing Efficiency in Puerto Rico,* Cambridge, Mass.
5. Katzin, M.
   1959 "The Jamaican Country Higgler", *Social and Economic Studies,* Vol. 8, No. 4. University College of the West Indies, Jamaica.
6. Mintz, S. W.
   1957 "The Role of the Middleman in the Internal Distribution System of a Caribbean Peasant Economy", *Human Organization,* Vol. 15, No. 2, pp. 18–23.
7. Nurkse, R.
   1953 *Problems of Capital Formation in Under-developed Countries,* p. 48. Oxford.
8. Rottenberg, S.
   1953 "Note on Economic Progress and Occupational Distribution", *Review of Economics and Statistics,* Vol. XXV, pp. 167–70.
9. Smith, M. G.
   1956 *A Report on Labour Supply in Rural Jamaica,* p. 14. Jamaica.

CAROLINE J. LEGERMAN

18. Kin Groups in a Haitian Market

This article will deal with the significance of kin groups in a developing market situation in Haiti. Since the kin groups were only among women selling specific products—eggs and live fowl—I will try to point out the relation between the nature of the products and the organization of selling.[1]

SETTING

Within the largest 'bourgeois'[2] market place in Port-au-Prince, Haiti, most of the market women have stands and are full-time sellers; most of them are permanent residents of the city as well. A woman selling fruit may have a sister selling rice next to her, or a daughter who helps her, or a brother who is a butcher in this same market place. These types of arrangements are fairly consistent throughout the market place except among the women dealing in poultry and eggs, where I found a significant number of kinswomen selling the same product, but further organized into groups. Out of some 40 sellers, a group of seven and another group of 17 claimed to be kinswomen. This article is concerned with the latter group. It describes the group composition; how the women are organized into smaller working units; the specific rights and reciprocal duties expressed in kin ties; changes over time; and the relation of this situation to urban conditions.

NATURE OF THE PRODUCT

The Haitian peasants keep poultry unpenned so that the birds can scavenge in the yard. Since they require little feeding, and they re-

SOURCE: Reprinted from *Man,* Vol. 62 (1962):145–49, by permission of the author and the Royal Anthropological Institute of Great Britain and Ireland.

produce quickly, fowls become a convenient and traditional means of storing wealth. Poultry and eggs

> are important items of middle class consumption in Haiti. Such foods are rarely eaten by the peasantry, since their sale brings cash to buy relatively large quantities of basic grains and starches as well as condiments and other necessities. Hence the flow of poultry and eggs to the larger cities and Port-au-Prince is significant.[3]

Like most local produce which is grown or raised on a small scale by peasants, poultry is marketed by women, and there may be several intermediaries involved.

MARKETING OF POULTRY

Women who market these items do not treat them as speculative goods; there is a low freight charge to bring them to the market place, and there is generally sufficient demand for poultry for the seller to have a fairly regular turnover. Though the market situation varies from season to season, month to month, week to week and even day to day, all the poultry-sellers whom I interviewed and those interviewed by Mintz stated that the selling of poultry and eggs is very safe, barring the death of a bird or breakage. Although I did not get enough data on wholesale and retail prices, the following examples indicate the margin of profit on three sales made on the same day in the 'bourgeois' market place studied. A chicken bought wholesale at 2.25 *gourdes* ($.45) was sold retail at 2.50 *gourdes* ($.50); a turkey bought wholesale at 12 *gourdes* ($2.40) was sold retail at 15 *gourdes* ($3.00); and a cock bought wholesale at 4 *gourdes* ($.80) was sold retail at 5 *gourdes* ($1.00). There were occasional days when the women were forced to sell their stock at wholesale prices, but I never witnessed a day when the women sold below the price which they had paid. It would be perhaps too much to say that poultry-selling continuously constitutes a sellers' market; but there seems to be a steady demand which, in relation to supply, does favour the sellers.

Country women, who are often part-time or very-small-scale sellers, will bring several birds to their local market places. Here they are generally bought up by other local women, who buy in bulk for further wholesale trade in larger rural market places. These women may sell to another wholesaler who may sell in turn to a retailer who comes from the city to buy at the large rural market place, or the wholesaler may take stock right into the city to sell at a wholesaling depot. Owing to the shortness of time in the field, I cannot document seasonal variations in the supply of fowls reaching Port-au-Prince. But it is clear that different regions vary in their production of fowls and eggs at different times. Mintz found that in the country during spring planting season the peasant sells his poultry to keep them out of the fields.[4] Variation in demand may also be related to the coffee harvest, when there is generally more money available, and probably an increase in the consumption of poultry in the city at least. All the city poultry-retailers agree that the demand is greatest and the price highest during Christmas and Easter. This suggests the festive and sacrificial nature of poultry—which is as true for the 'bourgeois' as it is for the peasants.

Poultry-sellers in the city buy in bulk at rural market places outside the city, or from middlemen who come to the city's wholesaling depots, and break bulk by wholesaling and retailing. All the poultry-sellers occupy a specific area within the market place studied, paying 1 *gourde* ($.20) a day and 1.50 *gourdes* on Saturday to municipal officials for a selling place. But this also entitles them to storage rights for their stock which they leave overnight in the market place. During some weeks, I counted from 26 to 32 paid places daily. This is a six-day market place and fluctuations in the number of paid places were due to the differences between the main market days, which are Monday, Wednesday and Saturday, and other market days. However, I counted up to 40 sellers on some days. The discrepancy between the number of paid places and the number of sellers can be explained through an analysis of the groups of kin selling together.

FIGURE 19   Genealogical Relations in a Haitian Market

The unbroken black lines denote working arrangements, the dotted lines kin groupings. *x* and *xx*, ritual kin ties. *A*, storing and selling arrangement avoiding the tax. *B*, buying and selling arrangement. *C*, storing arrangement avoiding the tax. *D*, buying arrangement. *E*, selling arrangement avoiding the tax. *F*, mother and daughter buy and sell together part-time. *G*, selling arrangement. *H*, mother with a young daughter who helps as she learns. *I*, selling arrangement

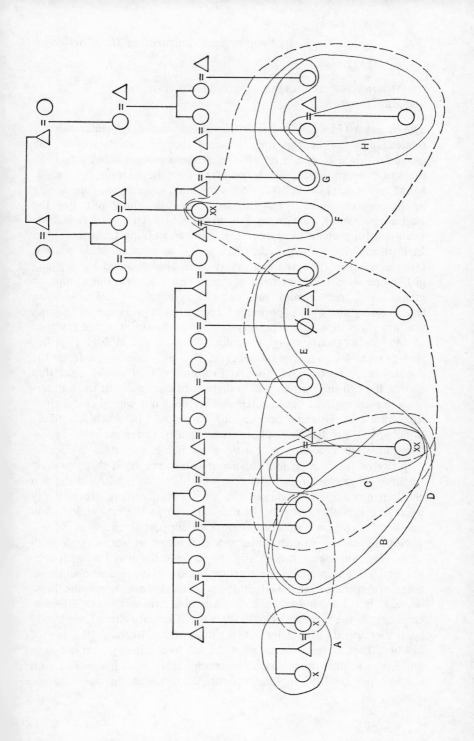

The diagram (Fig. 19) indicates how these women are genealogically related, and the broken lines indicate through which women the groups overlap. It should be noted that these women stand largely in the same generation. I would estimate that the average age is 45. Mintz in his rural studies found that the main kin relation functioning in the market situation was the mother-and-daughter unit. For the Haitian peasantry, marketing is a prestigeful occupation. It is conventional for women to market, the younger learning from the older. In Port-au-Prince, the poorer, often part-time or small-scale peasant seller coming in from the country is often accompanied by a young girl, more often than not her daughter. This girl serves as company, guards stock, runs errands and helps carry loads. At the same time, she is going through a period of apprenticeship. However, among the first generation urban poultry-retailers, I found only one instance of the mother–young-daughter selling combine (H in Fig. 19), but this woman was a marginal seller in the city, coming in from the country only several times a week. From my data, I would argue that among the full-time urban sellers there is discontinuity in the mother-daughter selling unit because the mother does not want her daughter to continue in the same occupation. This would be much less likely to occur in a rural setting. These women's aspirations for their daughters range from owning a *'boutique'* to being a doctor. While the majority of the women learned about commerce from their mothers or some other close female relative who also sold poultry, their own children are attending school. The women explain the discontinuity by saying that they grew up in the country. 'In the city children do not work with you because you work to support them.'[5]

Not all of the women have active working relations with each other. The unbroken lines in Fig. 19 indicate the way in which they are divided up into smaller working units. The women claim that there are specific rights and duties which exist among all the kinswomen, but I shall first discuss particular arrangements. The discrepancy in the number of paid places and actual sellers has already been mentioned. The daily tax is circumvented through the use of kin ties. That is, one woman pays the tax to sell in this market place and keeps a kinswoman's or kinswomen's stock with her own. Seven women are involved in this type of arrangement. In one instance

(C in Fig. 19), this is largely for storing purposes. A woman who sells full-time in the market place keeps her mother's and her mother's sister's stock with her own when these two, who are part-time sellers in the city, come in from the country to sell several times a week. (They also live with the paying woman while in Port-au-Prince.) However, the two who do not pay the tax sell in the street and not in the market place. In theory, women who sell in the street also pay a tax of a *gourde* per day, but there is a good chance of selling without paying because the women are constantly walking about as they sell. The kinswoman in this unit who pays the tax sometimes tears her sheet of tax tickets in half, giving part to her aunt or mother. If one is stopped by the inspectors, she will claim to have lost the rest of the tickets. When trading in the market place is slow, the women who sell in the street will help their paying kins-women sell, or take part of her stock out into the street. The reverse also takes place.

In another instance (A in Fig. 19), two women have a similar arrangement; one pays the tax, and the other sometimes keeps her stock, which she sells in the street, in the paid place. As in the previous example, the non-paying marketer only sells in the city several times a week. And both women occasionally sell for each other. Although they stand in affinal relationship, these two are also ritual co-parents.

The women in the third instance (E in Fig. 19), unlike the other two examples, both sell in the market place full-time. However, one is very old and does less selling. At first these two claimed cognatic ties but later admitted that this was not the case.

Casual avoidance of the tax does take place among the other kins-women, as when a woman with a small amount of left-over stock will put it in with her selling partner's when the tax-collectors come around.

Among these women there are key sellers around whom the rest are oriented. Two claim to have inherited their selling places from their mother. The elder of these two is the principal poultry-seller. She has the largest amount of capital, the largest number of credit arrangements with wholesalers, the largest stock and, as a result, the most buyers. However, she sells with several other women (B in Fig. 19), and together they employ a boy porter.

Although there are specific working units, women may be involved in several overlapping arrangements. A large group of women (D in Fig. 19) go to buy together once a week at a rural market just outside the city. This buying in a group benefits both sellers and buyers. Rather than individually searching out stock, the poultry-retailers station themselves in front of the one dry-goods store. Thus sellers know where to come, and have a better chance of finding a buyer among all of them, without having to spend time wandering around the market place. And by coming to buy in a group, these women can, to some extent, determine price through group bargaining, and through asking one another's opinion on the quality of stock. It is probably safer and surer for the sellers to deal with an established group. Buying of large amounts of stock is done on a credit basis, and I would suspect that the wholesaler might be more willing to sell on credit to one of the members of this established group than to an individual buyer. Yet another significant factor is that all of the 17 poultry-retailers are from this area originally, and all say that they have claims in family land here. But more important, they claim to have access to both loans and credit in the area. For instance, one borrows money from the local magistrate, another from the owner of the dry-goods store. On the day when I accompanied them, seven women bought approximately 50 turkeys, 60 chickens and 70 pigeons.

When these women sell in the city market place, they sit in a line along one side of a thoroughfare. Thus the prospective buyer is more likely to find what she wants in the stock of the group, viewed collectively, than in the stock of any single unaffiliated seller. These women do not compete for buyers. One of the sellers came in with a large stock of more than 50 fowls which she had just acquired on credit from a wholesaler, with whom she had a buying agreement. When a customer came by, she let her sister offer her left-over stock and even helped her bargain. She did not offer any of her own stock until the buyer asked to see it. There is an elaborate bargaining ritual, but the sellers say the buyer usually knows what she wants before she comes to buy, and my own observations corroborate this assertion of the sellers.

RIGHTS AND DUTIES EXPRESSED IN KIN TIES

Among all the sellers in this market place there is an imprecise but nonetheless genuine tendency towards oligopoly (*i.e.* group 'monopoly'), since sellers ask more when dealing with 'bourgeois' buyers than when dealing with the poor. A small measure of rice is sold for

40 *centimes* to the buyer who is recognized as 'bourgeois' and 30 *centimes* to the poor buyer. Since poultry is rarely bought by the poor in this market place, I had no opportunity of seeing a double set of prices at work in poultry sales. But the women did sell eggs for less to the poor buyer. Yet the degree of economic cooperation among the poultry-sellers who are kin is much greater than is generally true in the market place. There are certain statements which I can make about the rights and duties among these women which are based both on their explanations and on my direct observations. They say that it is good to have family selling together because they live together, and they love one another. If one has family, they will protect each other; they will lend each other money without interest; they will buy for each other and sell for each other if one is sick. And family will not rob each other. From my observations, kin will sell for each other if one is sick or unable to come. They also buy for each other. All the women say that one does not pay interest on loans from kin, though one does not like to borrow from a kinsman in the same trade. Women who are kin will lend each other stock if one is short, and several times one in need of cash sold several fowl to another.

There is a tendency for women not related to the group to try to claim cognatic ties with someone in it; within the group itself, women who are distantly related affines also may try to create fictitious cognatic ties. I have indicated in Fig. 19 instances of ritual kin ties where one woman becomes the co-parent of another by baptizing her child. The ritual ties are between two women who stand in an affinal relation to each other, and between a woman and a member of the group with which she has a working arrangement but no cognatic ties. I did find one case of strong friendship between a member of the kin group and a woman who sold next to her but who was not a kinswoman. However, they had also become ritual kin and this entitled the friend to come and buy with the large group (D), and the two women sold for each other, although they claimed that they would not lend each other money.

SUMMARY

These sets of kin, the members of which sometimes work so closely in coordination as to be termed groups, are bilaterally organized and appear voluntary. There is one woman who does not have any working arrangements. Yet she still would be extended certain rights and she would be expected to reciprocate.

The women say that the reason why there are so many kinswomen selling together is that one came, made a profit, and told another kinswoman to come. Since poultry-and-egg-selling appears to be less speculative than the marketing of perishable fruits and vegetables, there may have been more encouragement to establish stable kin-affiliated selling groups. These first-generation full-time urban sellers have found economic advantages in using kin ties. In a situation where there are no strongly established business ethics, these market women are using bilateral kinship network for security and trust in carrying out commerce. However, this seems a transitional situation in several ways, most important of which is that the daughters of these women are going into other jobs. By the very fact that they are urban dwellers, these poultry-retailers have given their daughters new opportunities *via* education. And rather than continue in their mothers' commerce, they are exerting some degree of choice in what they will do. However, their mothers, too, share their higher aspirations.[6]

Notes:

1. Field work was carried out during July, August and the beginning of September, 1961, when I was one of two students in the field with Dr. S. W. Mintz. I am very grateful to Dr. Mintz for his help and supervision in the field and for much of the supplementary material contained in this article on rural marketing of poultry and eggs and their relation to Haitian society.

2. 'Bourgeois' is the term used by the market women themselves to describe their customers, most of whom they consider to be of a higher class than themselves.

3. S. W. Mintz, 'A Tentative Typology of Eight Haitian Marketplaces,' *Revista de Ciencias Sociales,* Puerto Rico, Vol. IV, No. 1 (1960), p. 36.

4. *Ibid.,* p. 24.

5. A significant factor, but one on which I have not enough data, is that these women are largely responsible for the economic support of their children. None of the women have men living with them in the city; four of the 17 are still in some kind of union with a man, for three I have no information, but the other 10 are no longer in any kind of union. Certainly the ages of these women are significant, especially in the light of R. Smith's findings in British Guiana; those with young children claim to have some kind of arrangement with a man whom they call 'husband,' but even in these instances, at least one 'husband' contributes very little to the children's economic support.

6. I am indebted to Professor Firth, Mrs. Lorraine Lancaster and Dr. Mintz for their suggestions and criticisms of earlier drafts of this article.

DOUGLASS G. NORVELL AND R. V. BILLINGSLEY

19. Traditional Markets and Marketers in the Cibao Valley of the Dominican Republic[1]

The Cibao Valley is the most fertile region of the Dominican Republic. Formed by the Rio Yaqui and its tributaries, it is 150 miles long and 10 to 30 miles wide.[2] The valley supplies most of the fresh produce for its commercial center, Santiago, and provides a surplus that is distributed to other parts of the country. The valley also is a major producer of cacao and sugar which constitute the major export crops. Because agricultural products of the Cibao bulk large in the nation's economy, the marketing practices and problems encountered are strategic and significant to economic development. Also because less-developed nations are often strikingly homogenous, an analysis and description of marketing in the Dominican Republic will contain many caveats with wide application. The purpose of the following pages is to describe the food distribution system for fresh produce proceeding from producers to consumers. Attention will be focused on the people who ply this trade, as well as physical facilities.

The marketing area of Santiago has a rural population of over a million persons.[3] According to the 1960 census, seventy percent of the economically active population is engaged in agriculture, producing sugar cane, plantains, and tobacco along with a large variety of fruits and vegetables. Many are employed on, or own farms of less than four *tareas* in size.[4] Others are landless, or produce sporadically on *conucos,* which are plots farmed on land belonging to absentee or unmindful landlords, a category which often includes the government.

SOURCE: Original paper written for this volume. The authors are assistant professor of economics at the University of Tampa and associate professor of Agricultural Economics at Texas A&M University. This work was carried out as part of a Ford Foundation Task Force project directed by Dr. J. G. McNeely and administered by the Office of International Programs at Texas A&M University.

Many of the marketing practices of the farmers are modern, while others are primitive. Both are conditioned by their volume of production and the type of transportation facilities used. The Dominican Republic has a well-developed (if not maintained) system of primary roads, but secondary and connecting roads are either nonexistent or impassable in the rainy season.

Farmers living on or near main roads are able to market their produce in an efficient manner. Trucker-buyers call at the farm, often on alternating days, and pay prices which reflect the farmers' awareness of alternative outlets. Some farmers have integrated their operations vertically, and own trucks which are used to haul neighbors' produce as well as their own. Several of the larger farms are owned and operated by extended families, which wield considerable economic and political power.[5]

In comparison, farmers that live away from the main roads are functionally isolated. They are traditional in attitudes as well as in the way that they market their produce.[6] When their farms, which tend to be smaller than those nearer the main roads, afford a surplus they carry it to a roadside stand to be met by trucker-buyers or other transportation intermediaries. Their bargaining position is often eroded by a lack of price information or alternatives, thus they receive lower prices. In spite of the low prices very few farmers carry their goods all the way to the terminal market or directly to consumers. In summary, it can be safely assumed that the marketing function as carried out by these small farmers is costly both in terms of low prices and time diverted from production.[7]

Transportation intermediaries are modern day merchant adventurers who buy produce at the farm and sell at terminal markets. In the Cibao Valley they utilize equipment ranging from primitive to very modern. On most mornings before dawn, the trails and roads leading into Santiago will flicker from the lights of kerosene lanterns of market women as they come off the mountains—"La Loma"—carrying fruits and leafy vegetables by burro. At the same time, highways roar with the sound of large gas and diesel trucks coming in with loads of heavier fruits and vegetables. Other transportation intermediaries come haphazardly, carrying their goods by pickup, jeep, bus, or even walking.

Transportation intermediaries come into Santiago from a variety of locations. Forty-two percent come from less than 20 kilometers away, nineteen percent from between 20 and 40 kilometers, and thirty-nine percent from more than 40 kilometers.[8] When these sellers arrive, they pay an entrance fee according to the size and means of transportation and amount of product. Sellers carrying bags by foot or on burro are charged five cents a bag, a pickup normally pays seventy-five cents and larger trucks a dollar and a half. Trucks may enter and sell to wholesalers, or remain at the periphery of the market and sell. By selling at the periphery of the public market, the trucker-buyers assume the functions of and compete with market wholesalers.

There are two public markets in urban Santiago. The largest and oldest, Mercado Hospedaje, is primarily a terminal market where transportation intermediaries bring their produce to sell to wholesalers. The other, Mercado Modelo, is primarily a retail outlet.

Mercado Hospedaje began as a gathering place for buyers and sellers on the bank of the Rio Yaqui. Presently, it occupies a city block in a predominantly low income area where it was constructed at a cost of $75,000 in 1953. The market is simply constructed with a large open shelter in the center housing produce stalls and a variety of retail and service establishments at the periphery. In the early morning, pushcarts crowd the streets and gates, while sellers begin to pull bound hogs and goats from their overnight rest. As the morning progresses, pushcart vendors scatter to hawk their wares throughout the city, but are replaced by a variety of sellers and consumers. A gambler may appear as crowds of traders grow, and tempt the naïve with a version of the age-old shell game. All the while an ever-growing number of vehicles, animals, and consumers gather in the street to add to the morning medley that is characteristic of this colorful traditional market.

Mercado Hospedaje is supervised by an appointed administrator whose duties include the collection of taxes and maintenance of the physical facilities. In these endeavors, he looks to the municipal treasurer for leadership and is assisted by two collectors, three cleaners, and a night watchman. The tariffs, levied against the small owners, according to size and location, annually provide enough money to cover all salaries and other costs and in addition provide a surplus to the municipal treasury. Detailed records are kept of all tariffs, including those collected from vehicles entering the market and these records indicate an average daily revenue of about $45.00 R.D. Although in some cases minor officials in the Dominican Republic extract a small additional *picoteo* or "peck" for personal use, this practice does not seem to exist in Mercado Hospedaje. The administrator and his assistants collect and record receipts consistent with good bookkeeping practices. Each day sixteen cents is collected from most of the sellers, and more from others according to the size of their location which is generally directly related to volume.

Although traditional markets are often thought to be viable environments, sellers in the Santiago markets are the epitome of steady employ. While some sellers may enter and leave the trade on a casual basis, others have been working in Hospedaje, or its predecessor, for as long as twenty-four years. The sellers in Hospedaje at the time of this study indicated that they had been working in the market an average of 7.3 years. Tenure at a specific location in the market is extended because the institutional framework permits sellers to acquire a form of possession by default to sites in the market. The right to occupy these sites is acquired by physical presence. At night, sellers either remain in their locations, or post a guard in addition to those provided by the market administration. The right to occupy these sites is an economic good and has a market value. The value is functionally related to location and size and varies from seller to seller. In Hospedaje, part of the sites under this shelter had an average value of $156 and were occupied by sellers who had been in the market an average of 9.7 years. Sites outside the shelter, in the open yard of the market, were valued at an average of $77 by sellers who had been in the market for an average of 4.7 years. Even though sites under the shelter are more valuable, cleaner, and have better display facilities, they are taxed at the same rate as those outside. Stands outside the shelter have tables and facilities erected by the owner, or products are merely piled on the ground in the open.

The market at the time of the survey had forty-seven sellers of fruit and vegetables. The number of sellers varies according to the volume of trade because some sellers are distinctly marginal. These marginal sellers are retailers who merely gather a few goods to be sold at slightly higher prices. Their number is apt to fluctuate with the demand. Larger retailers are steadily employed, along with the wholesalers who buy directly from transportation intermediaries and sell to retailers and consumers. Even though some retail sales are made, Hospedaje is essentially a terminal market.

Mercado Modelo is similar to Hospedaje in setting, but serves a different function. While Hospedaje is a terminal market located in a low income area, serving only a small low income retail trade,

Modelo is located in a higher income area, and most of the sales are at retail. In this study it was found that only two percent of the lower income group spent most of their income at this market. Sellers in Mercado Modelo take advantage of this more effective demand to offer an array of products at a higher price than Hospedaje.

The Mercado Modelo is more elaborate, although smaller than Hospedaje. It was constructed new at a cost of $130,000 and is entirely enclosed. Like Hospedaje, the market is supervised by an administrator who is responsible to the municipal treasurer. Records are kept of taxes assessed, but unlike Mercado Hospedaje, these records were not made available for inspection either at the market or at the municipal offices. Most of the sellers paid eighteen cents daily rent, but some charges ranged as high as a dollar. Like Hospedaje, sellers entering or selling at the periphery of the market are taxed on a load basis. Total costs were $635.00 monthly for an administrator, two assistants for collection, two custodians, and a night watchman. Electricity and water were supplied by the municipality at no cost to the market.

There are sixteen sellers in the Modelo who deal in a variety of products that are bought mostly at Hospedaje, and sold at retail. Possession of sites is acquired by occupancy and the value of sites ranged from $100.00 to $400.00, and the number of years that sellers had been in the market ranged from a half to twenty-four. In addition to food sellers, the market was bordered by retail and service establishments and a number of lottery ticket sellers. Although active and busy, this market was more orderly and did not have the proliferation of small animal sellers and various entrepreneurs found in Hospedaje.

The sellers in the public markets used a variety of means to obtain funds to finance inventories, make change, and meet current obligations. In a survey of the sellers, fifty-seven percent relied on accumulated savings, thirteen percent on buying on credit, twelve percent borrowed from moneylenders (at annual interest rates ranging from fifty percent to one thousand percent) and the remaining twenty percent utilized a rotating credit association called *san*.[9]

The latter is particularly interesting because of its resemblance to similar institutions in other parts of the world.[10] A rotating credit association called *san* in the Dominican Republic is used predominantly by low income groups.[11] Rules for *san* follow a basic pattern from which several variations evolve. The practice first requires a specified number of participants, or players, one of which serves as a leader for the group. Each player contributes a specified amount of money at regular intervals such as once a week, and a winner is selected at random at each interval. The leader serves as an administrator by selecting winners, collecting the funds, and guaranteeing payment. In return for his services he usually extracts a toll which differs in amount according to the variation being played. At each drawing during the course of the *san,* the leader selects a number by a random nonrepetitive process, and the player whose number is drawn becomes the winner which entitles him to receive contributions of the other players minus the leader's share. Once a player's number has been selected, he continues to contribute but cannot win again.

To illustrate how *san* is played, assume that a *san* group is composed of ten players and a leader who sets the amount to be received by the winner at $100. In turn, players agree to contribute $11 at each of ten weekly meetings. On the Monday of the first week a number from 1 to 10 is assigned to each player. Each player gives $11 to the leader, who then selects one of the numbers. The player with the winning number receives $100. The remaining $10 is retained by the leader. The winning player's number is cast out, but he continues to contribute until the ten drawings have been held. Each Monday, the process will be repeated until the game has run its course. Eventually everybody wins so the advantage of being the winner is in acquiring funds early in the game. This form of *san*— even with the figures assumed above—is common, but by no means the only variation.

The cost of *san* as a credit mobilization scheme may appear excessive especially when you consider the fact that the probability of a player winning in the latter half of the game is equal to probability of winning in the first half of the game. This being the case it would appear to be more rational for the player to simply put away his $11 a week until he had saved enough money to finance his desired activity. However, one must consider the fact that low income people have extreme difficulty in saving money. The restrictions placed on the individual in playing *san* force him to save and when you consider the high interest cost that individuals must pay for credit in Santiago the expected interest cost does not appear to be excessive.

As an indication of the cost of credit in the Santiago market, information was collected in a 1966 survey which showed that the cost of credit adjusted to an annual rate, ranged from eighty to a thousand percent. The cost of credit in the markets may be called interest rates only in a vague sense; however, they still bulk large in the final price of food. In all probability, these costs—as represented by the high "interest rate"—are principally returns to management in a moneylending industry that has developed because market sellers cannot obtain credit from conventional sources. At the time of the study neither the government-operated *Banco Agricola,* nor any of the commercial banks had direct lines of credit with the market sellers.

In addition to the sellers in the public markets, the fresh produce distribution system of Santiago contains a proliferation of small entrepreneurs that have neither form nor number. A *marchanta,* usually a woman, is a roving seller. These vendors generally carry lightweight goods by foot or burro from house to house, and sell to an established clientele, and to random buyers. Her male counterpart is a *caratillero,* or pushcart vendor, who deals in a heavier product in the same fashion. Either of the two are apt to become stationary and operate a *ventorillo* or makeshift stand on the street. The total number of these entrepreneurial enclaves varies and they are distinctly marginal, but they constitute an integral part of the fresh produce distribution system of Santiago.

Small retail stores called *colmados* and *pulperias* abound in urban Santiago. They are so common that the survey of 173 Santiago consumers indicates that they spend thirty-one percent of their total food expenditures at *colmados,* and eighteen percent at *pulperias.* The *colmado* is simply a larger and more permanent edition of the numerous *pulperia.* The *pulperia* is managed alone by the owner who conducts his business on an across-the-counter basis. Equipment usually consists of a scale, some bins, shelves, and an icebox. Stock ordinarily includes a limited line of unpackaged staples; some canned goods, including imported items; nonfood products such as soap, cigarettes, and the inevitable rum. Purchases by consumers are often made on a hand-to-mouth basis because of inability to finance home inventories, lack of storage space and refrigeration facilities. It is common to observe purchases of one cigarette or two cents' worth of ice. Haggling, or sliding price mechanism, is not as common as in the public markets. This absence is probably due to nonprice competition, such as varying quantity instead of price, and may be affected by common credit sales. Consumers often buy ten cents' worth of beans or ice and accept the amount given to them by the storekeeper. Like the *pulperia,* the *colmado* is characterized by the across-the-counter service, but may employ sales personnel other than the owner. In this form of retail outlet, emphasis is on nonprice competition, and no advertising is done by radio or newspapers. One large *colmado* in Santiago approaches small supermarket capacity, but does not carry an extensive line.

The last link in the marketing chain is the consumer. There are several distinguishing characteristics of the Dominican consumer in Santiago. With an average intake of 2020 calories per day, the Dominican Republic has one of the lowest calorie intake rates in Latin America and is well below the average in the United States of 2520 calories. The diets are low in protein and are heavily accentuated with cereal starches and fats. The wife in the family usually plans the meals and does the shopping. She is probably within walking distance of a public market and has daily access to numerous small food sellers which are scattered throughout the residential area of Santiago and the numerous street vendors, several of which go up each street every day. The close proximity of these outlets is a necessity because most Dominican housewives typically have neither a car or an icebox. Because of the low income and a lack of home storage facilities, her spending patterns favor the convenient small retail outlets. As reported in a consumer survey most Santiago consumers shop at a variety of retail food outlets. Most popular are *colmados,* which are general food stores larger than a *pulperia,* which also receives a large portion of the total food expenditure. Other more specialized outlets are *carnicerias,* small meat markets; *panaderias,* bakeries, and *lecherias,* milk stores. Fresh produce may also be purchased retail from street vendors, *ventorillos* and *marchantas,* and at the public market, *Modelo* and *Hospedaje,* or at a farm *granja.*

SUMMARY AND CONCLUSIONS

The marketing system of the Cibao Valley is of strategic economic importance to the Dominican Republic. This system is typical of many in the developing nations and the observations herein may be useful to a wide range of planners in government and industry, as well as the students of the social sciences.

The marketing system is dualistic in nature. Some marketers use efficient modern methods and equipment, but most employ traditional means. In a cursory examination, the traditional sector appears disorderly and to some extent inefficient. However, given a high labor-to-capital ratio and present facilities, the traditional sector may approach an optimum allocation of resources.

Substantial increases in marketing efficiency could be brought about, however, by improvements in the physical facilities. The increases in marketing efficiency would have twofold benefits by lowering the cost of food to consumers and raising the price paid to producers. The physical facilities in the Cibao could be improved by selecting strategic locations for improved public markets, and also providing serviceable ingress and egress routes. Also, marketing efficiency could be improved by the distribution of timely and accurate price information. All of these would enable the marketers of the Cibao Valley to perform their function more effectively.

Notes:

1. This paper is based upon a larger study entitled "The Internal Food Distribution System and Marketing Channels for Plantains and Tomatoes in the Cibao Valley of the Dominican Republic," International Programs, Texas A&M University, 1968.

2. Garland Marshall, *Background Information on Marketing Methods and Practices Utilized at Mercado Modelo and Hospedaje,* Santiago, Dominican Republic: Centro Científico para el Desarrollo Agrícola, 1965.

3. Hernández, Frank M., *Notas Acerca de la Población de la República Dominicana,* Santiago, Dominican Republic: Asociación para el Desarrollo, 1966.

4. One *Tarea* is equal to .156 acres.

5. The present Minister of Agriculture, a Purdue University graduate, is a member of a Cibao agricultural family.

6. This is developed in Douglass Norvell and Bardin Nelson, *Values and Aspirations of Some Dominican Out-Farmers: A Pilot Study,* Departmental Information Report No. 67-6, Department of Agricultural Economics and Sociology, Texas A&M University, October 1966.

7. On some small tobacco farms, producers have an alternative to low prices. When the price of leaf tobacco falls, they shift into a compressed form called *Andullo* which is made by binding palm leaves tightly about a roll of leaves. In this form the tobacco can be stored indefinitely, or until the price is right.

8. Garland Marshall, op. cit.

9. This term is used by Clifford Gertz in "The Rotating Credit Association," *Economic Development and Cultural Change,* Vol. 1, No. 3.

10. For a general discussion of rotating credit association, see Shirley Ardener, "The Comparative Study of Rotating Credit Associations," *Journal of the Royal Anthropology Institute,* Vol. 94 (July 1964), pp. 201–9.

11. A more detailed explanation of the uses and varieties of *san* can be found in an article by Douglass G. Norvell and James S. Wehrly entitled, "A Rotating Credit Association in the Dominican Republic," in *Caribbean Studies,* Vol. 9, No. 1 (April 1969), pp. 45–52.

G.
Domestic Organization

More than any other topic, the structure of marriage, family, and kinship has attracted the attention not only of Caribbean scholars, but also of politicians, social workers, and missionaries. This is curious as the intricacies of kinship are perhaps the most arid and least shared aspect of anthropological inquiry in any other part of the world. Melanesian art is exposed in our greatest museums, yet who but anthropologists care about cross-cousin marriage in New Guinea? Technical aid specialists in Africa claim a concern for local practices of cattle breeding, but reject the suggestion that the vesting of cattle ownership in lineages is somehow relevant to their interests. The reason is obvious. The West Indian family —and the family among rural and ghetto blacks in the United States—is thought of as something not exotic, but as pathologically deviant from some supposed "norm," itself characteristic of middle-class Western Europeans. The politicians' focus has been not on how the family functions, but on supposed indices of disorganization (reflecting a sociological orientation which has otherwise enjoyed declining fashion in recent years): high rates of illegitimacy, weak father-child and husband-wife relationships, and the strong position of women in the household (the so-called "matrifocal," "matricentric," "matripotestal," and even "matriarchal" family). Daniel P. Moynihan's famous paper "The Negro Family" is subtitled "The Case for National Action" (Washington, D.C.: U. S. Department of Labor [Office of Policy Planning and Research], 1965).

The articles which follow, all by anthropologists, are descriptions of how West Indian families function, and are not, in any sense, calls to action.

NANCIE L. SOLIEN

20. Household and Family in the Caribbean: Some Definitions and Concepts[1]

In recent years much attention has been directed toward the family system observed in Afro-American communities. Typical features of this system include the high percentage of "non-legal" or "irregular" conjugal unions, legal marriage being typical only of the upper classes and well-to-do. The separation rate is high and children almost invariably remain with the mother. Women occupy a prominent position in this system; some writers even describe certain household groups as being "matrifocal" (15), "mother-headed" (4), "matriarchal" (8), "maternal" (8), etc. Such designations have served to emphasize the fact that many domestic groups in these societies include no male in the role of husband-father. In spite of minor differences, especially in regard to quantitative data on the types of families found in any given community, it is apparent that the situation is fundamentally the same in such widespread areas as Jamaica, Trinidad, British Guiana, Haiti, Brazil, the southern United States, and the Caribbean coast of Central America.

The specific object of investigation in many of these societies has been the family (1, 7, 11, 14, 15). There has been a tendency to identify the family with the household, a procedure which, as we shall see, has some precedent in anthropological usage. However, the situation in these societies differs so much from those described in other parts of the world, that great difficulty often arises when one tries to apply the classical concepts of "family" and "household" in Afro-America. Unfortunately, too often the writer merely glosses over the conceptual difficulty, using the terms interchangeably without defining them, and as a result there is much confusion in the literature.

It is the purpose of this paper to examine various definitions and

SOURCE: Reprinted from *Social and Economic Studies,* Vol. 9, No. 1 (1960): 101–6, by permission of the author and publisher.

usages of the terms "family" and "household" in order to determine their usefulness in analyzing Afro-American society.

Few writers have distinguished between family and household on either a theoretical or a descriptive level. Empirically the two are quite often identical, especially when one is dealing with the nuclear family. There is general agreement in the literature that within a household one finds a family of one type or another. Thus, Murdock includes common residence, along with economic co-operation and reproduction, as defining characteristics of the family (*12*, p. 1).

Radcliffe-Brown, after defining his term, "the elementary family", as a father, a mother, and their children, says that this unit "usually provides the basis for the formation of domestic groups of persons living together in intimate daily life" (*13*, p. 5). He goes on to give several examples of such domestic groups, each of which could be classified as an extended family.

Lowie defines the family as "the association" that corresponds to the institution of marriage, recognizing that the character of the interpersonal relations among the members is of more importance than the actual membership. He notes that a household may include persons unrelated by kinship ties who are excluded from the family, yet presumably to him too the family forms the core of the household (*10*, pp. 215–16).

Linton distinguishes between what he calls "conjugal" and "consanguine" families. His definition of each implies common residence of spouses and their offspring, the primary difference between the two types being that in the consanguine family the inmarrying spouses are relatively unimportant (*9*, pp. 159–63).

It is apparent that most anthropologists think of a family as a co-residential group within which there is at least one conjugal pair plus at least some of the offspring of this pair. Various extensions of this unit may occur typically in different societies, such extensions being based upon kinship ties (consanguineal and/or affinal) between other persons and one member of the original conjugal pair. Conversely, the household generally refers to a group of persons who live together and co-operate in at least some if not all domestic affairs. A family unit of some type is generally assumed to be the nucleus of the household, though there may also be present some unrelated persons.

Outside of the Afro-American area there have been a few other societies described in which the above concepts do not prove useful.

Notable examples include the Nayars in South Malabar and Cochin in which the household unit traditionally contained as regular members only matri-lineal kin. Gough states that "the simplest traditional dwelling-group is therefore a sibling group, together with the children and maternal grandchildren of the women" (*6*, p. 85).

The Ashanti also exhibit a pattern of duo-locality, in which husbands and wives, especially during the early years of marriage, do not reside together. Fortes describes three types of domestic unit: (a) households grouped around a husband and wife; (b) households grouped around an effective minimal matrilineage, or part of it; and (c) households made up of combinations of the two previous types (*2*, p. 69). Type (b), containing no conjugal pair, would not be equivalent to a family.

Henriques says in regard to Jamaica, ". . . the best method of classifying family groupings appears to be the adoption of the term domestic group as the unit of family structure in the island" (*7*). Yet he also notes, "In Jamaica the domestic group is the residential unit which constitutes a household. The domestic group may, but does not always, consist of the elementary biological family." On the other hand, he says, "Family groupings can be divided into those with a conjugal and those with a consanguineous basis" (p. 105).

R. T. Smith (*16*, p. 67) states that ". . . most writers are agreed that the main functioning family unit in the Caribbean is a household group". He then defines the household as ". . . a group of people occupying a single dwelling and sharing a common food supply". His data, as well as those of many other writers show that very often the household group contains no conjugal pair. He does not further define the family, but instead uses the term interchangeably with household group.

Obviously, these usages do not correspond to the definitions ordinarily used by anthropologists. As we have seen, in spite of minor differences in phraseology, most writers insist upon some form of marriage as the basis of the family. A household, on the other hand, is primarily a residential unit, and although it *may* and usually does include some sort of family as its core, the definition does not insist upon this as a criterion.

Goody (*5*, p. 56) takes this view when he says ". . . the use of the blanket term 'family' to indicate groups which are specifically defined by residence and descent as well as those defined by the existence of the marriage bond may be adequate for Euro-American systems in which there is considerable overlap, but it can be highly confusing in terms of other societies".

Fortes too, has pointed out that in many cases it is useful to distinguish analytically between the elementary family and the domestic group. He notes that the actual composition of the two may be identical, but that the reproductive functions of the group may be separated from the householding and housekeeping functions. He differentiates the two units on the basis of the types of bonds obtaining among the members. An elementary family is constituted solely by the bonds of marriage, filiation, and siblingship, while the household or domestic group may include persons bound together by various kinds of jural and affective bonds other than these (*3*).

One aspect of the problem in the Caribbean has been well phrased by Clarke, who says:

> The anthropologist in search of the family *sees* (italics hers) first the house . . . Within that house, be it hut or cottage, is contained, for some part of the day or night, part of the group which he is about to study.
>
> But what part of it? Will he find the majority of these households to contain parents and their children, or mothers only with their daughters and their daughters' children; or a man and woman with some only of their offspring? Or, instead, will he find a heterogeneous collection of kin, brought together by some new pattern of association, based on a system of relationships fundamentally different from that found in other societies elsewhere? (*1*, p. 28).

In fact, all of these situations may be found within most Caribbean communities today. Clarke suggests a typology in which she distinguishes between "family" households and "consanguineous" households. The latter may be one of three types: (a) denuded family households in which there is only one parent, plus children, grandchildren, or other lineal relatives of the parent; (b) sibling households in which adult brothers and sisters live under one roof; and (c) single person households (common only in towns to which people travel to obtain wage-labour during part of the year) (*1*).

It is my view that some distinction between family and household such as that made by Clarke is not only useful but necessary in dealing with Caribbean society. It seems to me that the fact that some households contain no family as ordinarily defined by anthropologists is one of the most important characteristics of Caribbean society. Elsewhere I have stressed the consanguineal nature of these households as a key to their understanding (*17*).

It is, of course, perfectly legitimate to view the society in terms of household units as long as the investigator distinguishes these from families. Presumably, the universe may be completely divided with a classification like Clarke's, for all persons would belong to one or another type of household. Does this mean then, that some persons are members of families and others are not? Undoubtedly, this is sometimes the case, but I suggest that in order fully to understand Afro-American society it is necessary to view it in terms of household units on the one hand, and family units on the other. I would maintain that many, if not most, individuals belong to both a family and to a household. At times the two units coincide, but quite often they do not.

In order to illustrate this point I shall draw upon my fieldwork of a year's duration among the Black Carib of Livingston, Guatemala[2] —a group of people whose culture is similar enough to other Afro-American groups to warrant classifying them together (*18*). The nuclear family unit among the Carib may be scattered in several different households. For example, the husband-father may be living with his own mother, one or more children may be with their maternal relatives or with non-Caribs, while the mother may be working and "living in" as a maid in one of the port towns. Some may then assert that under such circumstances this no longer constitutes a family unit. However, if the nature of the personal interrelationships among the group members is considered, it may be seen that there exists a pattern of affective and economic solidarity among them. It is true that many such groups are extremely brittle and unstable, but they do exist for varying lengths of time. And for their duration the members think of themselves as a unit; when questioned as to their family connections they will immediately name and locate their primary relatives. Furthermore, there is some economic co-operation among them, the man generally contributing a part of his wages (or money from sale of cash crops) to the woman and the children. The woman too, if working, may give money to the man, and certainly sends clothing and money to the household(s) in which her children are living.

Another common arrangement is that in which the husband maintains a single-person household in one town, leaving his wife and children living together in another. The latter would appear to be Clarke's denuded family household. However, I think it is important to recognize that within this type of household one may find either of two fundamentally different relationship patterns. The man, though living elsewhere, may make frequent trips to visit his wife and children, contributing a large part of his wages toward their support. They consider that he "lives" with them, though he may not actually have resided there for a number of years. The man will return to his family immediately in times of crisis, or when important decisions must be made. He also returns whenever possible to assist the woman in clearing fields, to make repairs on the house, etc. He remains a highly important influence in the socialization of his children. I would call this group a non-localized family.

On the other hand, the single parent (most often the mother, although occasionally one finds a father alone with his children) may be completely unattached to any individual who might be called a spouse. She may receive a small amount of economic assistance from the father or fathers of her children, but for the most part she is dependent upon herself and her consanguineal relatives in maintaining and socializing her children. This situation, which on the surface appears identical to that described above, is obviously entirely different. Although Clarke's term, the "denuded family", is somewhat descriptive of the situation, it is nevertheless ambiguous since it may refer to either set of relationships described above. I would not call this unit a family at all; consisting only of a mother and her children, it is on a lower level of organization than a family which must include a conjugal relationship and what Fortes would call patri-filiation (3).

Another interesting and pertinent example is that of the Israeli *kibbutz*. Here we find a situation in which married couples co-reside, but their children live elsewhere. Although Spiro (19), following Murdock's definition of marriage (12), states that the relationship between these couples does not constitute marriage, it seems clear from his data that the society itself recognizes the relationship as such. He points out that these couples are eventually united in accordance with the marriage laws of the state. Furthermore, he goes on to state that the family does not exist within the *kibbutz* system, unless one wishes to consider the *kibbutz* itself as a large extended family. Again, Spiro has followed Murdock's definition of the family in arriving at this conclusion.

However, Spiro makes it clear that within the *kibbutz* there does exist a group which could, by another definition, be termed a nuclear family. He says: "The social group in the *kibbutz* that includes adults of both sexes and their children, although characterized by reproduction, is not characterized by common residence or by economic co-operation" (*19,* p. 840). He goes on to show that this group is characterized by psychological intimacy, affection, and joint recreational activities. Although the children's physical and mental development for the most part is supervised by persons outside this family unit, Spiro notes that, "Parents are of crucial importance in the *psychological* development of the child" (italics his). "They serve as the objects of his most important identifications, and they provide him with a certain security and love that he obtains from no one else" (*19,* p. 844). In view of the strength of the affective bonds among this group, which includes their own recognition of themselves as a separate, cohesive, and enduring unit, I suggest that the family as an institution *does* exist within the *kibbutz*. If one wishes to liken the entire *kibbutz* to an extended family, then why not consider these smaller units of mother, father, and children as nuclear families?

In conclusion, I propose that the family be defined as a group of people bound together by that complex set of relationships known as kinship ties, between at least two of whom there exists a conjugal relationship. The conjugal pair, plus their offspring, forms the nuclear family. Other types of family may be defined as extensions of the nuclear type, each being identified by the nature of the relationship between the conjugal pair (or one member of that pair) and other members.

The household, on the other hand, implies common residence, economic co-operation, and socialization of children. Although the members of the household may be bound by kinship relationships, no particular type of tie is necessarily characteristic. In any given society a particular family may or may not form a household. Conversely, a household may or may not contain a family. Although it is probably useful to make an analytical distinction between the two concepts in all cases, the investigator must be particularly careful to examine the structure and functioning of both types of units in those societies in which their membership does not coincide.

Notes:

1. This paper was read before the Third Annual Meeting of the Kroeber Anthropological Society May 16, 1959, in Berkeley, California. The writer is indebted to David M. Schneider for valuable comments and suggestions during the preparation of the manuscript.

2. This fieldwork was conducted from July 1956 to July 1957, and was sponsored by the Henry L. and Grace Doherty Foundation and the Dept. of Anthropology, University of Michigan. Grateful acknowledgment is made to both.

References cited:

1. Clarke, Edith.
   1957 *My Mother Who Fathered Me.* London.
2. Fortes, Meyer.
   1949 "Time and Social Structure: An Ashanti Case Study", in *Social Structure: Studies Presented to A. R. Radcliffe-Brown,* Meyer Fortes, ed. Oxford.
3. Fortes, Meyer.
   1958 Introduction to *The Developmental Cycle in Domestic Groups,* Jack Goody, ed. Cambridge Papers in Social Anthropology, No. 1.
4. Frazier, E. Franklin.
   1939 *The Negro Family in the United States.* Chicago.
5. Goody, Jack.
   1958 "The Fission of Domestic Groups among the Lodagaba", in *The Developmental Cycle in Domestic Groups,* Jack Goody, ed. Cambridge Papers in Social Anthropology, No. 1.
6. Gough, E. Kathleen.
   1952 "A Comparison of Incest Prohibitions and the Rules of Exogamy in Three Matrilineal Groups of the Malabar Coast", *International Archives of Ethnography,* XLVI, No. 1, pp. 82–105.
7. Henriques, Fernando M.
   1953 *Family and Colour in Jamaica.* London.
8. Herskovits, Melville J.
   1958 *The Myth of the Negro Past.* Beacon Edition, Boston.
9. Linton, Ralph.
   1936 *The Study of Man.* New York.
10. Lowie, Robert H.
    1950 *Social Organization.* London.
11. Matthews, Dom Basil.
    1953 "Crisis of the West Indian Family", *Caribbean Affairs,* Vol. 9. University College of the West Indies.
12. Murdock, George P.
    1949 *Social Structure.* New York.
13. Radcliffe-Brown, A. R.
    1950 Introduction to *African Systems of Kinship and Marriage,* A. R. Radcliffe-Brown and Daryll Forde, eds. London.
14. Simey, T. S.
    1946 *Welfare and Planning in the West Indies.* Oxford.

15. Smith, Raymond T.
1956 *The Negro Family in British Guiana.* London.
16. Smith, Raymond T.
1957 "The Family in the Caribbean", in *Caribbean Studies: A Symposium,* Vera Rubin, ed. University College of the West Indies, Jamaica.
17. Solien, Nancie L.
1958 "The Consanguineal Household Among the Black Carib of Central America." Ph.D. dissertation, University of Michigan.
18. Solien, Nancie L.
1959 "West Indian Characteristics of the Black Carib", *Southwestern Journal of Anthropology,* Vol. 15, No. 3, pp. 300-7.
19. Spiro, Melford E.
1954 "Is the Family Universal?", *American Anthropologist,* Vol. 56, No. 5, pp. 839-46.

YEHUDI A. COHEN

21. Four Categories of Interpersonal Relationships in the Family and Community in a Jamaican Village[1]

There are several aspects to the study of the dialectical relationships between the family and the total community, outstanding among which is the investigation of the functional-structural roles of the family in the organization of society. Characteristically, the prevailing approach in contemporary studies is to analyze these dialectical relationships from the point of view of the mutually supportive roles of the family and the total social structure. Following Lowie's classic analysis of the relationships between property and kin group organization,[2] Murdock has more recently studied the external influences to which the rules of residence are particularly vulnerable, and, in turn, the latter's repercussions throughout the total social fabric.[3] Another approach is concerned with the cultural and social "needs" fulfilled by the family as a discrete and unique institution. Thus, the family is viewed, in a "functional" sense, as the primary institutional instrument which mediates between the individual and the rest of his society. It is, almost universally, the primary focus of economic and other forms of cooperation;[4] it is the context in which the training of the young occurs, for it is "the family [which] largely transmits that portion of the culture accessible to the social stratum and groups in which the parents find themselves."[5] Still another approach is the psychological one of the roles of the family, and the individual's experiences therein, in personality development. Murdock and Whiting have given a somewhat new twist to this problem in an attempt to bridge the gap between the purely structural aspects of the family and the emotional experiences of the growing members of society.[6]

SOURCE: Reprinted from the *Anthropological Quarterly,* Vol. 3, No. 4 (1955):121–47, by permission of the author and the *Anthropological Quarterly.*

In the investigation of the structural-functional position of the family in society, however, the point often seems to be missed that the same emotional and motivational processes are operative both in the interpersonal relationships of the family and in those of the total community; that it is possible, in relatively simple and stable societies, to prognosticate, so to speak, from one to the other. We do not wish to imply that an individual cannot experience a conflict of roles when moving from a status within his family into a status which he occupies within the broader community.[7] Nor do we wish to contradict the idea of the uniqueness of the family as a discrete institution. In the present instance, however, *we wish to emphasize the regularities and constancies of certain categories of interpersonal relationships within a total framework.*

Our choice of four categories of interpersonal relationships to illustrate our thesis is primarily heuristic. The categories selected—economic and property relationships; authority and mechanisms of control; anxiety in interpersonal relationships; and sexual relationships—lend a sufficient range of variety and contrast within the individual culture with which to illustrate this particular type of cultural consistency.

THE COMMUNITY

Rocky Roads (a fictitious name) is a community in the central mountains of Jamaica, B.W.I., and is about one and a half to two miles in diameter. The 277 Rocky Roaders are English speaking Negroes, descendants of former slaves brought to Jamaica from Africa. Today, they are independent farmers raising varied crops which they sell for cash at weekly markets about 10 miles from Rocky Roads. Looking from the air, one sees a road of red gravel winding through a mountain. On either side of this road the land is thickly covered with green foliage. Somewhere in the bush are households, haphazardly placed and scattered over the mountain and in the valley. At first glance each household gives the impression of autonomy and independence of all other households in the community. Each appears to be self-sufficient, divorced from the affairs of all other families. Social relationships in Rocky Roads, as we shall see, correspond to this bird's-eye physical picture.

Economic and Property Relationships: Rocky Roads is an economically competitive community, the accumulation of money and land being the chief goal of the individual Rocky Roader. The people of the community are constantly anxious over their economic welfare. Specifically, this anxiety is the belief that one never has enough money, that one is poor, and that one's opportunities for earning a satisfactory livelihood are being undermined by threats of sorcery. It is important to note that about 80% of the Rocky Roaders live above a subsistence level and no more than 3% of the adult population are indigent.

No matter how "independent" (wealthy) a person might be, he generally believes that everyone else, no matter how obviously poor, is better off and has accumulated more money. The Rocky Roaders are not ignorant of each other's finances. While no person will divulge the amount of his savings, other Rocky Roaders are able to render a fairly accurate account of his finances. It is the belief that everyone is more independent than oneself—while at the same time attempting to outdo everyone else—which makes for an extremely high level of anxiety.

As a result of this secrecy, one of the strongest proscriptions in the culture is the rule that it is grossly improper to inquire of someone how much money he or she has or earns. At the same time, however, most Rocky Roaders are possessed by an insatiable curiosity about the economic affairs, activities, and standings of their neighbors, and they often go to remarkable lengths to satisfy this curiosity. A variety of rationalizations are entertained to justify this secrecy. The first is theft; were it to become known that one had money, thieves would be tempted. Actually, not even our oldest informant, who was more than 90, had any memory of theft within the district. If one maintains secrecy he can refuse to lend money or economic help, pleading that he is too poor. In reality, however, it would appear that this secrecy is maintained to avoid the arousal of jealousy in neighbors (see below). Characteristically, money is hidden in "the box under the bed," a euphemism for one's secret hiding place. The rigid secrecy surrounding the location of this cache is demonstrated by the fact that if a Rocky Roader dies suddenly and without warning his money is often lost to his survivors.

One's own perceived poverty and relative economic failure is generally attributed to some wealthier person who will not lease land, because he or she "doesn't want other people to make a living." There are wealthy Rocky Roaders who own many acres of land which are not under cultivation. These landowners claim that they eventually reap greater profits if they allow the land to lie fallow and then cultivate it themselves. Crop failures, while often admittedly the results of droughts and hurricanes, are more often attributed to the machinations of the sorcerer working at a neighbor's behest. Economic success, in addition to being a purely individual matter, is always a relative value in Rocky Roads; its measure is the size of a neighbor's crop and the number of his cows. The Rocky Roaders sum this up succinctly in one of their favorite maxims: "One man's fall is another man's rise," and conversely, "One man's rise is another man's fall."

There are few forms of collective labor in Rocky Roads. One such is a system of reciprocal exchange of labor. When a Rocky Roader needs help on his land or in repairing his home he will ask someone—always of the same economic and social standing, not necessarily a kinsman—to help him for the day. The recipient of this labor may now at any time be called upon by the donor to repay the day's work with another. If a particular job requires more than a day's labor, the helper is remunerated financially. The latter labor does not have to be repaid. These forms in the exchange of labor prevail between all men, be they "strangers," father and son, or siblings. The latter will not charge each other the same rates gotten from more distant relations or from "strangers," but it is a wage relationship nevertheless. As one man who netted a tidy sum by working on his son's land explained, "After all, a man must have something to live on." Another semi-reciprocal relationship exists in which two men share a single crop; there were only two such arrangements. One owns the land and does no work while the other provides the labor. In return, each receives an equal portion from the crop returns. A third reciprocal arrangement is that of the "best friend" (see below).

Land is the mainspring of life in Rocky Roads and as such it constitutes the only medium by which a Rocky Roader can visualize the achievement of "independence." Overt competitiveness is for money, but land is the primary medium for securing money. There is a tremendous inequality in the distribution of the land, but there are no mechanisms of censure in the culture of the community by which one can be compelled to rent or sell land. One widowed woman with no dependents owns 200 acres of land. She began by owning the local general store. For long periods of time she extended credit more than generously to customers. When the latter could not pay their debts she took their land in default of payments. The second largest landowner is a man with one dependent who owns 40 acres. At the other extreme, one man with 6 children owns about 4 acres; another couple with 12 dependents own about 8 acres. All one can hope for is that sorcery will be effective in making a landowner ill and unable to work his land; he will then be forced into selling his land for ready cash with which to pay for medical care and for the expenses of everyday living. There were several instances in which formerly large land holders became seriously ill and were forced to sell almost all their land. These illnesses were attributed to the sorcery of jealous individuals who were unable to rent or purchase land under normal circumstances. The scarcity of land has a further divisive effect in forcing a number of the younger people of the community to seek employment outside Rocky Roads.

All objects of ownership, whether in movables or in land, are privately and individually held. There are no joint, corporate, or collective types of ownership. Land is never lent or exchanged; it must be acquired either by will, purchase, or lease. Nor can a person erect a house or any other permanent structure on land which is rented, but only on land which has been bought or inherited.

Anxiety in Interpersonal Relationships: Most Rocky Roaders genuinely feel that their neighbors dislike them and are intensely jealous of them.[8] The anxiety and discomfort which most feel in physical and social proximity to others can be detected in several areas of behavior. The "scatter pattern" of settlement in Rocky Roads provides an excellent clue to the overall structure of interpersonal relationships in the community. The most outstanding sociological phenomenon in the social organization is that *the community is composed of isolated, independent nuclear families.* There is no inter-household discipline and control; nor is there any mechanism for the pooling of resources between households or similar social units. It is a truism that the survival and perpetuation or total extinction of a family in Rocky Roads would hardly affect the remaining households—save, perhaps, in the availability of purchasable land.

Paralleling this state of affairs is the absence of any inalienable kin groupings and the dearth of voluntary groupings. There are some voluntary associations, but their significance within the general social organization of the community varies from one type to another. While 80% of the families in Rocky Roads are related, the culture of the community has not worked out, even in ideal form, patterns of aid or systematized economic relationships along kinship lines. Even during the worst of food shortages some families manage to raise and sell a surplus of food, and the fortunes of a few multiply while the savings of most dwindle to almost nothing. Ties of kinship, including those between parents and children and siblings, are not totally exempted from this pattern. There is but one instance in Rocky Roads of two households sharing one plot of land for purposes of residence, yet even these two families, the heads of which are siblings, maintain this competitive relationship.

People are untrustworthy, say the Rocky Roaders, because no sooner are they told something than they go about repeating it to others and "causing a lot of trouble." It is true that Rocky Roaders gossip about whatever they are told. But it is also true that one will rarely divulge a piece of information which he does not want spread.

There is little visiting in Rocky Roads, and the culture makes no provision for hospitality or the treatment of guests in general. As a rule, Rocky Roaders do not like people to "come on their yards" and only rarely is one invited into the home of a Rocky Roader. Paralleling this is the absence of festive or recreational gatherings within the community.

Blood brotherhood is unknown to Rocky Roads, although the culture does provide that every person have a "best friend."[9] Actually, there are very few such friendships. The majority of these are among the men, some of whom form friendships in pairs. These friends spend considerable time together in a continual exchange of labor, but their relationships are subject to the same anxieties which pervade interpersonal relationships in general. Each member of the pair believes that he is a better friend than his partner, that he is the more devoted of the two, while the other is participating in the relationship for purely selfish reasons and will never grant a favor which he is not forced to. Characteristically, these accusations are not made one *to* the other but rather one *about* the other. These are premarital friendships and are discontinued after the marriage of one of the partners. Finally, it is interesting to note that secrecy over finances and feelings of competitiveness are maintained between such friends.

The frequency of such friendships is even smaller among the women of the community. For one thing, the women have no cause for economic unions and exchanges of labor as they do not habitually work in the fields. Housework is never brought under the category of exchanged labor. Where close friendships among young adult women do exist they are mainly homosexual unions in the absence of heterosexual outlets. These dissolve completely upon the acquisition by either of a heterosexual partner.

Every individual has a godfather and a godmother, but this relationship, too, is unelaborated. In addition to sponsoring an infant at the christening service, a godparent's paramount duty to his ritual child is to give the latter gifts, and the child is obligated to reciprocate. However, this rule is infrequently adhered to; nor do ritual parents and their children engage in any relationships of mutual aid in times of need.

Authority and Mechanisms of Control: Rocky Roads is a socially stratified community composed of lower, middle, and upper classes. Class position is determined primarily by how much money one has and how readily he can get money when he needs it. A lower class person—there are 4 such persons—is one who cannot meet his financial obligations and is dependent upon some outside agent—a wage relationship with an upper class person—for survival. Middle class persons are those who own or can afford to rent sufficient land to meet their obligations and manage to save varying amounts of money. An upper class person is one who does not exert any manual effort for the acquisition of food or money, but whose income derives from the rental of land and the sale of food cultivated and harvested by hired help. There are 4 such persons in Rocky Roads.

Allied to the system of social stratification is the almost complete absence of leadership arising from within the community. While there are differential degrees of prestige afforded individuals, by virtue of their economic (class) standings, prestige rarely takes the form of supreme importance within the group. Just as social status is achieved rather than ascribed, prestige cannot be transferred from one individual to another. As a result, there is no prestigeful status which is permanent and which is always occupied. For the community, prestigeful significance is derived almost entirely from an individual's economic success.

There are few situations in which spontaneous leadership arises from within the community. When leadership does become apparent, it is only in the person of an individual who was not born in the area. For example, cricket, of which the Rocky Roaders are very fond, requires the formation of teams which must be captained. As a result, very little cricket is played. Occasionally, teams will be organized, but they are chosen and coached by someone who is not a Rocky Roader. At the time of our investigation this leadership was in the person of a government employee who came from another region and whose residence in Rocky Roads was temporary. When his leadership was withdrawn the teams dissolved. This leadership is neither recognized nor effective in any sphere other than the one in which it originates. The leadership arises in the context of cricket, for example, and remains there. Furthermore, it is exercised by transient individuals who do not own land in or around Rocky Roads and who are, therefore, outside the community's system of economic competition. The same structural components could be discerned in other instances of leadership in the community, as in the Jamaica Agriculture Society, the Banana Growers' Association, and the like, groups set up by governmental agencies for the marketing of produce grown in the area.

The latter brings us closer to a fuller understanding of the dearth of leadership arising from within the community. In Rocky Roads true social and political authority can derive solely from economic power. There are no solidary kin groups which own the land to which the individual has but rights of lifelong use without attendant rights of alienation, permanent or otherwise. Nor are there any inalienable associations of individuals who have rights to each other's property and wealth. Instead, each individual stands in competitive relation to all other individuals, true economic power of one individual over the other being extremely rare.

The near identity of social and economic power can be seen in two separate phases of the culture. The only true locus of authority recognized by the Rocky Roader is parental authority. But even this is relative, for such authority ceases to function for an individual when he leaves his parental home and is completely independent financially of his family of orientation. Since, by virtue of the economic structure of the community, almost every man is economically independent he is also virtually independent of group and political authority.

In a few instances indigent persons are dependent upon others for their economic and physical survival. The dependent individual, in such cases, becomes an employee because he does not own sufficient land with which to meet his obligations. He does not possess definable and limited roles, for as far as his employer is concerned, everything falls within his obligations as an employee. The employer may at any time sever the relationship and render the employee and his family completely unable to survive. The employee is therefore at all times respectful, obedient, and prepared to grant any "favor" which the employer may request—even to the point of handing over part of his own food supply. But the employee alone is not the sole member of this end of the relationship, for the members of his family are equally subject to such demands. This is the only circumstance under which "strange" children may be put to a task—by their father's employer—without criticism by the children's parents. To be sure, this relationship rarely occurs, for most Rocky Roaders do own some land from which to support their families; its existence, however infrequent, illustrates the notion that true authority occurs in Rocky Roads under conditions of economic power. Since the clear majority of the members of the community are not subject to such economic power they are not subject to social authority emanating from within the community itself.

Despite the dearth of leadership and authority outside the family group, and a corresponding weakness of formalized and systematized mechanism of control, certain techniques of control are at work and are effective in minimizing overt signs of strife in the community. Essentially, these are of two sorts: internalized controls and individualized controls; the two are not unrelated. On the one hand, rather than existing in a patterned, externalized fashion, the pressures toward conformity are internalized within the individual. On the other hand, retribution and retaliation for offensive behavior, rather than being effected by communal endeavor, are always carried out by the affected individual. It is worth noting that the absence of a *sense* of community in Rocky Roads finds its extension in the fact that the perception of threat is never on the community level but rather on the individual level. That is, a Rocky Roader who perceives himself threatened by the behavior of another Rocky Roader views the threatening action as deliberately directed against his own self and has little interest in considering the effect of the action upon any of his neighbors.

The most significant internalized control is the inhibition of aggressiveness. Quarreling and outright malevolence are not unknown in Rocky Roads, but most often individuals attempt to avoid those situations which demand the expression of hostility. For example, when one is cheated by a neighbor in an economic transaction, one generally says nothing to the dishonest acquaintance but merely attempts to avoid future transactions with him. Predominantly, Rocky Roaders express their spontaneously induced anger with a wall of complete silence.

In addition to the internalized fear of behaving aggressively, action committed in the face of threatened aggression or retaliation is itself perceived as an aggressive act. Hence, Rocky Roaders are extremely law abiding. On occasion a woman will find it necessary to sue the father for support of her illegitimate child but she will not do so if the man threatens to retaliate with sorcery. The effects of sorcery are easily combatted, but the threat is one of aggressive retaliation and hence is not provoked.

A Rocky Roader's greatest fear is of his neighbor's jealousy. Rocky Roaders do not employ the phrase "evil eye," but are familiar with the idiom, and use "jealousy" as its equivalent. Great pains are taken to avoid its arousal, for once it is aroused, one's fortunes are certain to disintegrate. Most people, when seeing a successful crop which is not theirs, wish that something would happen to it. When the jealous wish itself is incapable of doing the task, the sorcerer may succeed.

The most frequently employed and most effective externalized mechanism of social control within the community is gossip. Its frequency can be accounted for in terms of its aggressive and malicious functions, and its effectiveness can be accounted for in terms of the dread and fear of being talked about. Gossip, on the part of the person who is its subject, is equivalent to criticism and criticism is intimately linked with sorcery. This equation is made by the Rocky Roader because, he reasons, only a jealous individual would gossip and criticize. It is the fear of gossip and the implied criticism, and the resultant fear of sorcery, which largely controls the display of wealth in Rocky Roads. The display of wealth, while not defined by the culture as an aggressive act, will threaten most Rocky Roaders, for such an action is meant to imply economic failure in everyone else, and it will arouse the jealousy of neighbors. Jealousy is the emotion which provides the very foundation for sorcery and its arousal will bring economic catastrophe to its object. One rarely admits to either jealousy or sorcery, but it is generally recognized as a deterrent to conspicuousness in wealth.

Sexual Relationships: The motivational undertones to sexual behavior provide an almost complete antithesis to those which impel economic and other interpersonal relationships in the community. Almost all Rocky Roaders first experience heterosexual intercourse at 14 years. Informants report that there are no particular anxieties surrounding this. Very little time is devoted to sexual activity, there is no preoccupation with it, and at no point in the life-cycle do there seem to be any anxieties surrounding coitus. For the first 2 or 3 years of adolescence there are few restrictions—aside from the rules of incest and the proprieties of time and place—on sexual partnerships between boys and girls; unions are struck up wherever and whenever convenient. But at about 17 or 18 years, definite patterns in sexual relationships take form and are adhered to. At this point, a boy and girl must be "friends" before they indulge in coitus. In the relationship the boy "owns" the girl and the girl "owns" the boy. Sexual relationships are never matters for gossip within the community and should a "boy friend" or "girl friend" prove unfaithful to his or her partner the matter is a problem for the affected individuals to work out; no one in the community will exhibit interest in the matter. Furthermore, there is no competition among the men for a girl or among the women for a particular man.

Aside from the motives of sexual gratification, there appear to be few emotions of any significance involved in the formation of sexual friendships. There is no requirement for affection between premarital sexual partners; one may have a sexual relationship with another while still nurturing a dislike for the person. There are no terms of endearment or expressions of affection between premarital sexual partners. The only criterion for the maintenance of the relationship is mutual physical gratification; if either fails to gratify the other sexually, the relationship is dissolved.

A final indication of the almost complete absence of anxiety surrounding sexual behavior is the phenomenon of homosexuality. Few Rocky Roaders are familiar with the term "homosexuality"; nor do they possess a substitute term for it. Similarly, the members of the community do not know the word "masturbation" nor have any single word or phrase to denote the activity. There is no known homosexuality among the men although they are aware of its occurrence in the capital and in the towns. Similarly, there is no prostitution in Rocky Roads and the men never visit prostitutes in the more urbanized sections of the island. There is some homosexuality among the women of the community, but only among those who must go for long periods without any heterosexual intercourse. In such instances, homosexuality never completely supplants heterosexuality but is a temporary substitute.

THE FAMILY[10]

Marriage in Rocky Roads serves two primary functions. It serves, first, to grant full adult status to the individuals who are marrying. This does not refer to cultural permission to engage in sexual intercourse and bear children; such freedom was gained at adolescence. Full adult status means final and complete emancipation—both in theory and in actuality—from one's family of orientation; it means, in short, the unqualified termination of parental control and jurisdiction.

The founding of a new household—the second primary function —is equally specific. In juxtaposing an economic upon a sexual relationship, marriage in Rocky Roads unites only the two individuals who have entered into such a permanent union, *not* their households of orientation. Whatever new economically cooperative relationships are inaugurated by marriage do not extend beyond the limits of the new individual family unit. When seen in relation to the overall social organization of the community, these two functions of marriage affect practically every aspect of Rocky Roads culture.

Marriage is strictly monogamous and the rule of residence is neolocal. Descent and inheritance are bilateral; kinship terminology is of the Eskimo type. There are no prohibitions covering the marriage of cousins; outside the range of primary relatives the rules of incest proscribe marriage to aunts and uncles and nephews and nieces.

In the overwhelming majority of cases the number of generations present in the Rocky Roads family is three, not two. The prevalence of the third generation is due almost exclusively to the phenomenon of illegitimacy. More than half the births recorded in any 12-month period in Rocky Roads are illegitimate. The culture assigns illegitimate children to the care of the maternal grandparents rather than to the unwed mother, and it thus turns out that almost every couple rears two generations.

Almost all the men of Rocky Roads voluntarily support their illegitimate children until the latters' 14th birthdays. The customary sum which these men contribute is 5 shillings a week—one-third the sum which the culture recognizes as minimal to survival. The willingness of men to support their illegitimate children is more an expedient than a principled fulfillment of an obligation, since, fearful of court action and too high an assessment by the judge, almost all the men resort to the voluntary contribution of 5 shillings per week.

In the families where there are two generations, namely, a married man and woman and their children, the status system is clearcut; the man is the ruler of the household. The children occupy the lowest status, while their mother maintains an intermediary position. Where there are three generations, the father occupies the highest status; progressively, below him, are his wife, the children they have in common, their daughters' illegitimate children, and, on rare occasions, the mother's illegitimate children by a man other than her husband. It is not infrequent for a man to marry a woman by whom he has had an illegitimate child. In such cases these children are brought along to the newly founded household and occupy the status of children the couple have in common, for after the marriage of their parents these children are no longer illegitimate. In *extremely* rare instances a man will permit his bride to bring along to her new home an illegitimate child by another man. These children are indeed the pariahs of the Rocky Roads family. Even when men do allow their wives to bring these children, the husbands live up to the traditional refusal to "feed other men's children." Their support is the obligation of the mother. When they reach late adolescence, at 17 or 18 years, they leave the immediate household and cease to be even nominal members of it. They usually move onto a piece of their mother's land, supporting themselves as best they can. They maintain almost no social intercourse with their families of orientation.

Economic and Property Relationships: Aside from the provision of foodstuffs by the father, there is no single practice in the distribution of money within the family. The most frequent practice is for a man to grant a small weekly allowance to his wife. Some men dole out money piecemeal for every household item which their wives must purchase. Some men keep all their money and insist that their wives provide whatever money is needed. The latter only occurs where a woman earns enough money to care for the family needs which are not provided for by cultivation.

Husbands and wives maintain absolute secrecy about their cash earnings from each other. The maintenance of such secrecy and of separate purses in the family must be viewed within a broader context of economic rivalry between spouses which is manifest in a number of ways: (1) Husbands and wives sell land (but not food) to each other. Buying and selling between spouses is as competitive as between unrelated Rocky Roaders. (2) Spouses compete in begging relationships. Almost all Rocky Roaders beg, both from neighbors and strangers, and it is not unusual for a Rocky Roader in a begging situation to compete with his or her spouse, just as one competes with non-relatives when begging. (3) Spouses pilfer money from each other. Women are generally assigned the task of carrying their husbands' produce to market for sale. The latter have no way of predicting the precise amount of money these items will net, and their wives capitalize on this fact and invariably pocket part of the proceeds. Men do the same when carrying their wives' produce to market. Rocky Roads culture defines this practice as stealing and condemns it.

Property, both real and movable, is rarely held within the family in common ownership, and is basically subject to the same patterns of ownership as money. The Rocky Roaders recognize three classes of property in land relative to the family: (1) The land which the man inherited from his parents or which he has purchased prior to his marriage. This is his exclusive property to do with as he pleases. (2) The land which his wife received from her parents or which she purchased before her marriage. She may never sell this land or dispose of it in any way without her husband's permission. But while he cultivates it, as he does his own land, he may not sell it without his wife's consent. (3) The land which was bought after marriage. Nominally, this land is held in joint ownership by both spouses. In reality, ultimate jurisdiction over it is in the hands of the man; he may dispose of this land without consulting his wife.

A man sells all the produce he has raised on all three types of land and the income is exclusively his, but he sells only the surplus which remains after providing for the needs of his family. Any produce which the woman raises on the second or third category of land is hers and the income is exclusively hers. A woman never cultivates on the first class of land. Generally, the husband has first call on any of the land which he wishes to use; all that remains from the second and third categories may be used by the wife.

Secrecy regarding financial matters prevails between parents and their children as between spouses. This is an important facet of parent-child relationships in Rocky Roads. Grown sons still residing with their parents must contribute about one-third of their incomes to their parents to help defray the cost of the food which the young men consume. Sons invariably capitalize on this secrecy and very often turn over to their parents a sum smaller than required. Daughters, even when they are wage-earners, retain all their money and need not make any contributions to the family coffers.

The culture of the community directs that sons must support their parents when the latter become too old to work. We did not know any men, however aged, who were incapable of working, but there were some aged women who were incapacitated. These women received little or nothing from their sons who claimed that they could not afford to help support their mothers. Interestingly, this rule applies to the men of the community, not to the women. As it turns out, many daughters help their parents in the latter's old age, while almost none of the men do.

Relationships between siblings at all age levels conform to the general patterns described thus far for the Rocky Roads family. Economic relationships are competitive, and social intercourse and emotional attachments are almost wholly absent.

Inheritance is a family affair and as such is illustrative of economic and emotional relationships between parents and children, as well as among siblings. Theoretically, a man is supposed to make out a will leaving his property to his wife; upon her death the land is to be distributed equally among all her legitimate children. These are the rules governing inheritance. However, when a man makes out a will he invariably keeps its contents secret lest some members of the family be disappointed with it and quarrel with him. Generally, men will their land and money to their wives, but occasionally land is willed directly to the children.

The land is not always divided equally among the children; sons almost always get a larger share than do daughters. On occasion poorer sons will get more than others. But favoritism in willing land is almost always present and generates feuds and animosities among siblings after the reading of the will. Although few of these wills would ever be legally binding in a Jamaican court of law, since they are rarely witnessed or properly certified, no Rocky Roader ever contests a will in a court of law. The folks of the community are fully aware of the legal status of their wills, yet tradition dictates that no one ever seeks legal action to nullify the legacy of a parent. The quarrels among siblings over the inheritance take place during the funeral. Residues of old quarrels and bitternesses emerge, and the quarrel continues until one of the two parties desists. During the quarrel one catches references to threats of sorcery and the feuding siblings are immediately hushed by onlookers.

Quarrels over the patrimony are not of the usual run of family disputes, for they are not easily forgotten; there are several related factors which militate against the reestablishment of peace between the family members. First, there is always the material expression and symbolism of the dispute: the divided land. This is directly related to the second factor, namely, that the nature and character of practically all interpersonal relationships are colored and usually determined by emotional attitudes toward the land. A Rocky Roader who is deprived of land, especially through a human agency, deeply believes that his deprivation is the result of some concerted effort directed at him which aims at his impoverishment. Hints of sorcery are very often discerned in such ideas. This is particularly important in family relationships, for quarrels and bitterness over inheritance, when added to the general competitiveness with which family life is fraught, often deal the final blow to the minimal cohesiveness of the family group.

As the children begin to leave home to establish themselves independently, the process of the disintegration of the Rocky Roads family, as a unit, commences and is hastened by quarrels over the division of the family property. In its extreme form this phenomenon is most clearly illustrated by the fact that siblings, after they leave their families of orientation, have no more contact with each other than they do with their neighbors. And, as we have seen, this contact is minimal. To be sure, there are exceptions to this, but they are few, indeed. Relationships among siblings within their families of orientation and among their respective families of procreation do not—at least as far as economic matters are concerned—form any exceptions to the dominant community patterns of fear, suspicion, mistrust, anxiety, competitiveness, and isolation.

Anxiety in Interpersonal Relationships: Most couples in Rocky Roads are unhappily married and admittedly regret, within a few years after marriage, having entered into such a permanent union. The reasons offered for this are almost always of an economic nature. The never ceasing task of supporting and providing for a family makes the men wish they had never married. The women marry with a view to greater economic security and comfort, yet they complain that they must "hustle" even more and work harder after marriage than before. Another complaint often registered is the frequent failure of spouses to make good the promises made before marriage. Men often promise to raise and support the illegitimate children of the women they are courting and usually refuse to do so after marriage. Young ladies being courted lay claim to proficiency in cooking, sewing, and farming, but are often without such aptitudes after marriage. Only secondarily do spouses mention that they have tired of each other's presence and yearn for a change of environment.

In a similar vein, quarrels between spouses are usually precipitated by matters centering about food and money. A man will fly into a rage if his meal is late or if his clothes are unwashed and unmended. A woman will complain bitterly that her husband does not provide adequately for her. A woman's refusal to work with her husband in the field is a frequent source of quarreling. Spouses often quarrel over the upbringing of their children, but here, too, the problem is of an economic nature. For example, a man will attribute the growing number of his illegitimate grandchildren to his wife's failure to keep proper watch over their daughters. His complaint on this score is soley that he must shoulder the burden of supporting his illegitimate grandchildren.

Family quarrels are usually waged with a stony silence after an initial outburst of verbal abuse on both sides. Such silence may last several days. In the meantime, if aggressive feelings are exceedingly intense, husband and wife might refuse to eat food which the other has grown, partaking only of his or her own food. No act can constitute a more deadly insult, for to refuse an offer of food by another Rocky Roader is tantamount to an open declaration of contempt. It should be pointed out that there is no divorce or permanent separation of spouses in Rocky Roads. No informant had any memory of divorce or permanent separation in the community.

Social intercourse between spouses is minimal. Husbands and wives do not share their leisure. Mutual recreation and relaxation are absent in family life. Nor is there any positive emotional interdependence between married people to serve as a foundation of the family partnership. There are no terms or overt expressions of endearment between husband and wife. In short, as most Rocky Roaders readily admit, husbands and wives are not particularly fond of one another.

Basically, interpersonal relationships between parents and their children conform to the patterns which constitute the modes of interaction between spouses. There is a minimum of social intercourse between parents and their children, and few patterns of mutual recreation in which they participate. Parents never attempt to elicit support from their children during family quarrels. Nor do parents ever vie with each other for the affection of their children.

Parents have their favorites among their children. When the latter are young, the most subservient and submissive is the favorite. Children who are singled out as more "meddlesome" or "rude" receive more punishment. As the children get older the favoritism is realigned, and the inheritance will often be divided according to it.

Authority and Mechanisms of Control: The Rocky Roads family is authoritarian in character. Theoretically, the father is the undisputed ruler of the household, and a woman may do nothing without her husband's permission. This authority is by virtue of his economic position in the household and does not necessarily rest upon his status as the eldest male in the home. The family ruler is answerable to no one; he can be overruled by no one either within his own household or any other household in the community. When making a decision he need not fear nor take into account the opinions of his spouse or children. And his decisions carry an implied finality. The women are conscious of their inferior status, primarily in terms of their economic dependence on their husbands, but deny that it arouses any resentment in them. They recognize the inequality of authority in the family as ordained by God and never to be questioned. They explain the restraints placed on their behavior with the statement that "I am a woman." The men are likewise aware of their superior status within the family, are proud of it, and often exploit it to its full advantages.

Within the family, the women are not without their private schemes and techniques for circumventing their husbands' authority, and resort alternatively to three characteristic techniques. If, for example, a woman decides to buy something for the home and if she knows or suspects that her husband would disapprove of the expenditure, she will wait until he is in the fields and then make her purchase. Confronted with the fact the irate husband can do nothing but chastise his wife for not having sought his permission. The second most frequent source of friction on this score arises when a woman decides that she would like to provide her parents with some food from her husband's crop. The men generally object to this. Having been forbidden to do this, a woman will be beaten by her husband if he discovers her action. The willingness of many of the women to help support their aged parents is one manifestation of the greater dependency of Rocky Roads women on their mothers. Girls frequently visit their mothers after having married, but they do not visit their parents' homes with the express purpose of visiting their fathers. Sons generally visit neither parent after their departure from home. A daughter going to live and work in a different section of the island is obliged to correspond with her mother, not her father, and she must always return to Rocky Roads at her mother's behest. Sons are never under such obligations, even when traveling to a foreign country. A third technique frequently employed is gossip about husbands' miserliness or unbridled authoritarianism. To be sure, not many women will go out of the way to volunteer unflattering remarks about their husbands, but that it does occur without arousing much censure— except, of course, from the affected husband—points to one wifely weapon which can be used effectively against a disliked spouse. A woman who gossips about her husband knows quite certainly that her remarks will reach his ears. As we have already seen, the Rocky Roader equates gossip with criticism and he links criticism with sorcery.[11]

In general terms parents maintain absolute authority over their children as long as they support them. Formulating this principle in another manner, a Rocky Roader owes his parents absolute obedience as long as he is being supported by them. Whatever degree of economic independence a Rocky Roader enjoys, he enjoys a corresponding independence from parental authority. Theoretically, parents are not obliged to support their children after the latter have finished their schooling (generally about the age of 14). Likewise, parents enjoy absolute authority in every sphere until their children have left school. Many parents, weary of the burden of providing for their children, adhere strictly to this rule and insist that their youngsters seek gainful employment. When a Rocky Roads youth commences his career as a breadwinner, he is left more or less to do as he chooses, and only on occasion will his father reprove him for errant behavior; only on the rarest of occasions will his father attempt to strike him. As he gets older and earns more money he enjoys greater freedom, and once he has reached premarital adulthood his parents enjoy minimal authority over him. But so long as he is living in his parents' home he is somewhat restrained, for he retains the luxury of having his mother cook for him. Often, in early adulthood, parents will threaten a son with deprivation of this luxury or with possible expulsion from the home if he does not comply with certain prescribed requirements enumerated by them.

This can be seen more clearly in the treatment of daughters. Girls are generally restricted from gaining the same economic independence as their brothers. As a result, the young women of the community are generally not permitted the same freedom of movement enjoyed by the young men. In those cases in which they are permitted to attain a measure of economic independence they enjoy a comparable measure of freedom from parental control. It is in these contexts of social learning that a Rocky Roader learns that economic independence is synonomous with social and political independence.

Sexual Relationships: Almost all married couples in Rocky Roads are sexually well adjusted. By the latter valuation we mean the attainment and maintenance of maximal mutual satisfaction and gratification by both parties involved in the sexual relationship.[12] As to whether sexual enjoyment and gratification is greater in one or the other spouse, informants found the question a difficult one to answer. Most agreed that sexual activity was mutually enjoyable and satisfying.

So far as we were able to determine, the denial or granting of sexual intercourse is never employed as a technique either to control or reward a spouse. As a matter of fact, a woman who behaved seductively toward her husband would be considered quite aberrant.

Extramarital sexual liaisons are frowned upon, but there are no proscriptions covering adultery which carry the force of a taboo. Adultery is considered neither a crime nor a sin in Rocky Roads. The attitude of the community toward adultery may be put another way. Should the knowledge of a person's extramarital affairs become public no one will criticize him or her. In fact, no one would say anything about the matter. The only one who would censure the act is the spouse. A man will seek an extramarital partner if his wife does not satisfy him sexually, and he will attempt to select an elderly woman who can no longer bear children. If a man cannot satisfy his wife sexually she will likewise seek another partner, claiming that her husband "leaves her in more pain than before."

CONCLUSION

Economic and property relationships in Rocky Roads must be thought of as competitive. Individual success in the accumulation of wealth, rigid secrecy surrounding the amount of money an individual has accumulated, and a frugality to excess are the outstanding characteristics of interpersonal economic relationships.

We are able to observe these traits in microcosm on the various levels of family relationships. The maintenance of separate purses of money within the family is as strictly adhered to as it is within the general community. The emphasis of "mine" as against "yours" continues to operate with unabated intensity within the family. And in the attempt to increase the volume of "mine" as against "yours" spouses employ many of the techniques of competition which are found in the general community. The maintenance of secrecy regarding financial matters is as much a cardinal rule in family life as it is between members of different households. It is to be found between spouses, between parents and their children, and between siblings. The almost complete absence of material generosity in Rocky Roads is manifest in extreme form in the manner in which the men dole out money to their wives for household expenses and in the adherence by many to the rule that one need not support a child after the age of 14.

When thinking of property the Rocky Roader can think only in terms of individual, private holdings. Competition for land is divisive in the general community, and this wedge in social relationships can be observed again in the family.[13] In its extreme form it is one of the primary catalysts in the disintegration of the family and its inability to exhibit continuity as a solidary entity from generation to generation. Competition for land in the broader community pits family against family, militating against inter-household unity and the pooling of resources between individuals and households. Similarly, the competition for land in the division of the patrimony destroys whatever bond might have existed between brothers.

On the score of anxiety in interpersonal relationships we note the individual's feelings of unpleasantness and discomfort in the face of close personal ties, an uneasiness which is probably a manifestation of mistrust and suspicion of others, specifically their economic motives and aspirations. In the broader community this discomfort in the face of close personal ties can be seen in several areas of behavior, as in ideas of being disliked, the belief that most people are untrustworthy and malicious, and the prevalence of anxieties even between "best friends." It is also to be seen in the failure of the culture to develop patterns of visiting and recreation as well as solidary and inalienable groupings of individuals.

These perceptions of the social world are equally present in interpersonal relationships within the family. It does not take long for married couples to tire of the marriage relationship nor do spouses relax together or share their leisure time. The anxieties which militate against the formation of close ties within the general community are also sources of frequent tension and quarreling between spouses. Just as within the broader community the Rocky Roaders believe that their fellows are attempting to deny them a comfortable livelihood through means of covert hostility, so do spouses quarrel when they believe that they are being deprived by each other. Part of the disappointment in marriage is a perceived failure on the part of the other person to fulfill all one's material and economic expectations. Similarly, the techniques of expressing and avoiding hostility in family situations are those which are employed in the broader community.

Perhaps the clearest and most succinct illustration of our thesis is to be found in the areas of authority and mechanisms of control. In the more diffuse relationships of the general community we noted the absence of either horizontal or vertical control and authority as these stemmed from the economic independence of the individual nuclear family; where there is no economic control there is hardly any political control arising from within the community. Similarly, where parents lose their economic control over their children their authority over them diminishes accordingly. Where they continue to support their children they continue to exercise a corresponding degree of authority over them.

Aside from internalized mechanisms of control the most effective means of restraining offensive behavior are anomic. Jealousy, gossip, and sorcery, while effective in controlling the behavior of others, are not recognized by their victims as normal and justifiable pressures toward conformity. Similarly, the techniques of control used between spouses are anomic, for the culture in no way justifies gossip about one's spouse or subterfuge as legitimate means to desired ends. Incidentally, the Rocky Roaders do not, as do other peoples, regard such techniques as matters for humor.

Finally, the basic motivations to sexual behavior are repeated with precise regularity in marital and non-marital situations. In both the primary concern is physical gratification. There appear to be no anxieties in either premarital or marital sexual relationships, just as there are no "romantic" or other pseudoemotional rationalizations for sexual behavior. Furthermore, the community treats marital infidelity with exactly the same lack of interest as it does premarital infidelity.

Rocky Roads is a relatively simple and stable community. A logical problem is whether such a hypothesis would hold true in similarly stable societies as well as in far more complex and rapidly changing societies. If it does hold true in other equally stable societies it might be possible to employ the degree of consistency of values and personality orientations in the family and in the broader society as an index or criterion of cultural and sociological disequilibrium in a process of change.

A corollary to this is our inability at this point to offer a qualitative statement as to exactly which categories of values in interpersonal relationships we would include in a broader hypothesis and which we would exclude. For example, we have the impression that competition for non-economic prestige symbols—such as competition in "counting coup" among the Plains Indians—while obviously a category of interpersonal relationships, is not one which is repeated microcosmically in the family institution. It is hoped that future research into the problem will provide a formulation which will enable us to state which categories of interpersonal relationships of the broader community are repeated in the family and which are not.

Notes:

1. The field work reported on here was made possible by grants from the Wenner-Gren Foundation for Anthropological Research, and was carried out during July 1950–February 1951. The writer is indebted to his wife, Vera Krassin Cohen, who participated in the field work. Part of this paper was read at the Annual Meetings of the American Anthropological Association, Detroit, Michigan, December 28–30, 1954.

2. Lowie, Robert H. *Primitive Society.* New York, 1920.

3. Murdock, George P. *Social Structure.* New York, 1949. The conflicting relationships of the family to other aspects of the social structure, as among the Hopi, is another problem in this general area of research. See Titiev, Mischa, *Old Oraibi: A Study of the Hopi Indians of Third Mesa,* Papers of the Peabody Museum of American Archaeology and Ethnology, Harvard University, Vol. XXII, No. 1, 1944, pp. 39–43. Also Aberle, David F., *The Psycho-Social Analysis of a Hopi Life History,* Comparative Psychology Monographs, Vol. 21, No. 1, 1951, pp. 63–75.

4. Linton, Ralph. *The Study of Man.* New York, 1936, p. 152. Murdock, *op. cit.,* pp. 7–9.

5. Merton, Robert K. *Social Theory and Social Structure.* Glencoe, 1949, p. 147.

6. Murdock, George P. and Whiting, J. W. M. "Cultural Determination of Parental Attitudes: The Relationship between the Social Structure and Parental Behavior," in M. Senn (ed.), *Conference on Problems of Infancy and Childhood,* 1950.

7. Linton, Ralph. "Problems of Status Personality," in S. S. Sargent and M. W. Smith (eds.), *Culture and Personality,* New York, 1949, pp. 163–73.

8. It is also true that most Rocky Roaders dislike their neighbors and are intensely jealous of them. However, we are confining ourselves at this point to but one facet of interpersonal relationships within the community.

9. See, for example, Herskovits, M. J., "The Best Friend in Dahomey," M. Cunard (ed.), *Negro Anthology,* London, 1934, pp. 627–32.

10. See Henriques, Fernando, "West Indian Family Organization," *American Journal of Sociology,* Vol. 55, pp. 30–37, 1949.

11. We do not know whether spouses ever actively employ sorcery against each other or whether, in view of the linkage between gossip and sorcery, this is the closest they do come to practicing sorcery against each other.

12. This valuation refers to physical, *not* emotional, gratification. As we noted in our discussion of premarital behavior, such liaisons seem to be lacking in emotional content.

13. Similar functional relationships and regularities are to be observed among the Yurok, a society comparable to Rocky Roads in their economic competitiveness. See Goldschmidt, Walter, "Ethics and the Structure of Society: An Ethnological Contribution to the Sociology of Knowledge," *American Athropologist,* Vol. 53, pp. 506–24, 1951; Kroeber, A. L., "The Yurok," in *Handbook of the American Indians of California,* Bulletin 78, Bureau of American Ethnology, 1925; Waterman, T. T. and Kroeber, A. L., *Yurok Marriages,* University of California Publications in American Archaeology and Ethnology, Vol. 18, No. 5, 1920.

22. Life Cycle in an East Indian Village in Trinidad

In the course of a normal lifetime, the East Indian of Amity will experience a patterned sequence of ceremonial and social events. There are certain things the villager will have to do or have others do for him. The sequence is different for males and females, but is the same for all castes in the village. This East Indian life cycle, involving as it does the almost certain expectation of marriage as well as the relocation of the girl to an alien village, represents one of the most striking ways in which Trinidad East Indian social structure differs from that of their Creole neighbors.

There are two or three men in Amity with considerable religious education who speak of the *sorā sanskār* (sixteen sacraments). They believe that all good Hindus in India observe all the *sanskār*. Among other things, the *sanskār* include the four traditional "stages" (*āsrāma*) of a holy Hindu life: *brāhmacārya* (the chaste student); *grihastha* (the householder); *bana-prastha* (the ascetic hermit); and *sannyāsa* (the holy mendicant). Few in Amity apart from these men have ever even heard of the *sorā sanskār*. As Lewis writes of the village of Rampur in India, after discussing some of the *sanskār*, "these ideal stages bear little resemblance to the present-day life cycle" (1958: 45–47; see also Stevenson 1920).

The following is a brief analysis of the Amity life cycle, including the *rites de passage*.

Birth: Most women travel to their parents' home for the birth of at least their first child. Since East Indian marriages are customarily village exogamous and virilocal, this means that a large part of the population of Amity was actually born elsewhere on the island. When

SOURCE: Pp. 117–31 of Morton Klass, *East Indians in Trinidad.* New York: Columbia University Press. Reprinted by permission of the author and publisher.

one asks a person the name of the village from which he comes, he gives the name of his father's village; it was there he was raised, and it is there that he belongs.

Soon after the baby is born the father visits a pandit, giving the latter the day and hour of the baby's birth. The pandit casts a horoscope for the child, and tells the father the only possible initial letter the child's name can have. Either the father or the pandit then chooses the name. This name, called the "pandit (or 'planet') name," will be kept secret by the child and his family—so secret, sometimes, that if the father dies or deserts the mother, the child may never know its "true" name! A second Hindi name is given—but one that has nothing to do with this particular child's "planet"—and will be the one used publicly, since this "calling name" will be of no use to any evil person who might wish to learn the child's "planet" and so injure him. Some people even feel uneasy about the use of "calling names," and to be on the safe side, substitute pet names, English names, or nicknames.[1]

For six days after the birth the baby and mother may not leave the house or be visited by the father. A midwife, usually of the Camār caste,[2] cares for them both during this period. On the evening of the sixth day the mother and baby are bathed and "purified" and a celebratory feast called a *catthī* is made. Female relatives and neighbors attend, and there is a long night of ribald rejoicing. No men are permitted in the house during a *catthī*, but the father, who will soon see his child for the first time, usually buys drinks for his friends at the rum shop.

Some of the wealthier families prefer to hold the birth celebration on the twelfth day, in which case it is known as a *barahī*, and is of greater magnitude. Once the mother and baby have been "purified" they may leave the house during the day. The night dew is feared by all, and mothers of newborn children are admonished not to go out at night; the dew could not only cause them to sicken, but through them might infect the child.

The baby's head is usually shaved at the time of the *catthī*, if it is done at all. If it is not, the baby's first haircut is given on the first Good Friday following its birth, near the Roman Catholic Church in Siparia in southern Trinidad. Hindus believe that the "Virgin of Siparia" is actually an incarnation of a Hindu deity, whom they call "Sopārī-mē."[3] Alternatively, the first haircut may be given during the celebration of Siw Rātrī.

Childhood: Weaning and toilet-training are often delayed until quite late, and for some children may not take place until the age of five when they begin school. With the presence of a nursery school in the village now, toilet-training is beginning to take place at an earlier age. Infancy ends and childhood begins with the entrance into school. Many date their first "serious beatings" from this point. For the first time the child's circle of acquaintance extends beyond the immediate family and its neighbors. Not only will the child learn new games, but the separation of the sexes, in terms of both association and type of play, begins at this time.

The young child has few duties at home. Both boys and girls will have to help with the fetching of water, and the girl may have to help with the smaller children. They may assist beyond that, the boys working in the garden and rice field and the girls in the kitchen, but there is no strong pressure on them.

Puberty: At about the age of twelve or fourteen, a boy of a Brāhman or Cattrī family may go to the pandit to receive the *janeo,* or sacred thread. Today many families do not bother with the ceremony. Generally, therefore, the boy's entry into puberty is not marked by any ceremony or sudden change in his life.

For the girl, however, the menarche usually marks the end of her schooling. From now on until her marriage, she will stay close to the house, leaving it only in the company of some member of her family. She will have more work to do at home, and it is important that she learn to cook and sew well, since these skills will be helpful in the search for a husband. In many families, however, there is a feeling that these are the last years of childhood for a girl; soon enough she will be a *dolāhīn* (bride) working hard in some alien household, and so not too great a burden of work is forced upon her.

Sexual intercourse is a subject of increasing interest and discussion among the adolescent boys. The boys are shy and uncertain and the girls are not too accessible, and many a man has told me that his first sexual experience was with an older married woman whose husband was away working. The boys claim they prefer girls of their own age, and they soon learn the techniques for getting the girls away from familial observation. It is a generally held assumption in the village that no female has any capacity to resist sexual advances. Only the continually watchful eyes of her family can protect her. Let a young man get her alone, and he and she automatically assume that sexual intercourse is inevitable.

Marriage: Years ago, in Amity, marriages commonly took place at the time of puberty, or even before. Today, a boy is considered of marriageable age from the time he is sixteen until he is around thirty —and even a man over thirty has no real difficulty in securing a wife if he should finally decide to marry. A girl, on the other hand, is really marriageable only between the ages of fifteen and seventeen, and an unmarried girl over the age of eighteen becomes a serious problem for her father. In rare cases, husbands have been found for girls as old as twenty. If the father delays too long, neighbors may begin to whisper disapprovingly that the girl's parents are keeping her to care for them in their old age. Gossips may even hint that the father is sexually interested in his own daughter. The pressure therefore is on the father of the girl. Time is short, and the longer he waits the greater the danger of the girl escaping the vigilance of her chaperones.

The girl's father literally sets out to find a boy. He cannot take one from his own village, and he prefers not to go to any village where he has family if he can help it. In the old days, he would probably have consulted an *āgwā*,[4] who traveled continually about the island noting the homes containing eligible young men. Today he must rely on his own efforts and on the advice of friends.

When he locates a boy, he must investigate the family. He will usually want a boy of the same caste as himself, or of a close caste of the same Varna. He must be certain that no kinship relationship exists between the two families; that the boy's family are decent people who are unlikely to mistreat his daughter; and that the boy himself is respectable and hardworking. Once the father of the boy becomes interested in the girl, he will have to make similar inquiries in her village, in an attempt to determine her character and behavior. Many modern young men like to make their own inquiries. With all this, the information received is likely to be of a highly dubious nature since few people would tell the truth about a member of their own village to a total stranger.

In the past, when marriages were arranged, the two fathers would make all decisions. Today, marriages are said to be made by free choice. This means that at some point in the proceedings the boy will be brought to the home of the girl, and the two will be introduced and allowed to whisper together privately for a little while. Later on each parent ascertains the willingness of his child to proceed with the match. If either child objects the matter is dropped and the father of the girl seeks another boy.

The business of finding a boy is a difficult, tedious, and expensive one. One informant estimated, on the basis of his own experience and that of friends, that a man usually interviewed around five boys before finally managing to "engage" one. With taxi trips, loss of work, a small fête each time, and other expenses, he estimated that each prospective bridegroom cost the father close to ten dollars. My informant, himself, had been through eight young men before finally securing one. Many young men, he said bitterly, look upon the "viewing" of a girl as a kind of sport, to be engaged in even when there is no real intention of getting married.

Assuming that all goes well, the boy continues to visit the girl for a number of months and slowly they become acquainted. Eventually, both sides satisfied, the *chēke* (engagement) of the boy takes place in his home, with the men of both sides present. The engagement of the girl, with a similar ceremony in her father's house, was once considered a custom of only Sudra people, but today it is practiced by many members of the higher castes as well. For Amity this represents the rare example of a custom moving upward, from low caste to high.

The date for the wedding is decided by a pandit, after consulting the horoscopes of both young people. Years ago the wedding might be held at any time during the week, and would be an all-night affair. In recent years, however, night weddings have been disappearing, and I observed none at all during my study. Today, weddings take place on Sunday afternoons.

A Hindu wedding in Amity is a lengthy, intricate, and expensive affair for both sides. It is becoming more and more customary to forego the *tīlāk* ceremony (giving of the dowry to the boy), formerly held two weeks before the wedding at the boy's home. *Tīlāk* is now given during the opening ceremonies of the wedding itself.

Each side must prepare an extensive feast for the people of its respective village. A "small wedding" is considered one in which food is prepared for only 200 to 300 people.[5] The minimum cost of such a "small wedding" is $60 to $75, for food alone. The wedding will be held at the home of the girl's father, and he will have to entertain the guests (all male) who come with the *barāt* (wedding procession). On the other hand, the boy's father will have to rent a car for the whole day. There are many additional expenses: *tīlāk* and *kicarī*[6] gifts from the girl's father and his family, presents of jewelry and clothing from the boy's family to the girl, gifts to the pandits, etc.

A "big wedding" is one in which preparations are made to feed

400 to 500 people or more. No one keeps records of the exact expenditures, but one informant, after marrying off his daughter in a "big wedding," estimated that he had had the following expenses:

One bag of flour (200 lbs.)	$20.00
One bag of rice (320 lbs.)	45.20
Potatoes ("Irish") (200 lbs.)	16.00
dāl (split peas) (50 lbs.)	8.00
	$89.20

In addition, the cost of the feast included money spent for "pumpkin" (squash), *māsālā* (curry), cooking oil, and other culinary incidentals. These brought the cost of the feast alone to well over $120, he estimated. He gave a *tīlāk* (dowry) of $120, which was a little more than the customary $100 for a "big wedding."[7] There were still further expenses. Among other things, he had to hire a "mike" (sound truck) to play records continually for almost twenty-four hours, and he had to give his daughter both a wedding *sārī* (gown) and a traveling dress. With *kicarī* and incidental gifts, the wedding cost him a minimum of $300, he said.

When it is realized that any man with annual income of over $1,000 to $1,500 is expected to make a "big wedding," it will be understood what a tremendous financial drain a wedding is for a Hindu family in Amity. Poor families may wind up seriously in debt. Even wealthy families who cannot stint in any way without losing the respect of their neighbors have difficulty meeting all the expenses unaided.

The family may save for years to prepare for the wedding, or it may take out a loan when the time comes. A favored way of meeting the expenses is by membership in a *dāheja*—a village organization of household heads pledged to assist one another at weddings. The largest one, on Beharri Road, has over one hundred members. There are smaller *dāhejas* on Lloyd Street and in Casecu. The normal contribution per member in the smaller *dāhejas* is fifty cents per wedding. In the Beharri Road *dāheja*, the normal contribution is at least one dollar, and wealthier men, who will need more when their times come, are expected to give more to others. A *dāheja* member can expect to be called upon to contribute to about fifteen weddings during the "wedding season" which lasts from March through July. A few wealthy men are not members of any *dāheja*. Proudly, they note possession of their own "pot and spoon."

Additional wedding expenses may be incurred by families that are neither making a wedding of their own nor fulfilling a *dāheja* obligation. One must make a special contribution at the wedding put on by a close friend ("bye-family") and contribute to the *kicarī* at the wedding of a daughter of any relative. Many people keep a record of who gives—and how much—at their weddings, as a guide to their obligations at the future weddings of their relatives and friends.

The wedding proper may be said to begin with the ceremony of *ūthāwe hārdī*, in which the boy and girl—each in his own home—is daubed with saffron. This takes place on the Friday preceding the Sunday wedding. From then until the third day after the wedding, the boy and girl are considered to be in a state of "danger." Neither may leave his house unaccompanied during this period, and both must wear amulet bracelets containing iron to protect them from malevolent spirits.

On the Saturday night before the wedding, the "cooking" for the next day's feast takes place. The family is assisted through the night by relatives, neighbors, and friends, and particularly by members of the *dāheja*. Entertainment is provided.

Preparations for the wedding ceremony begin early the next morning, as soon as the "cooking" is completed. There is hardly a noticeable break between the two activities. The *barāt*—a procession of taxis containing the male friends and relatives of the groom, and led by the *dolāhā* (bridegroom) in a decorated car—departs around 1 P.M. It returns around 7 P.M., carrying the new bride to her husband's home.[8]

Years ago, when boys and girls were married at the age of eleven or twelve or even younger, they were not permitted to sleep together until they were at least thirteen or fourteen. Today, when the girl is brought to the boy's home, she sleeps away from him for the first three nights. After a ceremony in which the amulet-bracelets are removed from both bride and groom, the bride is taken back to her home for a three-day visit. Her husband then brings her back to his home once more and the marriage is usually consummated that night. Next day she enters upon her full duties as a daughter-in-law. From now on her hair must always be covered by an *orhinī* (veil) when she is in the presence of her husband's male relatives and friends. She is a married woman.

From start to finish, the Hindu wedding is conducted in an atmosphere of mutual distrust, fear, and even hostility. The boy's family is worried about this stranger who is joining them. Will she be faithful to her husband and obedient to his parents? Will she work hard? Can she bear children? The girl's family is worried about the treatment the girl is likely to receive. The girl herself is most nervous of all. She is leaving her home and her family to take up residence with a strange family in a distant village. She has heard stories about the girls who have been starved, overworked, badly beaten, and even killed, by unfeeling mothers-in-law. She cannot help but wonder about her own fate.

Married Life: Marriage represents much more of a change in the life of a girl than it does in that of a boy. Before this he had to share a bed with one or more brothers; now he has a wife and together they have a bed in a room of their own. Beyond that, and the fact that he now has a sexual partner, his life has really not changed very much. He has his meals at the same times, perhaps served now by his wife instead of his mother, and he occupies the position he always did in his father's home. He will probably continue to give the major share of his earnings to his parents. His social life continues to be in the company of his male friends; playing cards, playing cricket, and going to the movies. It is still the rare *dolāhā* who will even occasionally take his wife to the movies.

The girl, on the other hand, is expected to shoulder the full burden of the household chores. Many a mother-in-law ceases all work the day her first son marries, and says triumphantly (as one did, in Amity): "Me have a *dolāhīn*, now!" The daughter-in-law must cook, clean, and do all the washing. She is the first to rise and the last to eat. If it is a large family, and she is the only *dolāhīn*, her life will indeed be hard. With all this, she is likely not to be accepted as a full member of the family until her first child is born.

As time goes on, life will get better for the *dolāhīn*. Once she has a child, her marriage becomes more secure and so does her position in the house. Her mother-in-law is likely to help her, at least with the care of the child. She may make friends with the sisters and female cousins of her husband, and the wives of his brothers and friends. Slowly the village becomes less alien. During the first year of her marriage she visits her family frequently (often every month or two) if finances permit but as the years go on the visits dwindle in frequency and duration.[9] As her husband's younger brothers get married, she will have sisters-in-law to share the work under the direction of their common mother-in-law. When her husband's parents die, the joint family usually breaks up. The wives are frequently responsible for the break-up, for each wants her own home and kitchen. When the woman's first son marries, *she* will be a mother-in-law, and can retire from active labor in the house.

For the man, on the other hand, life becomes more difficult as time goes on. Once children are born, his sense of responsibility increases and his freedom decreases. Children and parents of one nuclear unit share the same room and usually the same bed. As the man grows older, he must spend more time working and less time playing. His father grows old and now he must shoulder the family responsibilities: finding husbands for his younger sisters, jobs for his younger brothers, and money for household expenses. He will be expected to represent his family at the ceremonies and weddings of others. He must provide money for the education, medical care, and finally the marriage of his children. He has obligations to his relatives, in the temple, to his *hūr*-mates, and he is in debt to the shopkeeper and perhaps to the bank. Men in their thirties look back on their lives, only ten years before, as times of careless, irresponsible pleasure.

Old Age: Once the daughters have been married and the sons all have wives in the house the cares of both mother and father are lessened. They can work if they choose, or they can sit with their friends and gossip and smoke. The women play with their grandchildren, and the men often turn their attentions to religion. In old age, the woman frequently is more fortunate than the man, for she has daughters-in-law to rule over. A son will invariably side with—and care more for—his mother than his wife. In the case of the father, on the other hand, the reins of economic control pass to the stronger hands of his sons, and where he once ruled them with the "lash," they may now beat him for coming home drunk.

Death: If a child under six or seven dies there is little ceremony and a quick funeral. When an adult dies, taxis are immediately hired and members of the family set out in all directions to notify relatives in other villages of the funeral to be held the next day.

A wake is held during the night immediately following the death. Though not as extensive an affair, it resembles the wake described by Herskovits for the Trinidad Negro community of Toco (1947: 137–38). The body is prepared for burial, and the family pandit will come to make a brief prayer. A few friends will gather in the house with the family. They will read from the *rāmēyn* (*Ramayana*) until dawn, for no one is permitted to go to sleep. Neighbors swiftly erect a tent of bamboo poles and galvanized iron in the yard of the house, and people from the village will drop by during the night to pay their respects.

The Amity wake is comparatively quiet; some of the younger men play cards, and the older ones sit and talk softly. Those who wish to step into the house to view the body and to say a word of consolation to the family. Periodically, members of the family come out and serve coffee and cigarettes—and, very rarely, rum—to the men in the yard. Even this much in the way of refreshment is considered a recent innovation. People begin to drift home about midnight, and by 2 A.M. the wake is over, except for those in the house.

The funeral takes place about 4 P.M. the next day. Usually only men follow the coffin to the cemetery. People put on clean clothes to follow a funeral, but never a suit or a tie. Friends and neighbors help to dig the grave, and a carpenter will help build a simple coffin for the price of the wood. In Amity the dead are buried though cremation sometimes occurs elsewhere on the island. A little camphor is burned at the grave to symbolize cremation.

Expenses of the wake and funeral are not too high, since neighbors and friends help with the work, and even the carpenter does not normally charge. Refreshments are minor, and the family can shoulder all costs. No "Friendly Society" for funereal assistance has ever been formed in Amity.

The period of mourning is nine days for a woman and ten days for a man, during which time the men may not shave and no one may cut his or her nails. At the end of this time the "shaving" takes place on the bank of the river north of Amity. A member of the Nō (barber) caste comes to the house of mourning and cuts the nails of the women. He then walks to the riverbank with the men of the family, accompanied by the male friends of the family, and particularly of the deceased. Donning a *dhotī*, one male member of the family (the son of the deceased, if there is one, or a brother) is shaved —head, face, and armpits. One tiny lock of hair—the *cūrkī*—is left on the back of his head. Other male members of the family have their faces shaved, as do all men who wish to pay their respects to the dead.

The men then bathe in the river and a prayer is held on the bank. Properly, a *māhāpitar* Brāhman[10] should officiate, but usually, these days, the Nō conducts the ceremony. On the thirteenth day after the death, the family makes a dinner, called a *bhandārā*, for neighbors and friends and this ends the period of mourning. Some people make another *bhandārā* a year later, but most do not.

Hindus of Amity rarely visit the graves of their dead; it is said that a good Hindu should not. In recent years many have taken to visiting the cemetery on All Saints Night—as the Creole Roman Catholics do—to light candles on the graves.

Notes:

1. A villager usually considers that he has only one name, his "calling name," and he carries his father's "calling name" as his own "title" or surname. A woman uses her father's name as a "title" until she marries, after which she is called by her husband's "calling name." Thus, Bhola, the son of Sookdeo Gopal, would call himself Bhola Sookdeo. If he marries Soolin Baljit, she would become "Mistress Bhola."

2. Midwifery is looked upon by Hindus as an "unclean" occupation, and it is practiced in Amity usually by Camār women. The government requires such women to be licensed, however, and they exhibit their prestige-giving papers proudly.

3. This is an interesting example of what Herskovits has termed a religious syncretism, a form of reinterpretation. It may be compared with the identification of African deities with Catholic saints as in Haitian Vodun—but in this case the identification is reversed! (See Herskovits 1949: 553–54; and 1938: 38–39.)

4. Young people in Amity today refer to anyone who contributes to the arrangement of a successful marriage as an *āgwā*. Older people prefer to reserve the term for the professional marriage broker, no longer to be found.

5. In theory everyone is welcome at a wedding feast, but more people are likely to be attracted to a wedding in the home of a wealthy man than to one in the home of a poor man.

6. *Kicarī* consists of gifts of money presented by members of the girl's family to the boy, at the end of the wedding ceremony, to cajole him into tasting food and thereby declaring the wedding completed.

7. In the old days, it is said, *tīlāk* consisted of a cow or a few goats, rather than money, and *kicarī* rarely amounted to very much.

8. The wedding ceremony is protracted and involved, and space does not permit a detailed analysis here. See Smith and Jayawardena (1958) for an analysis of Hindu marriage customs in British Guiana. Trinidad Hindu marriage is essentially similar, though there are a few important small differences.

9. But they rarely stop completely. It is simply that other demands have become more pressing. Almost every Sunday, in fact, members of any village family are away visiting, or the family itself is entertaining relatives.

10. This would seem to be the same as the "Mahabrahmans" (Great Brahmins) who, according to Hutton, "officiate at the cremation of corpses" (1946: 69).

References cited:

Herskovits, Melville J.
  1938 *Acculturation: The Study of Culture Contact.* New York, J. J. Augustin.
  1949 *Man and His Works.* New York, Alfred A. Knopf, Inc.
Hutton, J. H.
  1946 *Caste in India.* Cambridge, Cambridge University Press.
Smith, R. T. and C. Jayawardena.
  1958 "Hindu Marriage Customs in British Guiana," *Social and Economic Studies* 7:178–94.

23. Culture and Social Structure in the Caribbean: Some Recent Work on Family and Kinship Studies

The territories of the circum-Caribbean region contain some of the most complex societies in the world. Their complexity lies not in their size, degree of internal differentiation or technological development, but in the dependent and fragmented nature of their cultures, the ethnic diversity of their populations, the special nature of their dependent economies, the peculiarities of their political development and the apparent incoherence of their social institutions. It has been suggested that many Caribbean societies have no history of their own but should be viewed as an extension of Europe. Dr. Eric Williams, Prime Minister of Trinidad and Tobago, has recently written in reference to his country:

> On August 31st 1962, a country will be free, a miniature state will be established, but a society and a nation will not have been formed.[1]

His words are an almost exact echo of those of a former Governor of Trinidad, Lord Harris, who wrote in 1848:

> As the question now stands a race has been freed but a society has not been formed.[2]

When Lord Harris wrote he was particularly concerned with the problem of creating a society out of a population consisting of recently freed Negro slaves, their white masters and an intermediate

SOURCE: Reprinted from *Comparative Studies in Society and History,* Vol. 6, No. 1 (1963):24–45, by permission of the author and the Cambridge University Press.

group of coloured persons created out of the irregular unions between white men and Negro women. By the time Dr. Williams came to face the same problem Trinidad had acquired a large population of East Indians and sizeable minorities of Chinese and Portuguese. Each Caribbean territory faces something of the same problem that faces Trinidad, but national unity is further compromised by sharp differences in standard of living between rich and poor—standards which often coincide with ethnic divisions. This incoherence of the national and societal image within each unit is to some extent a reflection of the recent growth of the very idea of national independence, and of an attempt to establish an image different from that of the metropolitan countries, but Haiti and some of the Latin American countries show that the condition is not cured by simple political autonomy.

The study of kinship and family structure reflects these difficulties and uncertainties; throughout the region we find ambiguity in normative prescriptions and variability in behaviour patterns even within ethnic and class units. Most of the work on kinship and family structure has been concentrated upon lower-class Negro groups and a number of recent publications continue this bias.[3] Some general descriptions of non-Negro groups in Puerto Rico have been published but as Mintz says,

> In Puerto Rico, in spite of a large number of papers and books dealing directly or tangentially with rural family life, there is nothing permitting rigorous comparison with the excellent studies of domestic social structure carried out in Jamaica, Trinidad, British Guiana and elsewhere.[4]

Studies of East Indian family structure in Trinidad and British Guiana have not really been brought into the same comparative framework as yet though they are crucial cases for assessing the relative effect of cultural tradition and structural constraint, and for the testing of other hypotheses.[5] Even if analysis is confined to Negro groups the number of variables that have to be taken into account is considerable. A brief discussion of the development of family studies in the region will show that some unsolved problems and unresolved conflicts still dominate present-day discussions.

The first real family studies to be made in the Caribbean were an offshoot of studies of the American Negro, and they were carried out as a result of Professor Herskovits's scheme for plotting the persistence of Africanisms in the New World.[6] They were not studies of Caribbean family structure, nor even of Haitian or Trinidadian family structure, but of family forms among the descendants of Africans, and of the relation of those forms to the general structural features of African societies. Professor Franklin Frazier had formulated some significant generalisations about the effects of slavery upon the family life of American Negroes.[7] Unlike Professor Herskovits he did not regard New World Negroes as being primarily displaced Africans, but rather as Americans trying to build a stable life after the almost total social disorganisation of slavery and in a society which continues to be hostile and discriminatory. He argued that deviations from normal American patterns of behaviour (including normal family patterns) can best be seen as a failure to achieve proper adjustment because of continuing obstruction. Gunnar Myrdal put it even more strongly when he said,

> *In practically all its divergencies, American Negro culture is not something independent of general American culture. It is a distorted development, or a pathological condition, of the general American culture.*[8]

Myrdal is making a deliberate statement of value which he proposes as a basis for practical action but the general point is similar to that made by Franklin Frazier.

This controversy between Herskovits and Frazier was introduced into the earliest studies in the British West Indies and it fitted itself into the emerging pre-occupation with welfare problems that came with the post-war movement towards greater political autonomy. It was very noticeable, for example, that Jamaica had an illegitimacy rate of over 70% of all live births and this caused considerable concern as soon as a more active interest began to be taken in the well-being of the lower-classes. Was this evidence of massive social disorganisation or was there something wrong with a view that measured 'legitimacy' according to 'English' or 'upper-class' standards? It had long been known that women exhibited a high degree of independence both in the West Indies and among Negroes in the United States and Frazier had referred to the 'matricentric' family based on a mother and her children, and to a 'type of matriarchate' based upon a group consisting of an old woman, her daughters and their children. The primacy of the relationships between mother and children was remarked upon by both Frazier and Herskovits. Frazier saw this unit of mother and children as the one primary group which had persisted throughout the slavery period while Herskovits derived its structural importance from the domestic organisation of African societies where the mother-children group forms a separate cell within the framework of the polygynous family. Both spoke of the destruction of male roles in relation to the domestic group during the slavery period and Frazier tried to show with a wealth of historical material that American Negroes had rebuilt a stable family life with strong paternal authority whenever they had been able to do so. That is, whenever they could get decent jobs which enabled them to provide the economic foundations for a reasonable family life in the American fashion. In looking at West Indian societies it was natural to adopt the points of view developed in these studies since the family arrangements seemed to be quite similar to those described by Frazier, and there was ample evidence of African cultural survivals. But there were other factors involved in the West Indies. The atmosphere of these developing societies was such that it predisposed students to examine the contemporary situation rather than its historical derivation. Professor Simey did as much as anyone to set the pattern for future studies by his use of simple distribution figures for various family 'types', taking his data from a survey conducted by Lewis Davidson in Jamaica.[9] Both Simey and Henriques[10] directed attention to the colour-class system and to the fact that there seemed to be a close relation between colour, occupational or economic level and family type. By the time Henriques' book was published in 1953 the idea was firmly established that there are a number of different family types each of which is 'normal' within the stratum in which it occurs. A slight variant of this idea was put forward by Dom Basil Matthews on the basis of a number of years' work in Trinidad.[11] Focussing attention upon what he called 'the non-legal union' he tried to show that the persistence of this form of mating in the New World is related to the continued importance of plantation agriculture which dominates the economies and the social life of so many territories. He wrote:

> The persistence of the non-legal union has to do essentially with the persistence in the social system of those elements which produced it in the first instance. On the impersonal or

material side, the effective agents or factors comprise the geographic, economic, moral and social conditions built into the free plantation economy, heir to the physical and social traditions of the plantation in slavery. On the personal and formal side, the deciding factor was and is, the free choice of the people. It must, however, be conceded that in their choice the people were confronted with an overmastering set of social and economic conditions which it was morally impossible, that is to say, extremely difficult, for them to overcome.

The social and economic setting and background of the non-legal union everywhere suffice to explain its social origins and its social structure. And this setting and historical background are the same for all peoples in the New World, even for those who did not themselves undergo the ordeals of slavery.[12]

This was an important variant upon the themes of colour and poverty because it introduced the idea that high illegitimacy rates and unstable family forms are not peculiar to the Negro lower-classes but are related to the existence of a form of social organisation found in the non-Negro areas of Latin America as well. There is also the suggestion here that the plantation economy produced a peculiar type of social system wherever it occurred, a type of social system with a distinct value configuration which would affect all those who became involved in it irrespective of their contact with plantation life itself.

Here then by the early 1950's the main shape of future studies had been blocked out. This is by no means a complete survey of the work that had been published up to that time. A fuller bibliography can be assembled from the summaries by Mintz and Davenport contained in *Working Papers in Caribbean Social Organization*.[13] No attempt has been made here to examine the often penetrating commentaries by contemporary writers for the slavery and post-slavery periods. Extracts such as the following show that many of the ideas we work with today are really quite old:

I have known them [the slaves] point to things of this description, for the purpose of shewing that it is impossible for them to marry. Over their children it is obvious that they could have no authority resembling that which parents in a free country possess: they could only leave them the same wretched inheritance which they received from their ancestors. Hence those who have children are careless in respect to the habits they form, and the lives they lead. They know they can never sink lower in the scale of society than they already find themselves placed, and they have no hope of rising. A regular line of orderly conduct may save them from the lash but it can effect no radical change in their condition.[14]

By the early 1950's a clear distinction had been made between cultural persistence as an explanatory device and the study of contemporary structural arrangements and inter-connections. Some writers like Simey, Henriques and Matthews adopted a two-dimensional approach but without pushing very far in either direction. The obvious need was for more detailed studies, both historical and of contemporary structure; the main emphasis in recent work has been on the latter for the simple reason that material is more easily available. Mr. George Roberts' work in demographic problems is perhaps an exception in that he has done considerable research on archival and census material but he too has been concentrating upon surveys to provide supplementary data in recent years.[15] Almost all recent discussions have been based upon the analysis of quantitative data of the kind presented in my own work on British Guiana and in Miss Clarke's study of Jamaica.[16] In the Mintz-Davenport volume, *Working Papers in Caribbean Social Organization,* four out of the five papers concentrate upon analysis of quantitative material on household composition while M. G. Smith's book, *West Indian Family Structure,* is an extended comparison of statistical data on household composition and mating from five samples, two in Jamaica, two in Grenada, and one in Carriacou. One of the reasons for the concentration upon domestic organization was that since it had been usual to speak of lower-class family life as being 'disorganised' it was important to establish whether any patterning existed at all, and whether the 'disorganization' was not primarily a matter of definition. From our general knowledge of other societies we know that unstable marriage, separate residence of spouses, or even the complete whittling away of the marriage relationship as among the Nayar, is not necessarily a sign of social instability or of pathological development. In an important paper published in 1949 Fortes had shown that a wide range of variability in household composition among the Ashanti could be understood as the result of the varying strength of two major forces; the pull of matrilineal kinship ties on the one hand, and the tendency for the nuclear family to establish itself as a separate unit on the other.[17] It was pointed out that while economic factors and missionary teaching tended to reinforce the claims of nuclear family relationships at the expense of the matrilineal tie, the conflict was not new, but must be rooted in the very nature of matrilineal systems. Audrey Richards made much the same point in an essay on Central African matrilineal societies published in 1950.[18] Fortes also demonstrated that the shape of households is bound to change over time since households are constituted around the process of physical and social reproduction and are therefore tied to biological birth, maturation and death—a point which he has made even more elegantly in a recent publication.[19] Much the same techniques of analysis have been used in recent studies in the Caribbean but the problem has been to determine the forces which are at work giving shape to domestic group structure. Another way to put it is to ask how social reproduction is accomplished and how it fits with other activities which in many societies are embedded in domestic organisation—activities such as mating, domestic services such as cooking, washing, the provision of economic support and so on. In my studies of three Negro villages in British Guiana, *The Negro Family in British Guiana*, I paid particular attention to the developmental cycle of household groups and tried to see the extent to which the ideal form of nuclear family domestic group is realised in practice and what patterning there is in the deviations from this form. Nancie L. Solien drew attention to the fact that in view of the many relationships which seem to exist in some Caribbean societies between individuals who reside in *different* households, including nuclear family relationships, more attention should be given to investigating these relationships and a clear distinction should be made between domestic organisation and family structure.[20] M. G. Smith takes this point and makes it the basis of his analysis, though the nature of much of his survey data, which was collected during brief interviews, makes it impossible for him to deal in depth with extra-residential relationships. As more field studies are made available it is becoming clear that we need to reconsider the whole question of the relation between nuclear family relationships, socialisation and domestic structure; new questions have arisen and new investigations will have to be carried out, but unless we are to revise the whole of current family theory it will not be possible to ignore nuclear family relationships as one important constellation of roles which has functional as well as formal implications.

Another major variable, or set of variables, that has been investigated for its effect upon family and domestic organisation is 'the economy' or economic factors. Earlier writers such as Frazier, Simey, and Henriques had discussed the effect of 'poverty' in producing or perpetuating unstable family forms. One of Miss Clarke's main objectives in conducting the West Indian Social Survey (which was actually a study of family life and child-rearing in Jamaica) had been to measure the effect of varying economic background upon family structure. In order to do this she chose communities in a) a sugar plantation area, b) a poverty stricken peasant farming area and c) a relatively prosperous community of citrus farmers.[21] Miss Clarke's collaborator in this study, Dr. Madeleine Kerr, transformed the idea of 'poverty' into that of 'social deprivation' by adding other dimensions to it and has since carried out comparative work in a Liverpool slum area which yields surprisingly similar conclusions about the effect of such deprivation upon personality.[22] Most of the conclusions of these studies are incorporated in Davenport's excellent discussion of the Jamaican family system.[23] Cumper's paper on Barbados and Wilson's on Providencia Island both treat of economic and status factors as the prime variable affecting domestic and family relations but none of the papers in *Working Papers in Caribbean Social Organization,* nor M. G. Smith's book, deal adequately with the whole question of status, societal and subcultural norms, mainly because all the studies limit themselves to Negro subsectors of these societies.

The other major variable to receive considerable attention recently is the organisation of mating relations. From one point of view this is an integral part of the discussion of nuclear family relationships. In the Caribbean it must receive special attention because of the prevalence of unstable mating, of a widespread distinction between legal and non-legal unions, and the existence of mating unions which do not involve common residence. Studies by Roberts and Braithwaite,[24] Judith Blake[25] and M. G. Smith's book *West Indian Family Structure,* focus upon the variability in making relations and its effect upon family structure, and M. G. Smith's book raises anew the whole question of African heritage versus slavery by his derivation of present mating forms from slavery. In the following discussion these

varying aspects of Caribbean family structure and its social milieu
are dealt with one by one in an attempt to take stock of recent
contributions.

THE NUCLEAR FAMILY AND KINSHIP STRUCTURES

Since Murdock published his *Social Structure* in 1949 there has been
considerable controversy over the question of the universality of the
nuclear family and over Murdock's statement that:

> The family is a social group characterised by common residence,
> economic cooperation, and reproduction. It includes adults of
> both sexes, at least two of whom maintain a socially approved
> sexual relationship, and one or more children, own or adopted,
> of the sexually cohabiting adults.[26]

It has been pointed out that in many cases husbands and wives habitually live in separate households, or that in some societies nuclear
families are so absorbed in wider units that they can hardly be said
to exist as separate organisational complexes at all. Despite these objections there has been a convergence upon the view that the basic
functions of the family are those of socialisation and the regulation
of personality whatever other activities the family may engage in,
and for these functions the role structure of nuclear family relationships seems to be both required and universally present in all societies.[27] According to some variants of this view it is not necessary
that every 'family' should be a concrete co-residential nuclear family
group, but the role system of nuclear family relationships should be
institutionalised and in the normal cases enough interaction should
exist to carry out the functions and to maintain the system. In particular cases nuclear family relationships exist across the boundaries of
household groups, household groups take on a great many other
activities than those of child-care and sexual interaction, and nuclear
family roles may be performed by individuals other than 'real' family
members, but empirically there seems to be a close correspondence
between 'family' activities and domestic group organisation. As Fortes
says, "In all human societies, the workshop, so to speak, of social
reproduction, is the domestic group."[28] These views would seem to
mean that the nuclear family is more than a fortuitous by-product
of sexual mating and physical birth; that it has positive functions and

is in a sense 'required' if societies of human beings are to continue. Even Leach in his discussion of the variability of ideologies of reproduction and genetic transmission seems to assume that underneath the differing types of relationship of incorporation and alliance actual nuclear family relationships exist.[29] Even if the theory exists that mothers and sons are like affines, they do not engage in sexual intercourse and there would appear to be more to it than the simple fear of committing adultery, even though this might fit very nicely at the formal structural level. There is something more than psychological dogma or the slavish copying of Freud to the idea that the relationship between a mother and her children is of a particularly close kind, even if at other levels of behaviour the relationship is played down. With the father-child relationship the position is rather different and even those theorists who base their arguments for the universality of the nuclear family upon personality theory admit a great deal of variability in this relationship. Apart from their domestic and familial roles, men in most societies have important statuses in wider social systems and therefore the husband-father role is particularly responsive to variations in the external situation.

Analysis of the Caribbean material is affected by these changing views of nuclear family functions and it provides evidence bearing upon those views. Solien's insistence upon the distinction between household and family arose out of her experience of family arrangements among the Black Carib of Guatemala. She says:

> The nuclear family unit among the Carib may be scattered in several different households. For example, the husband-father may be living with his own mother, one or more children may be with their maternal relatives or with non-Caribs, while the mother may be working and "living in" as a maid in one of the port towns.[30]

Her observations could be duplicated from every report that has ever been written on lower-class Negro family life, and it is quite true that the concentration of attention upon the household as a functioning unit of child-care and economic organisation has tended to divert attention from the networks of relationship linking households to each other. It is important that these relationships be studied with as much exactitude as possible but it would be ridiculous to regard the household in a purely negative way, or to forget that 'family' functions require frequent social interaction and not merely a token recognition of consanguineal or deactivated conjugal relationships. It is also important to know the frequency with which the patterns of divided residence occur and the intensity of the relationships which are maintained across household boundaries. This problem is discussed again below in relation to mating.

The study of household composition has shown that a variety of kinship ties may be activated to bring people together into the same dwelling unit, and considerable attention has been given to charting the shape of kinship systems and the strength of the various relationships within them. Both Davenport and Solien have analysed 'non-unilineal descent groups' as a structural type and Solien has identified such formations among the Black Carib as well as suggesting that they probably exist elsewhere in the Caribbean. M. G. Smith speaks of patrilineages in Carriacou (though his use of the term 'lineage' is somewhat idiosyncratic) and Bastien stresses the importance of patrilineal joint families in Haiti. Davenport's discussion of the lower-class Jamaican Negro kinship system is couched in general terms but provides an excellent overall view which is applicable to most British West Indian territories. He characterises it as being based upon 'kindred organisation'. By this he means that there are no corporate kin groups, as such, that kinship is reckoned bilaterally and that kinship rights and obligations are relative to individuals. What is equally clear is that "Parents, parent's siblings, first cousins, children, sibling's children (both sexes referred to as 'niece') and grandchildren form a hard core of close kin that is sometimes described as 'near family', in order to distinguish it from more distant relatives, called 'far family'. A person's kindred then will be defined as his near family, plus any other kin with whom he may have special relationships."[31] It is clear from this that kindred ties arise out of domestic relations, mating, and local community ties. Within the kindred, relationships are further modified by emphasis upon siblingship and mother-child relations in much the same way as previously described for British Guiana.[32]

So far as Carriacou and its 'patrilineage' organisation is concerned we are dealing with a miniature society with a whole series of special features. Carriacou is an island dependency of Grenada, which is itself dependent upon the British Government's grants even to balance its budget. Carriacou has a population of about 6,800 and an area of 13 square miles. A large proportion of its male inhabitants are off the island working at any one time. As M. G. Smith describes it there is no significant class differentiation within this small population, and of course the island is so small that most people must know each other personally. The majority of households are headed by women but since there are 2½ times as many adult women as men resident on the island this is perhaps not surprising. The 'bloods' or 'patrilineages' appear to be name groups consisting of those agnatic kin between whom extended family relations exist. The development of these groups seems to be related to the stability of local relations, the regulation of mating in a very small community and the performance of family rituals—the family being not only ideally but actually paternalistic. Not dissimilar name lines of even greater depth can be found in isolated and economically stagnant Guianese Negro villages, but the units carrying out ritual activities are the close kindred on the one hand and the whole village community on the other. It is clear from M. G. Smith's descriptions that it is not merely the existence of 'bloods' which makes paternity important within the family system, but also the strong emphasis upon legal marriage and the status conferring functions of paternity plus the channelling of male economic support through the husband-father role. In other words, it is not the 'lineage' that determines male domestic roles, but other variables.

More extensive groups of kin, settled on 'family land' as in Jamaica or constituting extended family clusters as in Haiti, arise out of common interests in land and Davenport offers an excellent summary of the situation in Jamaica. He stresses the fact that 'family land' represents a focus of interest for absent kindred and while rights in family land are vested in all the members of the kindred there is, inevitably, a number of mechanisms for limiting the actual exercise of claims.

To sum up. The kinship system is bilateral and not very extensive. The most important relationships within it arise out of co-residence, co-siblingship, and the coincidence of neighbourhood and kinship ties. The special strength of the mother-child relationship compared to the easy diminution of father-child ties has been noted by all writers but the reasons for this cannot be located merely in the definition of kinship relations. Similarly the emergence of short matri-lines consisting of mother, daughters, and daughter's children is an important feature of the system though M. G. Smith asserts that this has been greatly exaggerated in the literature.[33] Elizabeth Bott's comments on the conditions necessary for the emergence of these female solidaritics are interesting especially since they are based upon work in Britain rather than in the Caribbean. She says:

> . . . the psychological consequences of being brought up in a family having marked segregation of parental roles does not of itself produce groups of women within a kinship network. All it produces is a close emotional tie between mother and children, particularly between mother and daughter. Before there can be a group there must also be several related women in the same place at the same time. If groups of grandmother, mothers, and daughters are to be formed, women should get married young, they should have plenty of children, preferably girls, they should live for a long time, and all the women concerned should continue to live in the same local area. The formation of such groups also depends on certain negative factors—on the absence of rights to land or other economic advantages through the father and his relatives . . .
>
> To phrase the discussion in general terms: whenever there are no particular economic advantages to be gained by affiliation with paternal relatives, and whenever two or preferably three generations of mothers and daughters are living in the same place at the same time, a bilateral kinship system is likely to develop a matrilateral stress, and groups composed of sets of mothers and daughters may form within networks of kin.[34]

The special relationship between 'two sisters' children' which was reported for British Guiana[35] and which M. G. Smith has included under the more general term 'materterine' kinship (a term first suggested by Schapera[36]) is, in the societies we are dealing with, clearly derivative from the kind of female grouping within bilateral networks that Bott has described. The placement of children with their mother's sister or mother's sister's daughter is a logical procedure once such female groups have existed.

MARRIAGE AND MATING

What is the nature of the mating system and what is the significance of high illegitimacy rates? This is the most vexed question in the whole literature on Caribbean family systems. It would be impossible to discuss it fully here but certain broad features are clear. Legal, christian, monogamous marriage is everywhere accepted as the correct and respectable form of mating relationship by all sections of the population of Caribbean societies, with the exception of the East Indian groups in Trinidad and British Guiana. In practice the majority of children are conceived and born *outside* such marital relationships. Some of these children are born to couples who live together in non-legal unions, and some are born to women who are not in co-residential unions and who enjoy varying degrees of stability in their relations with the father of their children. M. G. Smith refers to all these latter as 'extra-residential unions', ignoring the differences between them except when they become so unstable as to constitute promiscuity, and he further maintains that a specific type of parental role is associated with such a form of mating though he does not tell us what it is. A more sophisticated treatment in quantitative terms has been carried out by Roberts and Braithwaite who use the term 'visiting' union and try to distinguish degrees of stability within this broad category.[37] A recent book by Judith Blake dealing with Jamaica discusses the whole question of extra-residential mating in a clear and lively way.[38] It is obvious that the existence of visiting unions and the birth of children to women in such unions must affect household composition and, despite Dr. M. G. Smith's assumptions to the contrary, this has been recognised by all previous writers on the subject. The problem is—why do extra-residential mating and co-residential non-legal unions occur and how stable are such forms of mating? Among the Ashanti extra-residential mating is a recognised form clearly associated with the strength of matrilineal ties, and it is based upon clearly recognised marital relationships which include properly defined mutual rights, duties and obligations. Among the Nayar it is again related to matrilineal ties and the need for their protection. In the Caribbean extra-residential mating is clearly associated with the *avoidance* of responsibilities and rights and obligations. Full acceptance of responsibility involves co-residence, but even here there is a variation in the degree of assumption of responsibility from the minimum amount involved in short-term unstable unions up to that of stable marital unions. M. G. Smith joins a long, and respectable, line of writers who attribute the non-legal mating patterns of West Indians to customs laid down during slavery, plus (in order to account for the absence of common-law marriage in Carriacou) the varying success of the churches in enforcing lawful marriage in different areas.[39] He is doubtless correct and there is no reason for not recognising also that there is an equal likelihood that West African patterns of extra-residential mating have persisted into the present. Mintz states very clearly the case for further historical research which will have as its object the elucidation of structural relations at various stages of Caribbean history; the progressive development of different types of structural arrangements has been worked out for Puerto Rico but very little along these lines has been done for the British Caribbean as yet. But even if more attention is devoted to historical research (as opposed to speculation) Schapera's point will remain valid—"I do not imagine that we shall ever abandon completely the study of the social present, and in a study of that kind history is at best an aid to understanding and not the only means of understanding."[40] If we recognise the existence of a direct connection between slave society and the present and between the present lower-class Negro family system and that of the slave plantation, what accounts for the persistence of those patterns? Is it cultural inertia or the existence of a separate folk-culture in a plural society, or is something else involved? Numerous answers have been given to this question and their consideration brings us to the next stage of the discussion.

ECONOMIC AND STATUS FACTORS

It has been a matter of common knowledge for a very long time that there is some sort of association between mating patterns and family structure on the one hand and the level of income and status on the other. Frazier made this association the basis of his analysis and both Simey and Henriques laid primary emphasis upon poverty and low status as causal factors in producing mating and family patterns which deviate from the societal ideals. It has always been assumed that in the 'middle' and 'upper' classes (however they may be defined) legal christian marriage is the rule, that it is an essential prelude to child-bearing, and that the typical domestic unit consists of a nuclear family group. As Davenport says, ". . . it will be assumed [for lack of data to the contrary] that the middle and upper-class family systems are homogeneous and indistinguishable from those of comparable class strata in England and the United States."[41] There is good reason to believe that this is not wholly true. In the first place we know that kinship ties are recognised to a much wider degree than in the U.S. or Britain, partly because of the immobility of the higher status groups and their concentration in a few urban centres. There is also a well marked pattern of extra-marital mating on the part of higher status males. Along with the middle-class emphasis upon respectable patterns of behaviour which differentiate them from the lower classes, there is an old and pervasive pattern of sexual licence for men. The idea of the Caribbean as a place of hot passions, sensuous music and provocative calypso is not something dreamed up by the tourist agencies. The Europeans set the pattern of mating outside marriage by their willingness to take black or coloured mistresses, and the existence of a large population of mixed-bloods testifies to the importance of the pattern set by the upper classes. The ambivalence about stable marriage, for men at least, is probably found at all levels of the society. Certainly more research needs to be done on attitudes toward marriage among the higher status groups in Caribbean societies, and its possible contribution to attitudes of permissiveness at all levels of the society. Judith Blake, in her recent book on Jamaica, argues that her interview data show that the vast majority of Jamaican women wish to marry, that everyone in the society regardless of class level or culture regards marriage as the right framework for mating, but that men are able to exploit the ignorance and the economic insecurity of women to enjoy regular sexual associations without the responsibility of marriage. She considers that the family structure is weak and that the present conditions reinforce this weakness, that there is no sub-norm of preference for non-legal unions, and that if "economic development and adequate opportunities within the system of social stratification" develop then it is possible that the family system will develop enough control to propel people into marriage at the proper time.[42] Before examining this idea further what sort of variation do we actually find according to economic and status differences?

Edith Clarke's work in Jamaica as presented in *My Mother Who Fathered Me,* showed that the variation in mating and household types between her three field centres was quite complex and depended upon more than simple differences in income level. The nature of the community structure and the type of economic base on which the family is erected also affect the picture. For example the high incidence of both concubinage and one-person households in Sugartown is not associated simply with low incomes, but with a whole pattern of mobility, casual labour, individualism, absence of wide kinship networks and a particular kind of community authority structure. In both Mocca (the peasant hill community) and Orange Grove (the prosperous farming area) the household group is a unit of agricultural production in addition to any other functions it may have. The extent of co-operation between families was small in Mocca and extensive in Orange Grove, according to Miss Clarke, and it is interesting that the type of community activity found in Orange Grove is that associated with 'development' and is therefore in conformity with wider societal values. The building of a Community Hall, organising a Savings Union, Agricultural Society Branch, Egg Co-operative, Cricket Club and so forth were obviously related to the level of agricultural prosperity and the striving after a greater sense of social worth. Marriage rates were higher in Orange Grove than in the other two centres, but there was also a higher proportion of extended families of all types, including those with a female head. This is related to the fact that in this community there is an adequate economic base for the growth of more extensive kinship units, so that older women as well as men are able to build up sizeable household groups. Without such a base, including a house, it is difficult for households to grow beyond a certain size, and once a family passes a certain socio-economic level there is presumably an incentive to reduce the size of the household in order to alter the style of life and to facilitate upward mobility.

The most detailed treatment of the relation between 'economic' data and household composition is provided by Cumper both in his earlier work on Jamaica and in his "Household and Occupation in Barbados" which is one of the essays in the Davenport-Mintz volume.[43] Although he works with a relatively simple model which relates the household to the occupational system through the boundary role of the household head, he is not simply dealing with 'economic' factors as Davenport suggests.[44] His sample of 1,296 Barbadian households (a random sample of 1 in 42 of the island's population) is divided into eight groups based upon the occupation of the household head. While not attempting to measure 'status' apart from income it is clear that in Barbados occupation is a good index to status. For example, the difference in income between skilled workers and non-farm labourers is very small, but skilled workers are probably a higher status group and this is reflected in the higher incidence of common-law marriages among labourers.

It would be impossible to summarise Cumper's very detailed data on Barbados here but certain key points are worth noting. The group of households in which the head is a white-collar worker conform reasonably closely to the societal ideal of a nuclear family group based upon stable legal marriage. Barbados has a large white population and it is possible that the picture for this white-collar group is affected by the fact that there is a large racially white element included. However, Dr. Cumper is of the opinion that the majority of families in this group are non-white though he has no statistical data on this point.[45] At the other end of the comparative scale Cumper places a group of 'peasant proprietors' whose households appear to be typically stable units, a high proportion of them based upon legal marriage, but containing a relatively high proportion of the children of unmarried daughters. (Peasant proprietors in Barbados, like those in British Guiana, generally live in close proximity to sugar plantations and depend upon them for part-time work.) In all peasant households, both male and female headed, male earnings constitute the bulk of household resources and female heads of households are usually widows or women whose spouses are away or have deserted them. Peasant proprietors are a stable population living in their own houses and able on this account, as well as the relative security of their economic base, to sustain three-generation domestic groups. Cumper shows very ingeniously that the intermediate occupational categories and their households can be dynamically related to each other and to the peasant types through a consideration of the life chances and experiences of their members. It is the same method of analysis which Cumper used so successfully in his study of the symbiotic relationship between sugar plantations, hill peasant communities, and urban migration in Jamaica, and it demands a consideration of development over time including occupational mobility.

The intermediate categories with which he deals consist of:
1) 'Renters'—a group of agricultural labourers who erect their own moveable houses upon rented land.
2) Landless labourers (agricultural).
3) Domestic servants.
4) Own account workers.
5) Non-farm labourers.
6) Skilled workers.

What Cumper suggests is that the 'renters' and landless labourer categories are being constantly augmented by young men with their way to make in the world—young men who are incapable of meeting the prescriptions of the role of married household head. Their compromise solution is to enter into non-legal unions of varying degrees of stability; the acquisition of a house without land is, for example, considered to be a sufficient basis for establishing a common-law marriage, or a young man may join the household of a woman and her mother where he can receive various kinds of domestic services as well as enjoy sexual relations in exchange for his contribution to the household economy. The instability of these unions produces female headed households of either the two or three generation type and of the same general nature as those termed 'denuded' by Miss Clarke. Some young men move from the agricultural labourer or peasant groups into skilled labour but in these cases the men concerned are likely to acquire new mobility aspirations and to adopt new cultural norms in relation to marriage and family formation. Or to put it another way they may feel, because of their higher status occupation, that they are better able to live up to the role prescriptions of the family norms accepted by the whole society as being correct. On the other hand many men and women remain in the renter and landless labourer groups for life, and as they grow older they too may try to meet the cultural prescriptions of the total society by getting married. The possession of even a moveable house on rented land seems to increase the potentiality of the household developing into a three generation group but among the landless labourers households are held together mainly by women, who, living in rented or free quarters manage by their own, their children's or their daughters' lovers' labour to provide an economic base for the continued existence of domestic units.

In the non-agricultural sector the categories of 'own account worker' and 'domestic' are in some senses the counterpart of 'renter' and 'landless labourer' occupations. The households with domestics as heads are naturally female headed, since domestic service is a female occupation in the West Indies, but many of these women have been, or are, in unions of some kind. About 10% of the households contain a common-law husband of the head and ". . . a third or more . . . receive some support from a man who is, or has been, the husband or lover of the head".[46] Other important contributions flow in from remittances and pensions. The own-account worker group contains a varied collection of people from small jobbing contractors to seamstresses, petty shopkeepers and female traders. This group is generally economically less secure than any other non-agricultural group despite its economic independence, and it contains a high proportion of older men living alone, and women from broken unions.

Cumper recognises that his material is limited in many respects, but he shows very clearly the sort of control that is necessary before one can generalise about 'urban' and 'rural' groups in the West Indies. If one compares Cumper's work with that of Dr. M. G. Smith, as set out in his *West Indian Family Structure,* one is immediately conscious of the shortcomings of Smith's generalisations about urban and rural patterns in Jamaica. By lumping together the sample populations on a geographical basis and speaking of status only in terms of a 'folk' typology, Smith confuses important differences within these groups if Cumper's arguments are correct. Davenport too recognises the importance of economic and occupational differences in Jamaica when he says:

> Land and wealth are almost synonymous to the lower-class countryman. When he is landless he is poor, with nothing to fall back on in time of need, and no place to go to when wage work is done. Under these dire circumstances, households, as we have seen, tend to be small or incomplete, with their members dispersed throughout related households which are better able to support them.[47]

SOCIAL CLASS AND THE PLURAL SOCIETY

So far we have dealt mainly with studies of family structure among lower status Negro groups for the simple reason that this is where most work has been done. In most societies in the Caribbean Negroes constitute the lowest status groups for historical reasons and it is therefore very difficult to determine whether the pattern of family and mating relations found among them is due to economic and status factors alone or whether residues of African and slave plantation culture constitute the determining factors. What complicates the matter further is that dark skin colour is itself a status factor in all Caribbean societies. This is a contemporary fact and not simply a 'survival'. Theoretically the study of family structure among East Indians should provide us with a crucial test since in Trinidad, British Guiana and Jamaica East Indians constitute (or did until recently) a special low status group. A number of studies have been carried out in recent years which show conclusively that the East Indian family pattern is quite distinct from that of the lower class Negro groups.[48] Morton Klass in his book *East Indians in Trinidad: A Study of Cultural Persistence* chooses a deliberately cultural bias in his analysis and sees the East Indians of Trinidad as people who have, in the face of considerable difficulty, re-established an Indian village way of life. Studies by Roberts and Braithwaite in Trinidad and by Smith and Jayawardena in British Guiana,[49] show that there are considerable differences between the kinship structure of Indians in these territories and a pure Indian system (if there is such a thing). What is distinctive about East Indian family and kinship structure is the early age at which marriage takes place, the absence of extra-residential mating and the position of the husband-father in the domestic organisation. All these factors are certainly associated with a continuing Indian sub-culture though all of them are also consonant with the ideal pattern of the total society. In practice they are considerably modified by circumstances. Early marriage takes place but it is usually customary religious marriage and not legal marriage and the incidence of break-up of first unions is high both in British Guiana and in Trinidad.[50] Even if these first unions are regarded as proper marriages and not equivalent to common-law marriages among Negroes, subsequent unions are apt to be simple common-law unions. There is also considerable variation in the internal relations of domestic units. Jayawardena shows that in the sugar estate communities paternal authority is considerably modified in situations where sons, wives and daughters contribute substantially to household income.[51] But the crucial point is that the role of husband-father among Indians is defined in a quite different way to its definition in the rest of the society. A household which does not have a man to represent it in community affairs, in religious organisations and at rites-de-passage is socially deficient. The authority and status of the husband-father within the family does not depend solely upon his ability to provide for his family and to achieve a certain standard of consumption, nor does it depend upon his ability to participate in activities characteristic of higher class groups; it depends upon his ability to represent his family within the Indian community and its specialised associations, though the man's earning capacity and his occupational status are becoming more important as Indians become more closely integrated in the societies of which they are now a part.

Various attempts have been made to place the discussion of

Caribbean family systems in a wider comparative framework; a framework not of historical comparisons designed to trace cultural derivations, but a structural framework in which cross-cultural comparisons could be made. Such a comparative framework was suggested in *The Negro Family in British Guiana* and a more elaborate comparative scheme was suggested some years ago by William J. Goode in his paper on "Illegitimacy, Anomie and Cultural Penetration".[52] Goode treats illegitimacy as an index to familial disorganisation under certain circumstances. In European countries where illegitimacy rates are high this is usually associated with freedom in courtship and delays in getting married rather than with casual or unsanctioned mating. In Africa the high illegitimacy rates are found mainly in urban areas and are to be seen as a result of the effects of migration and the subsequent weakening of tribal community sanctions. In the New World communities of Latin America, the Caribbean and the southern United States special conditions have been created by massive cultural penetration and the destruction of traditional social systems. Goode suggests that a four phase development is likely under such circumstances:

1) Pre-contact situation with low illegitimacy rates.
2) Intense contact in cities with high urban illegitimacy rates.
3) Beginnings of assimilation in the urban areas and spread of contact to rural areas results in a drop in urban illegitimacy rates below those of the rural areas.
4) The development of a unitary social system and uniformly low illegitimacy rates.

In the Americas south of the Rio Grande the destruction of traditional cultures was accompanied by a period of economic stagnation in which there was little opportunity for the development of upward mobility. A relatively integrated western group dominated many anomic communities in which the peasants had a low commitment to western values while their old values had been undermined. Goode also adopts Merton's idea that anomie can result from the failure to master instrumental norms which are necessary for adherence to cultural norms, so that low educational levels, absence of skills and so forth impede social integration around new norms. This paper is a reasonable attempt to generalise over a wide range of data but it necessarily by-passes many difficulties. The problem of measuring national integration is much more difficult than is suggested and continuing sharp status differentiations are often related to the maintenance of given economic and political systems rather than to some disembodied process of cultural contact and assimilation.

Goode's analysis raises the crucial question of what constitutes 'anomic'. Are we dealing with a state of normlessness in badly integrated societies; are these 'plural societies' in which the population segments "mix but do not mingle", as Furnival said; or are they societies of a peculiar type in which a special mode of integration of a differentiated population obtains? This is a fundamental problem for upon its solution depends the kind of analytical framework one adopts for the examination of family structure and mating. Dr. M. G. Smith takes a 'plural society' view so that for him extra-residential mating and common-law marriage are patterns of 'folk culture'—at least so long as they appear to have statistical stability. Miss Blake takes the opposite view and, as a result of attitude measurement, concludes that all Jamaicans hold the same values but many are prevented from realising those values in action owing to a breakdown in social control and to the unfavourable position in which women find themselves. The fact is of course that lower-class West Indian Negroes hold contradictory views about what is desirable or possible for them; otherwise one can hardly explain the fact that although couples live together without benefit of clergy they usually do marry eventually or in times of stress.[53] The problem is to uncover the source of this patterned deviance from societal values.

There is a fundamental dissonance between the accepted ideals of these societies and the objective possibility of their realisation by the majority of people. This is not due simply to a failure to master instrumental norms; it has to do with the mode of integration of colonial or ex-colonial societies around the acceptance of white superiority while at the same time political power was deployed for the maintenance of a relatively fixed pattern of social and economic relations. It was, and in many cases still is, a far more rigid stratification than that of nineteenth century England and it produced a family system much closer to Engel's picture of proletarian family life than Europe ever did. Even the special position of East Indians is due to their relative isolation on plantations and to a deliberately pursued policy of encouraging them to retain Indian customs instead of becoming christianised, educated and assimilated to creole society; a policy that was only partially successful.

CONCLUSION

The work reviewed here shows that the study of Caribbean kinship and family structure raises a host of general theoretical problems. Most obviously there is the problem of determining just what is the structure of family relations, how it fits into the domestic organisation and how it is related to generalisations about the family as a universal social institution. The adoption of statistical measures of frequency in types of domestic, kinship and mating relations and the use of developmental cycle models, has revealed some very complex patterns. It is to be expected that controversy will continue over the question of whether a number of discrete 'types' of family structure or of household composition are involved or whether actual variations can be seen as the resultant of the interaction of a limited number of organisational principles. There is room for considerable refinement in the application of statistical techniques. Most early studies were case studies of particular communities employing 100% surveys or using very large samples. Now that investigators are beginning to work with national samples or at least with samples covering very large populations it is imperative that proper tests of significance be applied. While the tendency to apply statistical measures over a larger area of the social map is a very welcome trend, it is also necessary to extend the study of family and kinship relations in depth by doing more case studies. Although the records of social agencies, mental hospitals and clinics may contain some interesting case material no systematic work has been done on such records. One suspects that the records are really inadequate. Because of the inarticulateness of the lower-classes, the relative dearth of literary work dealing with lower-class life, and the limited number of people who receive any kind of psycho-therapy we know little of a really intimate nature respecting the personal and family life of Caribbean peoples. Field anthropologists have so far been trying to understand a wide range of behaviour and have not had the time for a close study of a limited number of cases. The biographical studies by Mintz,[54] M. G. Smith,[55] and Oscar Lewis[56] are valuable but we need studies comparable to those carried out in England by Elizabeth Bott. This would deepen our understanding of lower-class motives, feelings, frustrations and values. Judith Blake is right in her contention that we do not understand people's values well enough but more is needed than

simple, short, attitude surveys especially since there is so much conflicting evidence.

The major problem is what it has always been; to relate patterns
of familial, domestic and mating behaviour to other factors in the
contemporary social systems and to the cultural traditions of the
people concerned. Here progress has been less impressive because we
are still unclear about the nature of these societies. William J. Goode
speaks about degrees of political integration, Dr. Eric Williams voices
his doubts about whether Trinidad is a society at all, and Dr. M. G.
Smith asserts that we are dealing with 'plural societies'. These are
not mere idle speculations; they determine what factors we shall consider important for their effect upon family relations. It is possible
to start with a close look at families and to move outwards, exploring
the systems of action in which family members are enmeshed and we
can construct theories of the middle range—or models of limited
mechanisms. But eventually we shall have to make decisions about
such questions as what is the meaning of blackness in societies integrated around the dominance of whiteness? or what is the meaning
of being Indian in societies where prestige is defined in terms of
Spanish culture? or what does it mean to be an East Indian in Trinidad? To answer these questions calls for models of total social systems no matter what kind of models they may be. It is an urgent task
to find out more about the mode of integration of these societies,
both for its intrinsic interest and as the proper framework for family
and kinship studies.

In the meantime it is a pleasure to record the considerable progress
that has been made in recent years and the growing interest in the
Caribbean to which the studies reviewed here testify. A special debt
of gratitude is due to the Research Institute for the Study of Man, and
to its Director Dr. Vera Rubin, for the assistance it has given to most
of the recent studies discussed here.

Notes:

1. Eric Williams, *History of the People of Trinidad and Tobago* (PNM
Publishing Co., Ltd., Port of Spain, Trinidad, 1962), p. 284.
2. W. L. Burn, *Emancipation and Apprenticeship in the West Indies* (Jona-
than Cape, London, 1937), p. 370.
3. Sidney W. Mintz and William Davenport (eds.), *Working Papers in Caribbean Social Organization*, being a special number of *Social and Economic
Studies*, Vol. 10, No. 4 (1961).—M. G. Smith, *West Indian Family Structure*
(University of Washington Press, Seattle, 1962).

4. Sidney W. Mintz, "A Final Note", *Working Papers in Caribbean Social Organization*, p. 528.

5. Among recent studies the following deal with family structure and mating: R. T. Smith & C. Jayawardena, "Hindu Marriage Customs in British Guiana", *Social and Economic Studies*, Vol. 7, No. 2 (1958).—R. T. Smith & C. Jayawardena, "Marriage and the Family Amongst East Indians in British Guiana", *Social and Economic Studies*, Vol. 8, No. 4 (1959).—Chandra Jayawardena, "Marital Stability in Two Guianese Sugar Estate Communities", *Social and Economic Studies*, Vol. 9, No. 1 (1960).—Morton Klass, *East Indians in Trinidad: A Study of Cultural Persistence* (Columbia University Press, New York & London, 1961).—G. W. Roberts & L. Braithwaite, "Mating Among East Indian and Non-Indian Women in Trinidad", *Social and Economic Studies*, Vol. 11, No. 3 (1962).—Chandra Jayawardena, "Family Organisation in Plantations in British Guiana", *International Journal of Comparative Sociology*, Vol. III, No. 1 (1962).

6. M. J. Herskovits, *Life in a Haitian Valley* (New York, 1937).—M. J. Herskovits, "Problem, Method and Theory in Afroamerican Studies", *Afroamerica*, Vol. 1 (Mexico, 1945).—M. J. & F. S. Herskovits, *Rebel Destiny: Among the Bush Negroes of Dutch Guiana* (New York, 1934).—M. J. & F. S. Herskovits, *Trinidad Village* (New York, 1947).

7. F. Frazier, *The Negro Family in the United States* (University of Chicago Press, 1939).

8. G. Myrdal, *An American Dilemma* (Harper Brothers, New York, 1944), p. 928.

9. T. S. Simey, *Welfare and Planning in the West Indies* (Oxford University Press, 1946), pp. 82–90.

10. F. Henriques, *Family and Colour in Jamaica* (Eyre & Spottiswoode, London, 1953).

11. Dom Basil Matthews, *Crisis of the West Indian Family* (Trinidad, 1953).

12. *Ibid.*, p. 104.

13. These summaries are contained in the "Introduction" and "Final Note" in the volume *Working Papers in Caribbean Social Organization*, edited by Mintz and Davenport, and referred to above.

14. Quoted in *Negro Slavery: or a view of some of the more prominent features of that state of society as it exists in the United States of America and in the colonies of the West Indies especially in Jamaica* (Hatchard & Son, Piccadilly, London, 1823), pp. 57–58.

15. G. W. Roberts, *The Population of Jamaica* (Cambridge University Press, 1957).—G. W. Roberts & L. Braithwaite, "Fertility Differentials in Trinidad", *International Population Conference* (Vienna, 1959).—G. W. Roberts & L. Braithwaite, "Fertility Differentials by Family Type in Trinidad", *Annals of the New York Academy of Sciences*, Vol. 84, Article 17 (1960).—G. W. Roberts & L. Braithwaite, "A Gross Mating Table for a West Indian Population", *Population Studies*, Vol. XIV, No. 3 (1961).—G. W. Roberts & L. Braithwaite, "Mating Patterns and Prospects in Trinidad", *International Population Conference* (New York, 1961).—G. W. Roberts & L. Braithwaite, "Mating Among East Indian and Non-Indian Women in Trinidad", *Social and Economic Studies*, Vol. 11, No. 3 (1962).

16. R. T. Smith, *The Negro Family in British Guiana* (London, 1956).—E. Clarke, *My Mother Who Fathered Me* (London, 1957).

17. M. Fortes, "Time and Social Structure: An Ashanti Case Study", *Social Structure: Studies Presented to A. R. Radcliffe-Brown* (edited by M. Fortes) (Oxford University Press, 1949).

18. A. I. Richards, "Some Types of Family Structure Amongst the Central Bantu", *African Systems of Kinship and Marriage* (edited by A. R. Radcliffe-Brown & Daryll Forde) (Oxford University Press, 1950).

19. M. Fortes, "Introduction", *The Developmental Cycle in Domestic Groups* (edited by Jack Goody), Cambridge Papers in Social Anthropology, No. 1 (1958).

20. Nancie L. Solien, "Household and Family in the Caribbean", *Social and Economic Studies*, Vol. 9, No. 1 (1960).

21. E. Clarke, *op. cit.*

22. M. Kerr, *Personality and Conflict in Jamaica* (Liverpool University Press, 1952).—M. Kerr, *The People of Ship Street* (Routledge and Kegan Paul, London, 1958).

23. W. Davenport, "The Family System of Jamaica", *Working Papers in Caribbean Social Organization* (edited by Mintz and Davenport) (1961).

24. Roberts & Braithwaite. See note 15.

25. Judith Blake, *Family Structure in Jamaica* (Free Press of Glencoe Inc., New York, 1961).

26. G. P. Murdock, *Social Structure* (Macmillan Company, New York, 1949), p. 1.

27. This view is most clearly expressed in T. Parsons & R. Bales, *Family, Socialization and Interaction Process* (Free Press, Glencoe, Illinois, 1955).

28. M. Fortes, "Introduction", *The Developmental Cycle in Domestic Groups* (edited by Jack Goody), Cambridge Papers in Social Anthropology, No. 1 (1958), p. 2.

29. E. Leach, *Rethinking Anthropology* (University of London, The Athlone Press, 1961), pp. 17–26.

30. Nancie Solien, *op. cit.*, p. 104.

31. W. Davenport, "The Family System of Jamaica", *op. cit.*, p. 422.

32. R. T. Smith, *The Negro Family in British Guiana* (London, 1956), pp. 151–59.

33. M. G. Smith, *West Indian Family Structure* (University of Washington Press, Seattle, 1962), p. 243.

34. Elizabeth Bott, *Family and Social Network* (Tavistock Publications Ltd., London, 1957), pp. 137–38.

35. R. T. Smith, *op. cit.*, p. 152.

36. I. Schapera, "Marriage and Near Kin Among the Tswana", *Africa*, Vol. XXVII, No. 2 (1957), p. 154.

37. G. W. Roberts & L. Braithwaite, "A Gross Mating Table for a West Indian Population", *Population Studies*, Vol. XIV, No. 3 (1961).

38. Judith Blake, *Family Structure in Jamaica* (Free Press of Glencoe Inc., New York, 1961).

39. M. G. Smith, *West Indian Family Structure* (University of Washington Press, Seattle, 1962), pp. 255–65.

40. I. Schapera, "Should Anthropologists Be Historians?", *Journal of the Royal Anthropological Institute*, Vol. 92, Pt. 2 (1962), p. 154.

41. W. Davenport, "The Family System of Jamaica", *Working Papers*, p. 420.

42. Blake, *op. cit.*, p. 147.

43. G. E. Cumper, "The Jamaican Family: Village and Estate", *Social and Economic Studies*, Vol. 7, No. 1 (1958).—"Household and Occupation in Barbados", *Working Papers, op. cit.*

44. W. Davenport, "Introduction" to *Working Papers, op. cit.*, p. 381.

45. Personal communication.

46. G. E. Cumper, "Household and Occupation in Barbados", *op. cit.*, p. 397.

47. W. Davenport, "The Family System of Jamaica", *op. cit.*, p. 450.

48. See note 5.

49. *Ibid.*

50. One of the reasons why East Indians in British Guiana are reluctant to accept automatic registration of customary marriages is that it would then be difficult to dissolve the union if the couple prove to be incompatible.

51. C. Jayawardena, "Family Organisation in Plantations in British Guiana", *International Journal of Comparative Sociology*, Vol. III, No. 1 (1962).

52. William J. Goode, "Illegitimacy, Anomie and Cultural Penetration", *American Sociological Review*, Vol. 26, No. 6 (1961).

53. There was a significant jump in the marriage rate immediately following the earthquake in Jamaica in 1907. See G. W. Roberts, *The Population of Jamaica*, Cambridge University Press (1957), pp. 287–88.

54. S. Mintz, *Worker in the Cane: A Puerto Rican Life History* (Yale University Press, New Haven, 1960).

55. M. G. Smith, "Dark Puritan: The Life and Work of Norman Paul" in two parts in *Caribbean Quarterly*, Vol. 5, Nos. 1 & 2 (1957).

56. O. Lewis, *Five Families: Mexican Case Studies in the Culture of Poverty* (Basic Books, New York, 1959).

24. A Decision Model of Conjugal Patterns in Martinique*

The sociology of the West Indies is rich in descriptions of the variety of mating patterns and domestic organisations found within the limits of bilateral kin relationships and a formal proscription of polygamy.[1] The most impressive of these studies is Michael G. Smith's (1962) demonstration of the relationship between conjugality and household organisation in five populations from three islands in the British Caribbean. In this article I shall attempt to explain why particular conjugal patterns are elected at specific points in the male life cycle, using descriptive material from a highland peasant village in Martinique. In particular, I shall show how the choice is an effort to maximise values within an arena of social and ecological restraints, and how these restraints change as a man matures. I shall then attempt to verify the asserted relationships with data from several of the samples analysed by Smith.

The kind of explanation here employed aims to understand frequentive or nonrandom behaviour as an aggregate of individual decisions. The focus of analysis is on the determinants of choice; in his Nuffield Lecture, Barth (1966a: 25) showed how frequentive behaviour can be explained:

> The model most readily available for this is one of utilities, and can be represented as one of choice under constraints. Such a model, incidentally, can also generate a *range* of behaviour, if assets and opportunities are distributed unequally between the members in the system—a condition that can be readily observed and depicted in any society.

There is a recurrent tendency in anthropological analysis to invoke two theories of human behaviour when the data to be explained divide unequally, for example where 92 per cent of men reside in their

SOURCE: Reprinted from *Man*, Vol. 2, No. 3 (1967):445–53, by permission of the Royal Anthropological Institute of Great Britain and Ireland.

fathers' compounds and 8 per cent do not. One theory focuses on the behaviour of most individuals, the modal or normal actors, and explains it as a response to moral imperatives; the other theory accounts for the statistically abnormal, 'deviant cases', whose behaviour is held to be the consequence of opportunistic assessments of the pay-offs from alternative actions. These deviants are supposed to find themselves less compelled than the others to conform to the rules of their society.

The model which Barth (1959; 1966*b*) developed is more parsimonious: the actions of both the statistically normal and the abnormal are considered to be strategic or opportunistic. The different results reflect the actors' different resources. By specifying the relationship between opportunities (or resources) and values, the processes whereby the varieties of action are generated are shown. Such a processual model is, of course, predictive, since a manipulation of the variables or change of their distribution affects the generated range of action.

In the Martinique highlands, four alternative mating patterns are available to adults: celibacy; extra-residential mating, in which the partners are not members of the same household; consensual cohabitation, so-called 'common-law' mating (called *en ménage* in Martinique); and marriage. Certain combinations are possible: a man may mate extra-residentially although married or consensually cohabiting; a married man separated from his wife may be celibate, mate extra-residentially or consensually. Plural cohabitation, either married or consensual, is not permitted. In a sample of about a third of the approximately 300 households in Morne-Paysan,[2] the following distribution of mating patterns among adults (persons 15 years of age and above) is found:

TABLE 1. DISTRIBUTION OF MATING PATTERNS.

	Men	*Women*
Single, childless	35	37
Single, parent	2*	13
Consensually cohabiting	18	20
Married	45	42
Widowed	4	15
Total	104†	127

* The number of single men reported to be fathers is surely understated. However, the fathers of children of single mothers may be single, consensually cohabiting, or married.

† No individual is counted more than once.

These patterns are not randomly distributed. Consensual cohabitation frequently follows a period of extra-residential mating, and is often deferred until the woman is pregnant or has borne children. Consensual cohabitation almost always precedes marriage, and marriage is usually delayed until some and often all children have been born. Thus older adolescents and young adults tend to mate extra-residentially; middle-aged adults are more likely to cohabit consensually, although a substantial number are married; and marriage is elected by older persons. The sequence is demonstrated in the following tables:

TABLE 2. MATING PATTERNS OF ADULT MALES CLASSIFIED BY AGE.

	Years of age								
	15–24*		25–39		40–54		55–69		70+	
	No.	%	No.	%	No.	%	No.	%	No.	%
Single, childless	26	92.9	5	16.7	3	10.7	1	7.1	0	0.0
Single, parent	0	0.0	2	6.7	0	0.0	0	0.0	0	0.0
Consensually cohabiting	2	7.1	13	43.3	3	10.7	0	0.0	0	0.0
Married	0	0.0	10	33.3	22	78.6	10	71.5	3	75.0
Widowed	0	0.0	0	0.0	0	0.0	3	21.4	1	25.0
Total	28	100.0	30	100.0	28	100.0	14	100.0	4	100.0

* mean: 18.9; median: 18.5.

TABLE 3. MATING PATTERNS OF ADULT FEMALES CLASSIFIED BY AGE.

	Years of age								
	15–24*		25–39		40–54		55–69		70+	
	No.	%	No.	%	No.	%	No.	%	No.	%
Single, childless	24	68.6	3	7.9	4	12.1	3	27.3	3	30.0
Single, parent	4	11.4	5	13.2	3	9.1	1	9.1	0	0.0
Consensually cohabiting	5	14.3	12	31.6	3	9.1	0	0.0	0	0.0
Married	2	5.7	17	44.7	17	51.5	5	45.5	1	10.0
Widowed	0	0.0	1	2.6	6	18.2	2	18.1	6	60.0
Total	35	100.0	38	100.0	33	100.0	11	100.0	10	100.0

* mean: 19.8; median: 20.0.

These figures alone do not rule out an explanation for the distribution in terms of social change, namely, that the older people in the sample are survivors of a time when marriage was more frequent and chosen by young persons. Interviews with married persons reveal, however, a prior history of consensual co-residence, and persons in the latter relationship claim an early period of extra-residential mating. As might be expected, the figures show that women enter each stage somewhat earlier than men. Of the five women in the youngest group cohabiting consensually, three live with men of the next older group, as do the two who are married. The direction of change is the same for both sexes.

An explanation for the association between conjugal patterns and age must take account of the changing incentives and opportunities by which values of persons are maximised as they proceed through the life cycle. We should be able to make sense of the patterns selected, in terms of values held by the actors and the possibilities for their achievement. In the following discussion I emphasise the man's point of view, since men and women in the village agree that the decisions to mate co-residentially and to marry tend to be the man's: most women mating extra-residentially prefer co-residence, and most women cohabiting consensually prefer marriage.

a. *Late adolescents and young adults: aged 15 to 24 years.* The data show that almost 93 per cent of men aged 15 to 24 do not live in sexual co-residence, although many may mate extra-residentially. Eighty per cent of women in that age category similarly live singly, of whom 14.3 per cent are mothers. Extra-residential mating is a very widespread phenomenon, of course, not at all limited to Martinique or the West Indies. Where it differs from its north-western European manifestation is that there is no necessary expectation that a household—either with or without marriage—be established with pregnancy, although there are incentives for co-residence at this age.

The 93 per cent of young men who do not reside with mates live in households containing one or both of their parents. They provide labour on their parents' land, and share in the returns of its productivity. Since land units in the village are small (Horowitz 1967: 29–32)—50 per cent of the holdings are less than one hectare—the household of parents and children is adequate for land exploitation, and supplementary labour for field preparation, planting, and harvesting is supplied by co-operative or exchange work groups (called *coups-de-main*). Therefore most households neither need additional adult labour on a residential basis nor have means adequate to support it.

Most of the larger holdings, the 45 per cent which exceed three hectares in size, are subdivided into smaller units, and are rented out for cash or shares. This system of tenure redistributes land widely among the villagers and renders the small household adequate for productivity. A few of the very largest holdings are maintained as integrated units, but most of these are devoted to pasturage on which a few salaried workers care for the cattle, rather than to garden cultivation which requires more intensive labour.

The authority which a man may exercise over his son-in-law, a woman over her daughter-in-law, and an older adult sibling over a younger adult sibling is not institutionalised, and these relationships are frequently accompanied by considerable friction. This is expressed in the strong opposition to extended or joint families, which precludes a conjugal couple sharing a house in which there is already such a couple, even in the few instances where additional labour could be effectively mobilised. No household in the village contains more than one conjugal pair, although many include persons of three or more generations. Conjugal co-residence is an assertion of autonomy, expressed in the establishment of a new household, and made possible by the acquisition of land or other means of support. Occasionally a couple lives with one parent, particularly with an elderly woman, but even this is not preferred. On the other hand, it is common to find extended family neighbourhoods, in which individuals build huts close to their parents and siblings. This represents the fragmentation of small holdings, and the members of each hut constitute a distinct management unit.

b. *Middle aged persons: aged 25 to 39 years.* Less than 24 per cent of the men in this category do not live in sexual co-residence. Forty-three per cent live consensually and 33 per cent are married. The corresponding figures for women are 21 per cent (almost two-thirds of whom are mothers), 32 per cent, and 47 per cent (including a widow).

The major factor in establishing co-residence is the acquisition of land. Many persons of this age have inherited or have been able to rent land. The co-resident couple is a productive unit, jointly exploiting the fields and consuming the returns. Children are early introduced to productive activities: as soon as they are able they bring food to their parents in the field and take care of the small animals, feeding the rabbits and chickens, and staking out the sheep and goats to fresh forage. They actively join in field work as they become old enough.

Having acquired land, a man has a second incentive to establish a household: to have assured and sanctioned access to the market. The Martiniquan peasant produces for household consumption and for sale in domestic markets, and the returns from these sales are used to pay rents and taxes, to entertain friends, to support church and political party, and to acquire the many necessities which he cannot produce himself. All over the West Indies (with the exception perhaps of East Indian areas) women have an almost exclusive monopoly of transactions involving domestic garden produce; the peasant needs a woman to supervise the distribution of his crop. Some men have available a mother or sister, and old men rely on a daughter. But the most certain arrangement is to have the exclusive commitment of a woman who is available full-time. She may either sell the produce herself, travelling with it to the market, or contract for its sale with a professional *vendeuse*. The former is considered shameful and the latter at least improper for a man.

By establishing a household, men assert their independence from their parents. A woman with land may tempt a man to set up a household with her if he has no land or no expectation of inheriting any. Since married couples legally share in each other's goods, a woman with property has a bargaining advantage to make her conjugal status legitimate (or to retain headship of the *ménage*). Residence tends to follow the availability of land on which to build a house: there are almost equal numbers of couples living uxorilocally, virilocally and neolocally.

Many men who are not concerned with the approbation of the church claim that they preserve their freedom of action and ensure good treatment from their women by not marrying. The folklore abounds with stories of good conjugal relationships which were ruined by marriage. *Un beau ménage est mieux qu'un mauvais mariage*, goes one *non sequitur*. ('A good consensual relationship is better than a bad marriage.') It is true that while marriage is generally preceded by consensual cohabitation, and many consensual unions result in marriage, many of them also dissolve, and the partners find new mates.

c. *Older persons: aged 40 years and above.* In the age group 40 to 54, about 11 per cent of the men live consensually and 77 per cent are married; at the age of 55 and older almost 100 per cent are married (or widowed). Similarly, no woman aged 55 or older lives consensually.

A man receives no direct economic gain from marriage over consensual co-habitation unless his mate owns land. Marriage then makes him an heir to her property. For most men the choice of marriage can be understood as the realisation of three values:

1. As a symbolic or token prestation, legitimation is an investment in the loyalty of children. The mother-child relationship has been seen by almost all Caribbean scholars as the durable one, the father-child relationship as fragile.[3] Persons too old to work must be supported by younger relatives, and the legitimation of children, even late in a career, is an effort to buttress the paternal bond.

2. Legitimation assures transmission of property, since illegitimate children have no rights of inheritance in French law. (The *Code civil* specifies an intermediate category, recognition, between legitimate and natural children. Recognised children also have guaranteed access to their father's property. However, marriage and legitimation are no more complex legal acts than recognition.)

3. Legitimation is an emulation of 'respectable people' and is strongly sanctioned by the church. The priests may favour marriage by excluding consensual couples from Communion, railing against them in sermons, and refusing to officiate at their funerals if they have shown no intention of marrying. Consensual couples are not permitted to serve as godparents, which restricts those who wish to build a political career from developing or reinforcing a clientele with ritual kin ties. Old people become increasingly aware of death and are sensitive to pressures from the church and from the examples of age-mates who have 'regularised' their conjugal statuses. A severe illness or fear of imminent death may also motivate younger persons to marry, and some marriages are celebrated at the sickbed.

Before attempting to verify the analysis with comparative material, I shall summarise the argument:

1. There is a variety of mating patterns among the adult population of Morne-Paysan, a highland village in Martinique.

2. These patterns are distributed sequentially: young adults tend to mate extra-residentially; middle aged persons cohabit, frequently consensually; older persons marry.

3. The sequence is explained in terms of men modifying their behaviour in an attempt to maximise values within the constraints

of their peasant economy.[4] This analysis is concerned with the connexions between values, economic conditions, and conjugal patterns, and not with their origins.

COMPARISON

I shall now confront the analysis with other data, turning to Latante and Grenville, the Grenadian villages analysed by Smith (1962). The historical, geographical and sociological features of Grenada approximate closely those of Martinique. The majority of persons in both islands are of African ancestry, Roman Catholic, and frequently French Creole-speaking. Their agrarian economies are divided between estate cultivation of cash crops for export, formerly worked by slaves, now by wage labourers; and highland peasant cultivation of food crops for subsistence and sale in local markets. Owners of the large estates, mostly white, dominate economic life.

> Of Grenada's 69,000 acres . . . 4,000 were held by the Crown as forest reserve, and the rest were privately owned; 116 parcels of more than 100 acres accounted for 40,000 acres together, while the remainder fell into 200 units between 20 and 100 acres each, 1,200 units of 5 to 20 acres, 4,900 holdings of 1 to 5 acres and 4,800 plots of less than 1 acre each (Smith 1965a: 14).

There is a similar concentration of land in Martinique, where estates of 40 hectares (*c.* 99 acres) and over, owned by less than 6 per cent of the proprietors, cover 75 per cent of the land.

Latante is a village of small peasant holdings, where the people raise nutmeg and cocoa for export, and fruits and vegetables for subsistence and sale in local markets. Although I have found no description of peasant productive organisation in Smith's (1962; 1965a; 1965b) writings on Grenada, I hazard that they share the general Caribbean reliance on their households, supplemented by occasional exchange labour groupings. As a consequence of similar values and opportunities for their maximisation, the distribution and sequence of conjugal patterns in Latante is strikingly like that of Morne-Paysan:

> These data reveal a single coherent pattern. Men may mate extra-residentially before their 24th year, but very few establish

domestic unions, and none of those who do so marry at this time. However, before they are 39 most men will be living in domestic unions, and the numbers who do so within and without marriage will be approximately equal. Moreover, the number of single men of this age group engaged in extra-residential unions will be much the same as of those living in marriage or in consensual domestic unions. By the time they are 54, four in every five men are married, and most of the remainder live in consensual domestic unions. Beyond this age point we find no men participating in consensual cohabitation, and only one in ten who remain single. In other words, men begin by mating extra-residentially; in the next phase they establish domestic unions, but at this point only about a third of the age group will marry, and consensual cohabitation is evidently the forerunner of marriage. By the time they are middle-aged, very few men remain single or in consensual cohabitation.

There are thus three recognised mating alternatives in this system, and these are arranged in serial order, the one succeeding the other as the individual matures (Smith 1962: 70–71).

We may note at this point a somewhat different emphasis in our analyses. Smith and I are both interested in the explanation of frequentive or patterned behaviour. He writes (1962: 198) that he seeks 'explanations of similarity or difference at the structural level, in the principles which regulate family relations within these samples'. But the principles appear to be the very patterns which are being explained:

> Marriage represents a status achievement appropriate to maturity; the married person who resumes cohabitation consensually is repudiating his own status. Conversely, the extra-residential mating form expresses immaturity and is appropriate to young persons, while the consensual domestic union is the appropriate prelude to marriage (Smith 1962: 73).

This statement translates the patterns into rules, implying that what is normal is also moral. The deviant behaves immorally, by repudiating his status. Smith convincingly shows covariations between mating forms and domestic organisation in a number of Caribbean villages. But his model requires acceptance of the existence of these forms without being able to explain their frequency or sequence, other than to assert their appropriateness. The values are not demonstrated independently of the forms they are held to explain. Thus the similarities between conjugal patterns in Morne-Paysan and Latante, which are predicted on the basis of our analysis ['an aggregate of people exercising *choice* while influenced by certain constraints and incentives' (Barth 1966b: 1)], appear to be merely fortuitous correspondences on the basis of his analysis.

The other Grenadian village, Grenville, shares an ethnohistorical background with Latante, but differs sociologically, being 'lower class urban' rather than 'peasant'. It thus provides a further test of the analysis, for the people act in relation to quite different incentives and restraints. While the kinds of conjugal patterns present in Grenville are the same as those in Latante and Morne-Paysan, their occurrences are different:

> Among both sexes, we find a random distribution of these mating forms within the reproductive age groups; and it is to this randomness that the marked instability of all forms of mating relation may most likely be due. Clearly if an individual has a free choice with regard to mating forms within the legal limit against bigamy, the distribution of these mating forms among persons of different age and sex may well be random; but this can only be the case if neither form of mating relation is permanent or defined by its place within a developmental series embracing them all (Smith 1962: 103).

The distribution, random, is accepted as a consequence of free choice. But an explanation of the distribution should show the utility of the choices as well as their display.

A final demonstration of the adequacy of the utility model may be offered by the data from rural Jamaica. Ecologically the people resemble peasants in Martinique and Grenada: they are small holders producing for household consumption and sale in domestic markets. Ten per cent of the households in Smith's sample of 550 are landless: '28 per cent had less than one acre, 16 per cent had between one and two acres, and 22 per cent had from 2 to 5 acres . . . less than 3 per cent had more than twenty acres' (Smith 1962: 126). There are numerous writings on the productive organisation of the Jamaican peasantry (e.g. Clarke 1957), which stress the household as the basic unit of production and consumption. If the major values are pan-Caribbean rather than specific to the French Creole areas, the analysis predicts that peasant regions in Jamaica will display conjugal forms and sequences parallel to their counterpart areas in Martinique and Grenada. Smith writes (1962: 130–31):

> We have here a developmental series of mating alternatives very like that of Latante. Mating forms for males are serially successive, and each has its mode at a particular point in the individual life cycle. . . . The analysis of male mating patterns accordingly demonstrates a serial arrangement of extra-residential mating, consensual cohabitation, and marriage, which has high actual observance. This mating order is thus clearly normative.

Smith's suggestion apparently is that since the sequence is frequentive it is also normative, and because people behave normatively the sequence is explained. But this is a rather limited kind of explanation, for while presenting the forms of behaviour, it tells us little of how these forms are generated. I have argued that an analysis of these forms should also reveal the incentives which lead individuals to behave in particular ways and the resources they can mobilise to make such behaviour possible.

Notes:

* Fieldwork in Martinique was supported by grants and fellowships from the Social Science Research Council and the Research Foundation of the State University of New York. The analysis was made during my tenure as Fulbright Professor of Anthropology at the University of Bergen; I am very grateful to my colleagues at Bergen, Fredrik Barth and Jan-Petter Blom, for their critical readings of the manuscript.

1. There is an enormous literature on New World Negro conjugality. Among the most prominent authors are E. Clarke (1957), E. F. Frazier (1939), and R. T. Smith (1956).

2. There are approximately 1,600 villagers distributed among some 300 households. The characteristics of the sample and the nature of domestic organisation in the village are discussed in detail in Horowitz (1967: 39–50).

3. It was partially this fragility which encouraged Herskovits's notion (e.g., 1947: 295–96) that there was a survival and re-interpretation of African polygyny in New World Negro domesticity.

4. On the basis of the analysis we predict a different distribution of conjugal patterns among salaried agricultural labourers, whose decisions to mate reflect a somewhat different set of incentives.

a. Because they contract for plantation work as individuals, the household is not a managerial unit, nor a means of mobilising labour.

b. Because they have no involvement in the distribution of the crop—sugar, rum, bananas, and pineapples are exported in bulk overseas—they need no access to the domestic market system as producers.

c. Because they rarely own land, they need not marry to assure transfer of property through inheritance.

Unfortunately we have no details of the distribution of conjugal patterns among these labourers in Martinique. I have done no systematic fieldwork on the plantations, and the Census of 1954, which comes closest to the fieldwork period, gives no detailed information on consensual cohabitation. The data do show that the percentage of persons who are married varies with relationship to land:

Occupational category for adult males	Per cent married
Land owners	56
Land tenants	54
Agricultural wage labourers	34

These figures are biased because of the concentration of agricultural wage labourers in the younger age categories, where few persons marry regardless of occupation. For example, while 15 per cent of land owners and 13 per cent of tenants are in the 15 to 24 year group, some 26 per cent of the wage labourers are in the category. Conversely, labourers are under-represented in the senior age groups. Nevertheless, when we control for age, the frequency of marriage does vary with occupation.

Percentage of males married (including divorced and widowed)		
Age group	Owners and tenants*	Labourers
20–29	16	11
30–39	51	41
40–49	66	51
50–59	77	64
60+	85	77

*These categories are combined to imply 'peasant', although a small number of great land owners is included.

References cited:

Barth, F.
   1959 "Segmentary Opposition and the Theory of Games: A Study of Pathan Organization." *Journal of the Royal Anthropological Institute* 89, 5–21.
   1966a "Anthropological Models and Social Reality." *Proc. R. Soc.* B, 165, 20–34.
   1966b *Models of Social Organization.* (Occasional Paper of the Royal Anthropological Institute 23). London: Royal Anthropological Institute.
Clarke, E.
   1957 *My Mother Who Fathered Me.* London: Allen & Unwin.
Frazier, E. F.
   1939 *The Negro Family in the U.S.A.* Chicago: Univ. of Chicago Press.
Herskovits, M. J.

1947 *Trinidad Village.* New York: Knopf.
Horowitz, M. M.
   1967 *Morne-Paysan: Peasant Village in Martinique.* New York: Holt, Rinehart & Winston.
Smith, M. G.
   1962 *West Indian Family Structure.* Seattle: Univ. of Washington Press.
   1965a *Stratification in Grenada.* Berkeley & Los Angeles: Univ. of California Press.
   1965b *The Plural Society in the British West Indies.* Berkeley & Los Angeles: Univ. of California Press.
Smith, R. T.
   1956 *The Negro Family in British Guiana.* London: Routledge & Kegan Paul.

H.
Religion and Folklore

The attempt to locate Africanisms in West Indian culture is exemplified in the first two papers in this section. Both Simpson and Bascom were closely associated with Herskovits, and both have had field experiences in West Africa as well as in the Caribbean. The assertions of African continuity are convincing because, as M. G. Smith has pointed out ("The African Heritage in the Caribbean," in V. Rubin, ed., *Caribbean Studies: A Symposium*. Mona, Jamaica; Institute of Social and Economic Research, 1957, p. 46), it is possible to assign a *specific* African provenience to the elements of the cults, as opposed to the more *general* attribution of, say, West African polygyny reinterpreted as serial monogamy in the Caribbean. (Morton Klass and I have attempted to locate elements of East Indian religious practice in Martinique to specific manifestations among Tamil-speakers in South India ["The Martiniquan East Indian Cult of Maldevidan," *Social and Economic Studies*, 10(1):93–100, 1961; and M. M. Horowitz, "The Worship of South Indian Deities in Martinique," *Ethnology*, 2(3):339–46, 1963].) The papers by Cook and Kitzinger take a different point of view. Rather than attempting to identify the particular historical connections of the elements of the cults, these authors show the meanings of them in the disprivileged lives of their lower-class adepts, a synchronous social-psychological interest in the culture of poverty. Miss Kitzinger expands this approach in a more recent paper, "Protest and Mysticism: The Rastafari Cult of Jamaica" (*Journal for the Scientific Study of Religion*, 8[2]:240–62, 1969).

GEORGE EATON SIMPSON

25. The Belief System of Haitian Vodun*

While it seems likely that the Haitian *vodun* cult began to take definite form between 1750 and 1790,[1] a full explanation of the origins of this hybrid religion cannot be given. The Code Noir prescribed baptism and instruction in the Catholic religion for all slaves (the rationalization of the slave trade was that the heathen blacks were being converted to Christianity), but it is doubtful if the new religion had much meaning for the transplanted Africans. The Code Noir also provided that assemblies of slaves for purposes other than Catholic worship were illegal, and masters could be punished for permitting such gatherings. Meetings of slaves were potentially dangerous to the colonials because of the possibilities they offered for plots and revolts. However, it was impossible to prevent all slave assemblages, and secret reunions during the night occurred frequently. If what is known to have transpired at the middle of the eighteenth century occurred earlier, and there is no reason to believe that it did not, the old men kept alive elements of African culture through tales, discussions, and religious and magical rites. Evidence of what happened at these nocturnal conclaves is found in *L'Essai sur l'Esclavage et Observations sur l'Etat Present des Colonies*, published by an anonymous author about 1750.

The dance called at Surinam *Watur mama*, and in our colonies "the water mother," is strictly forbidden to them. They make a great mystery of it, and all that is known of it is that it excites very much their imagination. They become excessively exalted when they meditate a wicked plan. The chief of the plot becomes so ecstatic that he loses consciousness; when he regains consciousness, he claims that his God has spoken to

SOURCE: Reprinted from *American Anthropologist*, Vol. 47 (1945):35–59, by permission of the author.

him and has commanded the enterprise, but as they do not worship the same God they hate each other and spy on each other reciprocally, and these plans are almost always denounced.[2]

Dr. Mars remarks that while different groups of slaves worshipped different intermediary gods, they all believed in a Great God above these secondary spirits.[3] In less than forty years revolutionary leaders, who had found rituals useful in promoting their cause, had brought about a religious compromise which included the essentials of the various beliefs. While it is impossible to indicate with finality those who were most responsible for the merging of Islamic, African, and Catholic elements into Haitian *vodun*, some of the most likely contributors may be designated.[4]

Little is known about the religious and magical activities of Macandal, a Limbé slave who was born in Africa, except that:

> He predicted the future, he had visions and an exceedingly strong and vigorous eloquence. . . . He had persuaded the Negroes that he was immortal, and he had instilled in them such terror and such respect that they considered it an honor to serve him on bended knee and to render unto him the worship that one owes only to the divinity whose representative he declared himself to be.[5]

Escaping from his master's plantation, Macandal spread terror throughout the North by pillaging plantations, sacking villages, stealing cattle, and poisoning both whites and blacks. Finally this audacious man was burned alive at the Cap Haitien army post in 1758.[6]

Jean-François, another fugitive in the North, took the title of Grand Admiral of France and of General-in-Chief. Biassou, his lieutenant, became Viceroy of the Conquered Countries. Madiou reports that they dominated their followers as much by the superiority of their intellects as through superstition. Jean-François inspired respect among the rebels by wearing elaborate costumes covered with stripes, braid, and medals taken from white officers, and by riding a richly bedecked horse or travelling in a carriage drawn by four white or black horses. Biassou surrounded himself with sorcerers, and filled his tent with cats of all colors, dead men's bones, and other symbolic objects. At night great fires burned in his camp, and nude women performed extraordinary dances. When the excitement had reached its peak, Biassou, followed by his magicians, appeared before the crowd, cried that the spirit of God was inspiring him, and said that he was instructed to announce that the fighters who succumbed in battle would return again to their tribes in Africa. Frightful shouts, singing, and drumming followed Biassou's dramatic appearances, and he seized upon these moments of exaltation to lead his men against the enemy in the middle of the night.[7]

In the West, Romaine Rivière, Hyacinthe Ducoudray, Halaou, and others spread terror. Rivière, a Spaniard who called himself Romaine the Prophetess, plundered Léogane. Claiming to be the godchild of the Virgin Mary, he used to say mass, torture the whites, and maintain all he did was in accordance with the orders of the Virgin.[8] Hyacinthe led 15,000 insurgents against the white dragoons and the national guard at Croix des Bouquets. The blacks fought fanatically because they had been told by their sorcerers that the dead would come back to life in Africa. Hyacinthe himself ran through the ranks waving the tail of a bull and crying: "Forward, forward! The bullets are as dust."[9] Halaou, the giant who headed the rebels of Cul-de-Sac, always carried a white rooster under his arm, claiming that it transmitted to him the desires of Heaven. He used to march preceded by drum music, by trumpets, and by his sorcerers who sang that he was invulnerable, that the cannon were only bamboo and the gunpowder dust. His guard carried long ox-tails which, it was claimed, could turn aside all bullets.[10]

But perhaps the insurgent leader whose rites came closest to the acts of the later cult was Boukman. Born in Jamaica, Boukman escaped from a plantation near Morne-Rouge. In order to produce greater unity among the rebels of that region he conducted an impressive ceremony during the night of August 14, 1791. After an enormous crowd had assembled a violent storm arose, and in the midst of thunder and lightning an old Negro woman appeared, danced wildly, sang, and brandished a huge cutlass over her head. Finally, the silent and fascinated crowd saw her plunge the cutlass into the throat of a black hog. The slaves drank the animal's blood and swore they would execute Boukman's orders.[11]

Six days later, led by Boukman, the slaves of the Turpin plantation, near Cap Français, indiscriminately massacred every white man, woman, or child upon whom they could lay their hands. This inaugurated a general insurrection, and within a few weeks the magnificent plantations of the Plaine-du-Nord were in ruins and the white population either murdered or cooped up in the larger towns.[12]

Dr. Mars has called attention to a description of the rites witnessed by Moreau de Saint Méry towards the end of the eighteenth century.[13] Judging from this account it would appear that the new cult took on definite form about 1790. At this time the first part of the ceremony consisted of the officiant's interpretation of the wishes of the divinity, symbolized by a snake. The dance followed this service, and included singing, fainting, intense nervous excitement and some rather violent behavior. At this point the Catholic elements in the ritual were practically non-existent.

Haitian *vodun* seems to be explainable in the light of certain religious and political conditions. Presumably Catholics, but finding the new religion none too congenial, the slaves continued to rely upon old tribal beliefs for their spiritual needs. During the latter half of the eighteenth century revolutionary leaders utilized nocturnal rites to dramatize their cause and to weld together diverse slave groups.[14] Gradually a more or less standardized set of rites emerged. During the next one hundred and fifty years the beliefs and rituals of the cult became more elaborate, the Catholic components increased, and regional differentiation developed.

THE PLACE OF THE LOAS IN THE VODUN CULT

In discussing the religion of the members of a non-literate group every effort must be made not to erect a mock theology by reading into their belief system the familiar concepts of one's own culture. In the account which follows we have tried to avoid bringing perfect consistency and order out of a situation which is filled with inconsistencies and contradictions. The lack of written formulations and the absence of an ecclesiastical hierarchy in Haitian *vodun* are conducive to variations in belief and ritual from region to region and even from temple to temple within a region.

By far the most prominent figures in the *vodun* cult's realm of the sacred are the *loas*.[15] Many of the *loas* are African deities who "have been inherited through succeeding generations by the descendants of those who brought them to Haiti."[16] Both Herskovits and Courlander report that some of the *loas* are indigenous to Haiti, and they agree that these *loas* are the result of the deification of powerful ancestors.[17] Evidence to support this contention was also found by the writer. One Plaisance informant, when asked if he had heard of the *loas* enumerated by another man, said that he did not know all of them, but added that that was not strange since each person knows special *loas* in addition to those recognized by all devotees.

All told there are hundreds of *loas*.[18] One peasant said that the number of the *loas* is infinite, another said that while one cannot possibly know all of the *loas* it is important during a ceremony to invite all of them. Still another, a *houngan's* assistant, said that he is not concerned with knowing the names of all the *loas*, but insisted that in a ceremony he can easily summon all of them.

No sharp distinctions are made in northern Haiti between the Arada gods and gods derived from other African cults. Separate ceremonies are not held for Arada, Ibo, Congo, and other African tribal gods. None of the vodunists near Plaisance could classify the gods they know according to these or any other categories. Some of these believers are acquainted with the names of non-Arada gods, as well as Petro *loas*, but in their thinking and in their ceremonies they treat them as if they were Aradas.[19]

In the Plaisance region there seem to be three schools of thought with reference to the relationships between the *loas* and the Catholic Saints. According to one point of view there is a spirit "under the water"[20] to correspond to each Saint in Heaven. The Saints and the *loas* are intermediaries between God, the creator of man and the master of the Universe, and man. God is too busy to listen to the pleas of men so the *loas* and the Saints meet at the halfway point on the road between Heaven and earth, and the *loas* tell "their brothers" what their human followers want. The Saints then return to God and report on the appeals which men have made to the *loas*, and God grants or refuses the various requests. This group of vodunists does not believe, however, that the *loas* are limited to those who correspond to the Saints. In addition, they know of *loas* who are independent and who have nothing to do with God and the Saints.

Some members of the *vodun* cult believe that the Saints are *loas*, although they hold that not all *loas* are Saints. One man said that the Saints and the *loas* are "la meme bagaille" (the same thing), but others said that while Saint Patrick is Damballa, and Mater Dolorosa is Erzilie, Sousou pannan is simply Sousou pannan and L'Inglésou is merely L'Inglésou.

PLAISANCE VODUN DEITIES*

Loa	Informants	
Adjassou-Linguetor	A.G.	Ar.
Adja or Adja Bosu, Courlander, *op. cit.*, 30; or Agasu, Herskovits (1), 267; or Aguasu, Dorsainvil, *op. cit.*, 174.		
Adjassou-Miroi	H.V.A.G.	Ar.
Agaone	O.U.	C.J.
Agaou	A.G.	C.J.
Agaou-Tonné and Agaou-Wédo, Dorsainvil, *op. cit.*, 174.		
Agarou	O.U.	Mar.
Agoué-Oyo	A.G.	B.V., Ar., C.J.
Agwe Woyo, Herskovits (1), 267; Agué or Agué Woyo, Courlander, *op. cit.*, 31.		
(Maitresse) Amelia	H.O.	Mar.

* This is a combined list of *loas* given by nine non-literate informants (Arsène Pierre Jean Baptiste, Termitus Boisier, Bertrand Velbrun, Terméus Joseph, Ulysse Joseph, Marguerite——, Cénous Jean, Madame Petit-Homme, and Anazine Merveilleux). Lists were obtained separately, from the first seven informants. The shortest list consisted of seventeen gods, the longest of forty-nine. No attempt was made to extend the lists by prompting, although a few names have been added here for some of these seven individuals because they mentioned other gods in songs and tales. Undoubtedly all of these persons know about additional *loas*. The names of a few gods referred to by the last two informants in conversations, possessions, and songs are included. There was no opportunity to get lists from these individuals, but since they were important members of the cult they certainly knew of dozens of gods.

Informants are indicated by initials. One hundred and thirteen *loas* were named by one informant only, seventeen gods were mentioned by two informants, thirteen by three informants, four by four informants, two by five informants, and three by six informants. Of the one hundred and fifty-two *loas* listed here, twenty-seven are African tribal gods, and are indicated above by the letters A.G. The sixteen Catholic Saints are labeled C.S. The names of six *loas* in this list are derived from African tribal or place names, and are listed as A.N. Nine of these *loas* probably are of African origin, and are given as P.A.O. Fifty-seven seem to be of Haitian origin, and are scheduled above as H.O. Eighteen *loas* appear to be variations in name for African tribal gods, and are listed as H.V.A.G. There are nineteen *loas* of unknown origin in this group, and they are indicated by the letters O.U.

The sources for the designation of African origin for certain of these *loas* are: M. J. Herskovits, (1) *Life in a Haitian Valley*; (2) "African Gods and Catholic Saints in New World Negro Belief," AMERICAN ANTHROPOLOGIST,

Loa	Informants	
Amminan	O.U.	Ar.
Anago	A.N.	Ar.
Nago tribe		
(Saint) Antoine	C.S.	Ar.
Arada	A.N.	T.J., U.J.
Arada tribe		
Assez-Media	H.O.	C.J.
(Mediateur ?)		
Atacrou	O.U.	Mar.
Ati-Dangné	P.A.O.	T.B.
Possibly Dangbe, Herskovits (3), 58, 75.		
Badé	A.G.	C.J.
Gbade, Herskovits (3), 21; Badé-si, Dorsainvil, *op. cit.*, 174.		
Baquicie	O.U.	Mar.
Baron Lacroix	H.O.	B.V.
Baron Minuit	H.O.	B.V.
Bazou or Bosu	A.G.	Mar.
Bosu-Cessé and Kadia-Bosu, Dorsainvil, *op. cit.*, 174.		
Bazou-Mainnain	H.V.A.G.	B.V., Ar.
Bois l'en Dingué	H.O.	An. M.
Bolodjoré	O.U.	Ar.
Borrommée	C.S.	C.J.
Brave	H.O.	Ar., U.J.
(Mait') Carrefour	H.O.	Ar.
Cassé Brisé	H.O.	C.J.
(Sainte) Catharine	C.S.	T.J.
(Sainte) Celia	C.S.	T.J.
Cibi	O.U.	Mar.
(Monsieur Difficile) Clérmeil	H.O.	C.J.
(Président) Clérmeil	H.O.	Ar., T.J., T.B.
Clermézine	H.O.	B.V., T.B., Ar.
Confrit (Confrère ?)	H.O.	C.J.
Congo	A.N.	Ar.

n.s. 39 (October–December, 1937), 635–43; (3) "An Outline of Dahomean Religious Belief," *Memoirs of the American Anthropological Association*, No. 41, 1933; H. Courlander, *Haiti Singing*; J. C. Dorsainvil, *Vodou et Névrose*.

Several of the *loas* listed here as indigenous to Haiti may be Catholic Saints, i.e., Laurentine may be one of the St. Laurences, St. Laurentia, or St. Laurentinus; Amminan may be St. Ammianus, St. Ammon, or St. Ammonius; Sylvanie may be St. Silvanus; Marie-Noël and Maitresse Madeleine may be derived from Sainte Marie Madeleine; and Solophine may refer to St. Solina. See *The Book of Saints* by the Benedictine Monks of St. Augustine's Abbey, Pamsgate, 3rd Ed., Macmillan, 1941.

PLAISANCE VODUN DEITIES*—*Continued*

Loa	Informants
Dagué	H.V.A.G. C.J.
See Agoué-Oyo	
Dagué-Amminan	H.V.A.G. U.J.
See Agoué-Oyo	
Dagué-Cala-Michaud	H.V.A.G. Ar.
See Agoué-Oyo	
Dagué Lissa	A.G. Ar.
Lisa, Herskovits (3), 14.	
Dahomain	A.N. Ar., C.J.
Kingdom of Dahomey	
Damballa	A.G. Ar., T.J., U.J., C.J.
Damballa, Herskovits (2), 638; Damballah, Dorsainvil, *op. cit.*, 174; Courlander, *op. cit.*, 33.	
(Pié) Damballa	H.V.A.G. C.J.
(Pierre) Damballa	H.V.A.G. U.J.
Danger	H.O. U.J., T.B.
Danger Mina	A.N. C.J.
Mina tribe	
Dan-Houézo	P.A.O. B.V., T.J., C.J.
Damballa Hwedo, Herskovits (3), 34, 75; Damballa Wédo, Courlander, *op. cit.*, 33. Herskovits refers to Damballa Hwedo as "the Da who surpasses all ancestors in power." (3), 58.	
Dan-Yi	O.U. C.J.
Dent-Friand	H.O. C.J.
(Monsieur) Desportes	H.O. C.J.
Dévis Pas Pressé	H.O. P-H
Diable Tonnerre	H.O. Ar.
(Monsieur) Dieujuste	H.O. C.J.
Dismiraye	H.O. Mar.
(Mamselle) Dispensa	H.O. C.J.
(Dispensatrice ?)	
Dji	A.G. Ar.
Dji, Herskovits (3), 14.	
Dosu-Dosa	H.O. B.V.
Erzilie	A.G. C.J., B.V., Ar., T.J., U.J., T.B.
Erzilie, Herskovits (2), 638.	
Erzilie Dantor	H.V.A.G. T.J., Mar., U.J., Ar., B.V.

Loa	Informants	
Erzilie Dosbas	H.V.A.G.	Ar.
Erzilie Kanzo	H.V.A.G.	Ar.
Erzilie Freda	H.V.A.G.	B.V., U.J., Ar.
Erzilie gé rouge	H.V.A.G.	B.V., U.J., Ar.
Erzilie Nain-naine	H.V.A.G.	B.V., U.J., Ar.
Erzilie Mainfort	H.V.A.G.	B.V., U.J., Ar.
Erzilie pied cassé	H.V.A.G.	B.V., U.J., Ar.
(Sainte) Etienne	C.S.	Ar.
Exzaie (Exact ?)	H.O.	C.J.
(Saint) Francois Bolomi	C.S.	U.J.
Fré Ti Jean	H.O.	P-H
Ganga	O.U.	Ar., T.J.
(Saint) Georges	C.S.	Ar.
(Saint) Glin (Gislain ?)	C.S.	Ar.
Gougoune	A.G.	B.V.
Gugune, Dorsainvil, *op. cit.*, 174.		
Grande Batala	A.G.	U.J., T.B.
'Batala, Herskovits (1), 267; Obatala, Courlander, *op. cit.*, 40.		
Grand Bois	H.O.	B.V.
Grand Bois Elie	H.O.	Mar.
Guéde Nibo	A.G.	B.V., Ar.
Gede, Herskovits (1), 267.		
Ibo	A.G.	Ar.
Ibo-Lélé, etc., Dorsainvil, *op. cit.*, 175.		
(Maitresse) Inomène	H.O.	T.B.
(Saint) Jacques Majeur	C.S.	B.V., T.J., U.J.
(Saint) Jean Baptiste	C.S.	Ar.
Jean Brigand	H.O.	Mar.
(Maitre) Jean Crabe	H.O.	U.J., Mar.
Jean Délé (Delire ?)	H.O.	T.B.
Jean Féro (Féroce ?)	H.O.	An., Mar.
Jean Petro	H.O.	T.B.
Jeune Gens Direct	H.O.	P-H
(Maitresse) Karous	O.U.	T.B.
La Silène-La Baleine	H.O.	T.J., C.J.
La Sirène is "a character derived from European mythology." Herskovits (2), 639.		
(Maitresse) Laoué-Dji	P.A.O.	T.B., Mar.
Alawe and Dji, Herskovits (3), 14.		
L'Afrique	A.N.	Ar.

PLAISANCE VODUN DEITIES*—*Continued*

Loa	Informants	
Laoka	P.A.O.	Ar.
Loko, Dorsainvil, *op. cit.*, 174; Loko Attiso, etc., Courlander, *op. cit.*, 37; Loko, Herskovits (3), 14.		
L'Arc En Ciel	H.O.	C.J.
Laurentine	H.O.	T.J.
La Victoire	H.O.	C.J.
Legba	A.G.	B.V., Ar., T.J., U.J.
Legba, Herskovits (1), 267; Dorsainvil, *op, cit.*, 174.		W
Lembélie	H.O.	Mar.
Limba	A.G.	Ar.
Limba-zaou, Dorsainvil, *op. cit.*, 175.		
Limba-Zaho	A.G.	T.J.
Limba-zaou, Dorsainvil, *op. cit.*, 175.		
Linglésou	A.G.	Ar., U.J., T.B., C.J.
Inglinsou, Dorsainvil, *op. cit.*, 175.		
Linglésou-Bassin-sang	H.V.A.G.	B.V., T.J.
Linglésou Guerre	H.V.A.G.	B.V.
Lomi Ago	P.A.O.	Ar.
Age, Herskovits (3), 14.		
Lorvana	H.O.	Mar.
(Maitresse) Madeleine	H.O.	C.J.
Mambo	O.U.	B.V., Ar.
Mambo La Salle	O.U.	C.J.
Mambo Zacca	P.A.O.	C.J.
Azaca-Si, Dorsainvil, *op. cit.*, 174; Azaka Baing Baing, Courlander, *op. cit.*, 32; Azaka Mede, Herskovits (2), 642.		
Mamba Ya Djoni	O.U.	Ar.
Marassa Jumeaux	A.G.	B.V., Ar., T.J.
Marassa, Herskovits (2), 642.		
Marie	C.S.	C.J.
(Sainte) Marie Madeleine	C.S.	Ar.
(Maitresse) Marie-Noël	H.O.	B.V.
Membo-Delahi	O.U.	B.V.
(Saint) Michel	C.S.	Ar.
Mouché Pierre	H.O.	U.J.
Nago Shango	A.G.	Ar.
". . . Shango, the god of thunder . . . of Nago [Yoruban] origin." Herskovits (1), 267.		

Loa		Informants
Nambo-Nansi	P.A.O.	T.B.
Anansi is the trickster-hero in Ashanti-Fanti folklore.		
Ogoum-Tonnere	A.G.	B.V., Ar.
Agomme Tonnere, Herskovits (2), 642.		
Ogun Balanjo	A.G.	B.V., Ar., T.J., C.J.
Ogun Balanjo, Herskovits (2), 641.		
Ogun Batala	A.G.	C.J.
Ogun Batala, Herskovits (1), 316.		
Ogun Ferraille	A.G.	B.V., Ar., C.J.
Ogun Ferraille, Herskovits (2), 641.		
(Mait') Ozoun Elou Mandja	O.U.	Ar.
Papa Ogoun	A.G.	Ar., U.J.
Ogoun, Herskovits (1), 316.		
(Maitresse) Philomène	C.S.	B.V., Ar., T.J., U.J., T.B.
Pié Anfalo	O.U.	C.J.
Papa Pié (St. Peter)	C.S.	B.V., Ar., T.J., U.J., T.B., C.J.
Pierre Marsiqué	H.O.	T.B.
(Monsieur) Polisson	H.O.	C.J.
Raphaèl	C.S.	Mar.
Ravagé	H.O.	T.B.
Sans-Manman	H.O.	Ar.
Shango	A.G.	T.B.
Shango, Herskovits (1), 267.		
Simba-La Source	H.V.A.G.	C.J.
Probably a variation of Simbi.		
Simbi Laoka	A.G.	B.V.
"Simbi. . . is a Congo god. . . ." Herskovits (2), 638. Simbi-ampaka, Dorsainvil, *op. cit.,* 175.		
Sine	O.U.	C.J.
(Maitresse) Siridja	O.U.	B.V.
Sobo	A.G.	Ar.
Sobo, Herskovits (1), 267; Sobo-si, Dorsainvil, *op. cit.,* 175.		
Solophine	H.O.	C.J.
Soussou-Pannan	H.O.	B.V., Ar., T.B.
Sylvanie	H.O.	Mar.
Taureau	H.O.	Ar.
Ti-Jean Dantor	H.O.	B.V., T.J., T.B., C.J., Mar., P-H

PLAISANCE VODUN DEITIES*—*Continued*

Ti-Jean Laurent	H.O.	B.V.
Ti Milette Porte	H.O.	C.J.
Ti Pierre Dantor	H.O.	Mar.
Ti Solé (Little Sun ?)	H.O.	Mar.
(Monsieur) Toussaint	H.O.	C.J.
Tracas	H.O.	Mar.
Trois Plumettes	H.O.	C.J.
Ya Tibois Quinto	O.U.	B.V., Ar.
Zadieu	P.A.O.	C.J.
Za, Dorsainvil, *op.cit.*, 174.		
Zahi	P.A.O.	C.J.
Za, Dorsainvil, *op. cit.*, 174.		

A blind *houngan*, Termitus Boisier, and all of the members of his family maintain that the *loas* and the Saints are bitter enemies.[21] The *loas* are fallen angels who are worshipped by those who have been chosen by them, but this worship is based solely on a fear of their power.[22]

The situation is made more complicated by the fact that those who believe that the *loas* and the Saints are on friendly terms, and those who maintain that they are enemies, sometimes talk about the Saints and the *loas* as if they were identical.

The Plaisance peasants are uncertain about the exercise of authority and power among the *loas* themselves. They believe that the government of the *loas* is similar to human governments, but that men cannot know what the hierarchical levels are. They imagine that there are such categories as: the *loas* of the first class, secondary *loas*, inferior *loas*, simple domestics, and those who have been condemned for their misdemeanors. One informant said that Erzilie is the Queen of the *loas*, but added that no one can boast that he knows the "chief of the chiefs," nor even the principal chiefs. According to him, the "chiefs" may be classified only by their conduct, that is, their conduct with respect to men. By the use of this criterion the most powerful *loas*, in his opinion, would be Président Clérmeil, Agoum-Tonnere (Saint John), Legba, Papa Pié (Saint Peter), and Agoué-Oyo.

THE ORIGIN OF HAITIAN GODS IN THE VODUN PANTHEON

Herskovits and Courlander both speak of the necessity of removing the *loa* from the head of a dead *serviteur* (a person who becomes possessed by one or more gods) in order to prevent him from becoming a *loa* himself.[23] On the basis of my discussions with Plaisance informants I have come to a somewhat different conclusion, namely, that it is not the *loas* as such which are removed but the ability to become possessed by the *loas*. This apparent difference may be explainable in terms of variations in regional beliefs. The Plaisance peasants spoke of the necessity of "degrading" all persons who are thought to have special abilities. According to them special talents are due to "les esprits" which these individuals have. "Spirits" in this context did not appear to mean *loas*, but rather some vague, mysterious power not unlike Polynesian *mana*. They claimed that musicians and sailors, for example, must be "degraded," and one informant said that I would have to be "degraded" because of my interest in photography. In their minds those who become possessed by the *loas* simply represent a category of persons with a special talent. This talent, like any other special talent, must be removed at death and transferred to someone else. One ceremony is held to "degrade" the dead man, and another ceremony is given to discover his successor (I collected examples both of the "degradation" and the "transference" ceremonies, but these are as yet unpublished). Since persons who are not servants of the *loas* are "degraded," it would seem that the "spirits" which are removed are not the *loas* of the *vodun* cult. If these "spirits" are not removed, the dead persons, regardless of whether or not they are servants of the *loas*, will return to plague their living relatives. I am sure that dead persons do become *loas*, and that in general those who attain this status are those who were prominent and powerful *houngans*. It is my opinion, however, that some who have been degraded, as well as some who have not received this treatment, have joined the ranks of the gods. I am not sure that persecution of the living is a necessary prerequisite to becoming a *loa*. Even if this were the case, the ceremony of "degradation" would not be a complete guarantee against the return of the dead man. The dead may intercede in the affairs of the living because they were dissatisfied with the funeral rites or with the offerings given to the dead at *vodun* ceremonies held after the burial. Perhaps the essential thing is that a *serviteur*, for whatever reason or reasons, has made an impression on his relatives or followers which is strong enough to cause them to think that he will surely outrank the ordinary dead and take his place among the important figures in the world which is known only imperfectly to the living.

THE FIDÈLES AND THEIR LOAS

Each *fidèle* has one or more *loas* who are important to him, but he has one principal *loa-protecteur*. Members of the cult in northern Haiti fall into four main, although not mutually exclusive categories: *houngans* (*vodun* priests), *badjicans* (assistants to *houngans*), *serviteurs* (those who become possessed by the *loas* during ceremonies), and *fidèles* (the rank and file believers who never become possessed at a ceremony). As nearly as the writer can determine from estimates given by informants, there were in 1937 approximately two hundred *houngans* in the Plaisance commune's population of thirty thousand. These were perhaps fifteen hundred to two thousand *badjicans*, three thousand *serviteurs*, and fifteen to twenty thousand *fidèles* of varying degrees of belief. In terms of deviation from *vodun* beliefs as culture norms it appeared that from one-fifth to one-third of the Plaisance peasants were non-conformists. A high correlation between position in the cult and general prestige or influence levels does not exist. An important *houngan* and the *badjicans* most closely associated with him are highly respected, but the lesser leaders are not held in particularly high esteem merely because of the roles they play during ceremonies. *Serviteurs* are popular on ceremonial occasions because successful rites require numerous possessions, but the standing of a *serviteur* outside the realm of *vodun* depends in part upon characteristics other than his ability to become possessed by a god. In the Bassin section of the commune of Plaisance the most prosperous, and before the onset of old age, the most influential peasant happened to be a man who was scornful of *vodun* and boasted that he had never believed in the *loas*.

A majority of the vodunists are Catholics, but most of these people do not seem very secure in their Catholicism. The old traditions persist, the African gods are still real to them, and they cannot rely solely on the Church. A number of my informants apologized for being vodunists, and insisted that Catholicism is more important to them than the *vodun* cult. Their explanations for their *vodunism* were: God has condemned *vodun,* but he permits the *loas* as a diversion; there is no difficulty in being both a Catholic and a servant of the *loas;* God forgives a member of the cult who is conscientious about his Catholicism; men need some religion, but they cannot afford to practice Catholicism; that they have *placées,* but since God disapproves of *plaçage*[24] they cannot go to the Church; that the *loas* are too powerful to be ignored. Several *houngans* claimed that they had become cult officiants against their own wishes. The *loas* had demanded that they become *serviteurs,* often with the sanction of sickness to enforce the demands. Only one peasant was encountered who seemed to feel that the *loas* are more powerful than God, but she was not willing to ignore God completely. The spiritual uncertainty of these people is summed up in a proverb—*Moceau Bon Dieu, Moceau solocotor* (A little for God and a little for the Devil.)

The peasantry near Plaisance believes that most of the *loas* are both good and bad, that is, that they alternate assistance to their followers with persecution of them.[25] In general the feeling is that if one observes the taboos imposed by one's chief *loa-protecteur,* as well as any other *loas* one may have, and if one is punctilious about offerings and ceremonies, the *loas* will be generous with their aid. Many peasants think of their relationship to the *loas* as a contractual one. They believe that the gods must be paid once or twice each year by the staging of an impressive *vodun* ceremony, and that small gifts must be presented frequently. One informant said that the *loas* like blood and that it is by means of sacrifices that favors may be obtained. If a *fidèle* neglects his *loas* punishment in the form of sickness, death, crop failure, or other misfortunes will surely follow.

The rationalistic orientation of the Haitian peasant towards the realm of the sacred is explainable in terms of their cultural background and their contacts with Western civilization. Many of the ancestors of the present rural dwellers came from Dahomey, a land where offerings and sacrifices to the gods was a matter of great importance, and where economic life was based on a money system. Practical African attitudes were reinforced and supplemented by the calculating way of life which the slaves and their descendants encountered in the New World. The fees of the Catholic Church for baptisms, confirmations, weddings, and funerals, as well as special gifts and offerings for the Saints, have also given support to the viewpoint of rational expediency.

In the North at least three *loas* are considered to be unqualifiedly malicious. These are Linglésou, Sousou pannan, and Limba. Linglésou is a harsh god who, through his servants, kills readily and without mercy. Sousou pannan is a very cruel *loa* who loves alcohol and blood. Limba is an arbitrary persecutor, a glutton whose appetite is insatiable, a *loa* who is said to kill and eat his followers. Several of the *loas* may take more than one form. Erzilie, the most versatile of the gods, may appear as any one of the following: Erzilie Dosbas, Erzilie Dantor, Erzilie Freda, Erzilie Mainfort, Erzilie gé rouge, Erzilie pied cassé, Erzilie Kanzo, or Erzilie Nain-naine. The chart which follows shows the preferred foods, drinks, clothes, and colors, as well as the physical characteristics, abodes, sacred days, powers, and behavior of *serviteurs* when possessed, for selected *loas*. The members of the cult strive to please the *loas* by providing exactly the right foods, drinks, songs and dances, and by wearing the proper clothing, at the various types of *vodun* ceremonies.[26] In addition, they avoid the performance of irreverent acts near the springs and other sacred places which the *loas* frequent. Examples of such acts would be the throwing of refuse near these abodes, lying down under sacred trees, and tying a horse in the immediate vicinity of one of these points. Since the *loas* may find it necessary to manifest themselves to the faithful outside of the ceremonies, it is essential that the devotees keep themselves pure and in a proper condition to receive their messages on sacred days.

THE DEAD

In the *vodun* cult of northern Haiti the dead rank second only to the *loas*. We have already stated that some of the dead become *loas*, but not all of them do, and those who do not achieve this distinction must also be treated respectfully. The dead are here, there, and everywhere. They are simply the invisible living. They retain an interest in this world, and, like the *loas*, they favor or destroy its inhabitants.

There are several categories of the dead. While the term *zombies* is used to cover all dead persons it is also used in a special sense, and there are other categories in the world of the dead. The term *zombie* is often employed to designate persons who have been killed by sorcerers, or those who have met death in other ways, and have been resurrected by "bad" *houngans*. Such *zombies* have no souls, are completely dominated by their masters, and are utilized by them for evil purposes. *Zombie errants* are the spirits of human beings who died in accidents. They inhabit the woods by day and walk on the roads at night, as they live out the periods of earthly existence assigned to them by God. *Diablesses* are evil spirits who must live in the woods for several years before they can be admitted to Heaven. These devil-women are being punished for the crime of being virgins at the time of their deaths. *Lutins* are the ghosts of children who died before baptism. *Bakas* are *zombies* who have been converted into animals, usually dogs, by sorcerers. These creatures are sent out to steal for their masters.[27] *Spectres* and *fantomes* are inhabitants of the other world who appear before the living stripped of their bodies. Ordinarily they disappear quickly and the living get only a glimpse of them. *Revenants* are the dead who feel that they have been neglected and who return to persecute their relatives. *Marassa-jumeaux* are dead twins, and are highly revered by the living.

In the North there is no separate cult for "Les Mort," nor one for the Twins. However, neither the dead in general nor the dead twins may be overlooked in any *vodun* service, and songs and rites for them are always included. Since the dead both protect and persecute the members of their families, according to the treatment they receive, it is essential that elaborate wakes, pompous funeral rites, numerous prayers, Catholic masses, and *vodun* ceremonies be given in their honor.

The peasants are not very clear about the soul. Most of them agree that in a "natural" death (death due to God's recalling a man's soul) the soul returns to God to receive its reward or punishment. Some good souls remain in the sky with God, others return to earth as "good" *loas*, and still other good souls are inherited by new-born babies in the family (but not the immediate family). Bad souls become bad *loas* and spend eternity suffering in Hell and doing evil on earth. If the *loas* kill a man he remains a captive "under the water" until a big ceremony is given. After that, presumably, the *loas* permit the soul to go to God for judgment.[28] There was considerable disagreement among the peasants concerning the fate of the souls of persons killed by sorcerers (*houngans* or *loup garous*) either at the instigation of enemies or without such incitement. Some claimed that the souls of *zombies* (special sense) never leave their bodies, while others believed that while the soul is detached from the flesh by means of bad magic, it is almost immediately reunited with the body

CHARACTERISTICS OF SELECTED LOAS IN NORTHERN HAITI

Loa	Physical Characteristics	Special Clothes of Servitors	Abode	Favorite Foods	Favorite Drinks	Favorite Colors
Legba (Saint Anthony the Hermit)	Handsome old man with flowing beard.	Kerchiefs of different colors tied around the body.	Under the fig trees and at the crossroads.	An abundance of meat.	Alcoholic drinks.	Black and yellow.
Erzilie (Mater Dolorosa)	Beautiful brown woman. Very amorous.	Silk clothes and fine cloths of brilliant colors.	"Les Roches au Gouffre" between Plaisance and Gonaives.	Delicate foods. White chicken, fine cakes and desserts.	Fine non-alcoholic liqueurs.	Rose and white.
Damballa (Saint Patrick)	Ugly and strong.	No elegant clothing. One or two simple colored kerchiefs worn diagonally across the chest.	Vicinity near Gonaives.	Likes much food, especially pork and goat meat.	Lover of alcohol. Often drunk.	Red.
Guédé	Resembles a dead person.	Black robe and a high hat.	Cemeteries and the crossroads.	Fish with much pimento. Black chickens. Fried plantains.	Kola and taffia.	Black.
Saint John (Saint John)	A stern and nervous loa.	Black and white silk robe.	Always moving. Does not have a fixed abode.	Black cattle and white sheep.	Champagne and fine liqueurs.	White.
Papa Pié (Saint Peter)	Military appearance. Never laughs.	Red and gray robe.	At the bottom of rivers and ponds.	Goat meat and cocks.	Taffia.	Red, black, and white.
Adjasou	Protruding eyes. Always in a bad humor.	No special robe.	Under the mombin tree near a spring.	Duck, turkey, pigeon, and goat meat.	Vermouth, rum, cognac.	No color preferences.

Sousou pannan	Very ugly. Body covered with sores.	Odd combinations of worn-out clothing.	No fixed abode. Lives in the air.	Blood, pork, and red cocks.	Clairin and taffia.	Red.
L'inglésou	Fierce looking *loa*.	No special robe. Red kerchief.	Abysses and large rocks.	Yellow pig.	Wine.	Red.
Limba	Coarse person.	No special robe. May make nude appearance.	In the rocks.	Pork.	Strong alcoholic drinks and liqueurs.	Red and black.
Maitresse Mombu	Stammerer.	No special robe. Red and white kerchief.	In springs.	Goat meat. Red cocks.	Rum and wine.	Red and black.
Nago Shango	Lively appearance.	No special robe. Yellow madras kerchief.	Under *badjis* and in abysses.	Beef, guinea fowl, chickens, birds.	Anisette.	White.
Président Clérmeil	A white man.	Multicolored robe.	River near Limbe, the sea, and under Cap Haitien bridge.	Delicate food. Good meat. Large cakes.	Good rum, champagne, and fine liqueurs.	Red.
Ibo	A handsome man.	Clean clothes of two colors. Madras kerchief.	Unknown.	Goat meat, chickens, vegetables.	Kola, wine, liqueurs.	Rose, and white.
Congo	Handsome enough, but apathetic. Almost idiotic.	Content with any clothing.	Guinee.	Mixed foods with much pimento.	Mixed drinks.	Mixed colors.
Ti Jean Quinto	Insolent appearance.	No special robe.	Bridge at Borgne.	Goat with white beard.	Taffia.	No color preferences.
Sobo	Handsome military officer.	Military apparel. White and lemon madras kerchiefs.	Found everywhere. Lives under trees.	Goat meat, mutton.	Cognac, champagne.	White, red, lemon.

CHARACTERISTICS OF SELECTED LOAS IN NORTHERN HAITI (cont'd)

LOA	Sacred Days	Powers	Behavior of Servitor When Possessed by LOA
Legba (Saint Anthony the Hermit)	Tuesdays and Thursdays.	Guardian of crossroads and barriers. Great power. Favors his servitors by giving them hidden treasures.	Acts like a limping grandfather. Carries a cane and walks carefully so that he will not be trampled on.
Erzilie (Mater Dolorosa)	Tuesdays and Fridays.	The powers of a queen.	The servitor's behavior is tranquil, aristocratic, and coquettish. Thought to be a learned person who can speak several languages. Shows dislike for alcohol, houngans, and bad people. Personifies gentleness, sensitiveness, and health.
Damballa (Saint Patrick)	All days except Mondays and Wednesdays.	Loa of snakes and floods. Very powerful. Can cure desperate illnesses. Gives favors according to recompense.	Drinks much alcohol. Violent behavior includes rolling on the ground.
Guédé	Mondays.	Important figure in black magic intended to kill human beings.	Talks continuously and through his nose. Is always armed with a knife which is used to beat possessed persons. Note: An interesting description in the West is given in Courlander, op. cit., 15–17.
Saint John (Saint John)	Fridays and the 24th of June.	Guardian of thunder. Causes earthquakes.	Behavior is both haughty and conciliatory. Shows great fondness of alcoholic drinks.
Papa Pié (Saint Peter)	Fridays and the 29th of June.	Great power. Makes rivers overflow.	Energetic, authoritative behavior. Speaks with a piercing voice.

Name	Description	Days	Behavior during ceremony
Adjasou	Very powerful. Makes water rise in springs.	Fridays.	Servitor runs around in an excited manner.
Sousou pannan	A wicked and cruel *loa* who is capable of doing evil without pity.	Always present.	Tries to break furniture and drums. Runs after sacrificial animals to suck their blood. Drinks much alcohol and also the blood of animal sacrifices.
L'inglésou	A killer.	Tuesdays.	Appearance is grave and harsh. Actions are menacing.
Limba	Arbitrary persecutor.	Thursdays.	Shows a gluttonous interest in foods and drinks offered to the *loas*.
Maîtresse Mombu	Causes great rains.	Fridays.	This gentle *loa* performs gay dances. Eats her favorite food (eggs, flour, and accasan) off the ground.
Nago Shango	An important administrator.	Thursdays.	This restless *loa* plays the role of a "bon garçon" during a ceremony.
Président Clérmeil	Absolute power of President. When angry he causes rivers to overflow.	Sundays, Tuesdays, Fridays, and festival days.	Domineering manner.
Ibo	A secondary *loa*.	Tuesdays, Thursdays, Fridays.	This friendly *loa* jests and pays special attention to children. Sometimes acts like a dog, and may eat dog meat.
Congo	A subordinate *loa* without power.	All days except Mondays and Wednesdays.	Quiet and shy during ceremony.
Ti Jean Quinto	Policeman.	Saturdays.	Enjoys himself at ceremonies, but noted for his quarrelsomeness.
Sobo	Military official.	Thursdays.	Calm, dignified behavior. Dislikes noise.

in its new, feeble, attenuated life. A few maintained that sorcerers withdraw the souls of these creatures from their bodies and hide them.

THE SOCIAL FUNCTIONS OF VODUN

Much has been written in recent years about the functions of religion in society and the functional analysis of culture.[29] A. R. Radcliffe-Brown and Bronislaw Malinowski are generally regarded as the principal proponents of this type of analysis, although they were preceded by Emile Durkheim and Robertson Smith. That these societal experts were not the first to expound this viewpoint can be seen from an examination of Polybius' remark about the Roman social order before the birth of Christ.

> But it seems to me the most distinctive superiority of the Roman political and social order is to be found in the nature of their religious convictions; and I mean the very thing which other peoples look upon with reproach, as superstition. But it nevertheless maintains the cohesion of the Roman state.[30]

This statement is not essentially different from the clearest definition of function given in recent years, namely: "The function of a trait complex is the sum total of its contribution towards the perpetuation of the social-cultural configuration."[31] This conception of function is followed in our discussion of the *vodun* cult.

The child gets his first notions about the *loas* and the dead from his relatives. Indoctrination concerning sacred things is acquired in conversations with his elders, in story-telling sessions on the family estate, and in the *vodun* ceremonies which his family sponsors.[32] These ceremonies are held on the family land, the expenses are paid by the family's members and all who can afford to contribute are solicited, and the relatives are supposed to attend and assist in the rites. This family participation in *vodun* affairs, plus the fact that the reasons for giving the ceremonies stress the common dangers which members of the family group are facing, or the thanks which all are giving to the *loas* and the dead for favors granted, tend to enhance family solidarity. Since the extended family is still the most important basis of social organization in non-urban areas, activities which maintain or strengthen kinship bonds contribute to the perpetuation of the Haitian peasant culture pattern and the Haitian social structure.[33]

The *vodun* cult contributes to the perpetuation of the folk society by providing supernatural sanction for such mores as the taboos on murder, incest, theft, and the showing of disrespect to the old. The most famous *houngan* in the Plaisance region stated that a vodunist must follow the laws of God and the *loas*. He learns the former laws in the Catholic Church, and the latter are obtained from the *loas*. The *loas* reveal the rules of right conduct to one during possession and in dreams. Those who are never possessed by the gods hear revelations from those who do have these experiences. The belief that the *loas* kill those who persist in violating the mores is undoubtedly an important factor in social control.

If one takes the *vodun* beliefs and rites as a whole and does not attempt to separate too sharply that which is religious from that which is magical, it is feasible to utilize Malinowski's and Evans-Pritchard's analyses of the functions of magic.

> Magic fills a gap left by a lack of knowledge in man's pragmatic pursuits; and it provides an alternative means of expression for thwarted human desires.[34]

These peasants are agriculturists who live on small tracts of land and cultivate the soil with simple technological devices. They are at the mercy of such natural disasters as floods, droughts, and insect pests. There is much uncertainty about farming under these conditions, and success and failure are often attributed to the *loas* and the dead. Hence the need for honoring, propitiating, and thanking those of the other world. Magico-religious acts are techniques which assist one in obtaining certain desired objectives in a difficult world. To the extent that they "work," or rather, to the extent that the peasant believes they are effective, they prevent him from utilizing other types of action to solve his problems. Thus these acts contribute to the perpetuation of existing technological patterns.

The peasant child also learns that it is well to be wary of neighbors, for he finds that his elders suspect them of causing some of the family's misfortunes. Sicknesses, deaths, and crop failures are almost as likely to be due to jealous neighbors as to the *loas* or the dead. While it is not usual for a family to call upon the gods during a regular *vodun* service to punish its enemies, one might ask a *loa* privately for assistance in striking back at a malicious neighbor. Thus if the *vodun* complex is considered in its entirety, it appears to be an important institutional device for the release of aggressive impulses. In this connection it is interesting to note that aggression (magical or otherwise) is seldom directed against those who have been responsible for much of the peasant's plight, namely, the members of the *élite*. The overwhelming majority of the peasants do not expect to improve their social positions materially. They would like to become Grand Dons, that is, large land-holders, but as a rule they do not look forward to becoming educated men, or even town residents. Under present conditions (which they do not expect to change soon) they prefer to live on the land if that is at all possible, and they have accommodated themselves to the station of peasant. There has never been a genuine revolt of the peasants against the government. Since Independence, Haiti's revolutions have been started by military leaders anxious to gain power for themselves. The peasant's struggle, then, is to hold what he has, prevent his situation from worsening, and make some gains economically if he can. Placing the blame for mishaps on enemies and directing magic against them provides an opportunity for the release of aggressive impulses. One feels that he is doing something about his troubles. The activity keeps him occupied and relieves tensions even if he gets poor or no results. If the results are good, so much the better. *Vodun* ceremonies and magical acts perform, therefore, a mental hygiene function for the individual, and thereby contribute to preserving the status quo.[35]

Another way that religion functions to perpetuate the "social-cultural configuration" in rural Haiti is its provision of entertainment and recreation for the hard-working peasants. A *vodun* ceremony is an occasion which brings together nearly all members of the family, and the attraction is not just the rites themselves but also the opportunity which they create for visiting, story-telling, feasting, card-playing, and dancing. In addition, these ceremonies have esthetic aspects. *Vodun* altars are decorated with flowers, chromolithographs of the Catholic Saints, and other objects to make them as attractive as possible. The ritual dancing, drumming, and singing also have an esthetic appeal. A successful ceremony, then, is not only one in which the *loas* and the dead are placated, but one which has been characterized by generous hospitality on the part of the host and genuine enjoyment for the participants. *Vodun* ceremonies are strenuous affairs, yet the revitalizing effect which they have on many of the faithful sends them back to profane tasks with new confidence and courage. For a minority of the believers the ceremonies may serve to increase rather than decrease accumulated tensions. We refer to those individuals who resent their obligations to the *loas* and who brood about the necessity of honoring them.

Finally, the *vodun* cult provides these peasants with a world view, an explanation of the universe and man's place in it which gives some meaning and direction to their individual lives.[36] *Vodun* does not have a monopoly in furnishing these folk with a cosmology and a philosophy of life, for, as we have stated previously, most vodunists are also Catholics. However, the peasants tend to be vague and confused about Catholic beliefs and to rely more heavily on the hybrid rather than the orthodox religion for their basic orientations.

We are not suggesting that religion is the only unifying force in Haitian peasant life. Kinship institutions, the social structure, the political system, economic practices, health customs, and educational procedures all function in ways which contribute to the continuation of the total culture pattern of these folk. The magico-religious complex reinforces most of the other major aspects of this peasant society, and culture, and these in turn tend to support it.[37]

THE DECLINE OF VODUN

The important role played by *vodun* rites in the War of Independence has been indicated in the introductory section. The attitudes of Haiti's rulers towards *vodun* have varied greatly, and more than one president has altered his policy with respect to the cult during his term of office.

Toussaint Louverture was a faithful Christian, but he was also an astute political leader who utilized *vodun* as a device for uniting the slaves. However, after coming to power he waged a merciless war against the cult. Dessalines boasted of his African ancestry, but ruthlessly suppressed the cult. Christophe was even more severe. He tolerated only one *houngan*, Louis Sangosse of Campeche, whom, according to tradition, he consulted about his own affairs. Pétion, in order to checkmate his rival, Christophe, philosophically allowed the existence of the cult. Boyer acted against *vodun* in 1826, but only on paper.[38]

The first leaders of Haiti opposed *vodun* for political reasons, for reasons of racial pride, and for purely personal reasons. Undoubtedly they believed that the *vodun* which had unified the slaves against the white masters might produce the same results against them. In addition, *vodun* was considered as an inferior religion which must be repudiated. It was regarded as an obstacle to civilization. It was an enemy which must be overcome. Finally, it was not suitable that there should be one religion for the mass and a different religion for the ruling class. The immediate successors of the first leaders of the new Republic imitated their predecessors. Many of the presidents and high political authorities secretly consulted *houngans* and offered sacrifices, while publicly they seemed to be taking rigorous measures against *vodun*.

The laws have been applied according to the sympathy or the hostility of the local authorities for the cult. Generally speaking, the *vodun* "societies" constituted until recently a part of all national holidays, and all religious festivals (in spite of the protestations of the priest), and in especially critical periods the law against *vodun* was put aside and freedom of action for the cult was proclaimed.

In the early days of the American Occupation (1915–1920) the military officials enforced the law strictly and conducted an unrelenting war against the *houngans*. *Houmforts* (temples) were destroyed, and the *houngans* were sentenced to hard labor on public works or given heavy fines. For a time it seemed that *vodun* would disappear. Later, however, the Marines began to take an interest in the cult and *vodun* flourished again. The "dance without sacrifices" was invented to circumvent the law. During Borno's presidency (1922–1930) *vodun* underwent an eclipse. In 1930, both as a reaction to the preceding government and because of political exigencies, the restrictions on *vodun* were lifted and it was widely and openly practiced. Later in President Vincent's term of office an attempt was made to suppress the cult by enacting a law (September 5, 1935) which provided for six months' imprisonment and a fine of eighty dollars for holding a *vodun* ceremony.[39] Some local officers who were on friendly terms with *houngans* ignored the new law, and others were bribed to allow ceremonies with sacrifices to be held on permits issued for *bals*. Sometimes members of a family held their ceremony in the privacy of a bedroom while a dance was in progress in the courtyard. Even where local officials were not opposed to the cult, the poverty of the peasants during the middle and late thirties prevented them from staging elaborate ceremonies.

During 1941, 1942, and 1943 both the Catholic Church and the

Haitian government carried on an intensive campaign against *vodun*. Close relationships exist between church and state in Haiti. Local priests are paid small salaries by the government. The new President, Mr. Elie Lescot, seems to be desirous of having the full support of the church. Dr. Alfredo Métraux, of the Smithsonian Institution, stated in October, 1941, that *vodun* shrines were being abandoned so rapidly that within a few months it would be difficult to find any trace of the cult except in the most remote sections of the interior. Many important *houngans* have brought ritual paraphernalia to the priests during the last three years and have taken a solemn oath that henceforth they will not participate in cult affairs. Some say that the *loas* themselves demanded that their servants go to the priests and submit to the Catholic Church. Others maintain that while the people profess that they are giving up their beliefs, actually they are not doing so. After receiving the first reports concerning the "movement of the *rejectés*," the writer published the following statement.

> According to recent reports from reliable informants a large number of *houngans* have renounced their connections with the *vodun* cult. However, I doubt if the whole belief-system of *vodun* will disappear quickly. Even though many officiants have given up their temples, one wonders if others will not take their places sooner or later, and in small ways if not openly and on a large scale. For while it is true that the *vodun* beliefs sometimes induce fear, they also inspire confidence in the peasant as he faces life's uncertainties and dangers. Until major changes occur in education, medical service, and economic conditions the *vodun* beliefs will be useful to the peasants.[40]

There seems to be no reason at present for modifying that conclusion.

Notes:

* This material was obtained on a field trip to Haiti which was made possible by a post-doctoral fellowship from the Social Science Research Council, New York City. The field data given in this article were acquired from peasant informants who were living in the northern part of the country near the village of Plaisance. I am indebted to Dr. Price Mars and to Mr. J. B. Cinéas for valuable assistance in the preparation of this article, and to Professor M. J. Herskovits for preliminary training and subsequent counsel. The writer wishes

to acknowledge the helpful criticisms of this paper which were given by Edward Abramson and Linvill F. Watson.

1. Price Mars, *Une Étape de l'Évolution Haitienne,* p. 142.

2. Cited by L. Leytraud, *L'Esclavage aux Antilles françaises avant 1789* (Paris, 1897), and quoted by Price Mars, *Ainsi parla l'Oncle,* p. 113.

3. P. Mars, *Une Étape de l'Évolution Haitienne,* p. 141.

4. "Il n'est pas possible d'avoir des détails sur la vie de la plupart de ces hommes avant les troubles révolutionnaires étant donné qu'ils étaient sans état civil, de simples numéros d'ordre dans la foule anonyme des esclaves. Mais il est non moins certain qu'ils se révélèrent des personnalités de premier ordre dans l'action par la puissance prodigieuse et leur influence religieuse sur les masses." Letter from Dr. Price Mars.

5. *Memoire sur la création d'un corps de gens de couleur levé à Saint Domingue,* 1779, A.M.C., Corr. Gen., Saint Domingue, 2e série, C9 carton XXIX.

6. Moreau de Saint Méry, *Déscription topographique, physique, civile, politique et historique de la Partie Française de l'Isle de Saint Domingue,* I (Philadelphia, 1797), pp. 651–53.

7. Thomas Madiou, *Histoire d'Haiti,* I, pp. 72–73.

8. *Ibid.,* p. 97.

9. *Ibid.,* pp. 100–1.

10. *Ibid.,* p. 181.

11. J. C. Dorsainvil, *Manuel d'Histoire d'Haiti,* pp. 77–78; V. Schoelcher, *Vie de Toussaint Louverture,* I, p. 30.

12. H. P. Davis, *Black Democracy,* p. 36.

13. P. Mars, *Ainsi parla l'Oncle,* 114–18.

14. It is interesting to note that once in power the former revolutionists prohibited the practice of *vodun* because they feared that political enemies might utilize it for counter-revolutionary purposes. See Dorsainvil, *Vodou et Névrose,* p. 166.

Also, it is interesting that one of the means used by an oppressed group to attain the goal of independence has become an end in itself. Instead of full freedom, which the overwhelming majority of the peasants never gained, a kind of substitute goal has been accepted. This objective is to make the best possible adjustment to a bad situation by honoring, placating, and seeking favors of the dead and the gods.

15. Known also as *Les Esprits,* and the *Zanges.* In the South and West the term *Les Mystères* is also used, but this is less common in the North. It is interesting that *Zanges* is a contraction of *"les anges"* of Christian faiths.

16. M. J. Herskovits, *Life in a Haitian Valley,* p. 142. One of my informants (Boisier, a *houngan* or cult leader) stated that all of the *loas* came from Guinée.

17. Herskovits, *op. cit.,* pp. 150, 268–69; H. Courlander, *Haiti Singing,* pp. 26, 29.

18. J. C. Dorsainvil, *Vodou et Névrose,* 36, says: "Ces loa à la verité sont si nombreux qu'on pourrait placer chaque jour de l'année sous le vocable de l'un d'eux."

19. In the West, and perhaps in the South and in some parts of the Artibonite, special ceremonies are held for the Petro gods. At Mirebalais Herskovits found that the worship of Congo and Ibo gods was restricted chiefly to individual families. See Herskovits, *op. cit.,* p. 149, and Courlander, *op. cit.,* p. 29.

20. The phrase "under the water" refers to the capital of the *loas,* and is sometimes called "Ville au Camp." The peasants are vague as to the exact location of this city. Apparently not all of the *loas* live "under the water" because in

the ceremonies the *"Zanges* of the forest" and the *"Zanges* of the sky" are also addressed. It is impossible to say whether this tripartite division of the *loas* is a continuation of the Sky, Earth, and Water pantheons of Dahomey, or whether the *"Zanges* of the sky" indicates a confusion of the *loas* and the Catholic Saints, or whether the *vodun* priests simply are not taking any chances of offending any of the spirits by failing to include them in the invitation to the ceremony.

21. When told that *houngan* Boisier had said that the *loas* and the Saints are passionate enemies who are engaged in a perpetual battle over mankind, with the Saints trying to attract men to God, and the *loas* striving to lead them to the devil, and that the *loas* do not make reports to the Saints about the deeds of men, one peasant clung to his previously expressed belief, and asserted that Mr. Boisier could not prove that he was right.

22. Dorsainvil, *op. cit.,* p. 37, reports the same belief. "Dans certaines régions du pays, les loa deviennent les anges, particulièrement les anges rebelles, ces révoltés du Paradis que Dieu frappa comme jadis Jupiter dans la légende grecque foudroya les titans orgueilleux escaladant le ciel."

23. Herskovits, *op. cit.,* pp. 213–14; Courlander, *op. cit.,* pp. 237–38.

24. *Plaçage* is a socially but not legally sanctioned relationship between a peasant man and woman. There are several types of *placées,* or concubines, and a man may have one or more *placées* without or in addition to a legal wife.

25. Dorsainvil, *op. cit.,* 38, writes: "Les Vodou sont encore considérés suivant leur action bienfaisante ou mauvaise. Il y en a, parait-il, qui sont condamnés à faire le mal comme par une fonction native. En réalité, tous sont des petits êtres jaloux, vindicatifs, réclamant de leurs serviteurs plus qu'ils ne peuvent donner, aussi ennemis de leur repos, de leur prospérité. . . ."

26. No ceremonial details are included in this article. For a generalized description of the *vodun* service near Plaisance, see G. E. Simpson, "The Vodun Service in Northern Haiti" (*American Anthropologist,* Vol. 42, No. 2, 1940), pp. 236–54. The service near Mirebalais is described by Professor Herskovits in *Life in a Haitian Valley,* Ch. 9. The writer hopes to publish later accounts of several special *vodun* rites.

27. For a discussion of the *baka* concept in another section of Haiti, see M. J. Herskovits, *op. cit.,* pp. 239–43.

28. This belief seems to be an adaptation of the concept of purgatory in Roman Catholic doctrine.

According to some informants a *houngan* who has been properly degraded may enjoy eternal happiness at the Ville au Camp, the residence of the *loas.*

29. For a recent study along these lines see A. I. Hallowell, *The Role of Conjuring in Saulteaux Society.*

30. Polybius, VI, p. 56. Quoted in T. Arnold, *The Folklore of Capitalism,* p. 46.

31. R. Linton, *The Study of Man* (New York, 1936), p. 404.

32. There seem to be no formal initiation ceremonies in northern Haiti for the induction of individuals into the *vodun* cult. Young people seem to acquire their knowledge of the gods, the mores, and the rites gradually and unsystematically. Eventually a dream experience, a vision, spirit possession, or a message from one of the *loas* through a *houngan* or a *serviteur* informs one of his *loa-protecteur.* The extent of a peasant's participation in the cult appears to depend upon his personality traits, the turns which his fortune takes, and the amount of interest which his family has in *vodun.*

33. Data on the Haitian social structure have been published previously— G. E. Simpson, "Haiti's Social Structure" (*American Sociological Review,* 6,

1941), pp. 640–49. For material on the Haitian peasant family see M. J. Herskovits, *op. cit.*, Chs. 5–7, and G. E. Simpson, "Sexual and Familial Institutions in Northern Haiti" (*American Anthropologist*, 44, No. 4, 1942), pp. 655–74.

34. E. E. Evans-Pritchard, "The Morphology and Functions of Magic" (*American Anthropologist*, 31, 1929), p. 621. See also B. Malinowski, "Magic, Science and Religion," in J. Needham, *Science, Religion and Reality* (New York, 1925), pp. 82–83.

35. Another interesting possibility in connection with the release of the peasants' aggressive impulses is that *vodun* affiliation may also constitute a mild form of indirect aggression against the Catholic Church. This is suggested both because of the Church's antagonistic attitude toward the cult, and because Catholicism stands for certain moral principles which are not altogether congenial to the peasants.

36. In this connection another possible function might be suggested, namely, that of providing a sense of a long-continuing tradition, the African heritage. Whether *vodun* is regarded as a source of racial pride, as a distinctive racial achievement by some peasants, is a matter which needs further investigation.

37. Some of the functions of the family and the social structure are discussed in the author's articles on these subjects referred to in note 33. Some functions of the peasant economy are discussed in G. E. Simpson, *Haitian Peasant Economy* (Journal of Negro History, 25, 1940), p. 499.

38. Section VI . . . Code Pénal. Sixième classe. "Des Sortilèges."

Art. 405. Tous faiseurs de ouangas, caprelatas, vaudoux, donpèdre, macandals et autres sortilèges seront punis de trois mois à six mois d'emprisonnement et d'une amende de soixante gourdes à cent cinquante par le tribunal de simple police; et en cas de récidive, d'un emprisonnement de six mois à deux ans et d'une amende de trois cents gourdes à mille gourdes, par le tribunal correctionnel, sans préjudice des peines plus fortes qu'ils encourraient à raison des délits ou crimes par eux commis pour préparer ou accomplir leurs maléfices.

Toutes danses et autres pratiques quelconques qui seront de nature à entretenir dans la population l'esprit de fétichisme et de superstition seront considerées comme sortilèges et punis des memes peines.

Art. 406. Les gens qui font métier de dire la bonne aventure ou de deviner ou de pronostiquer, d'expliquer les songes ou de tirer les cartes seront punis d'un emprisonnement de deux mois au moins et de six mois au plus et d'une amende de cent gourdes à cinq cents gourdes.

Tous individus condamnés pour les délits prévus au présent article et en l'article 405 subiront leur peine dans les prisons maritimes et seront employés aux travaux de la marine.

Ils seront, en outre, à l'expiation de leur peine, placés sous la surveillance de la haute police de l'État, pendant deux ans, par le fait seul de leur condamnation.

Art. 407. Les instruments, ustensiles et costumes servant ou destinés à servir aux faits prévus aux deux articles précédents seront de plus saisis et confisqués, pour être brulés et détruits.

39. Décret-Loi du 5 Septembre, 1935.

Art. 1. Sont considérés comme pratiques superstitieuses: (1) les cérémonies, rites, danses et réunions au cours desquels se pratiquent en offronde a des prétendues divinités, des sacrifices de bétail ou de volailles; (2) le fait d'exploiter le public en faisant accroire, par des moyens occultes, qu'il est possible d'arriver soit à changer la situation de fortune d'un individu, soit a le guérir d'un mal quelconque, par des procédés ignorés de la science medicale; (3) le fait d'avoir en sa demeure des objets cabalistiques servant a exploiter la crédulité ou la naiveté du public.

Art. 2. Tout individu, convaincu des dites pratiques superstitieuses, sera condamné à un emprisonnement de six mois et à une amende de quatre cents gourdes, le tout à prononcer par le tribunal de simple police.

Art. 3. Dans les cas ci-dessus prévus, le jugement rendu sera exécutoire, nonobstant appel ou pourvoi en cassation.

Art. 4. Les objets ayant servi à la perpétration de l'infraction prévue dans l'article 3 seront confisqués.

40. G. E. Simpson, *Loup Garou and Loa Tales from Northern Haiti* (Journal of American Folklore, 55, 1942), pp. 219–20.

26. The Focus of Cuban Santeria[1]

The worship of African deities, as it is practised in Cuba today, is known as *santeria*. The deities and the men and women who work with them are known by the Spanish words *santos, santeros,* and *santeras,* or by the Yoruba words *orisha, babalorisha,* and *iyalorisha.* Santeria is a vital, growing institution, practised throughout the entire length of the island, in both rural and urban areas; in the latter, in fact, it is probably the strongest. In recent years it seems to have been expanding, recruiting additional members from the Negro, the mixed, and even the white population.

The African elements of santeria are predominantly Yoruba, or Lucumi, as the Yoruba of Nigeria are called in Cuba. In the town of Jovellanos, Matanzas province, where most of the material on which this paper is based was gathered,[2] the importance of Yoruba religion in santeria is clearly apparent. The Yoruba influence is also recognizable throughout Cuba, despite regional variations, in the names of the Yoruba deities, in similarities to Yoruba ritual, in the Yoruba cities named by Cuban Negroes as homes of their ancestors, and in individuals who can still speak the Yoruba language. On a quick trip in the summer of 1948, more than eighty years after slavery, it was possible to find Cuban Negroes in towns from one end of the island to the other, and in Havana itself, with whom I could talk in Yoruba.

Certain features of santeria have become well known through the work of Herskovits and other scholars in the field of New World Negro studies. In Cuba they have been discussed in the valuable contributions of Ortiz and of Lachatanere, Castellanos, and Martin. These features include the syncretism of African deities with Catholic saints, commonly represented by chromolithographs; the African pat-

SOURCE: Reprinted from the *Southwestern Journal of Anthropology,* Vol. 6, No. 1 (1950):64–68, by permission of the author and the editors of the *Southwestern Journal of Anthropology.*

tern of possession which has attracted interest as a psychological phenomenon; and the retention of animal sacrifices and African drumming, singing, and dancing in the New World Negro rituals. All of these are important elements in Cuban santeria, but in the mind of the cult members in Jovellanos, those which are the foundations of their form of worship are the stones, the blood, and the herbs.

In discussing these basic elements of santeria, there are two problems in the field of acculturation to be considered. First, are they derived from Africa or from Catholicism? And secondly, if the traits themselves are African in origin, is their position as the essential elements of the Afro-Cuban cults also African, or has it developed in Cuba under a situation of culture contact? A final answer to the second question may have to wait on a fuller knowledge of West African cultures, but it is of far greater theoretical importance. It will show whether or not the "focus" of an institution or culture pattern—to transfer a term from culture as a whole to a part of culture —has been retained, in addition to the retention of individual cultural traits or items. This point is of more than academic interest, since the preponderance of African retentions in the field of religion among the New World Negroes, over all other aspects of culture, has been interpreted as evidence that religion is the focus of African culture.

The fundamental importance of the stones in Cuban santeria was stressed consistently by informants. While chromolithographs and plaster images of the Catholic saints are prominently displayed in the shrines and houses of the santeros, they are regarded only as empty ornaments or decorations, which may be dispensed with. The real power of the santos resides in the stones, hidden behind a curtain in the lower part of the altar, without which no santeria shrine could exist. The stones of the saints are believed to have life. Some stones can walk and grow, and some can even have children. Informants told of their own experiences with stones which they had thrown into the streets or otherwise disposed of, only to have them reappear in the house. The most powerful stones are said to have been brought from Africa by the slaves, who concealed them in their stomachs by swallowing them.

The power of the stones is conceived as an invisible fluid, whose force at times can be felt. This is the power which protects the santero and the members of his cult house, and through which the "guardian angel" or saint manifests its blessings. This miraculous power is given to the stones by treating them with the two other essentials of santeria, herbs and blood. This treatment is known as "baptism" (*bautismo*). Stones which have not been prepared in this way, as well as any item of cult paraphernalia which has not been "baptized," are called "Jewish" (*judia*); they are said to be distasteful to the saints, as well as completely powerless.

When he acquires his stones, each santero takes an oath to protect them constantly and to feed them at least annually. When the saints are fed, the warm blood of the sacrificial animals is allowed to flow onto the stones. The blood must be *caliente* or warm, so that the invisible fluid of the stones may be increased. Following the blood sacrifices there is drumming, singing, and dancing, usually for three successive nights, during which the possessions take place. A large number of possessions is desirable because it is a sign that the saints are well fed and satisfied, and also because the fluid and power of the stones are increased by the presence of saints in possession. The major cult rituals of santeria center about the annual feeding of the saints through the stones.

Resguardo or protective charms are also prepared with herbs and blood in direct contact with the stones from which they acquire some of the invisible fluid. By wearing prepared strings of beads or other objects on the body, the protective power of the saints can be kept nearby at all times. Before and after the annual feeding of the saints, the stones are washed in herbs and the *resguardo* of the cult members may be washed at the same time. The cult members themselves are prepared for possession by washing their heads with herbs and "feeding" their heads with blood. The head may be washed at other times without herbs, but before it can be "fed" it must be treated with herbs. Herbs are also used for brews and baths, and for the cleansing of the house that follows the annual feeding of the saints. A knowledge of the properties and uses of the herbs is as important to a santero as a knowledge of the rituals, the songs, or the language.

To strengthen the fresh mixture of herbs and water used in washing or baptizing the stones and the *resguardo,* a little of the infusion containing the herbs and blood from the sacrifices made in previous years may be added. This infusion, known by the Yoruba name *omi ero,* is the most powerful liquid in santeria, and is said to contain all seven "*potencias.*" It is added to after each annual feeding and preserved for future washings and baptisms, for removing evil influences, and for washing the hands of the *matador* and his assistant before they begin the killing of the sacrificial animals. Unless the hands of the *matador* have been washed in *omi ero,* and unless his knife and the stones themselves have been washed in herbs, the gods will not drink the blood through the stones.

Each saint has its own particular herbs, its own type of stone, and special animals which are its favorite food. The function of the herbs is to cleanse and refresh and to prepare individuals or objects for contact with the saints. The blood is the food of the saints. The stones are the objects through which the saints are fed, and in which their power resides. One might perhaps find parallels to these three elements in the consecrated stone (*el ara*) in the Catholic altar, in the blood of Christ as symbolized in the Eucharist, and in the burned palm leaves used on Ash Wednesday. The differences, however, are so marked that one may safely say that the blood, the stones, and the herbs as they are employed in santeria are foreign to Catholicism.

Among both the Lucumi in Cuba and the Yoruba in Africa there are certain saints for whom objects other than stones are actually fed, e.g. Ogun, for whom iron is used. The Cuban concept of the stones (*piedras*) is equivalent not to the Yoruba *okuta* (stone) but to the Yoruba *iponri,* which is the material object which represents the power of a deity and to which its sacrifices are actually presented. The place of blood sacrifices in African religion and of herbs in African magic is widely recognized, although the use of herbs in the worship of the African deities is less well documented. Nevertheless, "the three hundred and seventy-six different kinds of leaves which are used for the making of a *vodu*" are mentioned for Dahomey, with the following footnote

> whatever the exactitude of the figure, that leaves are of great importance in the *vodu* cult has been seen in the description of the making of a *vodu* and in the quoted phrase, "If you knew the story of all the leaves of the forest, you would know all there is to be known about the gods of Dahomey."[3]

Until further work has been done on the religious use of herbs in Africa, it is not possible to show specific similarities between Africa and Cuba in the particular herbs associated with each saint comparable to those found in the types of stones and the animals whose blood is most appropriate for individual saints. Specific correspondences are also to be seen in the types of beads and colors associated with the individual saints; the names, characteristics, and mythological interrelationships of the saints; the techniques of divination; the prayers and songs in the Yoruba language; as well as in the patterns of drumming, dancing, and possession previously mentioned. The details of these and other elements of santeria ritual and belief, however, do not concern us here.

We may then, take the use of stones, blood and herbs in santeria as African in origin and turn to the second and more important problem. Is the emphasis on these three elements as the focus of Cuban santeria also derived from Africa? Here we can speak with less assurance in terms of our present knowledge of West Africa. On the basis of my own field work among the Yoruba, stones (or *iponri*), blood, and herbs do not seem to assume the importance that they hold in the minds of Jovellanos worshippers. The mythology or theology of the gods, the prayers and the verbal formulæ, and the rituals themselves seem of equal, if not greater importance. In the full reports of Herskovits and Rattray on the neighboring Dahomeans and Ashanti these three elements are discussed, but again not in such a way as to indicate their importance as the focus of religion.

We may here be confronted by an illustration of a point made by Herskovits,[4] that the study of Negro cultures in the New World not only provides leads for further research in Africa, but also throws into relief the important values of the African cultures from which they are derived in a way that cannot be seen in Africa because of the wealth of institutional and ritual detail. It is possible, but not highly probable, that the real focus of West African ritual has so far escaped the scholars working in Africa, while it stands in clear relief in Cuba. This can be finally settled only by a reëxamination of the importance of stones, blood, and herbs in Africa through further field work.

Another possibility, however, presents itself: that in contact with Catholicism, the distinctive features of African religion, which set santeria apart from the rituals of the Church, have been given additional emphasis and have come to be regarded as the core of the religion. In other words, the focal elements of Cuban santeria may not represent a carry-over of the focus of West African religion, but a shift in emphasis which has occurred as a result of culture contact. In this instance, acculturation would have resulted, not in a coalescence of beliefs, such as is represented by the syncretism of African deities and Catholic saints, the use of plaster images, chromolithographs, candles, and holy water, or the recitation of the Lord's Prayer and Hail Mary in santeria rituals, but a shift in the opposite direction.[5] The present evidence is largely negative, but this interpretation is at least plausible.

If it is correct, an interesting psychological point is raised, since the members of santeria cults regard themselves as Catholics. All informants, without exception, stated unqualifiedly that they were Catholics, yet they stressed the importance of those very elements of their faith and ritual which set it apart from that of the Catholic Church. This would seem to be another illustration of Herskovits' concept of ambivalence in New World Negro cultures. While Catholicism is outwardly embraced, it is inwardly rejected; and the stones, the blood, and the herbs have become, perhaps unconsciously, a rallying point for the defense of the African religious tradition.

Notes:

1. Read before the meeting of the American Anthropological Association in Toronto, Canada, December 30, 1948.

2. Field work in Cuba for three months during the summer of 1948 was made possible by a grant from the Viking Fund, which also assisted in the preparation of this manuscript. Field work among the Yoruba in 1937–38 was made possible by the Social Science Research Council of New York City. The sponsorship of both of these field trips by Northwestern University is also acknowledged.

3. Melville J. Herskovits, *Dahomey* (New York, 1938), p. 195.

4. Melville J. Herskovits, "The Contribution of Afroamerican Studies to Africanist Research" (*American Anthropologist*, Vol. 50, pp. 1–10, 1948).

5. This would be no less significant as far as the dynamics of culture is concerned if further work in Cuba should show that it is not true throughout the island, or even elsewhere in the New World.

27. Carnival in Nineteenth Century Trinidad¹

The following is a discussion of the form and content of the institution of Carnival in Trinidad, viewed from the point of view of the changing culture and social structure of that island.

PRE-EMANCIPATION SOCIETY AND ITS CARNIVAL—1783-1833

We are not here concerned with the origins of Carnival outside Trinidad, and so on account of the insignificance of the population before 1783, and the lack of evidence of any institution of Carnival before that date, we may use it as a zero-point. The population was as follows:—

	White	Coloured	Slave	Indian
Spanish	126	245	310	2,000

During the next 14 years following the opening of Trinidad, a Spanish colony, to Catholic settlers of all kinds, the main immigrants were (a) French colonists and their slaves from Dominica, St. Vincent, Martinique and Grenada, unsettled on account of hostilities between Great Britain and France, (b) French white and coloured planters and their slaves upset by the revolutionary disturbances in St. Domingo, Guadeloupe and Martinique and (c) republicans, and other unsettled persons from islands temporarily held by the French and at that time (around 1794) returning to British rule. These included Jacobins, and "Brigands" as they were called by the British, i.e., bands of ex-slaves who resisted or fled to Trinidad when the

SOURCE: Reprinted from *Caribbean Quarterly*, Vol. 4, Nos. 3 and 4 (1956): 176–93, by kind permission of the author and *Caribbean Quarterly* (University of the West Indies, Mona, Jamaica).

British re-took their islands. The slaves were mainly Creole. Thus, in 1797 the population was:

	White	Coloured	Slave	Indian
Spanish	150	200	300	1,127
French	2,250	4,700	9,700	

In the period which followed, changes took place: (*a*) a considerable number of French white and coloured free citizens left the island for the Spanish Main (*b*) English carpet baggers, merchants, a few planters bringing slaves, and free coloured from British islands entered (*c*) a large number of slaves was imported direct from Africa (*d*) a large immigration of coloured people from the Spanish Main entered the island.

	White	Coloured	Slave	Indian
Spanish	505	1,751		
French	1,093	2,925	20,464	?
British	663	599		

The most marked additions to the population in the period which followed were (*a*) the arrival of American freed slaves who had served with British Forces 1812-13 in Virginia, (*b*) the settlement of disbanded African soldiers of the West India Regiment and of freed slaves taken from slave-trading vessels, (*c*) a large influx of peons from the Spanish Main, a proportion of whom returned thither.

By 1826 the population was:

	White	Coloured	Slave	Indian
Spanish or Colonies	450	2,154	Creole:	
French or Colonies	617	2,150	15,291	655
British or Colonies	938	1,594		
African		1,450	African:	
American		1,056	7,832	

The nature of Trinidad society just before capitulation is important because, despite the many and varied immigrations, a pattern of rural life was firmly drawn by the French, whose exceptional pioneering work established, between 1783 and 1797, 468 plantations, covering 85,000 acres, of which 37,960 were already cultivated, with 159 sugar mills, and 130, 103 and 70 undertakings growing and processing coffee, cotton and tobacco respectively.

The most reliable account of this society is given by Borde in his *Histoire de la Trinidad.*

He depicts the French planters of Trinidad as a true rural aristocracy, "authorised to wear the sword of Louis XIV . . . , a veritable aristocracy of colour no whit less urbane or distinguished than an aristocracy of blood". They appear to have been a close-knit group, and they sought their rewards in their country of adoption, establishing a fairly comfortable standard of living and maintaining "vastes mais modestes manoirs champêtres", usually near rivers, with orchards and pasturage near the house. Whilst they continued to import their wines, they adapted the cuisine of Bordeaux to creole fish, meat, fruit and vegetables and learnt the use of the local flora for making "tisanes" and medicaments. The women, following the style of Bordeaux, wore white, but adorned their heads and necks with the brightly coloured "madras" and foulard. The older men continued to wear culottes, with pigtail or powdered hair, though the young men took to the pantaloon which was becoming popular in France at the end of the century. The cordial relations existing between the French plantocracy were expressed in varied "divertissiments", concerts, balls, dinners, hunting parties and "fêtes champêtres", and these were especially concentrated into the Carnival season, which lasted from Christmas to Ash Wednesday. This was in the dryest and coolest time of the year, before the worst rush of the cutting of the canes begins, and when least attention needed to be given to agriculture. The gatherings of the Carnival season were characterised by "a contagious gaiety, brilliant verbal sallies, and comic buffoonery which made the subject of the morrow's conversations."

We must be on our guard against a tendency natural in Borde's description to idealise French society in Trinidad, but there are clear indications that its members, emerging from their homes, or entertaining therein, sought and found recognition amongst their peers by excelling in elegance, sophistication and ability in the arts, conversation, dress, music and hospitality, according to provincial French standards, rather than regarding the West Indian colonies as places to be tolerated for the sake of a quick fortune, the fruits of which might be enjoyed in the metropolitan country, as was often the outlook of the English planter or absentee owner. It was characteristic of the French through most of the Nineteenth Century, that they should send their children to school in France *at all costs.* Certainly Port-of-Spain seems to have had blossoming pretensions to a gay and cultural urbanity during the first three decades of the Nineteenth Century, based on a considerable prosperity. Eckstein, some of whose notes were published posthumously in the *Port-of-Spain Gazette* during 1840, speaks facetiously of this development as follows: "At this period of the history" (approximately 1806) "of our Experimental Island, the town Society could not yet boast of sufficient stock of elegants to assume a *bon ton* and the *haut ton,* to which it has since so rapidly aspired, and was scarcely suspected. The seductive soirées at Mademoiselle Annie's—the fascinating Ninon of Trinidad, collected at this time the male beau-monde round her sofa, or the harpsichord . . ." and of the 1820's "Satiated with the ordinary indulgences of the human appetite, the relish of higher society became so exquisite, that while scores of old pianofortes stand silent . . . , nothing less will now soothe the modern ear than Parisian-tuned harps, from the Atelier of an Ekhard. None other must touch the bosom of the finished boarding-school Miss, except a pedal lyre . . . By the sacred honour of the lovely muses I aver, that the Apollos and the Amphions of Musical Antiquity never consumed so many strings as are snapped at one soirée of the tight-laced dilettantes of our Port-of-Spain". And Colonel Capadose, who was in Trinidad during the 1830's, reports in his *Sixteen years in the West Indies,* that at one period (probably early 1820's) there were three theatres and five companies in Port-of-Spain, two of which were professional, one being French and the other English.

Although the French upper class suffered dilution at the hands of the British Planters who entered Trinidad on a large scale, particularly after 1802, they remained in the ascendant in the country areas, and in the City they seem to have set the tone. The "English Party" continued to be regarded by the Governors and the British Government as "adventurers" and their request for the replacement of Spanish Law by English Law was not acceded to until much later. Governor Woodford (1815-26) was at great pains to preserve cordial relations with the Roman Catholic authorities (most of his subjects being such) and was a personal friend of the Roman Catholic Bishop.

But while the pattern of the white upper class was modified somewhat, the position of the Free Coloured underwent great changes following the Capitulation.

Under the Spanish Regime, they ranged from the coloured and black slave-owning planters and traders to artisans and petty cultivators. Some of the planters came from families which had been substantial property holders in their place of origin, and were similar in language, customs, dress, &c., to the French, though smaller in number. In their new homeland, these planters predominated in the Naparimas (South Trinidad), and it was they, according to Borde, who built the best of the early town houses in Port-of-Spain. According to earlier Spanish law the Free Coloured were a legal class subject to a variety of legal restrictions as against whites, but nevertheless having certain rights secured to them. But the Cedula of Population (1783), and later the terms of Capitulation to Great Britain superseded this discriminatory legislation and endowed them with legal status almost equal to that enjoyed by the whites. Chacon, the Spanish Governor, undoubtedly administered the law in this spirit. Free Coloured were commissioned in the Militia, and, although they lived socially separate from the Whites, yet Borde insists that "il est de tradition authentique la plus parfaite entente existait alors entre . . . les deux fractions de la societé coloniale".

The artisan class, though definitely of more humble condition, were much favoured in a decade of exceptionally rapid entrepreneurial development, involving new buildings, installation of machinery, &c., and enjoyed good wages, respect and responsibility. They became owners of artisan-slaves, and were able to acquire other property in land and real estate so that they or their children could progress towards entry into the *societé de couleur*.

By 1826 the content of the Free Coloured section was radically different. It still included these two classes of culturally-French, amounting to a quarter of the legal category of Free-Coloured. A further quarter were from the Spanish Main, consisting of unsettled peons, who worked by contract as woodcutters, or hunted for livelihood, or frequented Port-of-Spain, and others uprooted by Civil War. Coloured artisans, overseers, bookkeepers, cultivators, &c., from the British West Indian Colonies amounted to about a fifth, freed American Negroes and Africans from the West Indian Regiment about one-eighth each.

This varied assortment of free coloured presented a serious problem to successive Governors, but all appeared to share a common policy in one respect, namely, they sought to remould the society into a clearly hierarchical structure in which the élite should be exclusively white, and the free coloured excluded from the social and political privileges of the élite. The successive steps in implementing this policy were: (1) They no longer received commissions in the Militia; (2) The office of Alguacil, or police, feared by slave and despised by white, was ascribed exclusively to them; (3) The "Fandango licence", a discriminatory regulation, was passed making it necessary for "any free coloured proprietor wishing to give a dancing party in the night" to "first obtain permission to do so from the Commandant of the Quarter", and at the same time they were "forbidden under penalty of a fine of $25 to admit any slave to the party"; (4) During the long struggle to decide whether Trinidad should continue to be governed under Spanish law, or should adopt a form of British Colonial Constitution, the free coloured felt themselves particularly threatened by the demands for the latter, not merely because they feared the loss of privileges, but because they feared the racist temper of the "English Party". In 1810, knowing that the introduction of British Laws was being proposed, they addressed the Governor in the most loyal and respectful manner requesting permission to forward to H.M. the King "a dutiful, loyal and affectionate address imploring him to extend unto them, under whatever system of jurisprudence His Royal wisdom may deem most expedient for the future government of the colony, such a participation in its operation as may secure to them their personal security and social happiness". This request was repressed curtly by Hislop the Governor, who proceeded to appoint a Commission to enquire into the personal characters and antecedents of the signatories, several of whom were subsequently banished on flimsy pretexts.

Spanish laws remained in force, but in 1822 Orders in Council were published which produced profound dissatisfaction, amongst the provisions of which was the establishment of an open Court of Alcaldes-in-Ordinary to try summarily and inflict punishment, including corporal punishment, street labour in chains, &c., for petty theft, and numerous breaches of regulations, on free persons of colour.

Dr. J. B. Phillip, accepted leader of the free coloured, headed a deputation to Sir Ralph Woodford on this above subject on behalf of 13,392 citizens in 1822.

In 1826 a Royal Proclamation was published removing "certain vexatious regulations", respecting free people of colour. Thereafter, although the legal status of the free man, the slave, and later the apprentice and the indentured labourer were differentiated, race and colour were no longer legally crucial factors.

Throughout the period under consideration (1784-1833) Carnival was an important institution for Whites and Free Coloured, particularly in the towns. But it was threatened by the special position of Christmas under British rule, which, during the first three decades of the nineteenth century seems to have predominated at the urban apex of society as the leading festival of the year.

This was due to the existence of a tradition in the colonies that Martial Law was enforced during the Christmas season. Amongst the English, Christmas—and amongst the Scots, New Year—were seasons of rowdy merry-making and licence, and in the older British West Indian colonies, the slaves were given considerable freedom for dancing, pageantry, parades and traditional good natured strife between plantation bands. Two concomitants of this tradition were (1) that while the practice of duelling was contrary to Civil Law, it was permitted under military law, and there was a tendency to put inter-personal conflicts which demanded duels into cold storage until Christmas; (2) the Christmas season came to be a time at which the whole status system was given outward expression through the vehicle of the Militia. All free persons were obliged by law to enrol. On account of the mustering of the militia, business was at a standstill, and the occasion became one not only for serious military duties, but also for balls, al fresco pleasures, and a variety of other amusements. In 1821—the Editor of the *Port-of-Spain Gazette* apologises on January 10th for his failure to comment on recent events, but pleads "military duties" in extenuation. In that year Martial Law lasted from December 23 to January 8. In the Militia General Order issued on January 1, the Governor and Commander-in-Chief says he had wished to relieve "the Militia from their permanent duties on 2nd instant. The assembly of the General Court Martial, which unfortunately became indispensable, and the duties which crowded upon it, prevented this intention; and the Commander-in-Chief laments that so many well conducted officers and men should have been exposed to a protracted and severe duty by the heedlessness of a few". In that year the First Division of Militia was reviewed on the Cabildo Pasture on December 30. A day each was allotted for the review of the Second and Third divisions, belonging to Diego Martin and St. Joseph areas respectively, and the First Division was reviewed along with the regular Third West Indian Regiment. "His

Excellency with his usual liberality, caused tents to be erected on the
ground for the accommodation of spectators, who were plentifully
supplied with refreshments . . . The Regiments going through their
manoeuvres and firing, and the charging of the Cavalry, together with
the novel appearance of the tents, and the assemblage of ladies formed
a scene highly interesting". "On Saturday evening (Jan. 6) an elegant
Ball and entertainment was given to a select party by H. E. the Governor at his seat at St. Ann's . . . the Band of the 3rd West Indian
attended. There were fireworks on the lawn . . . and dancing up till
a late hour . . ."

Or, to quote an anonymous rhymester of 1846 (*Port-of-Spain
Gazette,* 20th January, 1846):

"When Xmas came in former days
The time for Martial schoolery
Three guns from Fort George battery were
The signal for Tomfoolery.

Then all our towns folk turned as red
As lobsters in hot water;
And, had there been an enemy
There might have been much slaughter!

But after vapouring a week
The scarlet fever vanished,
And till next Christmas Martial thoughts
Were from each bosom banished."

Carnival, as the end of the social season, was also marked at the
apex of society by elaborate balls to which was added the custom of
masking and disguising. But the major part of the Carnival activities
consisted of house to house visiting and street promenading, on foot
or in carriages, witticisms, playing of music and dancing, and a variety
of frolics and practical jokes.

An English officer in 1826 writes to his friend: "I wish, Bayley,
you had been here in the time of the carnival; you have no idea of
the gaiety of the place in that season. Ovid's Metamorphoses were
nothing compared to the changes that took place in the persons of
the Catholics of Trinidad. High and low, rich and poor, learned and
unlearned, all found masking suits for the Carnival. A party of ladies,

having converted themselves into a party of brigands, assailed me in my quarters and nearly frightened me out of my wits. I was just going to cut and run when Ensign *——— who was with me, not knowing the joke, and thinking they were so many devils come to take him before his time, drew his sword . . ." (Bayley: *Four Years in the West Indies.*)

Fraser, in a memo to Governor Freeling on *History of the Origin of the Carnival.* [Colonial Office Original Correspondence Trinidad (Co. 295) Vol. 289—Trinidad No. 6460. On the outside of the Memo is written "This might go to Mr. Hamilton." (Commissioner sent out in 1881 to enquire into the Canboulay Riots) "Mr. Fraser I have understood was a very inefficient Head of the Police and he naturally stands for masterly inactivity. E.W. 14.4.] after referring to the surprising anomaly that "in an Island which never belonged to France even for a single day the French element so largely predominates", continues, "Such being the original elements of the population it will be easily understood that the habits and customs of the people of the Colony resembled those of the mother countries from whence they were derived and amongst these was the Carnival."

In former days and down to the period of the emancipation of the slaves the Carnival was kept up with much spirit by the upper classes. There are many persons still living who remember the Masked Balls given at St. Ann's by the Governor, Sir Ralph Woodford, and also that the leading Members of Society used on the days of the Carnival to drive through the streets of Port-of-Spain masked, and in the evenings go from house to house which were all thrown open for the occasion.

It is necessary to observe that in those days the population of the Colony was divided into the following categories, Whites, Free persons of Colour, Indians and Slaves.

The free persons of Colour were subjected to very stringent Regulations and although not forbidden to mask, were yet compelled to keep to themselves and never presumed to join in the amusements of the privileged class. The Indians kept entirely aloof, and the slaves except as onlookers, or by special favour when required to take part, had no share in the Carnival which was confined exclusively to the upper class of the community."

Fraser's account is supported by the evidence, including that of Borde, and that of Ofuba the Chantwell, a slave, who sang of the "nèg dèyè pòtla"—the slave behind the door, mentioned in Mitto

Sampson's article. Sampson also heard tell of Jack Bowell, a slave, famous for his marionette dance, who was called in to dance at Carnival parties, and who was advertised as a "marron" or runaway from January 14, 1826, in the *Port-of-Spain Gazette* at the end of that month (during the Carnival season).

It is most difficult to find out the nature of the disguises used at that period. The Ball at Mrs. Bruce's in 1831 was attended by "the beauty and fashion of Port-of-Spain composing a motley assemblage of elegantly dressed ladies, lovely Swiss damsels, French Marquises, English noblemen, grooms, postillions, priests and Friars . . .", but apparently there was a local creole element in Carnival at this time also. Writing in 1881 (*Port-of-Spain Gazette* 26. 3. 1881) an anonymous correspondent, in discussing the origin of "Canboulay" or "Cannes Brulées" tells us that in those days (1820's) "the élite of our society took an active part in the carnival. The favourite costumes of our mothers and grandmothers was the graceful and costly one of the "mulâtresse" of the time; whilst gentlemen adopted that of the "nègres de jardin", or in creole "nègre jardin" or field labourer. In that costume, the gentlemen often figured in the "bamboola", in the "giouba" and the "calinda". It is traditional in our old families that General P. aide-de-camp to Governor Woodford, and Commander in Chief of the militia, with the P.G. who, though then 70 years of age, was still strong and robust, both excelled in the above-mentioned dances. These pretended *nègres de jardin* were wont to unite in bands, representing the camps of different estates, and with torches and drums to represent what did actually take place on the estates when a fire occurred in a plantation. In such cases the gang of the neighbouring estates proceed alternately accompanied with torches at night to the estate which had suffered to assist in the grinding of the burnt canes before they became sour."

Fraser makes no reference to an aristocratic version of Canboulay, but traces the later Carnival Canboulay to the same original source in the plantation. "In the days of slavery whenever fire broke out upon an Estate, the slaves on the surrounding properties were immediately mustered and marched to the spot, horns and shells were blown to collect them and the gangs were followed by the drivers cracking their whips and urging them with cries and blows to their work."

"After Emancipation the negroes began to represent this scene as a kind of commemoration of the change in their condition, and the procession of the 'cannes brulées' used to take place on the night of the 1st August, the date of their emancipation, and was kept up much for the same reason as the John Canoe dance in Jamaica.

After a time the day was changed and for many years past the Carnival days have been inaugurated by the 'Cannes Brulées'."

There are certain contrasts and similarities as between the two festivals of Christmas and Carnival of the pre-emancipation era which are relevant to the study of both during the subsequent 120 years. (1) Martial Law was declared at Christmas, and this not only broke the routine of daily work and allowed time for parties, but it also compelled participation of all free people in ceremonies (musters) which exactly demonstrated the order of social prestige after the pattern which the élite chose to enforce, thus stressing the downgrading of the middle and upper class free-coloured who still cherished the recollection of formal equality of status before capitulation, and, they claimed, guaranteed to them by its articles. On the other hand, Carnival enabled all the non-slave population to adopt fictitious social rôles, and indeed, in masking on the street at least, to overstep the social boundaries of colour. (2) The celebration of Christmas was closely associated with Church attendance, whereas Carnival was not, though observance of Lenten abstinences during the period following Carnival, appears to have been meaningful and acceptable to large sections of the population. Thus Carnival was more out of reach of this second superstructural agency. (3) The slaves were excluded from Carnival, but whether in African, or in Creole and European style were universally given licence at Christmas time, for dancing, feasting at the master's expense, some freedom of movement, and elaborate costuming.

After Emancipation, Christmas Martial Law lingered on, but with the suspension of the Militia Laws in 1846, the public aspect of Christmas pomp disappeared. What remained were the house-to-house visiting in the French tradition, with the singing of "quesh" or "Cantiques de Noel, and in the Spanish tradition, with the serenading with stringed instruments, and the family feasts on Christmas Eve.

Carnival however, had a different development.

POST-EMANCIPATION CARNIVAL

"After the Emancipation of the Slaves things were materially altered, the ancient lines of demarcation between the classes were obliterated and as a natural consequence the carnival degenerated into a noisy and disorderly amusement for the lower classes". (Fraser).

Immediately before Emancipation the free community was split sharply and the various factions were quarrelling. The *Port-of-Spain Gazette* of 1832 makes no mention of Carnival, the masquerade itself invades the columns of the newspaper as correspondents refer to one another as "Sir Richard Donkey", "Demon of Dullness", "Printer's Devil", "Sir Petulant Penman", &c.

In 1833 during January, "an attempt was made by Mr. Peake (Assistant to the Chief of Police) to check the shameful violation of the Sabbath by the lower order of the population, who are accustomed about this time of year to mask themselves and create disturbances on a Sunday. He arrested two persons who were in masks and lodged them in the Cage. On his return from performing this necessary duty his house was assaulted by a large concourse of rabble, who broke all the windows, and attacking Mr. Peake, pelted, beat and otherwise ill treated this officer" (*P.O.S. Gazette* 22.1.1833).

Shortly after this incident, there appeared in the *Port-of-Spain Gazette* a peremptory Police notice forbidding the wearing of masks before 18th February, ending "Any person being found masked in the streets" (before this date) "will be immediately arrested and dealt with according to the Law". After Carnival 1834 the Editor of the *Port-of-Spain Gazette* comments "Nothing can more decidedly mark the great change which has taken place within this Colony than the want of spirit, and we might add, deficiency of elegant bustle, which was to be seen during the Carnival week in olden times". The writer walks through the town looking for persons *in character*. All he found deserving notice was a party of negroes intended to represent the Artillery. He looks for an imitation or caricature of reality, and has little praise for what he sees except "the two jolly Subs., (subalterns) who were done to the life". Marching and wheeling were "defective" and "the mockery of the best Militia Band that has ever been embodied in the West was in very bad taste". He decides, however, that there was no attempt at ridicule, but that the whole thing was a piece of fun. What is noticeable is the complete change of tone with regard to Carnival, from the former unctuous self-congratulation (expressed in phrases such as "the morning breeze of wit, usually breaking with the dawn of day, the periodical flaws of punning puffs . . . . . . were carefully concentrated in that more spirited epic style of jocosity to which character and dresses give the pantomimic zest") to the apprehensive expectation of disgust tempered by condescension in case of disappointment.

During the next 30 years, the morphology of Carnival is difficult to trace. Certain facts, however, stand out clearly. The white élite of the society withdrew from public participation, and the comments of their journalistic representatives became increasingly hostile and condescending right through till the 1890's. It is true that on a few occasions brilliant fancy-dress balls were held, but the connection of these with the traditional Carnival became remote.

At the other end of the social scale, however, participation in Carnival increased, resulting in a change of content. The first public reaction to this appears in 1838, when Carnival was still permitted to run for three days (Sunday, Monday and Shrove Tuesday) by "Scotchman" who writes to the *Port-of-Spain Gazette* indignant over the "desecration of the Sabbath", and on whose letter the Editor comments: ". . . . . We will not dwell on the disgusting and indecent scenes that were enacted in our streets—we will not say how many we saw in a state so nearly approaching nudity as to outrage decency and shock modesty—we will not particularly describe the African custom of carrying a stuffed figure of a woman on a pole, which was followed by hundreds of negroes yelling out a savage Guinea song (we regret to say that nine-tenths of these people were Creoles)—we will not describe the ferocious fight between the "Damas" and the "Wartloos" which resulted from this mummering —but we will say at once that the custom of keeping Carnival by allowing the lower order of society to run about the streets in wretched masquerade belongs to other days, and ought to be abolished in our own".

By 1843 the threat to the Sabbath had been broken by an order restricting masking thereafter to two days instead of three, and one of the results of this was that from this period on, Carnival was to begin on Sunday night. (*See* above on origin of Canboulay); but the only substantial comment during the decade came from the *Port-of-Spain Gazette* in 1848 when it is complained that "since midnight on Sunday, this festival has broken the slumber of our peaceable citizens with its usual noisy revelry and uproarious hilarity". No mention is made of obscenities, brawls or threatening behaviour, but a valuable reference is made to "bands of music (soi-disant) including those inelegant instruments, the tin kettle and salt box, the bangee and shack shack.[2]

The degree of participation by the coloured middle-class is difficult to ascertain. The evidence seems to point to the following situations: (1) Carnival remained for them an important season of festivity and sociality, consisting of house to house visiting with small combinations of musical instruments, playing in the tradition of the Spanish Main, and also a variety of 19th Century Dances from Europe. It was cherished on account of the traditions of an earlier period when the standing of the class was less overshadowed. (2) Whilst avoiding association in the streets with the masses, this class was deeply resentful of any interference with Carnival by the Government, and was ready to use it if necessary as a means of indirect attack on the Governor and the upper (white) class whenever the tension rose.

In 1846, on account of the general unrest in the city and the numerous cases of arson, the practice of appearing masked in the streets for Carnival was expressly forbidden by the Governor, the writer in the *Port-of-Spain Gazette* commenting "we trust this will prove a final . . . . stop to the orgies which are indulged in by the dissolute of the town at this season of the year, under pretence of Masking", and then, three days later, presumably in response to representations, the paper points out that the prohibition does not prevent bands of maskers dressing up and going from house to house, putting on the masks as they get to the houses. This seems to suggest a tardy realisation by the paper that Carnival *in toto* could not be threatened, and that at least the house-to-house visiting by the respectable class should be tolerated.

Carnival in 1847 was fortunately witnessed by Day, who gives us quite useful details of the various masquerades in *Five Years Residence in the West Indies.* "I was residing", he writes "in Trinidad during the Carnival, which commenced on Sunday, the 7th of March, at midnight. I had seen the Carnival at Florence, at Syra in Greece, and in Rome; and was now about to witness a negro masquerade, which, from its squalid splendour, was not unamusing, cheapness being the grand requisite. The maskers parade the streets in gangs of from ten to twenty, occasionally joining forces in procession. The primitives were negroes, as nearly naked as might be, bedaubed with a black varnish. One of this gang had a long chain and padlock attached to his leg, which chain the others pulled. What this typified, I was unable to learn; but, as the chained one was occasionally thrown down on the ground, and treated with a mock bastinadoing it probably represented slavery. Each masker was armed with a good stout quarterstaff, so that they could overcome one-half more police than themselves, should occasion present itself. Parties of negro ladies dance through the streets, each clique distinguished by bodices of the same colour. Every negro, male and female, wore a white flesh-coloured mask, their woolly hair carefully concealed by handkerchiefs; this, contrasted with the bosom and arms, was droll in the extreme. Those ladies who aimed at the superior civilization of shoes and stockings, invariably clothed their pedal extremities in pink silk stockings and blue, white, or yellow kid shoes, sandled up their sturdy legs. For the men, the predominating character was Pulichinello; every second negro, at least, aiming at playing the continental Jack-pudding. Pirates too were very common, dressed in Guernsey frocks, full scarlet trowsers, and red woollen cap, with wooden pistols for arms. From the utter want of spirit, and sneaking deportment of these bold corsairs, I presumed them to have come from the Pacific. Turks also there were, and one Highlander, a most ludicrous caricature of the Gael, being arrayed in a scarlet coat, huge grenadier cap, a kilt of light blue chintz, striped with white, a most indescribable philibeg, black legs of course, and white socks bound with a dirty pink ribbon. There were also two grand processions, having triumphal "wains", one of which was to commemorate the recent marriage of a high law-officer; the other, judging from the royal arms in front (worth a guinea of anybody's money, if only for the painting —the lion looking like a recently drowned puppy), and a canopy of red glazed calico, trimmed with a silver tinsel, shading a royal pair, who, in conscious majesty, sat within, represented the Sovereign pair of England. This brilliant cortege was marshalled forward by a huge negro, in a celestial dress, made after the conventional fashion of the angel Gabriel; and who stalked along spear in hand, as if intent on doing dire deeds. The best embodiments were the Indians of South America, daubed with red ochre; personified by the Spanish peons from the Main, themselves half Indian, as testified by their exquisitely small feet and hands. Many of these had real Indian quivers and bows, as well as baskets; and, doubtless, were very fair representatives of the characters they assumed. In this costume, children looked very pretty. One personation of Death, having what was understood to be a skeleton painted on a coal-black shape, stalked about with part of a horse's vertebra attached to him, and a horse's thigh bone in his hand; but his most telling movements only elicited shouts of laughter. I noticed that whenever a black mask appeared it was sure to be a white man. Little girls dressed à la jupe, in the *vrai créole* negro costume, looked very interesting. All parties with the assistance of bands of execrable music, made a tremendous uproar; and most of us were glad when the priestly saturnalia was over."

In this list of masqueraders we can distinguish the persisting elements, of both European and Creole provenance, and we can note the apparent absence of the characteristic elements of the late Nineteenth Century Carnival. Pulichinello, model for the typical costume of a number of different later masquerades, the pirates, the Highlander, the Turk and Death are all out of the European tradition. The first of these is the guise of foolery, but it also came to be regarded as simply suitable for Carnival. The pirates, the Turk, and Death are incursive forces which threaten social life, while the Highlander is the strange and exotic. The representation of Royalty is as much in vogue today for Carnival as it was in then, and the marriage of the law-officer is in the same spirit in that it offers homage to a great one, a theme which became popular again at the end of the Century. *Little girls à la jupe* presumably refers to the costume of the late eighteenth century planters' wives and which remained the festival costume of the country women until a few years ago. It is certainly interesting that "red" Indians were played by peons themselves with a high degree of naturalism. At the turn of the century, Red Indians were played mainly by Negroes, were extremely combative and had a repertoire of songs and speeches in what purported to be the language of the Guarahoons or Warraus. As for the primitives, it is not at all clear what masque is referred to here, but the chained man (representing the slave?) may well be the father of the Beast in the Devils' Band. The prevailing elements of the Carnival which was to follow, however, are not remarked by the observer. Whilst maskers carry staves symbolic of a defensive-offensive posture in case of trouble, there is no suggestion that conflict between bands was institutionalised, as was happening 25 years later, nor that individual conflicts were to be expected as previously during Christmas festivities. Transvestism is not noticeable, though masking in the opposite colour is usual, i.e. black as white and white as black. Obscenity is not mentioned.

During the next ten years, Carnival comes to be regarded as increasingly disreputable. The use of Carnival as a means of ridicule and derision of the pretentious emerges, and a demand grows amongst the dominant town group for its abolition. "None but the vilest of the vile . . . now think of appearing in public streets" to play mask, "why not forbid it altogether?" asks *A friend to mirth but enemy to folly* in the *Port-of-Spain Gazette* of January, 1856.

In 1858 Governor Keate, himself something of a bon-vivant, forbade masking. According to the *Gazette,* wearing masks in the streets had become a nuisance, and a pretext to other nuisances and offences against decency. More than two weeks before Carnival, a correspondent calling himself "DUTY" is complaining that "the noise, tumult and barbarian mirth which fill our streets every evening is greater than anything experienced hitherto even by the oldest member of the community". He notes that shopkeepers, in deference to the Governor's Order, are refraining from selling masks, but suggests that the police should stop the yelling and howling as well. The Order, however, was not obeyed. The police managed to arrest some maskers, and even persons who were not masked, as aiders and abettors, but the resistance was so turbulent that they were forced to withdraw. The crowds were finally dispersed by the arrival of the military. That resistance to authority on this occasion took an organised form is apparent from the fact that after the "defeat" of the police a band of Negroes 3,000-4,000 strong passing the police station, armed with hatchets, woodmen's axes, cutlasses, bludgeons and knives ". . . had the bold temerity to give a derisive shout of triumphant defiance to the police . . ." Another correspondent makes it tolerably clear that "Canboulay" had by this time become an established part of Carnival: "In our towns . . . commencing with the orgies on Sunday night, we have the fearful howling of a parcel of semi-savages emerging God knows where from, exhibiting hellish scenes and the most demoniacal representations of the days of slavery as they were 40 years ago: then using the mask the two following days as a mere cloak for every species of barbarism and crime . . ."

Like the Canboulay crisis, the incidents of Carnival 1858 became the occasion for the expression of various latent hostilities and the crystallisation of viewpoints. *The Trinidad Sentinel,* a paper owned and edited by a Negro group, attacks the administration of Governor Keate for acting on the assumption that this English Colony should be made English in language, custom, manners, religion and habits of thought, if necessary by force. The *Port-of-Spain Gazette* rebutting the charge of colour prejudice (resulting from a letter by a passing traveller in facetious yet insulting terms about Negroes) takes the view that Carnival is undesirable because Messrs. A and C down to R and S in the alphabet of respectability are exposed to the vagaries of X, Y and Z, i.e., the lowest class. It also points out that "our respectable community would dwindle down small enough if it was deprived of coloured and black, and the list of rogues sadly lessens if deprived of some few of white skin."

After the upsurge of pro-Carnival feeling which followed Governor Keate's attempt at suppression, there is a marked decline in its social magnitude. In 1861 "those who had formerly exercised their right of masking . . . to protest against the interference of the authorities with such a time-honoured absurdity had no incentive this season to appear, and the display fell entirely into the hands of the idle and the vagrant". While "not the usual number of unclad creatures who sometimes take advantage of the general laxity to outrage public decency" appeared on the streets, there was "the usual ostentatious promenade of those ladies whose existence is usually ignored or accepted as a necessary evil". The only costumes to be mentioned are "the fantastic mummers who represent the continental pierrots". In 1866, at the west end of the town, there was "a fair burlesque of a recent trial before the Supreme Court here, in which the law was somewhat stripped of its dignity by the extravagant imitation given of one or two of the legal and lay personages who were engaged on that trial". In 1870 there is a clear reference to Canboulay: "an unremitting uproar, yelling, drumming and blowing of horns", starting on Sunday night, by the *fundus* of the population. And the year after we are told that Carnival, which becomes yearly "more thoroughly contemptible" is "dying a natural death".

JAMETTE CARNIVAL

But Carnival did not die a natural death, and within six years the *Gazette* could write: "The thing which with the majority of the lower classes here goes under the name of masquerading acquires a new strength and fresh vitality every year that it is tolerated"; and ten years after, in 1881, occurred the famous Canboulay Riots, a pitched battle between the Police and the organised masqueraders, in which the interests of many groups within the community became involved, and which was a national issue of the greatest importance. We are not here concerned with the issues raised by the Riot, some of which were well dealt with by the Commissioner, Mr. Hamilton, who was sent out from Britain to investigate the "causes and disturbances in connection with the Carnival in Trinidad". It is, however, a matter of special interest that during this period Carnival, not only in Port-of-Spain but in other parts of the Island, came to have a distinct character and significance for the society as a whole. It is described as "Jamette Carnival" because of the wide currency at that time of the word (diamètre or diamèt) which was applied to what almost amounted to a class in the community, the people below the diameter of respectability, or the "underworld".

The newspapers of the period give a clear picture of the features of Carnival which disturbed the authorities most, and comments, exhortations and criticisms about appropriate counteraction by police, church, and other public authorities.

In 1874 two important features appear, one of which was to be a public concern for the next 40 years, namely "vagabondage" and "bands". The *Gazette* calls for a Vagrancy Law and a Reformatory School, asserting that the Government has allowed the situation to deteriorate so far that "the present order of things does not permit our mothers, wives and sisters to walk the streets and promenades without having their senses shocked by sights and sounds in the fullest sense of the word 'disgusting'". The leading article speaks about "herds of disreputable males and females . . . organised into bands and societies for the maintenance of vagrancy, immorality and vice, and some of the most noted members are those who have paid their footing by an unlimited number of visits to the Royal Gaol". A week later, immediately after Carnival, warfare between bands is denounced . . . "all around, the dwelling houses and shops had to be closed so as to keep out the stones and broken bottles and other missiles which were set in constant motion by the contending bands. There are, we are informed, about treble the number of bands as before and all were in active operation at the Carnival". To this writer, Carnival has indeed died out, owing to the loss of interest in it by the better classes, but "the name and season is but a cloak . . . . . for the shameless celebration of heathenish and vicious rites of some profligate god whose votaries rival in excesses the profligacies and brutalities of Pagan Rome or Heathen India".

In 1875 Fraser, who was then Inspector of Police, realising the threat to public order in these organised bands, proposed that the Habitual Criminals Act provisions should apply to persons guilty of offences and belonging to "the bands, which under different names infest the colony and are fruitful sources of immorality and crime". (*Royal Gazette* 15/6/75).

In 1876 the police are mildly criticised for unnecessary harshness especially in the use of batons, whilst in San Fernando Fitz Simmons, in charge of the Police, swore in 24 of the local gentry to intervene between two rival bands reported to be squaring up for war on Canboulay night.

In 1877 Fraser was dismissed as too weak, and was replaced by the redoubtable and famous Capt. Baker. It appears that he succeeded in controlling the Carnival in 1878 and 79 sufficiently to avoid breach of peace by the "savage and ferocious hordes", and the *Gazette's* wrath is concentrated on obscenities. With these successes behind him, he proceeded to attempt the suppression of Canboulay in 1880 by calling on the participants to surrender their sticks, drums and flambeaux, to which demand they agreed. It seems to have been widely believed that the police action of 1880 was a step towards the suppression of Canboulay and Carnival, and there is good reason to credit the conclusion of Hamilton that an organisation was formed to resist police interference, and that the bands planned to operate in concert in 1881, should the police take action against them. In the event, Capt. Baker, contrary to the wishes of the Governor, once again attempted to extinguish the torches carried by the Canboulay bands, and met organised and vibrant resistance which the police succeeded in quelling, though 38 of the detachment of 150 police were injured. On the following day the Governor, having ordered the confinement of the police to barracks, reinforced their numbers with 50 soldiers, and swore in 43 volunteer special constables, and then, at the instigation of the City Council, addressed the people at the Eastern Market, telling them that Government had no desire to interfere with their customs, and enjoining them to keep the peace.

By making a personal appeal to the masqueraders, the Governor took an important step towards re-establishing a relationship based on mutual consent between the populace in its Carnival formation and the authorities. The progress of Carnival towards its present position as a national festival, in which the total society is involved, is marked by similar accommodation. Fitz Simmons in San Fernando consulted with the leaders of the bands in San Fernando in 1881. In 1882 twelve band leaders in Port-of-Spain made a deputation to the *Port-of-Spain Gazette* asking the paper to use its influence on "some Bands, composed mostly of strangers" to prevent them inciting rioting and disorder. Indeed, Hamilton (the Commissioner) draws attention to the dangers inherent in the gap between the authority of a non-responsible colonial Government and the consent of the populace—"In my view it is of great importance, more especially in a Crown Colony where the people are not represented in the Government that they should as it were be taken into council in a matter of this *port,* as by this means I fully believe they may often be got to acquiesce in a course which they would resent if it were forced upon them".

From this point onwards, and most noticeably during the 1890's Carnival is gradually upgraded socially, and brought under more effective control by the Police. First Canboulay is stopped by forbidding street parading before 6 a.m. on the Monday morning. Bands of more than 10 men carrying sticks are forbidden, pierrots are obliged to get a police licence, *pisse-en-lit* bands, transvestism, obscene words and actions are prohibited. The paving of the roads and more effective collection of old bottles deprived the warlike traditional weapons. The white élite once again attend glittering Fancy Dress Balls at Government House, and the middle class citizens turn out in the afternoons, masked and disguised in their carriages, and accompanied by music bands. College boys form up in street bands, and store clerks organise Fancy Bands. The Carnival competition in Marine Square organised by Papa Bodi (or Councillor Bodu, author of *An Historical Account of Trinidad,* and a noted teetotaller) had the express aim of "improving the moral tone of Carnival". Lord Executor, still regarded as perhaps the greatest of Calypso singers, was a balladeer consistently moralising and didactic in tone. The business men of Port-of-Spain, San Fernando and Arima were now fully alive to the commercial benefits which Carnival showered upon them. From 1890 onwards Carnival moved spasmodically forward to the place it holds to-day.

Thus Carnival has changed its social form three times. After Emancipation the element which had predominated formerly withdrew from active participation, and those who had hitherto been debarred from participation joined in tentatively and experimentally. About thirty years later, Canboulay became established as the midnight overture to Carnival, and for the next twenty years its dominant element, whilst the moving spirits were the jamettes of the underworld. Towards the end of the Century the festival re-emerged and began to move "upwards" towards the position it occupies today, namely, acceptable to and practised by all the main sections of the community with the exception of the older generation of stricter Protestants and the less acculturated East Indians.

Of the first of these changes we have spoken already. The second arises out of the peculiar features of Trinidad's development. This can best be understood by use of the concepts "superstructure" and "folk", and their interaction. By *superstructure* we mean the interwoven administrative, legal, economic and religious institutions stemming from the colonising power (or its predecessor) and supported by it. By *folk* in this case we mean the people living within the above framework, the major part of whose culture has been transmitted to them from sources other than those of the superstructural institutions, though they may have appropriated some elements of the latter. The controlling positions in the superstructure are manned by an élite, usually having broad common interests including a shared general policy with regard to the society as a whole. In Trinidad the superstructure was by no means monolithic. There were persistent antagonisms between the British administration and the French landed gentry, and sharp collateral competition between the Catholic and Protestant religious institutions. But there was agreement as to public order, a hierarchical status system grouped beneath the office of Governor, a recognised system of behaviour as between one class and another, and the existence of an effective and productive labour force, Christianisation and "civilisation".

As for the folk, by 1860 its composition was extremely heterogeneous. There was a nuclear group consisting of (*a*) ex-slaves and their children, nurtured in both French and English plantation traditions, and speaking Patois and English respectively, mainly Trinidadian but including many immigrants from Barbados and other islands, and a few born Africans, (*b*) descendants of the non-slave small settlers, labourers and artisans of African and mixed descent, (*c*) free Africans to the number of about 7,000 who had immigrated during the preceding 20 years, and (*d*) Spanish speaking Peons. In spite of linguistic and other cultural differences, these four groups moved towards a form of Creole folk culture, symbolised by the tendency of most to adopt Patois (the area around Princes' Town, firmly settled by the descendants of the American Negro refugees, remained English speaking). Beyond this nucleus were other folk groups, Indians, Chinese and Portuguese all less ready to merge. Whilst estate work was being taken over increasingly by the East Indians, the nuclear group described above lived as occasional labourers, gardeners, semi-subsistence squatters, artisans in town and country, and fishermen. They were not under heavy economic pressure nor subject to tight control (as in the smaller islands without land resources) but were subject nevertheless to the influence of the institutions of the superstructure, such as law, churches and schools, and also to the influence of the manners and customs of the élite. Thus a type of rural life established itself in which law and custom, the African drum and the fiddle, the country doctor and the bush healer, the Catholic liturgy and the cults of Yorubaland and Dahomey, school English and Patois, lived side by side in easy accommodation, and a dual acculturative process took its course—creolisation, and accommodation to the institutions and standards of the superstructure.

The conditions of urban life in Port-of-Spain, however, give a characteristic twist to this process which is highly relevant to the history of Carnival. During the twenty years which followed 1860 the city prospered and the population grew from 16,457 to 29,468, of which latter figure 40 per cent were born outside Trinidad. The city itself was compact and well laid out in blocks fronted by tolerably well built houses and shops. But behind the perimeter of each block were barracks, often simply long wooden structures set against the walls dividing lots, and chopped up into rooms each of which might contain a family grouping belonging to the labouring classes. Just beyond the confines of the town were scattered ill controlled settlements, some of whose inhabitants worked in the city.

The barrack yard community, which still exists in Port-of-Spain, has a certain character. Accommodation is such that there can be little privacy, and the yard in the centre becomes a common living place. Water and latrines are common facilities, and there is competition for their use. Deep antagonisms develop which burst out at times, but are largely restrained. A sensitive public opinion develops in the yard and expresses itself sharply. Few actions escape its scrutiny. An order of domination is built up in a series of encounters between rivals. In many respects the barrack life of the city is closer to the life in the plantation barracks, except that the superimposed order and control of the latter is missing. Antagonisms are relaxed from time to time by fêtes, when the traditional pastimes of dancing, singing and stick-fighting are enjoyed, with liquor and food. At other times the antagonisms are projected into hostility to the outside world, particularly into sharp conflict with rival yards. Thus in the pre-Carnival period, during the rehearsals of the yard bands, the "chant-well" or leading singer was expected to insult and provoke rival bands in his "carisos" or Carnival songs, and when the yard stick-men went out into the streets, they sought out their rivals and single combats ensued. As a development from this, the bands of a region, led by the champions, would form up together. Canboulay itself was a fight between regional bands in which the rules of single combat were forgotten, and sticks, bottles and stones, &c., became the weapons of the bands and their followers both male and female. And finally Canboulay, in 1881 and on a few other occasions, took on a class character, with the disappearance of band rivalries in united action against the police. It was the singers, drummers, dancers, stickmen, prostitutes, matadors, bad-johns, dunois, makos and corner-boys, that is to say the jamette class, who dominated the Carnival of the day. It must be borne in mind that barrack-yard society was not isolated in one quarter of the town, but back to back with the houses of the middle and upper classes. Its members were not only constantly confronted with the display of cultural standards of the higher social ranks, and thus aware of their distance from them, but paradoxically closely associated with them, especially through the women who were servants and often the predominant influence in the lives of the children. On the other hand, middle-class men would seek liaisons with the women of—and on the fringes of—the jamette world, and some of them became patrons of yard bands and even stickmen themselves, or "jacket-men" as they were called on account of their superior class which was suitably marked in their dress.

Thus there existed a jamette sub-culture the ethos and myth-making character of which finds expression in Mitto Sampson's article. Its bearers were often recognisable by gait and dress, and were organised in bands for gambling, stickfighting and exploiting women. The qualities they boasted included skill and bravery in "bois" or stickfighting, sharpness of wit and repartee in conversation and in song, talent in dance and music, indifference to law and authority, and great sexual accomplishments. Some even were blasphemers and claimed to be of the Devil's party. Thus they represented the reversal of the values of respectability and a flamboyant rejection of the norms of the superstructure. The labouring classes generally, to which they belonged, aspired to respectability, but they felt excluded from enjoyment of the fruits of their aspirations by their colour, traditional mores, lack of education and poverty, and took vicarious delight, both covert and overt, in seeing it overturned and ridiculed by the jamettes.

It is not difficult to see why for 20 years Carnival was in the hands of the jamettes. The festival itself is the occasion for licence and the reversal of rôles and values. But after it ceased to be a significant part of the culture of the élite at Emancipation, it had no clear direction, content or organisation, and while its content accumulated from the folklore of the diverse groups in the island, its organisation fell to the organised bands of the underworld. The Canboulay clash was the logical outcome of this, and it had two important results. On the one hand, the government finally became aware of the importance of Carnival, and the implications of a licence to reverse values for a few days each year, so they set about purging and controlling it, whilst they attacked and broke the power of the jamettes' bands. On the other hand, police intervention on Canboulay night brought to a head several different types of existing hostility to the administration, causing new social groups to identify themselves nominally "the People" and the people's festival, so that Carnival began to be a symbol for a national sentiment shared by a broad section of the community, and in opposition to the administration, manned largely by British (i.e. "foreign") officials. Given the exclusion of warfare and practical obscenity from Carnival, these social groups began to participate, and Carnival has since moved forward to its present position as the most important and characteristic national festival of Trinidad.

Notes:

1. The main sources of information on which this article is based are the newspapers of Trinidad which are to be found in the vaults of the Registry at the Red House and the Trinidad Public Library. My thanks are due to the Registrar General, Mr. Hector Deeble, and the Librarian of the Public Library, Mr. Carlton Comma, for the help they gave, and to Miss Ursula Raymond for her help in excerpting information from the late Nineteenth Century papers.

2. bangee: probably the banja, or sanza, known to have been played in Trinidad by Africans, consisting of a box with steel or bamboo tongues of different pitches, grasped between the palms and plucked with two thumbs.
   shack-shack: maraccas.

ANNEMARIE DE WAAL MALEFIJT

28. Animism and Islam Among the Javanese in Surinam

During the last decades there has been a growing body of theory about the relationship between the "little tradition" of peasant and folk communities and the "great tradition" of major civilizations. Kroeber (1948:284) wrote that peasant societies are always "part-societies with part-cultures." Redfield (1956:68) added that "to maintain itself, peasant culture requires continual communication to the local community of thought originating outside of it." It may be validly asked what happens in a "part-culture" when "continual communication" is absent.

My fieldwork among the Javanese immigrants of Surinam, (Dutch Guiana), brought me in contact with such a culture. The Javanese came to Surinam between 1891 and 1939, in successive, almost yearly shipments. Their immigration was part of a large-scale effort of the Surinam Government to cover the existing labor shortage on the plantations which had developed after the abolition of slavery in 1863. Other groups of people had been brought to Surinam for the same purpose, notably Chinese and Indians, the latter locally called Hindustans. The importation of these Asiatic groups added to the large variety of ethnic groups already present in Surinam, including Carib and Arawak American Indians, African Bush Negroes and Creoles, and, of course, the ubiquitous Europeans, mostly now Dutchmen.

The Asiatic groups, the recruited laborers, all came on a five-year contract. After successfully concluding this contract, the workers had a choice between free transportation back to their countries of origin, or remaining in Surinam. The latter alternative was encouraged by the Government by giving the settlers a small plot of land and some money, so that they could start as independent rice farmers. Of the

SOURCE: Reprinted from the *Anthropological Quarterly*, Vol. 37, No. 3 (1964):149–55, by permission of the author and the *Anthropological Quarterly*.

33,000 Javanese who entered Surinam, approximately 10,000 returned to Indonesia. The others remained in Surinam, and the majority of these settlers still live primarily in the rural areas as small rice farmers. At present they number about 43,000.

The most salient feature of the Javanese culture in Surinam is its relative absence of acculturation, accompanied by the overt expression of the ideal to retain the cultural practices in as far as they were remembered from Java. Indeed, on the surface the difference between the Javanese culture in Surinam and the mother culture of Java appeared to be one of scale, of complexity. From this point of view the culture may thus be designated as incomplete, or "broken." But there were also processes of mending and of adjustment. The culture of the Javanese in Surinam was yet a whole culture, although one of smaller dimension and of lesser complexity. The Javanese in Surinam have found new ways for dealing with the new problems in a different environment, without large-scale borrowings from the cultures surrounding them. Rather, the remembered features of the Indonesian culture were reinterpreted, given new meanings where the older ones were lost. This process of adaptation was at work in all their cultural institutions, as I have shown elsewhere (1963). But it appears most lucidly in their religious system, which contains elements of both Islam and Animism.

Animism and Islam seem to stand far apart. Even if we no longer accept Tylor's evolutionary scheme of religion with animism as the earliest and monotheism as the highest development of religion, it appears yet incongruous that both should appear in one culture, not side by side, but rather hand in glove; not in disjunction, but in wedlock. Even if we know that the contents of religious beliefs are, by their very nature, not verifiable in the scientific sense, it yet appears contrary to all common sense that people call themselves Moslem, proclaiming, *"La illaha illa'llah"* ("There is but one God"), and simultaneously have at the core of their religious system a ritual explicitly held for the establishment of the proper relationship to the spirits, those invisible beings, present everywhere, who rule the life and the destiny of the people. But this was exactly the condition as I found it to exist among the Javanese in Surinam.

The Javanese in Surinam call themselves Moslems, and they pronounce the *shahada,* the Moslem confession of faith at all their rituals. Yet, the most important of their rituals has no counterpart in any form of orthodox Islam. These are held, consciously and explicitly, for the spirits. In general, there is a much greater emotional involvement with the spirits than with Allah. Allah, it is true, created the world, and he knows and sees everything, but he is remote; he is transcendent but not immanent. But Creation, omniscience and omnipotence are of minor importance if one considers that it is not Allah, but the spirits who maintain the general welfare of the community; not Allah, but the spirits who can make the crops thrive or fail; not Allah, but the spirits who can make children healthy, or take them away. The spirits are immanent: they are present in rivers, trees, flowers, rain, and rice fields; in items of clothing and in religious paraphernalia, and they are also associated with the recently deceased. The spirits are not considered to be evil, but they are strongly anthropopsychic, much like human beings in their desires. Thus, to give but one example, the spirits are as fond of children as the Javanese themselves, and therefore, even if the spirits take away some children, it is sad and regrettable, but also understandable.

The relationship to the spirits is maintained in a ritual, known as the *slametan*. It is a very simple ritual, and usually it does not last longer than half an hour. Slametans are held in every crisis situation— *i.e.*, at the third, seventh, and ninth month of pregnancy; at birth; 5 days, 36 days, 3 months, 7 months and one year after birth; at circumcisions, weddings, and funerals; at 10, at 100, at 1000 days after a death; and at various calendrical and other important occasions, such as at harvest time, or when moving into a new house.

A slametan is always held at home, and the host invites a number of families to participate. The adult females of these invited households come together during the daytime and prepare the sacred food, which is then ritually consumed in the evening by the adult males of the participating households. The slametan is opened by the *ka'um,* the religious leader, with the *Bismillahi* formula—"In the Name of Allah, the Compassionate, the Merciful"—after which Koranic passages are recited and Islamic prayers chanted. Then the host, or more often the ka'um himself, states the specific reason for the slametan (pregnancy, birth, etc.), now addressing the spirits: "Thou invisible ones, you see us here united in harmony and brotherhood: we invite you to partake in our food, so that we will receive *slamet*: health, happiness, well-being; through your participation." The food which has been placed before them on the ground is then uncovered, partially consumed, the spirits partaking in it by smell. The leftover food is wrapped in banana leaves, and brought home, to be shared with wife and children.

There are also, in every community, specialists who have particular powers: the *dukuns,* male and female, who are curers, sorcerers, and ceremonial specialists. There are many kinds of dukuns: those specializing in childbirth, in wedding ceremonies, in circumcision, in the curing of man or beast, in love magic, and several others. It is also more often than not a dukun who directs women in the preparation of the ritual food for the slametans—each type of slametan having its own specific dishes, sometimes in great variety. Usually, a dukun has more than one specialty, but in every community we find more than one dukun present, sometimes as many as five or six; although some are more active than others. These dukuns receive their special powers from the spirits but they do not disregard Allah completely. Every spell, every curing ceremony, every ritual is opened with the words: "In the Name of Allah, the Compassionate, the Merciful" and, in the magic formulae, both Allah and the spirits are entreated.

There is also, in every community, a small group of mostly elderly men, the *santri,* who take the Islamic prescripts more seriously than the rest of the community. The ka'um is the leader of this group, and they come together on Fridays in the *langgar,* the humble counterpart of a Mosque, for praying and reciting parts of the Koran. The santri also pray regularly at their homes—not five times a day as the Koran demands, but at least once or twice daily, at fixed hours. The non-santri do not conscientiously perform the ritual prayers. Santri are also the ones who keep the religious fast in the holy month of Ramadan, almost as vicarious sufferers for the whole community. Their presence within a community is considered of the utmost importance —several informants told me earnestly that they themselves would become santri if there were not enough left. But the ka'um and the santri also take the spirits very seriously. We have already seen that it is precisely the ka'um—or in his absence another santri—who presides over the slametans, and they address both spirits and Allah.

If we look at this situation structurally and functionally we notice that it is through the ka'um and the santri that the socio-religious community receives its sense of being a community. There would be very little community structure without the office of the ka'um. It is true that the Surinam government has set up administrative village designations, but these have often very little meaning to the Javanese, and the borders appear to them rather arbitrarily chosen. Also the Government has appointed a Javanese headman, or *lurah*, in every such village. But the lurah has no legal authority, no powers whatsoever, and very few significant duties, and the Javanese are fully aware of this. The lurah may be consulted on occasion, if a problem arises in a family, but the Javanese prefer to settle their problems themselves rather than seeking outside help, because it is rather shameful to have problems in the first place, and the lurah can do nothing else but give his opinion.

Also the dukuns cannot serve as a steady reference point. There are always several dukuns in one village, and although most communities tacitly recognize one dukun as the village dukun, it by no means follows that this is the dukun in whom one has the greatest faith. Many of the functions of the dukun are magical, directed to a specific and practical end—curing, or love magic—and therefore people naturally tend to seek the services of such dukuns whom they believe to have the greatest powers. In many cases the people travel, sometimes for several days, to other villages to consult dukuns, because among the Javanese too a prophet is often less honored in his home.

It is thus through the ka'um that the community receives a sense of unity. The ka'um forms "congregations," because all families pay their yearly *zakat* to the ka'um. Although, according to Islamic prescript this money is meant for the poor, it is kept by the ka'um as payment for his services at the slametans over the year. Moreover, the langgar, the house of prayers, is a visible structure which gives therefore a visible point of reference. Neither the lurah nor the dukun has an office in the material sense of the word. In front of the langgar, moreover, stands the *bedug,* or sacred drum, announcing both secular and religious events, thus reminding the people of the core and binding force of their community, whether they heed the call for prayer, or disregard it, as most do.

But whereas the ka'um and santri give the framework, to the community, the slametans give it content—not only because the people are emotionally closer to the spirits than to the distant, otiose Allah, but also because in and through the spirit-centered slametan all people can and do participate in the religious sphere, and no one, not even a woman, is excluded from it. Women may not enter the langgar and if they would want to pray to Allah they may do that at home. Women cannot be santri, nor may they participate in the slametan itself; but they greatly contribute to the success of the slametan by the preparation of the right kind of food in the right kind of way—an importance of which they are well-aware, and which gives them a strong sense of participation.

It is important to note that the two traditions, Animism and Islam, have been reinterpreted in such a way that they do not disturb the cultural ideal of internal cohesion. To the contrary, the new form both augments and sustains the social solidarity that is such an important value for the Javanese. On Java, Islam and Animism are segregating forces rather than uniting ones. Clifford Geertz, in his important book *The Religion of Java* (1960), describes the stress on animism, *Abangan,* possessing many similar features as in Surinam; and the same holds true for his description of the Santri, the Islamic tradition. But they find their representatives primarily in different groups; the *Abangan* is related to the peasant element in the population, while the Santri is represented by the traders and shopkeepers. Geertz gives, moreover, several examples of hostility and strife between the two groups. This is decidedly not the case in Surinam. The two elements are so closely intertwined that one could not exist without the other, and this will probably remain so as long as the Javanese abide by their ideal to be, and to remain, "one big family," a family in which it is shameful to quarrel, or to try to be different from your brothers.

The editor of this magazine has asked me to add a paragraph on the question of how far the religion of the Javanese in Surinam may be called a new form of religion, or if it is a form of syncretism. I believe that it is both. It is syncretistic in as far as we understand syncretism as a reconciliation of different principles into a new whole. From the foregoing presentation it is clear that this is the case in the religion of the Javanese in Surinam. But what is more, most religions appear to be syncretistic in this sense. Islam itself is a reinterpretation of elements of Judaism, Christianity, and Arab tribal religion. Christianity is a reconciliation of Judaism and Hellenism. But every reinterpretation brings with it some new elements: for Islam it was the power of Mohammed, for Christianity the power of Christ, with all its implications, and for the Javanese it was simply the Santri as vicarious sufferers for the rest of the community.

The question then remains: when do we call a religious system "new." The decision cannot be based upon the appearance of outwardly similar traits or elements. The New Guinean Messianic or millenarian cults show sometimes a number of external similarities with Christian elements, but no one would deny these are separate forms of religion. This is so because they play entirely different roles within the cultures where they appear. Just exactly because religion is a strong force in society—regardless of the individual beliefs or the absence thereof—religion is reflecting social change. As soon as religious reinterpretations have become systematized in a different cultural situation, it appears to me that we may call it a "new" religion, even if it has deep roots in the older traditions, as is the case in Surinam.

References cited:

Geertz, Clifford.
   1960 *The Religion of Java.* Glencoe, The Free Press.
Kroeber, Alfred L.
   1948 *Anthropology.* New York, Harcourt, Brace and Company.
Redfield, Robert.
   1956 *Peasant Society and Culture.* Chicago, University of Chicago Press.
Waal Malefijt, Annemarie de.
   1963 *The Javanese of Surinam: Segment of a Plural Society.* New York, The Humanities Press.

SCOTT COOK*

29. The Prophets: A Revivalistic Folk Religious Movement in Puerto Rico

INTRODUCTION

The purpose of this paper is to outline some basic structural and functional features of a little-known revivalistic folk religious movement in Puerto Rico—the "Prophets"—through a description of the beliefs, rituals, ceremonies and organizational structure of one of its local groups known as Cilicia Temple. In the course of this essentially descriptive account the writer hopes, by implication, to relate the Prophet movement in Puerto Rico to the general sociocultural phenomenon of revivalistic folk religion as it appears among the 'have-not' peoples—the "detribalized", the "deculturated", the "disinherited"—throughout the world in both rural and urban settings who are experiencing rapid and fundamental changes in their traditional modes of existence. To describe the Prophet movement in its Cilician context will perhaps furnish some clues to the nature of the more generalized phenomenon.

The occupation of the Caribbean island of Puerto Rico by the United States in 1898 laid the groundwork for subsequent penetration of North American cultural values, norms, and ways of life. Among these intruding traits were those connected with the missionizing and proselytizing activities of Protestant Christianity—as this was interpreted and propagated by North American churches and missionary societies. So effective were Protestant efforts during the years following occupation that by 1941 the combined Protestant groups on the island had a "total registered membership of 32,122 upon their rolls and . . . a constituency estimated at 81,854"

SOURCE: Reprinted from *Caribbean Studies,* Vol. 4, No. 4 (January 1965): 20–35, with slight modifications made by the author, by permission of the author and The Institute of Caribbean Studies. Copyright by the Institute of Caribbean Studies, University of Puerto Rico.

(J. Merle Davis: 13). At the present time, according to a recent estimate (Lewis: 279), there are more than 500 active local Protestant groups in Puerto Rico with a total membership of approximately 250,000 constituents amounting to some 10% of the island's total population.

To a large extent this impressive increment in Protestant membership is attributable to the efforts of the fundamentalist sects[1] with their more aggressive proselytization techniques, their emphasis on literal biblical interpretation, and their insistence on an ecstatic conversion experience as a validation of one's religious involvement, rather than to those of the more conservative established denominations.[2]

The greatest appeal of religious revivalism in Puerto Rico, as is true wherever this phenomenon takes seed and spreads, has been among the landless wage workers in rural and urban areas. The class character of revivalistic movements in Puerto Rico is concisely summarized in the following passage from a recent comprehensive study of Puerto Rican society and culture:

> The more popular pentecostal groups have . . . flourished in response to the emotional needs of a people too uninhibited in their attitudes to be satisfied with American Protestant middle-class norms. They have not acquired, of course, the colorful eccentricity of such cult religions as the Jamaican Rastafari or the Trinidadian Shango groups . . . Rather their prime function is to provide for the cash-dependent Puerto Rican poor, both rural and urban, a sense of emotional security in a changing world. They thus reflect, like the more quaint cargo cults of Melanesia, the cultural disturbance of more backward peoples as they are driven to comprehend the modern Western technology that is gradually overwhelming them (Lewis: 273).

While it may be true in a global, comparative sense that the revivalistic religious groups in Puerto Rico have not acquired the "colorful eccentricity" of their counterparts in other Caribbean societies, there is at least one Puerto Rican group which in beliefs, rituals and organizational structure does approximate the model of the bizarre cult groups of Jamaica, Trinidad, and Haiti.[3] This is the movement which is popularly known in Puerto Rico as "Las Profetas".

The distinguishing trademarks of this movement are the ceremonial wearing of veils by its female members and the centrality of prophesying in its belief and ritual system. As a uniquely Puerto Rican folk religion this movement incorporates elements derived from four separate sources: 1) North American fundamentalist Protestantism; 2) Puerto Rican Spiritualism;[4] 3) lower-class Puerto Rican folk culture; 4) Catholicism. From fundamentalist Protestantism comes a considerable number of Prophet beliefs and rituals including Holy Ghost possession, spiritual gifts, the faith healing complex, a strict ethical code, literal biblical interpretation, and admiration of the Primitive Christian church. The local variety of Spiritualism has provided a model for the peculiar role of prophesying in the Prophet movement's belief and ritual system, as well as for the style and function of the prophet or prophetess who may best be described as a sort of Protestantized Spiritualist medium.[5] Lower-class Puerto Rican subculture has also contributed several elements to Prophet religion including beliefs in "evil spirits" and "bad air", spontaneity and freedom of emotional expression, and folk music patterns and instruments (i.e., guitar, güiro, pandareta, and maracas). The only Prophet trait which can be directly traced to Catholicism is the ritual wearing of veils by female members. This custom is modeled on the Catholic practice.

It is obvious from the preceding discussion that the Prophet Movement has a syncretic religious system, thus, placing it in a category with most of the folk religions of the New World. The remainder of this article will consist of a description of certain essential features of one Puerto Rican Prophet group—Cilicia Temple.

ORIGIN AND MEMBERSHIP OF CILICIA TEMPLE

Cilicia Temple is the name of the local Prophet group in Caguas, Puerto Rico, a city of some 50,000 inhabitants located approximately thirty kilometers from San Juan. The group was founded in 1953 by a Korean War veteran who was converted to the Prophet religion in San Juan shortly after his return to the island from Korea. He received no formal theological instruction and his becoming a pastor rested solely on the profound nature of his conversion experience, on his "spiritual" qualifications,[6] and on his deep religious commitment.

In response to the writer's queries concerning the process through which the Caguas Prophet group came to be identified as "Cilicia", the pastor paraphrased a passage from the Biblical book of Isaiah to the effect that "God will call His chosen people by a new name since their old name was given in a state of evil and damnation".[7] The pastor went on to explain that Cilicia is the name of a town mentioned in the Bible which existed during the time of the Apostle Peter. It was reputedly a commercial city which had five routes of departure to other towns. Since Caguas is a commercial city and also has five routes of departure, the pastor reasoned that "God chose to name the Caguas temple Cilicia".

The spiritual naming incident occurred around eight years ago and is described by the pastor as follows:

> I went to San Juan one afternoon and happened to find a person in our temple there who I knew had prophetic powers. I told this prophet that I had a personal problem which required divine guidance for solution. We both knelt by the altar in the temple and began to pray. During our prayer, the holy Spirit possessed the prophet and the word "Cilicia" was uttered. After the prophecy was over, the prophet told me that he had no idea of the meaning of the term Cilicia. I told him that my problem was to find a name for our temple in Caguas and that Cilicia was apparently the name which God had chosen for that purpose.

The Prophet temple in Caguas is located in the midst of a slum area and occupies one side of a humble single story duplex-like structure with wooden walls, concrete floor and a corrugated tin roof. Simple wooden benches, without back supports, line the side walls of the meeting room, which is approximately fifty feet long and thirty feet wide, and two crude doors open directly onto the sidewalk at the end of the room fronting on the street. Three rows of wooden benches are arranged horizontally across this side of the room. Against the wall, at the opposite end of the room, is a small elevated platform with space for the pastor's chair and podium. In front of the platform, on floor level, is a wooden table which serves primarily as a speaker's stand. The central floor area of the room is vacant and serves as the area for collective ceremonial activity. Five unshielded light bulbs, suspended from electric cords running along the ceiling beams, provide the only source of light for Cilician ceremonies. The heat generated by these light bulbs coupled with the poor ventilation of the room contributes to the hot and stuffy atmosphere which typically prevails at worship meetings.

The interior decor of the temple reflects the iconoclastic orientation of Prophet religion, and no religious pictures, symbols, or icons are on display. However, the walls are decorated with bunches of artificial flowers, and cardboard placards with prayers and Biblical sayings are displayed, at intervals, around the room. A large maroon-colored curtain, decorated with Christmas tree ornaments, is draped on the wall to the rear of the elevated platform, and a large calendar is hung on the opposite side. A blackboard, used for posting schedules of weekly activities and other announcements, is mounted on a side wall near the front of the room—directly across from a commercial-style electric clock hanging on the opposite wall. High on the wall to the rear of the platform is a placard which reads: "Santidad a Jehova" (Holiness to Jehovah). Another placard, attached to a ceiling beam in the center of the meeting room reads: "Venid a mí los trabajados y cargados que yo os haré descansar" (Come on to me all ye that labor and are heavy-laden and I will give you rest). This, then, is the physical setting in which Cilicia Temple comes to life in ritual and ceremony.

Cilicia has a total membership of about forty active constituents who regularly attend group activities. A glance at the sociological data summarized in Table 1 for ten of the active male members of the group will indicate that its support is drawn basically from the urban proletariat (i.e., wage-earners employed in non-agrarian occupations). It should also be mentioned that several of the female members of the group hold jobs in local factories, mainly on production lines.

The principal requirements for active membership in Cilicia Temple, following an initial conversion experience in which the individual accepts Christ as his exclusive Savior and repents of all sins, were succinctly described by the pastor to the writer as follows:

> The active member must cease to indulge in vice. If living in consensual union he must immediately arrange for a lawful Christian marriage. Also, he must faithfully comply with the tithe.

The pastor is the final judge of the moral and spiritual qualifications of prospective members but all Cilicians carefully scrutinize the conduct of aspirants during a trial membership period. Vice, in Cilician terminology, includes a wide range of entertainments and leisure

TABLE 1

BACKGROUND DATA FOR TEN FULL STATUS "ACTIVE" MALE
MEMBERS OF CILICIA TEMPLE

MEMBER	AGE	YEARS OF SCHOOLING	TYPE OF EMPLOYMENT	MONTHLY INCOME IN DOLLARS
1.	45	8	warehouse foreman	100–200
2.	25	11	factory machine operator	100–200
3.	21	4	cutter in sweater factory	100–200
4.	19	7	lacer in wallet factory	less than 100
5.	22	7	laundry machine operator	100–200
6.	27	12	private chauffeur for family	250–300
7.	38	0	bakery worker	less than 100
8.	40	12	warehouseman	300
9.	30	5	disabled veteran's pension	less than 100
10.	25	6	tile floor polisher	less than 100

time activities such as smoking or using tobacco; drinking alcoholic beverages; fornication out of wedlock; attending or participating in athletic events; gambling or attending cockfights; strolling in the town recreation plaza for social purposes; dancing or attending parties; and such feminine practices as the use of artificial beauty aids (i.e., cosmetics, padded brassieres, stylized hairdos, etc.) and wearing provocative clothing.

ORGANIZATION OF CILICIA TEMPLE

Two distinct structural patterns can be abstracted with regard to the organization of Cilicia Temple: 1) a formalized, explicit, non-ritual structure, and 2) a non-formalized, implicit, ritual structure. The former is composed of those official appointive and elective positions which enable the group to function effectively on a day to day basis as a religious organization and in its necessary transactions with the outside world. The most important of these positions is that of pastor followed, in order of decreasing importance, by those of missionary (i.e., the pastor's wife), the presiding officers of the men's and women's societies, and the lesser officers of these societies. It is through these offices that the routine operative and "business" activities of the group are performed.

However, it is the non-formalized, ritual structure which is of central importance in the functioning of Cilicia Temple as a religious cult group. Although Cilicians do not explicitly recognize the ritual structure of their group, such recognition is implicit in their ceremonial conduct. Within this informal structure status is attained neither by election nor by appointment but, rather, in accordance with the "spiritual" qualifications of individual members or according to the duties they perform in the ceremonial life of the group. From the standpoint of this informal structure, the Cilicia group can be considered as a kind of spiritual community of equals, with distinctions between individual members being based primarily on what each contributes in the way of a specialized task to the ritual and ceremonial proceedings of the group. Therefore, Cilicia can be conceived of as a socio-religious sub-system within the framework of the larger

FIGURE 20

INFORMAL RITUAL STRUCTURE OF CILICIA TEMPLE

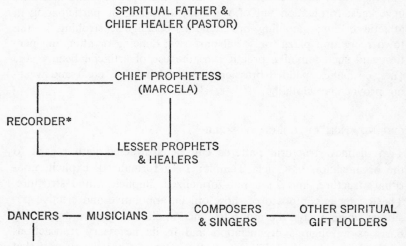

SPIRITUAL FATHER &
CHIEF HEALER (PASTOR)

CHIEF PROPHETESS
(MARCELA)

RECORDER*

LESSER PROPHETS
& HEALERS

DANCERS — MUSICIANS — COMPOSERS — OTHER SPIRITUAL
& SINGERS   GIFT HOLDERS

GUARDS**

* The "recorder" is a person who stays near to the prophet during prophecy sequences and makes a hand-written transcription of the prophecy. This role is performed by the pastor's wife who has several spiral notebooks filled with transcriptions of prophecies delivered in Cilician ceremonies over the years. The recorder often assists in the interpretation of prophecies.

** Guards are those persons who prevent spiritual dancers from bumping into obstacles during dance sequences.

social system—with its own set of values, norms, status and roles, and behavior patterns competing with and to some extent replacing those of the larger social system in the lives of individual members. The ritual structure of Cilicia is represented schematically in Figure 20.

BELIEF SYSTEM, RITUALS AND THE HEALING COMPLEX

The most important Cilician beliefs cluster around a group of phenomena known as "spiritual gifts" which manifest themselves in the form of trances, visions, and demonstrative motor behavior, and are often associated with special personal talents. Spiritual gifts are conceived of as "blessings" of the Holy Spirit or as endowments emanating from the Supernatural, and are thought by Cilicians to represent undeniable expressions of God's approval of actions by His Chosen People (i.e., the Cilicians themselves).

Official spokesmen for the Prophet religion (i.e., the pastor or other officers) consistently agree that there are nine spiritual gifts all of which are so categorized in a passage contained in the Biblical book of Corinthians (1 Corinthians 12: 4-11). These are: prophecy, discernment, revelation, vision, speaking in unknown tongues, interpretation of tongues, healing, operation of miracles, and faith. Most Cilicians, however, will classify the following items as spiritual gifts in addition to those cited above: repression of demons, exhortation, dancing in the spirit, preaching, guitar-playing and hymn-composing. Since there is no formal codification of beliefs associated with Prophet religion, disagreements as to what should properly be included in the spiritual gift category never arise. Indeed, concern with doctrinal issues is anathema to the Prophet brand of religion with its emphasis on spontaneity of individual expression. Obviously, the discrepancy between the text of the Holy Gospel and the beliefs of the typical Cilician concerning spiritual gifts reflect, to a large degree, the extent to which certain aspects of Puerto Rican folk culture have been incorporated into the Prophet belief system.

In this short article it will be impossible to discuss the role of each of these spiritual gifts in the Cilician religious system.[8] Consequently, attention will be focused on faith healing and prophesying the two most significant elements in the ceremonial and ritual functioning of Cilicia.

Faith healing, both with regard to beliefs and rituals, is second in importance only to prophesying in the overall structure and functioning of Cilicia's religious system. What may be termed the Prophet "healing complex" is basically modeled on a procedure described in James, the New Testament book (James 5: 14-16), and involves the following ritual elements: anointing with olive oil, exhortative prayer, laying on of the hands, and massaging. Ten of the Cilicians reputedly possess healing powers, but most members of the group employ the ritual acts of the healing complex whenever the need arises in their daily lives. Accordingly, Cilician meetings often include personal testimonies by individual members such as the following:

> Yesterday morning, I had to stay home from work because my wife had a severe headache and was unable to get out of bed. I took up my bottle of olive oil and rubbed her head. Then I knelt by the bed and prayed. Within a short while, my wife got up from bed saying that her headache was better. She immediately began to work at her usual daily tasks and I was able to leave for my job.

As this example illustrates, Cilicians sincerely believe that the oil and prayer sequence can result in the healing of physical maladies. Most members of the group would agree with one of their number who gave the writer the following explanation for his attendance at meetings: "I come here to the Temple in search of healing for the body."

Cilician healing beliefs, however, go one step further than this and, in so doing, reflect an interesting syncretism of Puerto Rican folk beliefs and Biblical Christianity. Anointing with oil and prayer is also believed by Cilicians to provide the recipient with protection from evil spirits and "malicious airs"—the first of which local spiritualists are reputed to manipulate—in addition to curing bodily ailments. Spiritualism and the spirit world are topics of significant concern to Cilicians. Fallen angels, spirits of the world, demons, and evil spirits are some of the terms which they apply to those phenomena which they believe are manipulated by the spiritualists. During a lively group discussion on the topic of spiritualism the pastor made the following statement:

> We (i.e., Cilicians) are not spiritualists; we are servants of God. However, I wouldn't put on gloves with a demon unless I had the help of Christ. These fallen angels are effective. There isn't

an army anywhere that is more effective than the Devil's army. His demons come through open windows and strike one in the head, the stomach, or the legs. At times, they fasten themselves to the wheels of a car or enter the mind of the driver. When a man attacks a woman, it is an evil spirit which has possessed and motivated him.

In spiritualism these evil spirits take away the minds of the mediums and inhabit their flesh. The flesh takes over and the mind is no longer in control. The demons of spiritualism are dangerous since it is a science created by the Devil to confuse souls. It is a work of the fallen angels, the demons. The Holy Spirit, on the contrary, works only for the well-being of mankind.

The writer was present at several Cilician meetings held in private homes during the course of which the pastor sprinkled oil at various "strategic" points throughout the house (i.e., windows, doorways, closets, and corners) for the avowed purpose of protecting the host family from undisclosed dangers which the pastor warned "might attack them in the near future." At one of these meetings the purpose of the oil sprinkling ceremony was to disinfect the host family's house of evil spirits which were believed to have been left behind by a spiritualist family which had previously resided there. During this particular ceremony, each member of the family was anointed with oil and prayed over prior to the sprinkling of strategic points. If such ritual precautions were not taken, Cilicians believe that the evil spirits would manifest their presence by causing the family illness or bad luck.

The pastor's role as spiritual leader of Cilicia rests in part on the fact that he is the group's most prestigious healer. His healing powers are often solicited during ceremonial meetings and outside of the ceremonial context. One young adult male member who often goes to the pastor for oil application and prayer explained his behavior to the writer in the following terms:

> I often feel a load on top of me. I feel badly. Evil spirits in the air want to enter into one, but oil and prayer protect him. I go to the pastor for this protection and not because I feel pain.

Some readers might be inclined to infer, at this point, that Cilician beliefs and practices related to healing are simply a function of selfish motivation and or fear of supernatural evil. A more rewarding approach, however, is to relate these beliefs and practices to the sociocultural environment within which Cilicians—as representatives of the Puerto Rican proletariat—operate on a day-to-day basis. It seems justifiable to infer from the data presented that healing beliefs and practices among Cilicians reflect their sincere mistrust of and lack of confidence in the medical and public health services in the wider social system to which they have access. The following example will serve to illustrate this: One evening Sr. Reyes (he and his family are active Cilicians) arrived at the Temple near the end of the worship meeting to solicit the pastor's immediate healing services for his daughter who was seriously ill with a high fever. As Reyes explained to the writer: "The doctors examined my daughter earlier this week but found nothing wrong with her. They prescribed some pills, as always, and told us to confine her to bed." The girl was in immediate need of the pastor's healing powers, according to Reyes, because the "doctor's pills are not doing her any good—her fever is higher than ever." To sum up the Cilician position, at the risk of oversimplification,[9] they believe more firmly in the healing efficacy of holy oil and prayer than in the impersonal treatment and routinely distributed pills from the public health units. As one Cilician phrased it: "The Great Doctor above has the power to heal our illnesses. He can succeed where medical science fails."[10]

The prophetesses (i.e., female members endowed with the spiritual gift of prophecy) play a significant ceremonial role in the healing complex—thus supplementing the healing services of the pastor. This may be illustrated by means of the following description of a special meeting involving twenty Cilicians who gathered in the Reyes' home to participate in a healing ceremony on behalf of the young girl mentioned above:

> During the opening phase of lively hymn singing, shouting, and clapping, the "bedridden" girl suddenly appears in the doorway of her bedroom and, in a trance-like state, comes dancing into the main room where the ceremonial activity is centered. Sr. Reyes comments as his daughter enters the main room: "The Lord has raised her from the bed dancing."
>
> As the girl moves toward the center of the room, the pastor begins applying oil to the fingers of several members who then cluster around her, each one placing an oily finger either on her

ankle or intertwining it with one of her fingers. When everyone is in position, a fervent healing prayer is initiated and, shortly, a prophetess begins to prophesy: "Devils going away—you will see shelter—don't be afraid my child—there is magic—I will be removing everything on time."

A second prophecy sequence follows during which the word "circle" is mentioned. Following up this cue, the pastor immediately instructs the group to form a circle around the four members of the Reyes family. A prophetess, in trance, enters the circle and begins to massage Sr. Reyes on his chest, arms, and back. She then falls to her knees directly in front of Reyes and begins massaging his thighs and legs. At this point the prophetess calls out: "Joel! Joel! (the spiritual name of the pastor)—You anointing him everywhere—kidneys, legs, stomach, head, brain —a satanic work—occult—walking" (i.e., present in the immediate situation).

The pastor, following the prophecy, immediately begins to rub Sr. Reyes with oil. The prophetess begins again: "Ay! Ay! Ay!—I take away everything—I am doctor—I am doctor—all pain is diabolical—you will have to remain bed many days." Interrupting the sequence here, the pastor proclaims to the assembled group: "God is in our midst promising to heal this family's illnesses."

RITUALS, CEREMONIES, AND THE PROPHECY COMPLEX

One of the most notable aspects of Cilician worship meetings is the informality and uninhibitedness of the ceremonial atmosphere. A concomitant ceremonial element is spontaneous and total audience participation coupled with a high degree of emotionalism which pervades most proceedings. Prophecy sequences, ceremonial dancing, unrestrained hymn sequences entailing singing, shouting, and demonstrative motor behavior, together with personal testimonials, form integral parts of the typical Cilician worship service. All of these ceremonial and ritual elements are characterized by a maximum degree of individual emotional expression.

Another aspect of these meetings is the equalitarian nature of ritual participation. Every member is expected to perform some ritual task such as giving a testimony, singing a hymn, playing the guitar, reading from the Bible, preaching a sermon, etc. as often as possible.

Manifestations of shyness or fright on the part of persons performing these activities are rare since Cilicians perceive each other as "brothers" in a spiritual community of equals. The performance of one member is for the spiritual benefit of all. In keeping with the informality and spontaneity of the ceremonial atmosphere, Cilicians generally wear casual dress to worship meetings—men with sport shirts and slacks or dungarees, and women with skirts and blouses or simple dresses.

During worship meeting, guitar players customarily stroll around the ceremonial area while they play. Music sequences often culminate in widespread manifestations of demonstrative behavior (i.e., dancing, twirling or spinning, crawling or rolling on the floor, bodily twitchings, and seizures or trances). Often, as a hymn sequence progresses, the lyrics become less and less intelligible while the rhythm and tempo of the music become more forceful and pronounced. The music, in combination with other stimuli present in the ceremonial situation, invariably triggers a series of ritual behaviors such as "danceo espiritual" (i.e., stylized twirling and spinning movements resembling dancing activity which Cilicians interpret as manifestations of the Holy Ghost), speaking in unknown tongues, and prophesying. Women are often seen to remove their shoes and maneuver about the ceremonial area in their bare feet during such sequences, and few members remain seated with most making positive contributions to the perpetuation of the festive atmosphere.

The ability to prophesy is considered to be the most valuable and prestigious spiritual gift with which a Cilician can be endowed. Its centrality in the Prophet religious system is assured by the fact that it serves as the means by which the Supernatural communicates with the group, as well as the means by which all other spiritual gifts are allocated. As is true of all principal Cilician beliefs and rituals, the centrality of prophecy is based on Biblical authority (1 Corinthians 14). What is termed here the "prophecy complex", as it regularly occurs during Cilician worship meetings, incorporates three discrete behavioral traits which typically appear in the following order: spiritual dancing (danceo espiritual), speaking in unknown tongues, and prophesying. In other words, the "prophecy complex" is an interrelated cluster of three separate and distinct motor behavioral patterns. The "prophecy sequence", on the other hand, refers to that portion of a prophecy complex in which the prophecy itself is delivered.

A prophecy complex is typically initiated when a prophetess begins to dance with a series of twirling, spinning movements. Her eyes are usually closed and her hands are either clasped tightly behind her back or are held over her eyes. After a brief interval of speaking in tongues to which scant attention is paid, the prophesying activity itself begins. This consists of a series of coherent words and phrases uttered between pauses of varying length, and is most often delivered in a dramatic monotone of urgency, warning and mystery. The prophetess always shows signs of strain, tension and exertion, with each exhortation expelled at the expense of a groan, grunt or sigh. There is customarily a great deal of repetition of words, phrases and sounds, both during discrete prophecies and from prophecy to prophecy.

The prophetic message itself is often one of impending danger expressed as a warning.[11] While delivering a prophecy the prophetess appears to be in a half-inebriated, half-epilectic condition—bobbing and weaving constantly as she prophesies. During the early stages of a sequence she moves around freely within the confines of the ceremonial area, occasionally bumping into bystanders, walls, benches, or tables and constantly, without prior warning, shifting the direction of her movement. Her posture, during the early stages of the sequence, is upright. However, toward the later stages, she ordinarily assumes a crawling or kneeling posture. Other members guide the possessed prophetess; certain girls and women follow her around during the ceremony to keep her veil in position and to prevent her collision with various obstacles. Below is a description of one Cilician prophecy complex as witnessed by the writer:

> The pastor explains to the assembled members of the group that sister Luisa is passing through a crisis due to certain personal and family problems, and that she needs prophetic assistance. He then asks that all of the prophets present in the Temple form a circle around Luisa, who is kneeling in the center of the ceremonial area with head bowed. The pastor then directs the group to "pray with faith and with interest." All those forming the circle immediately begin to shout and gesticulate urgently. Intelligible words such as "Problem! God! Resolve!" occasionally filter through the ceremonial tumult and shouting.
>
> Many Cilicians are still seated on the benches along the walls. Some are engaged in prayer, others are reading the Bible; but all are attentive to the proceedings taking place in the center of the room. The voice of the pastor momentarily soars above the

others: "Manifest yourself God! Your voice strengthens our souls!"

Next the pastor implores the group to concentrate more intensively: "Perhaps some mind is not here with us. Let's all kneel and try to clear our minds of preoccupations with jobs, housework, etc." All Cilicians in the circle immediately kneel and, shortly, motor behavioral manifestations become more demonstrative. Members who were previously seated along the walls are now on their feet participating more directly in the proceedings.

Abruptly, one of the younger members of the prayer circle, a guitar player begins to speak in unknown tongues, the muscles of his neck and shoulders twitching nervously. This signifies to all Cilicians that the Holy Spirit is now present. Similar behavior appears among others in the circle. Finally, a male prophet initiates a short, incoherent prophecy. Everyone present falls silent at the pastor's signal to do so.

Only a few moments lapse until Marcela, the chief prophetess, begins to prophesy:

> Santo—hay obra—viene a ti Luisa—
> viene abrigo—trabas—pasos hay unos—
> no temas—abrigo habrá—no temas tú—
> orando—hay obras rodándote a ti—
> alértate—obra satánica—abrigo
> hay—tendrás tu victoria—caminos
> se ve—no temas tú—espérame—
> obra viene—paredes vienen—cambiando
> todo están—obras satánicas, pero tú
> no temas—Satán está rodando—ya
> quitarétodo—trabas serán aquí—
> hay una obra—paredes—que vienen
> avisos más—abrigo habrá—esperas
> y no temas—orando más—brisas
> caen y chocan—no mires nada—
> trabas vienen—consejos hay antes—
> una obra pasando—sonrisas—quítalos—
> yo estoy abrigándote—hay alertas—
> no temas—mansedumbre—obra se ve.[12]

Following the termination of Marcela's prophecy, the pastor

leads the entire group in a prayer of thanks. The circle breaks up some thirty minutes after its formation.

The prophecy sequence presented above typifies those delivered during Cilician worship meetings in several respects. First, it contains a warning of imminent but unspecified danger, coupled with assurances of divine protection. Next, this prophecy contains certain Cilician code words which appear often during prophecy sequences (i.e., "trabas" = obstacle: "abrigo" = protection; "pared" = something that divides people; "brisa" = gossip). As far as the writer could determine, these code words are understood by most Cilicians without pastoral interpretation. Also, in this prophecy the person toward whom it is directed (i.e., Luisa) is promised that additional prophetic advice will be forthcoming in the future. Finally, the prophecy is delivered in the familiar (tú) form of Spanish and the prophetess speaks in the first person singular—the "I" referring not to the prophetess, but to the "Holy Spirit" who, in accordance with Cilician belief, is actually doing the prophesying.

CONCLUSION

From the functional standpoint, it is the prophecy complex which gives the Prophet movement its uniqueness among Puerto Rican revivalistic folk religions and distinguishes it from run-of-the-mill sect groups. Most sociological analyses of sectarianism agree that it is a working class phenomenon which arises out of and is sustained by the working class sectors of society. Usually, the strong eschatological content of typical sectarian belief systems is explained in terms of the compensation which such doctrines purportedly offer sect members for economic deprivation and psychological frustration experienced in their relationships with the wider social system. As the author of a recent study has expressed it:

> The eschatology of sects is perhaps the most emphatic expression of their basic orientation . . . it compensates both the economically disinherited, and those disillusioned and embittered by their experience . . . The present, with its shortcomings, is discounted for the future, and the disabilities suffered in this world are themselves an assurance of future blessing. Worthiness now is also assured by judgement, within the group, in terms of

those criteria which the sect has elevated as canons of ultimate justification (Wilson: 317-18).

It is certainly not true that eschatology is the most emphatic expression of the basic orientation of the Prophet movement. Although the concepts of Heaven, Hell, and the Second Coming are present in its belief system, they do not play an important role in the average member's world view. It follows, then, that the functions often attributed to the strong eschatological elements in sectarian belief systems are performed elsewhere in the Prophet system. In the latter case, as was described in the discussion of the Cilician system, ritual and ceremonies focused on healing and anxiety-allaying prophecy sequences serve to cushion the impact of economic, social, cultural and psychological deprivations suffered by its constituents.

However, other factors must be considered to fully explain the continued existence of the Prophet movement as a functioning socioreligious system. Owing to its extensive incorporation of traits from lower-class Puerto Rican culture, the Prophet movement can unequivocally be classified as a folk religion. Prominent in its belief system are concepts such as "evil spirits" and "bad air" which, as in Puerto Rican folk belief, are said to cause bodily and mental afflictions, as well as bad luck and other misfortunes. Also, Prophet ceremonies are highly informal and intimate affairs conducted in the Puerto Rican folk idiom and utilizing folk rhythms and dances in the music sequences which are played on standard folk instruments.

Finally, among the Prophets, there is no detectable evidence of attitudes toward thrift and frugality, hard work and productivity which could be considered as factors that might contribute to changes in individual or group socio-economic status. On the contrary, the Cilician leader repeatedly expressed the view that a small group consisting of poor, humble members was more "Christian", in his opinion, than a large group of affluent middle-class members. As far as he was concerned, rapid and progressive growth in membership and the concomitant accumulation of wealth represent steps in the de-Christianization of a religious group.[13]

All of these factors, considered together, suggest that the Prophet religion provides a milieu conducive to the satisfactory, if temporary, resolution of problems related to the social, psychological, and cultural adjustment of its constituents. Firmly rooted in lower-class Puerto Rican folk culture, this religion has incorporated ritual, ceremonial, and ideological mechanisms which enable its class-bound constituents to cope effectively with their frustrated aspirations and multiple deprivations. In essence, the Prophet movement represents one means by which a small segment of the Puerto Rican folk population confronts changing conditions in a society in the throes of urbanization and industrialization.

Notes:

* At the time this article was written, the author was a National Institute of Mental Health Predoctoral Fellow in the Department of Anthropology, University of Pittsburgh. At the time of the collection of the data upon which the article is based, he held a Pan American Union Training Fellowship at the Institute of Caribbean Studies, University of Puerto Rico.

1. Among these fundamentalist groups in Puerto Rico are: the Assembly of God, the Church of God, the Pentecostal Church of God, the Mennonites, and Jehovah's Witnesses.

2. The denominations include: Methodist, Baptist, Presbyterian, and Lutheran.

3. This statement is not meant to imply any direct linkage between the Prophet religion and the Africanoid cult groups found in other areas of the Caribbean. So far as the writer knows, there is no published evidence of African survivals among extant Puerto Rican folk religious groups. The similarities are purely structural and functional, not historical.

4. Spiritualism—a belief in the causation of many events by spirits and an attempt to manipulate or discover such causation through the mediation of a medium—in Puerto Rico, like fundamentalist Protestantism, began to flourish and establish its separate identity as a religious movement after 1898. Of course, beliefs in "evil spirits" were characteristic of the aboriginal Arawak and Carib, the Spanish, and the African traditions which preceded the North American as significant components of Puerto Rican culture. (Steward et al.: 88.)

Spiritualism also resembles fundamentalist Protestantism in Puerto Rico in that it "seems to occur primarily among socio-cultural groups which are losing or have recently lost their traditional way of life. It attracts socially maladjusted individuals—those who are attempting to maintain their traditional social role and status in a changing society and those whose special psychological organization makes it impossible for them to function smoothly in their own socio-cultural group and who seek contact with the supernatural to restore or achieve status" (ibid.).

For further information on Puerto Rican spiritualism refer to the following: J. Bram, "Spirits, Mediums, and Believers in Contemporary Puerto Rico", New York Academy of Sciences, *Transactions,* Series 2, Vol. 20, 1957, pp. 340–47; L. Rogler and A. Hollingshead. "The Puerto Rican Spiritualist as a Psychiatrist", *American Journal of Sociology,* Vol. 67, 1961, pp. 17–21.

5. There are a number of interesting parallels between the roles of the Spiritualist medium and the prophet in the structure and functioning of their respective groups. Both maintain positions of power and prestige in the organizational structure; both are vessels of the supernatural (i.e., are possessed by the supernatural) and manifest similar patterns of trance behavior; and both serve as the sole communicants between the other members of their religions and the supernatural.

6. For members of the Prophet movement "spiritual" qualifications refer to special endowments or powers which a person receives from the supernatural (i.e., from the Holy Ghost or God). Examples are prophecy and healing.

7. In accordance with this belief many Cilicians have spiritual names which were assigned to them during a prophecy sequence. These names are utilized only in the ceremonial context and are usually of Biblical origin. For example, the pastor's spiritual name is Joel.

8. Those readers who are interested in pursuing this matter further can consult Cook, pp. 105–52.

9. For instance, it is likely, that psychosomatic factors are deeply involved in the Cilician healing complex. However, comment or even speculation upon these is beyond the scope of the present article and the data upon which it is based.

10. Cilicians, like most believers in faith healing, maintain that it is only effective with those persons who truly believe and have faith in its efficacy.

11. The danger itself usually remains unspecified, except in allegorical form.

12. This is a transcription of an actual Cilician prophecy sequence. It should be noted that a prophecy is never delivered in a smooth-flowing, uninterrupted fashion. On the contrary, the majority are choppy and are characterized by many pauses. Rarely are complete sentences of more than five words uttered by the delivering prophetess without pause. In the transcription presented here each dash represents a pause in the prophet's delivery. Below is a free translation of this prophecy into English:

Holy—there is something in the offing—it is coming to you Luisa—protection is coming—obstacles—there are some steps—don't be afraid—praying —there are "works" surrounding you—be on alert—satanic works—there is protection—you will have your victory—ways are seen—don't be afraid— wait for me—a work is coming—there are things that separate—they are changing everything—satanic works but don't be afraid—satan is near— soon I will take away everything—obstacles will be here—there is a work— things that separate—more advice is coming—there will be protection—wait and don't be afraid—more praying—breezes are falling and crashing—don't look at anything—obstacles are coming—advice will come before—a work passing—smiles—take them off—I am protecting you—there are alerts—don't be afraid—meekness—a work is seen.

13. Although compliance with the tithe was mentioned by the pastor as one of the necessary conditions for active Cilician membership, this is not subject to strict enforcement and regulation. As far as the writer could ascertain, the pastor applies no direct pressure for monetary contributions and is guided by a belief that Cilicians will contribute what they can when circumstances permit.

References cited:

Cook, Scott.
1963 "Some Sociocultural Aspects of Two Revivalistic Religious Groups in a Puerto Rican Municipio." Graduate Thesis, Interamerican Program of Advanced Social Science Studies, Institute of Caribbean Studies, University of Puerto Rico.
Davis, J. Merle.
1942 *The Church in Puerto Rico's Dilemma.* New York: International Missionary Council.
Hogg, Donald W.

1964 *Jamaican Religions: A Study in Variations.* Ph. Dissertation, Yale University.

Lewis, Gordon K.
1963 *Puerto Rico: Freedom and Power in the Caribbean.* New York: Monthly Review Press.

Mintz, Sidney.
1960 *Worker in the Cane.* New Haven: Yale University Press.

Steward, Julian et al.
1956 *The People of Puerto Rico.* Urbana: University of Illinois Press.

Wilson, Bryan R.
1961 *Sects and Society.* Berkeley: University of California Press.

The Holy Bible.
Revised Standard Version (1952). New York: Thomas Nelson & Sons.

SHEILA KITZINGER

30. The Rastafarian Brethren of Jamaica

The Rastafarians have been a social problem for Jamaica ever since 1933, when one of their earliest leaders, Howell, sold 5000 postcards of the Emperor Haille Selassie at a shilling each making them out to be passports to Ethiopia. They gained greater publicity in 1941 when the police raided Howell's community at Pinnacle and arrested seventy of his followers on charges of growing ganja (marijuana) and of violence. In the 1950's many more were arrested, and—Rastas assert—flogged and forcibly shaved by the police; some were imprisoned on charges of rioting, and there were two separate cases charging that children were sacrificed by fire in Trenchtown, a slum area of the capital.[1]

In the course of anthropological field-work among peasant Jamaicans during the past year, I made friends with individuals in three Rastafarian "camps" and interviewed them intensively. They are the first to admit that there is a criminal fringe to the movement, but say that these are not "true" Rastas.

Members of the movement worship the Emperor Haille Selassie of Ethiopia, and insist that, as their African ancestors were brought unwillingly to Jamaica as slaves, it is now time for them to be "repatriated" to the land of their origin—Ethiopia, where reigns "the first Asian King of Creation, the Conquering Lion of the Tribe of Judah, God of the Black Race"—or more generally to any part of Africa. "All our aim is to go back to Africa, our ancient land, where we know we will live in happiness and plenty."

Periodic uprisings occurred between 1955 and 1958 when groups of these very poor and largely illiterate slum dwellers became impatient with waiting, and under the leadership of a prophet sold or gave

SOURCE: Reprinted from *Comparative Studies in Society and History,* Vol. 9, No. 1 (1966):34–39, by permission of the author and the Cambridge University Press.

away all their goods and swarmed the docks and airport. When the hoped-for transport did not appear, riot often resulted. Large numbers were arrested by the police—the "babylon" of the Bible—and thus was justified the Rasta's claim that the Jamaican Government is "Sodom and Gomorrah", though they assert that they are "nonpolitical" in the sense that they are not interested in Jamaica's internal politics.

Many accept no aid offered by welfare agencies and will not attend clinics or hospitals or use the midwifery service. They distrust all social workers, ministers of religion, and others who symbolize for them middle-class affluence, deceit, and the assumption of innate superiority. They join no Jamaican associations—and this includes trade unions. Political leaders among them have been making overtures to the Government of Ethiopia to obtain its consent for mass repatriation. The Ethiopian Government, which in 1955 set aside 500 acres "for the Black Peoples of the West" who wished to settle there, showers gifts on the emissaries, and returns them to Jamaica.

The more able of the Rastafarians are craftsmen—potters, carpenters, tailors, cobblers, wood-carvers, even artists; some are fishermen and a few till the land; a number are ganja pedlars and healers. The Rasta herb par excellence is ganja, which is included in many medicines and is used as frequently as we do aspirin. One Rasta informant remarked, with some insight, "The name 'ganja' and 'Rastafari' is the two terriblest names in Jamaica." They are in fact almost synonymous. Rastas themselves do not usually speak of "ganja". To them it is simply "the herb". They use it as a green vegetable, much like spinach, very good, they say, for children, make ganja tea by boiling the green leaves in water and, reducing the liquid, flavor stews with it, and smoke it in order to induce a state of euphoria or as a treatment for various illnesses. "We use the herbs for medical and spiritual conception. They help us to overcome disease, sickness, and death . . . We use our herbs in our church—the incense of God, like the Roman Catholics who use incense in their church. We burn our incense toward worshipping our God with spiritual conception . . . It give us spiritual comfort, to praise God in peace and love, without violence . . . When we are oppressed, when we are hungry, we smoke our little herb and we meditate on our God . . . Herbs to us is a comfort truly; through God (they are) our second comforter." They consider ganja—which is a drug of habituation rather than of addiction—far less dangerous than hard liquor.

Unemployment is high in Jamaica, and the Rastafarians tend to be "the last hired and the first fired", unless they find work with employers who value them simply because they will not join unions. To many, habits of concentrated and regular work and of dividing the day into hours of work and periods of leisure are utterly foreign. This is in part a reflection of the transitory nature of their remaining stay in Jamaica, in part a result of the economics of unemployment in the island, and to a large extent simply an extension of more general Jamaican attitudes towards work, which is considered a not entirely necessary evil, and time, which is an ever-flowing stream that cannot be dammed.

Two main categories of Rastafarians have emerged, physically indistinguishable, the political and the religious, with a large area common to both in between. The political Rastas are primarily concerned with the ways and means of getting back to Africa and the negotiations to obtain this end. The primarily religious Rastas criticize them for being personally ambitious to the detriment of the movement as a whole and for being opportunists. The political Rastas see the religious ones as ineffective and apathetic. Occasionally fights break out between conflicting groups at the headquarters which they both share.

In appearance Rastas can be clean shaven, but are usually recognized as Rastas by their beards (*Beardsmen*; in Jamaica a bearded man is either an intellectual or a Rasta)—and in the case of "the men of Dreadlocks" or *Locksmen* by their long, thick, matted thatch of hair, which they smear with lard and allow to grow down over their shoulders and often over their faces as well, so that one may see only an inch or so of their jaw region. To cut it would be to cut off their strength, like Samson. One sect of Locksmen should be mentioned —the *Nyabingi*, who make and play the Nyabingi drums, which, when they talk, say, "Death to the white oppressor and his black ally". The Nyabingi are reputed to be the most violent of all the Rastafarians. Those I met were courteous, dignified, and friendly, and took me to their shacks and introduced me to other of their brethren.

Rastas will not wear second-hand clothing, nor eat food prepared by anyone outside the faith. Some groups do not drink except for medicinal purposes because they are "waiting to drink the palm wine". As a general rule they refer to themselves always in the nominative case: "Hear I when I call!"; it is similar to the royal plural. Many of them possess a strange dignity of bearing which lifts them apart from other of Jamaica's slum-dwellers. Some Rastafarians live in camps from which women are excluded, and rear their sons there. Their horror of homosexuality—the worst sin of all—may be an indication of a heterosexuality which is not markedly pronounced. Women are, indeed, peripheral to the movement as a whole. "A woman can just leave the Rasta. They are not Rasta in heart. The man is head of the church. Women have to obey the principles of the Elders of the movement." They are quick to leave when they see opportunities of greater security for themselves or their children elsewhere.

Rastas live in rural and urban areas, but the largest number of known Rastamen is concentrated on Government-owned waste land, where they are squatters in wood hovels, many of them on a swamp reclaimed by tipping the filth from the Kingston refuse carts into the holes, so turning the swamp into a vast and mosquito-infested rubbish dump. It is on this rubbish dump that they have built their homes. On the Foreshore Road alone, a notorious slum settlement near the harbour, Rasta friends told me there live 1000 children, but as births are rarely registered this is impossible to check. The inhabitants call this area "the Dungle", the name of their last slum, which has been officially cleared. To the Jamaican the word "Dungle" signifies all that is most vicious, despairing and ugly in human life. Rastafarians take a certain pride in explaining that though they live there, they will never sink to its level. "Though we the Rastafaris live on the Dungle, we are not *of* the Dungle. We don't eat off the Dungle" (that is, gather condemned food stuffs and other rubbish tipped from the refuse trucks). "We do not eat like John Crow" (the vulture, which in Jamaica is an efficient and necessary scavenger). "It is below the integrity." Although some courageous social workers and nurses work in the area, on the whole it is avoided by those outside, and is certainly not a place where outsiders linger.

In spite of social conditions like these, there has occurred during the last few years an evolution of religious doctrine, so that it is now markedly different from that described by M. G. Smith, Roy Augier and Rex Nettleford in their report on the movement in 1960.[2] As the hope of returning to Africa has receded further and further into the distance with recurrent disappointments, Rastafarians have evolved a system of belief compatible with their lives of extreme poverty and need, the essence of which is a mystical experience similar to that found historically in certain other minority "protest" religions.

The initial Rastafarian concept of God owes much to Old Testament theology. In part the Jehova of Israel "returned as in former days, so terrible and dreadful amongst the wicked, Ja Rastafari, our Almighty God", a God of vengeance who "will break in pieces the horse and rider", He is made manifest upon earth in the form of the Emperor, and some affirm that he is in fact the reincarnated Messiah, but this time a true representative of the Black race. In the formal prayers and chants it is this aspect of God which is predominant.

Rastafarians speak scornfully of the white man's God in the sky and laugh about the Jesus of Sunday School books. "They say that Jesus is a white man with blue eyes and He lives in the sky," said one religious leader amidst hilarious laughter, but you have to *die* before you can see that God . . . Yet the Bible say . . . 'I am a God of the living.' Not a God of the dead!" They do not see that a God in Ethiopia is just as ridiculous, but this may be partly because to them the physical person of the Emperor is but one manifestation of the Godhead. Some even speak of a Trinity of the Creator, Haille Selassie and "the Breath within the temple". Hence, although they affirm that the Emperor will never die, there is unlikely to be a collapse in their faith when he does.

In many respects Rastafarians have now progressed beyond the concept of God as lawgiver, king and judge, and essential to an understanding of the mystical experience which many now seek is the concept of "*nature*". Man must have faith in God's Nature, which is beyond human comprehension. Faith is essential to redemption, for our minds cannot possibly grasp and encompass Nature. The word "nature" implies not only the cosmic creative force, "the light of this world, the first without last, the beginning without end" and the fruits of that creation, but also the inner power and vitality of all created things, including man and the spirit of man, and the force of sex. The Nature of God is not only made manifest in His world, but is the germinal power of all that is in the mind of man. As one Nyabingi leader told me, "Before the tree comes to this perfection it was seed, and it was in itself. The seed were in itself. And so with us. In the beginning was the Word." The Word is the seed from which all men spring and they cannot go beyond the potentialities contained within the seed. "We could not go beyond the power of God." Men must remain conscious of the seed and hence of their relation to God. And deliberately—with purpose and consideration—they must use language —"words"—to relate their living to the Word from which their own powers of communication are derived—for "words develop Nature."

Thus, although they believe that a man and woman must not hesitate to beget children, however impoverished they are, for the Lord will provide, they are highly critical of sexual relations "in the flesh only". "We are not of the flesh, but of the spirit." In the act of creation it is essential that both man and woman should relate their individual natures to the Nature from which they spring, so sanctifying intercourse. "The woman may not feel in the mood, but the man does it with words. When the man go into the woman, the first thing he do is say, 'I like you bring forth a child for me.'" Whenever a man and woman have intercourse, they must do so "knowing that within oneself that was the thing upon earth to be". Each must have pride and glory in himself or herself as he or she is, with no doubts.

Sexual intemperance and the high birth rate are explained in terms of "nature", as they are by all peasant Jamaicans. It is something uncontrollable and mighty which human beings suffer passively, as God's will. A man fearing impotence (a frequent dread) speaks simply of losing his "nature". Rastafarians disapprove strongly of contraception, which is "internal murder" and which they believe to be sterilisation or "stop altogether", rather than "space between"—a distinction which I found of primary importance in teaching peasants about birth control. This is partly because "we want to populate Africa" and partly because "it interferes with the true vision of women. Your inspiration tell you you have done wrong"—and not because of the slogans scrawled up on walls: "Birth control—white man's plan to kill off the black race". Indeed, so far is this from being a racial issue that friendly Rastafarians were deeply concerned when I, obviously white, told them that I used "the control", and pleaded with me not to harm myself. They disapprove of *coitus interruptus* for the same reasons and say, "If you don't use your nature, you lose your nature". In fact it is the duty of men and women to "bring forth seed" and the relationship between them dissolves if they fail to do so. One Nyabingi leader, himself childless, who "adopted" children, as so many Jamaicans (and even others with large families of their own) do, said that having children brought a new awareness of life and was a necessary part of becoming mature. "Some never think themselves responsible until they have a child. This Government believes when a person marry they become responsible. We believe it is when they have children. Responsibility comes through obligation"—and he paused. "Sometimes even through oppression."

Education does not start with schooling, nor even in infancy. "The child can be educated inside the womb—the way the father and mother live"—a highly sophisticated concept of parental influence. "The parents must first live the life that their children seek." Rastafarians are not monogamists and change their "Queens" when they wish. They do not bother with legal marriage, but in this they are no different from the majority of peasant Jamaicans for whom marriage is a sign of a successful relationship established over the years, rather than the ticket to one. Marriage exists "when two people come to each other to support each other". It needs no symbol or ritual.

Intricately involved with the mystical experience is the concept of *"art"*. "Not every man with a beard and locks is a Rastaman. We take a man with art, not because he carry a beard." "Some have all the zeal of God, but not the knowledge." That is, they stress the need for inward grace, not outward symbols. "Art" is the inherent ability to know the things of God, to see through the apparent to the real, to discern between the false and true, and to communicate this knowledge. A man may discover it in himself after living the major part of his life in dissolute unawareness—"in the flesh pots". It was there all the time, but he did not know it. When a man expounds doctrine excellently, prays movingly, or argues a point convincingly, his listeners call out, "Art! Mighty art! Rastafari!"

As time passes Rastafarians are faced with the necessity of developing beliefs which, although the core is the longed-for return to Africa, have deeper personal significance and hold out hope for the mass of Jamaicans who will never live to see the promised land. Although protesting that Rastas never die (they never attend the funeral of a member unless it can be argued that he was murdered), members of the movement are well aware that they do, and that this cannot be put down entirely to the machinations of white evil, white medicine, the depredations of "Babylon", or personal sin.

It may well be that since about 1954, when emigration to Britain became a practical possibility of making good for large numbers of Jamaicans with sufficient initiative, repatriation to Africa has lost some of its charms—although Rastafarians would be the last to admit it. Although Africa can offer racial triumph and the chimera of security in the land from which their fathers came (and Rastafarians assiduously pore through every travel folder they can get hold of about Africa and savor every item of news which stems from that continent), it has little to offer in the way of material advantages. Hence the "return to Africa" movement by itself is lacking in substance, and, aware of this, Rastafarians have become concerned about the content of their religion—and it is this concern which seems to me to have value and to indicate that the movement has a future.

However much middle class and peasant Jamaicans alike may laugh at the Rastas, when they are not expressing overt hostility to them—and one or other is the behaviour norm—their beliefs contain the seeds of a mystical faith comparable to that held in times of religious revival amongst more sophisticated peoples. When one is actually with them on the Dungle it seems extraordinary that their faith and philosophy can be as profound as it doubtless is for many of them. They feel marooned on a small island in the middle of the Caribbean Sea, cut off from their homeland, and deprived of the right to practise their religion as they believe God commands them to do (which, of course, includes the smoking of ganja). They long to communicate their ideas and to have the education to do so.

The early Quakers were not looked at with more misgivings by a society which saw them as coming "from the very rabble and dregs of the people", as individuals who differentiated themselves from more sober citizens by their odd appearance, the peculiar nature of their devotions, and their habit of quaking and trembling when filled with the "spirit". Seventeenth-century Quakers, like present-day Rastafarians, did not modify their beliefs when confronted by a hostile society, often used highly abusive language, and employed similar martial metaphors of pitching tents, drawing swords, and making ready for battle against the enemy. Rastamen would have understood George Fox's concern in walking around Litchfield shouting at the top of his voice, "Woe to the bloody city!"

It seems to me that the Rastafarian faith too bears within it the possibility of sincere and valid religious experience. If so, the task for the Jamaican Government would appear to be to offer facilities for the institutionalisation and social acceptance of this religion, so that the aggression springing from poverty and the Rastas' position at the bottom of the social pyramid is effectively canalised into satisfying ritual, to assist the Rastas to develop all that is most worthy and reasonable in their faith, and to provide educational opportunities for school-age children and in the form of adult classes, so that they can acquire habits of logical thought and be able to resist rabble-rousers and verbalize their protest in a non-violent manner. These are all aims which the Rastafarians themselves share.

Notes:

1. For further background material, see the three articles by G. E. Simpson: "Political Cultism in West Kingston, Jamaica", *Social and Economic Studies,* June 1955, 133–49; "The Rastafari Movement in Jamaica", *Social Forces,* December 1955, 167–70; and "The Ras Tafari Movement in Its Millennial Aspect", *Comparative Studies in Society and History,* Supplement No. 2 (1962), 160–65.

2. Published by the Institute of Social and Economic Research, University of the West Indies.

Index